THE
PROMISED MESSIAH

WHAT THE BIBLE TEACHES ABOUT

THE PROMISED MESSIAH

by

James E. Smith

THOMAS NELSON PUBLISHERS
Nashville

Published in Nashville, Tennessee, by Thomas Nelson, Inc.

Library of Congress Cataloging-in-Publication Data

Smith, James E. (James Edward), 1939–
   [What the Bible says about the promised Messiah]
   What the Bible teaches about the promised Messiah / by James E. Smith.
   Originally published: What the Bible says about the promised Messiah. Joplin, Mo. : College press, c1984.
   Includes bibliographical references and index.
   ISBN 0-8407-4239-8
   1. Messiah—Prophecies. 2. Bible. O.T.—Criticism, interpretation, etc. 3. Prophecy—Christianity. I. Title.
   [BT235.S59 1993]
   232'.12—dc20
                                             93-4591
                                                CIP

Printed in the United States of America

3 4 5 6 7 8 — 00 99 98 97 96 95 94 93

To

Three Preachers Par Excellence

My Brothers

In the Flesh and in the Faith

Fred W. Smith Jr.

Gerald C. Smith

John H. Smith

Table of Contents

Preface

Every Christian has publicly confessed, "I believe that Jesus is the Christ, the Son of the living God." To say that Jesus is the Christ means that he is the Messiah promised in the Old Testament. The average Christian would probably be at a loss to defend this confession of Jesus' Messiahship if called upon to do so. This study is designed to help Christians make that "good confession" intelligently and confidently.

The Old Testament contains a network of interrelated predictions and anticipations of a Coming One who would be both God and man, who would be prophet, priest, and king *par excellence*. The passages discussed on the following pages contain dozens of predictions about him. Some of these are general to be sure; but others are quite specific. The prophetic artists paint a rather complete picture of the Coming One. Nonetheless, Riehm is correct when he observes that the Old Testament picture of the Messiah falls strikingly short of the New Testament God-man. "The actual execution of God's saving purpose in Christ goes far beyond the contents of Messianic prophecy."[1]

Jesus of Nazareth was the first to claim that he was the one promised in the Old Testament. But he was not the last. Over forty others have made the same claim. One has only to place the personal Messianic prophecies of the Old Testament alongside the claimants to see that one and all they were impostures. Only in Jesus of Nazareth will a serious student find a Messianic claimant who does not wilt before the withering array of Old Testament specifications regarding the Messiah.

During the nineteenth century a number of works on Messianic prophecy appeared. Among the more important were the studies of Hengstenberg, Delitzsch and Riehm in Germany, and R. Payne Smith, David Baron, Alfred Edersheim, and Adolph Shaphir in England. The latter three of the above named were Christian Jews, men who were brought to Christ by a study of Messianic prophecy. Excepting the works of Mowinckel (ET, 1956), and Becker (1977), both of whom represent the modern critical school of interpretation, not much of importance has been written on the subject in the twentieth century. The works of the Christian Jew Kligerman (1957) and Kac (1975) are not very helpful.

No general agreement exists about what passages should be regarded as personal Messianic predictions. Overzealous believers have applied many passages to Christ which closer examination and honest interpretation proved not to lie within the compass of the prophecies of the Messiah. Modern scholars, however, have tended toward a reduction in the number of passages regarded as predictive of Christ.

---

1. Riehm, MP, pp. 271, 296.

Applying the principles of grammatico-historical criticism, many scholars have come to the conclusion that genuine Messianic predictions can be numbered on one hand. Becker speaks for the modern school when he writes, "Messianic prophecies cannot be considered visionary predictions of a New Testament fulfillment."[2]

In this work some seventy-three passages are classified as personal Messianic prophecies. No effort has been made to discuss every text adduced by interpreters as referring to Messiah, but only those which, according to criteria to be set forth in Chapter One carry certain, or at least probable, evidence of having been properly so designated. The degrees of that evidence will, of course, vary. But if the passages which appear to be least convincing are stricken from the list, enough will remain to establish that Jesus of Nazareth is the Messiah. The weight of the argument is not diminished by the reduction of the number of passages.

The omission of a passage from consideration does not constitute a rejection of that passage as a reference to the Coming One. Passages which speak, for example, of a coming of Yahweh for judgment or redemption are probably to be interpreted Messianically. The focus here is on passages which make explicit that the Coming One is the agent of Yahweh in the world.

The bibliography at the conclusion of this volume indicates that the author is in debt to numerous authors who have commented on the Messianic prophecies before. On the pre-monarchial predictions the works of Maas and Briggs have been most helpful. In the Psalms, Dickson, Kirkpatrick, Albert Barnes and Alexander have been invaluable. For the Minor Prophets Laetsch, Leupold, Keil, Pusey, Baron and Moore have been most stimulating. Leupold and Young are most helpful on Isaiah and Daniel.

The chronological principle for the most part has dictated the order in which the Messianic passages are discussed. The Book of Job may constitute an exception to this rule. It seemed best to treat Job in conjunction with the Solomonic wisdom literature even though there is a real possibility that Job is much earlier.

With regard to each prophecy the same format has been followed. Background material is followed by a translation of the text. That in turn is followed by an exegesis of the passage.

The titles of works cited have been reduced to the first letters of key words. Full bibliographic information can be found under the author's last name in the bibliography at the conclusion of the volume.

---

2. Becker, MEOT, p. 93.

Chapter One

INTRODUCTION TO THE STUDY

Background material essential to an understanding of Messianic prophecy is offered in this chapter. Key terms are defined. The methodology employed in the exegesis to follow is set forth. Herein is contained an overview of the material to be covered and a discussion of the purpose which such material serves in the Scriptures. The classical argument based on fulfilled Messianic prediction is developed. Some basic issues in the study of Messianic prophecy are explored. The chapter concludes with a discussion of the reasons Jesus has been rejected, for the most part, by the Jews as their Messiah.

Definitions

The Term Messiah

Messiah is the special title of the Savior promised to the world through the people of Israel. This title only appears twice in the New Testament. Andrew (John 1:41) and the Samaritan woman (John 4:25) referred to Jesus as the *Messias*, a Grecized form of *Messiah*. In the Authorized Version the term *Messiah* also only occurs twice in the Old Testament, in Daniel 9:25, 26.

The term *Messiah* is not used in early Jewish literature as often as one might think. It is used once in the Apocrypha, and is used but once in the Mishnah (*Sot.* 9.15). It is found in the Qumran literature (seven passages), about a dozen times in the Pseudepigrapha, in old Jewish prayers, the Targums of the second Christian century, and later in the Talmud.

The term *Messiah* is derived from the root *mashach* which almost always points to the consecration of objects to sacred purposes by means of anointing oil.[1] The verb is used of the anointing of objects such as the Tabernacle, altar and laver. The noun *mashiach*, however, is used only of individuals.[2] Etymologically, then, the Messiah is the Anointed One. Anointing in Old Testament times denoted the two ideas of consecration and endowment.

---

1. Isa. 21:5 and Jer. 22:14 are the possible exceptions to this meaning of *mashach*.
2. In II Sam. 1:21 *mashiach* is ambiguous. It was taken by the LXX to refer to Saul's shield. The verse is, however, best understood in the following way: The king had fallen at Gilboa like one of the common soldiers "not as the one who had been anointed with oil."

The term *mashiach* (anointed one) occurs thirty-nine times in the Hebrew Old Testament. In each case it is rendered in the Greek version by the term *Christos,* Christ. The Hebrew term *Messiah* and the Greek term *Christ* are synonyms.

The "christs"—anointed ones—of Old Testament times consisted of three classes of leaders:

1. Priests were anointed (Exod. 28:41) and in consequence one who served in this office was called "the anointed priest" (Lev. 4:3, 5).

2. As a substantive the term is used of kings, often with a posessive pronoun: "my anointed" (I Sam. 2:35), "your anointed" (Ps. 84:9), and "his anointed" (I Sam. 12:3, 5). The formal title of the king of Israel must have been "Yahweh's Anointed" (I Sam. 24:6, 10) or the Anointed of the God of Jacob" (II Sam. 23:1). Once the title *mashiach* is applied to the Persian king Cyrus because he had been appointed to carry out the designs of the Lord (Isa. 45:1).[3]

3. Prophets were also anointed, at least on occasion (I Kings 19:16). Patriarchs are called *anointed ones* (Ps. 105:15) because they were regarded as prophets, and because they played such an important role in the program of God.

It is sometimes said that the term *mashiach* is never used in the Old Testament of the Promised One.[4] Such an assessment is based on a critical view of the Old Testament which disallows any Messianic concept prior to the exile. In seven passages the term seems to be used of the Anointed One *par excellence,* and in two other places it is used in such a way as to embrace him. The chart on the following page gives an overview of the use of the term in the Old Testament.

The title *Christ* is wondrously appropriate for the Savior of New Testament Scripture. He embraced and exhausted in himself the offices of prophet, priest and king. He was infinitely superior to Old Testament priests like Aaron, prophets like Elijah, or kings like Saul. In Melchizedek the offices of king and priest were combined; in David the offices of king and prophet. But only in Jesus of Nazareth were the three offices combined. Perhaps this is why the prophet David described him as "anointed above his fellows" (Ps. 45:8).

---

3. Cf. also I Kings 19:15 where a heathen is to be anointed king over Syria because Yahweh intends to use him as an instrument of judgment.

4. E.g., Mowinckel, HTC, p. 4.

USE OF *MASHIACH* IN THE BIBLE		
USED OF	NO. TIMES USED	REFERENCES
1. Saul	12	I Sam. 12:3, 5; 24:6, 6, 10; 26:9, 11, 16, 23; II Sam. 1:14, 16, 21
2. Messiah	9	I Sam. 2:10, 35; Ps. 2:2; 89:51; 132:10, 17; Hab. 3:13
3. David	6	II Sam. 19:21; 22:51; 23:1; Ps. 18:51; 20:6; 28:8
4. Priest	4	Lev. 4:3, 5, 16; 6:22
5. Reigning King	3	Lam. 4:20; Ps. 84:9; 89:38
6. Patriarchs	2	Ps. 105:15; I Chron. 16:22
7. Solomon	1	II Chron. 6:42
8. Prospective King	1	I Sam. 16:6
9. Cyrus	1	Isa. 45:1

If the ancient offices of prophet, priest and king were typical, so also was the anointing oil itself. Christian tradition has seen in the oil of consecration a symbol and type of the Holy Spirit. Prophecy makes clear that Messiah would be anointed with the Holy Spirit (Isa. 41:1), and Jesus expressly claimed for himself fulfillment of this prophecy (Luke 4:16-21). When the Spirit descended on him at his baptism Jesus was anointed to his prophetical office. To his offices of everlasting King and Priest he was fully consecrated at his resurrection and ascension (Acts 2:36).

The Term Messianic

The term *Messianic* is used with a much wider range of meanings than *Messiah*. All anticipations in the Old Testament of a glorious future, a golden age, a grand redemption, are commonly designated *Messianic* even when they do not speak directly of a personal savior. Christian writers generally interpret such passages as referring to the coming and

3

work of Christ or to the church. The use of the term *Messianic* seems justified if a passage has some relationship to the work which the Redeemer would accomplish. Nevertheless, some writers insist that the term Messianic should be restricted to passages which speak of the Promised One.[5]

Perhaps it is best to distinguish between Messianic prophecy in general and *personal* Messianic prophecy. In the former category one would place all anticipations of a new age to come, and in the latter category, prophecies which speak of a glorious Prophet, Priest or King around whom that new age would center.[6]

Messianic prophecy—both general and personal—is not confined to the official prophets. It is not limited to any particular form of Old Testament literature. It is found in the history and devotional books as well as in the prophetical books. It is spread all over the literature of the Old Testament as the thread of light that binds its writings into an organism of redemption.[7]

Identification of Messianic Prophecy

Identifying passages which are properly interpreted as personal Messianic is not easy. No two authorities agree upon the number of such prophecies. Edersheim listed 456 passages which were interpreted as Messianic in ancient Jewish literature.[8] Payne lists 127 personal Messianic predictions involving 3,348 verses. Non-typical predictions, i.e., direct personal Messianic predictions, he finds in 574 verses. The following paragraphs are designed to indicate the principles which guided the writer in the selection of passages to be treated in this work.

The Starting Point

Some writers are quite frank in their denials of the reality of Messianic prediction. According to them, there are no original predictive references to Jesus Christ in the Old Testament and consequently no actual fulfillments of predictions referring to him in the events of the

---

5. E.g., C. W. Emmet, HERE, XIV, 570.

6. Terry (BH, p. 237) divides prediction into (1) those which present "an impersonal portraiture of a coming kingdom of power and righteousness in which humanity attains its highest good"; and (2) those which announce "a person, the Anointed One, with whom all triumph and glory are connected." Both he regards as "Messianic."

7. Briggs. MP, p. 61.

8. Edersheim (LTJM, II, Appendix IX) lists 75 Messianic prophecies in the Pentateuch, 243 in the Prophets, and 138 in the Writings.

New Testament. C. R. North commenting on the direct Messianic view of Isaiah 53 represents this point of view:

> Moreover, if this implies that he 'sees' in advance One who was not to come for another five or six centuries, it raises the difficult philosophical problem whether there can be an actual prevision of history.[9]

The reality of Messianic prophecy rests upon two basic presuppositions: (1) the possibility of prediction, and (2) the omniscience of God.

Rationalists tend to belittle or ignore the predictive element in Scripture. They insist that one must distinguish between prophecy and prediction. Prophecy is restricted to ethical teaching. Emphasis is placed on the prophets as preachers, as *forthtellers* rather than *foretellers*. What traditionally have been regarded as predictions are treated as (1) vague hopes regarding the future, (2) descriptions of events in the prophet's own day, or (3) post-dated utterances, i.e., "predictions" recorded after the events had already taken place. The prophets, it is said, had no greater insight into the future than any other astute political observers of the day.[10]

It is now clear that the old rationalistic denials of genuine prediction in the Old Testament prophecy simply do not square with the facts. In his classic study, *Encyclopedia of Biblical Prophecy*, J. Barton Payne identifies some 1239 predictions in the Old Testament involving some 6,641 verses or 28.5% of the Old Testament text. In the New Testament he finds 578 predictions in 1,711 verses or 21.5% of the New Testament text.[11] These statistics are not surprising to those who have taken seriously the Bible's own teaching concerning prediction.[12] Dewart was surely right when he argued that "the idea of prediction is essentially embedded in the word *prophecy*.[13] Rowley concurs: The prophets "regarded the foretelling of the future as the essence of their function."[14] Furthermore, "whether modern scholars like it or not, prediction was the way the New Testament writers themselves related the Testaments."[15]

---

9. North, SS, p. 207.

10. Cf. R. H. Charles (*Critical Commentary on the Book of Daniel*, p. xxvi): "Prophecy is a declaration, a forthtelling, of the will of God—not a foretelling. Prediction is not in any sense an essential of prophecy, though it may intervene as an accident—whether it be a justifiable accident is another question."

11. Payne, EBP, pp. 675-76.

12. See Deut. 18:22; Isa. 45:21; 46:9-11; Hab. 2:2-3; Jer. 28:9; John 14:29.

13. Dewart, JMPF, p. 36.

14. Rowley, RA, p. 34.

15. Brown, JBC, II, 615.

Principles of Identification

The entire Old Testament is Messianic in the sense that it prepared the way for Christ. The focus of this study is on direct Messianic prediction which imparts information of a factual, propositional sort about the Coming One. Most scholars would allow that prophecies of this kind do exist in the Old Testament, but no two writers agree as to their number. Payne finds 103 such predictions in eighteen books,[16] but there are others which should be placed in this category.

Typological Messianic prophecy has not been discussed in this study,[17] nor have what Culver[18] calls "the divine *parousia*" passages. These latter passages connect salvation with the coming of God himself (e.g., Micah 1:3; Ps. 50:3; Ps. 93-94). Israel never thought of Yahweh's rule without human representation.[19] Therefore, the ultimate representative of God cannot be excluded in passages where the coming of Yahweh is promised. Nonetheless, in this study the focus is on those predictions where Messiah is depicted as separate from and sent by God.

In seeking to determine what constitutes a personal Messianic prophecy six principles have been employed. These are:

1. The contextual principle. The common rule of all rational interpretation is this: A personal Messianic prediction is involved when the sense afforded by a careful examination of the terms of the passage be such as properly refers to Messiah, and cannot, without violence, be applied to any object exclusive of him. The writer himself defines the nature of the fulfillment within his own immediately surrounding declarations. The context may provide assistance regarding the manner or the time of the fulfillment. Help regarding figurative language is often provided.

This first principle must be applied with caution. The use of hyperbolic language in the ancient royal courts may give the interpreter pause. Even language implying deity of pagan kings is attested. One must

---

16. Payne, EBP, pp. 667-668. He finds twenty-five such predictions in Isaiah, twenty-four in Psalms and twenty in Zechariah.

17. A *type* is a description of an event, institution or person designed by God to be distinctly prophetic of the Messiah and his kingdom. Most of the Book of Leviticus and large sections of Exodus and Numbers reporting the sacrificial ritual are typological.

18. R. D. Culver, "The Old Testament as Messianic Prophecy," *Bulletin of the Evangelical Theological Society* 7(1964): 91-97.

19. Ellison, CMIOT, p. 8.

reckon with the possibility that in some of the Psalms, for example, the language of the royal court is being used to describe the reigning king, not the Messiah.

2. The Jewish principle. Another clue to the identity of personal Messianic prophecy is the most ancient Jewish interpretation of the Old Testament. Jewish interpretation, especially if it is pre-Christian, establishes the fact that personal Messianic prophecy is not the product of Christian wishful thinking. The application of the contextual principle above is strengthened when Jewish scholars concede a Messianic reference.

Jewish interpretation, however, as a clue to Messianic prophecy has drawbacks. First, one must reckon with the source problem. The written Jewish sources which are pre-Christian are not numerous. The post-Christian sources sometimes contain pre-Christian interpretations, but one cannot always be sure these interpretations have been untainted by Jewish-Christian controversies. Then there is this fact: Jewish interpretation is not always consistent, nor is it infallible. Jewish authors have no greater sagacity than Christian scholars when it comes to interpreting the Old Testament.

3. The analogy principle. Some passages can be identified as Messianic prophecies because they are very similar to other predictions which are admittedly Messianic. Simply stated, the Bible is the best interpreter of the Bible. An earlier prediction is often picked up by a writer and used in such a way that the Messianic thrust of the language of the first passage is recognized to be the original intent of the writer.

In the application of this principle there is also a danger. Similar predictive language does not always demand identical fulfillment. Girdlestone, for example, has pointed out that the expression "The Lord comes" indicates a range of various visitations and actions of God, some past at the time they were written, and some still future even from this present day.[20]

4. The transcendence principle. If a prophetic description of the greatness of an illustrous person, and the blessings conferred by him or on him be more exalted than can belong to any king, or prophet, or Old Testament circumstances; and if it be clearly foreign to anything in the situation of the writer, then it is proper, and even necessary, to consider it as belonging to the more noble dispensation of the Messiah.

---

20. Girdlestone, GP, pp. 56-57.

If the expressions employed by the prophet cannot, with any propriety, be applied to himself or his situation, it is legitimate to regard these expressions as declaring the dignity, character, and history of the Messiah.[21]

5. The event principle. Horne states: "The event is the best interpreter of a prediction."[22] Girdlestone agrees: "History is the best commentary on prophecy."[23] Carnell states the matter this way:

> It is part of the character of the Scripture prophecies not to be so framed as to be fully understood before the event. . . . It is not to have its full sense made out (like any other kind of composition) by the study . . . of each prophecy itself, but it is to be interpreted by the event that fulfills it.[24]

The God who ordains the course of history and who inspires men to inscripturate certain events, is the God who inspired the predictions in the first place. The ambiguities of figurative and symbolic language and cultural patterns are thus often removed and the original intent of the prediction made the more obvious. According to Luke 24:25-27, only in the light of the death and resurrection of Jesus was it possible for the disciples to recognize and understand the Old Testament predictions.

6. The authority principle. Those passages are personal Messianic prophecies which the inspired writers of the New Testament declare to be such. This involves some passages which modern readers would scarcely imagine were speaking about Christ were it not for the New Testament usage. The same Spirit inspired both prophet and apostle. Surely the Spirit speaking through the latter must possess the right to explain what he meant when he spoke through the former. New Testament citations often clarify and expand upon the meaning of the Old Testament predictions and open up whole new categories of Messianic prediction. Predictions, for example, which speak in generalizations of divine activity are declared in the New Testament to be the work of Christ.

To further clarify the authority principle the following thoughts from John Pye Smith[25] are helpful. The ground of authority is "the sense

---

21. Doedelein, cited by Dwart, JMPF, p. 186.
22. Horne, ICSS, p. 388.
23. Girdlestone, GP, p. 172.
24. Carnell, COT, pp. 54-55.
25. John Pye Smith, STM, I, 144-145.

assumed, positively averred, or manifestly implied, by the writer of the New Testament in citations from the Old." Why must this be the case? When an Old Testament citation is introduced in the New Testament explicitly as an assertion of fact or doctrine, or as a prophecy of the event to which it is applied, one must either admit the propriety of the application, to the full extent to which it is carried by the sacred writer, or he must attribute to him mistake or presumption, notwithstanding his professions of inspiration.

The above principle is easier stated than applied. Sometimes New Testament writers use Old Testament prophecies merely because they see an analogy. They borrow Old Testament language without intending to suggest that the prediction-fulfillment relationship exists between the two statements. Even when they declare that a prophecy was *fulfilled* there is sometimes a question as to whether or not they mean that the Old Testament statement was a direct prediction of that which is said to fulfill it (e.g., Matt. 13:14, 15).

The New Testament cites a wealth of Messianic passages ignored by scholarly apologetics as instances of purely external accommodation. Sometimes only the single line of a Psalm is quoted and said to be predictive of New Testament events. Is the apostolic writer supplying a clue to the interpretation of the entire passage? or is this a way of pointing out similar circumstances, history repeating itself as it were? Are modern scholars so confident in the exegetical methodology, and their knowledge of the background and circumstances of each prophecy that they can immediately label apostolic intepretation "accommodation" when it points in another direction?

There are yet other factors to be considered. Some of the most obvious Messianic prophecies are never cited in the New Testament. Was it precisely because they were so obvious that no citation is made? The instances of New Testament elucidation are relatively few. Is one justified in declaring a prediction to be Messianic which is very similar to one which the apostolic writer explicitly declares to have been fulfilled in Christ?

Obviously the authority of the New Testament cannot be employed against a Jewish apologist; but in any controversy among Christians it ought to be the ultimate court of appeals.

The Purpose of Messianic Prophecy

Predictive prophecy is not intended to be history written in advance. "God does not propose to gratify idle curiousity by writing history beforehand. . . . God has been able to write prophecy so it can be read after it is fulfilled, but not generally before."[26] What then is the purpose of such prophecy to those who first received it and to those who treasured it through the centuries?

Continuing Value

One may distinguish at least six purposes for Messianic prophecy. The continuing value of the study of Messianic prophecy is made clear by the enumeration of these purposes.

1. The chief purpose, of course, was to prepare the way for Christ so that when he should come, he might be identified by a comparison of the prediction with its fulfillment. Jesus regarded the evidence of prophecy as sufficient in itself to prove his claims. He reproved the Jews for failure to recognize the fulfillment as it unfolded before them. At the triumphal entry he so ordered things to make them harmonize with the prediction of Zechariah (Matt. 21:1; John 12:14). By so doing he was making a strong affirmation regarding his identity and the necessity of precise fulfillment of Old Testament Messianic prediction.

2. Messianic prophecy also served to prepare Israel for the grafting in of Gentile peoples; that is, it kept the Jews from becoming totally narrow and provincial. Even before the formation of the Old Testament theocracy at Mt. Sinai and many times thereafter God's prophets announced that the special relation between God and ethnic Israel was temporary. With the coming of Messiah peoples from all nations could and would be incorporated into the family of God. The child Israel was trained by the pedagogy of prophecy for the manhood of Messianic times.[27]

3. The promise of the Messiah was a means of sustaining the faith of God's people in times of great calamity. The fall of Jerusalem and destruction of the Temple in 587 B.C. was a dangerous time for the faith of Old Testament saints. Jeremiah, and especially Ezekiel, helped to put this tragedy in proper perspective as part of the long-range plan of God. The promise of return from distant lands of exile was for them the prelude to the glorious age of Messiah.

4. Messianic prophecy was also one means of promoting genuine piety and true devotion to God. Messiah would punish the ungodly

---

26. Zollars, KK, p. 34.
27. Briggs, MP, p. 63.

and reward the godly. This conviction helped sustain the faithful remnant throughout Old Testament history. The prophets all share in this characteristic feature of presenting their predictions as near of realization. The *nearness* and the *at handness* of prophetic prediction indicated the certainty of the events to come but the uncertainty of the time of fulfillment. "The interval between the today of prophecy and the tomorrow of prophecy is but a night-time of uncertain duration, so uncertain that today is and must ever be of supreme importance."[28]

5. As with all prediction, Messianic prophecy "testifies to its Author's wisdom and sovereignty over the future."[29]

6. Messianic prophecy—and indeed all predictive prophecy—lends strong support to the claim of the Scriptures to be the Word of God.[30] An older generation of scholars[31] did not hesitate to press the evidence from fulfilled prediction in their disputations with unbelievers. Modern scholars, faced with a multitude of anti-supernaturalistic explanations, are far from enthusiastic about the evidential value of fulfilled prophecy.[32] For them, Old Testament prophecy only prepared the way for the coming of Christ, though it did not anticipate it. Even Kirkpatrick cautions that the argument from fulfilled prophecy "is more properly addressed to believers for the support of their faith than to unbelievers for the removal of their doubts."[33]

Within the wide range of Biblical prediction there are passages most difficult to explain which might cause problems in any confrontation with unbelievers. There remain, however, more numerous examples of fulfilled prediction which those who oppose the Biblical claims to inspiration must find difficult to explain on naturalistic grounds.

Culminating Expectation

The absence of strong Messianic hope in Jewish literature before A.D. 70 suggests that the hope was mainly an element in the popular

---

28. Briggs, MP, pp. 53-54.

29. Payne, EBP, p. 13.

30. Cf. Zollars (KK, p. 33): The real purpose of predictive prophecy is "to confirm or establish the inspiration of the prophetic speaker or writer, after the events foretold have occurred."

31. E.g., John Urquhart, *The Wonders of Prophecy*, 4th ed. (New York: Gospel Publishing, n.d.)

32. E.g., E. A. Edghill, *An Enquiry into the Evidential Value of Prophecy* (London: Macmillan, 1906).

33. Kirkpatrick, DP, p. 11.

religion. Nonetheless, ". . . in the time of Jesus, the hope of a proximate appearance of the Messiah was part and parcel of the Jewish common belief. . . ."[34] Such is the clear testimony of the Gospel records.

Josephus bears testimony to first century Messianic fervor (*Wars*, VI.v.4) as do the Roman writers Tacitus[35] and Suetonius.[36] Pretenders arose during this period to take advantage of the Messianic excitement (*Ant.* XX.ii.6; *Wars* VI.v.4). Some evidence exists that Jewish Messianism even influenced the Gentile world. Klausner holds that Virgil's Fourth Eclogue which speaks of the birth of a child who would bring peace to the world was written under Jewish influence.[37]

How is the first century Messianic emotionalism to be explained? Roman oppression certainly was a contributing factor. But popular chronology was a more important element. Messianic fervor was provoked by the realization that the fulfillment of Daniel 9:24, 25 was near at hand. Counting from some order to rebuild the walls of Jerusalem, sixty-nine heptads (483 years) must elapse before Messsiah appeared. Whether the commencement of that period is dated from the decree of Cyrus (Ezra 1:1, 2) Darius (Ezra 6:8) or Artaxerxes (Ezra 7:11), the period of sixty-nine heptads had expired, or nearly so in the first century. Jesus may have had reference to this passage when he came to Galilee saying "the time is fulfilled and the kingdom of God is at hand" (Mark 1:14, 15).

Another chronological factor is important to note. The Jews in the first century believed they were living on the threshold of the Millennium.[38] On the basis of the creation week the Rabbis believed that the world would last 6000 years and then would be in chaos 1000 years (*San.* 97a). The thousand years prior to the destruction of the world (5000-6000) would be a millennium of blessedness. In the first century there was no fixed tradition regarding the age of the earth. But

---

34. von Orelli, NSHERK, VII, 327.

35. "The majority were deeply impressed with a persuasion that it was contained in the ancient writings of the priests that it would come to pass that at that very time, that the East would renew its strength and they that should go forth from Judea should be rulers of the world." *History* V.13

36. "A firm persuasion had long prevailed through all the East that it was fated for the empire of the world at that time to devolve on someone who should go forth from Judea. This prediction referred to a Roman emperor, as the event showed, but the Jews applying it to themselves broke out into rebellion." *Vespasian*, 4.

37. Cited by Jocz, ZPBE, IV, 203.

38. Silver (HMSI, pp. 16-17) develops this point at length.

testimony abounds that in the first century Jews believed that they were very near to the year 5000.[39]

The almost universal expectation was that the Messiah would be a temporal prince. Even the apostles were infected with materialistic notions of the kingdom until after Pentecost (Matt. 20:20, 21; Luke 24:21; Acts 1:6).

Did Messianic prophecy then fail in its intended purpose? The answer must be an emphatic No! Luke reports the existence of what seems to have been a considerable number of persons "that looked for redemption in Israel" (2:38). Strict adherence to the Law was the identifying mark of these pious believers. Among them were Mary and Joseph, Zacharias and Elizabeth, and Simeon and Anna. The dedication of these men and women is attributed to the Messianic hope which they shared. They were "waiting for the consolation of Israel" (Luke 1:6; 2:25, 37, 38). What profound and far-sighted faith was exhibited by them at the birth and infancy of Jesus; and they were not alone. At least some Gentiles displayed a no less marvellous faith when "the wise men from the East" did homage to the babe of Bethlehem (Matt. 2:2, 11). With the eye of faith they were able to see beyond the disguise of humiliation which obscured the true glory of the infant.

Even when the dark hour of his death came there were acknowledgments of the Messiahship of Jesus. Joseph of Arimathea "waited for the kingdom of God." He may have been impelled to seek an honorable burial for Jesus because of the great prophecy of Isaiah 53:9 which stated that the suffering Servant would be buried with the rich (Mark 15:43). A similar faith in Jesus' Messiahship compelled the dying thief to make his remarkable confession (Luke 23:42). His faith in turn brought even the Roman centurion to the conviction that Jesus was not only innocent (Luke 23:47), but even the Son of God (Matt. 27:54; Mark 15:39).

From the above it can be seen that Messianic prophecy did accomplish its purpose of preparing the world for Christ and providing the tools with which devout Jews could identify him for what he was. When it is said that the Jews rejected Christ, that is only a half truth. Many thousands were convinced through the exposition of Messianic prophecy in the light of Gospel facts that Jesus was the Messiah. Even prominent Pharisees like Paul and Nicodemus as well as many priests (Acts 6:7) were among the earliest converts.

---

39. IV Esdras 14:48; II Baruch 23:7; 68:4; 85:10; Josephus *Against Apion* I.1.

The Origin of the Messianic Hope

When did the hope of a Savior—a Messiah—originate? Emmett argues that "data are wanting whereby we might fix with any certainty the period in which the hope arose."[40] Edersheim, however, employs the process of elimination to arrive at a very early and supernatural origin for Messianic hope.[41] The paragraphs which follow expand upon his basic outline of this topic.

Inadequate Explanations

1. The Messianic hope did not originate in the New Testament period. There can be no question about the existence of Messianic ideas and expectations in the time of Christ. Christianity appealed to an existing state of expectation which was the outgrowth of a previous development.

2. The Messianic hope did not have its point of origin in the inter-testamental period as alleged by Becker and others.[42] A great part of that period is shrouded in darkness. Only one work, Ecclesiasticus, can indisputably be dated between the close of the Old Testament canon (Malachi) and the Maccabean revolt (c. 165 B.C.). Neither Ecclesiasticus, nor any book of the Apocrypha for that matter, contains any distinct references to the Messianic hope.[43] The Pseudepigraphic writings of the intertestamental period prove that after the Maccabean period the Messianic hope awakened to new life. One finds in this literature a variety of Messianic hopes and addition of detail but no trace of development in the underlying conception of Messiah and his kingdom. Commenting on the status of Messianic hope in the intertestamental period Delitzsch writes: "The development of the Messianic idea after the conclusion of the canon remains . . . far behind that which precedes in the time of the Old Testament prophecy. It affords no progress, but rather a regress."[44]

---

40. Emmett, HERE, VIII, 575.

41. Edersheim, PHRM, pp. 5ff.

42. Becker (MEOT, pp. 50, 87): "There is no evidence of true messianism until the second century B.C.. . . . It is on the threshold of the New Testament that we first encounter real messianism."

43. There may be a hint of the Messiah in I Macc. 14:41 in the "faithful prophet" who was to come. In I Macc. 2:57 the restoration of the Davidic kingdom is mentioned with no reference to the Messiah. In the rest of the books of the Apocrypha, though there may be hints of the Messianic kingdom in the wider sense (e.g., II Macc. 2:18; Bar. 4:21; Eccles. 44-50), nothing is said about a personal Messiah.

44. Delitzsch, MPHS, p. 119.

The Messianic doctrine of the Qumran sect is not quite clear. The literature speaks of two Messiahs, one of Aaron and one of Israel. The relationship of the one to the other is not spelled out (cf. 1QS IX.11). How the Qumran Teacher of Righteousness fits into the Messianic scheme is also unclear. There are allusions to "the Man" and "the Prophet" (IV.18; IX.11). In some of the Qumran hymns "the Man" is described as "a marvellous mighty counselor" (Hymn III.4).[45]

3. The origins of the Messianic hope are not to be sought in the exilic or post-exilic periods of Old Testament history.[46] Few would deny that the books of Daniel, Ezekiel and Zechariah have a fully developed concept of Messiah and his kingdom. Some have therefore argued that the hope of a glorious future ruler was born in this period when God's people were scattered and without a royal leader.[47] But if this were the case, why did the hope center in the house of David? The house of David in its pitiful state after the fall of Jerusalem in 587 B.C. gave no promise of rebirth. Yet Davidic descent is always a prominent element in the Old Testament Messianic portrait.

Intertestamental literature is virtually silent about the Davidic descent of the Messiah. This indicates a tendency to "play down" that which seemed to be at variance with political realities. It is very difficult to believe that the concept of a Davidic eschatological ruler could have been born at the close of Old Testament history when the fortunes of the house of David were at low ebb. After examining the exilic and post-exilic prophetic literature, Ellison observes:

> . . . it would far rather seem that there was a scaling down in the concept of the Messianic king during and after the exile, than the reverse. Passages like Isaiah 9:2-7, Micah 5:2 link far better with Psalms 2 and 100 and the pre-exilic monarchy than with the post-exilic community with its changing scale of values.[48]

---

45. Jocz, ZPBE, IV, 202-203.

46. Critics like Becker (MEOT, pp. 44-45) see Messianic implications in Pss. 2, 45, 72 and 110 but date these psalms to postexilic times. So also Micah 5:1-5. Isaiah 9:1-7 and 11:1-5 are given "a present-oriented interpretation." This in effect removes all Messianism from the preexilic period.

47. Mowinckel (HTC, p. 17) allows for no Messianic prophecy before the prophetic books. Only two or three of the passages which he regards as Messianic does he date to pre-exilic times. Based on his highly questionable dating scheme, Mowinckel states: "The overwhelming majority of the Messianic passages belong to the postexilic age, when the monarchy no longer existed."

48. Ellison, CMIOT, p. 10.

4. The Messianic hope was not born in the time of David. Starting with the premise that "kingship is the foundation of the messianic expectation," Becker contends that the notion of an early Messianic expectation that continued through Old Testament times is an "illusory hypothesis."[49] Even in the monarchy period Becker is unwilling to concede "a visonary preview of Christ." The Messianic element here, he thinks, is the expectation of a future royal savior, not at the end of the age, but within the monarchy period.[50] Becker must therefore regard Genesis 49:8-12 and Numbers 24:15-24 as "fictive prophecies of David's monarchy," "*vaticinia ex eventu* of a later writer who had the Davidic empire before his eyes."[51]

David was not the Messiah, nor was he the perfect model for what the Messiah would be. The union of religious and civil leadership seen in the "divine kingship" of the Fertile Crescent was dissolved in David. As the conqueror of Jerusalem David could have continued the tradition of the priest-kings of that city (cf. Gen. 14:18), but he did not. He looked forward to a royal priest "after the order of Melchizedek" (Ps. 110:4) who would perfectly unite the two offices. Thus the writers who argue that each king who followed David was a *present* savior and Messiah are incorrect. The word Messiah implies eschatology, the last days.[52] David himself looked for a ruler of a different kind as the Savior of his people. It would appear, then, that the Messianic conception was "a necessary concomitant of the peculiar Israelite conception of kingship from the first."[53]

To be sure the promise made to David constituted a significant *advance* in Messianic revelation. The Coming One is thereafter linked ancestrally to David and to a number of ideas which cluster about his dynasty. Each Davidic king, because of his personal shortcomings, and the shortcomings inherent in the Old Testament royal office pointed forward to the Coming One, not backward to an ideal king (i.e., David).

Even some liberal writers now concede the possibility of the expectation of a savior "which would be anterior to and independent of, the Davidic kingship."[54] Jenni, for example, gathers a number of scattered traces of Messianic hope which he regards as most likely pre-Davidic.

---

49. Becker (MEOT, pp. 14, 17)
50. Becker (MEOT, p. 38) calls this "protoeschatology" as opposed to the "imminent eschatology" which he sees in the post-exilic age.
51. Becker, MEOT, pp. 33, 37.
52. Mowinckel, HTC, p. 3.
53. Ellison, CMIOT, p. 12.
54. Jenni, IDB, K-Q, 361.

Among these are the concept that the Messiah had his origin in primeval times (Mic. 5:2), a mysterious birth and special diet (Isa. 7:14; Mic. 5:3), and the restoration of conditions of paradise (Isa. 11:6-8; Gen. 49:11f.). Jenni suggests that the unifying element among these scattered traces is "the mystical figure of original man or the king of paradise."[55]

The roots of Messianic prophecy are frequently traced to the Royal Psalms.[56] In these Psalms the ideal Davidic king is described. This ideal was transferred again and again, from one king to another. Such a process, declares Jenni, "presupposes a certain eschatologically adjusted attitude."[57] Some king who ascended that throne would be the ideal. The disappointments created by the failures of one king after another only served to sharpen the perspective and temper the hope. Some day the ideal king would come![58] Jocz writes: "The Messianic hope was born from the recognition that no human king is able to fulfill the high level."[59]

5. The Messianic hope did not originate in circles outside Israel. Gunkel and Gressmann have studied Messianic prophecy in the light of comparative religion. They have urged that Old Testament eschatology including the Messianic hope is not a new development of the prophetic or Exilic periods, but goes back to a far earlier time. Hope of a semi-divine Deliverer or *Heilbringer,* was a common possession of the ancient world especially in Egypt and Babylon, so they say.[60]

In response to this approach Maas[61] points out that among many ancient peoples there existed in antiquity a sense of general misery and a hope for deliverance. When the general expectations of the pagan world failed to materialize, a kind of universal despair took over with a consequent focus on the end of the world. Though many of the concepts which are part of the picture of the Messiah are also

---

55. Ibid.

56. Pss. 2, 45, 72, 110 are given serious consideration as Messianic by Becker (MEOT, p. 37); Pss. 89 and 132 "might be considered messianic at most in the indirect sense of the Nathan prophecy, whose themes they incorporate." Other royal Psalms (18, 20, 21, 101, 144) are usually not considered Messianic.

57. Jenni, IDB, K-Q, 361.

58. Emmett (HERE, VIII, 571): ". . . Precisely in proportion as the actual occupants of the throne proved themselves unworthy would it be natural to look for some one king who could realize the ideal."

59. Jocz, ZPBE, IV, 200.

60. Emmett, HERE, VIII, 575.

61. Maas, CTP, I, 76.

found among the Egyptians and Babylonians, the Old Testament Messiah has no real counterpart in the ancient Near Eastern milieu.[62]

The few correspondences between the pagan "messianic" ideas and Biblical concepts may be remnants of primeval revelation. In the promise of Genesis 3:15 lies the germ of a universal blessing. The deliverance intimated here was no doubt understood by Adam and Eve to be universal, like the injury sustained by the sin. It is no absurdity to suppose that this promise was cherished afterward by thoughtful Gentiles as well as believing Israelites; but "to the latter it was subsequently shaped into increasing precision by supplementary revelations, while to the former it never lost its formal vagueness and obscurity."[63]

6. Israel's Messianic hope cannot be accounted for by naturalistic explanations. Only by forcing the predictions into some preconceived evolutionary pattern can any semblance of naturalistic development be maintained. Taken as they stand chronologically in the text Messianic predictions defy political or psychological explanation. What possible combination of circumstances in the second millennium B.C. would account for the firm conviction in the line of Abraham that through his seed all nations of the earth would be blessed?

It has been asserted that in the Messiah Israel looked for an earthly king, and that the existence of the hope of a Messiah may thus be accounted for on natural grounds and without divine revelation. The prophecies, however, refute this. He is depicted there as Prophet and Priest as well as King, one whose business it would be to set the people free from sin and teach them the ways of God. Contrary to the exclusive notions of Judaism, the authority of the Coming One was to extend to Gentiles. A fair consideration of all the passages will convince one that the growth of the Messianic idea in the prophecies is owing to revelation from God not natural development.[64]

7. Messianic hope did not arise as a logical conclusion of Old Testament theology. Jocz, for example, claims that Old Testament Messianism is the logical result of the claim that Yahweh is Lord of heaven and earth. He explains: "The tension between historic experience and faith in the omnipotence of the benevolent God of the patriarchs can find no solution except in Messianic fulfillment."[65] The Biblical doctrine,

---

62. Jenni, IDB, K-Q, 362. Also Emmett, HERE, VIII, 575.
63. McClintock and Strong, CBTEL, VI, 135.
64. Ibid.
65. Jocz, ZPBE, IV, 201.

however, is that promises of the Coming One contributed to the understanding of God as benevolent, not vice versa.

Supernatural Origins

To say that Israel's Messianic hope grew out of her faith[66] is to state a half truth. Israel's faith was the result of divine revelation. Thus Israel's Messianic hope originated in God. It was not the product in whole or in part of *speculation* but of *revelation*. Men did not grope and guess regarding the ultimate future; God revealed it to them through chosen vessels.

The revelatory building blocks of Israel's Messianic hope are found in Genesis. This is not the place to enter into exegesis of the four foundational passages. It is, however, important to point out here that long before the formal organization of Israel at Mt. Sinai the foundation stones of Messianic hope were already in place. These were:

1. Satan ultimately would be crushed (3:15). Implication: If Satan is crushed, so also his seed, the enemies of God's people.
2. The agent of this crushing world come from the ranks of the seed of woman (3:15).
3. This victory over Satan would only be possible through suffering on the part of the Crusher (3:15).
4. Yahweh would come to dwell in the tents of Shem (9:27).
5. Through a descendant of Abraham, Isaac and Jacob all nations of the earth were to be blessed (12:3, etc.).
6. He who comes will appear before the scepter (rule, authority) departs from the tribe of Judah (49:10).
7. The one from the tribe of Judah would be a Rest-bringer (49:10).
8. Peoples would give allegiance to the Rest-bringer (49:10).
9. His coming would introduce a time of great abundance (49:11-12).

Upon these nine foundational predictions God constructed Israel's Messianic hope. Of the dozens of specific Messianic predictions which followed over the next 1400 years, scarcely one can be found which is not but a further amplification of these original predictions. It should be noted also that the first four of these predictions come from the primeval period of Bible history, long anterior to the call of Abraham.

These verbal revelations were accompanied in Genesis by a visional revelation of no little importance. To Hagar first (16:7) and later to

---

66. Jenni, IDB, K-Q, 362.

Abraham (ch. 18) and Jacob (32:24) Yahweh manifested himself in what appeared to be a flesh and blood body. These theophanies (or Christophanies)[67] would continue throughout Old Testament history. Here is a figure who at one time is Yahweh's messenger, at another time his double. The "angel of the Lord," as this theophany is often called, is a dramatic demonstration of God's determination "to reveal himself and to be personally present with his own, without, however, losing his supernatural character or destroying man by his unveiled presence."[68] Passages which speak of the coming of Yahweh should be interpreted Messianically. Messiah is Yahweh in some passages;[69] in other passages he is subordinate to Yahweh.[70] This dual nature of the Messiah would have been interpreted by astute Old Testament saints in the light of the angel of the Lord manifestations.

The Growth of Messianic Revelation

Various figures have been proposed to illustrate the progressive growth of Old Testament Messianic prophecy—the growth from seed promise to beautiful tree or flower; an ever-widening stream fed by tributaries of different concepts; a glorious edifice built block by block over centuries of time. Each prophetic announcement was designed to sustain human hope in the midst of human misery "as a light that shines in a dark place" (II Pet. 1:19). How great must have been the longing for their Deliverer which such persistent and progressive promises excited in the hearts of faithful men and women.[71]

The Interpretation of Messianic Prophecy

One of the most difficult problems in hermeneutics is the interpretation of prophecy. Disagreement about the meaning of this type of revelation has divided interpreters into warring camps.[72] Why is there no unanimity in the interpretation of prophecy? Why is there often disagreement as to what constitutes a prediction? In most cases, there is no disagreement about the original text, or the meaning of Hebrew words, or the syntactical relationship of clauses and phrases. In less than a half dozen

---

67. James Borland, *Christ in the Old Testament* (Chicago: Moody, 1978).

68. Jenni, IDB, K-Q, 362.

69. E.g., what is said of Yahweh in Zech. 2:10ff. is applied to the Messianic king in 9:9-10.

70. Cf. Jer. 23:5-6; Ezek. 34:23; Micah 5:4.

71. McClintock and Strong, CBTEL, VI, 137.

72. Ramm, PBI, p. 155.

prophecies Jewish authorities debate with Christian expositors over the meaning of the words. Controversies which have raged between unbelievers and believers, between Christians and Jews, and even between various schools of prophetic interpretation within the Church involve broader issues than verbal criticism.

New Testament Light

Hengstenberg distinguished between the "sense the prophets attach to their own utterances and what God intended in these utterances." The prophets sometimes said more than they intended to say or thought they were saying. Riehm, however, argued that "the contents of a prophecy can include only the sense in which at the time of its utterance . . . the prophets themselves intended to be understood by their contemporaries."[73] Beecher[74] suggested this criterion: "What did this mean to an intelligent, devout, uninspired Israelite of the time to which it belongs?" This emphasis guards against reading into the text things which are not there. There may be some usefulness in distinguishing between what a passage meant and how it subsequently was interpreted. This approach, however, meets with the following difficulties:

1. Scripture affirms that the writers themselves did not always fully comprehend their own utterances. One should not underestimate the prophetic foresight of a prophet like David who "because he was a prophet, and knew that God had sworn to him with an oath to seat one of his descendants upon his throne, he looked ahead and spoke of the resurrection of Christ" (Acts 2:30-31). But Daniel admits his failure to understand his own vision (8:27) and the outcome of a revelation he received (12:8). Peter claims that prophets searched diligently in attempting to fathom their own predictions (I Peter 1:10-11).[75]

2. Several examples can be cited of predictions where God's originally intended purpose (as revealed elsewhere in Scripture) seems most unlikely to have been ascertained by the prophet's contemporaries. Beecher, for example, concedes that some "Messianic prophecies" as first spoken contain "no hint of referring to a coming person who is to appear some centuries in the future."[76]

---

73. Riehm, MP, pp. 6-7, 19.
74. Beecher, PP, p. 14.
75. Kaiser (OTCP, pp. 35-37) has argued that it was ignorance over the time of fulfillment, not over the meaning of the predictions which is the point of I Peter 1:10-11. While this may be a possible interpretation of this passage, the Daniel citations seem conclusive that prophets did not always comprehend their predictions.
76. Beecher, PP, p. 403.

It is legitimate to inquire what a prophecy may have meant to the prophet or his contemporaries. It is, however, an unwarranted assumption that the intended meaning, the perceived meaning and the true meaning are all the same. One could raise the question whether it is even possible to ascertain certainly how the contemporaries of some prophet understood his predictions. In any case, it is not possible for a Christian to study the Old Testament as if he had never known what is revealed in the New.

Raymond E. Brown suggested the term *sensus plenior* to describe "the deeper meaning intended by God but not clearly intended by the human author, that is seen to exist in the words of Scripture when they are studied in the light of further revelation or of development in the understanding of revelation."[77] John Bright insists that theology informs the text.[78] Berkhof denies the validity of the position of Riehm, Beecher and others when he writes:

> There is no truth in the assertion that the intent of the secondary authors, determined by grammatico-historical method, always . . . represents in all its fullness the meaning of the Holy Spirit.[79]

Payne states the case this way: "Prophecy is transcendent as well as historical; and what its contemporaries may have thought must remain secondary to what God's inspiration may determinatively reveal as His primary intention."[80] In some cases it may have been the original auditors rather than the later writers who accommodated passages to circumstances not encompassed in the prediction.

The supreme object of studying prophecy is to find out what it means, rather than the sense in which the prophet or his contemporaries may have understood it. To one who believes that the prophets spoke under influence of the Holy Spirit, the obvious question is, What is God's thought in this passage? Everything else is secondary to this. Discovering what the prophet meant is only a means of finding out what God meant. The study of prophecy is not a mere intellectual exercise like the study of an arithmetic problem where the object would be defeated by looking first at the answer. Rather it is a search for light and truth which should be accepted wherever it is found.

---

77. Brown, JBC, II, 616.
78. Bright, AOT, pp. 143-144; 170-171.
79. Berkhof, PBI, p. 60.
80. Payne, EBP, p. 5.

Many of the Messianic prophecies can never be harmonized and understood without the light thrown upon them by their fulfillment. Prophecy is a lock. It needs the Master Key. The first advent unlocks a number of chambers. The key to the entire system is not given until the second advent.[81]

Briggs[82] has suggested a three-step process in the interpretation of Messianic prophecy. It is the responsibility of the interpreter to (1) study each prediction by itself with the most patient criticism and painstaking exegesis in all the details; (2) study it in its relation to other predictions in the series, and note the organic connection; and (3) study it in relation to Christ and his redemption.

Element of Obscurity

Nearly all ancient and modern writers have complained about the exegetical difficulties in Old Testament prophecy. A certain obscurity characterizes Biblical prediction. Those to whom prophetic visions were granted often did not know what they meant (Dan. 8:15-16; 12:9). Peter commented:

> Of which salvation the prophets have inquired and searched diligently, who prophesied of the grace that should come unto you, searching what, or what manner of time the Spirit of Christ which was in them did signify, when it testified beforehand the sufferings of Christ, and the glory that should follow (I Peter 1:10, 11).

It is also clear that the people who first heard the Biblical predictions were mystified by them. The prophecies of Isaiah were like the words of a sealed book to his generation (Isa. 29:11). Only in the last days would the people fully understand Jeremiah's predictions (Jer. 23:20; 30:24). When Ezekiel's predictions came to pass then people would know that a prophet had been in their midst (Ezek. 33:33). Zechariah and Daniel needed an angelic interpreter to explain to them the significance of their visions. In some cases predictions are clearer and more intelligible today than they were to the original recipients.

Even those who witnessed the fulfillment did not always comprehend what was taking place. The two men on the road to Emmaus had to be instructed regarding the significance of Jesus' death in the light of prophecy (Luke 24:27). John confesses to the lack of perception of the disciples regarding the significance of the triumphal entry: "These

---

81. Briggs, MP, p. 64.
82. Ibid., p. 65.

23

things understood not his disciples at the first; but when Jesus was glorified. then remembered they that these things were written of him . . ." (John 12:16).

Several factors account for the element of obscurity in Messianic prophecy:

1. Some predictions have not yet been fulfilled. Only at the second coming will all the details of these predictions become clear.

2. Some predictions may have been fulfilled, but the facts of history as they are now known do not permit verification of the fulfillment.

3. Some prophecies are dealing with sublime mysteries. Some, for example, deal with the dual nature of Messiah. Even doctrinal affirmations of the New Testament regarding the dual nature of Christ are not easy to understand.

4. Some predictions have been presented in the form of visions or dreams and consequently are couched in highly figurative language.

5. The Hebrew verb tense system obscures predictions. What is future is often represented as having already occurred. Thus, "He was wounded for our transgressions" is a prediction so certain of fulfillment that it can be described as an accomplished fact.

6. The fragmentary character of predictions results in emphases which must be correlated and harmonized. Rationalists delight in pointing to what they perceive to be contradictions among the prophets in their expectation. Because of the fragmentary character of Messianic predictions Jewish teachers expounded a dual Messiah theory. It was given to no prophet to paint the complete portrait of the Coming One. A prophet could not predict future events more clearly than he had been instructed to do. But even a rude sketch may reveal the likeness of a person even though a thousand minutiae which make up that person's countenance be wanting.

7. The absence of chronological perspective creates obscurity. The prophets often saw future events as one sees the stars in the night sky. The stars are millions of miles apart, but they appear to the observer to be contiguous. Thus in prophecy the fall of Assyria is blended with the coming of Messiah (Isa. 10-11). The redemption through Messiah is blended with redemption of Israel from exile (Isa. 40-46). Briggs describes this facet of prediction when he writes:

> The prophet stands as it were upon a lofty mountain. Far in the distance, beyond the range that bound the horizon of his generation, he sees the goal of the journey. But he cannot see all the hills and valleys, the rocks

and streams and the lesser mountain ranges which intervene between him and the predicted goal.[83]

Vos called this "foreshortening of the beyond-prospect."[84] Others refer to it as "prophetic telescoping."

Sometimes Messianic promises are missed because they occur in the midst of references to contemporary events. Partly because of a failure to recognize this principle some writers have charged that the prophets believed in the arrival of the Messianic kingdom in their own time.

Sometimes "telescoping" reverses two chronological elements. More often the prophet mentally leaps forward from his own day (or some near point in the future) to the glorious kingdom age. First and second advents are blended as if they were one. Jesus himself gave the clue to this in the way he read Isaiah 61:1-2 at the synagogue in Nazareth (Luke 4:18-21). He stopped his reading with the words "to proclaim the favorable year of the Lord" without adding the next phrase, "and the day of vengeance of our God," which applies only to his second coming.

8. Use of prophetic imagery has created misunderstandings. Messianic predictions often include *types*. A type is an historical person, place or object which was designed by God to foreshadow the future age. Zion, priests, Levites, feasts are projected into the Messianic age. Not only types, but also symbols and figures of speech abound in the Old Testament prediction. The prophets were poets and one must interpret them accordingly. Failure to recognize types and symbols in prophecy caused the Jews to reject their Messiah.

9. Lockyer[85] points to the paradoxes in Messianic prophecy which also create obscurity. The Messiah is Father of Eternity, yet a son born in time. He is chosen of God and elect, yet despised by men; born king of the Jews, yet rejected by them. He was to come from Bethlehem, Egypt, and Nazareth. He was David's son, yet at the same time David's Lord. He was the chief cornerstone, yet the rock of offense. He would be a priest, yet a king upon his throne. He would be pleasing to God, yet abhorred by his own nation; priceless, yet sold for thirty pieces of silver. He would be wounded and pierced through, yet not a bone of his body would be broken. He would be cut off, yet his days were to be prolonged.

---

83. Briggs, MP, p. 56.
84. Vos, BT, p. 311.
85. Lockyer, AMPB, p. 18.

10. Within Biblical prophecy there is a certain measure of intentional indefiniteness. Meyrick theorizes: "God never forces men to believe, but there is such a union of definiteness and vagueness in the prophecies as to enable those who are willing to discover the truth, while the willfully blind are not forcibly constrained to see it."[86]

Double Fulfillment

The theory of double fulfillment[87] holds that prophecy had two meanings: it meant one thing to the people who originally heard it, and also had a higher meaning as applied to the life of Christ. John Davison presents the classic defense of this concept. He regarded the predictions concerning the kingdom of David as a "conspicuous" and "unquestionable" example. Davison limits double fulfillment to the more distinguished monuments of prophecy, where the force and clearness of the description, and the adequate magnitude of the subjects, concur in giving simplicity to the combined view of them, and render the divided application at once necessary, rational, and perspicuous.[88]

A number of authorities in the field of hermeneutics, however, have warned about the dangers of this approach. Ramm states: "One of the most persistent hermeneutical sins is to put two interpretations on one passage of Scripture. . . ."[89] Terry adds: "If the Scripture has more than one meaning, it has no meaning at all."[90] Berkhof agrees: "It is absolutely foreign to the character of language that a word should have two, three, or even more significations in the same connection. If this were not so, all communication among men would be utterly impossible."[91]

The question of the multiple sense of prediction arises in connection with the New Testament interpretation of certain passages. When the apostolic understanding does not seem to square with the "natural" or "obvious" interpretation of the Old Testament passage some writers resort to the concept of double fulfillment. The options as they see them, are (1) to accept a double sense to the passage, or (2) to admit

---

86. Meyrick, SBD, III, 2596.

87. Other language amounting to the same thing: double reference, double meaning, manifold fulfillment, antitypical fulfillment.

88. Davison, DP, pp. 144ff.

89. Ramm, PBI, p. 87.

90. Terry, BH, p. 384.

91. Berkhof, PBI, p. 58.

that the New Testament writers were misappropriating the words of Scripture. A third alternative is, of course, possible *viz.*, that the prediction has but one sense, and the New Testament is the authoritative statement of what that sense is.

That the third alternative alone is correct is obvious from the following considerations:

1. Dual fulfillment is incompatible with objective interpretation.

2. In some cases the argument used by the apostolic writer excludes any possible dual meaning. Psalm 16, for example, is commonly regarded as having primary application to David and a "higher" application to Christ. Peter argues that David could not possibly have been referring to himself in Psalm 16 (Acts 2:29-31).

3. The larger Old Testament context does not lend support to the dual fulfillment theory. Regarding Psalm 2 and Isaiah 7:14, two passages often regarded as having a "higher fulfillment" in Christ, Terry writes:

> The language of Psalm 2 is not applicable to David or Solomon, or any other earthly ruler. . . . Isaiah 7:14 was fulfilled in the birth of Jesus Christ (Mt. 1:22), and no expositor has ever been able to prove a previous fulfillment.[92]

There can be no question that David and other Hebrew characters are used in Scripture as types of Messiah. This has contributed to the popularity of the double reference theory. It may be true that many prophecies were *applied* by the contemporaries of a prophet to their own circumstances, just as they may have been *applied* by subsequent generations to different circumstances. This in no way discounts the authoritative exegesis of the New Testament writers who declare those passages to have been fulfilled in the life and ministry of Jesus of Nazareth. One must distinguish between human application and divine intention. Only with the aid of the New Testament can the divine intention in many prophecies be ascertained.

There is no double sense to Hebrew prediction, no "succesive fulfillment." The prediction always has but one sense. But prediction grows out of temporal redemption and points toward eternal redemption of Messiah. It is part of a system of predictions in which the experience of redemption is advancing. This fact makes it inevitable that some of the elements of the predicted redemption would be realized in historical experiences before the ultimate goal of Messianic redemption was attained.

---

92. Terry, BH, p. 384.

Even though there is only one fulfillment for each prophecy, all Old Testament history prepared the way toward that Messianic fulfillment. Briggs states the case this way:

> As prediction is rising in successive stages to higher and broader and more extensive views of the Messianic redemption, the history of redemption is advancing with it towards the same end. Thus we ought to expect that the Messianic ideal should be realized in some of its phases ere the ideal itself is attained, and that the later predictions should base themselves on these partial realizations. But we should not be willing to acknowledge fulfillment in these historic and predictive approximations.[93]

Ideal or Precise Fulfillment?

Briggs sets forth the position of a number of authorities when he writes: "We are not to find exact and literal fulfillments in detail or in general, but the fulfillment is limited, as the prediction is limited, to the essential ideal contents of the prophecy."[94] With this Terry agrees. He pleads for "not literal but substantial fulfillment of the great ideas of prophecy."[95] Riehm goes still further: "We do not suppose the Spirit to have in some exceptional way concretely envisaged to the prophets certain individual historical facts of the New Testament fulfillment. . . . Revelation refuses to be magical."[96]

It is true that Old Testament prediction clothes and represents that which is to come in the scenery and language familiar to it in the present and in the past. The most suitable events, persons, and objects of the past and present are projected into the future. "Hence the type or symbol lies at the basis of all genuine prediction."[97] Hebrew predictive prophecy, in its view of redemption in the future, springs from the past and present experience of redemption.[98]

A number of questions are raised by the assertion that precise agreement between the event and the prediction is unimportant. Why did the apostles show the coincidences of the prophecy with its fulfillment in the life of Christ? Why did Jesus explain to his disciples after his resurrection the Old Testament Scriptures which pertained to him?

---

93. Briggs, MP, p. 66.
94. Ibid., p. 45.
95. Terry, BH, p. 337.
96. Riehm, MP, p. 310.
97. Briggs, MP, p. 45.
98. Ibid., p. 62.

And why did Jesus arrange his entry into Jerusalem in such a way as to bring about the coincidence of the prophecy and the event?[99]

Literal vs. Figurative

A modern school of interpretation insists that all prophecies must be interpreted literally. Those for which no literal fulfillment is attested are said to relate to events yet future. This would include especially predictions of the Messianic kingdom. Alexander McCaul presses for consistency in interpretation. One cannot prove, McCaul says, that Jesus is Messiah by the literal method, and evade the difficulties by adoption of the figurative method. Carry through the figurative exposition and there is no suffering Messiah; carry through the literal and a large portion of prophecies are not yet fulfilled. McCaul writes:

> To receive those prophecies which foretell Messiah's humiliation and atoning death in their plain and literal sense, and to seek to allegorize those which deal with His glorious reign on earth and over restored and blessed Israel, is to place an insurmountable stumblingblock before every Jew of common sense, and to hold up prophecy to the scorn of the infidel.[100]

A few observations regarding this very popular approach to Old Testament interpretation are in order:

1. How else could Jesus of Nazareth be verified as Israel's Messiah other than through precise and "literal," observable, demonstrable fulfillment of Old Testament predictions? One or two predictions which seemed to be fulfilled in his life could be brushed aside as coincidental. But as examples of predictions fulfilled in his life are multiplied, the law of probability would favor his Messianic claims. Having reached that point where probability approaches certainty, no harm is done to the Christian apologetic to recognize that certain predictions were not fulfilled in a physical, mundane, earthly way.

2. A prophecy may be fulfilled literally but not physically or materially. There is a dimension to reality which is not physical and consequently must be perceived by faith and not sensory perception.

3. If one takes the New Testament statements regarding the kingdom and church literally, he is forced to interpret the Old Testament predictions spiritually. For example, if the church is literally the Israel of God, then one must always reckon with the possibility that prophecies pertaining to Israel are fulfilled in the church. If Christians have literally

---

99. Questions raised by Hengstenberg, COT, p. 11.
100. Cited in Baron, RMG, p. 81.

come to Mt. Zion (Heb. 12:22) then one must reckon with the possibility that prophecies pertaining to Mt. Zion are fulfilled in the New Testament age. If this be allegorizing, so be it. The spiritual realities of the present glorious dispensation compel the Christian interpreter to view the Messianic predictions regarding Judah, Israel, Jerusalem, Mt. Zion, the land of Canaan, etc. as fulfilled in the church of Christ.

4. Whether certain prophecies are "allegorized" (interpreted spiritually) or projected into the future for literal fulfillment at the second coming, the net result in respect to Jewish evangelism is the same. In either case, the Jewish prospect is confronted with a body of prediction which cannot be demonstrated to have been fulfilled materially or physically by Christ or the church. It takes no greater faith to believe that those predictions are fulfilled in the spiritual dimension, than to believe that they will be fulfilled in the physical dimension in some future age.

5. Inspired New Testament writers seem to interpret large chunks of Old Testament prophecy spiritually.

6. The presence of figurative language in the Bible is usually self-evident as demonstrated by the nature of the subject or the nature of the context. The figurative style which is so characteristic of prophecy is explained by the visionary mode of revelation.

7. It is important to realize that most Old Testament prophecy is cast in the poetic form. "Poetic phraseology may thus take the form of embellishment, or hyperbole, in which more is said than is literally meant."[101]

8. Divine revelation comes in a specific historical context. "The prophet spoke of future glory in terms of his own society and experience."[102] For this reason some speak of "fulfillment by equivalents"[103] or "cultural reinterpretation." Assyria, Moab, Edom are depicted as playing a significant role in the Messianic age. Yet these nations were extinct long before the birth of Christ. These nations must then represent all enemies of God's people in the Messianic age.[104]

---

101. Payne, EBP, p. 18.
102. Ramm, PBI, p. 157.
103. Mickelsen, IB, p. 296.
104. It will not do to argue that *Assyria* refers to the geographical area once occupied by the Assyrians, for the passages refer to the Edomites, the Moabites, and the Assyrians as well as their lands.

Progressive Fulfillment[105]

Some predictions are stated in very general terms. Genesis 3:15 depicts the defeat of Satan, the crushing of the head of the Serpent. The fulfillment commenced with the resurrection and ascension (John 12:31-32; Rev. 12:5, 10), is continued in the church (Rom. 16:20), and will culminate in the abyss and lake of fire (Rev. 20:3, 10). Progressive fulfillment should be distinguished from (1) reapplications of general principles which might be stated in a prophecy; and (2) cumulative fulfillment, which is Beecher's way of affirming that predictions had many fulfillments before the ultimate Messianic fulfillment.[106] Progressive fulfillment is comparatively rare in Scripture.[107]

PROGRESSIVE FULFILLMENT ILLUSTRATED			
Single Focus:	"He shall crush your head" (Imperfect = continuous)		Ultimate Defeat of Satan
Progressive Fulfillment	In His Resurrection Rev. 12:5, 10 John 12:31-32	Through His Church Rom. 16:20	At His Coming Rev. 20:3, 10
	Commences	Continues	Culminates
PERIOD OF THE CRUSHING OF SERPENT			

The Argument From Messianic Prophecy

The prediction of future events, followed by the accomplishment of these predictions, has always been one of the divine methods of authenticating divine revelation. Perhaps some have unduly magnified the evidence of supposed fulfillment. But the real question is, Are there any real fulfillments? One genuine fulfillment of a genuine prediction would be sufficient to establish the validity of the Christian system.

The agreement between prophecy and the history of Jesus is not a forced one, but so obvious that it lies on the very surface, and is

---

105. Payne (EBP, p. 135) prefers the terminology "developmental fulfillment."
106. Beecher, PP, p. 130.
107. Payne (EBP, p. 136) sees only nine genuine examples in the whole of Old Testament prediction.

perceivable even by the simplest. "If the exercise of any ingenuity be required it is altogether on the part of those who try to conceal it."[108]

Not one Messianic prophecy has remained unchallenged. Rationalists seek to break the force of the argument for supernaturalism by attempting to eliminate the predictive element from the Old Testament. Jewish apologists attempt to break the force of the application to Jesus of Nazareth.

Jesus and the Jews

That the Jewish leaders of the first century were hostile toward Jesus of Nazareth is made clear on almost every page of the Gospels. Why did the majority of Jews of the first century reject the claims of Jesus? Why do they continue to reject him? Of course many Jews have embraced the Messianic claims of the Nazarene. But the majority has now rejected him, and for the following reasons:

1. Jesus' attitude toward the oral law caused many to stumble. Jewish sources blame Jesus for all sorts of crimes but never for claiming that he was Messiah.[109] Some use this negative evidence to set aside the clear claims of Jesus to be the long-awaited One. The claim to Messiahship, however, was never regarded as a crime. A man became a "false Messiah" only after he had failed. Jesus' conflict with the Pharisees was not because of the Messianic overtones in his message but because of his attitude toward the oral law.[110] A Messiah who treated the oral law lightly could be only a false Messiah in their estimation.[111]

2. Jews of the first century were unable to reconcile Jesus' claims to a divine nature with the contention of Deuteronomy 6:4, "Hear, O Israel, the Lord our God is one Lord." The trinitarian emphasis has been a stumblingblock to the Jews.

3. Jews have been unable to reconcile the humble life-style of Jesus, his sufferings and ignominious death, with the promises of a glorious and powerful Ruler. The cross has been to them a major stumblingblock.

---

108. Baron, RMG, p. 50.

109. Kramer, cited by Jocz, ZPBE, IV, 203.

110. Jesus did not oppose the written law in part or in whole. He did not seek to abrogate it or to substitute for it. That was not necessary. The kingdom age—the world to come—was at hand in which there would be no need for the law. The contemporaries of Jesus would have shared this view. Nid. 61b states: "All commandments are abolished in the world to come."

111. Jocz, ZPBE, IV, 203.

4. The predominating aspect under which prophecy spoke of the expected Messiah was that of a King coming for the purpose of occupying the throne of David. The Jews ask, Where are the signs of his royal state and dignity? Is it not true that many evangelical Christians, comparing what was predicted with what has been done, firmly maintain that Jesus has not yet taken possession of the throne promised to him?[112]

The alleged want of a kingdom lies across the threshold, a stumbling-block to the acknowledgment of Jesus as true Messiah. The Christian contends that the kingdom prophecies did not fail of fulfillment. The kingdom over which Jesus rules is not of this world. He does indeed sit on David's throne, because David's throne is in reality God's throne.

Jesus did not need to display the outward trappings of kingship in order to legitimately claim possession of David's kingdom any more than he needed a material Temple in which to conduct his priestly ministry. Why should the throne and kingdom be any more physical than the Temple? He proved that he possessed kingly authority far in excess to that which David or Solomon possessed "in every authoritative word He uttered, every work of deliverance He performed, every judgment He pronounced, every act of mercy and forgiveness He dispensed, and the resistless control He wielded over the elements of nature, and the realm of the dead."[113] These signs of royalty during his earthly stay, great as they were, are only tokens of the power which David himself foresaw when he saw him seated at the right hand of the Father.

5. Jews have been unable to accept the Christian doctrine of two advents of Messiah. As Jews see it, Isaiah 11 warrants no distinction in point of time between the clearly defined occurrences which were to mark Messiah's advent. Universal peace and the ingathering of Israel and Judah were to inaugurate, not result from, Messiah's reign.

History of the Argument

1. Jesus used the argument based on the fulfillment of Old Testament prophecy. At Bethlehem the Christ of prophecy became the Christ of history, and through his brief career he was forever laying hold on Old Testament predictions and relating them to himself.

---

112. Commenting on this regrettable fact Fairbairn (IP, 234) says: "The adversaries here have their quiver filled for them by the hands of friends."

113. Ibid., p. 236.

Search the Scriptures, for in them you think you have eternal life; and these are they which testify of me.

It is written in the prophets, And they shall be all taught of God. Every man therefore that has heard, and has learned of the Father, comes unto me.

Then he said unto them, O fools, and slow of heart to believe all that the prophets have spoken. Ought not Christ to have suffered these things, and to enter into glory? And beginning at Moses and all the prophets, he expounded unto them in all the Scriptures the things concerning himself (John 5:39; 6:45; Lk. 24:25-27).

In the latter passage Jesus is virtually claiming that Old Testament theology has a unifying theme, *viz.*, the witness of all parts of Scripture to him.[114]

2. The apostles used Old Testament prophecy to prove that Jesus was the Messiah. Consider these words of Peter:

Men and brethren, this Scripture must needs have been fulfilled, which the Holy Spirit by the mouth of David spoke before concerning Judas. . . . But this is that which was spoken by the prophet Joel. . . . for David speaks concerning him. . . . He seeing this before spoke of the resurrection of Christ. . . . But those things, which God before had shown by the mouth of all his prophets, that Christ should suffer, he has so fulfilled. . . . Yes, and all the prophets from Samuel and those that followed after, as many as have spoken, have likewise foretold these days (Acts 1:16; 2:16, 25, 31; 3:18, 24).

Matthew, it is thought, wrote his Gospel for the Jewish reader. Twenty-one prophecies are cited in this Gospel which were fulfilled in circumstances surrounding the life of Christ. Matthew himself quotes eleven passages to point out fulfillment using such introductory formulas as "That it might be fulfilled which was spoken through the prophet" (8 times), or "then was fulfilled that which was spoken by the prophet" (2 times).

Space does not permit analysis of all the apostles in their use of the argument from prophecy. Suffice it to say that the range of citation is amazing. Isaiah is cited between fifty and sixty times in the New Testament, and Psalms at least seventy, frequently as predictive. Of the prophets, only Obadiah, Nahum, Zephaniah and Ezekiel were not directly cited. It is strange, however, that some of the greatest Messianic predictions (e.g., Isa. 9:5f.; Jer. 23:5, 6; Zech. 6:12, 13) are not quoted by New Testament writers.

---

114. Consider also Matt. 26:54; Mark 9:12; Luke 18:31-33; 22:37; John 5:46.

3. The Church Fathers relied upon the argument from fulfilled prophecy. One of the earliest, the so-called Epistle of Barnabas (A.D. 71-120), sets the trend among the Fathers. Justin's dialogue with the Jew Trypho (before A.D. 163) exhibits a more extensive and systematic treatment of Old Testament prophecy. Justin was at a disadvantage in this discussion in not knowing Hebrew. Origen (d. A.D. 254), however, was better equipped. His eighth book against Celsus is filled with Old Testament citation. Unfortunately Origen was given to fanciful and arbitrary allegorization. The Antiochian school probably went too far in the opposite direction. Direct Messianic prophecies (e.g., Micah 5:1ff.) were applied to leading figures before Christ. These writers saw, however, a "higher fulfillment" in Christ. Theodore of Mopsuestia (d. A.D. 428) was a leader in this school of interpretation.

Liberal writers find only indistinct longings, expressions of the need of redemption such as one might find among the heathen. But Christ, the apostles, and the Church Fathers all believed that genuine predictions concerning Christ existed in the Old Testament.

Proof of Jesus' Messiahship

The intent of this entire study is to demonstrate the Messiahship of Jesus. Here by way of introduction, and unsupported by detailed exegesis, is the broad outline of the argument for the Messiahship of Jesus of Nazareth.[115]

1. Messianic prophecy necessitates that Messiah has already come. Proof for this proposition comes from three prophecies:

a) "The scepter shall not depart from Judah, nor a ruler's staff from between his feet until Shiloh come; and to him shall be the submission of peoples" (Gen. 49:10).

The date here fixed for the coming of Shiloh was not to exceed the time that the descendants of Judah were to continue as a united people, that should be governed by their own laws, and should have their own judges from among their brethren. Such was the case up to A.D. 70, but not since. The scepter (legislative and ruling power) has departed from Judah. For centuries that tribe has been broken up scattered, lost. The conclusion is irresistible: Messiah must have long since come!

---

115. Following McClintock and Strong, CBTEL, VI, 140 and Kitto, CBL, II, 331ff.

b) . . . from the going forth of a word to restore and to build Jerusalem unto Messiah-Prince shall be seven and sixty-two sevens (Dan. 9:25).

In the Talmud there is this tradition from earlier times: "In Daniel is delivered to us the end of the Messiah," i.e., the term in which he ought to come. Daniel's sixty-nine heptads (483 years) must have long since elapsed, whether the commencement of the period is dated to the decree of Cyrus (Ezra 1:1, 2), Darius (Ezra 6:8), or Artaxerxes (Ezra 7:11).

c) I will shake all the nations, and the Desire of all Nations shall come. . . . Greater shall be the glory of this latter house than the former (Hag. 2:7-9).

The glory here is most likely a reference to the Messiah, for in physical glory the second Temple was far inferior to the first. The symbols and tokens of God's special presence were also missing in the second Temple. That the Desire of Nations here is Messiah is supported by Malachi 3:1 where he comes suddenly to his Temple. The Messiah, then, must enter the second Temple. But that Temple has been destroyed for almost two thousand years.[116]

By A.D. 70 every mark that denoted the time of the coming of Messiah in the flesh was erased and could never be renewed.[117] Many Jews today will frankly admit that the time when their Messiah ought to have appeared according to the prophecies is long since past and they attribute the delay in his coming to national sinfulness.[118]

2. That Jesus of Nazareth is the Messiah is indicated by the following facts:

a) He was of the right lineage. He was of the tribe of Judah, of the family of Jesse, and of the house of David. No Messianic pretender today could positively establish his lineage. The prophecy: Mic. 5:2; Gen. 49:10; Isa. 11:10; Jer. 23:5. The fulfillment: Luke 1:27, 69; Matt. 1:1.

b) He appeared at the right time. He commenced his public ministry in the days of the Roman empire, the second Temple, while Judah as the nation of Judea was still intact. This fell within the range of the

---

116. The force of this passage is not greatly reduced even if "desire" here is not taken to refer to Messiah personally. In that case, the prophecy looks forward to a glorification of the second Temple which cannot be looked for under any "Messiah" yet to appear.

117. Keith, ETCR, p. 18.

118. Ibid., p. 19.

seventy heptads announced by Daniel. The prophecy: Dan. 2:44; 9:24, 25; Hag. 2:7-9; Gen. 49:10. Fulfillment: John 18:20; Luke 3:1ff.

c) He appeared with the right credentials. He was able to perform miracles (Isa. 35:5, 6; Matt. 11:4, 5). He rose from the dead (Ps. 16:10, 11; Acts 2:25ff.).

d) His appearance provoked the predicted response. He was despised, rejected, and slain. (Ps. 22; Isa. 53). "The very man who betrayed him, the price for which he was sold, the indignities he was to receive in his last moments, the parting of his garments, and his last words were all foretold of the Messiah, and accomplished in Jesus."[119]

The Law of Probability

Pierson[120] finds over three hundred predictions about the Messiah in the Old Testament. According to the law of compound probability the chance of their coming true is represented by a fraction whose numerator is one, and the denominator eighty-four followed by nearly one hundred ciphers. According to Pierson, one might almost as well expect by accident to dip up any one particular drop out of the ocean as to expect so many prophetic rays to converge by chance upon one man, in one place, at one time.

---

119. McClintock and Strong, CBTEL, p. 141.
120. Pierson, *God's Living Oracles* cited by Lockyer, AMPB, p. 17.

Chapter Two

MESSIANIC FOREGLEAMS

The several centuries between creation and the call of Abram (Gen. 12) are divided by the Flood into (1) the Antediluvian and (2) the Postdiluvian periods. Nothing like precision dating is possible for these early periods. Little is known about the Antediluvian period (Gen. 1-6) and even less about the Postdiluvian age (Gen. 9-11). Nonetheless, from these earliest days two prophecies have been preserved which were, it would appear, the fountainhead of Messianic hope. These prophecies are (1) the protevangelium in Genesis 3:15 and (2) the blessing on Shem in Genesis 9:26, 27.

Prophecy No. 1

THE GOSPEL IN THE GARDEN

Genesis 3:15

Genesis 3:15, the first promise of the Bible, is the only Messianic prophecy to survive from the Antediluvian period. This is the most general and at the same time the most comprehensive foregleam of the Messiah. All subsequent Messianic promises are but amplifications of that which is implicit here. The verse is commonly called the *protevangelium* (first Gospel). Here in embryo state is the whole of God's program for the human race.

Genesis 3:15 is the seed from which the Old Testament promise of a coming Savior grew like a mighty tree. Here is the fountainhead of the Messianic stream which over the centuries would swell to a mighty river fed by an ever increasing number of conceptual tributaries. Here is the mother prophecy which gave birth to all the rest. Herein is "the germ of promise which unfolds in the history of redemption."[1] The passage stands sphinx-like at the entrance of the Temple of sacred history. The solution to the riddle of the sphinx begins to emerge in Old Testament literature; but it is fully solved only in Jesus of Nazareth.

That Genesis 3:15 should be interpreted Messianically is supported by the following points:

1. The opinion of the Church Fathers is all but unanimous in favor of the Messianic view.[2]

---

1. Briggs, MP, p. 73.
2. Several Fathers, however, regard Eve as typical of the virgin Mary. See Maas, CTP, I, 207.

2. The Jerusalem Targum and the Targum of Jonathan speak of a healing from the bite of the Serpent "in the days of King Messiah."

3. The Mishnah (Sotah 9.15) introduced the phrase "in the footsteps (heels) of Messiah" to designate the nearness of the advent. This terminology, borrowed from Psalm 89:51, may rest ultimately on Genesis 3:15.

4. The Septuagint version translated the verse in such a way as to underscore its Messianic implications.[3]

5. Paul's statement, "The God of peace shall bruise Satan under your feet shortly" (Rom. 16:20) is undoubtedly based on Genesis 3:15.

Translation of Genesis 3:15

An enmity I will put between you and the woman, and between your seed and her seed; he shall crush you with respect to the head, and you shall crush him with respect to the heel.

Discussion

It is ironic that the first announcement of the Gospel occurs within the context of a curse of Satan. A gleam of grace shines through the gloom of divine retribution. That old satanic Serpent is cursed above all animals upon the face of the earth (v. 14). The crawling on the belly and eating dust are metaphors signifying the deepest humiliation.

Some scholars in their comments on Genesis 3:15 reveal the absurdity of their antisupernatural bias. Gunkel sees the verse as being nothing more than the explanation of why men hate snakes. Skinner in the same vein sees here only the promise that men will be victorious over snakes. Faithful Jewish and Christian commentators, however, have seen in this verse the most profound significance. Here God is unfolding the various stages in the conflict of the ages. Three levels of battle can be distinguished.

A. *Level One: The Personal Battle.* God declares: *Enmity I will put between you* (Satan) *and the woman.* The direct object (*enmity*) stands first in the Hebrew sentence for emphasis. The term is never used in relation to dumb beasts.[4] The verse, therefore, is not merely a primitive tale designed to speculate about the origin of the dislike most people feel toward reptiles. God is speaking here of hostility—active hatred—

---

3. R. A. Martin, "The Earliest Messianic Interpretation of Genesis 3:15," *Journal of Biblical Literature* 84 (1965): 427.

4. Leupold, EG, p. 164.

between two intelligent beings, satanic Serpent and Eve. Dewart comments:

> It is absurd to suppose that these words of blame, inflicting punishment upon the serpent, were addressed to an irrational animal, and not to an intelligent, accountable being.[5]

It was God himself who placed this enmity in the heart of the woman. Before her sin she had listened sympathetically to satanic Serpent and had placed her confidence in him. Now her attitude had changed. She knew by personal experience the shame, guilt, and fear that he had already brought upon her. Now she recognized Satan as her malevolent enemy who was determined to destroy her. She would need help in battling him in the future, and God promised to give her that help. He would help her hate Satan.[6] From this time on she would fight determinedly against every temptation.

By disposition, attitude and perhaps by petition Eve had made clear her desire to resist the encroachments of satanic Satan. In this promise God responded to her desire. He will not force anyone to hate Satan; but he will give this enmity to those who ask him for it.

B. Level Two: The Posterity Battle. On level two Genesis 3:15 predicts a perpetual warfare between serpent-kind and mankind. *Enmity I will put between your* (Satan's) *seed and her seed.*

In the word seed there is marvelous prophetic ambiguity. The term sometimes is a collective noun embracing a whole collection of peoples. In other cases *seed* refers to a single individual (e.g., Gen. 4:25; 15:3). The term usually refers to physical posterity; but on numerous occasions the term is used for one's spiritual or moral descendants.[7] In what sense is the term *seed* used in Genesis 3:15?

Satan's seed certainly embraces evil men—those who consistently choose to do the bidding of that old Serpent. Probably the evil spirits are also included in serpent-kind.

Physically speaking, all human beings (except Adam) would be the seed of woman. But on level two the term *seed* is a limited collective embracing all those in the world who share Eve's God-given enmity against satanic Serpent.[8] The term is used in its spiritual and moral

---

5. Dewart, JMPF, pp. 90-91.

6. It is obvious that God does not place enmity in the heart of Satan for the woman, for Satan already had manifested his hatred toward her.

7. See Isa. 1:4; 57:4; Matt. 3:7.

8. Others see the *seed of woman* on level two as an unlimited collective. The idea would then be that through Christ all men obtain the power to successfully combat Satan though most never avail themselves of it.

sense rather than in its physical sense. All bad men are excluded because they are the seed of Satan.

On level two Genesis 3:15 sets forth that the personal warfare between Eve and Satan will be perpetuated in the spiritual/moral progeny of the two rivals. As in any warfare, sometimes there are defections from one side to the other. By God's gracious plan of redemption any individual who is among the seed of Satan may find forgiveness and thereafter may request God's enmity against Satankind. By the same token, sometimes individuals among the seed of woman surrender their enmity toward Satan and begin to follow the dictates of the master deceiver. The following diagram illustrates the two directions which individuals travel in relationship to the two groups here denominated *seed of Satan* and *seed of woman.*

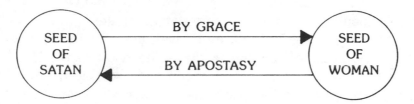

C. *Level Three: The Paramount Battle.* Genesis 3:15 points to the final outcome of the battle between the seed of Satan and the seed of woman. The outcome of the contest is settled by the great champions of the respective antagonistic groups. *He[9] will crush you as to the head, and you will crush him as to the heel.*

Here satanic Serpent is singled out as one of the final combatants in the conflict of the ages. The pronoun *you* emphasized two things: (1) the individuality of this combatant; and (2) the fact that the Serpent of the original temptation and the Serpent of the final showdown are one and the same.

Since the malevolent combatant is a solitary personality, it is most likely that his opponent on level three should also be regarded as an individual—some great champion from among the seed of woman mentioned on level two. It is true that the masculine singular pronoun *he* refers back to the word *seed* which is used in a collective sense. Yet the last two clauses of Genesis 3:15 give the impression that a *personal* combat and a *personal* victory are in view. The *he* and *him*

---

9. The rendering of the Vulgate, *she,* must be rejected. It is true that in the Pentateuch often no distinction is made between masculine and feminine. The suffix *nu* on the last verb, however, makes the masculine rendering of the pronoun imperative.

in these two clauses refer to an individual son of woman who becomes the ultimate victor over the satanic Serpent.

A terrible battle between the satanic Serpent and the Savior is implied in this verse. The outcome of that battle, however, was not in doubt. The promised Savior would crush (*shuph*)[10] the head of satanic Serpent. The Hebrew construction of this clause stresses the violent nature of this crushing.[11] A blow to the head of satanic Serpent would be a mortal blow. That blow was administered by Jesus Christ when he died on the cross and subsequently rose victoriously over death.

Jesus said that the Comforter would convict the world of judgment "because the prince of the world is judged" (John 16:11). Shortly before offering himself as a sacrifice for the sin of the world Jesus said, "Now is the judgment of this world; now shall the prince of this world be cast down" (John 12:31). The antagonism between Christ and satanic Serpent is indicated in the statement Jesus made in John 14:30 "Hereafter I will not talk much with you; for the prince of this world comes, and has nothing in me." The reign of the Devil came to an end in Christ's death, resurrection and ascension: "And having spoiled principalities and powers, he made a show of them openly triumphing over them in it" (Col. 2:15). It was, declares the Apostle John, "for this purpose that the Son of God was manifested, that he might destroy the works of the devil" (I John 3:8).

Satanic Serpent would not go down without a bitter struggle. He would *crush the heel* of the Savior. As a reptile writhes and twists and sinks his fangs into his adversary, so satanic Serpent tries to defend himself against the deadly tread of mankind's Savior. Here the important point is that the victory over satanic Serpent would be accompanied by, if not accomplished through, the suffering of the Savior.

Many examples can be cited from the Gospel records where Satan wounded, or at least attempted to wound, the heel of Christ. The attempt to slay the infant Christ child was a satanically inspired effort to eliminate the Savior at the outset of his mission. In the wilderness following his baptism Jesus was put to the test by the insidious temptations of the Devil. In Nazareth a mob attempted to stone the Savior (John 8:59). Satan engineered the betrayal of Christ by Judas (John 13:27). The scourging, the crown of thorns, the nails, and the cross were, at the outset, evidence of the bruising of Christ's heel.

---

10. *Shuph* does not mean "lie in wait" as it is rendered in the Septuagint version.
11. A double accusative after a verb always indicates violent action.

The promised Savior is said to be *the seed of woman.* It would perhaps be going too far to say this is a prophecy of the virgin birth. Yet the prophecy does say he would be born of *woman.* Genesis 3:15 is consistent with the later prediction (Isa. 7:14) that Messiah would be born of a virgin. Of what woman the Messiah would be born is left open. No doubt from creation onward Satan waited in constant dread of his confrontation with this conqueror from the seed of woman.

Throughout the long centuries of the Antediluvian period Genesis 3:15 was the only star of hope. That men accepted and clung to this acorn of promise is indicated by the following factors:

1. Adam named his wife Eve (*chavvah*) because she was to be the mother of all subsequent human-kind. In so doing Adam is expressing confidence that physical death would not snatch away the woman until she had at least commenced the birth chain which would culminate in the Savior.

2. When the first child was born Eve named him Cain (*qayin*) because she had acquired him with the help of the Lord.[12] Did Eve expect this first son to be the Savior? If so, she was to be disappointed, for after a few years it became obvious that Cain was of the seed of Satan (I John 3:12).

3. In the days of Enosh the grandson of Adam "men began to call on the name of Yahweh" (Gen. 4:26). The name Yahweh signifies God in the role of redeemer or savior. To call upon the Lord is generally understood to refer to public worship. This public worship of God as redeemer suggests that at least among the descendants of Seth the promise of coming salvation was very much alive. They were worshiping the God of promised salvation.

4. The translation of Enoch so that he did not see death (Heb. 11:5) was a token graciously bestowed upon early believers. The spiritually perceptive would see in this miracle more than a hint that ultimately death would be conquered. It seems that the crushing of satanic Serpent and the conquest of death became conceptually linked (cf. Heb. 2:14).

5. Lamech the ninth from Adam seems to have believed in the promise. He named his son *Noah* ("breathing out, rest") and said as he did so: "This child shall comfort us[13] from our labor and from the toil of our hands because of the ground Yahweh has cursed." The comfort expected by Noah was one of deeds, not words. Later in

---

12. Literally, *I have acquired a man with the LORD.*
13. *Piel* of *nacham,* to rest.

the Old Testament the pregnant concept *comfort* sums up all that is anticipated of God in the Messianic redemption. Yahweh is comforter (Isa. 49:13; 52:9); the Messianic Servant of Isaiah 61:2 brings comfort. Noah is a forerunner of the Comforter anticipated by the Antediluvian patriarchs. "Comforter" was an old Jewish name for the Messiah. By implication Jesus appropriated the term Comforter to himself when he said, "I will send you *another* Comforter (John 14:16).

Prophecy No. 2

GOD IN THE TENTS OF SHEM

Genesis 9:26-27

In the judgment of most Old Testament scholars, it is impossible to compute the time lapse between the expulsion from the garden and the Deluge. If the genealogies of Genesis 5 are meant to be taken consecutively—and that is a big *if*—the *minimum* time lapse between Creation and the Flood would be 1656 years. Probably the time lapse was much greater.

Noah lived 350 years after the Flood (9:28). The second Messianic promise comes at the very end of Noah's life. That would mean that *at least* 2006 years elapsed between the first and second Messianic predictions in the Bible.

Genesis 9:18-24 relates the sad story of the second fall of the race—Noah's drunkenness and Ham's parental disrespect. Most commentators assume that Noah's prophecy regarding his sons followed immediately Noah's return to sobriety. Often in Scripture, however, lengthy time gaps appear without any formal notice of the passage of time. What follows in 9:25-27 gives every indication of being Noah's last words—his patriarchal pronouncement—regarding the fate of his descendants. Since Noah lived 350 years after the Flood, there may have been a considerable time gap between the transgression of Ham and Noah's prophetic pronouncements. The parallel between these words of Noah and the last words of Jacob (Gen. 49) are striking. Jacob waited many years before ever condeming Reuben, Simeon, and Levi for the sins by which they had shown disrespect for their father. On his deathbed, however, Jacob strongly rebuked these sons for their crimes.

Noah's last words contain a triple prophecy regarding Canaan, Shem and Japheth. Space does not permit a discussion of the vexing question of why Noah leaves Ham out of his prophecy and curses instead Canaan. It is, however, important to note the structure of Noah's discourse:

A. Three Curses on Canaan

　　1. A servant of servants to his brethren (v. 25).
　　2. Canaan shall be his (Shem's) servant (v. 26)
　　3. Canaan shall be his (Japheth's) servant (v. 27).

B. Two Blessings on Shem

　　1. Blessed be the Lord God of Shem (v. 26).
　　2. He shall dwell in the tents of Shem (v. 27).

C. One Blessing on Japheth: God shall enlarge Japheth (v. 27).

Translation of Genesis 9:26, 27

(26) And he said, Blessed be the LORD, the God of Shem, and Canaan shall be a servant to him. (27) God shall enlarge Japheth, and he shall lodge in the tents of Shem, and Canaan shall be a servant to him.

Discussion

Briggs is certainly correct when he identifies Shem as "the central figure of the prophecy."[14] Presumptive evidence in favor of a Messianic interpretation of Genesis 9:26, 27 is found in the Messianic revelations connected with other Old Testament mediators, *viz.*, Adam, Abraham and Moses.

Yahweh, the God of redemption, is the God of Shem (v. 26). The implication here is that redemptive blessing and salvation would come through the line of Shem. Noah pronounces a curse on Canaan and he blesses Japtheth; but he blesses *the God* of Shem. Salvation ultimately is of God alone, and he alone deserves the praise!

Let him dwell in the tents of Shem (v. 27). This clause is somewhat ambiguous because the antecedent of the pronoun is not clear. Is it Japheth who is to dwell in the tents of Shem? or is it God who dwells there? Grammatically either of these interpretations is possible.

The view that Japheth is to dwell in the tents of Shem has much to commend it.[15] It is best, however, to regard *God* as the subject of

---

14. Briggs, MP, p. 81. He refers to Canaan as the "dark background" and to Japheth as the "distant perspective" of this prophecy.

15. This view is developed by Delitzsch.

the clause.[16] This, then, would be a second blessing on Shem. In the previous verse Yahweh is called the God of Shem. It is altogether proper that the God of Shem should be depicted dwelling in the tents of Shem. God is the portion of the Shemites; they were those entrusted with preserving the knowledge of the true God in primeval times.

In Genesis 9:27 the central idea is that of the advent of God. Here is the seed of the doctrine of the incarnation. Contentwise, the second Messianic promise is at the opposite pole from the seed of woman in Genesis 3:15. The former passage stresses the humanity of the Redeemer; the present passage speaks in terms of a day when God himself would come to identify with his people.

During the long centuries of the Postdiluvian era the saints of god had two basic promises to sustain their faith: (1) a human deliverer would come to crush the head of satanic Serpent (Gen. 3:15); and (2) God himself would come to dwell in the tents of Shem (Gen. 9:27). The Shemites were the chosen race through which God would make his entrance into the world. Later prophets would take up these two strands of Messianic expectation, develop them, first separately, and then weave them into the tapestry of divine truth.

MESSIANIC DEVELOPMENT IN GENESIS

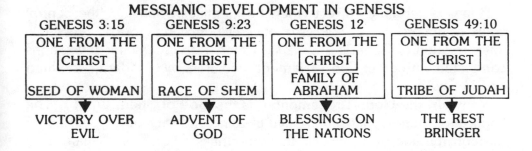

GENESIS 3:15	GENESIS 9:23	GENESIS 12	GENESIS 49:10
ONE FROM THE	ONE FROM THE	ONE FROM THE	ONE FROM THE
CHRIST	CHRIST	CHRIST	CHRIST
		FAMILY OF	
SEED OF WOMAN	RACE OF SHEM	ABRAHAM	TRIBE OF JUDAH
VICTORY OVER EVIL	ADVENT OF GOD	BLESSINGS ON THE NATIONS	THE REST BRINGER

---

16. Briggs (MP, pp. 82-83) gives a lengthy argument for this view.

Chapter Three

THE CHOSEN LINE

About the year 2092 B.C. God initiated a new stage in the drama of redemption. God called Abram to leave his hometown of Ur of Chaldees to embark upon a pilgrimage in search of that city whose maker and builder was God (Heb. 11:10). No one can precisely compute the time lapse between the Flood and this call of Abram. If there are no gaps in the genealogy of Genesis 11, the minimum figure between these two events would be 427 years.

In a cluster of predictions during the Patriarchal era God defined clearly the chosen line through which Messianic blessing would come into the world. It becomes clear in Genesis 12-28 that the channel of blessing would be Abraham, Isaac and Jacob. Toward the end of the Patriarchal period Jacob singled out Judah as the chosen one among his twelve sons.

Prophecy No. 3

THE PATRIARCHAL PROMISE

Genesis 12:3

The Patriarchal promises were enunciated on six occasions to Abraham.[1] Twice those promises were given to Isaac,[2] and twice to his son Jacob.[3] To the seven promise statements[4] made to Abram in Haran, an eighth[5] was added after he had entered the land of Canaan. This man of God was to receive an eightfold blessing for his faith and obedience. The original promises of Genesis 12 underwent development and amplification during the 215 years of Patriarchal wandering. The promises were sharpened and clarified as subsequent revelations were received.

The seventh of the eight promises made to Abraham has Messianic implications. Both the Church Fathers and Jewish Rabbis so interpreted it. The New Testament specifically quotes the seventh promise and regards it as embracing the blessings available in Christ Jesus.

---

1. Gen. 12:1-3, 7; 13:14-18; 15:4, 5, 13-18; 17:1-8; 18:17-19; 22:15-18.
2. Gen. 26:4, 23-24.
3. Gen. 28:14-15; 35:9-12.
4. These promises were: (1) I will make of you a great nation; (2) I will bless you; (3) I will make your name great; (4) be a blessing; (5) I will bless them that bless you; (6) I will curse him that curses you; (7) in you shall all clans of the earth be blessed.
5. The eighth promise: To your seed I will give this land.

The Messianic element within the Patriarchal promises appears five times. Abraham heard it three times, Isaac once and Jacob once. The chart below summarizes the data about this great declaration.

THE PATRIARCHAL PROMISE

	Gen. 12:3	Gen. 18:18	Gen. 22:18	Gen. 26:4	Gen. 28:14
Speaker	Yahweh	Yahweh	Angel of Yahweh	Yahweh	Yahweh
Auditor	Abram	Abraham	Abraham	Isaac	Jacob
Location	Haran	Mamre	Moriah	Gerar	Bethel
Approximate Date	2092 B.C.	2068 B.C.	2047 B.C.	1955 B.C.	1930 B.C.

Translations:

Genesis 12:3: In you shall all clans of the earth be blessed.
Genesis 18:18: All nations of the earth shall be blessed in him.
Genesis 22:18: In your seed all nations of the earth shall regard themselves as blessed.
Genesis 26:4: In your seed all nations of the earth shall regard themselves as blessed.
Genesis 28:14: In you and in your seed all clans of the earth shall be blessed.

Discussion

With regard to the blessing which would come into the world through the seed of Abraham four particulars need to be explored: (1) the beneficiaries, (2) the action, (3) the channel and (4) the nature of the blessing.

A. *The Beneficiaries of the Promise.* All the clans (*mishphechot*) of the land ('*adhamah*) were to be blessed through Abram according to Genesis 12:3. This promise is perhaps broadened in 18:18 to include all nations (*goyim*) of the earth ('*erets*). All of these terms may have a limited or restricted sense, and some have given these words their restricted sense here. According to this view, God was doing no more than telling Abram that he would be a blessing to the Canaanites in the land of Canaan.

It is best to regard the terms *all nations* and *earth* in their unrestricted and literal sense. There is not the slightest hint in the text that God meant in any way to restrict these terms. Jewish tradition favors the unrestricted or universal application of this promise. Furthermore, Abram's descendants were promised *dominion* over the Canaanites in Genesis 15:18. Servitude would be a dubious blessing for them!

According to Galatians 3:8 *Scripture* foresaw[6] that God would justify the heathen through faith. This promise is called by Paul "the Gospel" which was preached to Abraham. When Abraham received this promise he was as much a Gentile as the Gentile Christians to whom Paul wrote in Galatians. He was still uncircumcised (Rom. 4:10-12). What God spoke to that Gentile directly and in person was what all nations were to read as good news. Abraham was the forerunner and type of all Gentiles who would one day hear the Gospel of blessing in Christ.

B. The Action of the Blessing. In the statements regarding the future blessing of all nations two different forms of the verb *to bless* are used. The *Niphal* form is used in 12:3; 18:18 and 28:14. The *Hithpael* form is used in 22:18 and 26:4. Some commentators attempt to obscure the differences between these two verb forms.[7] It would appear, however, that the Holy Spirit intended to communicate two very different thoughts by guiding the penman of Scripture to employ these two distinct verb forms.

The *Hithpael* is a reflexive verbal form in Hebrew. Genesis 22:18 and 26:4 are not to be interpreted as a salutation with which people would greet each other in the future (e.g., May the Lord bless you as he blessed Abraham).[8] The basic idea conveyed by this form is that the nations would regard themselves as blessed in the seed of Abraham. They would realize how fortunate they were to have some association with this seed.

The *Niphal* form is most naturally rendered by the passive voice in English in Genesis 12:3; 18:18 and 28:14. The notion is not that the nations will be blessed *as* Abraham was blessed.[9] Rather, the idea is that nations will, as a matter of fact, be blessed *in* or *through* Abraham. The *Niphal* form thus states the objective fact of blessing, while the *Hithpael* form sets forth the subjective impression which this blessing will have on the recipients.

---

6. God and Scripture are here closely identified. God is in Scripture. It is his Word.

7. Some have attempted to make the voice of the verb uniform in all passages. They would attempt to give the *Hithpael* stem a passive sense in 22:18 and 26:4. Others to achieve the same end give the *Niphal* forms a primitive reflexive meaning. It is best, however, to give to each stem its customary connotation.

8. The *Hithpael* of the root *barach* does not mean "to wish one another prosperity" as alleged by some.

9. The Hebrew preposition *beth* is sometimes translated *as* (e.g., Exod. 6:3; Num. 26:53; Ps. 37:20; Hos. 10:15). This, however, is not the normal meaning of this preposition.

C. The Channel of Blessing. The blessing upon the nations is said first to come through Abram. God promised Abram: *In you shall all clans of the earth be blessed* (12:3). In a later divine monologue the Lord said concerning this patriarch: *All nations of the earth shall be blessed in him* (18:18). In a still later development of this promise, however, God made it clear that the blessing would come through Abraham's seed (22:18).

What is meant by *seed*? The word has a marvelous ambiguity about it that makes it prophetically appropriate. Seed *could* be an unlimited collective noun embracing all of a man's biological progeny. On the other hand, *seed* might be a limited collective referring only to a chosen portion of the descendants. Genesis 3:15 already has made a clear distinction between biological and spiritual progeny, between unlimited and limited collective use of the term *seed*. Paul was not imposing upon the text a concept which was foreign to it when he insisted that those who shared Abraham's faith were his true descendants.

Paul's inspired interpretation of the word *seed* in the Patriarchal promise is instructive. He wrote: "Now to Abraham and his seed were the promises made. He does not say, And to seeds, as of many; but as of one, And to your seed which is Christ" (Gal. 3:16). The Apostle saw significance in the fact that the promise was made to Abraham's *seed* (singular), not *seeds* (plural). That seed—that individual—of whom God spoke in the promise was Messiah.

Paul goes even further. "The promises[10] were spoken to Abraham and to his seed" (Gal. 3:16). Paul employs here a simple dative. It is not *for* Abraham and his seed, nor *through* Abraham and his seed. Rather "the seed is characterized as the party to whom the promises were uttered or given."[11] Paul reveals the wonderful truth that God made this promise with Abraham, but also with Messiah! Until Christ came the promise was unfulfilled. Even after the law was given and Canaan occupied, the promise of universal blessing awaited fulfillment.

Paul's argument here has been challenged. It is commonly asserted that Paul was using Rabbinical argumentation[12]—that he was resorting to sophistry—that his argument is without linguistic justification. Paul, however, was an inspired apostle and what he says here must be

---

10. It is not clear whether Paul means *many promises* or one promise repeated in varying terms.

11. Eadie, CEPG, p. 256.

12. Pinnock, (TF, p. 43) see Paul's argument as Rabbinical in origin and addressed *ad hominem* to his opponents.

regarded as the true intent of the statement in Genesis 22:18. In response to the attack on Paul's intelligence and/or inspiration the following points must be made:[13]

1. Without doubt the promise made to Abram included in some sense the Messiah and the blessings which would be dispensed through him. To dispute this would be to call into question repeated declarations of New Testament writers. (See e.g., Rom. 4; John 8:56).

2. The promise made to Abram cannot refer to all the seed of the Patriarch taken collectively. There is no sense in which Abram's son by Hagar or his sons by Keturah have been a blessing to all the families of the earth. On any supposition, therefore, there must have been some limitation of the promise; or the word *seed* was intended to include only some portion of his descendants. *Seed* must have referred to a part only of the posterity of Abram, but to what part can be determined only by subsequent revelation.

3. It is obvious from Genesis that it was the intention of God to confine the blessing to one branch of the family, to Isaac and his descendants. The promised blessing was to be through him, and not through the family of Ishmael. See Gen. 17:19-21; 21:12; 25:11. (Cf. Rom. 9:7; Heb. 11:18). Thus the original promise of a blessing through the posterity of Abraham became somewhat narrowed down, so as to show that there was to be a limitation of the promise to a particular portion of his posterity.

4. The promise was subsequently narrowed down still more, so as to include only one portion of the descendants of Isaac. Thus it was limited to the posterity of Jacob, Esau being excluded; subsequently the blessing was promised to the family of Judah (Gen. 49:10), then David, then Solomon, until it finally terminated in the Messiah. By being thus narrowed down and limited by successive revelations, it is shown that the Messiah was eminently intended—which is what Paul is saying in Galatians.

5. It is sometimes argued that the term *zera'* is never used in the plural to denote a posterity, and thus Paul's argument based on the singular use in Genesis is not legitimate. It is true that *zera'* does not occur in the plural in this sense in the Old Testament; but the Old Testament is but a fragment of a much larger corpus of material written in Hebrew. It cannot be proved *zera'* was never used in the plural to denote sons, or races. The equivalent Greek term *sperma* is used in

---

13. Following Albert Barnes, NNT, II Cor. and Galatians, p. 341.

the plural to denote several sons of the same family.[14] Paul elsewhere used the collective singular of *sperma* (Rom. 4:18; 9:7). Paul knew his Greek, and he knew his Hebrew no doubt better than those who are his modern day critics. It should, therefore, not be necessary to defend him against the charge that he misread the collective *zera'* and imagined it to be the individual person Christ.

6. The posterity of Abraham was embodied in Jesus Christ. He was biologically and spiritually the son of Abraham. He was the summation and crown of the Abrahamic line. The entire purpose for the selection and call of Abraham and his descendants was to prepare the way for Messiah's coming. Abraham's destiny was to be a blessing to all nations, and that could only be fulfilled in Christ.

D. *The Nature of the Blessing.* That the promise of blessing through Abraham's seed is Messianic in implication is the clear teaching of the New Testament. The full scope of the blessing which would be granted to all mankind through the seed of Abraham can only be ascertained from a study of the apostolic writings. Five overlapping involvements of the blessing can be seen:

1. The birth of Christ. Zacharias, the father of John the Baptist, under the influence of the Holy Spirit, related the birth of Jesus to the oath of God made with Abraham in these words:

> Blessed be the Lord God of Israel for he has visited and redeemed his people, and has raised up an horn of salvation for us in the house of his servant David; as he spoke by the mouth of his holy prophets, which have been since the world began: that we should be saved from our enemies, and from the hand of all that hate us; to perform the mercy promised to our fathers, and to remember his holy covenant; the oath which he sware to our father Abraham, that he would grant unto us, that we being delivered out of the hand of our enemies might serve him without fear, in holiness and righteousness before him, all the days of our lives (Luke 1:68-75).

2. The resurrection of Jesus. Paul made the connection between the resurrection of Jesus and the Patriarchal blessing in his sermon at Antioch of Pisidia.

> And we declare unto you glad tidings, how that the promise was made unto the fathers, God has fulfilled the same unto us their children, in that he has raised up Jesus again; as it is written in the second Psalm, You are my Son, this day have I begotten you (Acts 13:32-33).

---

14. See A. Barnes (Ibid., p. 342) for references in classical Greek literature.

3. The conversion of sinners. Peter argued in his second Gospel sermon that the blessing offered in Christ was the very blessing contemplated in the well-known promise to Abraham. Because of their relation to the prophets and Abraham, God had sent his risen Son to bless the Jews before visiting the rest of mankind. Peter declared:

> You are the children of the prophets and of the covenant which God made with our fathers, saying unto Abraham, And in your seed shall all kindreds of the earth be blessed. Unto you first, God, having raised up his Son Jesus, sent him to bless you, in turning away every one of you from his iniquities (Acts 3:25, 26).

McGarvey comments on these verses:

> We here have an authoritative interpretation of the promise to Abraham. It was fulfilled, according to Peter, in turning living men away from their iniquities. Those only who turn away from their iniquities are the recipients of the promised blessing; and the fact that all the kindreds of the earth were to be blessed, does not affect this conclusion, except by extending its application to those among all kindreds who shall turn from their iniquities.[15]

4. Justification through faith In Galatians Paul refers to the Abrahamic promise as "the gospel." The blessing which is embraced here is that of justification for the heathen. "And the Scripture, foreseeing that God would justify the heathen through faith, preached before the Gospel unto Abraham, saying, In you shall all nations be blessed" (Gal. 3:8).[16] God foresaw his own gracious and uniform process of justifying Gentile races through faith. God made this known to Abraham even while disclosing certain promises which pertained to that patriarch's biological descendants. It is Paul's contention that the blessing of Abraham came upon Gentiles through the death of Christ (Gal. 3:14). The Edenic curse of death and the Babel curse of division which fell upon all the families of mankind are removed in Christ. Justification is the central blessing without which no other spiritual blessing comes to anyone.[17]

5. The gift of the Holy Spirit. Paul argues that Christ died on the cross to redeem men from the curse of the law "that the blessing of Abraham might come on the Gentiles through Jesus Christ; that we might receive the promise of the Spirit through faith" (Gal. 3:14).

---

15. McGarvey, NCAA, I, 65-66.
16. Paul does not quote exactly either Genesis 12:3 or 18:18 but combines the tw
17. Lenski, IGEP, p. 138.

The world-wide blessing in the seed of Abraham in Christ was put in the form of a promise. That promise put Christ before Abraham, and he believed God, and it was accounted to him for righteousness (Gal. 3:6). Jesus declared that "Abraham rejoiced to see my day and he saw it, and was glad" (John 8:56).

Prophecy No. 4

SHILOH THE REST BRINGER

Genesis 49:10-12

The fourth and final development in the Messianic theme in Genesis is found within the context of Jacob's final predictions regarding his sons. This prophecy can be dated to about 1860 B.C. To this point God had indicated that the Savior would be one born of woman (Gen. 3:15); that he would be divine and would dwell in the tents of Shem (Gen. 9:26); that he would come from the line of Abraham, Isaac and Jacob (Gen. 12:3, et al). In the present prophecy the channel of blessing further narrows to one particular tribe—the tribe of Judah.

Normally in Patriarchal times the eldest son received special consideration at the time of inheritance. Such, however, was not the case among the descendants of Abraham. Isaac was not Abraham's firstborn and Esau was by some minutes older than his twin Jacob. Under direction of the Holy Spirit Jacob here makes clear that his three oldest sons would lose their rank. Reuben (because of his incest), Levi and Simeon (because of cruelty) are here downgraded. Primacy in the history of salvation and leadership among the tribes would belong to Judah.

The Judah oracle opens with four statements concerning the exaltation of Judah among the tribes of Israel: (1) Judah will be praised by the other tribes; (2) Judah will be victorious over his enemies; (3) the other tribes would recognize the leadership of Judah; and (4) like a lion, Judah will strike fear into the hearts of those round about (vv. 8-9).

Translation of Genesis 49:10-12

(10) The scepter shall not depart from Judah, nor a ruler's staff from between his feet until Shiloh comes, and to him shall be the submission of peoples. (11) He will tie his donkey to a vine, and his colt to the choice vine; he will wash his garments in wine, and his robe in the

54

blood of grapes. (12) His eyes will be dark because of wine, and his teeth white because of milk.

Discussion

Concerning the coming of Shiloh four particulars must be discussed: (1) the time of his coming, (2) the meaning of his name, (3) his ancestry, and (4) his rule.

A. *The Time of Shiloh's Coming.* The leadership among the tribes would come to Judah and would continue to reside in Judah until the appearance of Shiloh. *The scepter*[18] *shall not depart from Judah, nor a ruler's staff*[19] *from between his feet.* The scepter and the ruler's staff should not be restricted to *royal* power. The royal dignity resided in Judah until 587 B.C. when Zedekiah was captured and deported to Babylon and the *kingdom* of Judah ceased to exist. In the Postexilic community, however, from 538 to at least 516 B.C. Judah was governed by Zerubbabel of the tribe of Judah. During the intertestamental period the entire land was called Judea after the name of this tribe. The political power of Judah came to an end when Judea was made a Roman province in A.D. 6. The political demise of Judah coincided with the physical growth of Jesus of Nazareth.

B. *The Name Shiloh.* The expression *until Shiloh comes* has "exercised the ingenuity of interpreters considerably."[20] The word appears to be a proper name and thus is properly capitalized in some English versions.[21] Shiloh appears to be the subject of the verb *shall come* and hence is to be regarded as a personal name.[22] Shiloh would then be the first proper name given to the Messiah in the Old Testament. This name is etymologically related to the Hebrew root *shala* which means to be secure, to rest. As a proper name Shiloh then would mean Peaceful One or Rest Bringer.

As early as the days of Lamech the father of Noah a longing for one who would bring comfort to the world was manifested. See comments page 43 on the meaning of the name *Noah.*

---

18. Hebrew *shebheth* usually is translated *tribe.* About forty times, however, the word means *scepter.* The Septuagint and other Greek versions and the Aramaic Targums render *shebheth* by words suggesting scepter or royal power.

19. So rendered by NASB and NIV. In KJV the word *choqeq* is rendered once *decree*, once *governor*, six times *lawgiver.* BDB renders, *prescriber of laws; a commander's staff.*

20. Maas, CTP, I, 291.

21. Shiloh is a proper noun in KJV, NASB, ASV, BV, and in the margins of the NIV and RSV.

22. See special note at the end of this chapter.

C. The Ancestry of Shiloh. The phrase *until Shiloh comes* may imply that Judah's tribal dominion and political influence were to extend only until the appearance of Messiah. It is perhaps better to give *until* (*'ad*) the inclusive sense which it often has in the Old Testament.[23] Judah's capacity for rule would extend up unto Shiloh and beyond. Judah's leadership would climax in a ruler who would be able to achieve real rest for God's people. If the promised Shiloh were not to be of Judah's descendants, this prophecy would actually be hostile to Judah. It would announce that at some point in the future Judah would lose his leadership to the Messiah, and in him to the tribe of his birth. Manifestly, however, it was Jacob's intention to bless Judah and to paint a picture of his future without negative stroke. Thus it is best to see in this statement the implicit promise that Messiah would come from the tribe of Judah. Later prophecies will make the tribal ancestry of Messiah crystal clear.

D. The Rule of Shiloh. With the appearance of Shiloh tribal dominion expands into world dominion, for *unto him shall be the submission of peoples.* The term *peoples* here could refer to the tribes of Israel; but nothing in the context gives any hint that God intended to restrict the word to Israelite tribes. It is therefore best to take the word in its widest connotation. The peoples of the world would render homage to Shiloh. That homage would not be forced servitude to some tyrannical oppressor, but "inner submission cheerfully rendered."[24]

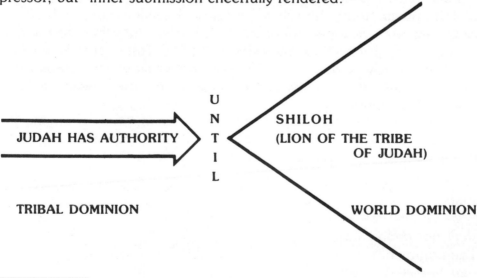

---

23. E.g., Gen. 26:13; 28:15; Ps. 112:8; 110:1.
24. Leupold (EG, p. 1180) commenting on *yiqqehath.*

Under Shiloh's rule the land would enjoy great prosperity. That seems to be the thrust of verses 11-12, although there is a legitimate question as to whether these verses refer to Shiloh or Judah. The following expressions point to the prosperity which would attend Shiloh's rule:

1. *He ties his foal to the vine* (v. 11). This would only be done in a situation where there was such a profusion of vines that it did not matter whether or not one vine was damaged.

2. *He washes his garments in wine* (v. 11). The profusion of vines yields winepresses full to overflowing. Those who tread the grapes have their garments, as it were, bathed in juice.

3. *His eyes are dark from wine . . . his teeth white from milk* (v. 12). The thought here seems to be that the abundance of nourishing food and drink imparts a healthy color.

Note on Shiloh

Four major views of *Shiloh* have found support in the history of the exegesis of this passage:

1. Some scholars prefer to change the text (e.g., Orelli; Driver; Briggs). They suggest the reading was originally *shello* or *sheloh* which would properly be translated *which is to him* or *which belongs to him*. Thirty-eight Hebrew manuscripts support the reading *sheloh*. This reading is also reflected in several ancient versions. The Septuagint and Theodotion rendered: *until that come which belongs to him* (Judah), i.e., dominion over the world. Aquila, Symmachus and the Targum of Onkelos read: *Until he comes to whom it* (the scepter or rule) *belongs*. Some think that Ezekiel 21:27 (21:32 in the Hebrew text) reflects this understanding of Genesis 49:10.

Maas feels that the reading *shelloh* "presents no unanswerable difficulties."[25] This emendation of the Hebrew text, however, is unjustified, and that especially so when it is unnecessary. A transcriptional error has to be postulated if one is going to insist on the view that *shiloh* is a combination of a relative pronoun, a preposition, and a pronominal suffix.[26]

2. Others see Shiloh as a geographical designation. *The scepter shall not depart from Judah . . . until he (Judah) comes to Shiloh.* The argument is that Judah is the subject in the following two verses,

---

25. Maas, CTP, I, 293.

26. It is alleged that *sh* is an abbreviation for *'asher*, *l* represents the preposition *lamedh*, and *oh* is an unusual form of the third masculine suffix.

and so he should be regarded as the subject of the last clause of verse 10. After conquering Canaan Israel erected the Tabernacle at Shiloh (Josh. 18:1). According to Delitzsch, this is the fulfillment of Jacob's prediction.[27] Did Judah, however, have the primacy among the tribes during the Egyptian, Wilderness, and Conquest periods before the Tabernacle was set up at Shiloh? Moses and Aaron were from the tribe of Levi, while Joshua was an Ephraimite. Furthermore, the Canaanites did not submit to Judah any more than to the other tribes during the Conquest period. There does not appear to be any adequate fulfillment of this prediction if Shiloh is taken as a geographical designation.

3. Others take *shiloh* here in Genesis 49:10 to be a common noun meaning peace or tranquility. Judah maintains the leadership among the tribes *until peace comes*. Those who adopt this interpretation do not believe that there was any concept of a personal Messiah during the Patriarchal period. This, of course, is an erroneous assumption. Furthermore, if *shiloh* be taken as a common noun the concluding statement—*unto him shall be the submission of peoples*—"comes limping along rather lamely."[28]

4. The fourth and most likely interpretation of *shiloh* is that the term is a personal Messianic title. The spelling here is unique in the Old Testament.[29] It is sometimes objected that the interpretation of *shiloh* as a proper name is a rather recent development, appearing for the first time in the last century. Jewish tradition, however, has long held the verse to be a personal Messianic prophecy. Targum Onkelos reads: *Until Messiah come*. The Jerusalem Targum reads: *Until the time that King Messiah shall come.*[30]

---

27. Delitzsch, MPHS, p. 51.
28. Leupold, EG, p. 1179.
29. A few Hebrew manuscripts have the more familiar spelling of *Shiloh*.
30. Further citations of ancient Jewish sources can be found in Maas, CTP, I, 286, 292-293.

Chapter Four

MOSES AND THE MESSIAH

One can scarcely read the Book of Exodus, so replete with typological foregleams, without thinking of that better Priest and better Sacrifice which God in the fullness of time provided for his people. The same can be said for the Book of Leviticus. Both books are to be read Christologically, i.e., read with a view of antitypical fulfillment in the spiritual realities of the present age. Neither book, however, adds any specific predictions regarding the person and work of the Messiah. The sacred record reveals only three Messianic prophecies which date to the age of Moses. One of these came from the mouth of God himself, one from Balaam the hypocritical prophet, and one from Moses.

Prophecy No. 5

THE STAR AND THE SCEPTER

Numbers 24:17

The Balaam oracle can be dated to the fortieth year after the Exodus from Egypt, to about the year 1407 B.C. This is the fourth prophecy spoken by the soothsayer Balaam when he was employed by Balak, king of Moab, to curse Israel in the plains of Moab. It appears that Balaam really desired to pronounce a curse on the people of God. Three times he tried, but God turned his curse into a blessing. Before leaving Balak, Balaam volunteered to portray prophetically the future of Israel. In this fourth and last oracle the personal Messianic element appears. Through the mouth of the two-faced prophet God continues to develop the theme of royal Messianism which found its fountainhead in Jacob's prediction regarding Shiloh's world rule (Gen. 49:10).

That the fourth Balaam oracle contains a personal Messianic prophecy is supported by the following considerations:

1. The prophecy describes what Israel would do to Moab in *the last days* (v. 14). This phrase frequently in the Old Testament points to the Messianic age.

2. The passage focuses attention on a great Israelite king who would crush the enemies of God's people.

3. Verses 20-24 seem to establish the chronological framework for the rise of this great king. He would arise after the defeat of the Greek empire, i.e., in the days of the Roman empire.

4. The Church Fathers saw in this passage a reference to the advent of Christ.

5. Jewish Rabbis regarded the star and scepter as a reference to the Messiah.

Translation of Numbers 24:16-24

(16) An oracle of the one who hears the sayings of God, and who knows the knowledge of the Most High. A vision of the Almighty has been seen, falling and with eyes uncovered. (17) I see him, but not now; I observe him, but not near. A star shall go forth from Jacob, and a scepter shall arise from Israel, and shall crush through the corners of Moab, and tear down all the sons of noise. (18) And Edom shall become a possession, the gate of his enemies shall be a possession, and Israel shall .act valiantly. (19) And from Jacob shall come the one who shall have the dominion, and he shall destroy him that remains of the city. (20) And he saw Amalek, and he lifted up his proverb and said: The first of nations was Amalek, but his end shall be destruction. (21) And he saw the Kenite, and he lifted up his proverb and said: Your dwelling place is enduring, and your nest is set upon the rock. (22) For Kain shall surely not be destroyed[1] until Asshur shall carry you captive. (23) And he lifted up his proverb and said: Alas, who can live except God has ordained it? (24) And ships shall come from the coasts of Kittim, and they shall afflict Asshur and shall afflict Eber; but he also shall perish forever.

Discussion

In his fourth oracle Balaam presents a vision of the Messiah. He foresees the Messianic kingdom, and foretells the various events which must transpire before his coming.

A. *The Visionary Description of the Coming Messiah.* In prophetic vision Balaam saw "him," obviously some outstanding leader of Israel. Three things are stated about this Ruler:

1. The Ruler was not to arise in the near future. He is the distant one. The phrases *not now* and *not nigh* make this clear.

2. This Ruler would be a glorious one. He is likened to a star. *A star shall arise in Jacob* (v. 17). Some of the early Church Fathers suggested

---

1. The particle *ki* and *'im* here probably should be separated and the latter regarded as having the strong negative force which it has in oaths.

that the Magi of Matthew's Gospel found in this passage the basis for their belief that the birth of the Messiah would be marked by the appearance of a wondrous star in the heavens. The eastern Magi would have been especially interested in the prophecies of Balaam for he came from "the mountains of the east" (Num. 23:7). But the idea that Balaam was predicting the star over Bethlehem has this against it: Matthew, who carefully gathers Messianic fulfillments does not apply this passage to the Christmas star. Furthermore, in what meaningful way can it be said that the star which led the wise men arose out of Jacob? The star in the heavens was a visible sign that the real Star had made his appearance at Bethlehem. The heavenly star signaled the fulfillment of Balaam's prophecy. The "bright and morning star" (Rev. 22:16) became clearly visible in the dark night of Israel's spiritual and political situation.[2]

3. This Ruler would be a mighty one. He is figuratively called *scepter*.[3] Jacob saw him as Shiloh, the peace bringer; but Balaam saw him as Scepter, the mighty conqueror. Jacob focused his attention on the relationship of this Ruler to Israel; but Balaam describes his reign as it affects those who are outside his kingdom.

B. *The Victorious Conquests of the Coming Messiah.* This one who is the Star and Scepter of Israel will be victorious over the enemies of God. Two examples of his mighty conquests are here foreseen.

The Ruler will crush Moab whose inhabitants are contemptuously referred to as *sons of noise*.[4] The king of Moab had shown his hatred of God's people when he tried to hire Balaam to curse them. The Edomites who recently had refused to allow Israel to pass through their territory would also be numbered among the conquests of Israel's Star and Scepter.[5]

The subjugation of Moab and Edom by the royal house of Israel began with the conquests of David.[6] Yet toward the close of Old Testament history Jeremiah took up Balaam's oracle and made it future (Jer. 48-49). It is therefore clear that the crushing of Edom and Moab

---

2. One false Messiah was called Bar-cochba, son of a star. This further underscores the fact that in the first century Balaam's prophecy was given Messianic application.

3. Briggs feels that *scepter* here is generic and points to Israel as the kingdom of God.

4. The Septuagint and other ancient versions render *sons of Sheth*. Some commentators understand Sheth to be some Moabite prince. Others think the reference is to Seth, the son of Adam, who is here a symbol for all mankind. Jeremiah 48:45 quotes this verse substituting for the Hebrew word *sheth*, the word *sha'on* which means *din* or *noise*.

5. Edom is the people, Seir the country.

6. I Sam. 14:47; II Sam. 8:1, 14.

cannot have been fully accomplished by David. John Hyrcanus, a Jewish leader in the intertestamental period, conquered Edom in 129 B.C. He forced circumcision upon them and incorporated them into Israel. The Edomites disappear from history after A.D. 70.

The various blows struck by Israel against Edom and Moab may be regarded as progressive accomplishments of what Balaam foretold. Every defeat experienced by those two hostile neighbors was a token and pledge of the final defeat of the wicked. Edom and Moab are here types and forerunners of all those nations which war against the Israel of God. It is common in Messianic prophecy to depict some ancient enemy being defeated by the Messiah. The Hebrew mind preferred the specific to the general, the concrete to the abstract. The defeat of Edom, Moab and other long-deceased nations is the Old Testament way of saying that God in the end will triumph over all his adversaries.

In the struggle against Edom and Moab Israel *shall act valiantly* (v. 18). The struggle between the seed of woman and the seed of Serpent (Gen. 3:15) will continue down to the end of time. Until that climactic moment when Christ returns to take vengeance on them who know not God, the Lord will fight in and through his people to hold in check the forces of evil.[7] God's present-day Israel, the church of Christ, must wage valiant battle against modern Edomites and Moabites who would withstand the forward movement of God's people, or who would try to lure them into sin. With the sword of the Spirit previous generations of the King's men have won impressive victories over the pagan peoples of this world. Every sinner who surrenders to King Jesus betokens the ultimate fulfillment of this prophecy that some day all forces of wickedness will submit to the Star and Scepter of Judah.

The victory over God's enemies is accomplished by the divinely appointed Ruler (v. 19). The Star and Scepter of verse 17 is now identified as a Ruler who will arise out of Jacob, i.e., the descendants of Jacob, or Israel. He will *destroy him that remains of the city*. Every stronghold of the enemy will fall to him. No fugitive will escape the day of his wrath. The Ruler from Jacob—God's Messiah—achieves total victory.[8]

It is both ironic and appropriate that Balaam the Gentile seer is the

---

7. See Num. 24:5-9 for additional thoughts on how and why God gives victory to this people.
8. Cf. Ps. 72:8; Zech. 9:10.

one who first proclaims Messiah's triumph over hostile Gentiles. To the nations of this world Balaam's oracle should serve as a warning. At the same time, God's people can take comfort here in the ultimate victory of the Messiah.

C. *The Various Events which Must Precede the Coming of Messiah* (Nu. 24:20-24). Old Testament prophets never held out the hope that the Messianic age was just around the corner. For them the golden age was in the distant future. The coming of Messiah was for them the climax toward which history was moving. At times they speak of specific events which must transpire before Messiah appears. Balaam here, under direction of God, lists five mile markers by which spiritually alert Old Testament saints might gauge the progress of God's grand plan of the ages:

1. He speaks first of the destruction of Amalek (v. 20). Amalek is described as *the first of nations* because it was the first heathen nation to attack Israel after the Exodus (Exod. 17:8ff.).[9] *His end shall be destruction* (lit., even to perishing). God commissioned King Saul to wipe out the Amalekite nation (I Sam. 15:1ff.). Although he struck a devastating blow against these ruthless marauders, Saul did not completely carry out his assignment. It remained for good King Hezekiah some three hundred years later to inflict the death blow against Amalek (I Chron. 4:39-43).

2. Balaam speaks next of the protection of the Kenites (v. 21). Moses' father-in-law Jethro was a Kenite. Throughout their history the Kenites and Israelites had cordial relations. Balaam predicts that through the vicissitudes of history the Kenites would be safe because *your dwelling place is enduring and your nest is set upon the rock.* The Kenites left their mountain home in the Horeb range to travel with the people of God who were looking for a home (Num. 10:29ff.; Jud. 1:16). That act of faith gave them a habitation on a far safer Rock, even the God of Israel (Ps. 18:2). Unfortunately the Kenites never entered fully into fellowship with Israel, but sought rather to maintain their independence throughout Old Testament history.

3. The next historical milestone mentioned by Balaam is the Assyrian captivity (v. 22). The Kenites would maintain their distinctive existence until *Asshur shall carry you captive.* It was almost seven hundred years after Balaam that the Assyrians became an imperialistic power which dominated subject peoples by dispersing them throughout their empire.

---

9. So Keil. Others see in this descriptive phrase an allusion to the power of Amelek in the time of Balaam.

The term *Asshur* in the Old Testament sometimes is used in the broad sense to embrace all powers which dominated the Mesopotamian river valley. Even the king of Persia is called the king of Assyria (Ezra 6:22). In the broadest sense, the captivity period began in 745 B.C. with the conquests of the Assyrian King Tiglathpileser, and ended in 538 B.C. with the royal edict of Cyrus the Persian which allowed captive peoples to return to their homelands. This "Assyrian" captivity was only a passing phase in Israel's history; but for the Kenites the captivity meant the end of national existence.

4. Balaam speaks next of the demise of the Mesopotamian powers (vv. 23-24). Balaam seems to have some premonition of the tumultuous international upheavals he is about to describe. He introduces this oracle with the word *alas*, which is an expression of deep emotional distress. Only those ordained to survive the world-wide catastrophe would do so.

A great invasion of the Near East from the west is prophesied here. *Kittim* is Cyprus and the islands of the Mediterranean sea. Similar terminology is used in I Maccabees to refer to the invasion of Asia by the armies of Alexander the Great in 332 B.C. (I Macc. 1:1; 8:5).[10]

The Greek armies *shall afflict Asshur and shall afflict Eber.* The term Asshur refers to eastern Shemites (descendants of Shem) who lived in the Mesopotamian river basin. Eber embraces the western Shemites of Syria, Phoenicia and Canaan. The Near East is thus to be dominated by the armies of Alexander the Great.

5. Balaam seems to allude to the eventual fall of the Greek invader from the west. *He* (the Greek invader) *shall also perish forever.* The successors of Alexander the Great dominated the political scene in the Near East until about 63 B.C. when the Roman armies became masters of the region. It was during the Roman occupation of Judea that the Star and Scepter spoken of by Balaam appeared on the scene of history. Thus with broad strokes of his brush, Balaam painted the picture of some of the major events which had to transpire before the coming of the Messiah.

Prophecy No. 6

A PROPHET LIKE MOSES

Deuteronomy 18:15, 18

The fountainhead of a new tributary of the Messianic stream is found in Deuteronomy 18. The Messiah would be a prophet as well as a king.

---

10. The phrase *ships of Kittim* in Dan. 11:30 seems to refer to the coming of the Romans.

The revelation that God would give to Israel a prophet like Moses was originally given at Mt. Sinai. The people had been overcome by fear because of their direct confrontation with God. They no longer wished to hear directly the voice of God. The Lord put his stamp of approval upon this attitude of the people. In this context God revealed privately to Moses his intention to bring a very special prophet into the world.

This revelation was made public some forty years later in Moses' second discourse to the nation in the plains of Moab (Deut. 5-26). In this discourse Moses deals with obligations towards judges or kings (16:18—17:20), priests (18:1-8) and prophets (18:9-22). The section dealing with prophets opens with a strong prohibition against the employment of occult acts. Israelites were forbidden under penalty of death to attempt to seek guidance for the future by means of any kind of pagan divination. God would provide Israel with a Prophet like Moses who would tell them all they needed to know about the future.

The Scriptures state that no other Old Testament prophet can be compared to Moses (Deut. 34:10-12). Therefore, the prophet like Moses must be someone who in some significant way transcends the line of Old Testament prophets. It is quite evident that the Jews of the first century understood the passage as referring to a single person. After seeing the miracle of the feeding of the five thousand the Jews began to say: "Surely this is the Prophet who is to come into the world" (John 6:14). When they heard him teaching at the Feast of Tabernacles some said: "Surely this man is the Prophet" (John 7:40). It is evident from John 1:20-21, 24, however, that the Jews were not entirely sure that the Messiah and the Prophet would be one and the same.

Samaritan tradition held that the Messiah would teach them all things (John 4:25). Since the Samaritans recognized only the Pentateuch as sacred literature, it is obvious that they interpreted Deuteronomy 18 as referring to the Messiah.[11]

Peter in his second Temple sermon (Acts 3:11-26) quoted this passage in reference to Jesus. In this sermon Peter spoke first of the crucifixion of Jesus and the criminal responsibility of the Jewish leaders in this heinous deed (Acts 3:13-14). He then goes on to demonstrate the resurrection and glorification of Jesus (Acts 3:15-16). All of this,

---

11. For other evidence on Samaritan attitude toward Messiah, see Maas, CTP, II. 25.

said Peter, fulfilled what the Old Testament prophets had predicted. In crucifying Jesus the Jewish nation had unwittingly fulfilled those passages which predicted that Christ would suffer (Acts 3:17-18). He then called upon his audience to repent so that they might experience the blessings of the Messianic age (Acts 3:19-20).

However persuasive Peter's arguments about the resurrection may have been, a Jewish audience would not have embraced Jesus as Messiah unless the Apostle could establish his case from fulfilled prophecy. Twice in the sermon Peter referred in general to Old Testament predictive prophecy (Acts 3:18, 24). He cites, however, only two specific passages, the first of which is Deuteronomy 18. Here then is the proper interpretation of "the prophet like unto Moses." If all that Peter said about Jesus in Acts 3:12-21 were true, then only Jesus could fulfill the terms of the ancient Mosaic prediction. J. W. McGarvey comments:

> This proved that he alone was the prophet spoken of by Moses, and it showed the audience that in obeying Jesus they would be obeying Moses, while in rejecting him they would incur the curse which Moses pronounced.[12]

To this evidence may be added, for what it is worth, that Patristic testimony weighs in favor of the personal Messianic interpretation of Deuteronomy 18:15.

TRANSLATION OF DEUTERONOMY 18:15, 18

THE ORIGINAL REVELATION TO MOSES	THE PUBLIC PROCLAMATION BY MOSES
A prophet I will raise up for them from the midst of their brethren like you, and I will place my words in his mouth, and he shall speak unto them all which I command.	*A Prophet from your midst, from your brethren, like me shall the Lord your God raise up. You shall hearken unto him.*
Deuteronomy 18:18	Deuteronomy 18:15
AT SINAI 1447 B.C.	IN THE PLAINS OF MOAB 1407 B.C.

---

12. McGarvey, NCAA, I, 64.

Discussion

These verses bid the student to explore (1) the appearance, (2) the analogy, and (3) the authority of the special prophet.

A. *The Appearance of the Special Prophet.* It is taken for granted in this passage that people need to know something about the mysteries of life, or at least that they will earnestly desire such information. God promises here to provide his people with a source of special revelation infinitely superior to pagan divination or witchcraft. He would raise up for them a Prophet. A prophet is one who receives direct communication from God through dreams, visions or other means, and who then communicates that revelation to his contemporaries.

Throughout the passage the singular "prophet" is used. The term "prophet" stands in the place of emphasis in front of the Hebrew verb in verses 15 and 18. A single individual is intended here. (See the Special Study at the end of this chapter.)

Some Jewish commentators (Rashi, Iben Ezra) thought that the reference in Deuteronomy was to Joshua. By the time this prophecy was made Joshua had already been raised up (Num. 27:18-23). Besides, Deuteronomy 34:10-12, which was most likely written in the days of Joshua (and possibly by him), explicitly states that no prophet like Moses had arisen.

The nationality of the Prophet is indicated in the phrase *from among your brethren.* More specific information was given as to the tribe of the Messiah in Genesis 49. (See prophecy No. 4.) Nothing in the present passage suggests that the Prophet and the Ruler of Genesis 49 and Numbers 24 are one and the same. That fact will become clear in later prophecies.

B. *The Analogy of the Special Prophet.* The main point in this prediction is that the future Prophet will be like Moses in some distinctive way (vv. 15, 18). It is clear that in the first century there was a general expectation that the Messiah would be a second Moses. In John 6:30-33 the multitudes challenged Jesus to perform a miracle which would be comparable to the manna provided to Israel by Moses in the wilderness. Jesus corrected their impression by saying it was God not Moses who gave them bread from heaven. Jesus suggested that the manna was but a preview of the true bread from heaven (John 6:32-33). The manna sustained men physically for a time, but the true bread from heaven, Jesus himself, grants to those who partake of him eternal life (John 6:48-51).

Messianic impostors arose in the first century who persuaded multitudes to follow them into the wilderness pretending that they would there exhibit wonders and signs.[13] One of them, Theudas, claimed that he would divide the waters of the Jordan.[14] These historical examples give evidence that many in the first century were looking for a leader like Moses who would duplicate the miracles of the wilderness period.

Philip may have been reflecting the second Moses expectation when he reported to Nathaniel: "We have found the one Moses wrote about in the Law, and about whom the prophets also wrote" (John 1:45). Jesus capitalized on this popular expectation when he stated: "As Moses lifted up the serpent in the wilderness, so shall the Son of Man be lifted up" (John 3:14); and again when he charged: "If you believed Moses you would have believed me, for Moses wrote of me" (John 5:46).

Moses was unique among the Old Testament prophets. It is not clear at what point the last three verses of Deuteronomy were written. These verses declare that no prophet had arisen in Israel like Moses. If these verses were written by Joshua as some think, then this assessment of the greatness of Moses was made before the rise of the great prophets of the monarchy period. But what was written here at the end of Deuteronomy could have been appended just as well to Malachi. In all the long history of Israel no prophet like Moses arose. Only of Jesus of Nazareth can it be said that a greater than Moses is here. In five specific areas Moses was a forerunner and type of the Messiah:

1. Moses enjoyed intimate communication from God. The Lord spoke to him "face to face" (Deut. 34:10). With other prophets God spoke through dreams and visions, but with Moses God communicated in this more intimate manner. The intimate association between the Son and the Father is stressed throughout the New Testament, as for example in the following two verses: "All things are delivered to me of my Father; and no man knoweth who the Son is, but the Father; and who the Father is, but the Son, and he to whom the Son will reveal him" (Luke 10:22). "No man has seen God at any time; the only begotten Son, who is in the bosom of the Father, has declared him" (John 1:18).

2. Moses was a miracle worker. His miracles of punishment—the ten plagues—brought Pharaoh to his knees. His miracles of preservation sustained Israel during the forty years of wandering (Deut. 34:11-12).

---

13. Acts 21:38; Josephus, *Ant.* XX.viii.6.
14. Acts 5:36; Josephus, *Ant.* XX.v.1.

Among the other Old Testament prophets only Elijah and Elisha were great miracle workers. But most of their miracles were of a more private nature whereas the miracles of Moses were national in scope. Jesus had the reputation of a prophet "powerful in word and deed before God and all the people" (Luke 24:19). When John the Baptist was imprisoned he sent his disciples to ask, Are you the One who is to come, or should we look for another?" Jesus replied: "The blind receive sight, the lame walk, those who have leprosy are cured, the deaf hear, the dead are raised, and the good news is preached to the poor" (Matt. 11:2-5). Jesus is saying that his miracles were adequate credentials of his Messiahship.

3. As a mediator, only Jesus compares with Moses. Moses prayed earnestly for the preservation of Israel on several occasions (Exod. 32:11ff.; 32:31-35). Jesus is the one mediator between God and man (I Tim. 2:5). He sits today on the right hand of the throne on high making intercession for his own (Heb. 4:14-16).

4. As a lawgiver no other prophet compares to Moses save Jesus. None of the great prophets of the Old Testament attempted to introduce any new law code to replace the Mosaic law. No other prophet would have dared to set aside any provision of Moses' law. But Jesus of Nazareth set forth a new code of conduct for his followers, and a new pattern of public worship as well. He was the mediator of a new covenant (Heb. 8:6; 9:15; 12:24). The law which governs his kingdom is contained in the twenty-seven books of the New Testament.

5. Moses was a deliverer and so was Jesus. No other Old Testament prophet was responsible for leading so many people out of bondage. Moses led as many as two million people out of slavery in Egypt to the edge of the promised land. Jesus was like Moses in that he came as a deliverer, proposing a far more glorious deliverance than that effected by Moses. He was destined to lead countless millions all over the world out of sin's bondage onward and upward to a celestial Promised Land (Luke 4:18; Heb. 2:10).

Other parallels between the lives of the two great prophets can be observed. Moses spent forty years in the wilderness of Sinai (Acts 7:30), and Jesus spent forty days in the wilderness of Judea (Luke 4:2). The seventy spirit-filled elders who prophesied in the days of Moses (Num. 11:16ff.) find their counterpart in the seventy spirit-filled disciples Jesus sent forth to evangelize (Luke 10). The cloud which enveloped the Mt. of Transfiguration is reminiscent of the cloud which hovered over Sinai when Moses was in the mount (Exod. 24:15).

While Moses stood head and shoulders above any prophet of the old economy, Jesus is infinitely superior to Moses. Such is the argument of Hebrews 3:1-3. The author likens the Old Testament worship system to a house. Moses was faithful to God as a servant in that house; but Christ is God, one with the Father (Heb. 1:8). God built that Old Testament house. It follows then that Christ, who is one with the Builder, is superior to the Old Testament house itself and all who served in it. Furthermore, Moses was but a servant in the symbolical house of God; but Christ as Son presides over the true house of God, the New Testament Church.

C. *The Authority of the Special Prophet.* The main issue in Deuteronomy is that of authority. The Israelites were not to listen to those who practiced witchcraft in any of its many forms (v. 14). Prophets who spoke in the name of another god were to be executed. The same was true of prophets who presumed to speak in the name of Yahweh when he in fact had not spoken to them (v. 20). Moses realized that it would be difficult to identify prophetic deceivers of this third category. Therefore, he set forth a simple criterion for judging whether or not God had spoken to a man. If what the prophet proclaimed in the name of the Lord did not come to pass, then that was proof positive that the man was a fraud.

Israel must listen to the special Prophet that God would raise up (v. 15). God would put his words on the lips of that Prophet, and he in turn would pass on to God's people everything that God commanded him. He would both know and faithfully proclaim God's word (v. 18). Those who give no heed to the words of this Prophet will be accountable directly to God (v. 19). Jesus was reflecting the language of Deuteronomy 18 when He said:

> He that rejects me, and receives not my words, hath one that judges him. The word that I have spoken, the same shall judge him in the last day. For I have not spoken of myself; but the Father which sent me, he gave me a commandment, what I should say, and what I should speak. And I know that his commandment is life everlasting. Whatsoever I speak therefore, even as the Father said unto me, so I speak (John 12:48-50)

70

Prophecy No. 7

THE OBJECT OF ANGELIC WORSHIP

Deuteronomy 32:43a

On the basis of Hebrews 1:6[15] Deuteronomy 32:43a must be regarded as personal Messianic. The writer of Hebrews was utilizing the Septuagint text which differs somewhat from the traditional Hebrew text which simply reads, "Rejoice, O you nations, with his people." A pre-Christian Hebrew manuscript discovered at Qumran[16] makes clear that at this point the Greek translation represents the original text.

In accordance with divine direction (31:19) Moses composed a prophetic poem (32:1-43) which he recited to the people just before his death. The written record of that song remained with Israel through the years as a witness against them. The aim of the song is to place in juxtaposition the unchanging faithfulness of God and the anticipated corruption and unfaithfulness of Israel.

Beginning in verse 20 the Lord speaks in the first person to warn of the punishments which he is about to heap on Israel. Ultimately he would punish them by means of a Gentile nation (v. 21), scattering them into distant lands (vv. 25-26). In verses 29-33 Moses interjects his wish that the people in that day would recognize their predicament and the reason for it (vv. 29-33). God speaks again in verses 34-35. He is a God of vengeance. The calamity will soon befall his sinful people.

Moses begins to describe the deliverance of God's people in verse 36. God speaks in verse 37 and reminds his people of the folly of their allegiance to false gods. He declares that he alone is eternal; he alone has power to kill and to make alive, to wound and to heal (vv. 39-40). God will make his arrows "drunk with blood" when he punishes those who exiled his people (v. 42).

Translation of Deuteronomy 32:43 (LXX)

Rejoice, you heavens, along with him, and let the sons of God worship him. Rejoice, you nations, with his people, and let all the angels of

---

15. The quotation, "Let all the angels of God worship him" is referred by some (e.g., Milligan) to Ps. 97:7. According to Payne (EBP, p. 212) this is not likely because of the differences in wording and because of the non-predictive character of Ps. 97 in which Yahweh himself is the object of worship.

16. P. W. Skehan, *Bulletin of the American Schools of Oriental Research,* 136(1954): 12-15.

God ascribe might to him.[17] For he will avenge the blood of his servants, and will render vengeance to his adversaries, and will be merciful unto his land, and to his people.

Discussion

Who is the speaker in this verse? God is the speaker in verses 37-42. Since there is no indication of a change of speakers in verse 43, Yahweh must still be speaking. The writer of Hebrews seems to regard God as the speaker: "And again when he brings the Firstborn into the world, he says, And let the angels of God worship him" (Heb. 1:6).

Four commands or exhortations are contained in the verse: (1) The heavens are called upon to *rejoice. Heavens* here by metonymy stands for the inhabitants of heaven, i.e., angels. (2) The *sons of God* are told to worship him. Sons of God are the angels of glory. (3) The nations (Gentiles) are also called upon to rejoice. Passages which speak of Gentiles joining in praise of the God of Israel are Messianic in implication. (4) All the angels are called upon to ascribe might to him. By implication Israel is also to join the joyful praise which is here urged upon the angels and nations.

Who is the person who is the object of this worship by angels, nations and Israel? The pronoun could not refer to Yahweh, for Yahweh is himself the exhorter. Nor could the pronoun refer to Israel, for Israel is called upon to join in the worship-praise for *him*. The interpretative options thus narrow. Who, other than Messiah, is worthy of worship-praise by angels, nations and Israel? The fulfillment according to the author of Hebrews, is seen in the worship of Christ by angels. Hebrews assigns this verse to the time when God brought "the Firstborn into the world" (Heb. 1:6). Most likely this refers to the advent of Christ when angels sang praises in honor of Christ (Luke 2:13-14).[18] The main point of the author of Hebrews is that angels in the Messianic day are only worshipers, not like the Son, sharers of the throne.

A twofold reason is given for the praise of him, i.e., Messiah. First, he administers a righteous judgment, a judgment in which the blood of his servants is avenged and his foes repaid. *His servants* include all those who loved and served God because of the Messianic hope.

17. Following the translation of Payne, EBP, p. 211.

18. Because of the association with angels and the use of the word "again" some commentators see here a reference to Christ's second advent. Others think the reference is to the resurrection of Christ (A. Clarke), or the establishment of his kingdom on Pentecost (Milligan).

These faithful servants were often persecuted, oppressed, and put to death by the ungodly. *His adversaries* are those who in any way try to thwart the Messianic program. In particular, *his adversaries* are those Jews and Gentiles who have shed the blood of the faithful servants.

On the other hand, *he* i.e., Messiah, will be merciful to his land and his people. This he does by removing all those who corrupt the land from within and oppress God's people from without. His land (kingdom) will be a pure realm.

Viewed in the light of later prophecy, this triumph is identified with that of the Messianic kingdom. This is why the writer of Hebrews refers the verse to the time of the bringing of the Firstborn (i.e., Messiah) into the world. In Romans 15:10 the same verse is applied to the time of Christ.

Special Note

PROPHET OR SUCCESSION OF PROPHETS?

The personal Messianic view of the Prophet of Deuteronomy 18 has not commended itself to many modern writers. It is commonly stated that Moses is here predicting the rise of the prophetic institution which culminated in the Messiah. The term "prophet" here is taken to be a collective noun[19] embracing all the prophets from Moses to Christ. The reasons offered to support this view are six in number.

1. The idea of a personal Messiah was not so fully developed in the days of Moses. Answer: In the light of the discussion of previous passages in Genesis and Numbers this argument can be dismissed as worthless. The concept of a personal Messiah is as old as the garden of Eden.

2. Maas argues that the coming of the Messiah would not have been a valid reason for not consulting diviners and soothsayers.[20] Moses must, therefore, have been referring to something that would take place more or less immediately. Answer: Old Testament saints lived by faith. The Messianic hope was designed to keep true faith burning in the hearts of God's people. They would not need to consult diviners and soothsayers because some day God would make known to them all they would need to know about the mysteries of life through the Prophet like unto Moses.

---

19. Beecher (PP, p. 351) holds another variation of this view which sees the word "prophet" used distributively rather than collectively. Each prophet becomes a type of the final prophet.

20. Maas, CTP, II, 26.

3. Moses has spoken of Israel's obligations to God and his ministers —judges, kings, priests and prophets. This order is destroyed if instead of the "prophets" one must understand "Messiah." Answer: The contrast here is between the Prophet like Moses to whom absolute obedience is required and the man who was already a prophet who will speak when God has not commanded him (v. 20). To the former God required absolute obedience (v. 19); the latter God required to be executed (v. 20). God does not deal here with the prophet who is raised up and who faithfully preaches the Word. But it is implicit here that if God will require absolute obedience to the Prophet like unto Moses who speaks forth faithfully the Word of God, he would require equal obedience to any prophet who spoke similarly. Thus, the prophetic office is *implicit* here.

4. Maas offers this argument:

> The description of the promised prophet well agrees with what we know of the Israelite prophets, of their divine election, of their influence on the life of the Hebrews, political, religious, and social, of their legislative authority, and, in fine, of their whole official character in the synagogue.[21]

Answer: But what prophet prior to Jesus Christ was "like unto Moses" in any but the most general and superficial ways?

5. In Hebrew the singular number is often used collectively.[22] Answer: This is true, but that does not prove that in this passage the singular is used collectively.

6. Maas argues: "The passages in the New Testament require only that Christ should be comprehended in the series of prophets predicted."[23] Answer: In Acts 3:22 Peter seems to be saying that the Mosaic prediction of the coming Prophet was fulfilled in Jesus Christ.

Moses is not predicting the rise of a succession of prophets because such a succession already existed. According to Peter, prophets had been active "from the foundation of the world" (Acts 3:21). Enoch prophesied (Jude 14, 15). Abraham is called a prophet (Gen. 20:7). Indeed, all the patriarchs are called "prophets" in Psalms 105:15. Moses was a prophet (Hos. 12:13), and his sister was a prophetess (Exod. 15:20). Seventy elders within the camp of Israel prophesied (Num. 11:16ff.). Furthermore, Deuteronomy 13:1, 5 seems to presuppose the existence of an order of prophets.

---

21. Ibid.
22. Cf. Gen. 1:26; Ps. 37:7; Deut. 17:14-20; Dan. 9:24.
23. Maas, CTP, II, 27.

Those who argue that a succession of prophets is in view in Deuter-onomy 18 have overlooked the principal circumstance in the description, the likeness to Moses. Moses was the law-giver, teacher, deliverer, and ruler of the people of God. A prophet "like unto Moses" can only be predicated of Jesus of Nazareth, who, like Moses, was the founder of a new dispensation of religion, a legislator, as well as a prophet, and, though in a much higher sense, a mediator between God and man.

SUMMARY OF MESSIANIC PROPHECY
IN THE PENTATEUCH

Biblical Periods	Thought Development	Specific Predictions	Scripture
Primeval	Two Messianic Lines	1. Messiah would be human	Gen. 3:15
		2. Messiah would be divine	Gen. 9:27
Patriarchal	Two Results of Messiah's Coming	1. Blessing to the Nations	Gen. 12:3
		2. Authority over Nations	Gen. 49:10
Mosaic	Two Functions of Messiah	1. He functions as King— crushing His enemies	Num. 24:17
		2. He functions as Prophet— Revealing God	Deut. 18:18

Ancestry of Messiah

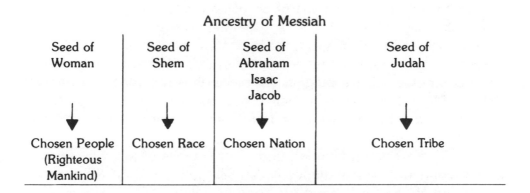

Seed of Woman	Seed of Shem	Seed of Abraham Isaac Jacob	Seed of Judah
↓	↓	↓	↓
Chosen People (Righteous Mankind)	Chosen Race	Chosen Nation	Chosen Tribe

Messianic Titles

SHILOH   STAR   SCEPTER   KING   PROPHET

Chapter Five

A RAY OF HOPE IN A DARK AGE

The Book of Joshua relates the thrilling story of the Israelite conquest of Canaan. The book covers about twenty-seven years (1407-1380 B.C.). Though rich in spiritual lessons and typology, the Book of Joshua contains no personal Messianic prophecy.

The period of the Judges lasted 335 years (1380-1045 B.C.). The Book of Judges and the first seven chapters of I Samuel give the record of these dark days. Very little in the way of positive revelation occurred during these years. Nevertheless, toward the end of this period two significant Messianic prophecies are recorded. The first comes within the prayer of an exultant mother, the second is found within an anonymous judgment oracle.

Saul's kingdom was preliminary. It was a failure. Saul was not really a theocratic king. In David the scepter passed over to Judah. The spotlight of Messianic revelation fell upon the son of Jesse in an oracle delivered by the prophet Nathan. This oracle came about eight years into the reign of David just after he had conquered Jerusalem and made it the capital of his united kingdom.

Prophecy No. 8

THE PRAYER OF HANNAH

I Samuel 2:10

Hannah suffered the stigma of childlessness for many years. When at last she was able to take her son Samuel to the Tabernacle to fulfill the vow she had made to God, she burst forth into a magnificent hymn-prayer. Critics complain that a simple farmer's wife could not possibly have composed such a magnificent piece as is recorded in I Samuel 2:1-10. Maas, however, has pointed out that nearly all the expressions that are used in this poem can be found in the inspired writings existing in Hannah's day.[1]

In her prayer-poem Hannah finds four sources of joy. She rejoices in her wonderful (1) experience (v. 1), (2) God (vv. 2-3), (3) observation about life (vv. 4-8), and (4) hope (vv. 9-10). The poem reaches its climax in the last lines which appear to have Messianic implications. Four factors support this view:

---

1. Maas, CTP, II, 32.

1. Hannah speaks here of universal judgment against the enemies of God and the exaltation of God's anointed.

2. Her words are very similar to Psalms 2 and 110, both of which are personal Messianic prophecies.

3. The Aramaic Targum renders verse 10 "And magnify the kingdom of his Messiah."

4. Some Church Fathers (e.g., Augustine and Gregory) supported the personal Messianic character of the passage.

Translation of I Samuel 2:10

The LORD will shatter his opponents, against them in the heavens he will thunder; the LORD will judge the ends of the earth, but he will give strength to his king and shall raise up the horn of his anointed one.

Discussion

Since the Lord governs the world, the righteous have nothing to fear. The Lord keeps the feet of his saints so that they do not tremble, so that they will not fall into adversity and perish therein. But the wicked—those who persecute the righteous—will perish in darkness. They will be swallowed up in adversity when God withdraws the light of his grace (v. 9).

Hannah is confident that they who fight against the Lord will be destroyed. He will thunder against them from heaven as a warning that his judgment is approaching. At this point Hannah's song becomes predictive. Two grand facts are set forth: (1) Ultimately the Lord will judge the whole world; and (2) God will give strength to his king.

Hannah's reference to "the king" indicates that the faithful in Israel had expectations of someday being part of a monarchy. God had promised Abraham that kings would come from his loins (Gen. 17:6, 16). Balaam had predicted the rise of a royal personage in Israel (Num. 23:21; 24:7). Moses set forth regulations to govern the rule of future kings (Deut. 17:14ff.). It was always God's intention that his people some day have a king.

According to many authorities, the "king" in Hannah's prayer is not any particular king, but an "ideal" king. According to this view, the passage is Messianic only in the sense that the royal line culminated in Christ. The fulfillment of the prediction is viewed as having four phases. The fulfillment *commenced* with David's victories over the enemies of Israel. It *continued* in every victory over the enemies of God and his kingdom gained by David's successors. The fulfillment *culminated* in the advance of the kingdom of Christ. The fulfillment *concludes* with the judgment of the last day through which all the enemies of Christ are made his footstool.

This may well be the proper explanation of the passage. Hannah's prediction would then be undergoing almost continuous fulfillment from her day to the present. Such an approach, however, robs Hannah's prayer hymn of specificity. Perhaps the matter can better be explained like this: Hannah's *prediction* concerns the exaltation and final victory of the Messiah. But her prediction also embraces a *principle,* viz., that God supports his anointed ones. This principle finds illustration in dozens of situations.

Rightly understood, Hannah's prophecy is the fourth stage of development in the gradual unfolding of royal Messianism. The following chart summarizes this aspect of Messianic prediction as it has thus far unfolded.

Basic Promise	Jacob	Balaam	Hannah
Gen. 17:6, 16 Gen. 35:11 Gen. 36:31	Gen. 49:10	Nu. 24:17	I Sam. 2:10
Kings to Come from Promised Seed	Judah to have Scepter until Shiloh Comes	Star/Scepter to Arise	Messiah/King
Blessing	Obedience of Peoples	Crush Enemies	Exalted

Prophecy No. 9

THE FAITHFUL PRIEST

I Samuel 2:35

At Mt. Sinai God designated Israel as a kingdom of priests (Exod. 19:6). This seems to be the further development of the directive given to Abraham that he was "to be a blessing" to others. So Israel as a priestly nation was to be a blessing to other nations of the world. Within that generic national priesthood, God ordained that the family of Aaron would officiate as priests (Exod. 29:9). Towards the end of the wilderness period God made with Phinehas "the covenant of an everlasting priesthood" (Num. 25:12-13). Briggs sees in the word *everlasting* the germ of priestly Messianism which culminates in the everlasting priesthood of the Messiah.[2] In I Samuel 2:35 God announces the removal of the Aaronic priesthood and the institution of a new priesthood under the leadership of a faithful priest.

Aaron, the first high priest, had two sons who survived him, Eleazer and Ithamar. God ordained that Eleazer should succeed his father in the high priesthood (Num. 20:25-28). Because of his zeal for the Lord in the religious crisis at Baalpeor the Lord designated Phinehas as heir apparent to his father Eleazer (Num. 25:12-13). Sometime during the period of the Judges the high priesthood line shifted to the line of Ithamar. The circumstances of this shift are not recorded, but Eli was of the priestly line of Ithamar.

The sons of Eli, who assisted him in the priestly ministry at Shiloh, were extremely wicked. They did not know the Lord in their own hearts (v. 12). They robbed the people of their share of the sacrificial offerings (v. 14), and took advantage of the women who served at the door of the Tabernacle (v. 22). Eli verbally chastised his wayward sons (vv. 22-25), but they paid no heed to their aged father. An anonymous man of God appeared to pronounce the divine sentence against the house of Eli.

In his discourse the man of God made the following observations:

1. The Aaronic priesthood enjoyed the highest privileges. God had revealed himself to Aaron (v. 27) and had chosen him as his first priest (v. 28). The sons of Aaron had the right to portions of sacrifices as payment for priestly service (v. 28).

2. The sin of the house of Eli was inexcusable (v. 29).

3. Divine promises of an eternal priesthood for the sons of Aaron were conditional. God would not continue to honor the house of Aaron if they would not honor him (v. 30).

4. Three punishments were immediately to befall the priesthood: (1) degradation of Eli's house (vv. 31-33); (2) the distress of Eli's soul (v. 33); and (3) the distress of the Tabernacle (v. 32).

5. In the more distant future God would cut off *the arm of your father's house,* i.e., the strength of the Aaronide priesthood.

---

2. Briggs, MP, p. 110.

6. Eli would know that all the predictions of the man of God would be fulfilled when he saw his two sons killed in one day (v. 34).

Translation of I Samuel 2:35-36

(35) And I shall raise up for myself a faithful priest who will do according to all that is in my heart and my soul; and I will build for him a lasting house, and it shall walk before my Messiah forever. (36) And it shall come to pass that everyone who is left of your house shall come to bow down to him for a piece of silver and a morsel of bread, and shall say, Put me I pray into one of the priestly offices that I may eat a piece of bread.

Discussion

The strength of Eli's house and that of the whole house of Aaron would be broken (v. 31). But that would not be the end of the priesthood. God would raise up a faithful or tried priest. Two points merit discussion: (1) the identity of the new priest and (2) the house of the new priest.

A. *The Identity of the New Priest.* Who is the faithful priest raised up by God? Four major views have been proposed:

1. Some think that the "faithful priest" was Samuel.[3] But a legitimate question can be raised as to whether or not Samuel was a priest. Furthermore, there is no adequate sense in which Samuel had "an enduring house" with respect to the priesthood even if it could be proved that he did function as priest for a time.

2. Some think Zadok was the "faithful priest."[4] The author of the Book of Kings makes this statement:

> So Solomon thrust out Abiathar from being priest to the LORD to fulfill the word of the LORD which was spoken concerning the house of Eli in Shiloh (I Kings 2:27).

Zadok and Abiathar seem to have shared the high priesthood in David's day. When Solomon deposed Abiathar, Zadok was left in sole possession of this honor. Abiathar was the last direct descendant of Eli to serve as high priest.

There can be no doubt that the deposing of Abiathar fulfilled the threat against the house of Eli. But I Kings 2:27 does not state that Zadok was "the faithful priest."

---

3. R. Payne Smith, PC, I, 56.
4. Goldman, SBB, p. 15.

3. Others take the "faithful priest" to be a collective embracing all the priests whom the Lord would raise up as faithful servants at his altar culminating in Christ.[5] According to this view the prophecy of the faithful priest found first fulfillment in Samuel, a new fulfillment in Zadok, and its highest fulfillment in Christ.

4. The fourth view is that this passage prophesies the abrogation of the Aaronic priesthood by Jesus Christ. The faithful priest would carry out all that was in God's heart. Of what person, however righteous, can it be said that he did all that was in the heart of God. But Jesus of Nazareth could say, "I do always those things that please him" (John 8:29).

B. *The House of the Faithful Priest.* The prophecy also states that God will build for the faithful priest a faithful house. The term *house* usually[6] refers to numerous offspring (Exod. 1:21; II Sam. 7:11). Other prophecies speak of the seed or descendants of Messiah (e.g., Isa. 53:10). The writer of Hebrews indicates that God set this faithful priest over his house (Heb. 3:5, 6).

The expression *he will walk to and fro before my anointed always* (v. 35) has exercised commentators no end. The usual interpretation is that the faithful priest would be under the observation and approval of the anointed one—the king or the Messiah.[7] For most commentators this sentence eliminates any possibility that the faithful priest could be the Messiah, for in what meaningful sense could the Messiah (faithful priest) walk under the supervision[8] of the anointed one—the Messiah?

The immediate antecedent of the verb *walk* is the noun *house.* It is the *house* of the faithful priest which is under the supervision of the anointed one, the Messiah. The idea of a walking house is already found in verse 30. The Faithful Priest and the Anointed One (Messiah) in verse 35 are one and the same person. The Messiah's house is the New Testament royal priesthood (I Peter 2:9).

Members of the old priestly house would submit to the authority of the Faithful Priest. The Aaronic priests would bow down to him. They would be dependent on him for sustenance (*piece of silver or loaf of bread*). Since the Aaronic priests would be defrocked, they would

---

5. Keil, BCOT, Samuel, pp. 46-47.

6. In some passages the term *house* is used metaphorically of assured prosperity. To those who dwell in tents, a fixed and permanent dwelling was a mark of greatness. For *house* in this sense see I Kings 2:24; 11:38.

7. Jamieson, Fausset and Brown (CCEP, II, 141) argue that since priests are never said to walk before kings the term *anointed one* (*mashiach*) must refer to the Messiah.

8. The Hebrew *liphney* as used in I Sam. 3:1.

depend upon the Faithful Priest for appointment to the priestly office (v. 36).

Jesus said to the leaders of the Jewish nation: "Your house is left unto you desolate" (Matt. 23:38). Many of the leaders of the Jews— members of the Sanhedrin like Nicodemus and former priests (Acts 6:7) —surrendered to the authority of Messiah and found a place of service in the new covenant priesthood.

Prophecy No. 10

THE NATHAN ORACLE

II Samuel 7:12-16

At the outset of his reign David sought to make Jerusalem, his new capital, the religious center of the nation. The Tabernacle was located at Gibeon in those days, and the ark of the covenant was located in the village of Kiriath-jearim about nine miles west of Jerusalem. David ordered the ark to be transported to the capital to be placed in a special tent which he had prepared for it. Great celebration accompanied the installation of the ark on Mt. Zion.

With the help of Hiram, king of Tyre, David built for himself a beautiful palace in Jerusalem. It bothered this man after God's own heart that while he lived in relative luxury, the ark of God was housed in a tent. Eventually David sought the permission of his prophetic friend Nathan to construct a house of God. Nathan thought the idea was superb. But God instructed the prophet that David was not to construct the Temple. His hands were stained with blood. The proposed task was noble, but it must be undertaken by David's son. David spent his last years gathering building materials for the project, but he died not having seen the first stone laid in that Temple.

The foundation of all that the Bible says in relation to David and the Messiah is found in the prophetic oracle delivered to David by Nathan. This passage marks the beginning of a new direction in Messianic expectation.

Nathan's oracle began with a question: Will *you* build a house for Me? (v. 5). The pronoun *you* is here emphatic in Hebrew. God pointed out that (1) there was no precedent for such a permanent dwelling (v. 6); and (2) there had been no request by God for such a dwelling (v. 7). The implication is that the construction of a permanent place of worship was not an urgent necessity.

God reminded David of all that had been done for him. God had (1) made David ruler over Israel; (2) enabled him to win victories over his enemies; (3) made David famous; and (4) given Israel a hitherto unknown tranquility (vv. 8-11). David had more than his share of divine blessing. But he would not be accorded the privilege of building the Temple of God. A more gentle prohibition is nowhere found in the word of God.

While David is not permitted to build a house for God, the Lord promised to build a house for David. David's house is the line of descendants which God would give him. Twenty kings were destined to follow David on the throne in Jerusalem in Old Testament days. The Davidic kings foreshadowed the rise of the son of David, Jesus, who would rule for ever and ever.

Translation of II Samuel 7:12-16

(12) When your days are fulfilled and you lie down with your fathers, then I will raise up your seed who has gone out from your loins after you, and I will establish his kingdom. (13) He shall build a house for my name, and I will establish the throne of his kingdom forever. (14) I will be his father and he shall be my son. When he commits iniquity, I will chasten him with the rod of men, and with the stripes of men. (15) My lovingkindness shall not depart from him as I took it from Saul whom I removed before you. (16) Your house and your kingdom shall stand forever before you; your throne shall be established forever.

Discussion

In these verses God points out five things which he will do for and through David's seed. The term *seed* here as in Genesis 3:15 and 28:14 is a collective noun which embraces the whole line of David's descendants including Christ.

A. *David's Seed Will Succeed him on the Throne* (v. 12). Saul's son Ishbosheth tried but failed to follow his father on the throne of Israel. But David's natural offspring (*from your body*) would follow him on the throne. The kingdom over which David's descendants would rule is Israel (7:23, 24, 26, 27) or God's kingdom (I Chron. 17:14).

B. *David's Seed Would Build a House for God's Name* (v. 13). There is no explicit reference to Solomon here as the builder of the

Temple, but to David's seed in general. In his final address to the leaders of the nation David applied the Nathan oracle to Solomon:

> And he said to me: Solomon your son shall build my house and my courts, for I have chosen him for myself for a son, and I will be a father to him, and I will establish his kingdom forever if he consistently does my commandments and my judgments as at this day (I Chron. 28:6, 7).

At the dedication of the Temple Solomon reflected on what he had been told by his father:

> And the LORD said unto David my father, Because it was in your heart to build a house for my name, you did well that it was in your heart. Nevertheless, you shall not build the house, but your son who goes out from your loins, he shall build the house for my name. Now the LORD has established his word which he spoke and I have arisen to replace my father, and I sit upon the throne of Israel as the LORD spoke, and I have built the house for the name of the God of Israel (I Kings 8:18-20).

It is clear, then, that both David and his son regarded the construction of the Solomonic Temple as the fulfillment of the Nathan oracle. Nathan, however, did not specifically mention Solomon. The *seed* of David would build a house. Toward the end of Old Testament history the prophet Zechariah would pick up this theme and announce that the Messiah would also be a Temple builder. Ezekiel would devote a large section of his book to a description of that Messianic Temple (Ezek. 40-48). The Temple of Solomon and the Temple erected upon return from Exile were both built by descendants of David. But like all the physical features of the Old economy, those two Temples were but types or previews of the glorious temple which is constructed of living stones (I Peter 2:5).

In the Garden Paradise God had perfect fellowship with sinless man. But sin entered the picture, and the creature-Creator fellowship was broken. The story of the Bible concerns the restoration of that original fellowship. The first step in the development of this theme came in Noah's patriarchal blessing: Yahweh would some day dwell in the tents of Shem (Gen. 9:27). Later God chose to dwell in the Tabernacle in the midst of Israel (Exod. 40:34ff.). In the days of Solomon he condescended to make the Jerusalem Temple his earthly throneroom.

Solomon regarded his Temple as the everlasting abode of God (I Kings 8:13). He may have recognized that his magnificent edifice was but a humble replica of the more glorious eternal abode of the Lord. The Old Testament Temple was but a step in the direction of the incarnation.

A temple is a place where God manifests his presence in the midst of his people. Since Jesus was a perfect manifestation of God's presence, he is said to have tabernacled among us (John 1:14). He spoke of himself as a Temple (John 2:19).

The New Testament goes one step further. This one who was himself the Temple of God became the architect, and builder of a glorious temple of living stones carved out of the quarry of life (I Peter 2:5). The church of Christ is the Temple of the living God (I Cor. 6:19; I Tim. 3:15). Furthermore, God makes his abode in the life of every obedient believer (John 14:23).

The climax is yet to come. Once sin has been removed and the Father of Lies cast into the lake of fire, the original fellowship of Eden can be fully restored. Throughout eternity God will tabernacle with redeemed men (Rev. 21:3, 22).

C. The House, Throne, and Kingdom of David would be Established Forever (vv. 13, 16). The threefold repetition of the word *forever* in these verses should be noted. The Hebrew term *'ad 'olam* in certain contexts has the meaning of long duration as opposed to the idea of everlasting.[9] Psalm 89, however, makes it clear that here *'ad 'olam* means literally *forever*:

> I will establish his seed forever, and his throne like the days of heaven. . . .
> His seed forever shall continue, and his throne like the sun before me. . . .
> Like the moon it shall be established forever, and as a faithful witness in heaven (Ps. 89:29, 36, 37).

David is thought of as continuing to exist in his descendants, for his house and kingdom are said to continue forever *before you.*[10]

The throne and seed of David continue into eternity. No earthly kingdom and no posterity of any single man has eternal duration like the sun and moon. The posterity of David could only last forever by running out into a person who lives forever. Consequently, Nathan's promise refers to the posterity of David, commencing with Solomon and culminating in Christ.

When the angel Gabriel announced to Mary that she would be the mother of the Messiah, he made this significant statement:

> The Lord God will give him the throne of his father, and he will rule in the house of Jacob forever, and of his kingdom there will be no end (Luke 1:32-33).

---

9. E.g., Exod. 21:6; Deut. 15:17; Joshua 24:2; I Sam. 1:22; Isa. 42:14; 57:11; 58:12; 61:4.

10. The Septuagint version and a few Hebrew manuscripts have here *before me,* i.e., God.

The angel is reiterating crucial aspects of Nathan's prophecy and declaring that these would find fulfillment through Mary's Son. *D. The Seed of David Would be Recognized as God's Son* (v. 14). The entire nation of Israel is declared to be the son of God in Exod. 4:22-23. This national sonship is now narrowed to the seed of David. In a very special sense, the Davidic kings were sons of God. David interpreted the words of Nathan to refer to his son Solomon (I Chron. 28:6). Again Psalm 89 amplifies the present passage:

> He shall cry to me, You are my father, my God, and the rock of my salvation. Also I have made him to be firstborn, higher than the kings of the earth (Ps. 89:26, 27).

In the Old Testament the concept of "the son of God" unfolds in four stages. The descendants of Seth are apparently referred to as sons of God in Genesis 6:1. Then the nation Israel is designated as God's son among the nations of the world (Exod. 4:22, 23). Within that filial nation the seed of David collectively is spoken of as God's son (II Sam. 7:14). This sets the stage for the culmination of the sonship concept in a single person, Jesus of Nazareth, who was God's Son in a very unique sense.

Royal sonship involved government, rule and authority. This promise too receives its ultimate fulfillment in Jesus of Nazareth. "The Father loves the Son and has placed everything under his control" (John 3:35). *E. The Seed of David Would Receive Redemptive Correction* (vv. 14-15). Even the sins of David's descendants could not frustrate the promise that his kingdom would have eternal duration. This being the case, the prophecy of Nathan must extend beyond Zedekiah, the last Old Testament king to sit on the throne of David.

Chastisements for sin will fall upon the royal descendants of David as a manifestation of God's paternal love. God would use evil men throughout Old Testament history to bring about this chastisement. Even as they afflict God's people, the enemies of Israel would unwittingly be carrying forward God's program.

The Seed of Woman would suffer at the hands of the evil one in his struggle to crush the head of the Serpent (Gen. 3:15). Now that theme of suffering is picked up by Nathan. The royal Son of God will suffer chastisement for sin. Later Isaiah will further develop this thought by adding the glorious truth that God's Servant—the Messiah—will be chastised for the sins of his people (Isa. 53:5).

Summary

Taken as a whole, the Nathan Oracle is a dramatic development in Old Testament royal Messianism. God had promised to Abraham and Jacob that kings would come forth from their descendants (Gen. 17:6, 16; 35:11). In his patriarchal blessing Jacob had indicated that the leadership among the tribes would belong to Judah until Shiloh arose to command the obedience of all people (Gen. 49:10). Balaam had seen the rise of a royal figure who would crush all the enemies of God's people (Num. 24:17). Hannah foresaw the universal judgment by God's anointed (I Sam. 2:10). And now Nathan indicates that this great sovereign would be of the seed of David and that he would rule forever (II Sam. 7).

The passage falls into the category of "seed" or descendant prophecies. Genesis 3:15 predicted victory for the seed of woman (righteous souls) through a single great champion who would crush the head of the Serpent. In the second "seed promise" God announced that through the descendants of Abraham all nations of the earth would be blessed (Gen. 22:18). This third "seed promise" looks forward to the eternal rule of the descendants of David. Thus:

> Seed of Woman . . . . Victory over Serpent
> Seed of Abraham . . . . . . Blessing to All Earth
> Seed of David . . . . Eternal Rule

Special Note

THE COVENANT WITH DAVID

In his thanksgiving prayer (II Sam. 7:18-29) David understands that God through Nathan has promised the creation of a dynasty (v. 29). In a hymn composed after David settled on his throne he praised Yahweh "who shows mercy to his anointed, to David and his descendants (II Sam. 22:51). That David clearly regarded himself and his descendants as linked to God forever in a very special relationship is indicated in a passage entitled "the last words of David."

> Indeed my house stands firm before God; because he made an eternal covenant with me, one that is firm on all points and guaranteed (II Sam. 23:5).

One of the main themes in the Old Testament is the faithfulness of God to the promises in the Nathan Oracle. Ahijah the prophet made it clear that part of the nation would be governed by the son of Solomon "so that David my servant might have a lamp always before me in Jerusalem the city which I have chosen for myself to put my name there" (I Kings 11:36).

In reference to King Abijam the sacred historian writes:

> And he walked in all the sins of his father which he did before him, and his heart was not perfect with the LORD his God like the heart of David his father. Nevertheless, for the sake of David the LORD his God gave to him a lamp in Jerusalem to raise up his son after him and to establish Jerusalem (I Kings 15:3-4).

Judah deserved to be punished during the wicked reign of King Jehoram.

> But the LORD did not desire to destroy Judah for the sake of David his servant as he said to him that he would give to him a lamp and to his children always (II Kings 8:19).

Jeremiah the prophet indicated that God's covenant with David was as permanent as the laws of nature itself (Jer. 33:20-22).

The Nathan Oracle states that the Davidic dynasty would rule forever. It does not state that the kings of that dynasty would necessarily rule consecutively with no interruption of the rule. Athaliah killed the seed royal and seized power in Judah for some six years (II Kings 11:1-3). When Zedekiah was carried away into captivity the rule of the Davidic dynasty was suspended for over six hundred years. When Jesus of Nazareth ascended into heaven he resumed the rule of the house of David and fulfilled the ultimate implications of the Nathan Oracle.

Even when the house of David was sorely humbled, oppressed by foes, and powerless to defend itself, the Old Testament saints continued to affirm their confidence in the eternality of the Davidic dynasty. The great prophets Amos, Hosea, Jeremiah and Ezekiel related the Nathan Oracle to the Messiah. They clearly saw the Messiah as the highest fulfillment of the promises contained in II Samuel 7

Even during the intertestamental period after the family of David had been dethroned for centuries the saints of God clung to the hope of a son of David who would inherit the throne of his ancestors (see I Macc. 2:57: Psalms of Solomon 17:21. At the time of Christ it was the common belief among the Jews that the Messiah would belong to the family of David. When Jesus asked the Pharisees whose son the

Messiah would be they replied immediately, David (Matt. 22:42). The scribes also referred to Messiah as the son of David (Mark 12:35). After Jesus had healed a demoniac the astonished crowd exclaimed, "Is this not the son of David?" (Matt. 12:23).

Jesus of Nazareth was a descendant of David. On several occasions he was addressed as "son of David" (Matt. 9:27; 15:22; 20:30f.). At his triumphal entry they hailed him as the Son of David and his right to this title was not challenged by his enemies (Matt. 21:9, 15). The genealogies of Jesus make it clear that both through his mother (Luke 3:31) and his legal father (Matt. 1:6) he was the heir of David. An angel addressed Joseph as "son of David" (Matt. 1:20). Luke the historian also speaks of Joseph as a descendant of David (Luke 1:27). The Apostle Paul argued that Christ had come from the seed of David (Rom. 1:3; II Tim. 2:8), and John underscores his connection with David several times in the Revelation (Rev. 3:7; 5:5; 22:16).

Chapter Six

DAVID'S GREATER SON

The unique significance of the Davidic dynasty is celebrated in several psalms. These psalms are built upon the foundation of the Nathan Oracle (II Samuel 7). In this chapter two psalms which develop the theme of Davidic Messianism are examined.

Prophecy No. 11

THE DAVIDIC KING

Psalm 89

Great promises were made to David through the prophet Nathan. The author of this psalm believed fervently in those promises. At the same time he foresaw the day when it would appear that God had abrogated that covenant, a time when the Davidic dynasty would fall into shameful disrepute among the kingdoms of the world. The psalmist prays earnestly that those days of dynastic humiliation would be shortened, and that God would vindicate his Messiah. The Messianic impact of Psalm 89 lies in the fact that no one short of Messiah could claim fulfillment of all the promises made to David.

Psalm 89 is attributed to Ethan the Ezrahite who was, so it would appear, a contemporary of David and Solomon (I Kings 4:31).[1] Ethan may have been the adopted son of Zerah (hence his name *Ezrahite*) but the natural son of Korah.[2] If this is so, then Ethan the Ezrahite would be the same Ethan who played an important role in the organization of the music program in Solomon's Temple.[3] Ethan's other name, or perhaps official title, was Jeduthun.[4]

Psalm 89 is closely related to the preceding psalm which was written by Heman, the brother of Ethan. The former Psalm contains lamentations and complaints. To the rather pessimistic appraisal of his brother, Ethan adds this psalm which recalls the promise made to David in II Samuel 7. Ethan may have outlived Solomon and may have actually witnessed the breakup of the Davidic empire. On the other hand, he

---

1. The genealogies of Chronicles list three Ethans: (1) a son of Zerah of Judah (I Chron. 2:6); (2) a descendant of Gershom of Levi (I Chron. 6:42); and (3) a descendant of Merari the Levite (I Chron. 6:44). The latter Ethan was a leader in the Temple music arrangements.

2. Alexander, PTE, p. 369.

3. I Chron. 15:17, 19.

4. This inference is based on the fact that Ethan and Jeduthun are both mentioned with Asaph and Heman in Chronicles, but never mentioned together.

may be playing the role of a prophet in this psalm as he describes the difficult days ahead for the Davidic dynasty in spite of the promise made to David.

Translation of Psalm 89 (Selected Verses)

(3) I have made a covenant with my chosen one, I have sworn to David my servant, (4) Forever I will establish your seed, and I will build up your throne from generation to generation.

(20) Then you spoke in a vision to your holy ones, and you said: I have extended help to one who is a mighty one, I have exalted one chosen from the people. (21) I found David my servant; with my holy oil I anointed him. (22) With whom my hand shall be established, my arm shall strengthen him; (23) No enemy shall trouble him, no son of iniquity shall afflict him. (24) And I will beat down his adversaries from before his face, and those who hate him I will plague. (25) My faithfulness and covenant loyalty shall be with him, and in my name shall his horn be exalted. (26) And I will set his hand in the sea, and his right hand in the rivers. (27) He shall cry unto me, You are my Father, my God and the rock of my salvation. (28) Also I will put him in the position of firstborn, higher in rank to the kings of the earth. (29) Forever I will keep for him my covenant loyalty, and my covenant shall be firmly established for him. (30) I will set his seed for eternity, and his throne as the days of heaven. (31) If his sons shall forsake my law, and in my judgments shall not walk; (32) if my statutes they profane, and my commandments they do not keep; (33) then I will punish the transgression with the rod, and their iniquity with blows. (34) But my covenant faithfulness I will not cast away from him, nor will I be deceitful in respect to my faithfulness. (35) I will not defile my covenant, nor will I alter what has gone out of my lips. (36) Once I have sworn in my holiness, I will not lie to David. (37) His seed shall endure forever, and his throne as the sun before me. (38) As the moon it shall be established forever, as a faithful witness in the heavens. (51) Remember, O Lord, the reproach of your servants. I bear in my bosom the entire multitude of peoples. (52) That with which your enemies have reproached, O LORD, that with which they have reproached the steps of your anointed.

Discussion

Psalm 89 speaks of the (1) theme (vv. 1-4), (2) the praise (vv. 5-18), (3) confidence (vv. 19-38), (4) lament (vv. 38-45), and (5) appeal (vv. 46-51) of the Psalmist Ethan.

A. The Theme of the Psalmist (vv. 1-4). The psalm opens with praise for the *mercies* and *faithfulness* of the Lord (vv. 1-2). The term *mercies* (*chesed*) refers primarily to the special promises made to David regarding the eternality of his dynasty (cf. Isa. 55:3). It is clear that Ethan speaks not only for himself, but for all the faithful through the ages (*generation to generation*).

For the Psalmist the supreme illustration of the truth and faithfulness of God was the promise made to David. The Lord himself replies to the Psalmist's opening expression of faith by mentioning his pledge to David in II Samuel 7. David was God's *servant,* his *chosen one* to execute the divine program. With David God had *ratified* a covenant. David's descendants would be confirmed in permanent possession of the royal office in Israel. The *throne* of David would endure forever (v. 4).

B. The Praise of the Psalmist (vv. 5-18). On the surface verses 5-18 are devoted to praise to God. The reason for this praise, however, is perhaps not so evident. The Psalmist is setting forth reasons why he believes in the fulfillment of the promises made to David. He cites ten reasons for his faith:

1. The heavens are an evidence of God's power to keep his promises, and his faithfulness in doing so (v. 5).

2. God is superior to any being in the heavenly realm (v. 6). He, therefore, has abundant resources for carrying out his promises.

3. God is held in reverence by his people because of his power and faithfulness (v. 7). Therefore, the Psalmist has additional reason to believe what God promised concerning David.

4. God is Lord of Hosts, incomparable in strength and faithfulness by which he is, as it were, surrounded (v. 8). Men can, therefore, believe the promise made concerning David.

5. God is Lord of the raging sea.[5] The God who can calm the tumultuous sea can suppress any tumults and troubles which arise against his people (v. 9). There is reason, then, to have confidence in what he promised regarding his kingdom.

6. God has already done so very much for his people. He has crushed Rahab or Egypt. He has scattered his enemies from time to time (v. 10). What God has done in the past, he can and will do again in the future.

---

5. The tempestuous sea here may be a symbol of the conflicting powers of the world. See Ps. 46:2-3; 65:7.

7. The entire universe (*heaven and earth*) and all which it contains (*its fullness*) belongs to God (v. 11). Even the beautiful mountains of Tabor and Hermon rejoice to fulfill their roles in God's creative scheme (v. 12). If God cares for the kingdom of nature, how much more will he watch over the affairs of his people.

8. God's character underscores the certainty of his promises. Where he reigns there is perfect righteousness; mercy and truth are fore-runners preparing the way before him (v. 14).

9. God is omnipotent (v. 13). He will do even more for his people in the future than he has done in the past.

10. The blessedness of those who trust God is another reason for continuing to maintain the faith. Believers enjoy a number of privileges: (a) they walk in the light of God's countenance (v. 15); (b) they can rejoice in God's name (i.e., his self-revelation) all the day (v. 16); (c) they can take special delight in God's righteousness which punishes the wicked and exalts the faithful (v. 16); (d) God is for his people a beautiful adornment and mighty strength (v. 17); (e) because of his favor, God's people can triumph over enemies (v. 17); (f) God is the protector of his people (v. 18); (g) The Holy One of Israel is a king which believers can be proud to follow (v. 18).

C. *The Confidence of the Psalmist* (vv. 19-38). The Messianic impli-cations of these verses are set forth by Dickson in these words:

> The psalmist expoundeth the covenant of grace made with Christ, represented typically by David, because he must be looked upon as the shadow, but Christ as the chief party, and as he in whom the real sub-stance is accomplished perfectly.[6]

Through Nathan (*your holy one*) and other prophets, God revealed his purpose to send the Messiah into the world. This revelation came in the form of a *vision*. In describing the circumstance at the time this great revelation was given, Ethan makes five points:

1. God had helped David to help his people (*I have laid help upon one that is mighty*).

2. In his sovereign will, God had chosen David for exalted assign-ments among the people (v. 19).

3. Having made David his choice, God *found* David. The reference is probably to Samuel's mission to Bethlehem when David was found tending his father's flock.

---

6. Dickson. CP. II. 117.

4. David was God's *servant*.

5. David had been set apart to his office by the anointing of holy oil administered by Samuel the prophet (v. 20).

In verses 21-33 eleven promises made to David in the Nathan oracle are enumerated:

1. David (and David's Greater Son) would be given divine assistance in the administration of his kingdom (v. 21).

2. David's subjects would not be subdued, nor would wicked enemies succeed in making them so miserable that they renounce their rightful king (v. 22).

3. David's enemies both without and within would be destroyed, beaten down suddenly or subjected to plague (v. 23).

4. David will experience God's faithfulness and mercy for the benefit of his subjects. All impediments to the growth of his kingdom would thus be removed (v. 24).

5. David's *horn* (i.e., power) would be exalted because his battles would be fought in the name of God (v. 24).

6. David's kingdom would be enlarged over sea and land His kingdom must reach beyond the bounds of Canaan (v. 25).

7. David would have a special relationship to God. He would be able to cry unto him in times of difficulty and call him *My Father* (v. 26). Dickson comments:

> The . . . promise properly belonging to Christ, according as it is declared by the apostle, Heb. 1:4, from this place, and from II Sam. 22:2: for, albeit David and Solomon were God's sons by adoption, office, government, and chosen types, yet Christ (who came of David according to the flesh) was God's Son by personal union of the human nature with the Word, or second person of the Trinity.[7]

The Jews once regarded Jesus as a blasphemer because he called God his Father, thus making himself equal to God (John 10:36).

8. David would be exalted in rank over the kings of the earth. He would be made (declared to be) God's firstborn[8] (v. 27). The New Testament advances beyond this to declare that Jesus Christ is the firstborn over all creation, i.e., the one who holds the highest rank (Col. 1:15).

9. God's merciful covenant with David and his posterity would endure forever (v. 28).

---

7. Ibid., p. 121.

8. The term *firstborn* is also used of Israel (Exod. 4:22) and Ephraim (Jer. 31:9).

10. The *throne* and *seed* of David would endure as long as the world stands (v. 29). Only in the everlasting kingdom of Christ could such a promise find fulfillment.

11. God's promise to David would not be disannulled by the unfaithfulness of some of his descendants[9] (v. 30). Kirkpatrick comments: "Man's unfaithfulness cannot make void the faithfulness of God, though it may modify the course of its working."[10] Any of David's descendants who were disobedient to God would be punished with multiple blows (vv. 30-32). Yet even in those moments God would not turn his back on the commitment to David. God is faithful to his Word even when men are not (v. 33).

To the list of covenant promises, God adds in verses 34-37 additional confirmation that the Davidic covenant was immutable. He promises not to break or in any way alter that covenant (v. 34). God has sworn by his holiness, for there is nothing higher by which to swear. He cannot lie (v. 35). The sun and moon bear eloquent testimony to the faithfulness of God in covenant keeping. The endurance of David's kingdom is likened to the permanence of the celestial bodies (vv. 36-37).

D. *The Lamentation of the Psalmist* (vv. 38-45). Having expounded the great promise made to David, the Psalmist next presents a situation which seems to contradict what he just before confidently affirmed. Is he describing here conditions as they existed in his own day? or is he anticipating the lowly state into which the Davidic dynasty would fall? If Ethan is indeed the author, verses 38-45 must be regarded as prophetic anticipation. The verbs are "prophetic perfects" in which the future is so vivid and certain to the prophet that he can describe it as though it had already transpired.

In seven concise strokes Ethan paints the picture of the dilapidated condition of the house of David.

1. Times would come when it would appear that God had contemptuously rejected his anointed (v. 38).

2. It would then appear that the covenant was dissolved, and the kingdom and crown altogether ruined (v. 39).

3. In those days Judah would be defenseless (v. 40).

4. Neighboring nations would take their fill of spoil, and in various other ways show their contempt for Judah (v. 41).

---

9. Dickson (CP, II, 123) applies verses 30-33 to the subjects of Christ. Christians are disciplined and corrected by God when they go astray.

10. Kirkpatrick, CB, p. 539.

5. The enemies of the house of David would be assisted by God, and the king himself would be put to flight (vv. 42-43).

6. All privileges and prerogatives of the Davidic kingdom would seem to be abolished (v. 44).

7. The youthful vigor of the Davidic king would be cut short and he would be covered with shame (v. 45).

E. *The Appeal of the Psalmist* (vv. 46-51). The situation portrayed in the previous lament could not be allowed to continue. The Psalmist was convinced that God should, could, and would give relief in those dark days. To this end he offers seven arguments for speedy intervention:

1. The wrath of God against his people cannot last forever (v. 46).

2. The Lord's people are of short life. If any relief is contemplated, it must be given before they pass from the scene (vv. 47-48).

3. The mercies (gracious promises) which were part of God's promise to David, and the oath of God concerning those promises, compel God's intervention (v. 49).

4. Zion should not be allowed to experience humiliation.

5. Zion bears in her bosom the nations of the world. She is their spiritual mother. This is a way of saying that Zion figures in the long-range plans of God for the world (v. 50).

6. Israel's enemies are really God's enemies (v. 51).

7. The enemies have reproached the footsteps[11] of God's anointed, the Messiah. Although they have been told of Messiah's coming, yet they scoff at the delay in his coming. One is reminded here of the skeptical taunting of Malachi 2:17 ("Where is the God of judgment?") and of II Peter 3:4 ("Where is the promise of his coming?"). Nevertheless, the faithful saints cling to the promise of Messiah's coming and continue to praise God (v. 52).

Prophecy No. 12

DAVID'S HORN AND LAMP

Psalm 132

Psalm 132 is Messianic by implication. It reflects the glorious promises which had been made to the house of David. The ultimate implications of the Davidic promises culminate in the Messiah. Those who recited

---

11. This expression is explained in traditional Jewish sources to mean "the tardiness of his steps."

this prayer in ancient Israel surely could not have been ignorant of these implications.

The theme here is closely related to Psalm 89, with this difference. Psalm 132 has a note of confidence running throughout while Psalm 89 reveals a pessimistic outlook in places.

Psalm 132 is a prayer-psalm. It is called a pilgrimage psalm. Commentators as a rule place this psalm in the Postexilic Period along with the other psalms of pilgrimage. Some commentators, however, assign Psalm 132 to the United Monarchy period. It may have been composed for the dedication of the Temple. Solomon may have been the author. Still it is best to regard the prayer here as that of the people rather than the monarch.

Translation of Psalm 132:11-18

(11) The LORD has sworn to David in truth, he shall not turn from it; of the fruit of your body I will set a throne for you. (12) If your sons keep my covenant, and my testimony that I shall teach them, also their sons forever shall sit for a throne for you. (13) For the LORD has chosen Zion, he has desired it for his dwelling place. (14) This is my resting place forever; here I will dwell, for I have desired it. (15) Her food I will abundantly bless; I will satisfy her poor with bread. (16) I will also clothe her priests with salvation, and her saints will shout loudly for joy. (17) There I will cause the horn of David to sprout, I have prepared a lamp for my anointed. (18) His enemies will I clothe with shame; but upon him his crown shall flourish.

Discussion

The psalm has two main divisions. Verses 1-10 are a prayer by the people offered at the dedication of the Temple. Verses 11-18 contain God's answer to that prayer.

A. *The Prayer* (vv. 1-10). The prayer of the people recalls the steps which led to the building of the Temple. The thrust of the prayer is that all those things for which David yearned might be realized (v. 1).

The building of God's house was the top priority of David's reign. The king vowed that he would not enter his house to sleep until he found a suitable sanctuary for his God (vv. 2-5).

The ark had all but been forgotten. In Ephratha (another name for Bethlehem, David's ancestral home) the report was received that the

97

ark had been located in the house of Abinadab (I Sam. 7:1f.) "the fields of Jaar," i.e., Kirjath-jearim (v. 6). David and like-minded friends, set out for Kirjath-jearim to worship. The ark may have been housed in a humble tent at Abinadab's house, but to the true believer that was God's "exalted dwelling," his footstool (v. 7).

The prayer moves into petition in verse 8. An ancient prayer was revived: "Arise, O Lord" (cf. Num. 10:35). This prayer, which always involved the removal of the ark to a new site, would signal the transfer of the ark to Jerusalem (v. 8). The petitioner prays that all God's people might rejoice at the movement of the ark (v. 9). The prayer concludes with the request that David's petitions might not be rejected (v. 10).

B. *The Answer* (vv. 11-18). God answers the earnest prayer of his people. He elaborates on the promises he gave to David through the prophet Nathan (II Sam. 7:11ff.). God's zeal for the house of David is no less than David's zeal for God's house. God actually took an oath concerning David's dynasty. No oath is mentioned in II Samuel, but his solemn assurances there are equivalent to an oath. (On this point compare Psalm 89:3, 35, 49.) That solemn assurance was that God would set one of David's sons on the throne after him (v. 11). The dynasty of David would continue uninterrupted so long as his descendants observed the law of the Lord[12] (v. 12).

The permanence of the Davidic kingdom is based upon the divine choice of Zion. After the pestilence had been halted in Jerusalem, God commanded David to offer a sacrifice upon the threshingfloor of Araunah (II Sam. 24:18ff.). This was designed to assure David that this was the spot which God had chosen for his permanent dwelling among his people. The magnificent Temple erected there on Mt. Zion was a tangible proof that God had chosen the spot, and furthermore, that he had made a divine commitment to David and his family which built that Temple.

Zion is where God dwells. Zion is God's kingdom, and God's kingdom will not want for a king. The physical Zion is but a preview of the true Zion which is the kingdom of Jesus Christ (Heb. 12:22). Dickson comments:

> What is promised under typical figures, is really everlasting, not in regard of the figure, but in regard of the signification: *for this is My*

---

12. The condition of the literal fulfillment of the promise is implied in II Sam. 7:14, and explicitly stated in I Kings 8:25. In Ps. 89:30ff. the thought is developed that man's unfaithfulness cannot defeat God's ultimate purposes.

rest for ever, is true only in respect of the church, represented by Zion.[13]

In verse 8 the prayer was presented that God would come to his resting place. Now the Lord assures his people that Zion would be his eternal resting place and that this was so by his own choice (v. 14). God would bless the very food and drink of his people. He would have special regard for the needs of the poor of Zion (v. 15). In Zion the poor in spirit feast on the bread of life.

The people prayed for their priests in verse 9. God now gives assurance that he will do even more than they ask. He will clothe the priests in *salvation,* i.e., he will regard their priestly ministrations as effective to the salvation of the people.[14] God will make the saints shout aloud for joy over their salvation (v. 16). In the New Testament Zion administered by David's greater Son, all the citizens are priests who are clothed in salvation. All God's saints will rejoice to see that day, and they shall shout aloud for joy.

The petition had been presented in verse 10 that God would grant blessings "for the sake of David." God will do more than that. He will "cause a horn to sprout for David." *Horn* in the Old Testament is a symbol of power. The figure may mean no more than that Yahweh would grant prosperity and might to the house of David.[15] The verb *sprout,* however, suggests a relationship to the prophecies of Jeremiah and Zechariah where *tsemach* (sprout) is used as a title for Messiah.[16] In Daniel (7:7, 8, 24; 8:5) *horn* is a symbol for a powerful king. The combination of words here (horn/sprout) "may be intended to have a personal reference and point to the messianic king."[17] Zecharias appears to have had this passage in mind when he said:

> Blessed be the Lord God of Israel; for he has visited and redeemed his people, and has raised up an horn of salvation for us in the house of his servant David (Luke 1:68, 69).

God not only will cause David's horn to sprout, he will also make a lamp for David. The *lamp* indicates the continuance of the Davidic line which culminates in the One who called himself the light of the world. There may be an allusion here to the lamp which was kept burning perpetually in the sanctuary.

---

13. Dickson, CP, II, 445.
14. Kirkpatrick (CB, p. 768): "He will prosper those who minister faithfully."
15. Cf. Ps. 89:17, 24; Ezek. 29:21.
16. Jer. 23:5; 33:15; Zech. 3:8; 6:12.
17. Kirkpatrick, CB, p. 769.

While his enemies are put to shame, the crown on David (in the person of his descendant and representative) would flourish. The word crown (*nezer*) used here and in Psalm 89:39 means (1) consecration; or (2) the diadem which was the mark of consecration to an office. It is used not only of a king's crown, but of the high priest's diadem (Exod. 29:6). The verb *flourish* (*yatsits*) or glitter, or sparkle is cognate to the word *tsits*, which denotes the glittering plate of gold bearing the inscription "holiness to Yahweh" which the high priest wore on his turban. "This phraseology seems intended to suggest that David's representative will have high priestly as well as royal dignity."[18]

Thus Psalms 132 ends with the assurance of the demise of God's enemies and the flourishing of God's anointed. Dickson has correctly observed that "the more Christ is opposed, the more shall his splendor and glory grow in the world."[19] There is no more appropriate comment with which to close the discussion of this grand psalm than that of Leupold: "To ignore the glorious climax which a word like this reaches in the Christ is to cut out the very heart of what is here implied."[20]

Special Study

THE SAVIOR IN THE PSALMS

Jesus himself encouraged his disciples to look for Messianic prophecies in the Psalms when he told them, "All things which are written about me in the Law of Moses and the Prophets and the Psalms must be fulfilled" (Luke 24:44). Psalms stood at the beginning of the third of the three great divisions of the Hebrew Bible. Jesus is referring to the *Kethubhim* or Writings by making mention of the largest and first book of this section of the Jewish Bible. His reference to Psalms is also appropriate for another reason.

Virtually no Messianic prophecy is found in the other books of the *Kethubhim* of Jesus' day.[21] By way of contrast Psalms contains, according to Payne,[22] 101 verses which are directly anticipatory of Jesus

---

18. Ibid.

19. Dickson, CP, II. 447.

20. Leupold, EP, p. 916.

21. According to Josephus, the Hebrew Bible consisted of three divisions: (1) five books of law; (2) thirteen books of prophets; and (3) four books of psalms and hymns. *Against Apion* I. 8.

22. Payne, EBP, p. 257.

Christ. These verses occur in thirteen different psalms "and they constitute the greatest single block of predictive matter concerning the Savior to be found anywhere in the Old Testament."[23] Payne's figures are conservative, for there are at least two other psalms that have as much claim to being Messianic as those which he discusses in his work.

Liberal critics dispute the Messianic character of the Psalter. T. K. Cheyne said:

> All the psalms are (let me say it again, for it concerns modern apologetics to be frank) only messianic in a sense which is psychologically justifiable. They are, as I have shown, neither typically nor in the ordinary sense, prophetically messianic.[24]

Responding to this position, W. T. Davison contends that modern criticism must face the fact that "the evangelists and apostles held a view of the Psalter that cannot be defended if . . . Christ is not contemplated in the Psalms."[25]

David claims that "the Spirit of Yahweh spoke by me, and his word was in my tongue" (II Sam. 23:2). This does not mean that the Spirit placed in David's mind thoughts totally divorced from his historical situation. Each psalm, no doubt, grew out of some definite historical circumstance, although the specific occasion often cannot be determined. The teachings of Jesus were intended for men of all ages, but they were connected naturally with some present incident. "He strang his pearls on the thread of passing occurrences or conversations."[26] The same is true of the Book of Psalms. The Messianic psalms spring from things local and temporal, but pass on from that point to embrace all ages to come.

Christians have found it difficult to read the psalms without being reminded of their Lord. It was not that they superimposed on the Psalter some fixed theory of interpretation. Rather it was that they inevitably found their thoughts wandering to the Lord Jesus "as the one Person in whom these breathings, these praises, these desires, these hopes, these deep feelings, found their only true and full realization."[27] Augustine is reputed to have said in a sermon on Psalm

---

23. Ibid.
24. Cited by Payne, EBP, p. 257.
25. Davison, HDB, IV, 160.
26. Bonar, CHC, p. lx.
27. Ibid.

58 that "the voice of Christ and His church was well nigh the only voice to be heard in the Psalms."[28]

It is sufficient to underscore at the outset of the study of the Messianic psalms this principle: this book, being Scripture, is not of private interpretation (II Peter 1:20). These psalms did not originate with the authors themselves, but rather "holy men spoke as they were moved by the Holy Spirit." It is an error of enormous magnitude to suppose that the psalmists could only write about that which had direct relevance to their contemporaries, and which was in every instance accurately understood by them. "Not unto themselves but unto us did they minister" (I Peter 1:12).

In time past perhaps too much has been read into the psalms with respect to Messianic prophecy. Augustine regarded practically all the psalms as Messianic. Bonar has followed this approach in his classic work *Christ and His Church in the Book of Psalms*. Without question this approach goes beyond principles of sound exegesis established by the New Testament.

In more recent times, however, the pendulum has swung in the opposite direction. Gunkel writes:

> At the same time it becomes apparent that the eschatology of the psalms offers no Messianic features of a sort such as bygone generations have erroneously sought to find. . . . Furthermore, the hope for a Messiah is unknown. The psalms know nothing of a human deliverer-king. Their ultimate expectation knows only of acts of Yahweh, only of a future kingdom of the God of Israel.[29]

Another writer of the same school of thought puts it this way:

> The older view that the psalmists refer to an anointed personage who would have a share in bringing Israel's future blessedness, has had to be abandoned, for it is now generally recognized that the anointed one of the psalms is a reigning Hebrew king.[30]

The New Testament writers certainly see something prophetically Messianic in the psalms. Peter and Paul both put major stress on the predictions of David in developing their argument for the Messiahship of Jesus, Leupold comments:

---

28. Quoted by Bonar, CHC, p. ix.
29. Quoted by Leupold, EP, p. 20.
30. McCullough, IB, IV, 13.

This factor cannot be lightly disposed of by assuming that the New Testament writers merely used suitable expressions that they happened to find in the psalms as fitting expressions of the truth they were attempting to put into words. They themselves attribute the prophetic element to the writers of the old Covenant.[31]

How extensive is the personal Messianic predictive element in the psalms? Leupold, whose conservative stance is unquestioned, sees the strictly prophetic element expressed only in four psalms—22, 45, 72, and 110. The other Messianic psalms he thinks are prophetic only "by way of type." Payne lists thirteen psalms which are "definitely messianic." He arrives at this figure from "unambiguous New Testament statement, or in the case of Psalm 72, by clear Old Testament reference to the ruler of the eternal Messianic kingdom."[32] He does not include those psalms cited in the New Testament for the sake of general teaching, illustration or mere phraseology. Using these same criteria, at least two additional psalms must be added to Payne's list.

Some question exists about the dating of some of the fifteen Messianic psalms. Ten of the psalms are Davidic and four others were written by those associated with him in the United Monarchy period. Only Psalm 102 seems to come from another age, but that is by no means certain. It is appropriate, then, to treat the Messianic psalms as products of the United Monarchy period.

Payne organizes the Messianic psalms into three categories. The most obvious are those in which the psalmist, usually David, speaks in the third person about one who is to arise in the future. Psalms 89 and 109 would be examples here. In other psalms God or the psalmist speaks to the Messiah using second person pronouns. Psalms 110 and 102 fall into this category. The third category consists of those psalms in which the Messiah is apparently speaking in the first person. These are the "least obvious as to an exclusively messianic intent."[33]

Those who are reluctant to acknowledge the presence of Messianic prediction in the Psalter must come to grips with one hard fact, viz., contemporary Old Testament events generally fail to correspond to the Messianic foregleams of the psalms. A.F. Kirkpatrick comments:

The revolt of the nations, the royal marriage, the accession of a prince of unique promise, the installation of the king gave the inspired poets

---

31. Leupold, EP, p. 21.
32. Payne, EBP, p. 258.
33. Payne, EBP, p. 260.

opportunity for dwelling on the promises and hopes connected with the Davidic kingdom. But successive princes of David's line failed to fulfill their high destiny. . . . The kingdom ceased to exist; yet it was felt that the divine promises could not fail, and hope was directed to the future. Men were led to see that the divine promise had not been frustrated but postponed and to look for the coming One who should 'fulfill' to the utmost that which had been spoken of Israel's king.[34]

To what extent did the psalmist understand that he was speaking of the future Messiah when he penned his work? That is a question which is difficult to answer. Peter says that David was a prophet and knew that God would raise up Christ. With the prophetic eye he "saw this great event and spoke of it" in Psalm 16 (Acts 2:30, 31). In this case, at least, David had a deeper insight into the prophetic meaning of his words than most modern critics would allow. But the real issue is not what the human penman may have thought about his composition, but rather what the Holy Spirit had in view when he guided the psalmists in the choice of their words. The Spirit's intention is clearly revealed in the New Testament and that must be for Christian expositors the supreme rule of interpretation. Sampey spoke to this hermeneutical problem as follows:

Rationalistic critics insist that to apply part of a psalm to David and part to Christ introduces confusion. They contend that the language refers to the psalmist and to him alone, and that the application of certain verses to our Lord Jesus is only by way of accommodation. This theory ignores the presence and activity of the Holy Spirit altogether; and when men talk of psychological impossibilities, they may be talking nonsense; for who of us can understand fully the psychological experience of men while receiving revelations from God? The real author of inspired prophecies is the Holy Spirit. His meaning is that which the reverent interpreter most delights to find. . . . We ought not to be surprised that we should be unable to explain fully the method of the Holy Spirit's activity in guiding the thought of prophets and psalmists in their predictions of the suffering of Christ and the glories that should follow them.[35]

---

34. Kirkpatrick, CB, p. lxxix.
35. Sampey, ISBE, IV, 2493.

Chapter Seven

THE MYSTERY OF THE INCARNATION

Two psalms focus on the emptying of Christ as he journeyed down the ladder of love to tabernacle among men in human flesh. In Psalm 8 the Messiah appears as the last Adam who was made for a time lower than the angels. In Psalm 40 the curtain is pulled back to reveal some of the discussion which took place in the councils of heaven prior to Bethlehem.

Prophecy No. 13

THE LAST ADAM

Psalm 8

That Psalm 8 is Messianic in some sense is clearly indicated by the usage made of it in the New Testament. This psalm is quoted four times in the New Testament and each time it is applied to Jesus Christ. When Jesus presented himself in the Temple at the climax of his ministry, the multitude and the children cried: "Hosanna to the Son of David; Blessed is he that cometh in the name of the Lord; Hosanna in the highest." The leaders protested these accolades for they implied that Jesus was the Messiah. Jesus responded by citing Psalm 8:2: "Have you never read: Out of the mouths of babes and sucklings you have perfected praise?" (Matt. 21:16).

Ephesians 1:20-22 refers to the resurrection and exaltation of Jesus. He is now seated in the heavenly realms "far above all rule and authority, power and dominion." God has placed "all things under his feet." In I Corinthians 15:25-27 Paul sets forth the ultimate triumph of Jesus Christ, the last Adam. He must reign "till he has put all enemies under his feet; the last enemy that shall be destroyed is death." The most important New Testament reference to Psalm 8 is Hebrews 2:6-9 where the apostle sees in this psalm a description of the incarnation and exaltation of Christ.

In spite of these New Testament references to Psalm 8 it must be admitted that "this Psalm has less of a messianic appearance than almost any."[1] Furthermore, Psalm 8 has never been recognized by Jewish teachers as a Messianic prophecy. It is, therefore, not uncommon for commentators to argue that the psalm was not originally

---

1. Delitzsch. CEH, I, 104.

intended to be Messianic—that it is used by way of accommodation to Christ is the New Testament. Those who would discover what was truly intended in this psalm, however, must reckon with the fact that the Holy Spirit is the ultimate author of the passage. The true and correct interpretation of the words of this psalm can only be grasped when the Holy Spirit in the New Testament indicates the proper lines of interpretation.

The Davidic authorship of Psalm 8 is generally recognized.[2] Though David probably wrote this psalm in his mature years, it contains meditations from his early shepherd days. Directions are contained in the heading for the "chief musician" or choir director.[3] The term *Gittith* in the heading is a noun referring to some aspect of the musical accompaniment of the psalm. The word is related to the place name Gath, and probably means a tune song in Gath.[4]

Translation of Psalm 8

To the chief musician, upon Gittith. A psalm of David. (1) O LORD, our Lord, how majestic is your name in all the earth! which (glory) place above the heavens. (2) From the mouths of infants and sucklings you have established strength because of your adversaries to silence the enemy and the avenger. (3) When I see your heavens, the work of your fingers, the moon and the stars which you have ordained, (4) what is man that you would remember him, or the son of man that you would visit him. (5) You have caused him to be less than angels for a little while, but with glory and honor you shall crown him. (6) You shall make him to rule over the works of your hands, everything you have placed under his feet: (7) sheep, and oxen, all of them; and even the cattle of the field; (8) the birds of the heavens and the fish of the sea, and that which passes through the paths of the sea. (9) O LORD, our Lord, how majestic is your name in all the earth.

Discussion

This psalm is organized around a basic proposition stated in identical words in the opening and closing verses. The intervening verses offer

---

2. It is curious that in Hebrews 2:6 the citation of this psalm is introduced by the words "one in a certain place said."

3. Fifty-five psalms have this notation in their headings.

4. *Gittith* appears also in the headings of Psalms 81 and 84. Other authorities think *Gittith* refers to the particular kind of musical instrument employed with the psalm.

specific proofs or illustrations of the truth stated in the proposition. Thus the psalm may be discussed under the following headings: (1) the proposition, (2) the proof, and (3) the prophecy.

A. *The Proposition* (vv. 1, 9). The proposition is stated in the following words: "O LORD, our Lord, how majestic is your name in all the earth." The implications of this profound declaration can be set forth in a series of observations:

1. The name Yahweh (LORD) is itself a rich revelation of the character of God. Yahweh is the all sufficient, self-sufficient God of revelation and redemption. This name above all others stresses the role of God as covenant maker.

2. Yahweh is Lord; he is sovereign Ruler. He is boss. Such is the thrust of the title *'adhonay* used here. McLean comments on the connection of the name Yahweh and the title *'adhonay* in the opening and closing declarations of Psalm 8 as follows:

> And the conjunction of these two . . . may tend to remind us how faith and obedience, dependence on grace and surrender to authority, link themselves inevitably and inseparably together in all true saintly life.[5]

3. Yahweh is Lord of all. Such is implied in the possessive *our*. Should the possessive be limited to the Israelites? Probably not. David here is the mouthpiece for all humanity. *Our Lord* (Sovereign) is, of course, the language of believers. But *all* men are potentially sons and servants of God.

4. Yahweh has made his name glorious. The *name* of God here, as often in the Bible, stands for the person himself. It is God's character, his personality which is meant—"the prints of His foot, the impress of His hand, the stamp of His ineffable attributes."[6] He is glorious[7]—great, mighty, powerful, and splendid.

5. Yahweh's majestic attributes are recognized throughout *the earth*. This is not to say that every man recognizes the glorious God who created the heavens and the earth. But wherever one may go upon the earth he will find a consciousness of the power of a supreme being.

To this basic proposition is appended what appears to be a prayer: *which (glory) place above the heavens*. The verbal form translated

---

5. McLean, GTP, p. 27.

6. Ibid., pp. 28-29.

7. The Hebrew adjective *'addir* is used to describe the might of the waves of the sea (Ps. 93:4); a large ship (Isa. 33:21); powerful kings (Ps. 136:18), nations (Ezek. 32:18), gods (I Sam. 4:8), or political leaders (Neh. 10:29). In the moral sense, the word is used to describe the nobility of God's earthly people who excell in good qualities (Ps. 16:3).

place or *set* (*tenah*) is an imperative. The psalmist prays that the divine glory "may be made still more conspicuous."[8] To give or place glory on an object is an idiomatic expression used elsewhere to denote the conferring of honor on an inferior.[9] The implication here is that the glory of nature is not inherent, but is derived from the Creator.

B. *The Proof* (vv. 2-4a). The proof that God's name is majestic throughout the earth is supported by three witnesses: (1) infants, (2) heavens, and (3) man himself.

1. Infants testify to the glory of God (v. 2). The mouths of infants and sucklings testify to the majesty, power, divinity, and goodness of God. Young children sang vigorous praises of Christ when he made his way into Jerusalem on Palm Sunday (Matt. 21:15, 16). Add to their testimony that of the early disciples who in simple faith and child-like innocence embraced the Messiah (Matt. 11:25). Jesus reminded his auditors: "Except you be converted, and become as little children, you shall not enter into the kingdom of heaven" (Matt. 18:1-6).

Through these children of the flesh and children of the spirit *you* (Yahweh) *have established strength.* The Septuagint gives an interpretative rendering of this clause—*you have perfected praise,* and this is the version cited by the first Evangelist. The strength (*'oz*) referred to in the Hebrew is verbal strength or praise. The refusal to silence the hosanna-cry of Jerusalem's children proves indirectly that Jesus regarded praise for himself as in reality praise of the manifestation of Yahweh.[10] Maas' comment is to the point:

> . . . It appears evident that the words quoted by Jesus himself on the occasion of his solemn entrance into Jerusalem cannot be considered as a mere accommodation of a victory-hymn composed for a past triumph over Israel's enemies. The words of our Lord are argumentative, directed against his enemies, and must therefore have the full weight of an argument in their application. This they would have lacked had they not been fulfilled in Jesus, or had they not been expected to be fulfilled in him.[11]

Through the mouths of these children the enemy is silenced. The *enemy and the avenger* would include all malignant railers against

---

8. Alexander, PTE, p. 38.

9. Cf. Num. 27:20; I Chron. 29:25; Dan. 11:21.

10. Delitzsch, CEH, I, 104.

11. Maas, CTP, II, 139. Alexander (PTE, p. 38) thinks Jesus cited these words only because they were apropos to the situation, not because he saw himself as the focus of Psalm 8.

God. By his citation of Psalm 8:2 Jesus was suggesting that the religious leaders who were determined to thwart any public acclamation of the Messiah were the enemies of God.

2. The heavens bear testimony to the glory of God (v. 3). The more man probes the heavens with telescope and satellite, the greater wonder is generated. "The heavens declare the glory of God, and the firmament shows his handiwork" (Ps. 19:1).

The heavens are the work of God's *fingers*. This bold anthropomorphism stresses the beauty of the heavens, the careful workmanship which went into their design and construction. The word *ordain* (*konaneta*)[12] points to the orderliness of the heavens. The stars, vast in magnitude and innumerable in multitude march across the heavens in perfect array.

3. The condescension of God testifies to his glory (v. 4a). Contemplation of the vastness of the expanse of the heavens helps man keep himself in proper perspective. *What is man?* The word for man (*'enosh*) points to man in his creaturely weakness. Yet God is *mindful* of this weak creature of dust.

C *The Prophecy* (vv. 4b-8). In the first half of verse 4 *man* (*'enosh*) is man generically in his weakness. The *son of man* in the second half of the verse is Messiah. The author then is giving two illustrations of his marvel: (1) that God takes note of man generically; and (2) that he visits the son of man, the Messiah. The particular visitation of the Son of Man (Messiah) to which he has reference is then explained in the next verse.

1. The Son of Man was *made* for a time *to be lower* than the angels (v. 5). The verb *chasar* (to cause to want, lack) is not part of the creation vocabulary in the Old Testament. Had the Psalmist been speaking of the original creation of man one would have expected *bara'* (create), *'asah* (make) or *yatsar* (form) to be used. *Chasar* means to take away from something; to subtract or remove some of what already exists. In this case, to take away from the equality (or superiority) so that one is less than angels. Only one who was already superior to the angels could be made lower than the angels. Adam could not become less than an angel when he in fact had not previously been more than angels. While the language must be strained to refer to Adam, it fits

---

12. The word is used of the establishment of a throne (Ps. 9:7), the founding of a city (Ps. 107:36). It is also used of the directing of arrows (Ps. 7:13). In relation to the acts of God it is used of the formation of man (Deut. 32:6), the earth (Ps. 24:2), and heaven (Prov. 3:19).

perfectly the incarnation of Jesus Christ. Prior to entering the world he existed in the form of God, but did not deem equality with God a thing to be clutched; but he emptied himself and made himself of no reputation (Phil. 2:6-7).

Actually the Hebrew text states that God made the Son of Man to be less than *'elohim*, the usual Old Testament word for God. The plural *'elohim*, however, is sometimes used in a more vague or abstract sense for all who exist on a higher than human plane. The Greek version of the Old Testament translated *'elohim* by *angeloi* (angels).[13] The inspired author of Hebrews uses this version in 2:7.[14]

Delitzsch refers to Psalms 8 as "a lyric echo of the history of creation as given in the Torah (Gen. 1)."[15] But where in the Genesis creation narrative is there any suggestion that Adam was created lower than (i.e., inferior to) angels? To equate "made in the image of God" with "made lower than angels" is certainly unjustified. The former expression speaks of the nature of man, and the latter of his rank.

In what sense was the Son of Man made lower than the angels? At his incarnation the Lord of glory took upon himself the form of a servant and became obedient unto death. Angels are not subject to the limitations of a flesh and blood body. They have direct access to the presence of God. But the Son of Man, during the duration of his earthly ministry, was subject to the frailties of the flesh. He experienced hunger, weariness, and sorrow.

It is important to focus attention on the adverb *me'at* in Psalms 8:5. If verses 5-8 refer to man generically, then the adverb *me'at* must have the sense of "a little lower in degree or rank." Delitzsch says: The adverb expresses "an enduring inferiority of degree imposed by the law of his creation."[16] But the writer of Hebrews takes the adverb *me'at* to have a temporal significance which it sometimes has in Hebrew.[17] Thus, the Son of Man was to be lowered beneath the angels *for a little time*. No Scriptural evidence exists that generic man will *ever* rise in rank above the angels. Therefore, if *me'at* has the temporal significance as Hebrews declares, the passage could not refer to generic man. By the same token, if generic man is the subject of verses 5-8 then one has to conclude that the author of Hebrews has twisted the intended meaning of the adverb so as to make his Messianic application.

13. The Septuagint also renders *'elohim* by *angeloi* in Ps. 97:7 and 138:1.
14. The Aramaic Targum likewise understands *'elohim* here as angels.
15. Delitzsch, CEH, I, 104.
16. Ibid., p. 112.
17. See Ruth 2:7; Ps. 37:10.

2. The Son of Man was crowned with glory and honor (v. 5b). The nouns *honor* and *glory* are elsewhere put together to express royal dignity.[18] This is not a reference to the dominion given to Adam in the garden, but to the royal dignity bestowed upon the Son of Man after his passion. When he was taken up into heaven, in the presence of adoring myriads (Heb. 1:6) he was crowned Lord of all with "angels, authorities, and powers being made subject unto him" (I Peter 3:22).[19] Delitzsch states the matter this way:

> The suffering of death was the lowest depth of our Lord's humiliation, from out of which, and because He had descended into it, Jesus now is crowned with glory and honour, and so fulfills an ordinance of grace divine, by which He has tasted the bitterness of death in a way that should have a meritorious efficacy for the human race in all its members. His being now exalted in consequence of a previous voluntary subjection to the suffering of death, is a clear manifestation of divine grace, and at the same time puts a seal upon the meritorious character of that subjection.[20]

Here again is proof that, contrary to most modern interpreters, generic man is not the focus of Psalm 8:5. According to the traditional interpretation, Adam at his creation was made a little lower than angels. Yet, it is argued, man was given dominion over the earth at that time (See Gen. 1:26, 28). Angels, however, have never been given dominion over anything. Dominion would indicate the superiority of man with respect to angels. But how can that be reconciled with the thought of man being made a little lower than angels? This logical inconsistency underscores the appropriateness of the apostolic interpretation of *me'at* as having temporal significance, and the application of this verse to Jesus Christ.

The universal authority of the Son of Man is set forth in verses 6—8. All things were set under his feet. The imagery here is that of the victorious soldier placing his foot upon the neck of a vanquished foe. All creatures—domesticated or wild, fowl or fish—are also under his rule.

In the beginning Adam was given dominion over all creation (Gen. 1:26, 28). He lost a good measure of that dominion when he sinned in the Garden. It must have been obvious to David that the universal dominion envisioned in this psalm was not a present reality. Even

---

18. E.g., Ps. 21:5. Cf. Ps. 45:3; Jer. 22:18; I Chron. 29:25.
19. See also Acts 2:36; 4:10-12; 5:30-32; 10:36-42; Eph. 1:20-23.
20. Delitzsch, CEH, I, 115.

today with all the technological advances it is obvious that man does not completely dominate his environment. A single microbe can put a man on his back or in his casket! Ever since the expulsion from Eden man has been forced to do daily battle with nature to regain his authority over creation. In Jesus Christ that dominion has finally been realized. This is just the point of the apostle:

> You have put all things in subjection under his feet. For in that he put all in subjection under him, he left nothing that is not put under him. But now we see not yet all things put under him. But we see Jesus, who was made for a while lower than the angels for the suffering of death, crowned with glory and honor; that he by the grace of God should taste death for every man (Heb. 2:8, 9).

The power and authority of the Son of Man over creation was demonstrated during his earthly ministry. Wilson cites the following illustrations: his dominion over (1) the forces of nature (Mark 4:39-41; John 2:3-11; 6:5-14); (2) the wild beasts in the wilderness (Mark 1:13); (3) domesticated animals (Luke 19:30); (4) the fish of the sea (Matt. 17:27); and (5) the fowl of the air (Luke 3:22).[21]

3. All things have been put under his feet. Christ now reigns from his throne on high. Besides Hebrews 2, the expression "all things under his feet" is used two other times in the New Testament. In Ephesians 1:22 the reference is to the authority of Christ in his church and in I Corinthians 15:25-27 the second coming and consummation are in view. Thus the three passages speak of past, present and future. "All things were put under his feet" at his ascension; all things are under his feet in his kingdom reign; and all things will be put under his feet at his coming. Thus the incarnation, glorification and dominion of Christ are clearly set forth here.

That generic man is not the focus of Psalm 8:5-8 is indicated by the plain fact that man does not have dominion over all things. It is to Jesus and to all humanity redeemed by him that the world has been put in subjection. "The world in which we now live; and in which, when it shall have been purified from sin, the redeemed will live forever" is what the apostle speaks of in Hebrews 2:5.[22] M'Lean has eloquently stated the matter:

> Yes, the crown which our first father had let fall into the dust has lifted and set on the brow of Jesus, radiant with gems unkown, undreamt

---

21. Wilson, MP, p. 146.
22. Milligan, EH, p. 84.

of before. The reins of dominion which the first Adam had dropped, the second Adam has caught up, and is wielding with all wise, benignant invincible hand—Head of His body the Church, and Head of all things to the Church, Lord of all creatures and powers on the earth, and of all principalities in the heavenly places. And it devolves on us, and well behoves us now and ever, with loyal, joyful hearts, to ascribe to Him the kingdom, the power, and the glory.[23]

Prophecy No. 14

BEFORE BETHLEHEM

Psalm 40

Three verses from Psalm 40 are quoted in Hebrews 10:5-7. According to the inspired author of that New Testament book, in these verses the Lord Jesus is speaking to the Father at the time he left heaven to come into this world. For this reason "all Christian interpreters agree in ascribing a Messianic reference to the psalm, but they differ in explaining its prophetic character."[24]

In this psalm, as so often in this book, the interpreter faces the difficult problem of determining what should be assigned to the writer and what speaks of Christ. It would seem logical that if Christ is speaking in verses 6-10 then he should be regarded as the speaker throughout the psalm. Statements appear, however, in the latter part of the psalm which seem incongruous with a Messianic application. Verse 12 is usually regarded as a confession of sin which certainly would be inappropriate in the mouth of the sinless Son of God. Verses 14-15 contain imprecations which some regard as incompatible with the spirit of forgiveness manifested from the cross.

It is, however, most likely that Christ is the speaker throughout the psalm. Milligan puts it this way: "David speaks; but Christ, whose Spirit already dwells and works in David, and who will hereafter receive from David his human nature, now already speaks in him."[25]

Several psalms have the title which is found over Psalm 40.[26] *For the chief musician* shows "that the psalm was not, as might have been supposed from its contents, a mere expression of personal feeling, but

---

23. M'Lean. GTP. p. 41.
24. Maas, CTP, II, 155.
25. Milligan, EH, p. 271.
26. Psalms 13, 19, 20, 21, 31.

designed for permanent and public use."[27] Some commentators see in the psalm an allusion to David's deliverance from Absalom; others think the psalm reflects David's attitude following his sin with Bathsheba. Both suggestions must be labeled as mere speculation.

Translation of Psalm 40

To the chief musician. A psalm of David. (1) I waited patiently for the LORD, and he stretched out unto me and heard my cry. (2) He brought me up out of a pit of destruction, from the mire of clay, and he set upon a rock my feet; he established my steps. (3) And he has put into my mouth a new song, praise to our God; many shall see, and shall fear and shall trust in the LORD. (4) Happy is the man who makes the LORD the object of his trust, and does not look unto the proud, or such as turn aside to lies. (5) Many are your wonderful works which you have done, O LORD my God, and your thoughts to usward; there is nothing which compares with you. I would declare and I would speak of them, but they are more than can be numbered. (6) You do not delight in sacrifice and offering; you have opened my ears for me; whole burnt offering and sin offering you have not requested. (7) Then I said, Behold I come; in the scroll of the book is it written of me. (8) I delight to do your will, O my God, and your law is within me. (9) I have announced the good tidings of righteousness in the great congregation; behold my lips I have not restrained, O LORD, you know. (10) I have not hidden your righteousness within my heart; I have declared your faithfulness and your salvation; I have not concealed your covenant faithfulness and your truth from the great congregation. (11) As for you, O LORD, do not withhold your mercies from me; let your loving-kindness and your truth continually preserve me. (12) For evils without number have surrounded me, and the crimes done to me have caught up with me so that I am not able to see; they are more than the hairs of my head, and my heart has failed me. (13) May it please you, O LORD, to deliver me; O LORD, hasten to my aid. (14) Let them be ashamed and confounded together who seek my life to take it away; let them be driven backward and be put to shame who plot my calamity. (15) Let them be desolate on account of the reward of their shame who say to me, Aha, Aha! (16) Let all who seek you rejoice and be glad in you; let those who love your salvation say continually, May the LORD be magnified. (17) But I am afflicted and poor; the Lord

---

27. Alexander, PTE, p. 178.

thinks upon me; my help and my deliverer are you; O my God, do not delay.

Discussion

Most authorities see a clear division in Psalm 40 after verse 10. In fact some have questioned whether verses 11-17 originally were joined to verses 1-10 as one psalm.[28] For the purposes of the present discussion six divisions are used. The psalm speaks of a great (1) deliverance (vv. 1-4), (2) program (vv. 5-8), (3) message (vv. 9-10), (4) petition (vv. 11-13), (5) prediction (vv. 14-16), and (6) confidence (v. 17).

A. *A Great Deliverance Experienced* (vv. 1-4). The Messianic psalms emphasize how the Father responded to Messiah's cry for help. There was a period of patient waiting for Yahweh (the Father) to act. Then the Father inclined his ear and heard the cry of his Son (v. 1). The image is that of one leaning forward to catch a faint or distant sound.

Messiah describes the ordeal which he went through as a horrible pit (lit., a pit of noise) filled with miry clay in which there can be no firm footing. One thinks immediately of the pit into which Jeremiah was thrown by the princes during the reign of King Zedekiah (Jer. 38:6). Messiah was delivered from that difficult experience. His feet were set on a rock. He regained his footing, and went on about his ministry (v. 2).

Messiah's joy after the deliverance is expressed in song and praise. The same thought is found in the closing verses of Psalm 22. Many will take note of Messiah's victory and will come to fear and to trust Yahweh (v. 3). Growing out of the experience of Messiah a beautiful beatitude is pronounced on those who continue to trust in God (v. 4). Such do not *look to* arrogant rebels who spurn God (*the proud*) or to *lies*, i.e., idols or perhaps falsehood.

B. *A Great Program Launched* (vv. 5-8). Verse 5 is a prayer which expresses Messiah's praise to the Father. He speaks of the supernatural character of God's acts of mercy to his people (*your wonderful works*). These acts are the product of God's incomparable wisdom (*and thoughts to usward*) respecting his people. Examples of divine beneficence are so numerous they cannot be counted (v. 5).

---

28. Adam Clarke (CCN, III, 139-140): "From the eleventh verse to the end contains a new subject, and appears to have belonged to another psalm. It is the same as the seventieth Psalm; only it wants the first two verses."

Verse 6 points to the cessation of the Mosaic sacrificial system.[29] The various Levitical offerings were part of the curriculum in God's school for Israel. Through them God taught important lessons and principles, and through them he pointed forward to the perfect sacrifice of Christ. Whenever the sacrificial system degenerated into meaningless ritual, God repudiated the offerings.[30] The present passage agrees with several other Old Testament texts which place offerings in subordination to obedience and love.[31] On the eve of his descent into the world to provide the once-for-all sacrifice, Messiah indicates the divine attitude toward the sacrifices currently being offered to God (v. 6). That Messiah is the speaker here is clearly indicated in Hebrews 10:5-6. Clarke's comment is worthy of note:

> . . . All the offerings and sacrifices which were considered to be of an atoning or cleansing nature, offered under the law, are here enumerated . . . to shew (sic) that *none* of them, nor *all* of them, could take away sin; and that the grand sacrifice of Christ was that alone which could do it.[32]

Thus Christ accomplished by the one offering of himself what the numerous Old Testament offerings failed to accomplish, *viz.*, he fulfilled the will of God. The sacrifice offered on Calvary's altar not only removed any further obligation to offer the Levitical offerings, it also signaled the end of the entire system under which those Mosaic sacrifices were offered.

What is meant by the statement, "My ears you have opened" (v. 6)? The verb *opened* (*karah*) here seems to have the meaning *pierced*. This may be a reference to the law[33] by which a servant could, because of love, commit himself in perpetuity to the service of his master. The ear lobe was pierced as a badge of this commitment. But what would it mean for God to pierce the ear of the Messiah? The opening of the ear is equivalent to causing one to hear something. But more

---

29. Four technical expressions from the law are employed here: (1) *zebach*—anything slaughtered for a sacrificial purpose; (2) *minchah*—secondary offering of grain, oil, wine and incense which accompanied the animal oblations; (3) *'olah*—the whole burnt offering; and (4) *chata'ah*—the sin and trespass offerings.

30. See I Sam. 2:12-17; 15:22; Isa. 1:11-12; Amos 5:21-24; Prov. 15:8; Mal. 1:7-8.

31. See I Sam. 15:22; Jer. 7:21ff.; Hosea 6:6.

32. Clarke, CCN, III, 141.

33. Exod. 21:1-6; Deut. 15:12-18.

than that is involved. The statement is probably meant to emphasize the submissive obedience of the Messiah to the will of his Father.

The writer of Hebrews, following the Septuagint version, renders this clause, *a body you have prepared me.* How can this be reconciled with the literal translation of the Hebrew, *ears you have pierced for me?* Several observations are appropriate:

1. The Septuagint version was the common version of the first Christian century. Sometimes New Testament writers use this version in spite of its occasional inaccuracy, and even quote passages which were somewhat inaccurately translated in that version. They never, however, attempted to profit from its errors or logically attempt to deduce the tenets of Christian theology from the inaccuracies of the Septuagint.[34]

2. When the Septuagint does not express correctly the meaning of the original, the writer of Hebrews either modifies the rendering so as to make it correct, or offers a new translation of the Hebrew. In his citation of Psalm 40 several slight departures from the Septuagint translation are in evidence; but in the clause which is now under consideration, the writer of Hebrews follows the Septuagint exactly. He translates *a body you have prepared me* because this rendering correctly expresses the mind of the Spirit.[35]

3. If one insists on a logical connection between piercing the ear and preparing a body it may lie in this: where there is an ear there must also be a body. The piercing of the ear was a token that a servant belonged wholly to his master. When the ear of this heavenly servant is pierced in love, God gets the whole body.[36]

4. The thought of the original Hebrew is not altered by this rendering of the Septuagint and the Book of Hebrews. The Septuagint has given the whole (the body) while the Psalmist expressed only a part of the body, the ear.[37]

5. It may be that the Septuagint translators followed the interpretation of Psalm 40:7 which was current in their own day (about 200 B.C.) and that interpretation may have been handed down from the ancient Hebrew prophets.[38]

In verse 7 the words *Behold, I come* declare the Messiah's intention to enter the world of time and space. The connective *then* under

---

34. See citation of Roger Nicole in Payne, EBP, p. 269.
35. Milligan, EH, p. 269.
36. Wilson, MP, p. 27.
37. Maas, CTP, II, 159.
38. Milligan, EH, p. 270.

these circumstances indicates "the particular act of obedience" which the Messiah was to perform.[39]

Messiah understood that *in the scroll of the book it is written of me* (v. 7). The *book* can be none other than the Old Covenant Scriptures, especially the Pentateuch. The specific point of the testimony of the book is found in verse 8: *I delight to do your will, O my God.* David did not always delight to do God's will, but at the well of Sychar Jesus told his disciples: "My food is to do the will of him who sent me, and to finish his work" (John 4:34). Even in his darkest hour he prayed, "Not my will but your will be done" (Luke 22:42). The Law of God— the ancient Scriptures—was written on his heart. He knew the Word, believed the Word, utilized the Word constantly in his ministry. In his most difficult moments the words of Scripture poured from his lips. Psalm 40 as interpreted in Hebrews 10:5-10 pinpoints to the time of the incarnation the Messiah's covenant to always obey the Father.

Messiah addresses the Father in verse 8 as *God.* This is in perfect harmony with John 20:17, "I ascend to my Father and your Father, to my God and your God." Dickson's words are worth noting:

> That these words may be applied to David, and made use of by every believer in their own degree and measure, there is no question: but that they are principally and in the main intention to be applied to Christ speaking of himself, the matter itself doth evidence; for who but he can ascribe to himself the accomplishing of what the typical sacrifices fore-shadowed? who but he could satisfy for sin, which the sacrifices could not? Again the apostle Paul, Heb. x.5,6, cleareth the matter so, as no ground of doubting is left. In all the psalm, let David be the shadow, but let Christ be the substance.[40]

C. A Great Message Proclaimed (vv. 9-10). If verses 6-8 describe the priestly ministry of Christ, verses 9-10 give an account of his prophetic office. Christ did not merely undertake to suffer for the expiation of sin; he also undertook to apply to his people by preaching the fruits of his sufferings, for their righteousness and salvation. The *great congregation* is either the whole of mankind, or the whole of the visible church.[41] Wherever and whenever opportunity arose he did not refrain from proclaiming God's righteousness (v. 9).

---

39. Maas, CTP, II, 159-160.
40. Dickson, CP, I, 223-224.
41. Clarke (CCN, III, 141) thinks that the great congregation means the Gentiles as distinguished from the Jews.

Verse 10 summarizes five key concepts of the public proclamation of Messiah: (1) the righteousness, (2) faithfulness, (3) salvation, (4) loving-kindness, and (5) truth of God. These Gospel gems could not be hidden. Messiah had to proclaim them.

D. *A Great Petition Presented* (vv. 11-13). Messiah begins to make petition in verse 11. The unchangeableness of God's lovingkindness, and the truth of promises made to and through his Messiah are a solid ground of assurance that the Father would not withhold his tender mercies from the Son.

Verse 12 is the crux in this psalm. Commentators are all but unaminous in arguing that this verse, containing what appears to be an admission of sin, disqualifies the psalm from being predictively Messianic. From the following two facts, however, there appears no escape: (1) the writer of Hebrews regarded Christ as the speaker in verses 6-8; and (2) there is no indication of speaker change in the psalm. If these two facts be conceded the conclusion is inevitable: Christ must also be the speaker in verse 12.

The all-but-standard answer to this dilemma among conservative commentators is to assert that David is speaking here in this psalm "as a type of Christ." Delitzsch, for example, writes:

> He speaks in typically ordered words which issue, as it were, from the very soul of the Antitype, the Anointed on the future, who will not only be the King of Israel, but also the Captain of their salvation, as well as that of the whole world. . . . David speaks; but Christ, whose Spirit already dwells and works in David, and who will hereafter receive from David his human nature, now already speaks in him.[42]

The argument seems to be that since David is a type of Christ, his words have a deeper meaning, a higher application to his descendant Jesus Christ. But does this approach really solve the exegetical problem in verse 12? If David speaks in this psalm as a type of Christ, then all of his words including the apparent confession of verse 12, would have typical significance. To say otherwise would open the way for the criticism that Christian interpretation of the Old Testament prophecy is subjective to the core. What is remotely applicable to the life of Christ and consistent with New Testament Christology is declared to have "typical" significance; what is deemed inappropriate to Messianic application is regarded as having application only to David.

---

42. Cited in Milligan, EH, pp. 270-271.

If the Messiah is the speaker in verse 12 how are his words to be construed? There are two possible lines of approach. Certainly the Messiah took upon himself the sins of mankind. It is possible that he has so closely identified with the sins of others that he can refer to them as his own iniquity.[43] Alexander, however, makes this observation: "This picture of complicated sufferings, produced by his own sins, is inapplicable to the Saviour, who neither in prophecy nor history ever calls the sins for which he suffered *my sins*."[44] To this argument Maas responds: "The contention of those interpreters who infer from this expression that the psalm cannot be messianic is groundless, since Messias bears the iniquities of us all (Isa. 53). . . ."[45]

Another avenue of approach to the problem of verse 12 is to view the entire verse as descriptive of what was done to the speaker. Verse 12 would not then be a confession at all. No one contends that the first line of the verse is confession. It is a description of the plight of the speaker. He is surrounded by *evils* or troubles (*ra'ot*). It is possible that the second line is repeating the same thought. The subject of the disputed line, commonly translated *my sins* could be translated, *the crimes* (or punishments) *done to me* (*'avonotay*).[46] The crimes committed against him caught up to and overwhelmed him (*hissiguni*).[47]

Three clauses further describe the plight of Messiah. First, he is not *able to see*. Obviously he is not blind physically. The expression denotes failure of sight, arising from distress, weakness or old age. The failing of the eyes is frequently linked with the assault of enemies.[48] In the second place, he declares that *they* (the crimes committed against him) were numerous—more than the hairs of his head. The unjust trials, the mockery, the buffeting, the scourging, the crown of thorns are just a few of the crimes perpetrated against the Son of Man. Messiah's plight is further indicated by the words *my heart has failed me* (lit., has left me). Strength and courage may fail, but God does not fail. In such an hour faith stands up and pleads for mercy and kindness.

In verse 13 Messiah calls on the Father to aid him. The first clause

---

43. Dickson, I, 227. Also Lewis. RP, p. 127.
44. Alexander, PTE, p. 182.
45. Maas, CTP, ii, 161.
46. Cf. Gen. 4:13 "My punishment (*'avoni*) is greater than I can bear"; Gen. 16:5 "My wrong (i.e., the wrong done to me) be upon you."
47. Cf. Deut. 28:15 "All these curses will come upon you and overtake you."
48. See Pss. 6:7; 13:3; 31:9-11; 38:10-16.

(*may it please you, O Yahweh, to deliver me*) is an acknowledgment of dependence on God. The second clause is reminiscent of Psalm 22:19.

E. *A Great Prediction Uttered* (vv. 14-16). The confident expectation of the Messiah regarding the fate of his adversaries is pointed out in verse 14. *Ashamed, confounded, turned back, disgraced* are the strong words he uses to predict their fate. On account of their shameful conduct with respect to Messiah—their mockery in his desperate hour—they would be *desolate* (v. 15). One is reminded of the prediction of Jesus regarding the Jewish national leaders: "Your house is left unto you desolate" (Matt. 23:38).

While the enemies of Messiah face a bleak future, true worshipers—those who seek communion with the Lord and love his salvation—rejoice and praise God. Loving salvation reaches beyond enjoying a personal relationship with the Lord, to embrace joy over the salvation bestowed on others (v. 16).

F. *A Great Confidence Expressed* (v. 17). The Messiah describes himself in the midst of his suffering as *afflicted and poor*. Yet he knows the Father will think upon him, i.e., remember him, or perhaps, make plans for his deliverance. The Lord is his *help, deliverer* and *God* consequently must come to his aid. He simply asks that God delay no longer in effecting the deliverance which he knows will be forthcoming (v. 17).

Chapter Eight

THE REJECTION OF THE MESSIAH

The prophetic psalmist paints a vivid picture of the rejection of the Messiah in Psalm 118. Part of the reason for his rejection was the teaching method which he chose. The fact that he would use parables and enigmatic sayings to convey the truth of God is the subject of the prediction found in Psalm 78:1-2.

Prophecy No. 15

THE REJECTED CORNERSTONE

Psalm 118

That Psalm 118:22 is Messianic is attested by the New Testament citation of the verse.[1] The stone which the builders rejected is not Israel (Hengstenberg) or the family of David (Maas), or the foundation stone of the second Temple. Jewish writers prefer to think of David personally as the rejected stone; but never is David depicted in any such condition as is presupposed in this psalm.

Thirteen verses in the psalm are in first person singular. Who is the speaker here? If the rejected stone in verse 22 is the Messiah, then the one who describes his suffering in the first part of the psalm must also be Messiah. The view that Psalm 118 proceeds from the voice of Messiah is at least as old as Eusebius. Most conservative scholars, however, have not adopted this view. According to Maas, the view that the Messiah is here the speaker is rendered untenable by verses 8, 10-12, 15 and 27, "for these verses can hardly refer to the Messias in their literal sense."[2] The Psalm can be applied only "in its typical sense to the Messias." He goes on to state: "The literal meaning of the stone may be referred either to the Jewish people or to the family of David."[3]

No insuperable difficulty stands in the way of identifying the first person singular speaker in this psalm as Messiah. In his classic commentary David Dickson states the case for the personal predictive character of this passage:

> The psalmist in this thanksgiving for bringing him so wonderfully to the kingdom, prophesieth in this psalm of Christ's troubles by his enemies, and of his victories over them, both in his own person, and in his mystical

---

1. Matt. 21:9, 42; Mark 11:9, 10; 12:10, 11; Luke 19:38; 20:17; Acts 4:11.
2. Maas, CTP, II, 148.
3. Ibid.

body. This psalm hath such an eye and respect to Christ and his church, that, whatsoever shadow of these things may be found in David, the main substance and accomplishment of all things herein contained, are to be found most clearly and fully in Christ's wrestling with his enemies, and his triumphing over them for the comfort of the church, and glory of the Father; and this the church of Israel perceived and acknowledged; as appeareth by their acclamation taken out of this psalm, and made to Christ at his coming into Jerusalem, as king riding, and by Christ's interpretation, and appropriating it unto himself, Mat. xxi.9-42. For this cause also the psalmist does not prefix his name to this psalm, whatsoever might be fit for his particular experience in it, but leaveth it to run the more clearly and directly toward the Messiah, or Christ, who is here mainly intended.[4]

The use of the first person singular to refer to someone other than the author of a poem is not unknown in Christian hymnody. When Christians sing the following words, do they understand them to be a reference to Frances Havergal?

> I gave my life for thee,
>   My precious blood I shed,
> That thou might'st ransomed be,
>   And quickened from the dead;
> I gave, I gave my life for thee:
>   What hast thou giv'n for me?

It cannot then be thought incredible that the first person singular in this psalm is, and was meant to be by the author, Messiah. Whether or not the Temple worshipers recognized this to be the case cannot be determined.

David most likely is the author of Psalm 118, but many regard it as a postexilic composition. The psalm is thought by some to be an antiphonal processional hymn. It portrays a joyous procession making its way to the Temple (vv. 1-18). The leader speaks for the whole group (v. 19), and the response comes from those within (v. 20). The procession sings antiphonally as it enters the gates (vv. 21-24); the whole procession sings in unison (v. 25); those within sing welcome (v. 26). The leader initiates sacrifice (v. 27) and the whole congregation sings (vv. 28-29).

Translation of Psalm 118:5-29

(5) From the distress I cried to the LORD, and the LORD answered me in a large place. (6) The LORD is mine, I shall not fear. What can

---

4. Dickson, CP, II, 331.

man do to me? (7) The LORD is mine with my helpers; and as for me, I will look on those who hate me. (8) It is better to take refuge in the LORD than to trust in man. (9) It is better to take refuge in the LORD than to trust in princes. (10) All the Gentiles surrounded me, but in the name of the LORD I will cut them off. (11) They compassed me about, yea they surrounded me, but in the name of the LORD I will cut them off. (12) They compassed me about like bees; they are quenched like a fire made of thorns, for in the name of the LORD I will cut them off. (13) You knocked me back to make me fall, but the LORD helped me. (14) The LORD is my strength and song; he has become my salvation. (15) The voice of rejoicing and salvation is in the tents of the righteous; the right hand of the LORD is performing valiantly. (16) The right hand of the LORD is lifted up; the right hand of the LORD performs valiantly. (17) I shall not die but live, and I shall declare the works of the LORD. (18) The LORD has chastened me severely, but he has not given me over to death. (19) Open for me the gates of righteousness; I will go in, I will give thanks to the LORD. (20) This is the gate of the LORD, through which the righteous may enter. (21) I will give thanks to you for you have answered me, and you have become my salvation. (22) The stone the builders rejected has become the head of the corner. (23) From the LORD this has come to pass, and it is marvelous in our eyes. (24) This is the day the LORD has made; let us rejoice and be glad in it. (25) O LORD save now, we beseech you; O LORD grant success. (26) Blessed is the one who comes in the name of the LORD; we have blessed you out of the house of the LORD. (27) The LORD is God and he has made his light shine upon us. Bind the sacrifice with cords unto the horns of the altar. (28) You are my God and I will give thanks to you, my God and I will exalt you. (29) Give thanks unto the LORD for he is good, for his lovingkindness is eternal.

Discussion

The psalm opens with exhortation to praise God for his mercy. Native born Israelites (v. 2), the priesthood (v. 3) and indeed all sincere believers (v. 4) should recognize in the great deliverance which has been effected another evidence of the everlasting mercy of God.

The prophetically significant portion of the psalm speaks to the theme of the deliverance of the Messiah. The psalm speaks of deliverance from (1) distress (vv. 5-9), danger (vv. 10-16), death (vv. 17-21), and disgrace (vv. 22-26).

A. Deliverance from Distress (vv. 5-9). The Messiah begins in verse 5 to describe a personal experience in which his Father came to his aid. He speaks first in general terms of the *distress* into which he had fallen. In this predicament the Father had done several things for him:

1. The Lord answered him *in a large place* (v. 5). A narrow place symbolizes distress, a wide place deliverance. Jesus spent much time in prayer during his ministry, and the more so when he faced that final crisis. The Father answered the agonizing prayer of Gethsemane. He delivered the Messiah, not *from* the ordeal, but *through* it.

2. The Lord sided with him during the distress. Literally the Hebrew reads, *Yahweh is to me among the helpers,* i.e., he is my great helper. The realization that the Father stood with him enabled Messiah to set his face stedfastly toward Jerusalem (Luke 9:51). He feared nothing which men could do to him (v. 6).

3. The Lord took his part, i.e., actively aided him. This enabled Messiah *to look on* those that hated him. He feared not to look the whole of them in the face (v. 7).

Before describing in more detail the distress and deliverance, Messiah pauses to press home a great principle: It is better to trust in the Lord than to put confidence in man (vv. 8-9).

B. Deliverance from Danger (vv. 10-16). The seriousness of the distress mentioned in verse 5 is amplified in verses 10-16. Three times in verses 10-12 Messiah describes himself as surrounded by enemies. They are identified as *all the Gentiles* (v. 10). Romans and Jews acting like Gentiles taunted, mocked, and threatened him. Because of the countless numbers of assailants, and furious desire to destroy, the enemies are likened to vicious bees. Angry and armed with stings (v. 12), they tormented him.

In verse 13 Messiah seems to be alluding to the malicious leader of the opposition, Satan himself: *You have knocked me back to make me fall!* Satan emptied his arsenal in his attacks upon Jesus of Nazareth. With his death on the cross Satan thought he had successfully destroyed Messiah. But Messiah has more than adequate resources for dealing with this multitude of enemies. The Lord—the Father—helped him (v. 13). Messiah acknowledges the Father as *my strength, my song* and *my salvation* (v. 14).

Three times in this unit Messiah expresses his confidence in ultimate victory: *I will cut them off* (vv. 10, 11, 12). The fire of rage and hatred against God's person and plan will be *quenched* (v. 12). Fire among thorns blazes up suddenly with intense heat, and then dies out, leaving no trace whatever. So the enemies of Messiah will certainly and suddenly come to their end.

All of this will be done judicially, properly, circumspectly *in the name of the Lord* (vv. 10, 11, 12). Judgment has been committed to the Son. All authority in heaven and earth has been given unto him. Through the authority granted to him, Messiah will be the final Judge of all, including those who with vengeance attacked him.

Messiah pauses anew to press home the application of what he has been saying. While Messiah's enemies are destroyed, there is the *sound of rejoicing and salvation* in the *tents of the righteous* (v. 15). What a stark contrast between the fate of the ungodly and the godly: destruction versus salvation. The joyful song of salvation centers around *the right hand of the Lord* (v. 15) which is exalted because he has fought *valiantly* (v. 16).

C. *Deliverance from Death* (vv. 17-21). Messiah expresses confidence in the ultimate victory over death when he declares *I shall not die, but live*. The argument is sometimes made that these words exclude the Messianic interpretation of the psalm because Jesus did in fact die. But if the words of verse 17 are pressed to the absolute literal limit, the statement would not be true of David either. He certainly died. The language must be interpreted in a restricted sense: David was confident he would not die in a particular situation. But if the words could be interpreted in a restricted sense in reference to David, they also can be understood in a restricted sense in reference to Messiah. Jesus did not die to stay dead. He was not abandoned to the power of death (v. 18b). He rose again to *declare the works of Yahweh* (v. 17).

The clause *Yahweh has chastened me sore* (v. 18) is pregnant with meaning. All the suffering of Gethsemane and Calvary are involved. This theme of divine chastening will be taken up by Isaiah and he will demonstrate that Messiah would suffer vicariously for the sins of mankind (Isa. 53). This suffering was part of God's grand plan, and in that sense the chastening can be attributed to the Father.

Returning triumphantly from his sacrificial mission, Messiah calls for the gates of the celestial city—*the gates of righteousness*—to be opened to him. He speaks here of gates which open only to the just, and which exclude all unrighteousness. Messiah returned to praise his Father (v. 19). His prayers had been answered; his salvation (deliverance) was complete (v. 21). Through this same gate of the Lord the righteous—those who have been declared righteous through faith in Christ—will follow their Redeemer (v. 20). "Whosoever lives and believes in me shall never die" (John 11:26).

D. Deliverance from Disgrace (vv. 22-26). Messiah refers to himself by a metaphor in verse 22. He is *the stone the builders rejected.*[5] The Jews, especially the priests, to whom was entrusted the task of building up God's spiritual Temple refused to recognize him as the rightful foundation upon which to build. According to Matthew 21:42 Jesus is this rejected stone. But what irony! That very stone cast aside as unfit for use became *the head of the corner*—the cornerstone or most important stone in the structure (v. 22).

The saints of God can only marvel at the circumstances which led to the exaltation of the rejected stone. On Friday afternoon the limp body of the teacher from Nazareth was removed from the cross. The hopes of the followers were shattered. But at sunrise on the first day they became eye witnesses of the most stupendous miracle of history (v. 23). The resurrection of Jesus of Nazareth ushered in a new day for the human race. *This is the day that the Lord has made.* Believers can rejoice and be glad in this day (v. 24). Death has been conquered. Jesus is on his throne!

The community of believers welcome the triumphant Messiah in verses 25-27. *Hoshe'a-na'*—hosanna—they cry. *O Yahweh, save now we beseech you!*[6] Where Christ comes salvation and spiritual prosperity come as well. To pray that this salvation and prosperity might come (v. 25) is the Old Testament equivalent of praying "Thy kingdom come, Thy will be done, on earth as it is in heaven."

Messiah came *in the name of the Lord.* In all that he did he was acting under a commission from his Father. The believing community pronounced a blessing on this one who was in fact a blessing to all mankind. Out of the house of the Lord—the spiritual Temple of II Peter 2:9—this worshipful blessing emanates (v. 26).

Yahweh is God (*'el*—the Mighty One). He has shown his power by resurrecting his Son from the grave. In so doing he brought new light to those who sat in the darkness of sin (v. 27). They who sat in darkness have seen a great light (Matt. 4:16).

Those who have been recipients of that Gospel light cry out in earnest petition: *Bind the sacrifice with cords even unto the horns of the altar*

---

5. Modern scholars usually regard the *stone* as (1) the capstone of the Temple being currently erected by Zerubbabel; (2) the nation Israel rejected by the nations of the world; or (3) a common proverb which could be applied to any situation in which someone despised is finally exalted. Accordingly, Christ was not giving an *interpretation* in Matt. 21:42, but merely an *application.*

6. This verse was chanted on the Feast of Tabernacles amidst the shaking of festive branches.

(v. 27). This is a prayer that the sacrifice made by the Christ might be a once-for-all-time offering. Sacrificial blood was smeared on the horns of the altar during the sacrificial ritual. For the sacrifice to be *bound* to the horns would make the effects of the offering perpetual. The prayer of the righteous is answered in the Johannine declaration that the blood of Jesus Christ keeps on cleansing us from all sin (I John 1:7).

Messiah speaks again in verse 28. Twice he declares his submission to the Father (*you are my God*). "The Father and Christ, both before he was incarnate and after, stand agreed in the covenant of redemption."[7] Twice the Messiah declares his desire to praise the Father. He is totally pleased with his earthly mission, with the grand deliverance which his sacrificial death and triumphant resurrection has made possible. The goodness of the Lord in sending Christ to be mankind's savior calls for everlasting praise. So the psalm ends as it began with an exhortation to express gratitude to God for his never-ending mercy (v. 29).

Prophecy No. 16

THE PARABLE TELLER

Psalm 78:1-2

That the first two verses of Psalm 78 are personal Messianic prophecy is suggested by Matthew 13:34-35.

> All these things spoke Jesus unto the multitudes in parables; and without a parable he did not speak unto them, that it might be fulfilled which was spoken by the prophet, saying, I will open my mouth in parables; I will utter things which have been kept secret from the foundation of the world.

Psalm 78 was written by Asaph who was a musician contemporary with David and Solomon. This claim of the heading is confirmed by the internal evidence of the psalm itself. It recounts the history of God's people down to the time of David and no further.

Conservative commentators struggle in their efforts to rescue Matthew from mere accommodation of the language of Psalm 78:1-2. The usual explanation is that Asaph was a prophet, and in his teaching methodology was a type of Christ. It would appear, however, that

---

7. Dickson, CP, II, 341.

Matthew regarded Psalm 78:1-2 as a direct prediction of the nature of the teaching ministry of Jesus.

Translation of Psalms 78:1-2

(1) Give ear, O my people, to my law; incline your ears to the words of my mouth. (2) I will open my mouth in a parable; I will utter dark sayings of old.

Discussion

Who is the speaker in verses 1-2? Most assume that the first person pronoun refers to Asaph, the author of the psalm. But this is only an assumption. First person utterances in prophetic literature often are direct utterances of God. According to the New Testament, first person utterances in the psalms as well as the prophetic books sometimes are to be attributed to Messiah.

Matthew, under inspiration of the Spirit, was keen to observe in Psalm 78:1-2 what most modern interpreters have missed, *viz.*, that Asaph could not possibly be speaking in these two verses. God is the speaker. The language admits of no other interpretation. The speaker addresses his readers as *my people*. Such direct address in the psalms is found elsewhere only two times, in both of which God is the speaker.[8] In Psalm 81, another Asaphic psalm, God refers to Israel as *my people* three times (vv. 8, 11, 13).[9] The use of the terminology *my people* is presumptive evidence that God is the speaker.

The speaker in Psalm 78:1 calls upon his people to hear *my law* (*torah*). The terminology *my law* or *laws* is found nineteen times in the Old Testament. Never does any one address the nation and urge them to obey *my law* (or laws) except God. It is true that *my law* is used three times in proverbs of the instruction of a father to his son. But for the nation only God could give *torah*. It would be blasphemy for any prophet or poet to insist that Israel heed his (i.e., the poet's) law. Thus the language *my people* and *my law* in Psalm 78:1 precludes the usual explanation that Asaph is addressing the nation.

If Asaph is not the speaker in Psalm 78:1-2, who is? The only answer can be, God. The divine utterance emphasizes five points:

---

8. Pss. 50:7; 81:8. In Ps. 49:1 the sons of Korah called upon all people to *hear*.

9. *My people* occurs nine times in the Psalter. Seven times God is speaking. There are textual problems with *my people* in Ps. 144:2. Only in Ps. 59:11, a Davidic psalm, is this terminology used by one other than God.

1. God will speak (*open my mouth*). The verb is cohortative in form and has the force of an emphatic future. God is determined to speak.

2. God will speak to his people.

3. God will speak in a *parable (mashal)*. The word "means (1) primarily a comparison, (2) a proverb, as frequently involving a comparison, (3) a parable, as the extension of a proverb, (4) a poem, either contemptuous or didactic."[10]

4. God will speak in *dark sayings*. The term *chidoth* denotes "(1) an enigma or riddle, (2) a parable or simile, (3) any profound or obscure utterance, a problem, dark saying."[11]

5. These dark sayings or parables express truths which are ancient, for they are *of old*. Matthew expands on this idea. Those truths which Jesus presented in parables had been hidden since *the foundation of the world*.

Matthew, observing that God was speaking in Psalm 78:1-2, and that the verbs were emphatic futures, quite properly assigns the fulfillment to the teaching ministry of Jesus. God announced that he would teach his people through the parabolic method. In Jesus God opened his mouth, as it were, and spoke ancient truths in parabolic form. God said he would teach in this fashion, and Jesus did it!

One point remains to be clarified. What is the relation of the predictive declaration of verses 1-2 and the lengthy narration of God's past involvement with Israel (vv. 3-72)? Whereas God speaks in mysterious utterances, Asaph and the pious within Israel speak those things which they have heard and known, God's wondrous deeds in the history of his people. The psalm presents a contrast, then, between the way God would teach and the way pious Old Testament teachers taught. Verses 3-72 do not contain the *mashal* and the *chidoth* mentioned in verse 2, but a flowing exposition of history.

---

10. Kirkpatrick, CB, p. 269.
11. Ibid.

Chapter Nine

THE BETRAYAL OF MESSIAH

According to New Testament authority, the betrayal of Christ by Judas is the subject of two prophetic psalms, Psalms 69 and 109. Both passages focus on the terrible judgment which would befall the betrayer.

Prophecy No. 17

PUNISHMENT FOR THE BETRAYER

Psalm 69

Psalm 69 is quoted seven times in the New Testament. No psalm, save Psalm 22, is more distinctly applied to Christ. Of course the mere quotation of a passage does not necessarily mean that direct prediction is involved. The manner of citation must be carefully examined.

Alexander expressed the common notion about Psalm 69 when he wrote:

> The subject of the psalm is an ideal person, representing the whole class of righteous sufferers. The only individual in whom the various traits meet is Christ. That he is not, however, the exclusive or even the immediate subject, is clear from the confession in verse 6 (5).[1]

It is, however, best to number Psalm 69 with the predictive Messianic psalms. The Sufferer in this psalm is Messiah. While the application of verse 5 is problematical, the New Testament evidence seems conclusive in pointing to Christ as the fulfillment of these predictions.

The psalm claims to be Davidic in its heading. The reference to the chief musician indicates that this composition was intended for public performance. Some interpret the *lillies* in the heading to be the title of the melody to which this psalm was put. Others think *lillies* refers to the "delightful consolations and deliverances experienced or hoped."[2]

Translation of Psalm 69

To the chief musician upon lillies. Of David. (1) Save me, O God, for waters have come unto my life. (2) I have sunk into deep mire where there is no foothold; I have come into the depths of waters and the floods overflow me. (3) I am weary in my crying; my throat is dry. My

---

1. Alexander, PTE, p. 292.
2. Ibid.

eyes fail while I wait for my God. (4) More numerous than the hairs of my head are those who hate me without reason; those who would cut me off, my enemies undeservedly, are strong. That which I did not steal I restored. (5) O God, you know my foolishness; my guilt from you is not hidden. (6) Let not those who hope in you be ashamed because of me. O Lord GOD of hosts; let not those who seek you be humiliated because of me, O God of Israel. (7) For I bear reproach on account of you, and shame covers my face. (8) I have become a stranger to my brethren, a foreigner to my mother's sons. (9) For the zeal for your house has consumed me, and the reproaches of those who reproach you have fallen on me. (10) When I weep with fasting for my soul, it becomes reproaches for me. (11) When I put on sack-cloth as my garment, then I become to them a proverb. (12) Those who sit in the gate speak of me, and I am the song of drunkards. (13) But as for me, my prayer is to you, O LORD, in an acceptable time; in your great lovingkindness, O God, answer me in the truth of your salvation. (14) Deliver me from the mire that I may not sink; deliver me from those who hate me, and from the depths of waters. (15) Do not let the floodwaters overwhelm me, nor let the deep swallow me up, nor let the pit shut its mouth over me. (16) Answer me, O LORD, for your lovingkindness is good; according to the multitude of your mercies, turn unto me. (17) Do not hide your face from your servant; because I am in trouble, answer me quickly. (18) Come near unto my soul, redeem it; because of my enemies deliver me. (19) As for you, you know my reproach, my shame, my humiliation; all my enemies are before you. (20) Reproach has shattered my heart, and I am sick; I looked for sympathy, but there was none, and for comforters, but I found none. (21) They put gall in my food, and for my thirst they gave me vinegar. (22) May their table become a snare before them, that which should have been for their welfare, let it become a trap. (23) May their eyes be darkened so they cannot see, and their loins shake continually. (24) Pour out your wrath upon them; let your fierce anger overtake them. (25) Let their habitation become desolate; let there be no one to dwell in their tents (26) For they persecute the one you have smitten, and they talk about the pain of those you have wounded. (27) Add iniquity unto their iniquity, and let them not come into your righteousness. (28) May they be blotted out of the book of life, and may they not be listed with the righteous. (29) But I am poor and afflicted; let your salvation, O God, set me on high. (30) I will praise the name of God with a song, I will magnify him with thanks-giving. (31) It is better to the LORD than an ox, a bull with horns and hoofs. (32) The humble shall see this and rejoice, those who seek God, and your heart shall live. (33) For the LORD hears the poor, and he does not despise his prisoners. (34) Let the heavens and earth praise him, the sea and all which move about in it. (35) For God will save Zion, and will build the cities of Judah that they may dwell there and possess it. (36) The seed of his servants shall inherit it, and those who love his name shall dwell in it.

Discussion

Psalm 69 is organized in three major divisions: (1) the prayer of the Messiah (vv. 1-27), (2) his prophecy regarding the enemies (vv. 22-28), and (3) his profession of thanksgiving (vv. 29-36).

A. *The Prayer of the Messiah* (vv. 1-22). Six times in the first section of the psalm the Sufferer presents his petition to the Father. Each time he strengthens his case by adding new reasons for divine intervention.

1. The first petition is simple: *Save me.* To support this petition he offers four reasons:

a) He was in serious danger (vv. 1-2). He uses the figure of near drowning to describe his plight in verse 1 and in verse 2 he employs the figure of deep mire in which there is no solid bottom.[3]

b) He had waited long and patiently on God (v. 3). He had become weary with calling upon God for help. His throat is parched dry by excessive exertion of the voice. His eyes are represented as exhausted, worn out by continued looking to God for aid.

c) He was facing numerous enemies who were malicious and mighty (v. 4). He was hated without cause. They were wrongfully his enemies. But these foes were out to destroy him. Though he was absolutely honest, he was treated as a thief—forced to restore that which he had not taken.

d) He was confident that God knew the true facts about his conduct (v. 5). God knew that he had been as foolish and sinful as his persecutors alleged. This obviously is the most difficult verse in the Psalm to interpret Messianically. Clarke comments: "How can such words as are in this verse be attributed to our blessed Lord however twisted or turned?"[4]

---

3. Cf. Jer. 38:6; Jonah 2:6; Ps. 40:2.
4. Clarke, CCN, III, 224.

From one point of view Christ was altogether free from the charges laid against him by his antagonists. From another point of view all the iniquities of mankind were charged upon him by imputation. By his suffering and death, that image of God which man had lost through his rebellion, he restored. This perhaps explains the last clause of verse 4: *that which I did not steal I restored.* Maas addressed the exegetical problem here when he wrote:

> We may add here that what the psalmist says of his own sinfulness may apply to Christ in so far as he has taken upon himself the sins of all; at the same time, the justice and righteousness of the sufferer are so much extolled that they cannot fully apply to anyone but the Messias.[5]

2. The second petition is that godly souls may not be hurt by the suffering which he experiences (vv. 7-12). This petition is strengthened by four reasons:

a) His sufferings were for God's cause (v. 7).

b) His friends had abandoned him (v. 8). (Cf. Matt. 26:56.)

c) His zeal for the honor of God's house has brought reproach upon him (v. 9). He had a jealous regard for the honor of the sanctuary, as the visible center of true religion. His strong desire to promote the glory of God's house consumed him, i.e., took precedence over all other desires. This verse is applied to Jesus in John 2:17. The latter part of the verse is applied to Christ in Romans 15:3.

d) He was greatly mocked for his religious commitment (vv. 10-12). The spiritual agony of Messiah is mentioned here, not in reference to his own suffering only, but to the sins of his people.[6] One thinks of the tears shed by the Master as he looked down upon the city of Jerusalem (Luke 19:41). People in positions of leadership (*those who sit in the gate*) and those rascals who compose drunken ditties made light of Messiah's earnest concern for the salvation of his fellows (v. 12).

3. In his third petition Messiah prays that God will hear him (v. 13). He adds three reasons in support of this petition:

a) He presents his petition *in an acceptable time*, i.e., before it was too late.

b) He makes mention of the multitude of God's mercies.

c) He speaks of the truth of God's promises of salvation.

4. The fourth petition is for deliverance (vv. 14-15). He supports this petition by again vividly describing his plight in terms of drowning and entrapment in a pit.

---

5. Maas, CTP, II, 206-207.
6. Alexander, PTE, p. 293.

5. To his fifth petition for deliverance (vv. 16-17) Messiah adds three additional supporting thoughts:

a) He refers to the multitude of God's tender mercies.

b) He again refers to the trouble he experiences.

c) He urges a swift response from God thus implying that his situation was desperate.

6. In connection with his sixth petition for deliverance (vv. 18-21) he mentions four facts:

a) God knows the reproach which has been heaped upon him (v. 19).

b) He is heavy hearted because of that reproach (v. 20).

c) He was able to find no comfort on earth (v. 20).

d) Tormentors had added affliction to affliction. Instead of meat they had given him *gall* (bitterness) and vinegar for drink (v. 21). Gall and vinegar are here put together to denote the most unpalatable forms of food and drink. In the passion of Jesus Christ circumstances were such that this verse received striking fulfillment. Romans usually gave those sentenced to the cross a sour wine with an infusion of myrrh for the purpose of deadening the pain. This practice was followed in the case of Jesus (Mark 15:23). On the part of the Roman soldiers this may have been an act of kindness; but considered as an act of the unbelieving Jews, it was adding anguish to one already overwhelmed with anguish. Matthew, therefore, suggests that the wine and myrrh offered to Christ are identical with the gall and vinegar of this prediction (Matt. 27:34).

B. *The Prophecy Regarding the Enemies* (vv. 22-28). The imprecations contained in verses 22-28 are not the outgrowth of a vengeful or selfish spirit. Jesus applied the words of these verses to the unbelieving Jews (Matt. 23:38) and Paul did the same thing (Rom. 11:9, 10). These imprecations should be regarded as predictions. Dickson[7] identifies ten plagues which are here pronounced against the persecutors.

1. God will curse all comforts of this life unto the obstinate adversaries: *May their table become a snare to them* (v. 22a). The place where they were accustomed to enjoy themselves would become for them an occasion of unexpected danger.

2. All things will work for the woe and torment of these enemies: *that which should have been for their welfare, let it become a trap* (v. 22b).

---

7. Dickson, CP, I, 419ff.

3. They shall not perceive the true intent of God's work:[8] *May their eyes be darkened, that they may not see* (v. 23a).

4. There shall be no peace: *their loins be made to shake* (v. 23b).

5. The wrath of God will be poured out upon them (v. 24).

6. The curse of God shall be on their houses and prosperity, and the place they have dwelt in shall be abhorred: *May their habitation become desolate; let there be no one to dwell in their tents* (v. 25). Before he quoted Psalm 69:25 Peter made this comment: "Brothers, the Scriptures had to be fulfilled which the Holy Spirit spoke long ago through the mouth of David concerning Judas, who served as a guide for those who arrested Jesus" (Acts 1:16). Thus the New Testament regards Psalm 69:25 as a God-given prophecy. The psalmist himself may not have been aware of the real import of this verse. Of course, the prophecy is not merely applied to Judas as an individual but as the representative of the Jewish people "in their malignant and perfidious enmity to Christ."[9]

7. The persecutors will go ever deeper into sin:[10] *Add iniquity unto their iniquity* (v. 27a). Deeper sin is sometimes made the punishment of sin.

8. They become so hardened in sin that they shall not come into God's righteousness (v. 27b).

9. They shall meet with an untimely death: *May they be blotted out of the book of life* (v. 28a).

10. These wicked enemies would not be numbered among the righteous (v. 28b).

What possible circumstances could justify these dire predictions? The answer is found in verse 26. They have heaped abuse on the one God had smitten. One thinks immediately of the verbal abuse to which Jesus was subjected on the cross where he was "smitten of God, and afflicted" (Isa. 53:4).

C. *A Profession of Thanksgiving* (vv. 29-36). In the closing verses of Psalm 69 there are four grand evidences of the Sufferer's victory.

1. The Sufferer utters a confident prayer (v. 29). He will not only be delivered, he will be exalted. *Poor and afflicted* describe the life

---

8. Alexander (PTE, p. 295) suggests two other possible interpretations for the dimness of eyes: (1) dimness of the eyes in death; (2) darkness as a figure for calamity in general.

9. Alexander, PTE, p. 295.

10. Others think that the meaning is that the punishment will be appropriate to their iniquity or that sin may be followed by the natural effects of sin.

of Jesus in his final agony. A later prophet will describe him as "a man of sorrows, acquainted with grief" (Isa. 53:3). His salvation or deliverance was the resurrection. The expression *set me on high* used by the psalmist means to be beyond the reach of danger—to be placed in a place of safety.[11]

2. The Sufferer utters his praise for the Lord (vv. 30-31). Messiah's praise for the Father following his deliverance from suffering and death is a major theme in Old Testament prophecy. The certainty of the future deliverance is indicated by this expressed determination to thank God for it.[12]

3. He utters a prophecy concerning the fruits of his suffering (vv. 32-33). The *humble*, i.e., true believers, shall rejoice over the victory of the Sufferer (Messiah). These committed ones shall find a life more abundant because of the victory of the Sufferer (*your heart shall live*). In view of the victory won by the Sufferer, all the poor in spirit can have confidence that their prayers will be heard (*for Yahweh hears the poor*). His deliverance from suffering will also establish once and for all that God does not despise *his prisoners,* those who are imprisoned by affliction or by oppressors for his sake.

4. The psalm ends with a prophecy of thanksgiving for blessings bestowed on God's people (vv. 34-36). In the mercy experienced by himself, the victorious Sufferer sees a pledge of gifts demanding universal praise. The deliverance of the Sufferer signals the salvation of Zion. The God who is faithful to the individual believer will also be faithful to the whole church. "It is characteristic of the ancient saints to regard every personal mercy as a pledge of greater favors to the body of God's people."[13]

When David wrote the cities of Judah were not in ruins. The implication here is that they *would* be destroyed. But that would not be the end. Those cities would be rebuilt. So it was in the years following the destruction of Babylon. Jews by the thousands returned to their homeland and built up the waste places. Once again they possessed the land of Canaan (v. 35). The *seed* (descendants) of God's servants inherited the land promised to Abraham (v. 36). Alexander catches the spirit of this promise when he writes:

---

11. Cf. Ps. 20:1; 59:1.
12. Alexander, PTE, p. 296.
13. Ibid., p. 297.

The foregoing promises are not restricted to a single generation, but extend to the remotest posterity. . . . As temporal and spiritual blessings were inseparably blended in the old dispensation, the promise of perpetual possession and abode in Palestine is merely the costume in which that of everlasting favor to the church is clothed in the Old Testament.[14]

Prophecy No. 18
JUDGMENT ON JUDAS
Psalm 109

According to the heading of this psalm, David is the composer. No good reason has been advanced to nullify this declaration. The psalmist portrays an individual crying out for divine help against a gang of merciless enemies who are attempting to bring about his ruin through false accusations and treacherous slander.

The history of David's confrontation with various enemies uniquely qualified him to paint this picture of a betrayed saint. The speaker in this psalm has many enemies, for he speaks of them in the plural number. Yet his main focus in on a single individual. In describing this archenemy David draws upon his own experiences with Saul who pursued him, Ahithophel who betrayed him and Shimei who cursed him.

Two basic exegetical questions face the interpreter of this psalm: (1) Who is the one who cries out to God for relief from abuse? and (2) who is the archenemy who attacks him? Nothing within the psalm itself gives a definitive answer to these questions. One might assume that the author, David, is speaking of himself, but that is only an assumption. The Apostle Peter, however, sheds light on the second of the two basic exegetical questions which in turn answers the first question. He declared: "This Scripture must needs have been fulfilled, which the Holy Spirit by the mouth of David spoke before concerning Judas" (Acts 1:16). Peter then goes on to quote one line from Psalm 69 and one line from Psalm 109: "For it is written in the book of Psalms, Let his habitation be desolate and let no man dwell therein (Ps. 69:25); and his office let another take (Ps. 109:8)." The persecutor, then, is Judas, and this necessitates that the sufferer must be Messiah. Dickson supports the Messianic interpretation of the Psalm when he points out that

---

14. Alexander, TPTE, p. 297.

David is not satisfying his own private revenge against Ahithophel, or any other such like traitor, but as a prophet foretelling what judgment was to fall on the desperate enemies of God, as a saint subscribing to God's righteous judgments, for the terror of all opposers of Christ's kingdom.[15]

Other arguments supporting the Messianic interpretation of Psalm 109 are these:

1. The psalm contains certain imprecations, or better still, pronouncements which cannot be justified in the mouth of mere man. Only God, or his Son, could make such pronouncements.

2. The petitioner in this psalm maintains throughout his absolute innocence. No one can challenge the sincere piety and godliness of the speaker. He humbly and devoutly bares his soul before God. Yet he is conscious of no wrong in his own life, nothing that would in any way have provoked his enemies. Such absolute innocence would be appropriate to the life of Jesus.

3. David was a prophet (Acts 2:30) and his psalms are frequently quoted by New Testament writers as personal Messianic predictions.

4. The Church Fathers saw in this psalm the sufferings of Christ.

Modern scholars reject the personal Messianic interpretation of Psalm 109. Leupold, for example, argues that the quotation of one verse in Acts 1 does not make the whole of Psalm 109 Messianic.[16] This, of course, is true. But the manner in which the one verse is quoted makes very difficult any other interpretation unless one wants to question the legitimacy of the apostle's Christological interpretation of the Old Testament. The one verse cited in the New Testament becomes a valid exegetical clue to the true meaning of the passage which the interpreter dare not ignore.

Translation of Psalm 109

To the chief musician. A psalm of David. (1) O God of my praise, Be not silent, (2) for the mouth of the wicked and the mouth of the deceitful are opened against me; they have spoken against me with a lying tongue. (3) With words of hatred they have surrounded me; and they have fought against me without cause. (4) In return for my love, they have made me an adversary while I am a man of prayer. (5) They have repaid me with evil instead of good, and hatred for my

---

15. Dickson, CP, II, 288.
16. Leupold, EP, p. 767.

love. (6) Appoint against him a wicked man; Satan shall stand at his right hand. (7) When he is tried, he shall be condemned, and his prayers shall condemn him. (8) His days shall be few, and another shall take his office. (9) His sons shall be orphans, and his wife a widow. (10) His sons shall be continually wandering about, they shall beg and seek their bread from desolate places. (11) A creditor shall seize all which is his, and strangers shall spoil his labor. (12) No one shall extend mercy to him; nor shall there be favor to his orphans. (13) His posterity shall be cut off; in another generation their name shall be blotted out. (14) The iniquity of his fathers shall be remembered with the LORD; and the sin of his mother shall not be wiped out. (15) They shall be before the LORD continually that he may cut off the remembrance of them from the land. (16) Because he did not remember to do kindness, and he pursued to death the poor, the needy and the broken hearted one. (17) He loved cursing, so it shall come on him; he did not delight in blessing, so it shall be far from him. (18) He clothed himself with cursing as with a garment, so it shall come into his body like water, into his bones like oil. (19) It shall be to him like a garment wrapped about, and like a belt continually girded about. (20) This shall be the payment of my adversary from the LORD, and of them that speak evil against my life. (21) But as for you, O LORD my sovereign, deal with me for the sake of your name; because your lovingkindness is good, deliver me. (22) For poor and needy am I, and my heart is wounded within me. (23) Like a shadow I fade away, I am shaken off like a locust. (24) My knees wobble through fasting, and my flesh lacks fatness. (25) And as for me, I became a reproach to them; they see me and wag their heads. (26) Help me, O LORD my God, save me according to your lovingkindness, (27) that they may know that this is your hand, that you, O LORD, have done it. (28) They may curse, but you will bless; they shall arise, but they shall be clothed with shame; but your servants shall rejoice. (29) I will praise the LORD exceedingly with my mouth; yes I will extol him in the midst of a multitude. (30) For he stands at the right hand of the poor one, to deliver from those who condemn him.

Discussion

The structure of Psalm 109 is simple. The petitioner—the Messiah—raises his cry for help in verses 1-5 and verses 20-31. His prayer is interrupted by the pronouncement of judgment against those who made Messiah an object of bitterness (vv. 6-19).

A. Messiah's Plight (vv. 1-5). In verses 1-5 the Messiah appeals to God to intervene on his behalf against ruthless persecutors. *Be not silent!* God is the object of Messiah's praise, for the Father has never failed him in times past.

God's silence is in stark contrast to the noisy clamor of the foe. His enemies "are scheming to effect his ruin by groundless charges supported by the false witnesses."[17] These vicious foes surrounded him like a pack of wild dogs. They fought against him without cause (v. 3).

Messiah loved men, even those who became his foes.[18] His love was proved by his prayers on their behalf (v. 4). But they had rewarded[19] his intercession and compassion with evil and hatred (v. 5).

B. The Judge Pronounces Sentence (vv. 6-19). The distinctive problem involved in this psalm begins to appear in verse 6. Here one finds "some of the strongest imprecation to be found anywhere in the Psalter."[20] Some regard verses 6-19 as a quotation of the words of the enemies against David. Another approach is to regard the verb forms as simple predictions rather than prayers or wishes.

In these verses God is no longer addressed in the second person; no vocatives appear. Nothing in these verses indicates that prayer is being continued. Nothing in the Hebrew grammar compels the conclusion that malevolent wishes are being here expressed. What are stated here are predictions, not wishes. Furthermore, the speaker seems to change in verses 6-19. These verses are best regarded as an answer to prayer, not as part of the prayer itself. God is responding to Messiah's pleas for help by pronouncing the doom of the enemy through the pen of his servant David. This is exactly what Peter declared: "The Holy Spirit spoke long ago by the mouth of David concerning Judas. . . . May another take his place of leadership" (Acts 1:16, 20).

The shift from the plural in reference to the persecutors, to the singular in verses 6-20 is also significant. One special adversary of Messiah is singled out for condemnation here. Ten details of that judgment are indicated:

---

17. Kirkpatrick, CB, p. 655.

18. The Hebrew word for *foes* is characteristic of this psalm (vv. 20, 29) and is found elsewhere in the Psalter only in 38:20 and 71:13. It may have the special sense of opponents in a court of law.

19. Literally, they have laid evil upon me.

20. Leupold, EP, p. 763.

1. The enemy comes under the influence of Satan[21] the wicked adversary of mankind (v. 6). John declares that the devil entered into the heart of Judas (John 13:27). Satan would stand at his side to urge Judas forward till he effected his intended crime.

2. The betrayer will be condemned in the judgment (v. 7a).

3. The betrayer's prayer before God will be to no avail. His prayer will be regarded as sin[22] (v. 7b). The first requirement of acceptable prayer is a penitent heart.

4. The betrayer's life will come to an end prematurely (*his days shall be few*) according to verse 8a.

5. The betrayer will be succeeded in his office by another person. This clause, together with Psalm 69:25, is quoted in Acts 1:20 in reference to Judas. It is commonly asserted that Judas is the antitype of the man who requited love with treachery.[23] But the explanation for Peter's citation is more than the similarity between David's opponents and Judas. The Holy Spirit speaks here of Judas. So declares Peter, and so must be the verdict of all those who take seriously the authority of apostolic interpretation of the Bible.

6. The betrayer's children will suffer by his death, for they will be fatherless. His wife will be a widow (v. 9). These dependents will be forced to roam about begging as their home falls into ruin for lack of upkeep (v. 10). This is not a case of the innocent suffering for the guilty, but a simple and obviously true prediction that the family of the betrayer will suffer when he dies.[24]

7. All that the betrayer had worked for would be taken from him by creditors (v. 11).

8. No one would extend compassion to the fatherless children of the betrayer (v. 12).

9. The betrayer's sons would die childless. Eventually the family name would be removed from the register of citizens (v. 13).

10. The punishment of the sins of his parents and ancestors, delayed and postponed in God's grace, would be brought to bear against the betrayer[25] (vv. 14-15).

---

21. Some explain the word here to simply mean "an adversary." But Satan appears as accuser in Job 1:6 and Zech. 3:1, 2.

22. Cf. Ps. 66:18ff.; Prov. 1:28ff., 15:8; 21:27; 28:9; Isa. 1:15.

23. Kirkpatrick, CB, p. 656.

24. Leupold (EP, p. 767) comments: "It is not very likely that the prayer would single out the children of the man involved if they had not given evidence of having the same spirit that controlled their father."

25. See Exod. 20:5. Cf. Matt. 23:32-36.

The terrible sentence against the betrayer is deserved. The Judge specifies the reasons for the sentence in verses 16-19. First, the betrayer showed no mercy toward that One who was preeminately *the poor, the needy, and the broken hearted.* He persecuted that One and was responsible for his death (v. 16).

A second justification for the sentence is found in the fact that the betrayer deliberately chose the policy of *cursing*, i.e., bringing calamity on others. As a result, blessing would be removed far from him (v. 17). His ill-will and negative conduct would be like a garment to him, and like substances taken into the body (vv. 17-19).

C. *Messiah's Prayer Resumed* (vv. 20-31). Having heard the just pronouncement of the Judge, Messiah indicates his acquiescence. He boldly announces the fate of all those who speak against him, of all who make themselves his adversaries. Their fate would be like that of the betrayer (v. 20).

Next, the Messiah enumerates the grounds upon which he implores the intervention of God on his behalf. They are eight in number:

1. He asks God to act for the sake of his name,[26] i.e., in his own best interest. Divine action on behalf of the agonizing Savior would prove God to be all that he ever claimed to be (v. 21).

2. He mentions God's good (i.e., abundant) mercy as a ground for intervention (v. 21).

3. He mentions his own pitiful condition: he is *poor and needy.* These words perhaps denote his physical condition. He is helpless in the flesh to resist his powerful adversaries (v. 22).

4. The inward spiritual agony of the Messiah is reflected in the words *my heart is wounded within me.* What an appropriate description of the garden agony of the Savior (v. 22).

5. He faces imminent death. His life is like a shadow when it stretches out towards evening. The dark hour of death is upon him (v. 23).

6. Without God's help he is as helpless before his powerful adversaries as locusts driven about by wind (v. 23).

7. In his distress Messiah had no appetite for food. Like a man in mourning he has abstained from the use of oil to soothe the skin in that harsh climate (v. 24).

8. He has become an object of reproach. The enemies greet him with a gesture of contempt and abhorrence. He is treated as though he were an object of the wrath of God (v. 25).

---

26. The name for the deity in this verse is the combination of Yahweh (GOD) and *'adonay* (Lord). This combination occurs in the Psalter three other times, and outside the Psalter only in Hab. 3:19.

Messiah's prayer for help intensifies in the closing verses of the psalm. Again he pleads for a deliverance which would be appropriate to the mercy of God (v. 26), a deliverance so stupendous that even his enemies would have to recognize the hand (i.e., power) of God in it (v. 27).

Messiah prays that the evil designs of his adversaries may fail. Even though they have cursed him with tongue and deed, let God override that curse with blessing. Let their moment of triumph (*they shall arise*) be turned to their shame. At the same time, Messiah prays, Let me, your servant, know the joy that comes with victorious deliverance (v. 28).

Messiah's prayer ends on a note of confidence. He is confident that his enemies will be *clothed with shame*; that their carefully conceived plots will be turned to confusion (v. 29). He anticipates the resumption of his former thanksgiving and praises (v. 30). He knows that his Father stands at his right hand to aid him in court, as it were, against those who condemn him to death (v. 31).

Chapter Ten

DEATH AND BEYOND

That the Old Testament prophets anticipated the "sufferings of Christ and the glory that would follow" is the affirmation of I Peter 1:11. Two clear examples of this dual theme are found in the Psalter. Psalm 22 focuses on the death of Christ and Psalm 2 on the glorious honor that was bestowed on Christ at his resurrection.

Prophecy No. 19

THE DEATH OF CHRIST

Psalm 22

Psalm 22 is the first and greatest of the passional psalms.[1] The psalm was written by David as is attested by the heading.[2] New Testament usage of the psalm makes it clear that it is to be numbered among the Messianic psalms.

The title of the psalm contains directions to the chief musician or choirmaster. It was to be sung to the tune called *Aijeleth Shahar,* the hind of the dawn. The early rays of light which preceded the dawn resembled the horns of a hind or deer. What an appropriate title this is. The light of morning pierces the darkened sky, like the horns of the hind, offering hope of rapidly approaching illumination. So in this psalm the black night of affliction and woe gives birth to the day of hope which hastens on towards the noontide of glory and gladness.[3]

Some of the specifications in the second half of the psalm do not seem to fit the personal Messiah in his resurrection and ascension glory. Yet in those very verses where one might be tempted to surrender the Messianic reference, the New Testament authority comes in expressly to confirm it. Verse 22, for example, states: "I will declare your name unto my brethren; in the midst of the congregation will I praise you." The author of Hebrews cites this verse word for word in the midst of a succession of kindred Old Testament quotations and gives the words a Messianic application. The apostle regarded these words as spoken by the Savior, showing Christ's intimate and tender relationship with his people.

---

1. In a passional psalm there is extreme and intense suffering. Other passional psalms are 69, 109, 35, 41 and 55.
2. Psalm 22 is cited many times in the New Testament, but the author is not named.
3. M'Lean, GTP, p. 103

In Psalm 22 the voice of a forsaken sufferer is heard loudly lamenting his lot and minutely describing his pain and shame. Not once, however, does the sufferer reproach God or accuse himself. This voice is silenced in death, but then is heard again celebrating with other voices the praises of the Lord.

Who is this innocent sufferer? David is the writer of the psalm. Is he speaking of the trials in his own life? David experienced much opposition during his life and more than once was at the point of death. But David's personal sufferings are not the focus of this psalm. So much of the language is inappropriate to David (cf. vv. 6, 11, 16, 18).

Who is the sufferer in Psalm 22? Certainly not the nation as a whole personified, or the pious saints within the nation. The sufferer and the congregation are clearly distinguished from one another throughout the psalm. The sufferer is despised by the people (v. 7), a mother gave him birth (vv. 10-11), he has bones, heart, palate, tongue (vv. 15-16), clothes (v. 14) and a soul (v. 21). Israelites oppose him and mock him for his trust in God, and Israelites are exhorted to rejoice in his deliverance.[4]

Who is the sufferer in Psalm 22? Jeremiah and even Esther have been nominated. But the truth of the matter is that no saintly person of Old Testament times was subjected to the mistreatment herein described. Briggs is right when he affirms that

> these sufferings transcend those of any historical sufferer, with the single exception of Jesus Christ. They find their exact counterpart in the suffering of the cross. They are more vivid in their realization of that dreadful scene than the stories of the Gospels.[5]

To this another point can be added. No Old Testament person could have imagined that his personal deliverance from death could be the occasion for the world's conversion. Such a hope must be restricted to the future Redeemer.[6] Under inspiration of the Holy Spirit David in Psalm 22 saw his descendant resembling, but far surpassing, himself in suffering. Furthermore, the deliverance of this descendant would have meaning for all mankind.

Psalm 22 reads as if it were composed at the foot of the cross. The evangelists, and Matthew in particular, have this psalm in mind as they pen the passion narratives. Although Jewish commentators did not

---

4. Heinisch, CIP, p. 66.
5. Briggs, MP, p. 326.
6. Heinisch, CIP, p. 66.

regard Psalm 22 as personal Messianic,[7] there can be little doubt that the early Christians so regarded it.

Translation of Psalm 22

To the chief musician. Upon the hind of the morning. A psalm of David. (1) My God, my God why have you forsaken me? Far from my deliverance are the words of my groaning. (2) O my God, I cry by day, and you do not answer, and by night, and I am not silent. (3) Nonetheless, you are the Holy One who sits upon the praises of Israel. (4) In you our fathers trusted, they trusted and you delivered them. (5) Unto you they cried, and they were delivered; they trusted in you and were not ashamed. (6) But I am a worm, and nobody; a reproach of men and despised of the people. (7) All who see me deride me; they open their lips,[8] they wag the head. (8) He trusts in the LORD[9] that he would deliver him; let him save him, for he delights in him. (9) For you are the One who caused me to burst forth from the womb. You caused me to trust upon the breasts of my mother. (10) Upon you I was cast from the womb; from the belly of my mother you were my God. (11) Do not be far from me, for trouble is near, for there is no helper. (12) Many bulls have surrounded me, strong ones of Bashan have attacked me. (13) They open wide their mouths against me as a lion tearing in pieces and growling. (14) Like water I am poured out and all of my bones are separated; my heart is like wax, it is melted within me. (15) My strength is dried up like a potsherd and my tongue cleaves to my jaws; you have brought me to the dust of death. (16) For dogs have surrounded me, an assembly of evil doers have encircled me; they pierced my hands and feet. (17) I count all of my bones; they look, they stare at me. (18) They have divided my garments among them, and cast lots over my apparel. (19) But as for you, O LORD, do not be far from me; O my strength, make haste for my help. (20) Deliver my darling from the sword, that which is most precious to me from the dog. (21) Deliver me from the mouth of the lion, answer me from the horns of the oxen. (22) I will declare your name to my brethren, in the midst of the assembly I will praise you. (23) You who fear the LORD praise him; all the seed of Jacob honor him and fear before him all seed of Israel. (24) For he has not despised nor has he

---

7. Only a ninth century A.D. midrash interprets the sufferer here to be the Messiah. See Heinisch, CIP, p. 68.

8. Lit., to cleave the lips, i.e., to open the mouth wide in scorn.

9. Lit., he rolled on the Lord.

regarded as an abomination the affliction of the afflicted one, nor has he hidden his face from him, but when he cried unto him he hearkened. (25) My praise shall be of you in the great assembly and my vows I will pay before them that fear him. (26) Meek ones shall eat and be satisfied; those who seek him shall praise the LORD: May your heart live forever. (27) All the ends of the earth shall remember and shall return unto the LORD, and all the families of nations shall bow down before you. (28) For the kingdom is the LORD's and he shall reign over nations. (29) All the fat ones of the earth shall eat and bow down before him, all who are going down to the dust shall kneel, and one cannot make alive his soul. (30) A seed shall serve him; it shall be recounted for the Lord for a generation. (31) They shall come and declare his righteousness to a people who shall be born, for he has done it.

Discussion

Psalm 22 has two major divisions. Verses 1-21 describe Christ's gloom on the cross, and verses 22-31 depict his glory following the resurrection. The first half of the psalm is suffering, the second part, song.[10]

A. *Christ's Gloom* (vv. 1-21). The darkness which shrouds the first half of this psalm is attributed to three major causes: (1) Christ has been forsaken by his Father (vv. 1-5), (2) he has become a reproach among men (vv. 6-10), and (3) he is experiencing intense physical agony (vv. 12-18). In spite of it all, the Sufferer continues to trust in God and to call upon him for deliverance (vv. 19-21).

1. Christ has been forsaken by his Father (vv. 1-5). Four points regarding this divine forsaking are made by the speaker:

a) The forsaking was very real (v. 1). The opening utterance of the psalm brings to mind the "Eli, Eli lama sabachthani" of Jesus' dying hour (Matt. 27:45ff.). The question is rhetorical. He expects no answer. The words are intended to express the agony of his separation from the Father. Even though he feels abandoned, yet Christ continues to speak of *my* God. A hint of the physical suffering of the Lord is found in the word *groaning,* a strong word used of the shrieking of a person in intense pain.

b) The forsaking seemed permanent (v. 2). Day and night his cry went up to God. There was no interposition on the part of God to

---

10. Wilson, MP, p. 58.

save him from the cross. The *night* here may refer to the darkness which covered the land at high noon, or perhaps to the gloomy night spent in the garden.

c) The forsaking was necessary (v. 3). *You are holy.* This is at once an affirmation of faith on the part of the Sufferer, and an explanation of the reason for the suffering. The holiness of God made it impossible for him to ignore sin. He had to punish sin. At the same time, his tremendous compassion desired to reach out to save lost mankind. The cross is the solution to the divine dilemma of how a holy God could forgive sinners and at the same time remain true to his holiness. It is the holiness of God, encompassing both his wrath and his mercy, which is most praiseworthy. God *sits* (part., continuous action) upon a throne constructed of the praises of his people. Having been redeemed from sin's bondage by the suffering of Calvary, the true Israel of God raises up continuous praise to God.

d) The forsaking does not suggest lack of power on God's part to deliver (vv. 4-5). The Old Testament is replete with accounts of how God's people trusted in him and how he rescued them from certain calamity. The key is *trust*. Three times the Sufferer refers to how the fathers *trusted* in God. He himself trusted in God. The Sufferer knew that God *could* deliver him. In patient trust he accepted his lot as the will of God.

2. The second paragraph of the psalm indicates another reason for the gloom of the speaker. He had become a reproach among men (vv. 6-10).

He is despised by the people (v. 6). In the eyes of those who looked upon his suffering, he was a *worm*[11] and not a man.[12] He was weak and helpless as a creature of the dust.

He was jeered by the people (vv. 7-8). All those who look upon him in his agony sneer at him, literally, they make faces at him and mock his cross-agony by wagging their heads (v. 8). The derisive taunt alluded to here is put nearly word for word into the mouth of mocking chief priests and scribes as they stood by the cross (Matt. 27:39-44). The crowds remembered his claims to divine sonship. They remembered the reports of the heavenly voice which said, "This is my beloved son

---

11. The word *tola'* also has the meaning *scarlet.* Beautiful dyes were made from blood of these worms, and the cloth dyed therewith was made into beautiful garments. Ironsides suggests that the glorious garments of our salvation are the garments that have been procured as a result of his death and suffering.

12. He was *lo' 'ish,* no man or nobody in contrast to being somebody.

in whom I am well pleased." The crowds mockingly urge him to cast (lit., roll) himself on Yahweh for *he delights in him* (v. 9).

Mockery is perhaps the most deadly missile in Satan's arsenal. Yet the Sufferer remained faithful. From the time of his birth he had learned to trust God. In spite of the cruel mockery hurled at him, he remained firmly committed in faith to his Father (vv. 9-10).

3. The third paragraph focuses on the physical agony which Christ endured on the cross (vv. 12-18).

a) His foes are vicious. He likens them to strong bulls (v. 12), lions (v. 13), half-starved dogs which roamed the streets of eastern cities (v. 16), and wild oxen[13] (v. 21).

b) He describes his utter exhaustion when he says, *I am poured out like water* (v. 14a).

c) His bones are disjointed (v. 14b).

d) His heart is failing (v. 14c). Like wax it has melted within him.

e) His thirst is raging (v. 15a). His tongue cleaves to his jaws. His strength is dried up like a broken piece of pottery. In his agony he lamented "I thirst," so that the Scriptures might be fulfilled (John 19:28).

f) He is nigh unto death (v. 15b). God has brought him to *the dust of death.* Obviously he is not yet dead. The meaning is that God has allowed him to approach the point of death.

g) His hands and feet have been pierced (v. 16b). This translation is supported by the ancient Septuagint, Vulgate and Syriac versions. The Hebrew text could be translated *like a lion, my hands and feet.* Jewish commentators prefer this reading. The enemies are mangling him as lions do their prey.[14]

h) His skin is taut, and he is so emaciated that he can count his bones. He is the object of the mocking glares of his enemies (v. 17).

i) He watches helplessly as his persecutors gamble over custody of his garments, his only earthly possessions (v. 18). The Evangelist quoted this verse and claimed that it was fulfilled when the Roman soldiers divided his clothing into four parts, and cast lots over his seamless robe (John 19:23, 24).[15]

---

13. Not *unicorns* as in KJV. Wilson (MP, pp. 60-62) has gone too far in suggesting that the bulls correspond to the chief priests and scribes, the wild ox to the mob, the dog to the Roman soldiers, and the lion to Satan working through Judas.

14. Cohen, SBB, p. 64. The textual difficulties in the passage perhaps explain why the evangelists do not cite these verses in their narrative of Christ's passion. There certainly is no justification for the translation of NEB: "They hacked off my hands and my feet."

15. Matt. 27:35 also notes this fulfillment, but there is some question about the textual integrity of the verse.

4. In spite of all his agony, the Sufferer continues to trust God and pray to him for deliverance in verses 19-21. *Do not be far from me . . . make haste for my help . . . deliver my darling*[16] (soul) *. . . deliver me!*

The similarities between Psalm 22 and Isaiah 53 are obvious. In the latter passage, however, the Suffering Servant dies and is buried. The world is converted because of his conquest of death. Psalm 22 speaks only of the brink of death. What is explicit in Isaiah 53, however, is implicit in Psalm 22.

B. *Christ's Glory* (vv. 22-31). After verse 21 the mood of the psalm changes. The prayers of the Sufferer have been answered. A great victory has been won. The writer of Hebrews writes:

> Who in the days of his flesh, when he had offered up prayers and supplications with strong crying and tears unto him that was able to save him from death, *and was heard* in that he feared (Heb. 5:7).

The loneliness and isolation of the first half of the psalm gives way to communal celebration in the second half. M'Lean comments:

> In respect of the *travail* foreshadowed in the former part of the Psalm, our Lord Jesus very peculiarly and emphatically held position of isolation. He trod the winepress alone, and of the people there was none with Him: none could divide with Him the woe; none could know in themselves the image and likeness of it. But it was otherwise with the *triumph* to follow. Out of the loneliness of the struggle He came forth not into possession of personal recompense merely, but as Forerunner into the joy of God's presence and fellowship of the multitude for whose sake He had undertaken the conflict.[17]

The sudden transition from prayer to answer is worthy of note. M'Lean again eloquently comments on the fulfillment:

> The deliverance when it comes, so mighty, so grand, in such height of contrast with the tribulation preceding, as to make interval of waiting to vanish into nothing. . . . Pass your eye up along the vista from the cross of pain and shame to that throne of joy and glory; measure the ladder of ascent from Joseph's sepulchre to the right hand of the Majesty on high: and then tell the force and significance of this that is spoken as from Messiah's own lips, . . . He hath not despised or abhorred the affliction of the Afflicted; neither hath He hid His face from Him: but when He cried, He hearkened unto Him.[18]

---

16. The RV translates "my only one." The LXX has *monogenes*. Wilson regards this as a Messianic title.

17. M'Lean, GTP, p. 124.

18. Ibid., pp. 127-128

Like the ever-widening ripples created by a stone tossed into a stream, the resurrection of Jesus first became a blessing to his brethren (v. 22), then to the seed of Israel (v. 23) and ultimately to the ends of the earth (v. 27). Four great thoughts dominate the second half of Psalm 22.

1. Christ's victory over death occasioned great joy (v. 22a). Christ knew that joyous victory lay just beyond the shadows of Calvary (Heb. 12:2). The key word in verses 22-23 is *praise*. Four things about this praise are indicated.

a) The first half of verse 22 speaks of the occasion for praise. After the suffering and agony of the cross, Christ rejoined his *brethren* to proclaim God's *name*. In the Bible the *name* of a person encapsulated the attributes of that person. To declare the *name* of God is to praise his attributes. The *brethren* here are those faithful ones who had followed him during his ministry of three and a half years (Matt. 28:10; John 20:17). The author of Hebrews makes the point that both the Redeemer and the redeemed are of one family. For this reason Jesus is not ashamed to call them (the redeemed) brothers (Heb. 2:11). Then the Hebrew writer cites Psalm 22:22. There can be no question, then, that the Sufferer in Psalm 22 is Jesus Christ, and the *brethren* are those he redeemed through suffering (cf. John 20:17).

b) The latter half of verse 22 speaks of the example of praise. *In the midst of the assembly I will praise you.* The triumphant Christ sets the example for his followers by praising the Father for the victory which had been won. The inspired author of Hebrews applies Psalm 22:22 to the savior and even puts these words into his mouth (Heb. 2:12). He identifies the assembly of this verse as the church.

c) Verse 23 contains the call for praise. Christ calls upon all true descendants of Jacob—those who fear the Lord—to honor and praise the Father.

d) The reason for this praise is stated in verse 24. Christ had not been permanently forsaken. The resurrection was the answer to Christ's cross petitions for salvation and deliverance. He was not delivered *from* death, for that was essential to the plan of God. But he was triumphant *over* death. For this reason God's people can and should forever praise the Lord.

2. Christ's victory over death is celebrated in worship (vv. 25-27). In verse 25 the triumphant Messiah shares in the worship of his people. God is the source as well as the object of praise. *My praise shall be of you in the great assembly.* The *great assembly* consists of all those who fear the Lord. Christ joins with his Church in praising the Lord.

Christ's people are sustained in worship (v. 26). *Meek ones shall eat and be satisfied.* Who are the meek ones? They are the poor in spirit, the humble, those who have surrendered their hearts to the Lord. Those who are here called *the meek* are those who can rightly claim to be members of the body of Christ. They are the *great assembly.* What will they eat? His body and blood! (John 6:33). Eating his flesh is appropriating the benefits of his atonement.

Since their spiritual needs are satisfied, the poor praise the Lord. They pray for one another: *May your heart live forever!* (v. 26). The earnest prayer of every Christian is that each brother and sister remain faithful unto death so that a crown of life may be received. All the ends of the earth join in this worship (v. 27). Paul echoes the same thought: "Every knee shall bow and every tongue confess that Jesus is Lord to the glory of God" (Phil. 2:10, 11).

3. Christ's victory over death ushers in his universal kingdom (vv. 28-29). *The kingdom is Yahweh's* (v. 28). His triumphant ascension to the right hand of God was his coronation procession. Daniel described prophetically that scene when one like unto a son of man came before the Ancient of Days to receive a kingdom (Dan. 7:13, 14). Obadiah ended his brief prophecy on the same optimistic note. John foresaw the days when the kingdoms of this world would become the kingdom of the Lord (Rev. 11:15).

Verse 29 further describes the extent of Messiah's kingdom. All the wealthy will someday worship him. John depicts the kings of the earth bringing their splendor into the New Jerusalem (Rev. 21:24). Every mortal man (*all those who are going down to the dust*) will one day yield to his sovereignty (Phil. 2:10).[19]

4. Christ's victory over death demands evangelism (vv. 30-31). God has a people in this world. *A seed shall serve him.* The seed of woman (Gen. 3:15), the true seed of Abraham (Gal. 3:16) will faithfully render service to him through the years. Many and strong have been the endeavors to silence the testimony. The church in one locale may be threatened in its testimony; but in another quarter it springs forth with fresh vigor and fruitfulness.

God's plan for world redemption involves the proclamation of God's *righteousness* as revealed in the death, burial and resurrection of Jesus.

---

19. M'Lean (GTP, p. 143) sees in verse 29 a contrast between two kinds of worshipers representing two extremes of social rank: the fat ones of the earth, i.e., the rich and honorable; and "he who cannot keep his soul alive," i.e., the outwardly destitute and afflicted.

He has done it! What a grand declaration. One single word in the Hebrew, a word which very closely anticipates the "It is finished" on the cross. The work of redemption is finished. Should the Lord tarry, generations yet unborn will learn of this great truth and respond to it. Praise the Lord! *He has done it!*

Prophecy No. 20

GOD'S GLORIOUS SON

Psalm 2

Psalm 2 is properly classified as a Messianic psalm because of the usage of it in the New Testament. This psalm is quoted seven times by the apostles, and in each instance it is applied to the Messiah.[20] The Church Fathers regarded the psalm as Messianic as did Jewish expositors even after the Jews' rejection of Jesus, which might have tempted them to seek another interpretation. It is thus clear who the central figure and subject of this psalm is. The king who in this psalm is the object of fiercest hostility from man and the highest honors from God was not David himself, but the Messiah, he in whom prophecy and history of the old world were to find their goal. M'Lean supports this view when he writes:

> This Psalm, in short, stands out clear and conspicuous, we might say chief and supreme, among those called *Messianic*; the personal history and surroundings and experience of the human author falling out of view, or supplying but dim, slender background; while by the Spirit of prophecy there becomes unveiled to himself, and through him mirrored to us in vivid panorama, 'the sufferings of Christ and the glory that should follow.'[21]

David was a prophet (Acts 2:30) and as such he made a rich contribution to Messianic expectation. Most likely all of Book One of Psalms (Pss. 1-41) came from the pen of David. Thirty-seven of the forty-one psalms in this "book" are attributed to David in their headings. Although Psalm 2 is anonymous, it is best taken as Davidic as well.

Psalm 2 pictures God's anointed king ruling upon Mt. Zion in spite of the efforts of Gentile rulers to overthrow him. What historical background, if any, prompted the writing of this psalm cannot be determined.

20. Acts 4:24-28; 13:33; Heb. 1:5; 5:5; Rev. 2:27; 12:5; 19:15.
21. M'Lean, GTP, p. 3.

Certainly the anointed one here is not David. David is often called God's anointed (II Sam. 12:7; Ps. 20:6), and he did wield power on Mt. Zion (I Chron. 15:1; 16:1). On many occasions he did face hostile Gentile foes. There is no indication, however, that David faced rebellion from Gentile foes which once had been subject to him. Furthermore, David was anointed at Bethlehem and Hebron, not Mt. Zion (v. 6). The same objections can be raised to the view that the anointed one is Solomon.

The truth is that David here is speaking as a prophet. The psalm is personal Messianic prophecy. The New Testament so interprets it (Acts 4:25-27; 13:33). The titles *anointed one* (Christ) and *son of God* which are used in this psalm were applied by the Jews of Jesus' day to the coming Redeemer (John 4:25; 1:49). Taken in its most literal sense the psalm fits perfectly with what is known of the life and ministry of Jesus of Nazareth.

Translation of Psalm 2

(1) Why do the nations rage and the peoples devise a vain thing? (2) The kings of the earth take their stand, and the rulers consult together against the LORD and against his anointed. (3) Let us tear their fetters apart, and cast away their cords from us. (4) The one who sits in the heavens shall laugh, the Lord derides them. (5) Then he shall speak unto them in his wrath, and in his fury he shall terrify them. (6) But as for me, I have anointed my king upon Zion, my holy mountain. (7) I will relate the decree: the LORD said unto me, You are my son, today I have begotten you. (8) Ask from me and I will give Gentiles as your inheritance, and the ends of the earth as your possession. (9) You shall break them with an iron rod, like a potter's vessel you shall smash them. (10) And now, O kings, act wisely, be instructed O judges of the earth. (11) Serve the LORD with fear, and rejoice with trembling. (12) Kiss the son lest he be angry and you perish in the way, for his wrath soon shall be kindled. Blessed are all who take refuge in him.

Discussion

Psalm 2 is a three act drama in which the psalmist depicts (1) the revolt of men against God (vv. 1-3); (2) the response of God to the revolt (vv. 4-6); and (3) the reign of Christ (vv. 7-9). To this is added

(4) an epilogue which sets forth the concluding remarks of the psalmist. A. *The Revolt of Men* (vv. 1-3). The psalmist paints a vivid picture of the efforts of sinful men to free themselves from the authority of heaven's king. In verses 1-3 he makes five points about this revolt.

1. The scope of the revolt. The revolt is world-wide in scope. It involves the *nations* of mankind. All ranks (*kings* and *peoples*) are involved.

2. The gravity of the revolt. The revolt is well organized. The enemies *consult together.* They carefully construct their plans to unseat the rightful king for they *imagine* or *devise*[22] their schemes. The revolt is resolute. The nations *rage*[23] (v. 1); they *take their stand* (v. 2). They are determined not to surrender to the authority of heaven's king.

3. The direction of the revolt. The revolt is directed against Yahweh and his anointed. The word *anointed* in the original is just the name Messiah, the exact equivalent in Hebrew to the name Christ which is derived from the Greek language. While not a title in this psalm, there can be little doubt that the anointed one here mentioned is the Messiah. M'Lean comments:

> Primarily from here, indeed, undoubtedly it is that the name Messiah came to be enshrined in Jewish thought and speech as the centre around which gathered hope and expectation for the nation and for the world.[24]

4. The objective of the revolt. Sinful man wants freedom from the restrictions which God would place on him. Such freedom is false freedom. The greatest freedom man can ever attain is submission to divine will. So the revolt here is against supreme majesty, rightful authority, infinite holiness, and goodness and righteousness and truth. How wicked were the hands which slew the Lord of glory and nailed the tender Teacher to the tree. How wicked the lips and lives which say to God and his Anointed, Depart from us. Here in prophetic anticipation is reflected the attitude of the mob in Pilate's judgment hall, We have no king but Caesar (John 19:14, 15).

5. The vanity of the revolt. According to verse one mankind's revolt against heaven is unreasonable (*Why*) and futile (*a vain thing*). Mankind shall never be able to dethrone heaven's King.

---

22. The root *hagah* means literally, *to murmur, mutter* and is used of those who plan their strategy by talking to themselves.

23. The root *ragash* is a hapax. The tense is perfect indicating that the psalmist has one specific act in mind.

24. M'Lean, GTP, p. 6.

Verses 1-3 are a poetic description of what would transpire in the rejection and execution of Jesus of Nazareth. Yet one has only to look to the prayer which comes from the apostles and disciples to see how close the fulfillment matches up to the predicton:

> For of a truth against your holy child Jesus, whom you have anointed, both Herod, and Pontius Pilate, and the Gentiles and the people of Israel, were gathered together, for to do whatever your hand and your counsel determined before to be done (Acts 4:27, 28).

Wilson refers to this fourfold coalition of power as the "confederacy at the cross."[25] Gentiles and Israelites, organized government (Herod) and judicial power (Pilate) joined forces to thwart the purpose of God. But even in their dastardly deed these enemies were unwittingly contributing to the scheme of redemption. M'Lean writes:

> And so, in this ancient Psalm, from across the interval of a whole millennium, we see mirrored beforehand, in these few clauses of vivid portrayal—mirrored and focused—the scenes of wrong and violence and blasphemy and blind fury which had their climax and issue in the death at Calvary.[26]

B. *The Response of God* (vv. 4-6). God reacts to the schemes against him in three ways. First, in majestic scorn he laughs at the feeble plot. While on earth the psalmist sees raging rebellion, in heaven he sees God reigning in dignity, majesty and composure. He *sits*, undismayed and unaffected by all that his opponents are doing. As he observes the efforts of his antagonists, he *laughs*,[27] he *scoffs* at them. The creature shall never unseat the Creator!

God's second reaction to the rebellion involves divine discipline (v. 5). He has but to speak a word and all those who arrogantly lifted themselves up against him are stricken with terror. God *speaks* to the plotters through circumstances, through natural disasters. Men quake before the awesome power of God. One can see this most vividly in the whirlwind of calamity which came upon that nation by whom Messiah was crucified in fulfillment of their self-malediction, "his blood be on us."

In his third response to the wicked scheme of the rebels, God declares his own purpose (v. 6). The *I* in verse 6 is emphatic. No matter what

---

25. Wilson, MP, p. 13.
26. M'Lean, GTP, p. 8.
27. On God laughing see Ps. 37:13; 59:8.

men attempt to do, God will carry out his purposes. His purpose is to install by anointing[28] his earthly representative on Mt. Zion.

Zion is the name of the hill in Jerusalem on which stood the sanctuary in David's day. Later the term was used to embrace the entire city of Jerusalem. The New Testament makes it clear that Old Testament Zion was but the type of real Zion, the church of Christ (Heb. 12:22). Here then is the promise and proclamation of Messiah's enthronement as head over all things to the church. The installation is so certain that God can speak of it as a completed action (perfect tense). Peter in his eloquent address on Pentecost announced that the enthronement had indeed taken place: "Being by the right hand of God exalted and having received of the Father the promise of the Holy Spirit, he has shed forth this which you now see and hear" (Acts 2:33).

C. *The Reign of Christ* (vv. 7-9). Verses 7-9 amplify the promise of God to install his king on Mt. Zion. He speaks here of three aspects of the future King's rule.

1. The position of Christ (v. 7). God speaks directly to the Messiah and declares him to be his Son. Twice during the ministry of Jesus of Nazareth—at his baptism and his transfiguration—the voice from heaven declared him to be God's Son. This heavenly declaration has as its counterpart the possessive "my Father" which so often appears in the recorded utterances of Jesus.

The words *Today I have begotten you* would at first glance seem to refer to the birth of the person addressed. But the term *begotten* in Psalm 2 does not refer to physical generation. It is not the incarnation and virgin birth which are being discussed here. This is clear from the fact that the words are addressed, not to an unconscious infant newly born into the world, but to an intelligent being. Paul applies Psalm 2:7 to the resurrection of Jesus:

> And we bring you good tidings of the promise made unto the fathers, how that God had fulfilled the same unto our children, in that he raised up Jesus; as also it is written in the second psalm, You are my son, this day have I begotten you (Acts 13:32-33).

Another New Testament text applies Psalm 2:7 in the same way: "So Christ glorified not himself to be made a priest, but he that spake unto

---

28. The basic meaning of the root *masach* is to pour out.

him, You are my son, this day have I begotten you" (Heb. 5:5). Now Christ was not a priest until he had died as a victim, and was prepared to enter heaven with his own blood. The words *begotten you* as used in Hebrews 5:5 must consequently refer to Christ's being begotten from the dead.

Whenever God gives a name to any one, he gives it in harmony with the rank and character of the person. Previous to the incarnation the name *Logos* (Word) is given to the second person of the Godhead, for he was the medium and substance of all the revelations made to fallen man (John 1:1). But after his resurrection it became necessary that he should receive a name corresponding to his new rank and dignity. Hence, he was called son of God.

Again in Hebrews 1:5 the thrust is the same: "To which of the angels said he at any time, You are my son, this day have I begotten you?" The Hebrew writer offers this statement as proof that Jesus was superior to angels. But at his physical birth he was made for a time "a little lower than the angels" (Heb. 2:7). When Jesus was begotten from the dead, however, he was thereafter exalted above all angelic beings (Phil. 2:9, 10).

2. The possession of Christ (v. 8). Sonship is followed by heirship. As a consequence of the exaltation of Messiah, his conquest of death and elevation to royal rule, God bestows on him as an inheritance the Gentiles living throughout the world. Paul echoes this thought in Philippians 2:

> Therefore God has highly exalted him and has given him a name that is above every name, that at the name of Jesus every knee should bow and every tongue confess that Jesus is Lord to the glory of God (Phil. 2:10, 11).

One condition is prefixed to this promise. *Ask from me*, says the Father, and I will give it. The chief part of the Redeemer's present work in heaven is this asking—intercession grounded in the work of atonement. That intercession shall prevail until its accomplishment in the glorious consummation.

3. The power of Christ (v. 9). Some have argued on the basis of verse 9 that Psalm 2 is not Messianic. The rule with an iron rod, the smashing of the opposition *like a potter's vessel* are alleged to be out of character for the Lord. For loyal subjects, for timely penitents he wields a golden scepter of tender grace, of loving welcome, of full and frank forgiveness. But the work of Christ is both constructive and destructive. The judgmental work of Christ in the New Testament is depicted in language just as severe as that employed by the prophet David.

In the Book of Revelation, John speaks of Christ as the one who rules nations with the rod of iron (Rev. 12:5). This iron rod rule is sandwiched between smiting the nations with the sword of his mouth and treading the winepress of the fierce wrath of God in Revelation 19:15. In Revelation 2:26, 27 Christ promises the one who overcomes the world that he will have power over the nations "and he shall rule them with a rod of iron; as vessels of a potter shall they be broken to slivers *even as I* received of my Father." Just as Christ rules over the nations and subdues all enemies under his feet, so shall believers judge the world at the side of Jesus their Lord.

Millennarian interpreters refer the ruling of Christ with a rod of iron to a time subsequent to the Second Coming. This approach is clearly contrary to the meaning of Psalm 2. Christ is ruling over raging heathen with his rod of iron *now*. From the moment of his exaltation to the throne on high he has been frustrating the counsels of evil men. The verb tense in Revelation 2:27 bears this out. The believer shall in the future rule "with a rod of iron *even* as I have received (perfect tense) of my Father."

D. *Concluding Remarks of the Psalmist* (vv. 10-12). In closing this beautiful psalm David does three things. First, he makes an appeal (vv. 10-12a). His readers need to know and do their duty. They need to serve the Lord, rejoice in the Lord and submit to the Lord. *Kiss the son*[29] reflects the custom of kissing the feet of a superior (cf. Gen. 41:40).

The second thing David does in these closing verses is issue a warning (v. 12b). Wrath will soon be kindled. Judgment is both a process and a crisis. Any judgment against a nation is called "the day of the Lord" in the Old Testament. There have been many such days in history, and each of them was a preview of the final day of the Lord. In that day every human soul will do homage to the Son (Phil. 2:10, 11).

David closes the psalm with a benediction (v. 12c): *Blessed are all who take refuge in him.*[30]

---

29. The word here is *bar* which in Hebrew has the meaning *pure* or *chosen* and in Aramaic the meaning *son*. David is probably using the word with its Aramaic connotation as in Prov. 31:2. If he meant the word to be taken in its common Hebrew sense, the reference would still be to Christ: Kiss the Pure One.

30. Psalms 1 and 2 form a double introduction to the Psalter. Attention has been drawn to the fact that the first Psalm begins with a beatitude, and the second psalm ends with a beatitude.

Chapter Eleven

VICTOR OVER DEATH

The victory over death which is set forth in Psalms 22 and 2 is further amplified in Psalms 16 and 102. In the former psalm Messiah blazes the trail for his followers through the grave to celestial realms. The latter psalm emphasizes the eternality of the Messiah.

Prophecy No. 21

CHRIST THE TRAILBLAZER

Psalm 16

Psalm 16 is quoted twice in the New Testament and applied by apostolic inspiration to the Lord Jesus Christ. In his first Gospel sermon, Peter cited verses 8-11 (Acts 2:25-28) and verse 10 was cited by Paul in his address in Antioch of Pisidia (Acts 13:35). Biblical authority, then, requires the personal Messianic interpretation of at least verse 10. Since there is no change of subject indicated, one must conclude that the entire psalm speaks exclusively of the Messiah. Such was the ancient view of the church.

Many modern scholars deny the personal Messianic character of Psalm 16. They think that David expresses here his conviction that God will deliver him from some present danger and save him from death. The psalm is Messianic only in the sense that it finds complete fulfillment in Christ. Briggs articulates this position when he writes:

> There is no thought of a personal Messiah in the psalm; yet in that David and none of his successors attained the realization of this blessed hope, it led to the Messiah who first was able to attain it for Himself and His people.[1]

Briggs sees no thought of a resurrection in Psalm 16. W. E. Barnes, on the other hand, sees the hope of resurrection as the main thrust of the passage. The psalm is Messianic in that one cannot speak about resurrection without reference to Christ.[2]

The question then is this: Is Psalm 16 Messianic in the primary or secondary sense? David was a prophet (Acts 2:30), and prophets frequently recorded first-person monologues in which they assumed the role of someone who was to appear in the future. That is what has

1. Briggs, MP, p. 152.
2. Barnes, WC, I, 66.

taken place here. The speaker in the psalm is the Messiah himself. M'Lean captures the thrust of the psalm in these words:

> . . . the Psalmist has been led on to climax of utterance which outran his own personal future, which reached its first adequate realization in the resurrection of Christ from the dead. . . . Under the inspiration of the Holy Ghost his own personality merges in the mysterious and glorious Personage in whom . . . all lines of Old Testament type and prophecy were to find their prime point of convergence.[3]

The title refers to this psalm as a *michtam* of David. Six psalms have such a title.[4] Among the numerous explanations of this obscure term, two opinions have some merit. The first is that *michtam* is to be traced to a root meaning "gold." The other opinion is that a *michtam* is derived from a word meaning "to hide." Hence a *michtam* is either a golden psalm, i.e., one of great worth, or a secret, mysterious psalm.

Translation of Psalm 16

A *michtam* of David. (1) Preserve me, O God, because in you do I put my trust. (2) (My soul) has said to the LORD, You are my Lord; I have no good besides you. (3) As for the saints who are in the land, they are the excellent ones in whom is all my delight. (4) Their sorrows shall be multiplied who hasten after another; their libation of blood I will not pour out, nor will I take up their names upon my lips. (5) The LORD is the portion of my inheritance and my cup; you maintain my lot. (6) The lines have fallen to me in pleasant places; yea I have a goodly heritage. (7) I will bless the LORD who gave me counsel; yea, all of my inward parts teach me in the night. (8) I have set the LORD before me always; because (he is) at my right hand, I shall not be moved. (9) Therefore, my heart rejoices, and my glory exults; yea my flesh shall rest safely. (10) For you will not forsake my soul to Sheol, nor will you give over your holy one to see corruption. (11) You will make known to me the path of life; in your presence is fullness of joy; at your right hand are pleasures forever.

Discussion

Psalm 16 follows a pattern which is characteristic of a whole class of psalms. M'Lean calls these "ladder psalms." They are like the mystic

---

3. M'Lean, GTP, pp. 47-48.
4. In addition to Ps. 16, Pss. 56-60.

ladder seen by Jacob, its foot resting upon the earth, its top touching the heavens. To change the figure, the psalm begins in a plaintive *minor* and ends in a jubilant *major.*[5]

One can distinguish four thought divisions in Psalm 16 which may be entitled (1) the cry of Christ (vv. 1-2), (2) the commitment of Christ (vv. 5, 7-8), (3) the confidence of Christ (vv. 6, 9-11), and (4) the consequence of rejecting Christ (v. 4).

A. *The Cry of Christ* (vv. 1-2). The opening verse of the psalm suggests that the Messiah is in the depths of trouble and danger.[6] *Preserve me,* he cried. He refers to his Father by the name *El* which underscores the strength of God. *El*[7] is the strong one, mighty to deliver in time of trouble. This name, usually found in combination with other divine names, here appears alone. The words *in you do I put my trust* underscores again the plight in which the Messiah sees himself. The word *trust* has in the original the connotation of a refuge to which one flees in time of danger.

B. *The Confession of Christ* (v. 3). From deep within the Messiah comes an acknowledgment: *My soul had said to Yahweh.* The affirmation in this verse is two sided. On the God-ward side Messiah affirms his submission to the Father: *You are my Lord,* i.e., my master (*'adhonay*). From a position of equality he had assumed the role of a servant (Phil. 2:7). This is why he declared, "My Father is greater than I" (John 14:28). Messiah goes on to declare: *I have no good besides you.* The translation and interpretation of this clause are disputed. The meaning seems to be that doing the will of God is the first priority of the Messiah.

On the man-ward side Christ's confession speaks of his high estimation of the *saints,* i.e., the holy ones—those who by commitment and conduct can be identified as God's people. In his estimation they are the *excellent,* literally, the nobles. True nobility is not so much a matter of purse and pedigree as it is of purity. When Christ came to earth he found a faithful and humble remnant waiting to receive him. *They are the excellent ones in whom is all my delight* (v. 3).

---

5. M'Lean, GTP, pp. 48-49.

6. Wilson (MP, p. 81) contends that *preserve* (*shamar*) "does not necessarily mean or imply threatening danger." Kirkpatrick and Leupold also question whether actual suffering or imminent danger is involved.

7. God is mentioned sixteen times in this psalm: Yahweh, four times; second person pronoun, nine times; El, Adonai, and third person pronoun, one time each. "Thus in nine out of sixteen instances God is directly addressed, showing that the eyes of the speaker are turned upward towards Him whom he trusts for protection, counsel, and guidance." Wilson, MP, p. 81.

C. *The Commitment of Christ* (vv. 5, 7-8). Four facts give evidence of the commitment of Christ during his earthly ministry.

1. He regarded God's will as his food and drink. *Yahweh is the portion of my portion* (v. 5). The ancient Levites had no earthly inheritance (Deut. 18:1-2). God was their portion. Jesus, the antitypical Levite, had nowhere to lay his head—no portion. Nonetheless, he was secure in the realization that he belonged to the Father and the Father belonged to him.

Yahweh was Messiah's *cup* as well as his portion (v. 5). Is this the cup that cheers and sustains—the overflowing cup of Psalm 23:5? Or is this the cup of suffering which he drank to the dregs? In either case, Messiah gained his strength, his sense of mission, his purpose from the relationship which he shared with the Father.

Throughout his ministry Messiah's *lot* was maintained by the Father. Messiah's lot was his ministry. The success of his ministry was in the hand of God.

2. Messiah knew God's will (v. 7). Messiah had received counsel, i.e., direction, from Yahweh. Even as a lad he knew his Father's business (Luke 2:40-52). By the time he launched his public ministry, and possibly long before, Jesus knew the will of God for his life. In his ministry whole nights were spent in prayer. During those night seasons he contemplated the joyous results of his sacrifical mission (Heb. 12:2-4). His heart instructed him in the sense that he found self-encouragement from deep within his soul.

3. Messiah set as his goal the execution of God's will (v. 8a): *I have set Yahweh before me always.*[8] He regarded himself as constantly in the presence of God. But more than that is meant. In all that he did, said, and suffered, he kept the glory of the Father and the accomplishment of his purpose constantly in view (John 17:4; Acts 2:23).

4. Messiah was determined to carry out God's will (v. 8b). He is confident in his mission because he knows that the Father is at his right hand. This would be the natural place for a defender in battle (cf. Ps. 110:5). At the right hand is also a post of honor and dignity. In view of this divine support he can boldly affirm: *I shall not be moved.*

D. *The Confidence of Christ* (vv. 6, 9-11). David places in the mouth of the Messiah the expression of a fourfold confidence:

1. Messiah is confident that he had a goodly heritage: *The lines have fallen to me in pleasant places* (v. 6). The speaker here is not

---

8. The Septuagint reads: "I beheld the Lord always before me."

David, but David's greater son. He contemplates the glorious kingdom which will be his as a result of his successful mission. His *goodly heritage* is the innumerable host of saints which is his church.

2. Messiah is confident that he would not be abandoned to the grave (vv. 9-10). His heart is glad, his soul (*my glory*)[9] rejoices over the glorious prospect. *My flesh* (body) *shall rest safely.* Christ knew that his stay in the grave would not be of sufficient duration to produce corruption. He would be in that tomb only sufficient time to prove the reality of his death.[10]

The stupendous assertion of verse 9 is amplified and defended in verse 10. *For you will not forsake my soul in Sheol.* The term *my soul* here is probably the equivalent to *myself*—the total person, not just the immortal part of a man which is distinct from the body. Old Testament Sheol is equivalent to New Testament Hades. It is the abode of the dead, the hereafter.[11] Messiah would enter the abode of the dead, but he would not remain under the power of death. The exact length of his stay in that dark realm is not specified here.[12]

In what sense would Sheol not hold sway over the person of Messiah? The second half of verse 10 seems to be synonymous with the first: *Nor will you give over your Holy One*[13] *to see corruption.* According to Acts 2:27 the holy one (*hosion*) in Psalms 16:10 is Christ.[14] This holy one will not *see corruption.* He would not be in the tomb long enough for his body to decay.

3. Messiah expresses confidence that he would walk the path of life (v. 11). The Father would show him that path—way of conduct—which would lead to life. Christ became the great pathfinder. He led the way out of the realm of death. He became the first fruits of the dead

---

9. The Septuagint renders, "my tongue."

10. Two alternative, but inadequate, interpretations of this line are worth noting: (1) during my life I will be under divine protection (Leupold, Kirkpatrick); and (2) I will lie down in my grave in the hope of eternal life and ultimately resurrection (A. Barnes).

11. G. M. Elliott (SR, III, 1957, pp. 58-59) establishes the fact that Sheol is never equated with the grave or sepulcher.

12. It is a weak interpretation of these words to assert with A. Barnes and others that these words are *ultimately* true of David. He would not be left *permanently* in Sheol. Such an interpretation flys in the face of Peter's assertion that David could not be speaking of himself in this psalm (Acts 2:25-31).

13. In the standard Hebrew text the word is plural. The singular, however, is supported by the ancient Aramaic Targum, the Latin Vulgate, the Septuagint, the Arabic, the Massoretic vocalization of the word, many Hebrew manuscripts and early printed editions, as well as Acts 2:27 There can be scarcely any doubt that the original reading was singular.

14. Christ is called Holy One (*hagios*) in Mark 1:24 and Acts 3:14.

(I Cor. 15:20), the first to exit from death's dungeon never to return. Joy mingled with heaviness and sorrow down here. But when he ascended to the right hand of the Father he experienced the fullness of joy which accompanies the successful completion of a significant mission. This was the joy which Christ anticipated prior to Calvary (Heb. 12:2).

4. Messiah was confident that he would assume his rightful place at the right hand of the Father (v. 11b). The perfect fellowship experienced prior to the incarnation is now restored. It gives the Lord Jesus the greatest pleasure to sit in that place of honor beside his Father and to rule over his kingdom of redeemed souls. In verse 8 it was the Father who was at the right hand of the Messiah to aid him in his mission. Now that the mission has been accomplished the Messiah occupies the place of power, priesthood, and pleasure.[15]

For the true interpretation of Psalm 16 the apostolic commentary should be consulted:

> For David speaks concerning him: I foresaw the Lord always before my face, for he is on my right hand, that I should not be moved; Therefore did my heart rejoice, and my tongue was glad; moreover also my flesh shall rest in hope, because you will not leave my soul in hell, neither will you suffer your Holy One to see corruption. You have made known to me the ways of life; you shall make me full of joy with your countenance. Men and brethren, let me freely speak unto you of the patriarch David, that he is both dead and buried, and his sepulcher is with us unto this day. Therefore being a prophet, and knowing that God had sworn with an oath to him that of the fruit of his loins, according to the flesh, he would raise up Christ to sit on his throne; he seeing this before spake of the resurrection of Christ, that his soul was not left in hades, neither did his flesh see corruption (Acts 2:25-31).

E. *The Consequence of Rejecting Christ* (v. 4). Three serious consequences follow the willful rejection of the saving work of the Messiah.

1. Multiplied sorrows will befall *those who hasten after another.* Another what? Another god? Clarke suggests that the word *Messiah* should be supplied for clarity. Unbelieving Jews who turned from Christ to look for another Messiah would experience multiplied sorrows. Such has been the history of the Jewish race after Calvary.

2. Those who reject Messiah will have no sacrifice for sin. *Their libation of blood I will not pour out.* The reference is to the libation of

---

15. Wilson, MP, p. 90.

blood poured out at the base of the altar during the sacrificial rituals. *Their libation* is then a libation offered on their behalf.[16] Those who turn after another Messiah cannot have any claim on the sacrifice made by Jesus Christ.

3. There would be no intercession on behalf of those who reject Messiah. *Nor will I take up their names upon my lips.* Whose names? Some say the psalmist here pledges never to invoke the names of pagan gods. Others think that it is the names of various sacrifices which will not be uttered. The Messiah, however, is the speaker throughout the psalm. He is warning that he will not make intercession for those who turn after another Messiah (cf. Matt. 10:32).

Prophecy No. 22

THE ETERNALITY OF CHRIST

Psalm 102

The justification for regarding Psalm 102 as Messianic is found in Hebrews 1. In this magnificent chapter the apostle quotes Psalms 45, 102 and 110 and declares that these citations were spoken by God to the Messiah.[17] To be specific, verses 25-27 of Psalm 102 are said to have been spoken by the Father to the Son (Heb. 1:10-12). Without the insight provided by Hebrews it would *appear* that the three verses quoted were addressed by the psalmist to Yahweh, as the self-existent One, who is before and above the world.

Some regard the Messianic interpretation of Psalm 102 as totally unjustified. The writer of Hebrews was supposedly misled by the Septuagint rendering of verse 25. This version inserts the word *kurie* (Lord) which is not attested in Hebrew manuscripts. Since *kurie* was the common appellation of Christ in the apostolic age, the writer of Hebrews jumped to the conclusion that the verse was addressed to Christ. Happily this attack on the inspiration and/or intelligence of the writer of Hebrews cannot be sustained. The author of Hebrews did

---

16. Other views: (1) drink offerings are repudiated because those who made them were guilty of bloodshed (Briggs); and (2) Jewish libations and sacrifices would cease (Clarke).

17. In Hebrews 1:10 the word *and* is used to connect vv. 10-12 with the two previous verses so that all five verses "are to be taken and construed as the testimony of God the Father, speaking by the mouth of one of his holy Prophets concerning his Son Jesus Christ." Milligan, EH, p. 69.

not as a matter of fact always regard *kurie* in the Septuagint as a reference to Christ. See for example Hebrews 8:8ff.; 12:6ff.

Others argue that the writer of Hebrews is not actually saying that Psalm 102:25-27 is addressed to Messiah. He is only using the language of the Old Testament to express his personal conviction about Jesus. Since Christians believed that Christ was before the world with God, then every passage which speaks of the eternality of *God*, can be applied also to Christ. In response, however, Milligan writes:

> His object here is, not to teach us what might be said of the Lord Jesus, but rather what the Father himself has actually said of him in the writings of the holy prophets. On no other hypothesis would our author be justified in quoting and applying this passage as he does.[18]

The following considerations support the Messianic interpretation of Psalm 102:

1. Certain expressions contained in the psalm (especially in verses 18-22) speak of the reign of Messiah over all the earth.

2. It is important to note that the other citations in Hebrews 1—from Psalm 2:7 and Psalm 45:7ff.—are unquestionably Christological. This being the case, would the middle citation of the triad of psalmic quotations be merely the expression of the Hebrew writer's own faith without regard for the original significance of the psalm? Most unlikely!

Thus the writer of Hebrews sees the hopes and longings of the psalmist fulfilled in the incarnation of the Son of God. He interprets what Psalm 102:25-27 says of the coming of Yahweh as a divine word concerning the Son, in whom the promised advent had been accomplished.

If, then, on sound principles of New Testament exegesis, the conclusion is sustained that in Psalm 102:25-27 God the Father is addressing the Son, what can be said of the rest of the Psalm? The speaker throughout must be Messiah, or, to be more precise, an Old Testament prophet who expresses in words approved by the Holy Spirit the inner thoughts of Messiah prior to his passion. "It is Christ, in the days of his humiliation, that is before us."[19]

The heading introduces the tone of Psalm 102. It is a prayer of one who is afflicted. Here he pours out his complaint before his God. The Psalmist makes use of material from earlier psalms.[20] He is, however, more than a compiler. He has absorbed the spirit of his predecessors.

---

18. Milligan, EH, p. 69.
19. Bonar, CHC, p. 300.
20. See list of earlier citations in Leupold, EP, p. 707.

The *afflicted one* or *needy one* of the heading is not necessarily the psalmist himself. He may or may not have been experiencing personal suffering. The speaker in the first twenty-four verses of the psalm is Messiah. This is the inevitable conclusion which the New Testament usage of verses 25-27 compels one to reach. The *needy one* of the heading is therefore Christ who "though he was rich, yet for our sakes became poor, that we through his poverty might become rich" (II Cor. 8:9). That there may be here an application, an illustration, a lesson for suffering saints of all ages can be cheerfully admitted. But the Holy Spirit himself has indicated the primary *meaning* of the passage in the New Testament.

It is generally thought that Psalm 102 comes from the Exilic period of Israel's history. The human author is unknown.

Translation of Psalm 102

A prayer of the afflicted one when he faints and before the LORD pours out his meditation. (1) O LORD, hear my prayer, and let my cry come unto you. (2) Do not hide your face from me in the day of my distress; incline your ear to me; in the day I call answer me swiftly. (3) For my days are consumed in smoke, my bones are burned as dry wood. (4) My heart is smitten like grass and is withered, for I have forgotten to eat my bread. (5) Because of the sound of my groaning, my bones cleave to my flesh. (6) I am like a pelican of the wilderness, like an owl of the waste places. (7) I watch, and I am like a bird alone upon a roof top. (8) My enemies reproach me all day long, and my adversaries are sworn against me. (9) For I have eaten ashes like bread, and my drink with weeping has been mixed, (10) because of your indignation and your wrath; for you have lifted me up, and cast me aside. (11) My days are like a lengthened shadow and I am withered like grass. (12) But you, O LORD, sit forever, and you will be remembered throughout all generations. (13) You shall arise, you shall have compassion on Zion, for it is time to show favor to her, the appointed time has come. (14) For your servants delight in her stones, and her dust moves them to pity. (15) So the nations shall fear the name of the LORD, and all the kings of the earth your glory. (16) When the LORD has built up Zion, he shall appear in his glory. (17) He shall turn unto the prayer of the destitute, he will not despise their prayer. (18) This shall be written for a later generation, and a people which shall be created shall praise the LORD. (19) For he has looked down from the height of his sanctuary; from heaven the LORD did behold the earth. (20) To hear the groan of the prisoner, to free those who are appointed to death. (21) To declare in Zion the name of the LORD, and his praise in Jerusalem. (22) When the peoples are gathered together, and the kingdoms, to serve the LORD. (23) He consumed my strength in the way, he cut short my days. (24) I said, O my God, do not take me away in the midst of my days; your years are throughout all generations. (25) Of old you laid the foundations of the earth, and the heavens are the work of your hands. (26) They shall perish, but you shall remain; all of them like a garment shall wear out; as a garment you shall change them, and they shall be changed. (27) But you remain the same, your years shall never end. (28) The sons of your servants shall abide, and their seed before you shall be established.

Discussion

Psalm 102 contains four major thought units: (1) the Messiah's appeal to the Father (vv. 1-2); (2) the Messiah's agony (vv. 3-11); (3) the Messiah's anticipation (vv. 12-22); (4) the Messiah's agony (vv. 23-24); and (5) the assurance to the Messiah (vv. 25-28).
A. *The Appeal of the Messiah* (vv. 1-2). The psalm opens with five separate but similar petitions. The Messiah asks to be heard. "Asking to be heard is not the outgrowth of expecting not to be heard but rather an effective way of recalling that God is ready to hear."[21]
B. *The Agony of the Messiah* (vv. 3-11). In verses 3-11 the Messiah sets forth his reasons for the fivefold appeal of the opening verses. The tone of these verses is like the deep pathos of Psalm 22.

The effects and signs of his sorrow can be seen in his body. Truly he was a man of sorrows. He feels he is wasting away as smoke. His bones feel as though they had been charred on a hearth (v. 3). The heart, the seat of the deepest thought and emotions, has withered like grass before the heat of the sun. Food is tasteless and undesirable (v. 4).[22]

The Sufferer gave vent to his agony in loud groans. This physical effort made him conscious of his emaciated condition (*my bones cleave to my flesh* (v. 5). Like the pelican and the owl who seek lonely haunts so the Sufferer endured his agony alone (v. 6). Sleeplessness added to the affliction (v. 7). But the greatest pain of all was the mockery of heartless enemies who poured out a continual stream of taunts. His

21. Leupold, EP, p. 708.
22. Cf. Hannah's and David's sorrow that took away all appetite for food (I Sam. 1:7; II Sam. 12:17).

name had become a term by which to curse, for he appeared to be a man cursed by God (v. 8).

The Sufferer sat or laid in the dust weeping when he should have taken refreshment for his body (v. 9). In those awful moments he felt that he was under divine wrath, cast off by his God (v. 10).[23] Because of this abandonment he felt his life gradually fading away like a lengthening shadow. In all this description of suffering there is no bitterness, no wild accusations against God. The Sufferer accepted his lot.

C. *The Anticipation of the Messiah* (vv. 12-22). The Sufferer comforts himself with nine arguments in verses 12-22. "As an angel strengthened him in Gethsemane, so the thought of his Father's purpose supports him here. At verse 12 he begins to look upward."[24]

1. However bleak the circumstances appeared to be, God was still on his throne. In all generations he will have those who will remember him (v. 12).

2. God is about to take action on behalf of his people. The appointed time has come, that time appointed since the fall in the garden to deliver God's people from the power of the oppressor.[25]

3. God's people loved the very ruins of Jerusalem, the *stones* and *dust* (v. 14).

4. The restoration of Zion sets the stage for the conversion of Gentiles (v. 15).

5. The restoration of Zion prepares the way for the appearance of God in his glory (v. 16).

6. God hears the prayer of his people even when they are in the most destitute conditions (v. 17). Christ was preeminently the Destitute One (*ha'ar'ar*)—naked of all things.

7. That which is about to happen—the climax of God's redemptive plan—will become a matter of perpetual record. Yet unborn generations would praise God for his action (v. 18).

8. The redemptive act of God indicates his grace. He looked down from his heavenly sanctuary (v. 18) to take pity on those who were prisoners[26] of sin, doomed to eternal death (v. 20). All that he had done he had done with the intent that God's name would be praised in Zion (Jerusalem), i.e., his kingdom (v. 21).

---

23. Leupold (EP, p. 710) argues that "there is an admission of sinfulness and guilt at this point."

24. Bonar, CHC, p. 301.

25. Commentators generally see here an allusion to the seventy years of captivity (Jer. 29:10) which had come to an end.

26. Since the word is singular, Bonar takes the Prisoner to be Christ himself.

9. As a result of the great redemptive act of God, all manner of people and kingdoms assembled in Jerusalem to join in the worship of the true and living God (v. 22). Leupold makes a pertinent observation on this verse:

> Though this statement seems to make the worship of God on the part of many nations in days to come center in the physical Jerusalem, this is only an incidental feature of the picture that need not be stressed as being essential.[27]

But as a matter of record, the worship of the true and living God by Gentiles is centered in Jerusalem, for the church of Christ is referred to as "the Jerusalem which is from above" (Gal. 4:26).

D. *The Agony of the Messiah* (vv. 23-24). His days are shortened, i.e., he was about to die in the prime of life (v. 23). He prays that this might not be so (v. 24a). One is reminded of the Gethsemane petition: "Let this cup pass from me."

E. *The Assurance to the Messiah* (vv. 25-28). According to the inspired author of Hebrews, verses 25-28 were addressed by God the Father to his Son, the Messiah (Heb. 1:10-12). Milligan writes:

> But whatever may be true of the principle on which this language is applied to the Son of God, the fact itself, as here stated, is indisputable. Guided by the Spirit of God, the author of our Epistle here deposes, that this is the testimony of God the Father himself with respect to the Son.[28]

The silence of the heavens is thus broken. The Father speaks words of comfort and strength to his Son. The comforting assurance is sixfold.

1. Messiah is superior to the created universe. The earth and heavens owe their very existence to Messiah. He laid the foundations of the earth; the heavens are his handiwork (cf. John 1:1-3).

At a certain epoch in eternity past (*of old*) the Son in connection and cooperation with the Father and the Holy Spirit created the material universe. *Laid the foundations* (v. 25) is equivalent to *created*. The connection of the earth with plural heavens is the Old Testament designation for the material universe. The anthropological phrase *work of your hands* (v. 25) points to the care which went into the original creation.

2. The Messiah is eternal. The heavens and earth will *perish*. The

---

27. Leupold, EP, p. 712.
28. Milligan, EH, p. 70.

word used here (*'abhad*) and the Greek equivalent in the New Testament (*apollumi*) does not mean that the universe will be annihilated, but rather destroyed with respect to the present state of existence.[29] They perish, Messiah remains. Messiah's eternality "stands forth all the more clearly in the light of the impermanence and frailty of the whole framework of this old earth."[30] As a garment gradually wears thin with use and must be discarded and replaced by another, so the visible universe in due time wears down and must be replaced. Scriptures consistently testify that the old order will perish to usher in the new heavens and earth.[31]

3. Messiah will preside over the destruction of the present order. *As a garment you shall change them, and they shall be changed* (v. 26).

4. Messiah will usher in a new heavens and earth. The word *change* (*chalaph*) connotes "succeeding to another having in it the radical idea of substitution."[32]

5. Messiah is unchangeable and ageless. *You are the same;*[33] *and your years have no end* (v. 27).

6. Messiah will have servants throughout generations to come (v. 28). The church will never be barren, but from age to age will bring forth children of God.

SPECIAL NOTE ON PSALM 16:10

The key word in Psalm 16:10 is the word *corruption* (*shachat*). The word is used of a ditch (Job 9:31); corruption (Job 17:14; Ps. 49:9; Jonah 2:6); pit (Job 33:24, 28, 30; Ps. 9:15; 30:9; 35:7; Prov. 26:27; Isa. 38:17; Ezek. 19:4; 28:8); grave (Job 33:22); and destruction (Ps. 55:23). Kirkpatrick contends that *shachat* must mean *pit* in some passages and may have that meaning in every case. To see the pit, then, means to experience death. Briggs sees *shachat* as a pit in Sheol— a deeper place than Sheol. W. E. Barnes and Cheyne accept the rendering *pit* but argue that this does not impair the Messianic impact. Christ did not *see* the pit in the sense that he did not experience the corrupting power of the pit or grave.

---

29. Milligan, EH, p. 71.
30. Leupold, EP, p. 713.
31. See Isa. 54:10; Matt. 24:35; Luke 21:33; II Peter 3:7, 10, 11.
32. Bonar, CHC, p. 303.
33. The Hebrew has literally, "you are he."

That *shachat* has the sense of corruption in Psalm 16:10 is essential to the argument of Peter in Acts 2:31 and Paul in Acts 13:35. It appears necessary to call into question the intelligence and/or the inspiration of these apostles if *shachat* is rendered *pit*. Sutcliffe argues that there are two nouns spelled *shachat* in Hebrew. One is derived from the root *shucha* (to sink down) and means *pit*. The second is derived from the root *shachat* (to go to ruin) and means *corruption*.[34]

Sutcliffe points out three passages where *shachat* seems to clearly mean corruption or destruction. In Psalm 55:23 the expression *the pit of destruction* appears. It would be an obvious redundancy to translate *the pit of the pit* here. Most probably Ps. 49:9 uses *shachat* in the sense of corruption: *to live forever and not see corruption*. The verb *to see* (experience) in Hebrew is commonly used with abstract nouns. In Job 17:14 *shachat* also appears to have the meaning *corruption*: *I have said to corruption (shachat) You are my father; to the worm, You are my mother and my sister*. Scholars who dogmatically deny that *shachat* can mean *corruption* have gone beyond the evidence. It cannot be shown that *shachat* cannot mean *corruption*.

The pre-Christian Greek version of the Old Testament (the Septuagint) rendered *shachat* with the word *diaphthoran*, corruption. The Syriac and Latin Vulgate followed suit in their respective languages. In Rabbinic tradition David's body was miraculously preserved from decay, thus reflecting Rabbinic interpretation of *shachat* in Psalm 16.

The case for understanding *shachat* in Psalm 16:10 to mean *corruption* then rests on three pieces of evidence: (1) the Holy Spirit inspired logic of Peter and Paul in their sermons in Acts; (2) the passages in the Old Testament where *shachat* clearly seems to have the meaning *corruption*; and (3) the rendering of the word *shachat* in the ancient versions.

---

34. Sutcliffe, FLOT, p. 77.

Chapter Twelve

MESSIAH'S MARRIAGE AND MINISTRY

The beautiful Messianic portrait painted by the psalmists is further embellished in Psalms 45 and 110. The former psalm focuses attention on the marriage of the divine king and the latter on his ministry.

Prophecy No. 23

THE MARRIAGE OF THE DIVINE KING

Psalm 45

Psalm 45 has been called "the center and crown of the messianic psalms"[1] Jewish tradition is united on the Messianic interpretation of this psalm. The writer of Hebrews cites verses 6-7 of Psalm 45 as a declaration of the Father to the Son. For those who take the doctrine of inspiration seriously, this should settle the matter. Psalm 45 is definitely Messianic. The language far transcends any language that could be used of the best earthly kings. From the earliest times in Jewish and Christian circles Psalm 45 has been understood to refer directly to Messiah.

Kirkpatrick represents those scholars who argue that the psalm is *typical* Messianic. According to this view the psalmist is addressing an actual king from the house of David. The Davidic kings were representative of Yahweh, the true King of Israel. Thus:

> The poet-seer can boldly greet the reigning monarch in the light of the great prophecies to which he was the heir. Bidding him rise to the height of his calling by the exercise of a just rule which should be a true reflection of the divine government, he can claim for him the fulfillment of the promise of an eternal dominion.[2]

Milligan sets forth correctly the scope of Psalm 45. It is

> . . . a simple allegory designed to celebrate, primarily and exclusively, the perfections, conquests, and righteous administration of Christ; to illustrate the intimate and sanctified union which exists between himself and his church; and to set forth, in the most pleasant and impressive manner, the happy and eternal consequences of this very holy and endearing relationship.[3]

---

1. Wilson, MP, p. 106.
2. Kirkpatrick, CB, p. 243.
3. Milligan, EH, p. 67.

With the above assessment Delitzsch agrees:

> To me, then, it appears quite undeniable that the author in the first place regards the forty-fifth Psalm as a not merely typico-messianic, but as a directly prophetico-messianic psalm; and secondly, that he finds there that now exalted Messiah who has appeared in Jesus addressed as *ho theos*, God.[4]

Psalm 45 is a marriage song. A great warrior and mighty king of Israel is married to a beautiful princess. Commentators vie with one another in their ingenious suggestions as to the identity of the two principal characters. Some see here one of David's marriages—his marriage to Michal, to Maacah of Geshur or to Bathsheba. These suggestions can quickly be set aside, for David was not king when he married Michal; he was not king of all Israel when he married Maacah; and Bathsheba was not of royal blood as is the bride in the psalm. More common is the suggestion that Solomon's marriage to the Egyptian princess is here being celebrated.[5] Solomon, however, was no warrior as depicted here, nor were his sons made princes over the whole earth (v. 16). Besides, this marriage was loathsome in God's sight (I Kings 11:1-13). Perowne has correctly observed that "a greater than Solomon is here."[6]

The truth is that none of the persons[7] proposed has all of the features stressed by the psalmist. "The hero of the psalm has not been successfully identified with any of these earthly kings."[8] If the poem had any relation at all to a concrete historical situation, that is now lost. Certainly no king of ancient Judah became the object of such universal and everlasting praise as this psalm envisions. The psalm is a prophetical-messianic picture of Christ's marriage to his bride the church. Spurgeon's famous comment is worthy of citation here:

> Some here see Solomon and Pharaoh's daughter only—they are short-sighted; others see both Solomon and Christ—they are cross-eyed; well-focused spiritual eyes see here Jesus only. . . . This is no wedding song of earthly nuptials, but an Epithalamium for the Heavenly Bridegroom and his elect bride.[9]

---

4. Delitzsch, CEH, I, 76-77.

5. I Kings 3:1; 7:8; 9:16, 24; 11:1.

6. Perowne, BP, I, 368.

7. Besides David and Solomon, these kings have been nominated: Jehoram of Judah who married Athaliah of Israel; Ahab who married Jezebel; Jehoshaphat; Jehoiachin, Jehu and Jeroboam II.

8. Leupold, EP, p. 351.

9. Spurgeon, TD, II, 351.

Even in the Old Testament times Psalm 45 was accounted by the prophets as Messianic. Isaiah applies certain language of this psalm to the Servant of Yahweh, the anointed one who gives the oil of gladness "for mourning" (Isa. 61:1-3). Isaiah 9:5 combines the *gibbor* (mighty one) of verse 3 and the *'elohim* of verse 6 in the composite Messianic name *'el gibbor* (mighty God). Zechariah 12:8 prophesies that in the latter day the house of David would be "as God" and "as the angel of Yahweh" before (or at the head of) his people.[10]

The psalm is attributed to the sons of Korah.[11] Sons of Korah are mentioned in connection with the reign of David (I Chron. 6:33-37) as leaders in the music program of the Temple. They reappear in the same role in the early Divided Monarchy Period (II Chron. 20:19). The likelihood is that Psalm 45, as part of the second book or collection of psalms, belongs to the United Monarchy period.[12] The phrase *to the chief musician*[13] indicates that this psalm was part of the Temple liturgy.

The Hebrew title provides three other bits of information about this psalm. The tune to which it was sung was called *Shoshannim*, i.e., upon the lillies.[14] The psalm is classified by its author as a *maskil*, a Teaching Psalm.[15] Twelve other psalms bear this title. The nature of the psalm is described in the words *a song of beloved ones*. According to Jeremiah 12:7 "beloved ones" signifies *love*. Therefore, Psalm 45 is a song of love.

Translation of Psalm 45

To the chief musician upon *Shoshannim*. By the sons of Korah. A *maskil*. A song of beloved ones. (1) My heart bubbles over with a good word! I speak things I composed concerning a king; my tongue is the pen of a ready writer. (2) You are fairer by far than the sons of men; grace is poured upon your lips; therefore God has blessed you forever. (3) Gird your sword upon your thigh O Mighty Hero, your splendor and your majesty. (4) In your majesty ride on successfully on

---

10. Delitzsch, CEH, I, 78.

11. Eleven psalms have this title.

12. Cf. Leupold who dates Psalm 45 after Isaiah 9:6, or in the eighth century B.C.

13. Fifty-five psalms have this phrase in their headings. Asaph, Heman and Ethan are mentioned as music directors in the Temple.

14. Others think Shoshannim refers to the instrument which accompanied the singing of the psalm. Four psalms have this heading.

15. A didactic element appears in verses 10ff. where instruction is offered to the Bride.

behalf of the cause of truth, meekness and righteousness; and your right hand shall teach you awesome things. (5) Your arrows are sharp— may peoples fall under you—in the heart of the enemies of the king. (6) Your throne, O God, is forever and ever; the scepter of your kingdom is an upright scepter. (7) You love righteousness and hate wickedness; therefore, O God, your God has anointed you with the oil of gladness above your associates. (8) Myrrh, aloes and cassia are all your garments; from the palaces of ivory stringed instruments have made you rejoice. (9) Daughters of kings are among your honorable women; at your right hand the queen has stationed herself in gold of Ophir. (10) Hearken, O daughter, and consider and incline your ear; forget your people and the house of your father. (11) So shall the king desire your beauty; because he is your lord, bow down to him. (12) And the daughter of Tyre is there with a gift; the rich ones of the people shall seek your face. (13) All glorious within is the daughter of the king; her garment is embroidered with gold. (14) In garments of needlework she shall be brought to the king; virgins, her friends who follow her, are brought to you. (15) They shall be brought with joy and gladness; they shall enter the palace of the king. (16) In the place of your fathers shall be your sons; you shall place them as princes over all the earth. (17) I will cause your name to be remembered in all the generations; therefore people shall praise you forever and ever.

Discussion

After a brief preface (v. 1), Psalm 45 focuses on (1) the bridegroom (vv. 2-9a), (2) the bride (vv. 9b-12), and (3) the marriage (vv. 13-16). The psalm concludes with a remark by the psalmist.

A. *The Preface* (v. 1). One verse suffices for the introduction to this grand psalm. In it the psalmist states his theme: *I speak things I composed concerning a king.* He then uses two figures to describe his eagerness to share his composition. His heart is a bubbling fountain, overflowing. He cannot restrain himself. He has a *good word* to share with his readers. In the second figure he compares his tongue to the pen of *a ready writer,* i.e., it is prompt to express and record the thoughts with which his mind is overflowing. He seems to realize that he is the instrument of a higher power.

B. *The Bridegroom* (vv. 2-9a). The psalmist's description of the bridegroom takes four directions. He discusses (1) the perfection; (2) the achievements; (3) the identity; and (4) the joy of this leading character.

1. The perfection of the bridegroom (v. 2). In his person and in his ministry, the bridegroom is perfect. Personal attractiveness was always regarded as a qualification for ancient rulers, for the outward appearance was regarded as the index of a noble character.[16] Messiah was *fairer* than the sons of men. It was not, however, Messiah's physical countenance, but his character that made him so supremely attractive.

The bridegroom is perfect in speech. *Grace is poured upon your lips* (v. 2). "That gracious smile upon his lips gives promise of the gracious words which proceed from them."[17] The term *grace* refers to everything that is attractive, everything that is *graceful* in character and form, in feature and expression. Grace here is what made him attractive in the eyes of others.[18] The winsomeness of his teaching ministry is in view here. "And all were bearing him witness and wondering at the gracious words which proceeded out of his mouth" (Luke 4:22).

His attractive character and graceful speech were not natural endowments. They were gifts of God. The conclusion is inevitable. God has blessed Messiah with these attributes, and he would possess them forever (v. 2).

2. The achievements of the bridegroom (vv. 3-5). The bridegroom is awesome in majesty. He will be compelled to use his God-given endowments in strenuous combat. He is well-armed and capable of doing mighty things. He carries a sword at his side. He is called a *mighty hero* (*gibbor*). This term by itself does not necessarily indicate deity, but it is used in conjunction with El (God) in Isaiah 9:6. It is possible that the terms *splendor* and *majesty* refer to his glorious armor. In any case the bridegroom is adequately equipped for battle. Glory and majesty are divine attributes reflected in the person of the victorious king.[19]

The bridegroom is victorious in his cause. He rides forth on warhorse or in chariot to the conflict for which he is destined. Yet unlike so many world monarchs, he has no interest in bloody battle or imperialistic conquest. He marches forth on behalf of truth, meekness, and righteousness.

The bridegroom is triumphant over his enemies. *Your right hand shall teach you awesome things.* The right hand, the source of power, is here personified. The right hand *teaches* the king. This is a way of saying that the king shall demonstrate tremendous powers.

---

16. Cf. I Sam. 9:2; 10:23; 16:12.
17. Kirkpatrick, CB, p. 246.
18. Bonar, CHC, p. 146.
19. Kirkpatrick, CB, p. 246.

Verse 5 depicts the conflicts of the royal bridegroom. The psalmist can visualize the battle scene. The arrows shower down on the opposing forces, piercing the hearts of the king's enemies. The prospect of this victory leads the psalmist to insert his prayer that people (enemy troops) would fall beneath the royal warrior (v. 5).

3. The identity of the bridegroom (vv. 6-7). Four facts about the bridegroom are set forth in verses 6-7 which render his identity beyond dispute.

a) The bridegroom is a divine ruler. He is addressed by the vocative *O God*. This rendering of the verse has indeed been challenged, but "interpretation is lifted out of the realm of speculation by Hebrews 1:8."[20]

b) The bridegroom is an eternal ruler. *Your throne, O God, is forever and ever.* The reference to the king as divine is incidental in verse 6. The major point of the verse is that the throne of this king is an everlasting one. Obviously, the only throne which could legitimately be called everlasting would have to be occupied by deity. Nathan's oracle which promised to David an everlasting throne (II Sam. 7:12ff.) finds fulfillment in this Ruler. "He shall reign over the house of Jacob forever; and of his kingdom there shall be no end" (Luke 1:33). For this reason Peter speaks of the "everlasting kingdom of our Lord and Savior Jesus Christ" (II Peter 1:11).

c) The bridegroom is an anointed ruler, anointed by God. *Therefore, O God, your God has anointed you.* God anoints God! Hebrews 1:8, 9 has these words spoken by God to or concerning the Son. This shows without question the deity of the king in Psalm 45. He would be anointed *with oil*. Oil is generally regarded as symbolic of the Holy Spirit. Jesus of Nazareth was twice literally anointed with oil, at the beginning of his ministry (Luke 7:38) and at the conclusion of it (John 12:3). But more important, at his baptism Jesus was anointed with the Holy Spirit (Luke 4:18).

Messiah would be anointed with the *oil of gladness.* The reference is not to ordinational anointing of a king or priest, but to the use of oil on occasions of great festivity.[21] Leupold thinks the reference is to "an ineradicable joy" which is "inherent in the entire being of this Hero."[22] It may be that the gladness refers more specifically to the joyful effects of his coronation of marriage celebration.

---

20. Wilson, MP, pp. 110-111.
21. Cf. Ps. 23:5; 104:15. The "oil of gladness" is contrasted with mourning in Isa. 61:3.
22. Leupold, EP, p. 356.

He was anointed over his fellows. Jesus was truly man as well as God. He is the only person in Scripture said to have the Holy Spirit without measure.

> For he whom God has sent speaks the words of God, for God gives him the Spirit without measure. The Father loves the Son, and has given all things into his hand (John 3:34, 35).

The *fellows* here are not angels, for they are not anointed beings. The reference may be to his fellow kings. To no other king is equal happiness granted, for his is the most blissful and glorious of all kingdoms.

d) The bridegroom is a righteous ruler (vv. 6b-7a). The scepter is the symbol of royal authority. The authority of the future king, like that of his heavenly Father, will be exercised in righteousness. Unlike so many who have been born to royalty, this king will not abuse his power. His scepter would be the symbol of uprightness.

4. The joy of the bridegroom (vv. 8-9a). The joyous festivities are envisioned by the psalmist in three ways:

a) The garments of the bridegroom are fragrant, woven, as it were, with myrrh, aloes, and cassia.[23] At his birth the wisemen brought frankincense and myrrh. At his burial Nicodemus brought myrrh and aloes to place by his body. His birth and death were fragrant with physical spices; but to the believer his royal robes are fragrant in a far more wondrous way. All that he does on behalf of the citizens of his kingdom is pleasing.

b) The bridegroom is made glad by the music of stringed instruments which are playing as he leaves[24] the ivory palaces to attend his own wedding. Palaces inlaid with ivory panels are attested elsewhere in Scripture.[25]

c) Kings' daughters attend the bridegroom. In Oriental nuptial celebrations virgin friends of the bride would greet and accompany the bridegroom to the marriage celebration. The fact that these friends of the bride are kings' daughters may serve to underscore the rank of the bride.

---

23. According to Leupold (EP, p. 357): myrrh is "an aromatic resin from Arabia that is used mostly in powdered form." Aloes is "a sweet smelling wood from India." Cassia is "a dried cinnamon blossom that is used for incense."

24. Another interpretation is that the music greets him as he approaches the palace of the bride.

25. I Kings 22:39; Amos 3:15.

C. The Bride (vv. 9b-12). The use of the husband-wife relationship to describe God's relationship to his people is common in the Old Testament.[26] The New Testament speaks of the church as the bride of Christ.[27] If the bridegroom in Psalm 45 is the Messiah, then the bride must be Messiah's people, the church of Christ.

1. The attainment of the bride (v. 9b). The psalmist envisions the beautiful bride at the right hand of the divine king. Even now before the marriage the bride is accorded royal dignity. She wears the title *queen*, and is attired in gold. In God's sight the bride is very precious. The word used here for *queen* (*shegal*) is a rare and unusual designation of a consort of the first rank.

Even now Christ's bride, the church, is reigning with him.[28] God's people are a *royal* priesthood now, but the royal dignity accorded the bride in this world will be amplified a hundred fold when Christ returns.[29]

2. The admonition to the bride (vv. 10-11). The bride prepares to make the transition from the single to the married state. To break old ties and establish a new home is difficult. The church is called out of the world and espoused to Christ. The psalmist assumes the role of a marriage counselor or wise teacher. He advises the bride to sever the old ties and give Messiah whole-hearted allegiance. So the bride is addressed by the psalmist or by God in five imperatives: (1) *Hearken*: Mark well what is bridegroom says to you; (2) *Consider*: Take note of all he has done in love for you; (3) *Incline your ear*: Be obedient to him and accept his gracious invitation; (4) *Forget*: Leave all for the sake of the one who loves you. Cast no lingering looks of regret behind. (5) *Bow down*: Render homage to your divine Lord. These five exhortations seem strange until it is remembered that the marriage was probably a matter of state policy, and that the bride probably had never even seen her future husband.[30]

3. Admiration for the bride (v. 12). The bride is admired, first, by the king himself. *So shall the king desire your beauty.* Christ's loving admiration is mirrored in the face of every groom who watches his beloved walk down the matrimonial isle. The Lord will love his people the more if they turn their backs on this world, and give themselves wholeheartedly to him.

---

26. E.g., Hosea 1-2; Ezek. 16.
27. Rev. 21:2, 9; 22:17. Cf. Eph. 5:22ff.
28. See Rom. 5:21; 6:12; 12:21.
29. Rev. 21; 22:5.
30. Kirkpatrick, CB, p. 250.

The *daughter of Tyre*[31] honors the bride by bringing a gift. It is not an individual Tyrian princess who is in view here, but the city and people of Tyre personified as a woman. Isaiah 23:18 prophesied the conversion of Tyre. Eusebius and Jerome declare that the wealth of Tyre was brought into the church. But that was only a token and foregleam of the enormous wealth which has come into the church from those converted out of the world through the preaching of the Gospel (cf. Isa. 60:11).

The rich among the people also bring gifts to the bride. If the daughter of Tyre personifies the Gentiles who render tribute to the church, then the rich among the people may be a reference to the Jews in their restored prosperity,[32] This, however, is uncertain.

D. *The Marriage* (vv. 13-16). As he describes the marriage, the psalmist focuses his attention on four matters.

1. The marriage attire (v. 13). The bride is the daughter of a king (v. 13), the wife of the king (v. 9) and the mother of kings (v. 16). These designations serve to emphasize the royal dignity of the bride. She is *all glorious within* and her outer garments are woven with gold. The day of the marriage of the Lamb will be most glorious also for the church.

2. The marriage procession (v. 14). In the manner of Oriental marriages, the bride is conducted with pomp and ceremony to meet her husband. She is accompanied by virgins. Here the bride is the church collectively; the virgins are individual believers.[33] Christians must be pure in heart, life and doctrine[34] and so the designation *virgin* is appropriate for them. The virgins follow the bride gladly, willingly here below. Ultimately they follow the bride to the mansions in heaven.

3. The joy of the marriage (v. 15). The bride and her maids enter the palace of the king in a mood of gay festivity. Weddings in Biblical times were occasions of great happiness marked by music, dancing and every mark of rejoicing.

4. The fruit of the marriage (v. 16). The king[35] will have sons. The king's fathers according to the flesh are the Patriarchs, prophets and priests of the old law. They will give way to the king's sons—the apostles

---

31. Leupold (EP, p. 358) thinks the daughter of Tyre symbolizes the new associates who will take the place of the old friends and relations left behind by the bride.

32. Bonar, CHC, p. 148.

33. The situation is the same as in Galatians where the church is the mother and individual Christians are the children.

34. Rev. 14:4; II Cor. 11:2.

35. The pronouns in the verse are masculine.

and evangelists of the New. These sons of the king will share the royal dignity, just as David's sons shared political dignity with their father (II Sam. 8:18). The New Testament emphasizes this very point. Christians constitute a royal priesthood (I Peter 2:9; Rev. 1:6). They shall reign on the earth (Rev. 5:10). It is the purpose of the Lord Jesus to bring "many sons to glory" (Heb. 2:10).

E. *Conclusion* (v. 17). The writing of the psalmist will perpetuate the memory of the king throughout the generations. Other peoples besides Israel will praise this king. The word *praise* (*yadah*) commonly is applied to God, and only rarely to men.[36] The names of the world's mighty monarchs may be forgotten; but God's Messiah shall be remembered by his loyal subjects forever.

Prophey No. 24

THE ROYAL PRIEST

Psalm 110

Psalm 110 has been styled the pearl of the Messianic psalms. Christ is here presented not only as King and Ruler of this world, but also as eternal priest. Under Old Testament law the wedding of royal and priestly lines was impossible. Priests were to be sons of Aaron; kings were descendants of David. One who did attempt to bridge the constitutional chasm between the two offices met with stern rebuke and physical affliction (II Chron. 26:16ff.). Yet in Psalm 110 the wedding of royal and priestly functions takes place naturally.

The authorship of Psalm 110 has been assigned by the critics to almost every prominent person from Abraham to Judas Maccabee. The evidence, however, is clear that David is the author of this psalm. The heading of the psalm testifies to Davidic authorship, and the New Testament supports the accuracy of this testimony. In fact, in Matthew 22:42f. the whole significance of the reference to Psalm 110 hinges upon David being the author and the Messiah being the subject of the psalm. To deny either Davidic authorship or Messianic interpretation is to call into question the intelligence and/or authority of Jesus of Nazareth.

No specific event is mentioned in the psalm which would give any clue as to its background. David here is functioning as a prophet. His

---

36. Kirkpatrick, CB, p. 252.

attention is focused on the Messiah. Albert Barnes states the matter this way:

> The Psalm has no particular reference to anything in his (i.e., David's) history, and as it is wholly prophetic of the Messiah, it might have been composed at any period of his life.[37]

Arguments of critics such as Driver who attempt to offset the prophetical Messianic character of this psalm are weak. The fact is that no merely human king merits to be associated with Yahweh on his throne. Furthermore, no Old Testament king was ever at the same time priest according to the order of Melchizedek. Only in the Messiah do these details find fulfillment.

The Messianic interpretation finds overwhelming support in the fact that this psalm is quoted fourteen times in the New Testament. In each instance the psalm is applied to Jesus Christ. No psalm finds in the New Testament an echo voiced so many times as this one.[38] Christian tradition follows the lead of the apostolic teachers. While Jewish tradition is not consistent, at least some Rabbis explained the psalm along Messianic lines.[39]

Translation of Psalm 110

A psalm of David. (1) An oracle of the LORD to my Lord: Sit at my right hand until I set your enemies as the footstool of your feet. (2) Your strong rod shall the Lord send forth from Zion; rule in the midst of your enemies. (3) Your people shall be willing in the day of your warfare; in the beauties of holiness, from the womb of the dawn, you shall possess the dew of your youth. (4) The LORD has sworn, he will not relent, you are a priest forever according to the manner of Melchizedek. (5) The Lord is at your right side; he shall strike through kings in the day of his anger. (6) He shall judge among Gentiles, piling up dead bodies; he shall smite the head over the whole earth. (7) From the brook in the way he shall drink; therefore shall he lift up the head.

Discussion

Psalm 110 has a simple organization. The two key statements are found in verses 1 and 4. The rest of the psalm expands on these statements. David depicts (1) the enthronement of the Messiah (v. 1); (2) the

---

37. Barnes, NOT, Psalms, III, 136.
38. See Matt. 22:41-46; Mark 12:35-37; Luke 20:41-44; Acts 2:34, 35; Heb. 1:13; 5:6; 7:17, 21
39. Maas. CTP, II, 53.

rule of Messiah (vv. 2-3); (3) the priesthood of the Messiah (v. 4); and (4) the conquests of the Messiah (vv. 5-7).

A. *The Enthronement of the Messiah* (v. 1). The solemnity and significance of the utterance which is made in verse 1 is indicated by the words *ne'um Yahweh* (oracle of Yahweh). This is the only place this poignant expression occurs in the Psalter. It is part of the vocabulary of Israel's prophets and constitutes the strongest possible claim to inspiration. Verse 1 is not the declaration of the people concerning David, but rather the declaration of God concerning David's Lord.

The first exegetical crux in the psalm is the identity of David's Lord. With irresistible logic Jesus argued that the word *Lord* implied one superior to David. David's Lord would have to be a predecessor, a contemporary or a successor of the great king. Some ancestor of David (Abraham, Moses, for example) who might conceivably be depicted as David's Lord is eliminated by the formula *ne'um Yahweh* which never introduces depictments of past events. Who among David's contemporaries would qualify for the title *Lord* (master) by the most powerful king of his day? Among David's successors who would possibly qualify for the title *Lord* except the Messiah? Delitzsch is surely correct when he says: "The type (David) lays his crown at the feet of the anti-type (Messiah)."[40]

The authority of David's Lord, the Messiah, is indicated by two considerations in verse 1. First, Messiah's position in respect to God indicates his authority. He is at the *right hand* of Yahweh. This was the place of honor, but not idle honor. The Messiah actually shares the power and dignity of Yahweh himself.[41] Jesus probably had Psalm 110 in mind when he declared: "Henceforth shall the son of man be seated on the right hand of God" (Luke 22:69). The enthronement took place following the ascension (Dan. 7:13, 14) and embraces the whole reign of the Messianic kingdom. Clarke comments:

> Jesus Christ, as God, ever dwelt in the fulness of the Godhead: but it was as God-man that after the resurrection He was raised to the right hand of the majesty on high, ever to appear in the presence of God for us.[42]

Four times in the Book of Hebrews Jesus Christ is depicted as sitting down at the right hand of the Father: (1) he sat down after he had purged our sins (Heb. 1:1-5); (2) he sat down as high priest, a minister of the sanctuary, the true Tabernacle which the Lord pitched (Heb.

---

40. Delitzsch, MPHS, p. 90.
41. See I Kings 2:19; Acts 2:34; Eph. 1:20-22; Heb. 1:13, 14.
42. Clarke, CCN, III, 361.

8:1-2); (3) he sat down after he had offered one sacrifice for sin (Heb. 10:1-12); and (4) he sat down as pioneer and perfecter of faith (Heb. 12:1-3). As priest on his heavenly throne Christ serves as advocate (I John 2:1), intercessor (Heb. 7:24-25), and high priest (Heb. 4:14-16).

The second indication of Messiah's authority in verse 1 is his position in respect to his enemies. They become the *footstool* of Messiah's feet. The allusion is to the custom of conquerors placing their feet upon the necks of captured enemies as a symbolic token of total victory (cf. Josh. 10:24).

B. *The Rule of the Messiah* (vv. 2-3). The command *sit* in verse 1 is followed by *rule* in verse 2. He sits as king as well as priest upon that throne. Five aspects of Messiah's rule are brought out in these verses.

1. The duration of his rule is suggested by the word *until* in verse 1. Satan the archenemy was dealt a crushing blow at the time of the resurrection and subsequent enthronement. But the victory won at the enthronement, important as it was, only signaled the ultimate and complete overthrow of all that oppose God. Christ's reign will not terminate before the total victory has been won. The last enemy that shall be destroyed is death (I Cor. 15:25ff.).

What happens then? According to Paul, Christ delivers over the kingdom—the mediatorial kingdom or church—to the Father. One grand phase of God's scheme of redemption will thereby be concluded. But even then Christ will not relinquish his basic, regal dignity. His reign will continue throughout eternity.[43] The word *until* then here, as in Genesis 49:10, only points to a climactic event within his reign without necessarily implying that the reign ceases at that point.

2. The center of his rule is indicated by the phrase *from Zion* (v. 2). The term *Zion* is used in several different ways in the Old Testament. To insist that Zion must always be the geographical city of Jerusalem is to fly in the face of Hebrews 12:22. Geographical, physical Zion (Jerusalem) was a type or preview of that heavenly city, that city not made by hands. Since Psalm 110 is Messianic throughout, Zion must refer to the Messianic Zion which the writer of Hebrews regarded as a present reality. This Zion—the kingdom of heaven—is Messiah's base of operations.

3. The means of his rule is indicated in the promise, *your strong rod shall Yahweh send forth*. This rod is the shepherd's rod. On his

---

43. See Eph. 5:5; Rev. 11:15; 21:1, 3.

coronation day this rod was set in his hand as a symbol of his authority in the kingdom. He is absolute monarch. He rules with a rod of iron (Ps. 2:9; Rev. 2:27). The term *rod* here may be metaphorical for Messiah's *word*, the Gospel, the sword of the spirit (Eph. 6:17), the mighty power of God (Rom. 1:16).

4. The commission under which he rules is suggested by the imperative *rule* (v. 2). His place at the right hand of God is not one of idle honor. He is active in the government of the kingdom. He has been delegated all authority in heaven and earth (Matt. 28:18). Under this divine proclamation he exercises the prerogatives of kingship. He is to exercise that rule in the midst of his enemies "converting all such as believe his Gospel, and confounding those who will not have him to reign over them."[44] *In the midst of his enemies* is equivalent to "in spite of his enemies."

5. Verse 3 speaks of the subject of Messiah's rule. The verse is difficult to translate and interpret; but at least seven essential ideas are presented here:

a) Messiah would have a people who follow him.

b) This people would be in willing subjection to him.

c) The existence of this people would be a result of Messiah's power.

Clarke comments:

> Whenever and wherever the Gospel is preached in sincerity and purity then and there is the day of Christ's power. It is the time of his exaltation. The days of his *flesh* were the days of his weakness; the time of his *exaltation* is the day of his power.[45]

d) This people would appear before Messiah in great beauty—in robes of holy adorning or priestly garments.[46]

e) From the *womb of the dawn*—from the very beginning of the Messianic age—the dawn of the Sun of Righteousness—Messiah would have such a group of followers.

f) The followers would display the vigor of youth. They would be filled with zeal for his cause.

g) The followers would bring refreshment to the barren world like the morning dew rejuvenates parched ground.[47]

---

44. Clarke, CCN, III, 361.

45. Ibid.

46. Cf. Exod. 28:2, 40; I Peter 2:9; Rev. 1:5, 6.

47. Some take *dew of your youth* to refer to Christ himself. He is forever young—the perfect man—bringing refreshment to all who meet him.

C. The Priesthood of Messiah (v. 4). Four specific facts are given regarding Messiah's priesthood.

1. It is a God-appointed priesthood. Messiah does not inherit his priesthood, but is appointed by God to this office. The truthfulness and solemnity of this appointment are underscored by a divine oath.[48] God will not change his purpose regarding this appointment. *He will not relent.* Christ will be incarnated, and the Gospel of his salvation will be preached over the whole earth. This is an irresistible decree of that God who loves mankind. Clarke comments:

> In the priesthood of Christ lies the main weight of our redemption; therefore, God swears that he will be a Priest to offer himself, and to intercede for us, without which he had in vain been our Prophet and King.[49]

2. This is a singular priesthood. The oath concerns one person— *you,* not you and your sons. No dynasty is envisioned here, but rather the priestly function of one individual.

3. This is an eternal priesthood. He is to be a priest *forever.* An eternal priesthood conferred on a single person can only be fulfilled in a person who lives forever.[50]

4. This priesthood is unique. It is *according to the manner of Melchizedek.* Melchizedek was king of Salem and priest of the Most High God (*'El 'Elyon*) in Genesis 14. Since nothing is said of his ancestry, it is safe to assume that he had been appointed to this dual office by the Lord. He had not inherited his priesthood. In terms of function. Jesus resembles the Old Testament Aaronide priesthood; but in terms of appointment he resembles Melchizedek.

D. The Conquests of the Messianic Priest-King (vv. 5-7). Verses 5-7 portray the overthrow of the foes of David's Lord. It would appear that the position of the Father and Messiah have been reversed. In verse 1 the Messiah was seated on the right hand of the Father; but in verse 5 the Father is stationed at the right hand of the Messiah.[51] The scene is one of battle. The Messiah and his Lord—the Father— *strike through* the adversaries. This day of wrath is the final showdown with the forces of evil.[52]

---

48. Cf. Heb. 6:17; 5:6; 7:17, 21; 10:13.

49. Clarke, CCN, III, 365.

50. See Heb. 5:6, 10; 6:20; 7:17, 21.

51. The suffix *your* in verses 1-4 refers to the Messiah. Unless there is an abrupt change. the second person masculine pronoun would continue to refer to Messiah also in verse 5.

52. Rom. 2:5; Rev. 6:17; 19:11ff.; II Thess. 2:8.

Verse 6 continues the description of the victory in that day. He shall judge (rule over) Gentiles—those who have rejected his gracious priestly ministries. The corpses of those who attempt to withstand the conquering Messiah fill the land. The head (singular) of many countries will be mortally wounded. Could this be the final defeat of Satan? The initial Messianic promise of the Bible announced the crushing of the head of the Serpent. Ultimately Christ will destroy every thing which opposes the universal spread of his kingdom.

While the enemies fall, this Messianic warrior presses on to total victory. The picture in verse 7 is of a soldier chasing a fleeing army. He delays his pursuit only long enough to refresh himself at a stream.[53] He then immediately continues the relentless chase. So King Jesus presses the battle against the foe. There can be no truce, no ceasefire, until every last enemy has been destroyed. The head of Satan will be wounded (v. 6), but that head of Messiah, once crowned with thorns, will be uplifted in glory and majesty.

Special Note

THE USE OF PSALM 45 IN THE BOOK OF HEBREWS

Psalm 45:6-7 is cited as part of the grand argument in the Book of Hebrews for the superiority of Christ (Heb. 1:8-9). The inspired Psalmist spoke the words of God. For this reason the Hebrew writer ascribes these words to God as their ultimate author. The Father spoke here concerning the Son. If these words were in fact spoken to Messiah as Hebrews argues, then clearly the superior rank of Christ is established. Milligan[54] points to the following particulars supporting the Messiah's exaltation in Psalm 45.

1. Messiah is called *God* by the Father himself. It is true that angels and even magistrates are sometimes called *gods*, in a metaphorical sense. But in the literal and proper sense of this word it is appropriately applied only to the uncreated, eternal and omnipresent deity.

2. Messiah has a throne, i.e., he exercises power, rule and dominion. Not only does Messiah have a throne, his throne is *eternal*. This is but another way of saying that his dominion is an everlasting dominion (Dan. 7:14).

---

53. Clarke sees in the drinking from the brook an allusion to the sufferings of Christ.
54. Milligan, EH, p. 68.

3. Messiah holds a *scepter*, symbol of his authority. All authority in heaven and earth has been given unto him (Matt. 28:18). Because his entire administration is conducted in justice, his scepter is called *a scepter of righteousness*.

4. Messiah has a *kingdom*. Of what value is a throne and scepter without a kingdom? He is no royal pretender. Ten thousand times ten thousand loyal subjects bow in homage before him.

5. Messiah has been anointed by God himself. Of what angel could that be said?

6. Messiah was anointed above his fellow kings. They were anointed only as kings. He was Prophet, Priest and King. They were anointed with oil only, but he with the Holy Spirit and power (Acts 10:38).

Special Note

THE DEITY OF THE BRIDEGROOM

Psalm 45:6 has caused much discussion among commentators. The basic issue is whether or not *'elohim* (God) is a vocative. Is the bridegroom addressed here as God? Most modern authorities rule out this rendering *a priori*. The deity of the Messiah had not yet been revealed, so they say. But scholars are all but unanimous in the admission that *'elohim* could be rendered as a vocative here.

Rationalistic commentators vie with one another in the ingenuity they expend in attempting to circumvent the clear implications of the words of verse 6. Basically, three lines of attack have been launched against the deity of the bridegroom here.

1. Proposed alternate translations. At least four translations of verse 6 have appeared which remove the deity of the bridegroom. These are:

a) *Your throne is the throne of God.* This translation is found in the American Standard Version margin. It is disputed whether this rendering is grammatically legitimate, but good authorities decide in the affirmative. Kirkpatrick, for example, says: "It gives, if the text is to be retained, what is the most satisfactory explanation of it."[55] Leupold, however, calls this translation a departure from "the simple and obvious translation" which had been upheld by all prominent versions before 1901.[56] The first alternative translation, says Leupold, is "difficult

---

55. Kirkpatrick, CB, p. 248.
56. Leupold, EP, p. 361.

to defend and would scarecely suggest itself as an easy and natural rendering."[57]

b) The Revised Standard Version rendered the phrase *your divine throne*. Such a rendering is possible as is indicated by such passages as Numbers 25:12. But while this translation is possible, it is not necessary or natural.

c) Still others render the disputed phrase: *God is your throne*, i.e., your kingdom is founded upon God. In spite of various parallels which can be pointed out[58] Kirkpatrick says: "the expression, to say the least, would be a strange one."[59]

d) Still another proposed rendering is this: *Your throne is God*, i.e., divine. On this rendering Kirkpatrick comments: "But though Hebrew uses substantives as predicates in a way which our idiom does not allow, this particular instance seems scarcely admissible."[60]

The fact is that all ancient versions, and the prominent modern versions until 1901, rendered this verse by construing "God" as a vocative.

2. Others have attempted to circumvent the implications of verse 6 by changing the object of the address. The ancient Targum, for example, understands the words *O God* to be addressed to God, not to the king. But this interpretation seems excluded by the context. The king is addressed in the preceding and following verses: "and it seems hardly possible to suppose that in this verse alone Jehovah is abruptly addressed."[61]

3. Still others suggest that the word *'elohim* here has its more general sense of mighty one, or judge.[62] Whereas the ruling power in Old Testament times might properly be called *'elohim* (cf. Ex. 21:6; 22:28) yet never is a single representative of that power so addressed.[63] Furthermore, throughout the context of Psalm 45 *'elohim* is always used in its far more frequent meaning *God*.

In the Old Testament there are undeniable traces of the notion that the future Messiah would combine in his own person an unexampled

---

57. Ibid.

58. E.g., Ps. 91:2; Deut. 33:27.

59. Kirkpatrick, CB, p. 258.

60. Kirkpatrick, CB, p. 248.

61. Ibid.

62. Arguments for this view are listed and analyzed by Kirkpatrick (ibid.): "After all that has been urged in favor of this interpretation it seems hardly possible to suppose that the king is directly addressed as *'elohim*."

63. Exodus 7:1 is not a case in point.

union of the human and divine. True, the mystery of the incarnation is still veiled in the Old Testament. Yet here and there one can observe the convergence of the two great lines of prophecy—the one which announces an advent of Yahweh and the other the rise of a son of David. Messiah is clearly called "mighty God" in Isaiah 9:5. Delitzsch remarks: "It was already part of the faith under the Old Testament, that the mighty God, the captain of Israel, the just God and the justifier, would hereafter manifest himself in bodily form in the person of Messias. . . ."[64]

---

64. Delitzsch, CEH, I, 79.

Chapter Thirteen

THE REIGN OF THE GLORIOUS KING

Further information about the victorious reign of the Messianic king can be gleaned from Psalm 72 and Psalm 68. The former psalm deals primarily with the character of Messiah's reign, and the later psalm with the ultimate victory of that reign.

Prophecy No. 25

THE CHARACTER OF MESSIAH'S REIGN

Psalm 72

Two considerations lead to classifying Psalm 72 as personal Messianic. First, the psalm is cast in the future tense throughout; and second, the ideal terms of the prophecy were not fulfilled by any king subsequent to Solomon, except the Messiah. Bonar observes:

> Israel's poets and prophets know of no golden age of which the very center and life is not Messiah, God incarnate. Restored paradise has streams; Messiah is their fountain-head.[1]

Delitzsch is surely incorrect in regarding this psalm as "only indirectly prophetic."[2]

Solomon is the author of Psalm 72.[3] The imagery in the psalm is clearly borrowed from the peaceful and prosperous reign of this grand monarch. Delitzsch supposes that Solomon "cherished the wish that in his person the Messianic idea, and through his government the Messianic age, might be realized."[4] The hard evidence, however, points in a different direction. Solomon here speaks as a prophet. He anticipates the coming of the one who would be greater than Solomon (Matt. 12:42).

Translation of Psalm 72

By Solomon. (1) Give to the king your judgments, O God, and your righteousness unto the king's son. (2) He shall judge your people in righteousness, and your afflicted ones with justice. (3) The mountains

---

1. Bonar, CHC, p. 215.
2. Delitzsch, MPHS, p. 98.
3. Such is the implication of the heading. Verse 20 in no way negates this, for verse 20 is the concluding verse in Book II of the Psalter. It was not originally part of Psalm 72.
4. Delitzsch, MPHS, p. 97.

194

shall bring peace to the people, and the hills, in righteousness. (4) He shall judge the afflicted of the people, he shall save the sons of the needy; he will crush the oppressor. (5) They shall fear you with the sun, and before the moon throughout all generations. (6) He shall come down like rain upon a mown field, like showers that water the earth. (7) In his days the righteous will flourish, and an abundance of peace until the moon is no more. (8) He shall rule from sea to sea, and from the river unto the ends of the earth. (9) The desert tribes will bow before him, and his enemies will lick the dust. (10) The kings of Tarshish and the isles shall bring an oblation, the kings of Sheba and Seba will present gifts. (11) All kings shall bow down to him, all nations shall serve him. (12) For he shall deliver the poor who cry out, the afflicted who has no helper. (13) He shall take pity upon the poor and needy, and shall save the souls of the poor. (14) From oppression and violence he shall redeem their soul, and their blood shall be precious in his eyes. (15) And he will live, and there shall be given to him of the gold of Sheba; prayer on his behalf shall be made continually, and all the day shall he be blessed. (16) And there shall be an abundance of grain in the land upon the top of mountains, and its fruit shall sway like Lebanon; and those from the city shall flourish like the grass of the earth. (17) His name shall endure forever, and his name shall flourish as long as the sun; all nations shall bless themselves in him, and shall regard him as blessed. (18) Blessed is the LORD God, the God of Israel who alone does wondrous things. (19) And blessed be his glorious name forever; and may the whole earth be filled with his glory; Amen and Amen.

Discussion

Four great facts about the reign of Messiah are brought out in this psalm. Messiah's reign will be (1) righteous (vv. 1-7); (2) universal (vv. 8-11); (3) beneficent (vv. 12-14); and (4) perpetual (vv. 15-17). To these grand predictions the psalmist appends his own doxology (vv. 18-19).

A. *Messiah's Reign is Righteous* (vv. 1-7). The psalm opens with a prayer for the king and his son (v. 1). The prayer, however, is virtually a prediction, for Solomon[5] only asks what he knows God will give. Under the Old Testament system judicial powers were exercised in God's name. The king was the supreme court of the land. Messiah

---

5. Others prefer to see here (1) the church praying for Christ; or (2) the Messiah praying for himself.

was expected to exercise judicial powers in perfection. Alexander's comment is appropriate:

> By the king and the king's son we are not to understand the descendants and successors of David indefinitely, but the last and greatest of them in particular.[6]

Verse 2 expresses the necessary consequences of the granting of the prayer of verse 1. The word *judge* is equivalent to *reign*. The reign of Messiah is characterized by *righteousness*. Even the *poor*—those normally denied justice in the courts—would be treated equitably by the glorious ruler here envisioned.

The result of the righteous rule would be a harvest of *peace* on the *mountains and hills* of the kingdom. Peace is often mentioned as a characteristic trait of the Messianic age.[7] The peace here envisioned is that which results from righteous government (v. 3). The coming ruler would *judge the afflicted*. To judge them is to do them justice and vindicate their rights. He would save the children of the needy from slavery, and crush those who oppress them (v. 4).

In verse 5 prayer and prediction are joined. Throughout all generations—as long as the sun and moon endure—the name of God will be revered (cf. Rev. 22:4). The expressions *with the sun, before the moon* and *generation of generation* are all Scriptural expressions for perpetual duration.

Clearly verse 6 refers to the advent of the Messianic king. His coming is likened to *rain upon a mown field*. This beautiful figure pictures the gentle yet refreshing influence of the king. After the scythe of war and every form of ruin has done its damage to the grass of life, Messiah comes to bring renewal. Indeed, under the reign of the Prince of Peace the *righteous will flourish*. This reign is to continue so long as the moon endures (v. 7) and even beyond.

B. *Messiah's Reign is Universal* (vv. 8-11). Messiah's kingdom stretches from *sea to sea, and from the river unto the ends of the earth*. This is an obvious allusion to the boundaries of the Promised Land as defined in Exodus 23:31. But Messiah's kingdom would stretch from any sea around to the same point again, and from the river—the Euphrates or any other river as a starting point—to the end of the earth.

---

6. Alexander, PTE, p. 302.
7. See Isa. 2:4; 9:6, 7; 11:9; 65:25; Micah 4:3; Zech. 9:10.

Even those on the fringes of the civilized world—the roving nomads of the wilderness regions—will crouch in fear before him. In total humiliation and subjugation Messiah's enemies would *lick the dust* (v. 9). From distant Tarshish on the coast of Spain in the west, from the islands of the Mediterranean, and from the distant Sheba and Seba will come men bringing their offerings (v. 10). The term *minchah* (oblation) and the verb *qarabh* (present) in verse 10 are part of the technical Old Testament vocabulary of worship. This verse is then describing worship offerings, not tribute or the presentation of friendly gifts. The locations named are but samples of all nations. *Tarshish* on the coast of Spain represents the far west. The *islands* are all distant sea-coasts but especially those of the Mediterranean Sea. *Sheba* is a province of Arabia[8] in the far south and *Seba* appears to have been in Ethiopia. Verse 11 underscores the universal reign of Messiah of which there was a hint in the preceding verse. The verbs in this verse (*bow* and *serve*) may be applied to either civil or religious subjugation, and probably both ideas are involved.

C. *Messiah's Reign is Beneficent* (vv. 12-14). In verses 12-14 the prophet returns to the impartial justice of Messiah's reign. The great empires of history were founded by bloodshed and violence. Once established, these kingdoms were characterized by oppression and slavery. But in Messiah's kingdom there would be no miscarriage of justice. He uses his might on behalf of the unfortunate (vv. 12-13). He would not allow oppression and violence to be used against the humble. Each citizen of his kingdom is precious in his sight. He would not tolerate acts of violence against them (v. 14).

D. *Messiah's Reign is Perpetual* (vv. 15-17). In spite of the determined opposition of hell, Messiah will live. He will receive precious gold as tribute in spite of efforts to undermine his program. Prayers of thanksgiving will continually be made for him, and he, because of his beneficent reign, will daily receive the praise of his subjects (v. 15).

The prosperity of Messiah's kingdom is depicted in verse 15. There will be plenty of corn in the land. Even on the normally barren mountain tops the grain will rustle like the cedar boughs on the Lebanon. In this same period, they *shall flourish like grass of the earth* (v. 16). The city intended is probably Zion or Jerusalem, the center of Messiah's kingdom. That city flourishes in population "like numberless blades of grass, all holy, all praising their King."[9]

---

8. An obvious allusion to the visit of the Queen of Sheba (I Kings 10:1-10).
9. Bonar, CHC, p. 217.

The name of Messiah will endure forever. Through him men will be blessed. He is the fulfillment of the promise made to Abraham that in him all nations of the earth would be blessed (Gen. 12:3). Therefore, all nations will call Messiah blessed (v. 17). The prosperity of the Sovereign is inseparable from that of the subjects. If all nations call Messiah blessed, it is because he is the source of their prosperity and salvation.

E. *The Psalmist's Doxology* (vv. 18-19). The psalm closes with the psalmist's personal praise for the God who would bring such a wonderful king into the world. Truly these are *wondrous things* which the prophet has been describing (v. 18). Every believer can join this ancient saint in the desire for God's precious name to be universally and eternally praised (v. 19).

Prophecy No. 26

THE MARCH OF THE MIGHTY MONARCH

Psalm 68

Psalm 68 is notoriously difficult to translate and interpret.[10] One writer refers to it as the Titan among the psalms. Some of its verses are impenetrable. Simon De Muis said of it:

> In this Psalm there are as many precipices and labyrinths, as there are verses or words. It may not be improperly termed, the torture of critics, and the reproach of commentators.[11]

Yet Paul refers to it in Ephesians 4:8 and makes use of it to undergird his teaching of the ascension. The Psalmist depicts Yahweh ascending to his heavenly Temple and receiving gifts of men. On this Lenski observes:

> What Jehovah did the psalmist describes in figurative language because it was to fit Christ, his ascent to heaven and his dispensing of gifts. The passage is plainly Messianic.[12]

That this psalm is Messianic there can be no question. It looks forward to the defeat of all opposition in the future, and the time when all the kingdoms of the world own the God of Israel as their king and

---

10. Clarke (CCN, III, 217) calls it "the most difficult in the whole Psalter."
11. Quoted by Clarke, Ibid.
12. Lenski, IGEP, p. 518.

pay him homage. This is not groundless nationalistic aspiration. This is Messianic hope. This is inspired prediction. Since Eden history has been moving toward the grand climax sketched so beautifully in the language of this psalm. Psalm 68 has always been the favorite of those who felt that their cause was the cause of God, and that in his strength they were sure to conquer.[13]

Interpreters fall into two broad categories regarding the background of Psalm 68: those who accept Davidic authorship, and those who do not. The latter group indulges in baseless speculation in assigning the psalm to almost any date from the reign of Solomon to that of the Hasmonean rulers of the second century B.C. The psalm clearly claims, however, to be from the pen of David and there is no solid evidence against his authorship.

Among those who hold to Davidic authorship for Psalm 68, two occasions are suggested as likely background for the composition. The most popular choice of the interpreters is that grand occasion when David transported the ark from the home of Obed-edom to the special tent on Mt. Zion (II Sam. 6). The other occasion mentioned as possible background is the return of the ark to Jerusalem after the overwhelming defeat of the Ammonites (II Sam. 11:11).

While either one of these episodes in David's life may have been the catalyst for this composition, in truth neither occasion fits snugly the language of the psalm. David here in the Spirit is speaking about things far distant from himself. He, perhaps better than his modern interpreters, realized that Mt. Zion and the ark were but symbols— pale physical copies of the heavenly realities.

Translation of Psalm 68 (Selected Verses)

To the chief musician. A psalm, a song of David. (1) God shall arise, his enemies shall scatter, those hating him shall flee before him. (2) As smoke is driven, you shall drive (them); as wax is melted in the presence of fire, wicked ones shall perish in the presence of God. (3) But as for righteous people, they shall be glad, they shall rejoice before God that they may express joy with gladness. (4) Sing to God, sing praises to his

---

13. Kirkpatrick (CB, pp. 377-378): "To the crusaders setting out for the recovery of the Holy Land; to Savonarola and his monks as they marched to the trial of fire in the Piazza at Florence; to the Huguenots who called it 'the song of battles'; to Cromwell at Dunbar as the sun rose on the mists of the morning and he charged Leslie's army; it has supplied words for the expression of their heartfelt convictions."

name; cast up a (highway) for the one who rides through the deserts, by his name Yah, and exult before him. (5) Father of orphans, judge of widows (is) God in his holy abode. (6) God makes the lonely ones to dwell at home, makes prisoners come forth into pleasures; but rebels have inhabited deserts. (18) You have ascended on high, you have taken captivity captive, you have received gifts on behalf of[14] even rebels, that the LORD God may dwell (among them). (19) Blessed is the Lord who day by day loads us down, the God of our salvation (selah).[15] (20) God is for us, a God of abundant salvation, and to the LORD God[16] belong, with respect to death, escapes. (21) But God will crush the head of his enemies, and the hairy scalp of the one who continues in his guilt. (22) The Lord has said, From Bashan I will bring again, I will bring again from the depths of the sea. (23) In order that you may crush (them) with your foot in blood, the tongue of your dogs (in blood) from your enemies, (even) from him. (24) They have seen your goings, O God, (even) the goings of my God, my king, in the holy place. (25) Singers went before, afterward came instrumentalists in the midst of maidens with timbrels. (26) In the congregations, bless God, the Lord (you who are) from the fountain of Israel. (27) There is little Benjamin conquering (them), the princes of Judah stoning them, the princes of Zebulun, the princes of Naphtali. (28) Your God (O Israel) has ordained your strength; be strong, O God, who has done it for us. (29) Because of your Temple above Jerusalem, to you shall kings bring tribute. (30) Rebuke the beasts of reeds, the crowd of bulls with the calves of nations, crouching with pieces of silver; he has scattered peoples who delight in wars. (31) Princes shall come out of Egypt, Ethiopia shall soon stretch out her hands to God. (32) O kingdoms of the earth, sing to God; sing to God; sing praises to the Lord (selah). (33) to the one who rides in the ancient heaven of heavens. Behold, one gives forth with his voice, with a strong voice. (34) Give strength to God! Over Israel (is) his majesty, and his strength in the clouds. (35) Awesome, O God, (are you) out of your holy places; the mighty One of Israel is he who gives strength and powers to the people. Blessed be God.

---

14. The preposition *beth* has other possible meanings.

15. Selah occurs in verses 7, 19 and 32 after the first verse of a stanza. Selah probably indicates a musical interlude designed to underscore the thought with which the stanza begins.

16. *'Adonay* = Lord, master, sovereign.

Discussion

Most commentators divide Psalm 68 into two major parts. Part One (vv. 1-18) is supposed to deal with the past; part two (vv. 19-35) with the present and future. This analysis makes the Messianic verse 18 a poetic description of some event which had already transpired in David's day. A more careful analysis reveals that the entire psalm is future with the exception of vv. 7-17 which furnish illustrations of God's omnipotence and graciousness in Israel's past. Even these verses are predictive in the sense that David is looking to the past for pictures of what was yet to be.

A. *The Glorious Advent* (vv. 1-6). The structure of Psalm 68 is simple. The psalmist announces his grand theme in verse 1: *God shall arise,*[17] *his enemies shall scatter, those hating him shall flee before him.* The psalmist anticipates a glorious coming of God. Before him the wicked flee like smoke before the wind; their powers of resistance to God melt like wax before the fire.[18]

The righteous, on the other hand, not only stand *before God,* they rejoice in his presence (v. 3). The day of this divine visitation is a prominent pillar in Old Testament theology, and the psalmist bids his readers to prepare for the reception of the glorious visitor: *Cast up a highway for the One who rides through the deserts* (v. 4). God's advent is described under the figure of a journey of an oriental monarch before whose chariot engineers prepare the road.[19] Through faith, obedience and godliness the righteous prepare for God's advent.

The phrase *by his name Yah* (v. 4) tells something of the character of the coming one. *Yah* is an abbreviation of Yahweh. This common Old Testament name emphasized the redemptive nature of God. Yahweh is the covenant-making, covenant-keeping God of redemption who shows himself mighty in the deliverance of his people. Three phrases in verse 5 further describe the coming one: he is *father of orphans,* i.e., protector of the innocent and helpless. He is *judge* (i.e., vindicator) *of widows.* His *abode* whether on earth or in heaven, is *holy.*

---

17. Most versions ancient and modern render, *Let God arise;* but the form of the verb is against this rendering.

18. Smoke scatterd by the wind is an appropriate emblem for total disappearance (Ps. 37:20), the wax melted by the fire, for unresisting impotence (Ps. 97:5).

19. In Isa. 40:3 similar language is used in reference to the coming of the Lord. See also Isa. 57:14 and 62:10 where the expression "cast up a highway" is used for the return of Israel from Babylon.

The past and present actions of God are a clue to the future actions of the Coming One. God habitually (Heb. participle) *makes the lonely to dwell at home, makes prisoners come forth into pleasures.* Only those who rebel against God never experience the spiritual transformation which may be likened to homecoming after a long journey or freedom after extended bondage. The rebels remain in the barren wastes of life (v. 6).

B. *The Glorious Accomplishments* (vv. 7-17). In graphic language the psalmist sets forth the history of Israel from the Exodus to the Entry into Canaan. The thought here is that the past accomplishments of God are a key to his future actions. The glorious power which he manifested on behalf of his old covenant people is a pledge of even more astonishing feats in the future. Here the psalmist alludes to how God (1) led his people through the wilderness (vv. 7-10); (2) gave his people Canaan (vv. 11-14); and (3) occupied Mount Zion (vv. 15-17).

1. God led his people through the wilderness (vv. 7-10). The Exodus from Egypt is cited as an illustration of how God brings his people home. In language borrowed from the Song of Deborah (Judg. 5:4-5) the psalmist depicts God's leadership of the people at that time. He marched before his people in the wilderness in the fiery cloud as their Guide and Commander (v. 7). A great thunderstorm and earthquake marked his presence at Sinai (v. 8).[20] There the covenant was offered and accepted. Yahweh became from that time forward the God of Israel.

During the forty years of wandering the Lord showered down upon them *rain,* an emblem of abundant and refreshing gifts which included manna, quail, and water. Thus did he strengthen his inheritance (or people) when they most needed it (v. 9).[21] God's people—his flock[22]— were brought into the land of promise. This, of course, proves that God will prepare a resting place or home for those who are poor and afflicted (v. 10).

2. God led his people into Canaan (vv. 11-14). The poet next graphically describes the victories by which Canaan was won and retained. Over and over again the Lord gave to his people *the word*— the good news. "God's word is sovereign. He has only to command,

---

20. Cf. Exod. 19:16-18.

21. Kirkpatrick (CB, p. 383) thinks verse 9 refers to God's gracious preparation of the land of Canaan (*your inheritance*) by means of abundant rain.

22. The Hebrew word literally means, an animal; collectively, a herd or flock.

and the victory is won."[23] The publishers of that good news were a *great host* (v. 11). The allusion here is to the custom of women celebrating victories with song and dance.[24] What was there to cheer about? *Kings of hosts*[25] fled repeatedly. *She that tarried at home* (peaceful non-combatants) shared in the distribution of the spoils of the routed enemy (v. 12). Following the defeat of each enemy the land had rest—they would *lie down between the borders.*[26] The beautiful allusion in verse 13 to the changeable colors of a dove's plumage "seems intended to suggest the idea of a peaceful but splendid prosperity."[27] In verse 14 the change from war to peace is likened to the dazzling whiteness of a patch of snow in the midst of dark terrain.[28]

3. God occupied Zion (vv. 15-17). The hill of God (i.e., God's kingdom) is like *mount Bashan, a mount of peaks* (v. 15). Mount Bashan is the lofty range of the Antilebanon range also called Hermon or Sion (Sirion).[29] This verse underscores the invincibility of God's kingdom (not a detached mountain, but a chain with many lofty summits). It is possible that the many peaks which make up the hill of God may refer to the states or kingdoms which are part of the kingdom of God. Mountains are frequently symbols of kingdoms in Scripture.[30]

Mt. Zion—the hill of God—is described in verse 16 as an object of hostility or envy[31] to the moutains of the heathen world. God has chosen Zion as his dwelling and he—Yahweh—God of revelation and redemption actually dwells there. Zion is protected by the innumerable chariots of God, and by the personal presence of the Lord (*'adhonay*)

---

23. Kirkpatrick, CB, p. 383.

24. The word translated *publishers of it* is fem. plural. See Exod. 15:20; I Sam. 18:6, 7.

25. The unusual expression *kings of hosts* seems to be chosen with reference to the title Yahweh of hosts. "Vast as their armies may be they are powerless to resist One who has infinitely stronger armies at His command." Kirkpatrick, CB, p. 384.

26. KJV *ye have lien among the pots* is impossible. The Hebrew noun occurs only here and Ezek. 40:43 where it is equally obscure. Others have proposed *folds* or *sheepcotes.*

27. Alexander, PTE, p. 286.

28. Zalmon ("shadow, shade") was an eminence near Shechem covered with dark forests (Judg. 9:48). Others interpret *it snowed in Zalmon* to refer to a snowstorm which accompanied and completed the rout of the kings.

29. See Deut. 3:9; 4:48; Ps. 42:6; 89:12.

30. Alexander, PTE, p. 286. Leupold (EP, p. 494) sees the thrust of the paragraph in the comparative physical insignificance of Mt. Zion in contrast to its spiritual prominence.

31. The verb *ratsad* is a hapax, but its meaning has been preserved in Arabic—to watch as an enemy, to lie in wait, to view with envy. KJV *leap* is unwarranted.

among them. The expression *Sinai in the sanctuary* (v. 17) is obscure. The meaning may be that "the same glorious theophany which once took place on Sinai is now renewed on Zion."[32]

C. *The Glorious Ascension* (v. 18). Verse 18 is generally taken to be a reference to the movement of the ark to Mt. Zion. Leupold's interpretation is typical:

> In a connection as clear as that in which this verse appears God's 'ascending on high' cannot refer to anything other than His taking up abode on His holy mount of Zion. . . . God is pictured as coming from the conquest of the land to occupy the mountain at Jerusalem.[33]

Actually the climax of the psalm is in this stanza. All that precedes has led up to it, and all that follows flows down from it. The mighty God who descends to earth in verses 1-6, now returns to his heavenly abode.

Paul saw in this statement a prophecy of the ascension of Jesus (Eph. 4:8). Thus the Holy Spirit has guided the apostle to understand the true import of this verse. In some sense this speaks of Messiah. At the very least one would have to concur with Leupold that the psalmist "apparently regards the Lord's victorious entrance into Jerusalem as a type or figure of Christ's triumphant entry into the heavens. . . ."[34] Without the instruction of the Holy Spirit through Paul interpreters probably never would have seen the ascension of Christ in this verse. But once the ultimate author of Scripture has indicated what he had in mind, careful students can see how the entire psalm hinges on this verse. That verse 18 is a prophecy of the ascension of Christ is supported by the following considerations:

1. The verse is in the second person. It is in the form of a prayer addressed to God. It is God personally who has ascended. This verse does not mention either the ark or Mt. Zion specifically.

2. God *ascended*. This phrase does not describe some procession winding its way to Mt. Zion. No incident in the Old Testament history matches what is here described. This is prophecy pure and simple.

3. God ascended *on high* (*hammaron*). By itself and without further specification the Hebrew term never means merely the height of Mt. Zion.[35] The term *hammaron* means heaven. Kirkpatrick lamely attempts

---

32. Alexander, PTE, p. 287. Cf. Kirkpatrick (CB, p. 387): "The glory and majesty which were revealed at Sinai are now transferred to God's new abode."

33. Leupold, EP, p. 495.

34. Ibid.

35. The same word in the construct state is used of Mt. Zion in Jer. 31:12.

to circumvent the clear meaning of the verse when he says: "Probably the poet did not make any sharp distinction between the triumphant return of Jehovah to heaven . . . and the triumphant procession to His earthly abode which was the symbol of it."[36] Certainly the advent of the Lord predicted in verses 1-6 must refer to more than the removal of the ark from Mt. Zion. In those verses God personally comes to the aid of his people. God *arises* from his throne to enter the battle on behalf of his people. In verse 18 the conflict is over, and the conqueror is returning to his heavenly abode.

4. God ascended to heaven as a great conqueror: *You have taken captivity captive.* The language is again borrowed from Deborah's song (Judg. 5:12). The general import of these words is quite clear. A great battle has been successfully concluded. But what is meant by *captivity*? Is this an example of an abstract term being substituted for the concrete? In this case *captivity* would be equivalent to *a body of captives.* Is this a personification of all the hostile powers arraigned against God's people? Is the *captivity* the Israelites themselves?

The term *captivity* here is a plain accusative, and as such it is highly significant. Lenski's comments are appropriate:

> *Captivity* itself was taken captive (Col. 2:15). What captivity? The captivity in which principalities and powers, the hellish kingdom, held and tried to keep men.[37]

Christ has triumphed over and bound everlastingly Satan, sin, and death which once held men captive (cf. I Cor. 15:54).

What is implied in the action of *taking captive*? Certainly conquest or victory. Probably, in this context, abolishment. That which held God's people captive has been abolished (I Cor. 15:57).

5. God ascended into heaven to become a beneficent ruler: *You have taken gifts on behalf of men.* The verb here demands close attention. In Ephesians 4:8 the verb is rendered *gave.* The latter reading is also found in the Targum and Syriac. The Septuagint, however, follows the Hebrew in rendering the verb *received.*

Various explanations for Paul's rendering *gave* have been proposed. Some hold that Paul deliberately altered the text to make his point. Others see this as an example of faulty memory. Still other proposals are that (1) Paul used a different Hebrew text which actually read *gave*:

---

36. Kirkpatrick, CB, p. 388.
37. Lenski, IGEP, p. 521.

(2) Paul only gives an application, not a translation of the verse; (3) the verb *laqach* means to take in order to give to another; and (4) the words *he gave gifts to men* are words of Paul and not part of the Old Testament citation.

It seems on the surface that the verbs *received* and *gave* are direct opposites. The truth is that Christ at his ascension *did* receive gifts of men. He then passed on these gifts to those for whom they were intended. On this point Maas comments:

> The person who receives gifts from God is to be understood as a mediator between God and man. His receiving gifts from God and his distributing those gifts to men are, therefore, correlative terms; hence the Apostle could quote the passage 'he gave gifts to men,' though the psalmist only gives the correlative term 'thou hast received gifts in men.'[38]

The verb *receive* must then be understood in the pregnant sense of receiving in order to give to others.

There is yet one point to be made about the word *received*. When Yahweh ascends back to heaven he *receives* gifts. How could David say that *Yahweh* could receive gifts? David saw the God-man in *Yahweh*. He could receive gifts from his Father.[39]

What are the gifts which Yahweh-Christ received in heaven and then passed on to men? Some think that the gifts are the *charismata* which he bestowed upon his church. He was the victor over death, and these gifts were like the spoils of his victory over Satan, sin and death. Others think of the gifts as the captivity mentioned in the preceding clause. This string of captives taken by the power of the Gospel is given back to the Church as servants for the upbuilding of the body (Eph. 4:11).

For whom are these gifts intended? They are received on behalf of men. Even some who had been rebellious would be given these gifts. Are the rebellious the heathen? The word is generally applied to stubborn Israelites. Kirkpatrick comments:

> Even the successors (in spirit) of the stubborn and rebellious generation of the wilderness are subdued when they see Jehovah's triumphs, and are content to become His obedient subjects.[40]

In Gospel application, the human enemies subdued by grace are one with those unto whom the gifts are given, the rebellious being converted into the obedient.[41]

---

38. Maas, CTP, II, 411.
39. Lenski, IGEP, p. 520.
40. Kirkpatrick, CB, p. 388.
41. Jamieson, Fausset and Brown, CCEP, III, 242.

The ultimate goal of the advent, the ascension, the endowment of God's people is that *God may dwell,* i.e., with his people. God is now dwelling in his Church which is the Temple of the Holy Spirit (II Cor. 6:16). The Lord daily *loads down* his people with salvation[42] (v. 19). For his people the Almighty (*ha'el*) is truly almighty (*'el*). He conquered all enemies, then ascended back to his throne. The salvation which he supplies to his people is superabundant.[43] The Almighty now makes possible escape[44] even from death itself (v. 20).

All that the psalmist has said about the past and future actions of God makes him confident that God will ultimately *crush the head* of all his enemies.[45] The *hairy scalp* in verse 21 is parallel to *head.* The unshorn hair of a warrior was the mark of his consecration to the work he had undertaken. His locks remained untouched till he had achieved the victory or had perished in the attempt. Never mind the zeal of God's enemies. They would not succeed. Who are these enemies? All who habitually act in a sinful manner (v. 21).

E. *The Glorious Announcement* (vv. 22-31). The Lord speaks directly for the only time in the psalm in verses 22-23. He confirms the confident acclaim of the victory expressed in the preceding verse. Even when the enemy seems to have escaped, God brings them back for punishment and destruction. He will bring them back from Bashan, frontier province of the land; he will even retrieve them from the depths of the sea if necessary[46] (v. 22).

The great victory over the forces of evil is celebrated in solemn worship. The subject of verse 24 is uncertain: *They have seen your goings, O God.* Does the pronoun refer to men in general? to God's people who watched the triumph over the enemies? to the enemies who observed the triumphant return to *the holy place?* Probably *they* includes all men who have been spectators of the conflict between God and his enemies.[47] And what is the *holy place?* Is it heaven? the Temple mount? the nation as a whole? The *goings* refers to the festive procession celebrating God's victory. The victor returns to heaven to be haled as king.

---

42. Also proposed: Who daily beareth our burden, or, Who daily beareth us. The latter translation has the support of several ancient versions.

43. The plural denotes mighty and manifold deliverances.

44. Again the plural of abundance is used.

45. Cf. Gen. 3:15; Ps. 110:6; Num. 24:8, 17.

46. Cf. Amos 9:3. Others think that it is Israel which is brought back from the depths of the sea. Cf. Isa. 49:12; 51:11, 12; 11:11-15.

47. So Kirkpatrick, CB, p. 397.

The triumphant procession is accompanied by musicians (v. 25). In the solemn assemblies of God's people the triumph of God should be praised (v. 26).[48] Representatives of all the tribes share in the procession—Benjamin and Judah in the south, Zebulun and Naphtali in the north. Some commentators have called attention to the fact that Jesus and several of his apostles were of Judah, Paul was of Benjamin (Phil. 3:5), and the remaining apostles of Galilee, the ancient territory of Zebulun and Naphtali (Matt. 4:13).[49] The important thing is that the entire nation is united in this victory celebration.[50]

Verse 29 looks forward to the day when Gentiles would pay tribute to the God of Jacob. Mt. Moriah, the site designated for the Temple, overshadowed the city of David which was built on the lower elevation of Ophel. The sanctuary, yet to be built when this psalm was composed, would be the crowning glory of the city and its protection as well. To this glorious city the kings of the earth would bring their tribute.

Verse 30 consists of a prayer and a declaration that the prayer has in fact been answered. He calls upon God to rebuke the *beasts of the reeds*, the crocodile or the hippopotamus. Both of these animals are associated with Egypt which here is depicted as the most powerful of heathen states. The *crowd of bulls* may represent the leaders of the nations, the *calves* their subjects. The subjects crouch as one man.[51] to offer tribute (*pieces of silver*) to their conqueror. The war-like enemies have been scattered by the hand of God.

God's victory over tyrants is complete. Princes of Egypt and Ethiopia submit to his will (v. 31). This is best regarded as a prophetic declaration of the spread of Messiah's kingdom. Egyptians were present on Pentecost, who, according to Hilary, became the heralds of Christ's Gospel in North Africa.[52] The Ethiopian eunuch was one of the first Gentiles to receive the Gospel.

---

48. The latter part of verse 26 (*from the fountain of Israel*) is obscure. Probably the words *you who are* should be supplied and the whole clause interpreted as descriptive of the nation—God's people. The *fountain* of Israel is then God himself.

49. Some suggest that Zebulun and Naphtali were selected to represent the northern part of the nation because they would be the tribes to suffer most severely in foreign invasions from the north. Cf. Isa. 9:1.

50. The prophets from Amos (9:11ff.) and Hosea (3:5) forward foretell the restoration of Israel as well as Judah. and their reunion into one nation. The Israelites who returned from Babylon regarded themselves as representing the whole nation, and not the kingdom of Judah only. See Kirkpatrick, CB, pp. 392-393.

51. The participle *crouching* is singular.

52. Cited by Clarke, CCN, III, 220.

F. The Glorious Appeal (vv. 32-35). In view of the conquests here foreseen, the whole world is summoned to acknowledge the God of Israel as universal sovereign (v. 32). Yahweh rides as a conqueror in triumph through the heaven of heavens which existed long before the heavens as men know them. The psalmist seems to hear an audible response from heaven itself (introduced by *Behold*) booming forth (v. 33). *Give* (i.e., ascribe) *strength to God*, the voice urges. Acknowledge by the tribute of your praises the power which is his. He is entitled to such praise because of the greatness he displays in protecting Israel, God's people (v. 34).

The nations seem to respond to the appeal of the psalmist in verse 35. They acknowledge the awful might which God displays from his sanctuary in the midst of Israel. They recognize the Lord as the source of Israel's preeminence. They bless his name (v. 35). "Thus the Psalmist's outlook reaches forward to the final triumph celebrated in Apocalyptic song, Rev. 15:3f."[53]

---

53. Kirkpatrick, CB, p. 396.

Chapter Fourteen

MESSIAH IN THE WISDOM LITERATURE

The wisdom literature of the Old Testament (Job, Proverbs, and Ecclesiastes) contains a comparatively low percentage of predictive prophecy.[1] The contribution of these books to the Messianic expectation is minimal if judged by the number of personal Messianic predictions contained here. It is, however, one-sided and misleading to measure preparation for the New Testament age solely in terms of personal Messianic prophecy. "The progressive knowledge of God the Redeemer is just as important a side of the preparation as the progressive knowledge of the world-wide rule of the second David."[2]

In the wisdom literature aspiration takes on the garb of prediction. Only in Messiah would the spiritual longings of Old Testament saints find fruition. Geisler puts it this way:

> Much of what the poets wrote is not directly applicable to Christ, but beneath it all can be seen a longing look upward, an aspiration to something higher which, as a matter of fact, was only fully realized in Christ.[3]

In the Book of Proverbs the aspiration is for perfect wisdom to become incarnate (Prov. 8). Jesus Christ is the wisdom of God personified (I Cor. 1:30). "All the treasures of wisdom and knowledge" are embodied in him (Col. 2:3). The sages who speak in Proverbs attempted to reduce wisdom to precepts to guide Old Testament saints; New Testament saints have a person to exemplify how true wisdom behaves in *every* situation.

In Ecclesiastes Solomon exposes the futility of life without God *under the sun.* He bears personal testimony to the emptiness of wine, women, works, wealth and worldly wisdom. There is no happiness unless man places God at the center of life. According to Geisler, he discovered that happiness must be found beyond the sun, in the Son.[4] "Fear God and keep his commandments" was his final verdict on life. Heed the words of the one Shepherd (12:11, 13). He longs for a closer walk with the good Shepherd (John 10). How he would have rejoiced to hear Christ say, "These things I have spoken to you, that my joy may be in you, and that your joy may be full (John 15:11).

In Song of Songs Solomon describes the beauty of true love between a man and a woman. If the Song were an allegorical poem, it would

---

1. Payne found none of these books to contain more than three per cent predictive material.
2. Delitzsch, MPHS, p. 102.
3. Geisler, CKIB, p. 80.
4. Ibid., p. 97.

be a prophetical production. Indeed, there have been those who have tried to make it such. Among the Church Fathers there was no lack of support for the view that Solomon represents Christ and the Shulamite maiden prefigures the Church. Most modern commentators have concluded that the allegorical approach cannot be consistently applied throughout. The figurative interpretation of all details falls into "a boundless arbitrariness, and loses itself in scandalous absurdities."[5] Even the typical interpretation which sees broad parallels between Solomon and the Shulamite on the one hand and Christ and the Church on the other, though it has gained wide support in evangelical circles, is probably not the best approach to this book. What Messianic implication there is in this book can be stated like this: Solomon here aspires to the real love—the total commitment—he observes in the Shulamite. Jesus provides perfect love (John 15:13; I John 4:17-18).

While three of the wisdom books[6] are devoid of personal Messianic prediction, at least three passages in the Book of Job show that the ancient wisemen, as well as the prophets, helped prepare the way for the coming of the God-man.

The chronological placement of the Book of Job is difficult. Job and his companions were not Israelites, but probably Edomites.[7] Job was probably a contemporary of the Patriarchs antedating Moses by several years. In the older arrangement of the Hebrew Bible, Job was counted among the prophetic books.[8] Payne comments:

> . . . It is in the speeches of Job (at his high points of spiritual insight in chs. 14, 17, and 19) and that of Elihu (ch. 33) . . . that far-reaching aspects of God's design for history come this early to expression: aspects of human redemption, of resurrection, and of judgment for both the saved and the lost.[9]

---

5. Delitzsch, MPHS, p. 101.

6. Some dispute exists about the classification of Song of Solomon as wisdom literature.

7. Payne, EBP, pp. 252-253. On the location of Uz (1:1) see Lam. 4:21. Note also the connection of Eliphaz the Temanite with the names of some of the early descendants of Esau in Gen. 36:10-11.

8. Josephus (*Against Apion,* I, 8) says in his day (A.D. 90) there were five books of law, thirteen books of prophets and four books of hymns and precepts. Since his twenty-two books are simply a different way of counting the present thirty-nine Old Testament books, it is obvious that Job must have been included among the prophetic books.

9. Payne, EBP, p. 253.

Prophecy No. 27

THE DIVINE MEDIATOR

ANTICIPATORY ASPIRATION

Four times in the Book of Job there comes to the surface a longing for someone to intervene between God and man. These poignant aspirations are in reality prophetic anticipations. Three of the relevant passages are attributed to Job himself, and one to the prophet-like character Elihu. Here there is longing for (1) a mediator. (2) a heavenly witness/advocate, (3) a divine bondsman, and (4) an interpreter.

A. Longing for a Mediator

> There is not between us a mediator that he might place his hand upon the two of us (Job 9:33).

Job here feels inadequate in his dispute with God. He can neither initiate nor conduct the necessary negotiations which would produce some explanation for the sufferings which he is experiencing. Herein lies the fundamental problem in the Book of Job, not the problem of suffering as is popularly supposed, but the problem of attaining a right relationship with God. It is this right relationship with God which alone will make man's existence amidst suffering acceptable.[10] Job sees the need for a mediator[11] (an umpire, daysman; Heb. *mokhiach*)—one who brings both parties together by laying his hand upon them both as a common friend.

B. Longing for a Heavenly Witness/Advocate.

> Even now my witness is in heaven, and my advocate is on high. My friends scorn me, as my eyes pour out tears to God. O that one might plead for man with God, even as a man for his friend (Job 16:19-21).

Job is confident that he has a *witness*, an *advocate* in heaven. Job is clearly hoping for some agent to help him settle his dispute, to secure the right of a man with God. Verse 21 is one of the amazing peaks of

---

10. Andersen, TOTC, p. 151.

11. The meaning is the same whether one translates as a longing (NIV; NEB), or as a regret that there is none (RSV; NASB).

spiritual insight and human paradox that make the Book of Job immortal. At times in the book Job has viewed God as the One who had cruelly and wrongfully smitten him. Here he expresses confidence in the God of justice and loving mercy. It is as if the defendant implores the plaintiff to be his judge.[12]

There was no mediator between Job and God, so here Job says in effect, Let God be my daysman. This passionate longing for a heavenly witness on his side strikingly points forward to the Christian concept of an advocate with the Father, Jesus Christ the righteous (I John 2:1).[13]

C. Longing for a Divine Bondsman.

Set forth, please. Make me a surety with yourself. Who is he who will strike hands with me? (Job 17:3).

The passage in context again focuses on the aspects of God as seen by Job—God who persecutes and wrongs Job, and God who becomes surety for Job and undertakes to see his cause righted. The question, Who is he . . . ? implies that only God can be his bondsman. This supports the conclusion that God himself is the advocate Job is searching for in 16:19ff. and elsewhere. To strike the hands is an idiom frequently used in Proverbs to ratify an agreement. The surety or bond or pledge is an agreement to be fulfilled at a future time. Job wants God to pledge now that his innocence will be acknowledged later. That for which Job begs in 17:3 appears in II Corinthians 5:19 as performed through God in Christ for the whole world. Delitzsch comments on the verse as follows:

God is conceived of as two persons, on the one side as a judge who treats Job as one deserving of punishment, on the other side as a bondsman who pledges himself for the innocence of the sufferer before the judge, and stands as it were as surety against the future.[14]

D. Longing for an Interpreter.

(23) If there is alongside him an angel as an interpreter, one among a thousand, to declare to a man his uprightness: (24) then he would be gracious unto him and say: Redeem him from going down to destruction; I have found a ransom. (25) His flesh shall be as fresh as a child's;

---

12. Reichert, SBB, p. 85.
13. Heavenor, NBC, p. 397.
14. Delitzsch, BCOT, Job, I, 295. See also Delitzch, MPHS, p. 103.

he shall return to days of his youth. (26) He shall pray to God and he will be favorable to him; and he shall see his face with joy, for he will return to a man his righteousness. (27) He looks upon men when he says, I have sinned and perverted what is upright and it profits me nothing. (28) He will redeem my soul from passing over to the pit, and my life shall see the light. (29) Behold all these things God does often with man (Job 33:23-28).

The longing for a mediator between God and man comes to the surface again in the first speech of Elihu. He longs for an angel or messenger who acts as an interpreter. The term *interpreter* (*melits*) is applied to prophets (Isa. 43:27) who interpret the will of God to men or mediate between God and men. This mediator must not be any ordinary angel or human prophet, he must be *one among a thousand*, i.e., pre-eminent above a thousand.[15] This agent of revelation speaks for God and shows to man the way of salvation which he has to take to be free of sin and death (v. 23).[16]

The superhuman interpreter envisioned by Job would be gracious. He would pray for an afflicted man[17] and announce that he has found a ransom for the sinner, or means of atonement. Does the prayer of the angel continue in verse 26 (NEB), or is the now recovered sick man expressing his prayer of thanksgiving? (RSV). Andersen is probably right when he writes:

> The activities described here resemble the traditional thanksgivings of the healed man who joyfully praises God for his cure, and recounts to men his salvation in public testimony.[18]

The Book of Job is remarkable for its angelology. Here the redemption of man can only be mediated by means of a superhuman being. Delitzsch comments:

> The *angelus internuntius* is a preformation of the Redeemer going forth from the range of the Godhead. The angelic form is the oldest, which the hope of a mediator of salvation gives (Gen. 48:16).

---

15. So Delitzsch, BCOT, p. 230. Others see in the expression the idea that God has a large team of angels available for such a task.

16. Gordis (BGM, p. 289) thinks the idea here is "a spokesman to vouch for a man's righteousness."

17. Delitzsch thinks it is God who has compassion and speaks in verse 24 rather than the interpreting angel.

18. Andersen, TOTC, p. 250.

By way of anticipation it may be noted that this theme of the angel/messenger surfaces again in Malachi where the Messiah appears under the title, the angel of the covenant (Mal. 3:1).

Prophecy No. 28

THE COMING REDEEMER

Job 19:23-27

Translation of Job 19:23-27

(23) O that my words were written, O that they were recorded in the book. (24) With stylus of iron and lead forever in the rock inscribed! (25) And as for me, I know my Redeemer lives, and as the Last he upon the dust shall rise up. (26) And after my awakening, even though it is destroyed, yet from the standpoint of my flesh I shall see God. (27) I myself shall see him. and my eye shall behold and not as a stranger. How my inward parts are consumed within me.

Discussion

Job 19:23-27 is one of the peak passages in the book. The central affirmation here is *My Redeemer lives!* Unfortunately this grand declaration is followed by several lines which are virtually unintelligible in Hebrew. The range of translation for these lines is bewildering.[19] Eight aspects of Job's confidence are more or less clear in the passage:

1. Job was confident that he had a personal Redeemer. He called him *my* Redeemer. Verses 25-27 are so tightly knit that there can be no doubt that the Redeemer is God. The Vindicator who will arise to speak in court as Job's witness and defense counsel is none other than God himself. The Hebrew *go'el* is used of the next-of-kin upon whom fell the duties of avenger of blood, levirate marriage, and redeeming property in danger of expropriation. Job is confident that in the end God would permit him with the eyes of the next world to behold him as *go'el*, as

> . . . avenger of his blood which is regarded as that of a criminal, as ransomer of his honor which has fallen into disgrace, as redeemer from

---

19. See H. H. Rowley, "The Book of Job and its Meaning," in *From Moses to Qumran* (1963), pp. 180f.

the curse which rested upon him, above all things, from the consequences of divine wrath, whose decree seemed to have occasioned his suffering.[20]

Job's confident assertion was baptized into Christ by Paul and emerges in Romans 8:34 as follows: "Who is he that condemns? Jesus Christ who died and who was raised to life is at the right hand of God and is also interceding for us."

2. Job is confident that his Redeemer is alive. I know that my Redeemer *lives!* The most fundamental truth about God emphasized in the Bible is that he is the living God, not some impotent idol.

3. Job was confident that his Redeemer would *rise up.* The living God can and will intervene in human history. The inactivity of God during his personal calamity disturbed Job. But he was confident that inactivity would some day end.

4. Job was confident that his Redeemer would arise *upon the dust.* Does the word dust (*'aphar*) here stand poetically for *earth?* The context here speaks of Job's body. The idea seems to be that there will be a coming of God to the soil in which Job's body lies buried.

5. Job is confident that his Redeemer would appear on the earth as the Last. The term *Last* in verse 25 is adjectival, not adverbial.[21] The God of the Bible is the beginning and the end, the First and the Last.[22] He existed before all things; he shall survive after the present order of things has been swept away.

6. Job is confident that he will survive death. After death he has hope that in the condition of a genuine human being he will have a favorable meeting with God. This is most certainly a statement of faith in a personal bodily resurrection.[23] Rowley argues:

> . . . in the preceding verses Job had recognized that he would see no vindication in this life, and so had sighed for a record of his defence to be preserved for after generations. It therefore seems most likely that his hope was for vindication after death.[24]

The exact translation of verse 26 deserves attention. Job would see God *after my awakening.*[25] Even though it (the body or perhaps, the

---

20. Delitzsch, MPHS, p. 104.

21. See NASB margin and Rowley, NCB. p. 173.

22. Isa. 44:6; 48:12.

23. Job 14:13ff. shows that the hope of resurrection lies at the very heart of Job's faith.

24. Rowley, NCB, p. 173.

25. Following Payne (EBP. p. 255) in understanding *'ori* (my skin) as an infinitive. (*'uri*) meaning *my awakening.* Cf. 14:12; Ps. 17:15.

dust that once had been his body) be destroyed, yet Job is confident of seeing God. From the standpoint of his flesh he will see God. The Hebrew preposition *min* ("from") could signify "without my flesh) (ASV), indicating spiritual immortality rather than bodily resurrection; but the resurrection concept better accords with the previous "awakening" and with Job's thought about hope for his body that began in 14:12-17.[26]

7. Job is confident that he will see God. Heretofore Job had indicated a need to *hear* God. In verses 26f. three times he speaks of *seeing* God. The reference to *skin*, *flesh* and *eyes* make it clear that Job expected to have the experience of seeing God as a man would see him, not in a vision or as a disembodied spirit.

8. Job is confident that he will see God in intimate association. He will not see him *as a stranger*. God will no longer act as a stranger toward Job.[27]

Job stakes his honor on his future justification by desiring that his declarations of innocence be permanently written down (vv. 23-24). The *book* to which he refers may be a scroll, or a tablet of clay; but it might also be metal or stone. Andersen argues that the word *inscribed* (v. 24) suggests some kind of monument, probably of stone.

SPECIAL NOTE ON WISDOM IN PROVERBS

Three times Solomon represents Wisdom herself as speaking in Proverbs (1:20ff.; 8:1ff.; and 9:1-12). In chapter 1 Wisdom comes forth publicly like a traveling teacher roaming the streets of the city. Wisdom partakes of divine nature. She promises those who turn to her participation in her spirit (1:23). It is presupposed that prayers are offered to her, and that she has an influence on whether prayers are answered or unanswered (1:28).

Wisdom in Proverbs is more than a personified characteristic, more than a personified good. Wisdom was a divine attribute in the very beginning. In 8:22-31 Delitzsch points out five main thoughts: (1) Wisdom was born of God before the creation of the world. (2) Wisdom was present when the world came into being. (3) God made use of Wisdom's meditation in executing his thoughts of creation. (4) Wisdom delighted in rendering this service to the Creator. (5) Wisdom delights in functioning within the sphere of earth and man.[28]

---

26. Ibid.
27. Alternatively, Job will not be a foreigner to God.
28. Delitzsch, MPHS, p. 111.

Delitzsch sees the role of Wisdom as follows: Wisdom is a power born of God, which makes that a reality which is to be created in the manner willed by God, and which helps free creatures, especially men, to the attainment of the end divinely willed.[29]

The Wisdom of God in the wisdom literature is like the Spirit of God in the historical narratives. They are not separate divine existence, emanating from the original deity as in pagan theology. The doctrine of the unity of God is against any such notion. The true explanation is that God "discloses the Spirit and Wisdom from Himself as special ways of the manifestation of His being."[30] Spirit and Wisdom are powers originating in the being of the one God, and surrounded by his one being.

The very first page of Scripture distinguishes between God and the Spirit of God. Now Wisdom is pictured as the mediator between God and his world. The historical books speak of God, his Spirit, his Angel through whom his self-revelation is made. Wisdom literature speaks of God, his Spirit and Wisdom.

It is remarkable that the utterances of Wisdom in Proverbs 1 and 8 correspond so closely with the utterances of Jesus in the Gospel of John. Wisdom, according to Colossians 1:16, has appeared bodily in Jesus of Nazareth.

---

29. Ibid.
30. Ibid.

Chapter Fifteen

THE EARLIER MINOR PROPHETS

Following the death of Solomon in 931 B.C. the Hebrew kingdom was rent asunder. The period from 931-722 B.C. is known as the Divided Monarchy period. A number of prophets are mentioned by name during this period. With the exception of Elijah and Elisha, however, little is known about the activities of these prophets. Only seven of these prophets recorded their messages. Perhaps Delitzsch is right when he observes that "in all which these prophets do and say there is no occasion for a testimony of messianic significance. . . . Messianic proclamation of the prophets appears to have run dry."[1] Outside of two veiled Messianic hints[2] at the very outset of the Divided Monarchy, almost nine decades passed before there was further amplification of the Hope.

Obadiah was the first prophet since Moses to record his poetic predictions in an independent document. Obadiah wrote in the aftermath of a humiliating sack of Jerusalem by combined forces of Philistines and Arabians during the reign of King Jehoash. The date is approximately 845 B.C. Six other prophets of the Divided Monarchy period recorded their messages. In chronological order they are Joel (830 B.C.), Jonah (755 B.C.), Amos (755 B.C.), Hosea (752 B.C.), Isaiah (739 B.C.), and Micah (735 B.C.).

The theme of the concluding verses of Obadiah is the ultimate triumph of the people of God. Verse 17 offers three pictures of the future kingdom: It is (1) a refuge center, (2) a holy kingdom, and (3) a secure inheritance. Obadiah then writes three predictions concerning the kingdom. God's people will be (1) victorious (v. 18), (2) enlarged (vv. 19-20), and (3) ultimately supreme (v. 21). These verses speak of that spiritual kingdom over which Messiah rules. The Ruler himself, however, is not specifically mentioned. He is one of the *saviors* (v. 21), albeit the greatest of them all, who would ascend Mt. Zion to deliver his people from all oppressors. So while these final verses of Obadiah are Messianic, they are not personal Messianic.

The prophet Jonah was without question a type of Christ in respect to his preservation in the belly of the fish for three days and nights (Matt. 12:39-41). Typology is a significant manifestation of the Messianic hope. Nothing, however, in the four-chapter account of Jonah's

---

1. Delitzsch, MPHS, p. 108.

2. The hints are found in I Kings 11:36 where God is said by Ahijah to leave a lamp for David in Jerusalem always; and II Chron. 12:7 which speaks of a *measure* of deliverance in the days of Shishak, implying a greater deliverance to come.

mission qualifies as personal Messianic prophecy. Nevertheless, the book does teach the lesson that God cares deeply for Gentiles. God's response to the Ninevite repentance was offered to proud and self-righteous Israelites as an illustration of that which could and would take place on a larger scale in the Messianic age.

Amos, that rambunctious herdsman from Tekoa, answered the call of God to proclaim the divine warning in Israel, the northern kingdom. As he brought his book to a conclusion, Amos recorded a prediction which has Messianic ramifications. The fallen hut of David—the Davidic dynasty—would experience a glorious restoration (v. 11). The purpose and result of this royal restoration of power would be the conquest of the remnant of Edom, archenemy of God's people, and all the nations "which are called by my name" (v. 12). At the apostolic conference in Jerusalem, James interpreted these verses as a reference to the incorporation of Gentiles into the kingdom of Christ (Acts 15:13-18). Abundant blessing (v. 13), growth and security (vv. 14-15) would characterize that kingdom. But while Amos paints this beautiful portrait of the *kingdom*, he says nothing of the King himself.

Four prophecies in the earlier Minor Prophets fall into the category of personal Messianic prophecy. One of these is in Joel, the other three are in Hosea. The passages from Hosea will be discussed in the subsequent chapter.

Prophecy No. 29

THE TEACHER UNTO RIGHTEOUSNESS

Joel 2:23

The Book of Joel the son of Pethuel stands second among the Minor Prophets in the Hebrew Old Testament, fourth in the Septuagint. There are no conclusive clues as to the dating of the book, but it appears to come from the period of the minority of King Joash, 835-817 B.C. A date of about 830 B.C. for the book would not be far off.

When Joel began to prophesy the nation Judah was experiencing a devastating plague of locusts.[3] In the first half of his book (1:2—2:17) Joel interprets this plague as a judgment of God and a harbinger of an awesome day of national judgment which he calls "the day of

---

3. The plague has been interpreted symbolically of the Assyrian or Babylonian armies. Literal locusts are intended.

Yahweh" (2:1-11). He therefore calls upon the people of the land to repent (2:12-17).

The second half of the Book of Joel outlines the history of God's people from the last decades of the ninth century B.C. to the end of time. In response to the reformation led by Jehoiada the priest during the minority of Joash, God promises first to remove the plague of locusts (2:18-22). He will drive the metaphorical northern army into the desert (2:20). In response to this divine declaration Joel attempts to bolster the courage and expectation of his people.

Translation of Joel 2:23-27

(23) Also you, O sons of Zion, exult and rejoice in the LORD your God, for he will give[4] to you the Teacher for righteousness; and will send you down the rain, the early rain and the latter rain in the first place. (24) And the threshing floors shall be full of grain, and the vats shall overflow with new wine and oil. (25) So I will recompense you for the years which the locusts have consumed—the various kinds of locusts,[5] my great army which I sent against you. (26) Then you shall eat your fill and be satisfied, and you shall praise the name of the LORD your God who has dealt so wondrously with you; and my people shall never be ashamed. (27) And you shall know that in the midst of Israel am I, and I am the LORD your God and there is no other; and my people shall never be ashamed.

Discussion

Joel 2:21-23 is a "prophetic song of encouragement"[6] set in the midst of an oracle of assurance (2:19-20 + 24-27). Here there is a threefold exhortation to *land* (v. 21), *beasts* (v. 22) and *the sons of Zion* (v. 23) to rejoice and banish fear. In each case the exhortation is supported by a motive clause which indicates complete reversal in circumstances is about to take place.

The *sons of Zion*, i.e., covenant people, are exhorted to join the celebration of the animal and vegetable kingdoms. Their joy is first of all to be in Yahweh himself, and especially in the fact that he was, in a very special way, *their* God. The primary reason the sons of Zion can

---

4. Prophetic perfect.

5. Three Hebrew words are used indicating different kinds of locusts or locusts in various stages of development.

6. Allen, NIC, p. 86.

confidently endure the temporal calamities is because of the long-standing Messianic Hope. God would some day give to them the *Teacher unto righteousness*. None of the standard modern translations has accurately rendered the Hebrew text at this point,[7] although the correct translation appears in the margin of the New American Standard Bible. For a discussion of the translation problem, see the special note at the end of this chapter.

That this verse contains personal Messianic prophecy was the dominant view of the early Jewish and Christian writers. Modern authorities have tended to shy away from this view because of the problem of relating a personal Messianic interpretation to the context. What does this passage contribute to the Messianic expectation in Israel?

1. Messiah would be a teacher. The Hebrew text actually uses the definite article. The coming Messiah would be *the* Teacher *par excellence*. Some think that by *the Teacher* Joel intends a royal personage.[8] But in the Old Testament the term *moreh* (teacher) is most often connected with priests.[9] In some passages God himself is called Teacher (Job 36:22; Isa. 30:20) or is said to exercise the teaching function (Isa. 2:3; cf. II Chron. 6:27).

2. The coming of Messiah is viewed here as a gift from God to his people. This thought is later echoed by Isaiah: "Unto us a child is given" (Isa. 9:6); and "I have given him a Witness to the peoples" (Isa. 55:4).

3. The result and object of Messiah's coming is righteousness. The preposition *for* in the phrase *for righteousness* announces that the Teacher will be one who gives, or is in agreement with, or acts according to, righteousness. He is virtually a personification of righteousness. Later prophets will refer to him as the righteous servant (Isa. 53:11), and as one who will usher in everlasting righteousness (Dan. 9:24).

4. The blessing which results from Messiah's coming is depicted in terms of rain and resultant physical prosperity. Yahweh gives the people the Teacher, and then he will let the rain come down. The next line then explains what kind of rain it will be: *early rain* and *latter rain*. Through this rain he will give to the land fertility and life.

---

7. KJV=he hath given you the formerly rain moderately; ASV=he has given you the former rain; RSV=he has given you the early rain; NIV=he has given you a teacher for righteousness; NASB=he has given you the early rain.

8. Ahlström, JTCJ, p.102. On the role of the king as teacher, see G. Widengren, "King and Covenant," JSS 2 (1957):1ff.; 21.

9. See II Chron. 15:3; II Kings 17:28. Cf. Micah 3:11; II Kings 12:2; Lev. 14:57. By implication the term *moreh* is connected with prophets in Isa. 9:15.

The word for *early rain* (or autumn rain) is *moreh*, the same word which was translated *teacher* in the previous line. In no passage save here does *moreh* mean rain.[10] The usual word for former rain is *yoreh*. This deliberate play on words—in fact a creation of a new word—may be Joel's signal that the rain of which he speaks is metaphorical. It is Messiah's rain.[11]

To understand the present passage it is necessary to note several connections made with the rain concept in the Old Testament:

a) Physical rain is sent by Yahweh, not Baal the pagan storm god (Hos. 6:3).

b) Rain is depicted as accompanying various theophanies (e.g., Ps. 68:8ff.).

c) Rain is used metaphorically to depict the coming of God's righteousness upon the land. In Isaiah 45:8 righteousness drips down and the result is salvation and righteousness springing up. In Hosea 10:12 Yahweh comes and rains righteousness upon those who seek him.

d) Rain is connected with God's role as Teacher of his people. In Job 36:22, 27 God the Teacher "draws up the drops of water" and then pours them down in abundance. In the same context he is said to judge the people by flashes of lightning. Yahweh's "teaching the way" and rain are closely connected in Solomon's prayer in I Kings 8:35f.; and II Chronicles 6:27.[12] (Cf. Isa. 30:20ff.)

e) The double connection of rain with righteousness/justice and the coming of the Messiah has already been made in Psalm 72. The Messianic King was there depicted as the giver and upholder of righteousness (vv. 1-2, 7). In Psalm 72:4, 12f. Messiah defends the poor and needy, at the same time, he is the one who causes abundance of grain and fruit (vv. 3, 16). Messiah is depicted as rain which makes righteousness flourish (vv. 5-7). The basic thrust in Psalm 72 is that the Messianic King is the life-giver.

f) The absence of rain is used in an eschatological context in Zechariah 14:17ff. to indicate the curse which falls on those who do not choose to worship Yahweh in Messianic Zion.

---

10. In Ps. 84:6 *moreh* is translated *rain* in KJV and NIV. Even here the meaning *teacher* seems preferable.

11. Laetsch, (BCMP, p. 126) understands the passage to mean that the rain is sent on the people of Joel's day for the sake of the coming Messiah.

12. Ahlström (JTCJ, p. 105, notes 2 and 3) calls attention to the Teacher in the Qumran texts saying that God put something that is like early rain in his mouth. He also notes that *torah* (instruction/law) is compared with water and rain frequently in Jewish literature.

What a blessing the coming of the Teacher will be! Threshing floors and vats will overflow (v. 24). Jesus used a similar figure to describe the blessing which would come to disciples who generously shared in the work of the kingdom:

Give and it shall be given unto you; good measure, pressed down, and shaken together, and running over, shall men give into your bosom. For with the same measure that you employ it shall be measured to you (Luke 6:38).

In that day of great blessing, past judgments will be forgotten. The damage inflicted by the locusts on vineyards and orchards over the years would be recompensed a thousand fold (v. 25). Men would eat and be filled with the good things provided by the Teacher (v. 26a). Jesus claimed to provide through his teaching life-sustaining and life-satisfying food:

Labor not for the food that perishes, but for that food which endures unto everlasting life, which the Son of Man shall give unto you; for him has the Father sealed. For the bread of God is he who comes down from heaven and who gives life unto the world. I am the bread of life. He who comes to me shall never hunger; and he who believes on me shall never thirst. I am that bread of life. Your fathers ate manna in the wilderness, and are dead. This is the bread which comes down from heaven, that a man may eat of it and not die. I am the living bread which came down from heaven. If any man eat of this bread, he shall live forever; and the bread which I will give is my flesh, which I will give for the life of the world. Truly, truly I say unto you, Except you eat the flesh of the Son of man, and drink his blood, you have no life in you.[13]

It is interesting that in John 6:45 Jesus applied to himself Isaiah 54:13, a verse which underscores the importance of teaching. To partake of the bread of life is equivalent to believing in Jesus. See the special study on Jesus as teacher at the conclusion of this chapter.

5. The children of Zion will praise the name of Yahweh who provides through the Messianic Teacher such abundant blessing (v. 26). Those who heard the Teacher Jesus stood in constant amazement at his words (Luke 4:22) and his miracles (Matt. 15:30-31). Signs and wonders also accompanied the preaching and teaching of the apostles of Jesus (II Cor. 12:12; Heb. 2:4).

---

13. John 6:27, 33, 35, 48-51, 53.

6. Never again would God's people be put to shame (v. 26). Certainly this did not apply to fleshly Israel, for after the days of Joel they were put to shame numerous times. God's people, reconstituted by the Teacher and regenerated by his Spirit would through time and eternity enjoy divine protection and blessing. Never again would the people have reason to be ashamed because of the apparent withdrawal of divine favor. This thought is so important that it is repeated in verse 27. Jesus endured the cross, despising the shame thereof so that his followers might not be ashamed when they stand before God on judgment day (Heb. 12:2).[14]

7. It will become clear to all those who live to see that day that the Lord was in their midst (v. 27). Because of his words, his deeds, his death and subsequent resurrection the early Christians became convinced that God had visited them in a very special way in the person of Jesus of Nazareth. He was Immanuel, God with us (Matt. 1:23).

Joel says much more about the Messianic age. After the appearance of the Teacher would come the outpouring of the Spirit of God in a manner unknown in the Old Testament dispensation (2:28-29). Peter makes it clear that the pouring out of the Spirit was proof that the Messiah had successfully fulfilled his mission (Acts 2:33). Joel says that a dreadful day of judgment (the A.D. 70 Fall of Jerusalem?) would be heralded by signs in heaven and on earth (2:30-31). But even in those terrible days those who in faith called upon the name of the Lord in the appointed manner would find salvation in the New Covenant Zion (2:32; cf. Heb. 12:22). The New Covenant people of God would come under severe attack (3:9-12), but the attackers would meet with disastrous defeat (3:13-15). On this triumphant note Joel concludes his panoramic view of the Messianic age: God's New Testament people would emerge from that final conflict secure, and prosperous; but the enemies who attack them would be wretched and miserable (3:16-21).

Special Note

THE TRANSLATION OF JOEL 2:23

Caution is in order in any discussion of Joel 2:23, especially as regards the words *hammoreh letsedeqah*.[15] At least three basic positions

---

14. Other confident New Testament assertions: Phil. 1:20; I Peter 4:16; I John 2:28; Rom. 1:16.

15. Keil (BCOT, Minor Prophets, I, 205): "From time immemorial there has been a diversity of opinion as to the meaning of these words."

have been taken with regard to the translation of these words.

1. Some feel compelled to alter the Hebrew text, changing *moreh* to *yoreh* (early rain)[16] or *marweh* (saturation),[17] or *biryah* (food).[18]

2. Others[19] retain the reading of the standard Hebrew text and argue that in this context *moreh* must mean rain. The argument goes like this: The term *moreh* occurs in the very next sentence. In this second instance the term must have the sense of *early rain*. Therefore, it would be unlikely that in the first instance the word should be translated differently. The context, it is said, also supports the translation *rain* in the first instance of *moreh*. Joel mentioned first the inferior, material blessings which will come upon penitent Judah in 2:21-27.[20] Not until verse 28 does he proceed to the higher and spiritual blessings.

Those who hold that *moreh* means *rain* must adopt a somewhat unusual interpretation for *letsedeqah* (for righteousness). Four suggestions have been made: (1) rain in just measure (ASV); (2) rain for your vindication (RSV; NASB; (3) rain according to (God's) righteousness; and (4) rain according to (man's) righteousness.

3. The ancient[21] and natural interpretation of *moreh* is *teacher*. In favor of the personal view of *moreh* in the expression *hammoreh letsedeqah*, the following points can be made:

a) The almost uniform meaning of the word *moreh* is teacher.[22]

b) The term *letsedeqah* is inapplicable to early rain. The term is only used in an ethical sense of righteousness.[23]

---

16. E.g., Duhm, G. R. Driver, Rudolph. This change is supported by thirty-four Hebrew manuscripts, but this reading is generally recognized as an early attempt to eliminate the perceived difficulty in the verse. The majority of manuscripts read *moreh*.

17. A suggestion made by van Hoonacker.

18. The text of Joel translated by the Greek translators either read thus, or the translators were guilty of altering the text, for they render the word *food*. The NEB and Wolff follow this reading.

19. E.g., Deane, Fausett, and among Jewish commentators, Kimchi and Iben Ezra.

20. Cf. Deane (PC, 26): "Among the promises of repairing damage done by the locusts, it would be obviously out of place to introduce the notion of a 'teacher.'" So also Kapelrud, *Joel Studies*, p. 115.

21. Supported by the Vulgate, Targum, and the Greek translation of Symmachus as well as Rashi, the Jewish commentator of the Middle Ages. According to Keil, most of the Rabbins and earlier commentators preferred "teacher."

22. In the singular *moreh* occurs eight times. Only in Psalm 84:6 is the word rendered *rain* in KJV and NIV. Even here the proper translation is probably *teacher*. In the plural the word appears seven times. Three times it is rendered *teachers* and four times *archers*.

23. Leviticus 19:36 has been urged as proof that *tsedeqah* can be used in a non-ethical sense. Here scales and weight stones are described by the word *tsedeq*. But the stones and scales are called *tsedeq* (correct) because that is what corresponds to what is ethically right.

c) The poverty of the expression if translated *rain*: He has given you the early rain unto righteousness (i.e., that you may be righteous).

d) The word *moreh* has the article and sign of the definite direct object. This is not true of the latter part of the verse where rain (whether actual or symbolical of spiritual blessings) is spoken of. "No reason can be discovered why *moreh* should be defined by the article here if it signified early rain.[24]

e) The structure of the sentence makes the sending of the rain "a separate action, later, in order of time or of thought, than the former.[25] To translate *hammoreh* as *early rain* creates a redundance in the verse.

Those who hold *teacher* as the proper interpretation of the Hebrew are not agreed on the significance of the term. Hengstenberg and Keil think the teacher should be understood collectively of all God-given teachers. The latter commentator includes Messiah in the collective as the last and greatest of the prophets.[26] Von Orelli and Hoffman took the teacher to be Joel himself. Pusey and more recently Laetsch have argued cogently that the teacher is Messiah. Among the Jewish commentators, Abarbanel held this position. Ahlström has presented an impressive case for a personal interpretation. He sees the verse as a veiled promise of a new Davidic leader and teacher.[27]

It seems that once the translation *teacher* has been established, the Messianic application of the title is altogether appropriate. Pusey summarizes the matter in these words: "It seems then most probable, that the Prophet prefixes to all other promises, that first all-containing promise of the Coming of Christ."[28]

Special Note

JESUS AS TEACHER

Jesus of Nazareth was regarded as a teacher by his disciples, his opponents (e.g., Mark 12:14), and the people generally. All the

---

24. Keil, BCOT, Minor Prophets, I, 206. The ususal Hebrew word meaning early rain (*yoreh*) never has the article, nor does the related word *malqosh* (latter rain).

25. Pusey, MPC, I, 190. The arguments listed supporting the rendering of *hammoreh* personally have been adapted from Pusey.

26. Keil (BCOT, Minor Prophets, I, 206-207) argues that "direct or exclusive reference to the Messiah is at variance with the context, since all the explanatory clauses in verses 21-23 treat of blessings or gifts which were bestowed at any rate partially at that particular time."

27. Ahlström, JTCJ, pp. 107-109.

28. Pusey, MPC, p. 190.

evangelists except Luke preserve the Aramaic title Rabbi or its variant Rabonni. Of the sixty instances of the use of the word *didaskalos* (teacher) in the New Testament, more than thirty are in reference to Jesus, mostly in direct address.[29] The frequent use of these titles recognizes Jesus' status as the leader of a group, and perhaps also indicates a recognition of the authority of his teaching.[30]

Like contemporary Jewish teachers, Jesus gathered disciples, and passed on to them a distinctive hermeneutic by which they were able to recognize that he was the long awaited Messiah (Luke 24:27, 44-45). As a recognized Rabbi he was consulted on questions of conduct and doctrine (cf. Mark 10:1-12). Sometimes he gave lengthy discourses (Matt. 5-7); on other occasions his teaching consisted of a concise explanation of his own conduct (Mark 11:15-17).

Numerous similarities between Jesus and the teachers of his day can be pointed out. Jesus, however, was no ordinary teacher as is indicated by the following pieces of evidence:

1. The method of Jesus' teaching provoked popular astonishment. Though uneducated in the Rabbinic schools (John 7:15), he astonished the people with his teaching. He taught them with authority (Mark 1:22, 27), not as the scribes who searched for legal principles and precedents in the sayings of their predecessors. The practical wisdom of his words impressed itself upon all his auditors (Mark 6:2).

2. Jesus' work as a teacher was closely associated with healing.[31] When he was requested to perform some mighty act he was often addressed as Teacher.[32]

3. The sons of Zebedee addressed Jesus as Teacher when they requested privileged seats in the coming age (Mark 10:35-37).

4. Nathaniel recognized Jesus as Rabbi, Son of God and King of Israel all in the same breath (John 1:49).

5. In popular estimation Jesus was a prophet, a successor to John the Baptist, and the incarnation of the ancient prophetic spirit (Mark 6:15; 8:28). In those days the restoration of prophecy was viewed as signaling the beginning of the last days. The term Prophet was loaded with eschatological significance.[33]

---

29. John 1:38 equates the terms Rabbi and *didaskalos* (teacher).

30. See Matt. 7:29; Mark 1:22; Luke 4:32.

31. Luke 5:17; 6:6; 13:10-11.

32. Mark 4:38; 5:35; 9:17, 38; 10:51; John 3:2.

33. Cullman, *Christology of the New Testament* (Philadelphia: Westminster, 1963), pp. 13-23.

6. Jesus encouraged others to think of him as more than a Rabbi when he applied to himself the proverbial saying that "a prophet is not without honor, except in his own country" (Mark 6:4). That he regarded himself as a prophet is even more clear in his response to certain Pharisees who warned him of Herod's murderous intentions: "It cannot be that a prophet should perish outside Jerusalem" (Luke 13:33). All of this indicates that Jesus was something more than a teacher in the traditional sense of that word.

Chapter Sixteen

THE HOPE IN HOSEA

Hosea lived in the eighth century before Christ. It is generally thought that he began to preach shortly after Amos in the reign of King Jeroboam II (782-753 B.C.). His ministry extended over some thirty years. He is the only native-born prophet of the northern kingdom whose writings are part of the Scriptures. Hosea thinks of the Coming One in terms of great leaders of the past. The future leader would be a second Moses (1:10—2:1), a second David (3:5), and even a second Israel (11:1).

Prophecy No. 30

THE SECOND MOSES

Hosea 1:10—2:1

Hosea's marriage to Gomer the daughter of Diblaim produced three children.[1] Following instructions from God, Hosea gave the children symbolic names which were designed to forecast the fate which would shortly befall the northern kingdom of Israel (Ephraim). The first name, Jezreel, means "God scatters." There is a double significance to this name. First, the bloody crimes committed by the ruling dynasty (house of Jehu) in the capital city of Jezreel[2] would shortly be avenged.[3] The second significance of the name lies in the prophecy that the military power of Israel would be broken in the valley of Jezreel (1:4-5).

The second child was named Lo-Ruchamah, "Not Pitied." The northern kingdom had passed beyond the bounds of God's mercy. Whereas Judah would find deliverance from the ruthless power of Assyria (1:7), Hosea lived to see Israel totally destroyed by the Assyrians in 722 B.C.

The third child was given the name Lo-Ammi, "Not My People." The covenant relationship between north Israel and God would be

---

1. Laetsch (BCMP, pp. 18-19) and others agree that God commanded Hosea to marry a harlot, and that the children named in chapter 1 were not actually Hosea's. There is, however, no solid evidence that Gomer was an impure woman at the time of the marriage. *Wife of whoredom* is explained in verse 2 as meaning a woman who was a citizen of a nation which committed harlotry against God.

2. Whereas Jehu is commended for executing God's will in exterminating the house of Ahab (II Kings 10:30), his role in the bloody revolution of 841 B.C. is here condemned. His executions were excessive, underhanded and perhaps not properly motivated.

3. The house of Jehu came to an end with the assassination of Zechariah in 752 B.C.

severed. To all intents and purposes the former citizens of that apostate kingdom would henceforth be regarded as Gentiles in the sight of God.

What a gloomy future for the children of Israel is portrayed by the three symbolic names. Scattered! Rejected! Repudiated! But that is not the bottom line. A glorious future awaited the people of God beyond the judgment.

Translation of Hosea 1:10−2:1[4]

(10) Yet the number of the children of Israel shall be as the sand of the sea which cannot be measured or counted; and it shall be that in the place where they were told, You are not my people, there they shall be called sons of the living God. (11) Then the children of Judah and the children of Israel shall be gathered together, and they shall set for themselves one head, and they shall go up from the land; for great shall be the day of Jezreel. (1) Say to your brothers, Ammi, and to your sisters Ruchamah.

Discussion

In these verses Hosea lifts his eyes to look into a future far distant from his day to describe the blessed privileges of the people of God in the Messianic age. Eight thoughts are prominent here.

1. The multiplication of the sons of Israel: *Yet the number of the children of Israel shall be as the sand of the sea* (v. 10). God would not forget his promises to the Patriarchs.[5] His plan for the descendants of Jacob (Israel) would not be thwarted by the apostasy of the northern tribes and the total and final destruction of the kingdom of Israel. A vast host in the future age would belong to that select group known as the children of Israel.

2. This multiplication of the children of Israel would be due to a future and massive conversion of those who were not God's people: *In the place where they were told, You are not my people, they will be called sons of the living God* (v. 10). Those who are not God's people are in Scripture called Gentiles. Israel according to the flesh was cast off, repudiated, disowned. They were dispersed all over the Assyrian empire. They intermarried with the heathen and practiced the ways of the heathen. Israel according to the flesh became indistinguishable from Gentiles.

---

4. In the Hebrew Bible 2:1-3.
5. Gen. 12:3; 15:5; 22:17; 26:4; 28:14.

Whether one is of Israel or of the Gentile world depends not upon his family tree, but upon his relationship to God. When one becomes a child of God, he at that same time becomes a son of Abraham, Isaac and Israel (Jacob).[6]

Now the miracle of the multiplication of the sons of Israel becomes comprehensible. Out of the vast numbers of those who know not God, sons of Israel—true men of faith—would be raised up to become a true Israel of God according to the Spirit.[7] The living God could raise up children of Abraham from the very stones of the earth (Matt. 3:9), and that is exactly what God did, and what he is doing even today. The Gospel imparted life to hardened and lifeless Gentiles. What is more, the Gospel imparted relationship. New converts became children of God and sons of Abraham.

> Know therefore that they which are of faith, the same are the children of Abraham. And if you belong to Christ, then you are Abraham's seed, and heirs according to his promises (Gal. 3:7, 29).

Hosea foresees this very day when vast numbers of Gentiles are incorporated into the covenant community known throughout the Bible as Israel. Paul understood the passage this way (Rom. 9:25-26) and so did Peter (I Peter 2:10).

3. The conversion of vast numbers of Gentiles is said to happen *in the place where they were told, You are not my people* (v. 10). The preaching of the Word of God makes a clear demarcation between those who are, and those who are not the people of God. Wherever that Word is preached many who discover that they are not God's people will respond and pass out of the kingdom of darkness into the kingdom of his dear Son (Col. 1:13).

The use of the third person in verse 10 is deliberately ambiguous: *they* were told . . . *they* shall be called. Had Hosea used second person the scope of the passage would have to be limited to citizens of north Israel. As it stands, Hosea is making a broad statement about all those who properly can be said to fall into the category of Not-My-People.

Commentators debate whether the phrase *in the place where they were told, You are not my people* refers to the place where the curse was uttered (Canaan) or the place where the curse was fulfilled (Exile). This debate assumes that Hosea is speaking strictly of the citizens of

---

6. Gal. 3:7-9, 29; Rom. 9:6, 7.
7. Rom. 2:28, 29; 9:6-8; Gal. 4:28.

the northern kingdom in this passage. Actually he is speaking about Gentiles among whom are the citizens of the northern kingdom of Israel who have been disowned by God.

The title *living* God is used fifteen times in the Old Testament. As a rule this title is intended to point to the contrast between impotent heathen deities, and the God of the Bible. Living God is the Hebrew way of declaring the superiority of their God to all gods worshiped by the heathen.[8] For those who were Gentiles (Not My People) to become sons of the *living* God implies a total repudiation of idolatry and complete commitment to the God of revelation and redemption (cf. Acts 14:15).

4. Hosea foresees the unification of God's people in the distant future: *the children of Judah and the children of Israel shall be gathered together* (v. 11). Since 931 B.C. two rival kingdoms had co-existed, both claiming a special relationship to Yahweh. Such an arrangement had been inaugurated by God (I Kings 12:24) as part of his plan (1) to punish, but not totally remove the Davidic dynasty; and (2) to preserve Judah, the Messianic tribe, in relative isolation from heathen influence. But that divided condition was never meant to be permanent. There would be an amicable reconciliation between the children of Israel and the children of Judah. Gentiles who were not God's people became children of Israel and sons of the living God through faith in Christ Jesus. They would be united to the true sons of Judah (Rom. 2:28, 29) who recognized Jesus of Nazareth as Messiah and they— both Jew and Gentile—would become the nucleus of the New Covenant people of God. This is the thrust of I Peter 2:10.

The verb (*shall be gathered together*)[9] presupposes that Judah too will find herself in the same condition, rejected of the Lord. A lost Jew has no more standing with God than a lost Gentile. The verb further suggests that the unification of those who are not God's people is the result of divine action. Only God can make Gentiles children of Israel; and only God can repair the breach between Jew and Gentile. Paul uses a different figure but says the same thing when he writes:

> For he is our peace, who has made both one, and has broken down the middle wall of partition between us (Eph. 2:14).

8. The deity is called the living God (1) in speeches designed to urge courageous action against the heathen (Josh. 3:10); (2) in prayers urging God to show his superiority over those who defy him (II Kings 19:16); and (3) in speeches recognizing the superiority of Yahweh over other deities in consequence of some stupendous miracle which has been performed (Deut. 5:26).

9. Niphal of the root *qbts*.

5. The reason for the unification of God's people is the common allegiance which all members of the New Covenant community will render to *one head*. The term *head* is used of kings occasionally in the Old Testament;[10] but far more frequently the term is used of civil or military leaders.[11] At least once the term is used of a prophetic leader (II Kings 2:3, 5) and once it is used of God himself (II Chron. 13:12). In the days of the Exodus and Wandering Moses was apparently referred to as the *head* of the children of Israel.[12]

The next line of verse 11 suggests that Hosea had in mind here an Exodus motif and a Moses-type *head*. Since both reason and apostolic authority demand that these verses be viewed as Messianic in scope, the *one head* must be the Messiah himself. The headship of Christ in the New Testament community of faith is abundantly documented.[13]

6. Under the leadership of the second Moses, the people of God will be led *up from the land* (v. 11). A new Exodus will take place.[14] *The land* (ha-'arets) is any place in this old sinful world where God finds men. Old Israel was gathered and organized by Moses for the march up from Egypt, the land of bondage (cf. Hos. 12:13). The Egyptian bondage and Babylonian bondage are but pale shadows of the real bondage to Satan and sin in which men are found. Out of that land the second Moses leads his followers. Wherever the Gospel is preached some respond. By so doing they *go up from the land* to become part of that group of pilgrims whose true citizenship is in heaven (Phil. 3:20).

7. This great age to which Hosea looks forward is called *the day of Jezreel* (v. 11). Earlier in the chapter the name Jezreel had the ominous sense of *God scatters*. Here the name takes on the positive sense of *God sows*. Whereas before fleshly Israel was dispersed as an act of judgment, here spiritual Israel is dispersed with a view to producing a bountiful harvest of souls. That will be a *great day*, a day when God reaches out to every corner of the earth through his people to plant the seed of the Word in the hearts of men.

---

10. E.g., Isa. 7:8, 9. The terms *head* and *king* are linked in reference to Saul (I Sam. 15:17). In Lam. 5:16 "The crown has fallen from our head" may refer to the last king of Judah.

11. E.g., Exod. 6:14; Num. 1:16; Judg. 11:8-11.

12. In Num. 14:4 the people want to replace Moses with a *head* to lead them back to Egypt.

13. I Cor. 11:3; Eph. 1:22; 4:15; 5:23; Col. 1:18.

14. The new Exodus motif is further amplified in 2:14-23; 11:10-11.

8. Members of the New Covenant community will possess a spirit of brotherly love toward one another: *Say to your brothers.* They will recognize one another as belonging to God (*ammi* = my people) and as having mutually benefitted from the grace of God (*Ruchamah* = Compassion). This is what Paul is speaking about in Romans 15:7-13.

So the three ominous names of Hosea's children have now all been reversed.

APOSTATE FLESHLY ISRAEL	UNIFIED SPIRITUAL ISRAEL
JEZREEL God Scatters the People (for judgment)	JEZREEL God Sows His People (for harvest)
LO-RUCHAMAH No Compassion	RUCHAMAH Compassion
LO-AMMI Not My People	AMMI My People

Prophecy No. 31

THE SECOND DAVID

Hosea 3:5

The whole tragic episode of Hosea's unfaithful wife forms the background to the Messianic prediction of Hosea 3:5. That Gomer is the adulterous woman of chapter 3 has been the judgment of most commentators who have examined this text.[15] She had been unfaithful to her husband; but whether she had actually separated herself from Hosea is another question. In the common translation of 3:2 Hosea is made to say that he *bought* his wife, which would suggest that her wayward life eventually had forced Gomer to sell herself into slavery. This is probably the correct understanding. There is, however, some dispute over the meaning of the Hebrew verb in 3:2.[16]

---

15. The view of McGarvey that Hosea brings a second woman—an unnamed prostitute—into his home flies in the face of all that can be called sound exegesis.

16. The verb root *krh* can mean (1) to buy, or conclude a bargain; or (2) to provide for. Laetsch (BCMP, p. 37) opts for this second view in which Hosea gave provisions of silver and barley to his wife in spite of her obvious attraction to various lovers.

In any case, Hosea demonstrated here a love for his wayward wife which is beyond the capacity of most men to even imagine, let alone imitate.

Hosea did not—could not—merely overlook his wife's ugly violations of her sacred marriage commitment. He imposed upon her an isolation from all men, including himself. She would sit quietly[17] at home. This she was to do *for me*, "to show her changed attitude to her husband whom she had so shamefully betrayed, to prove her willingness to remain loyal to him."[18]

Hosea's actions with regard to his wife were parabolic. The symbolism is explained in 3:4. The northern kingdom would shortly cease to exist. The succession of nine illegitimate dynasties which ruled that kingdom would come to an end. The citizens of that kingdom for a long time would be without their king or prince. In foreign exile they would no longer be able to practice the rituals (*sacrifice*) of the counterfeit calf worship which was established in the northern kingdom by Jeroboam son of Nebat.

Translation of Hosea 3:5

Afterward the children of Israel shall again seek[19] the LORD their God and David their king; and they shall tremble unto the LORD, and unto his goodness in the latter days.

Discussion

Six key thoughts are brought out in this passage:

1 .The Messiah would only come after the conclusion of Israel's great exile. The deportation of the northern tribes into the lands of the Fertile Crescent began during the reign of the Assyrian king Tiglath-pileser III as early as 745 B.C. The climax came in 722 B.C. when the Assyrian king Sargon destroyed Samaria, capital of Israel, and dissolved that nation. Hosea 3:5, however, indicates that 722 B.C. would not be the final curtain for the former citizens of the northern kingdom. There would be a glorious *afterward*.

---

17. Hebrew *yashabh*, to sit, remain inactive (Isa. 30:7; Jer. 8:14); stay at home (Lev. 12:4; II Kings 14:10).

18. Laetsch, BCMP, p. 39.

19. Lit., They shall return and seek. To return to do something is a common Hebrew idiom meaning, to do again.

2. The children of Israel would not be in a position to share in the Messianic age until they came back to their God in genuine repentance. They *will seek* Yahweh, their God. They will *tremble* toward him in open manifestation of the godly sorrow which brings about repentance unto salvation (II Cor. 7:10). They will humbly cast themselves upon God's *goodness*, i.e., his grace. The only question here is whether this conversion of Israelites is a preparation for the appearance of the Messiah or a consequence of his appearance. Either interpretation is possible.

3. The Messiah would be a descendant of David, and more than that. He would be the culmination of the Davidic line and is given the name David. He is David's greater son.[20]

4. Messianic David would be a great *king* and he would rule over a kingdom peopled by those who had been reconciled to God. Those who had formerly been enslaved to earthly monarchs would own him as *their* king.

5. The children of Israel, who in 931 B.C. had broken away from the house of David (I Kings 12:16), would seek out this second David and render allegiance unto him. A true return to God must involve a return to David their king since the Lord had promised the kingship to David and his seed forever (II Sam. 7:13, 16).

6. Messiah is closely identified with Yahweh, and yet is distinguished from him. Conversion to God involves recognition of the Messianic David. "No man comes unto the Father, but by me" (John 14:6).

7. All of this is to take place in *the latter days* (*be'acharit hayyamim*). Kimchi the twelfth century Jewish commentator set forth as a basic principle of interpretation that whenever this expression is used, it refers to the days of the Messiah.[21] A host of New Testament passages refer to the Christian dispensation as the last days.[22]

Prophecy No. 32

THE SECOND ISRAEL

Hosea 11:1

Chapter 10 concludes with a strong appeal for repentance couched in agricultural metaphors (v. 12). The present course of the nation has

---

20. Jer. 30:9; Ezek. 34:23, 24; 37:24f.
21. Cited by Laetsch, BCMP, p. 40.
22. Acts 2:17; I Cor. 10:11; Heb. 1:2; 9:26; I Peter 1:20; II Peter 3:3.

proved to be disastrous (v. 13). All of their fortifications will be destroyed (v. 14). The apostate calf worship centered in Bethel will be the primary cause of the total annihilation of the northern kingdom (v. 15).

Translation of Hosea 11:1

Nevertheless, Israel is a lad, and I love him, and from Egypt I have called my son.

Discussion

Most commentators see this verse as a reference to the Exodus of Israel from Egypt. It is regarded as a statement of historical fact, not a prediction regarding the future. This interpretation of 11:1 is alleged to be harmonious with the context where God graciously leads and trains his people (vv. 3-4), but is rewarded with unfaithfulness (v. 2). The problem with this interpretation is that it seems to run counter to the plain declaration of Matthew 2:15.

Matthew, under inspiration of the Spirit, declared that the words *I called my son out of Egypt* referred to the return of the Christ child from Egypt after the death of Herod the Great. Joseph and Mary had taken the child there. They remained there until Herod's death "that it might be fulfilled which was spoken by the prophet."

Various solutions have been proposed for reconciling Matthew's interpretation of 11:1 with the interpretation apparently dictated by context. At least five positions have been taken:

1. Catholic scholars, who speak of a multiple sense of each Scripture passage, have the literal sense of the passage refer to the nation Israel. Only in its mystical sense does the passage refer to Christ. But the whole premise that there are multiple senses of Scripture does not square with the laws of thought which men apply in attempting to understand any document. Though a passage may have many legitimate applications, it has only one intended meaning. To say otherwise places the Biblical interpreter afloat on a boundless sea of subjectivity without compass, sail or rudder.

2. Liberal scholars charge Matthew with proof-texting at best, or twisting Scripture. Here, if any place, is a clear example of the abuse of Scripture by the early Christians in trying to establish the Messiahship of Jesus. This position is totally unacceptable to those who have a modicum of respect for the authority of the New Testament writers.

3. Another approach, adopted by most conservative scholars, is to suggest that Israel was a type of Christ. Just as Israel took refuge

in Egypt and subsequently returned to Canaan, so Christ as an infant took refuge in Egypt and subsequently returned to his own land. The deliverance of Israel from Egypt is thus called by Pusey "a prophetic act."[23] According to Plummer, Matthew regarded the history of Israel as "a typical anticipation of the life of the Messiah."[24] Delitzsch indulges in mind reading when he assures his readers that Matthew "certainly does not fail to recognize that that which is said in Hosea is in its first reference intended of Israel."[25]

Undoubtedly typology is involved in the very application of the name *Israel* to Messiah. But, as Laetsch points out, Matthew says nothing about a *type* being fulfilled. He speaks of that which was prophesied— an historical fact—being fulfilled in Christ.[26]

4. Laetsch alone among modern commentators sees a direct and personal Messianic prediction in Hosea 11:1. He, however, limits the predictive element in the second half of the verse. Laetsch expresses his view in this way:

> Since the Holy Spirit calls the return of Christ out of Egypt a fulfillment of what the prophet foretold, we accept His interpretation as authentic. The eternal God speaking of His love toward Israel in the distant past, foretells in the same breath an act of love in the distant future, calling His Son, an Israelite concerning the flesh (Rom. 9:5), out of Egypt.[27]

5. The position taken by the present writer is that all of Hosea 11:1 is personal Messianic prediction.

The main argument against the strictly predictive interpretation of Hosea 11:1 is that the context cannot be reconciled with this view. There are several points to be made about the alleged connection between Hosea 11:1 and its immediate context.

1. Chapters 4-13 of Hosea do not contain lengthy and logical sermons of the prophet, but rather sayings coming from different periods of his long ministry. The problem of discerning logical connection between the paragraphs of these chapters is a notorious exegetical difficulty. Sometimes determining what should properly be classified as paragraphs is extremely difficult. Therefore, one cannot rule out a *a priori* considering Hosea 11:1 as an independent utterance totally unrelated to context.

---

23. Pusey, MPC, I, 110.
24. Plummer, GAM, p. 17.
25. Delitzsch, MPHS, p. 133.
26. Laetsch, BCMP, p. 88.
27. Ibid., p. 89.

2. When one examines 11:1 carefully and tries to relate it to verses 2-4, certain difficulties arise. The subject of 11:1 is first person—God is speaking; the subject in verse 2 is plural—an anonymous *they*, probably referring to the prophets. The object in 11:1 is singular—*my son*; the object in verses 2-4 is plural. Hosea does not elsewhere use the Father-son figure to describe the relationship between God and Israel. In fact, that figure has not been employed since the days of Moses (Exod. 4:22, 23). Finally, no copula joins the two verses together.

Wolff[28] has argued strongly for the position that Hosea 11 is "a homogeneous unit separated from previous and following context." Yet, to smooth out the transition between verses 1 and 2 Wolff finds it necessary to emend verse 2 to make it fit with verse 1. Instead of *They called them* in the standard Hebrew text, Wolff substitutes *Yet as I called them*. The truth of the matter is that the transition from 11:1 to 11:2 is rough.[29] Hosea 11:1 is best viewed as the concluding statement to the previous paragraph which began in 10:9.

The unit begins with an accusation rooted in Israel's early history. Mention is made of Gibeah with obvious reference to the foul act committed in Gibeah in the days of the Judges (Judg. 19:30; 20:6). Israel had not changed. Like the Benjaminites of that episode, Israel stood proud and defiant in the face of undeniable sin and impending judgment. Unlike those Benjaminites Hosea's contemporaries had not, as yet, been adequately punished for their sin (v. 9).

The hour was coming when God would chastise these people by means of foreign nations (v. 10). Ephraim's present life of ease is compared to a heifer which likes to thresh because she is allowed to eat her fill of the grain. But harsh times were coming. Ephraim and Judah as well will have to plow rough ground (v. 11).

The dark prospects lead Hosea to appeal for repentance using agricultural metaphors of plowing and sowing (v. 12). At present however, the nation was only plowing wickedness and reaping its bitter and deceitful fruit. They were especially guilty of the sin of trusting in their own military strength (v. 13). But Ephraim will fall to a ruthless enemy which will spare neither women nor children (v. 14). The king of Israel will perish, the inhabitants of the kingdom will experience the most ruthless treatment. But Israel is a child and I will continue to love him and out of Egypt I have called my son.

---

28. Wolff, HCHC, p. 193.

29. The Septuagint translators also found it difficult to harmonize 11:1 and 11:2. They rendered, "I called his sons," in 11:1 thus harmonizing the singular *Israel* (v. 1) with the plural *them* (v. 2).

Hosea had a predilection for beginnings in the history of God's people.[30] Hosea's faith in a reconstitution of the people of God after discipline is generally conceded. His belief that they would have a king after the Exile is clearly affirmed in 3:5. The same verse establishes Hosea's usage of historical names (David) in an eschatological setting. In 11:1 Hosea is announcing a new beginning—an eschatological beginning—the coming of a second Israel who like his earlier namesake would also find himself an exile in Egypt.

Hosea 11:1 begins with *ki*, a word with a wide variety of meanings. The temporal use adopted by most commentators (*When Israel was a child*) is one usage of *ki*. But the word can also have an adversative sense—*nevertheless*[31] or *but*. In Hosea 11:1 *ki* introduces a noun clause in which the verb must be supplied in English. Usually the verb *was* is supplied; the present tense or even future tense could just as easily be supplied.

Taken as a genuine prediction, Hosea 11:1 adds several important points to the Messianic expectation.

1. Messiah would be an Israelite. More than that, of course, is involved in calling him *Israel*. The Old Testament character Israel (Jacob) and the nation named for him are thus made typical of the coming Messiah. The remainder of the verse indicates in what way this typology is manifested.

2. The Messianic Israel would come into the world as a child. Although this idea is latent in Genesis 3:15, this is the first prophecy to explicitly make the point.

3. God would have a special loving concern for this Messianic child, just as he had shown special loving concern for Israel (Jacob) during his youth (Mal. 1:2, 3).

4. Messianic Israel, like the man Israel and the nation Israel, would spend some time in Egypt. The Old Testament Israel migrated to Egypt to escape the famine which threatened to wipe out the chosen family. The propriety of this descent into Egypt was confirmed to Old Testament Israel (Jacob) by "visions of the night" (Gen. 46:1-4). So it was with Messianic Israel. Being warned of Herod's evil plot in a dream, Joseph immediately departed for Egypt. There he and Mary

---

30. Wolff (HCHC, p. xxvii) points to the following: (1) Jehu, first king of the ruling dynasty (1:4); (2) Gilgal and Saul, the beginnings of monarchy (9:15; 13:10f.); (3) Baal-peor—beginning of Baal worship (9:10); (4) the Jacob story—beginning of Israel's deceitfulness (12:4f.; 13f.); and (5) several times the mention of Israel's beginnings in Egypt and the wilderness period.

31. *ki* is translated *nevertheless* in I Sam. 15:35 and Isa. 9:1 in the KJV.

tenderly cared for the infant Israel (Jesus) until the danger was past and they were called by God to return to the land of Israel.[32]

5. Messianic Israel would be the Son of God. Israel as a nation is spoken of corporately as God's son in the Mosaic literature (Exod. 4:22f.), but after that time is not so designated again.[33] In Hosea's day the concept of royal sonship was already well established.[34] If Hosea is referring historically to the call of the nation Israel out of Egypt, he is the first person since Moses to use the corporate son imagery. Given the prior revelation regarding the Davidic ruler being the son of God, and given Hosea's own expectation that a Davidic ruler would rule over a unified nation in the future (3:5), it is more likely that Hosea intended the term *son of God* here to be taken personally and royally. That certainly is how Matthew interpreted it.

POSTSCRIPT

The climax of Hosea's Messianic hope is reached in 13:14. Here God announces that he will ultimately conquer death. Because 13:14 is nestled within a context of accusation and threat, most modern writers deny that the verse even contains a promise. Nevertheless, Paul so regarded it (I Cor. 15:54, 55), and the ancient versions support his interpretation. Hosea 13:14 will find fulfillment in the final resurrection of believers. The verse is Messianic, but not personal Messianic.

Special Note

THE TITLE SON OF GOD

The titles *Messiah* and *Son of God* are brought together in several New Testament passages. The connection is made in Peter's good confession (Matt. 16:16), Caiaphas' query (Matt. 26:63; Mark 14:61), the parting cries of demons (Luke 4:41), the affirmation of Martha (John 11:27), the statement of John (John 20:31), and Paul (Acts 9:20-21). The two titles were probably brought together because *son*

---

32. Matt. 2:20, 21. This is the only place in the New Testament which speaks of *the land* of Israel.

33. In some passages Israelites taken collectively are called sons (plural) of God (e.g., Isa. 1:2; 30:1; 63:16). The concept of corporate (as opposed to collective) sonship seems to be indicated in Jer. 3:19-22.

34. II Sam. 7:14; Ps. 2:7; 89:26f.

of God was the logical implication of the title *Messiah*.[35] It was not the early Christians who invested the title *son of God* with Messianic implications. That association is already attested in the pre-Christian Dead Sea Scrolls.[36]

Jesus' use of the term *Father* for God indicates that divine sonship was very fundamental to his self-understanding and self-disclosure.[37] The concept of the sonship of Jesus is prominent in Matthew and a high point in John's Christology.[38] Paul, strange to say, only uses the title *son of God* three times (Rom. 1:4; II Cor. 1:19; 15:28), but uses the title *son* at least a dozen times. All of these data led Longenecker to make the following observation:

> As Israel and her sons were understood to be uniquely God's own among the peoples of the earth and the anointed king God's Son—and in that relationship pledged to loving obedience—so Jesus as Israel's Messiah, who united in his person both the corporate ideal and descent from David and who exemplified an unparalled obedience to the Father's will, was the Son of God *par excellence* . . . . In Jesus . . . the corporate and royal Son-of-God motifs were brought together, whether or not they were ever so united before.[39]

---

35. Longenecker, CEJC, p. 94.

36. 4 Q Florilegium. Cited by Longenecker.

37. See Matt. 11:27; Mark 13:32; Luke 10:21-22; John 5:19-26; 6:40; 10:36; 14:13; 17:1.

38. John 20:31; I John 4:15; 5:5. Cf. John 1:34, 49; 10:36; I John 2:23; 3:23; 5:11f., 13, 20.

39. Longenecker, CEJC, p. 99.

Chapter Seventeen

SNAPSHOTS FROM ISAIAH (1)

Not without reason Isaiah has been called the Fifth Evangelist. According to J. Barton Payne, fifty-nine verses in the book are directly anticipatory of Jesus Christ. Forty-seven chapters of the book are directly quoted or alluded to in the apostolic writings. Something like four hundred allusions to this book appear in the New Testament. If usage is an indication of the value placed on an Old Testament book, Isaiah would rank second only to Psalms as the favorite of the early church.

Isaiah was the son of Amoz and it is thought that he was of the tribe of Judah. He served as court historiographer during the reigns of Jotham and Hezekiah (II Chron. 26:22; 32:32). Isaiah was called to the prophetic ministry in the year King Uzziah died (c. 739 B.C.) according to 6:1. Because the call account appears in chapter 6, some have postulated a ministry in Jerusalem prior to the call. This, however, is most unlikely. The first five chapters of the book are designed as a sample of the preaching of this man of God in the early phase of his ministry. The call account has been inserted in chapter 6 to validate his ministry and to explain the apparent lack of communication which characterized it.

Chapters 1-6 of the book contain mingled rebukes and promises. Amidst stern denunciations of Judah's social and spiritual life are some of the most beautiful and far-reaching promises in the Old Testament. In 1:26, 27, for example, Isaiah depicts the ideal or Messianic future. There will come a time, typified by the reign of David, in which true righteousness and justice will be found in the land. Jerusalem will be known as the city of righteousness, the faithful city.

Isaiah 2:2-4 depicts Zion's glorious future. In the last days[1] *the mountain of the Lord's house* shall be established above all other mountains (kingdoms or worship systems). That this passage has found fulfillment in the church of Christ is a clear teaching of the New Testament. Christians worship God on Mt. Zion (Heb. 12:22). The church is the house of God (I Tim. 3:15; Heb. 3:6; Eph. 2:19), the temple of the Holy Spirit (II Cor. 6:16). Gentiles will continually stream up that spiritual mountain that they might be taught by God. From this heavenly Jerusalem (Gal. 4:25, 26; Heb. 12:22; Rev. 3:12; 21:2, 10) the word

---

1. In the Old Testament this phrase is used for the time when Messianic salvation would be accomplished. In the New Testament the phrase clearly applies to that time after the first advent. See Acts 2:17; Heb. 1:2; James 5:3; I Peter 1:5, 20; II Peter 3:3; I John 2:18.

of God will be carried forth. That kingdom will be administered by God (through Messiah). Within that kingdom people of all races and national- ities will live harmoniously. Swords to plowshares and spears to pruning hooks is Isaiah's way of underscoring the peace which will characterize Messiah's kingdom.

In the section of mingled rebukes and promises only one personal Messianic prophecy is found, viz., the prophecy of the beautiful shoot (4:2-6). Chapters 7-12 are called by students of Isaiah "the book of Immanuel." Four great personal Messianic prophecies are found in this section. The first of these—the famous virgin birth prophecy (7:14)— is discussed later in this chapter.

Prophecy No. 33

THE BEAUTIFUL SHOOT

Isaiah 4:2-6

Following Isaiah's brief look into Zion's glorious future (2:2-4), the prophet comes down to earth to deal with the inglorious present. Judah had been forsaken by the Lord (2:5-9) and consequently must face his judgment (2:10-21). Isaiah brings a stern indictment against the leading men (2:22—3:15) and the leading ladies (3:16—4:1) of the nation. The emphasis in chapter 3 on the dearth of qualified leadership sets the stage for Isaiah's first personal Messianic prophecy, one which emphasizes the quality of Messiah's future leadership.

Translation of Isaiah 4:2-6

(2) In that day the Shoot of the LORD shall be for beauty and for glory, and the fruit of the land shall be for pride and for glory of the remnant of Israel. (3) And it shall be that he who is left in Zion and remains in Jerusalem shall be called holy, everyone who has been recorded for life in Jerusalem. (4) When the Lord shall have washed away the filth of the daughters of Zion, and shall have purged the bloodstains of Jerusalem from her midst by a spirit of judgment and by a spirit of burning, (5) then the LORD will create over the whole of Mt. Zion and over her assemblies a cloud by day and smoke and the shining of a flaming fire by night; for over all the glory there shall be a canopy. (6) And a shelter shall be for a shade by day from the heat, and for a refuge and hiding place from the storm and from the rain.

245

Discussion

Since 2:2-4 Isaiah has been dwelling on the bleak future for Judah. Now he again has some good news about the future (*that day*)[2] for his readers. He speaks here of the coming Messiah and the kingdom which he would establish. The Jewish scholars who produced the Aramaic paraphrase known as the Targum recognized the personal Messianic import of the passage. They rendered it: At that time shall the Messiah of the Lord be for joy and glory. . . .

A. *The Description of the Coming Messiah.* Two botanical figures are used in 4:2 to describe the Messiah: (1) the sprout of the Lord, and (2) the fruit of the land.

1. The expression *Shoot of Yahweh* appears to be based on the general statement made by David in II Samuel 23:5.[3] As David penned his last words the glorious promises which had been made to him had not yet *sprouted.* Isaiah is saying that all those blessings which had been promised to David would be concentrated in one person now designated as the sprout of the Lord. By placing Isaiah 28:5 alongside 4:2 it becomes clear that the sprout should be taken personally and not simply as a reference to the productivity of the land.[4]

That the Shoot is brought forth from the house of David is the clear teaching of later passages which employ this same figure (cf. Jer. 23:5; 33:15; Zech. 3:8). The use of the Shoot figure here in Isaiah presupposes that the Davidic tree (dynasty) would fall. From the stump of that tree God would bring forth a Shoot which would eventually cause that old tree to become more glorious than ever before (cf. Isa. 11:1).

2. The Messiah will be *the fruit of the land.* This second botanical figure underscores his humanity.[5] The phrase *fruit of the land* seems to be borrowed from Numbers 13:26 and Deuteronomy 1:25 where the land of Canaan is particularly in view. Thus Messiah would be raised up from the land of Canaan or Israel. The Hebrew writer may

---

2. This is the seventh time this phrase is used in this section of Isaiah (2:1—4:6). This phrase introduces pronouncements of judgment (3:18—4:1) as well as announcements of salvation.

3. So Young, NIC, I, 173.

4. Leupold (EI, I, 103) occupies a middle position between the personal interpretation offered here and the general interpretation of *sprout.* He takes *sprout* to embrace the whole work of God, with Messiah as an important part of that work.

5. Young (NIC, I, 176-178) lists several persuasive arguments for regarding this phrase as a reference to the humanity of the Messiah. Others limit the expression to the fruitfulness of the land in the Messianic age.

have had this passage in mind when he wrote: "For it is evident that our Lord sprang forth (*anatetalken*) out of Judah, of which tribe Moses spoke nothing concerning priesthood" (Heb. 7:14).

B. *The Centrality of the Coming Messiah.* Four expressions are used to underscore how important this future ruler will be to the remnant of Israel.

1. He will be *for beauty.* He will be regarded as beautiful. It is not his physical features or outward garb which the prophet has in view, but his character. He was the ideal man. Those who through the years have closely scrutinized his life have echoed the words of the Roman procurator: I find no fault in this man! To those who know him as savior he is altogether lovely, the fairest of ten thousand.

2. He will be *for glory.* That in which Israel might truly glory is the Messiah. In place of the false glory and ornament (2:5—4:1) the genuine and real glory and ornament will appear, viz., the Lord himself.

3. He will be *for pride.* Compared to his knowledge of Christ, Paul counted all else rubbish. Christ was the sole object of his pride (Phil. 3:7-8).

4. He will be *for glory.* Again the Apostle Paul captured the feeling of all believers when he wrote: "God forbid that I should glory, save in the cross . . . !" (Gal. 6:14).

C. *The Subjects of the Coming Messiah* (vv. 2b-3). Concerning those who would serve the Messiah four statements are made:

1. They are those who have escaped the judgment of God. They are the *remnant of Israel* (v. 2b), those who are left in Zion and those who remain in Jerusalem (v. 3a). Terrible judgments fell upon Jerusalem subsequent to the time of Isaiah.[6] By God's grace, some would escape. Israel would always have survivors, a remnant. Those who escaped the temporal judgments, because of their spiritual commitment, also had been chosen to escape a far worse judgment. The kingdom of Christ consists of those who have been saved from sin, death and hell.

2. They are those who put Messiah at the center of their lives. Not all see Christ as beautiful and glorious, the pride and glory of their lives. But Messiah's subjects see and love him for what he is.

---

6. The most prominent: The 701 B.C. invasion of Sennacherib; the 587 B.C. destruction of Jerusalem by Nebuchadnezzar; the 168 B.C. sacking of Jerusalem by Antiochus Epiphanes; and the A.D. 70 Roman destruction of the city.

3. They will be called *holy*. The term should not be limited to cultic purity, but includes ethical holiness. The verse is introduced by the phrase *and it shall be*. The thought is, "and this shall be the consequences." A consequence of the appearance of the Sprout would be that a holy people would exist in the world. That is precisely the meaning of the New Testament title *saints*.

4. They will be citizens of Zion and Jerusalem: *he who is left in Zion and remains in Jerusalem*. The remnant was mentioned in the previous verse. Now Isaiah gives a more detailed description of them. The saved are part of Zion, the city of God. The writer of Hebrews speaks of Christians coming to Mount Zion (Heb. 12:22). This usage proves that the Old Testament city was but a type of the true Zion, the church of Christ. In Messianic contexts *Zion* and *Jerusalem* should be interpreted in the light of Hebrews 12:22.

5. They are the people who have been written in the lamb's book of life: *everyone who has been recorded for life* (v. 3). They are the elect, the redeemed, the saved.

D. *The Prerequisites of Messiah's Coming* (v. 4). Judgment must precede Messianic blessing. The agent of cleansing is the Holy Spirit. Both men and women stand guilty. Judgment will, as it were, wash away the filth of the women. The fires of God's judgment wrath would purge the land of its bloodshed. The reference is to the slaughter of innocent children in idolatrous sacrifice.

E. *The Blessings of Messiah's Coming* (vv. 5-6). Five blessings of Messiah's coming are enumerated:

1. A new creation: *Yahweh will create*. The verb *bara'* is the same as used in Genesis 1:1. In the Old Testament only the deity is said to *create*. That which he creates is brand new, something which did not previously exist. No other word is so appropriate to emphasize the uniqueness of the Christian era. Pentecost marked a new beginning.

In Genesis 1:1 it is *'elohim* the transcendent, all powerful One, who created the physical world. But here it is *Yahweh*, the God of redemption, who is involved in this creation. The prophet speaks of a spiritual creation, a creation associated with redemption. "If any man be in Christ he is a new creation" (II Cor. 5:17).

2. A glorious mountain: *over the whole*[7] *of Mt. Zion*. This is the same mountain of which Isaiah previously had spoken in 2:1-4. The

---

7. Lit., over every place of Mt. Zion. The Hebrew term *mekon* (place) never refers to human dwellings, and so designates a divine place of abode.

prophet now adds additional reasons why that mountain, which in Old Testament symbolism represents the covenant people of God, will be the main attraction in the age of the Messiah.

3. A unique worship: *and over her assemblies.* The references is to worship assemblies. "The word is actually a forerunner of the New Testament *ekklesia.*"[8] Wherever these assemblies may be located, they are part of Mt. Zion, the kingdom of God, the church universal (Heb. 12:22).

4. The protective presence of God. The citizens of New Testament Zion will experience the glorious presence of God as certainly as did old Israel in its wilderness trek. A fiery cloud guided and protected Canaan-bound Israel from camping spot to camping spot for forty years (Exod. 13:21; 14:20). The cloud at times descended upon the Tabernacle to indicate the approach of God (Exod. 40:34). At the dedication of Solomon's temple there had been a similar manifestation marking that spot as one chosen by God. Isaiah here foresees a more glorious manifestation of divine presence in the New Testament age. In Old Covenant times the cloud was confined to the Holy of Holies. But in the Messianic age the cloud of divine presence would cover all of Mt. Zion. The Messianic fiery cloud would not move about as did the wilderness predecessor, but it would be like a fixed canopy over that glorious city (v. 5). In Exodus terminology Isaiah is describing God's eternal dwelling with his New Testament people.

5. An accessible refuge center. The practical result of God's presence with his people is indicated in verse 6. The awesome imagery of verse 5 is now softened. None, save Moses, in the Old Testament times would venture into the midst of the glorious cloud which indicated God's presence. But New Testament Zion would be accessible to all. Like the familiar booths or huts which shepherds and vineyard guardians used to escape unbearable weather, Mt. Zion would provide shade from the burning heat and protection from the storms of life. To such as futilely toil in worldly enterprises Jesus issued the great invitation: Come unto me all of you who labor and are heavy laden and I will give you rest (Matt. 11:28).

Prophecy No. 34

THE VIRGIN BIRTH

Isaiah 7:14-16

Chapters 7-12 of Isaiah have been called the Book of Immanuel.

---

8. Young, NIC, I, 186.

These chapters contain what Delitzsch calls "The Great Trilogy of Messianic Prophecy." In chapter 7 Messiah is about to be born; in chapter 9 he has already been born; and in chapter 11 he is reigning over his kingdom.

In 734 B.C. the royal house of Judah came under enormous pressure from surrounding nations to join an anti-Assyrian coalition. Ahaz, king of Judah, refused to buckle to the pressure and, as a result, found himself under attack. Syria, led by King Rezin, and Ephraim, led by King Pekah, invaded Judah with the purpose of forcing Ahaz off the throne (vv. 5-6).

Chapter 7 opens with Ahaz making preparations to withstand the assault by Rezin and Pekah. Isaiah was sent by God's directive to meet Ahaz as he was inspecting his water supply system. Isaiah was to take with him his son Shear-jashub whose name had symbolic significance for the moment. The boy's name means "a remnant shall return." The name is obviously intended to be an encouragement to Ahaz. There would always be a remnant of God's people no matter how terrible the judgment might be.

Isaiah dealt with this crisis by (1) encouraging King Ahaz to manifest quiet confidence (v. 4), (2) deprecating the two invading kings (*two smoking stumps of fire brands*), (3) announcing the futility of the plot against the house of David (v. 7), and (4) predicting the dissolution of Ephraim as a people within sixty-five years[9] (v. 8).

King Ahaz had not been moved by the specific promises of the prophet, so God, through his spokesman, graciously nudged him with an imperative: *Ask for a sign.* These words constitute both an invitation and a command. To ask for the sign here would be a manifestation of faith; to fail to do so would be tantamount to rebellion. Hardened unbeliever that he was, Ahaz refused the command of God. He wanted no part of signs. He preferred to work out his own salvation from the invading armies. His hypocritical excuse for disobedience was that asking for a sign constituted tempting God (v. 12). He was aware of the implications of Deuteronomy 6:16, "You shall not tempt the Lord your God." Hypocrites are not ignorant of Scripture! Ahaz had no

---

9. The Syro-Ephraimitic invasion took place about 734 B.C. By 670 B.C. Ephraim would cease to exist as a separate people. The northern kingdom (Ephraim) ceased to exist politically in 722 B.C. The Assyrian king Esarhaddon (681-669 B.C.) brought foreign colonists to Samaria to replace the last group of Israelites who had been deported. This step was the one that spelled the total end of the national existence of Ephraim. See II Kings 17:24ff.; Ezra 4:2, 10 and II Chron. 33:11.

wish for a sign, because he had no wish to believe in any other salvation than that which he and his counselors might devise.

In response to the arrogant refusal of the king, Isaiah addressed the royal court (*house of David*). He accused these political leaders of wearying men by refusing to listen to God's prophet; and (2) wearying God by disobeying God's command to ask for a sign (v. 13). In verse 11 Isaiah had called Yahweh "*Your* God"; but now that Ahaz had rejected God's gracious invitation the prophet refers to him as "*my* God."

Translation of Isaiah 7:14-16

(14) Therefore the Lord himself shall give to you (plural) a sign. Behold! The virgin is with child and shall bring forth a son, and she shall call his name Immanuel. (15) Butter and honey shall he eat until he knows to reject the evil and choose the good. (16) For before the lad knows refusing the evil and choosing the good, the land which you are destroying will be forsaken of its two kings.

Discussion

Terry speaks of this passage as "probably the most difficult of all Messianic prophecies."[10] Three matters receive attention in these verses: (1) the birth of a child, (2) the naming of the child, and (3) the infancy of the child.

A. *The Birth of a Child* (v. 14). Concerning the birth of a child, Isaiah makes two points.

1. As to the purpose of the birth, Isaiah says that it will be a sign: The Lord himself shall give you a sign. A sign in the Old Testament might consist of a prophecy that something will take place in the future,[11] or it might be a miracle.[12] In this context Isaiah has challenged the king to ask for a sign, for something spectacular in the heavens or in Sheol. Obviously the sign which the Lord himself gives could be no less spectacular.

The sign is intended for *you* (pl.). Previously Ahaz had been commanded to *ask for yourself* (singular) a sign. Isaiah now leaves Ahaz in the background and addresses the court (v. 13) and the nation.

---

10. Terry, BH, p. 331.

11. E.g., Exod. 3:12; I Sam. 2:34; II Kings 19:29; Jer. 44:29. This type of sign would "only have the effect of signs on those who witnessed their accomplishment." Rawlinson, PC, I, 127.

12. E.g., Exod. 4:8ff.; 7:8ff.; Deut. 13:2ff.; Judg. 6:36-40; II Kings 20:8-11; Isa. 38:7.

The sign is given by the Lord himself. Ahaz could have chosen a sign, but he had refused. So now the Lord—'adhon, the God of sovereign decision—will give a sign of his own choosing.

2. The importance of the birth is indicated by the use of the word *behold!* The prophet is using an ancient announcement formula which was used to signal births of unusual significance.[13] Ahaz and his court would have realized immediately that the announcement which was to follow was of supreme importance. It is not some ordinary birth which Isaiah foresees in 7:14.

Behold (hinneh) is an imperative. The prophet bids the dignitaries of the house of David and the nation they represent to look where he is looking and to see what he is seeing. It is not, of course, with the physical eye that he sees the birth of the wonderful child, but rather in prophetic vision.

3. The miracle of the birth is indicated in the words *the virgin is with child.* The word *'almah* (KJV *virgin*) has been a battleground through the centuries. The translators of the Septuagint version long before the Christian age saw clearly the implications of this context and rendered the word *parthenos,* virgin. This translation was adopted by the King James translators. On the other hand, the Revised Standard Version rendered the word *young woman.* In this rendering the RSV translators were following the lead of the radically anti-Christian Jewish translator Aquila.

In sifting through the scores of pages written on the meaning of the word *'almah* certain facts seem clear. The word is used nine times in the Old Testament, five times in the plural, and four times in the singular. Without dispute the word refers to an unmarried woman. No one has ever produced a text either in Hebrew or in the closely related Ugaritic language where *'almah* is used in reference to a married woman. That the word can be applied to a virgin is proved conclusively by Gen. 24:43. Rebekah is here called an *'almah* and the context clearly indicates that she was an unmarried woman who had not known a man (24:16). In Proverbs 30:19, however, the word *'almah* may indicate an immoral woman.

At this point a little logic must be employed. A woman is to bear a child. She must be either a married woman or an unmarried woman. Usage of the word *'almah* prohibits thinking in terms of a married

---

13. See Gen. 16:11; Judg. 13:3. The use of this formula has been attested in the closely related Ugaritic language. See Young, NIC, I, 285 n. 32.

woman. If she is to be an unmarried woman, she would either be a virgin or an immoral woman. Since the birth of an illegitimate child to an immoral woman would not constitute then or now a very definite sign, one has to conclude that the 'almah of Isaiah 7:14 is in fact a virgin.

The definite article attached to 'almah is frequently overlooked by translators and commentators. The Hebrew has, not "a virgin," but "the virgin"[14] which "points to some special virgin, preeminent above all others."[15]

The position has been taken that the 'almah was at the time of the prediction an unmarried maiden, but at the time of the conception and birth was a woman married to Isaiah or some other prominent figure of the time. This position fails to adequately come to grips with the following aspects of the prophecy: (1) The most obvious interpretation of the words the 'almah is with child is that the woman is in the state of being an 'almah at the time of the conception.[16] (2) No child named Immanuel is noted as having been born in the time of Isaiah. (3) the birth of a child to a woman who at the time of the prediction was unmarried and who shortly thereafter got married would hardly constitute a sign to a rationalist like Ahaz.

The argument is sometimes made that had Isaiah meant to prophesy a virgin birth he would have used the Hebrew word bethulah instead of 'almah. That bethulah can in some contexts refer to a virgin is indicated in Genesis 24:16 where Rebekah is called a bethulah. Yet if this word is so unambiguously clear in its meaning, why would the Genesis narrator add, and she had never known a man? If bethulah means virgin, then this redundant explanation is inexplicable. Furthermore, bethulah in Joel 1:8 clearly refers to a married woman. In the closely related Aramaic language, the equivalent of bethulah is used of a married woman.[17] Had Isaiah chosen to use the word bethulah it would be very difficult to determine whether he intended to prophesy the birth of a child to a married or to an unmarried woman. Although the term 'almah does not necessarily mean virgin (it can refer to an unmarried immoral woman), it is the only word which unambiguously refers to an unmarried woman. That this unmarried woman was a

---

14. So also the Septuagint.

15. Rawlinson, PC, I, 128.

16. The Hebrew does not employ a participle here which would be translated as a future, but rather a verbal adjective which describes a state of being.

17. Young, NIC, I, 288.

virgin is proved by the context. This the Jewish translators of the Septuagint were keen to observe, and so in this context they rendered '*almah* by the Greek *parthenos*, virgin.

4. The product of the birth is a male child. At first Isaiah saw the virgin pregnant. Now he announces concerning that virgin, *and she will bring forth a son.*

B. *The Naming of the Child.* The child's name was to be *Immanuel* (v. 14). The mother names the child. As a rule this was the mother's privilege,[18] although the name was formally bestowed by the father.[19] She calls him *Immanuel* (God with Us) for the child will indicate in a special way that God (El, the all-powerful One) was with his people. No one else in the Old Testament has this name. According to 8:8 Immanuel is the name of the one who owns the land of Canaan. From this it is clear that the child who is born is no mere man.

C. *The Infancy of the Child* (v. 15). Isaiah sees the child next in his infancy. He focuses attention on the child's diet: *butter and honey shall he eat.* A humble died indeed, and the mention of it seems to point to the lowly circumstances of the child's family. Such would be the infant's diet until the time *when he knows to reject the evil and choose the good.* A child learns to distinguish between what is physically helpful or harmful at an early age, perhaps as early as two. A very few years later a child begins to make moral decisions between good and evil. It is not clear in which sense Isaiah was using the terms good and evil. The basic thrust of the verse is unchanged in either case.

Who are the mother and child of Isaiah 7:14? Some have suggested that the '*almah* is a designation for Israel. Others have suggested that the '*almah* is Isaiah's wife. More common is the view that the '*almah* is the wife of Ahaz and the child Immanuel is Hezekiah. Matthew, however, interpreted the passage as a prediction of the virgin birth of Jesus of Nazareth (Matt. 1:22f.).

D. *The Time of the Child's Birth* (v. 16). Before the coming of Immanuel *the land shall be forsaken of its two kings.* The land here must be the land of Israel. The two kings would then be the king of Israel (Ephraim) and the king of Judah.[20] The verse threatens the end of the monarchy. "Messiah would replace once and for all the merely human kings of

---

18. Gen. 4:25; 16:11; 29:32-35; 30:6-13, 18-21, 24; 35:18 *et al.*

19. Gen. 16:15; II Sam. 12:24; Luke 1:62, 63.

20. It is unnatural to force *the land* to refer to north Israel and Syria. Isaiah thought in terms of two *houses* (dynasties) living in one land (8:14).

Ahaz's house and character."[21] The coming of Immanuel is presented in the context of threat to Ahaz and not promise.[22] This is made clear by the tone of the context from verse 13 through the end of the chapter.

---

21. Payne, EBP, p. 292.
22. Young has championed the view that v. 16 is a promise that the land of Judah would be forsaken by Rezin and Pekah within two or three years, i.e., the length of time it would take the future Messiah (or any child) to reach the age of discerning what is physically good and harmful.

Chapter Eighteen

SNAPSHOTS FROM ISAIAH (2)

Chapters 7-12 of Isaiah are known as the book of Immanuel. The birth of Immanuel is narrated in 7:14. He would be born of a virgin at some time subsequent to the demise of the Israelite monarchy. Three other personal Messianic prophecies are found in this section of Isaiah, and they are discussed in this chapter. The first (8:17-18) depicts the pre-incarnate Christ patiently waiting for the day of his manifestation. The second (9:1-7) stresses the deity of the Child who was to be born. In the third (11:1-16) the royal Child is portrayed ruling over his kingdom.

Prophecy No. 35

MESSIAH'S PATIENT WAIT

Isaiah 8:17-18

In chapter 8 Isaiah expressed his absolute confidence that the Syro-Ephraimitic attack on Judah would fail. That confidence is expressed in the name given to his youngest son, Maher-shalal-hash-baz (*plunder speeds, spoil hastens*). The king of Assyria, Tiglath-pileser III would crush both Damascus and Samaria and carry away the spoils of war (8:1-4). The Assyrian army would surge like a mighty flood from Syria and Israel on into Judah. The waters would reach to the neck of the nation—the capital Jerusalem—but Immanuel's land would survive (8:5-8). No nation or combination of nations could be successful in warfare against God's people (8:9-10).

In 8:11-16 Isaiah relates the grounds of his confidence in the future of the true Israel of God. God's power (*strength of hand*) had come upon the prophet to assure him of the truth of what had been revealed and to warn him not to follow the majority opinion (v. 11). Isaiah and others like him were preaching total dependence on God. The people regarded these prophets as enemy agents because they would not endorse royal policy of submitting to Assyria in order to gain a powerful ally against Syria and Ephraim (v. 12).

Isaiah speaks of two classes of people: (1) those who sanctify God, for whom God becomes a protective sanctuary; and (2) those who do not fear God, to whom he becomes a stumblingblock and a snare (vv. 13-15). Isaiah is to *bind up* God's revelation in the hearts of those who sanctified God. They are *my* disciples, i.e., God's disciples, those who are willing to be taught of God (v. 16).

Translation of Isaiah 8:17-18

(17) And I will wait for the LORD who has concealed his face from the house of Jacob, and I will look eagerly for him. (18) Behold, I and the children which the LORD has given me are for signs and wonders in Israel, from the LORD of Hosts who dwells in Mount Zion.

Discussion

In respect to the interpretation of this passage verse 16 is the crux: *Bind up the testimony, seal the law in my disciples.* Who is speaking here, and what is the nature of that which is spoken?

The prophet introduces the passage in v. 11 by noting that the utterance which follows, at least through verse 15, is the word Yahweh. What complicates the matter is that the imperatives in verses 12-15—four of them—are plural, and the two second person possessive suffixes in verse 13 are plural. The only conclusion is that the instructions in these verses, which were given to Isaiah individually, were intended for the entire believing community. Then in verse 16 the two imperatives are singular, and the possessive suffix is first person singular.

The following positions have been taken with respect to the interpretation of verse 16.

1. The speaker is still Yahweh, and he is directing Isaiah to implant God's revelation in the hearts of his (Yahweh's) disciples. "The disciples are those among the people who are truly enlightened in that they are taught of God Himself. . . . It may be that this activity was carried on through the prophet, so that in a certain sense these enlightened ones might also be called the disciples of Isaiah."[1] The passage to this point would then consist of general instructions to all the righteous (vv. 11-15) and specific instructions for Isaiah (v. 16). The ancient Jewish Targum interpreted the passage in this sense.

2. The speaker is Isaiah and he is offering a prayer on behalf of the faithful few who have been receiving instructions that they might remain steadfast (vv. 11-15). This explains the shift from plural to singular imperatives. *My disciples* would be those Isaiah gathered about him as his students. The problem with this view is that the most basic formal

---

1. Young, NIC, I, 313 n. 35.

characteristic of prayer is missing, viz., an address to God. Also there is the fact that the term *disciples* (*limmudim*) is used elsewhere in Isaiah of disciples of Yahweh, not Isaiah (Isa. 54:13).

3. The third view sees the Messiah as speaker in verse 16. He issues the command to Isaiah to keep on implanting the divine word in the hearts of my disciples, i.e., those who embraced the Messianic expectation.[2] This seems to have been the view of the author of Hebrews who quotes verses 17-18, at least, as being the words of Messiah.

The correct interpretation of Isaiah 8:17-18 can only be obtained by carefully studying Hebrews 2:10-18. The purpose of the Hebrew writer is to answer the Jewish objection that Jesus could not be the Messiah because of his suffering and humiliation. The sufferings and death of Christ were, in fact, an essential part of the scheme of redemption. In his suffering Messiah became one with those he died to save. Both the Sanctifier and the sanctified are sons of God, and therefore, he, Christ, is not ashamed to call his people *brethren* (Heb. 2:11). The writer of Hebrews argues that this relationship had been anticipated in the Messianic prophecies of the Old Testament. He cites in support of his case, Psalm 22:22 ("I will proclaim Your name to my brethren: in the midst of the assembly will I praise You"). This in turn is followed by the citation of Isaiah 8:17-18:[3] "And again, I will put my trust in him. And again, Behold! I and the children whom God hath given me."

The citation from Psalm 22:22 is used by the writer of Hebrews to prove that Messiah was (1) a brother; and (2) a fellow worshiper. The citation from Isaiah 8:17, 18 shows him also to be a fellow believer. During his incarnation the Son of God lived a life of faith. Later the Hebrew writer will refer to him as the author and perfecter of our faith (12:2).

The majority of commentators think that Isaiah 8:17, 18 contain the words of the *prophet*, not the Messiah. How then do they explain the usage of these words in Hebrews? The answer usually given is that the prophets were types of Messiah and therefore whatever they said about themselves is regarded by the New Testament as prophecy concerning Christ. Milligan summarizes this position in these words:

---

2. In a slight variation of this view, Young regards Yahweh as the speaker in v. 16, and Messiah as speaker in vv. 17-22. NIC, I, 315.

3. The Greek *ego esomai pepoithos ep auto* used in Heb. 2:13 is nowhere found exactly in this form in the Septuagint, but the phrase *pepoithos esomai ep auto* which is identical in meaning, occurs three times—II Sam. 23:3; Isa. 12:2 and 8:17. "The third place alone is from a strictly Messianic passage and is therefore certainly the one referred to." Delitzsch, CEH, I, 126.

As every divinely appointed high-priest under the Theocracy represented Christ in his priestly office; and as every king of the royal line of David represented him in his kingly office; so also did every true prophet represent him to some extent in his prophetical office. And whatever, therefore, was said of Isaiah and his sons, *as types*, has reference also to Christ and the children God has given him, *as antitypes*.[4]

The Hebrew writer seems to regard Messiah as the speaker in Isaiah 8:17, 18 and his position is supported by the following considerations:

1. This section of Isaiah is full of Messianic implication. The previous chapter described the birth of the virgin's son, Immanuel. In verses 6-8 Yahweh reveals that Immanuel's land (Judah) is to be overrun by the Assyrians. Because of Immanuel all pagan efforts to destroy the people of God would fail (vv. 9-10).

2. The speaker in 8:11-15 is Yahweh. No change of speaker is specifically indicated in 8:16—9:1. It is God who instructs Isaiah to implant within the hearts of his disciples the law and testimony (v. 16). It is Yahweh who waits on Yahweh during the period of Israel's gloom. In this Yahweh who waits on Yahweh the Hebrew writer sees the Messiah.

3. The Septuagint version, which was undoubtedly before the mind of the apostolic author, brings out the Messianic implications of the passage even more forcefully:

Then shall be made manifest those who seal up the law that one learn it not; and he will say, In God will I trust, who hath turned away his face from the house of Jacob, and will put my trust in him. Lo! I and the children whom God hath given me.[5]

It is easy to see the scribes and Pharisees in those who seal up the law, and the Messiah as the one who speaks.

4. First person speeches of Messiah are found elsewhere in Isaiah.

5. In the high priestly prayer of Jesus (John 17) the incarnate Word makes intercession in terms strikingly similar to those which Isaiah here employs.[6]

What are the implications of the fact that Messiah is the speaker in Isaiah 8:17, 18? In verse 17 Messiah announces that he will await expectantly while the face of God is hidden from his people.[7] The

---

4. Milligan, EH, p. 96.

5. Cited by Delitzsch, CEH, I, 127.

6. Young suggests the following comparison: Isa. 8:18 with John 17:6, 9, 11, 12, 24; 6:37, 39; 10:29; and Isa. 8:19 with Luke 17:23 and Matt. 24:4.

7. Bruce thinks this concept of God's hiding his face provides the Hebrew writer the link with Psalm 22 which he has quoted in the preceding line.

period of the hidden face would refer to all the calamities which befell Judah beginning with the Assyrian invasion of 701 B.C. and continuing until the time of Christ. The absence of divine revelation during the intertestamental period may also be in view here.

In verse 18 the word *behold* directs attention to the importance of the statement which follows. The speaker (Messiah) has children! The reference is not to the physical sons of Isaiah nor to the disciples of the prophet, but to the spiritual seed (Isa. 53:10) of Messiah. The description of Christians as *children* or *sons* of Christ is peculiar to the Hebrew letter among the New Testament writings.[8]

These precious souls (Messiah's children) have been *given* to him by the Father. Jesus echoed this thought when he prayed, "I have revealed you to those whom you gave me out of the world. They were yours. You gave them to me and they have obeyed your words" (John 17:6).

Messiah and his *children* serve as *signs*—tokens and pledges of those great eschatological events which bring down the curtain on the drama of redemption. At the same time, Messiah and his *children* are *wonders* —special manifestations of the power of God. The Messiah and his *children* as signs and wonders are *from the Lord who dwells in Mt. Zion.* It is ironic that most bitter opposition to the Messianic claims of Jesus and his apostles came from the Temple hierachy. Jesus could refer to the Temple on Zion as *my Father's house.*

Prophecy No. 36

THE WONDERFUL CHILD

Isaiah 9:1-7

The message of Isaiah in chapters 7-9 can be briefly summed up in the following thoughts: Judah has nothing to fear from the Syro-Ephraimitic invasion of 734 B.C.; her testing will come rather at the hands of the mighty Assyrian empire. The Assyrians will inaugurate a period of gloom and darkness for God's people which will only finally be dispelled by the dawn of the Messianic day of salvation.

Translation of Isaiah 9:1-7

(1) But gloom will be no more to her who had anguish. At first he made contemptible the land of Zebulun, the land of Naphtali; but in the

---

8. Bruce, NIC, p. 48.

future he will honor[9] the way of the sea, beyond Jordan, Galilee of the Gentiles. (2) The people who are walking in darkness shall see[9] a great light; as for the inhabitants of the land of death's shadow, a light shall shine[9] upon them. (3) You shall enlarge[9] the nation and increase[9] the joy;[10] they shall rejoice before you as the rejoicing in the harvest, as men rejoice when they divide the spoils. (4) For the yoke of his burden, and the staff of his shoulder, the rod of his oppressor, you have shattered as in the day of Midian. (5) For every boot used in battle and every garment rolled in blood shall be for burning, fuel for the fire. (6) For a child is born to us, a son is given to us, and the government shall be upon his shoulder. And he will be called Wonderful Counselor, Mighty God, Everlasting Father, Prince of Peace. (7) To the increase of his government and to peace there will be no end, upon the throne of David and over his kingdom to establish and to uphold it with justice and with righteousness, from that time and forever. The zeal of the LORD of hosts shall accomplish this.

Discussion

Two points are emphasized in this famous prophecy: (1) the promise of a new day (vv. 1-5); and (2) the reason for the new day (vv. 6-7). *A. The Promise of a New Day: A New Light* (vv. 1-5). The prophet speaks first in the section of the past and present suffering of the northern part of the Holy Land. The tribal regions of Zebulun and Naphtali and the area east of the Sea of Galilee had suffered oppression, first at the hands of the Arameans (I Kings 15:20), and later under the Assyrian tyrant Tiglath-pileser III (II Kings 15:29). That oppression is referred to as gloom (*muaph*), anguish (*mutsaq*) and contempt (*heqal*).

The distress and darkness for these regions will not last forever. A contrast is made in 9:1 between the *former time* (darkness, distress) and the *latter time*, the dawn of a glorious new day. The region near the Sea of Gennesaret was known as (1) Naphtali-Zebulun, (2) the way of the sea, and (3) the circuit (Galilee) of the nations. The latter title was derived from the influence of Gentiles in the region.[11] This district, so despised in the eyes of orthodox Jews, would be honored in the latter time, the Messianic age.

---

9. The verbs are prophetic perfects.
10. Some MSS read, *have not increased the joy.*
11. See I Kings 9:11; Josh. 20:7; 21:32; John 7:52.

The inhabitants of Galilee were walking in darkness—the outward darkness caused by foreign invasion, and the inward darkness of ignorance, misery and sin. To describe this darkness Isaiah uses the strongest possible word—*tsalmavet*—deep shadow.[12]

The death-like darkness could only be dispelled by a great light, the light of life. That light was yet future to Isaiah, but he describes it as having already appeared. The prophets often use the prophetic perfect to describe future events which are so vivid to their minds and so certain to occur that they can be described as having already occurred. Isaiah will later develop the theme of the Messianic light,[13] and Malachi will close the Old Testament revelation with assurance the Sun of Righteousness would arise (Mal. 4:2).

The light first penetrated the darkness of the world in Galilee of the Gentiles. For thirty years he lived in Nazareth, in Zebulun. There he made a great Messianic claim (Luke 4:16-21). At Cana of Galilee he performed his first miracle (John 2:11; 4:54). Capernaum "upon the sea coast, in the borders of Zebulun and Naphtali" became his head-quarters throughout his great Galilean ministry (Matt. 4:13-17).

Isaiah paints a beautiful picture of all that God's people would experience as a result of the rise of the Messianic light. He mentions four specific elements of blessing:

1. The nation will be multiplied (v. 3). This promise would be especially meaningful to the people of Isaiah's day. Hundreds if not thousands of citizens of north Israel had been carried away into captivity by Tiglath-pileser III (745-727 B.C.). In the new day anticipated by the prophet Gentiles would be incorporated into the true Israel of God. Thus was fulfilled the great nation promise made to Abraham (Gen. 12:2).

2. The joy of the nation would then be increased (v. 3).[14] The salvation of the lost brings greatest joy to the redeemed. The grafting of elect from among the Gentiles into the Olive tree of true Israel was a cardinal objective of God's scheme of redemption (Rom. 11:11-24). As in a day of harvest or of military victory, men would enjoy God as never before in the Messianic age.

3. The nation will be delivered from the oppressor[15] (v. 4). The

---

12. This word is used in Ps. 23 where it is translated *shadow of death* in the KJV.
13. Isa. 42:6; 49:6; 60:1-3.
14. The Masoretic text reads: *You have not increased.* Most commentators follow the Septuagint, Syriac and Targum in rendering this as a positive statement. See discussion in Young, NIC, I, 326.
15. Lit., his taskmaster. The same word is used of the Egyptian taskmasters in Exod. 5:6.

word *for* (*ki*) with which verse 4 begins explains the reason for the great joy of the preceding verse. Like a beast of burden God's people had to bear a burdensome yoke. The oppressors, the Assyrians, and later the Chaldeans, Persians, Greeks and Romans, administered the rod or staff to the shoulder (i.e., side or flank) of the troubled beast. The ultimate cause of the suffering of God's people, of course, was sin; the ultimate oppressor was Satan. The deliverance anticipated here is not merely the physical removal of some hostile power, but the ultimate defeat of the archenemy of God's people, Satan. Rawlinson captures the intent of the prophet in these words:

> The coming of the Messiah sets the Israelites free, removes the yoke from off their neck, breaks the rod wherewith their shoulders were beaten, delivers them from bondage into the 'glorious liberty of the children of God.' Not, however, in an earthly sense, since the Messiah's kingdom was not of this world. The 'yoke' is that of sin, the 'oppressor' is that prince of darkness, who had well-nigh brought all mankind under his dominion when Christ came.[16]

The mighty victory over the oppressor is described as *breaking* the *rod* and *staff*. The enemy will be defeated in a mighty confrontation, like that crushing defeat inflicted by the Lord upon Midian through the agency of Gideon. Unaided by God, the judge and his three hundred warriors would have been massacred by the mighty Midianites. The point is that the great deliverance anticipated here would be wrought by the power of God over a foe too powerful for human might. The text will shortly link this victory to the birth of a child.

4. The age of the Messiah would be characterized by complete peace (v. 5). The word *for* (*ki*) indicates a second reason for the great rejoicing of verse 3. All the paraphernalia of war will be burned because it will no longer be needed. Every boot which soldiers may have worn into battle will be burned. Such also would be the fate of the battle garb which had been rolled in the blood of the enemy. Weapons, as well, will be destroyed in the Messianic age (Isa. 2:4).

B. *The Reason for the New Day: A New Leader* (vv. 6-7). God's people would have a joyous future (v. 3). Their numbers would be greatly increased (v. 3). They would experience a great deliverance (v. 4) and a wondrous time of peace (v. 5). All of this would be brought about through the birth of a very special child. In verses 6-7 it is important

---

16. Rawlinson, PC, I, 166.

to note concerning this new leader (1) his identity, (2) his dignity, (3) his superiority, (4) his authority, and (5) his credibility.

1. The identity of the new leader. In the Hebrew the noun *child* stands first in verse 6. He is the focal point of consideration. In view of the threatened invasion by the mighty Assyrian army it must have seemed strange indeed to speak of Israel's Deliverer as a child.

Isaiah speaks of the child's birth as though it had already occurred. The prophet, however, is certainly not referring to a past occurrence. No birth prior to Isaiah's time accomplished what is attributed to this birth. The interpreter is forced to the conclusion that the prophet is again employing the prophetic perfect in which future events are so certain and so vivid to the mind of the seer that he can describe them as having already occurred.

The expression *a child is born* stresses the human origins of Messiah. The sex of the child is indicated by the gender of the noun (*yeled*— masculine), and by the word *son* in the parallel line.

Of what significance is the clause, *a son is given*? He would be a son of David for sure, for the reins of government would be his. Is more involved? Perhaps. As early as the time of David the Messiah was looked upon, not only as the son of David, but also as the Son of God (Ps. 2:7b).[17] It is John 3:16 which gives the key to interpreting the clause, *a son is given*. This clause points to his divine origins. He was a unique Son, *the* Son of God.

Those who are the chief beneficiaries of the child's birth are grouped with the prophet in the words *to* or *for us* (*lanu*). Messiah would be *for* us as well as *with* us (Isa. 7:14). Isaiah realized that he stood in need of the blessings of this child as much as any man to whom he preached.

2. The dignity of the new leader (v. 6). *The government*[18] *shall be upon his shoulder.* "Government was regarded as a burden, to be borne on the back or shoulders, and was sometimes symbolized by a key laid upon the shoulder."[19] Earlier Isaiah had indicated that child rulers would be a divine curse against the nation (3:4). But this Child would be a king *par excellence*. All the earth is the rightful domain of this Child. His subjects are those who have responded to his grace

---

17. The title *Mighty God* used here also forges a link to Ps. 2.

18. The word *misrah* occurs only here and in verse 7. It is probably to be connected with *sar*, prince. Rawlinson, PC, I, 166.

19. Ibid. Cf. Isa. 22:22.

and who have willingly submitted themselves to his authority. His kingdom knows no bounds.

3. The superiority of the Child is indicated by the titles which are conferred upon him by those who know him.[20] Isaiah does not mean that Messiah would actually be addressed by these titles, but rather that he would be worthy of them. Names in Old Testament times were designated to be accurate descriptions of a person's character or nature.

The Child will be called Wonderful Counselor or Wonder of a Counselor. The root of the word wonder (*pele'*) is used in Psalm 78:12 to describe the mighty miracles which God performed at the time of the Exodus. In Judges 13:18 the Angel of the Lord who appeared to Manoah stated that his name was wonderful, i.e., incomprehensible to man. The Hebrew term used by Isaiah does not merely indicate that the Child is wonderful. He is that, and much more. He is a Wonder Child, God's greatest miracle, incarnate deity.

The aspect of the wonder of the child particularly in view here is his wisdom. He is a Counselor. To effectively manage that kingdom over which he rules would require superhuman wisdom. Only the Wonder Child possesses such wisdom, for the Spirit of wisdom rests upon him (Isa. 11:2). In this Ruler will be all the treasures of wisdom and knowledge (Col. 2:3).

The Child will be called Mighty God. Clearly this description points to the deity of the future Child. The term *'el* (God) is used by Isaiah only of the Supreme Being, Yahweh.[21] The second word in this second pair, *gibbor*, means hero, or mighty one. This pair of names stresses the great power of Messiah.[22]

The Child will be called Father of Eternity. Yahweh was a father to his people in Old Testament times (Isa. 63:16; Ps. 103:13). As Father, God protected and provided for his people. Throughout eternity past and future he will be a Father to his people. This Child is a Son; he is also the Eternal Father. Later the One spoken of in this prophecy would say, "I and my Father are one" (John 10:30).

The Child will be called Prince of Peace. The prophecy of Isaiah 9 has its historical setting in a period of war and tumult. The fourth title is thus the climax of the prophet's thought. The Child will be a prince and he will rule over an ever-expanding kingdom. But this expansion

---

20. It is better to take the verb *is called* impersonally than to take God as subject.

21. Isa. 10:20-21; 31:3. "Whereas the word *'elohim* in the Old Testament may sometimes apply to beings lesser than God, such is not the case with *'el*. This designation is reserved for the true God and for Him alone." Young, NIC, I, 337.

22. In Isa. 11:2 the thought of strength or power also follows that of counsel.

will not be accomplished by military might. This ruler's reign will be characterized by peace. This genuine peace is made possible by the removal of sin, the root cause of human conflict. To the extent that the sovereignty of this Ruler has been humbly acknowledged there is peace on earth.

4. The authority of the new leader (v. 7). Messiah's government will continually increase. As men and women obey the Gospel and own him as Lord the kingdom of Christ grows. The Book of Acts describes the initial surge of the soldiers of the cross in which the whole Roman Empire was turned upside down (Acts 17:6). New beachheads of evangelism are being established every year.

Messiah's government will be perpetual. Messiah will have no successors. Every conceivable form of human government has been tried, each of them subject to overthrow by militants or the electorate. Men keep struggling to find a leader or political system which will be able to cope with the enormously complex problems of the present age. Messiah's government will endure because he alone can meet the needs of every person. In his interpretation of the great image in the dream of Nebuchadnezzar, Daniel emphasized the eternality of Messiah's kingdom in these words: "In the days of these kings shall the God of heaven set up a kingdom which shall never be destroyed" (Dan. 2:44). At the birth of Christ an angel echoed the same thought:

> He will be great and will be called the Son of the Highest. The Lord God will give him the throne of his father David, and he shall reign over the house of Jacob forever; his kingdom will never end (Luke 1:32, 33).

Messiah's government will bring an increase to peace wherever it extends. Peace here involves the total well-being and prosperity of each individual citizen.

Messiah's government will be legitimate. He will sit upon the throne of David. He is no usurper or upstart. The Child whose birth here is foretold is from the family of David. He was the heir to the throne, the fulfillment of the prophecies which promised an eternal throne to David (II Sam. 7:16). Young states:

> He who sits upon this throne . . . is a legitimate descendant of David. It had earlier been promised that David's throne would endure forever, and hence the description of Messiah's reign is identified with that of David. The identification of the two reigns is not merely due to an external resemblance or even to a typical relation, but to the fact that

Messiah's reign was really a continuation or restoration of David's kingdom. David was a temporary and temporal king; the Messiah an eternal King. Both ruled over the same kingdom.[23]

Messiah's government will be fair and just. Oppression and injustice have no place in the establishment or expansion of his government. This explains why this kingdom endures into eternity. The kingdom reflects the qualities of the King. He is just and righteous, and because this is so, men will subject themselves to his justice. Upon his subjects he bestows as a free gift the righteousness—right relationship with the king.

5. The credibility of the coming ruler (v. 7). These tremendous promises of an eternal kingdom ruled by a scion of the house of David were made at a time when the throne of David was in jeopardy. The Assyrians threatened the very existence of the tiny kingdom of Judah. Was Isaiah an unrealistic visionary? No, he was a man of faith. *The zeal of Yahweh of hosts* would bring to fulfillment every promise here recorded. He is determined to bring to fruition the kingdom which was part of his plan before the foundation of the earth. He deeply loves the remnant of his people and he has a deep desire to protect them.

Prophecy No. 37

THE MINISTRY OF MESSIAH

Isaiah 11:1-16

In chapter 10 Isaiah announced the eventual overthrow of the great Assyrian empire. In its long career of conquest Assyria had become proud and boastful (10:5-14). God now intends to bring down the pride of Assyria by a sudden destruction (10:15-19). The downfall of that empire would be followed at some unspecified time by the return of the remnant of Israel to God (10:20-23). In the more immediate future God will engineer a stunning setback to the Assyrians when they swoop down against Jerusalem. Isaiah likens the downfall of the invader to the felling of a mighty forest (10:24-34).

Translation of Isaiah 11:1-5

(1) And a shoot shall come forth from the stump of Jesse, and a sprout from his roots will bear fruit. (2) And the spirit of the LORD

---

23. Young, NIC, I, 343.

shall rest upon him, the spirit of wisdom and perception, the spirit of counsel and might, the spirit of knowledge and the fear of the LORD. (3) His delight shall be in the fear of the LORD. He will not judge by what he sees with his eyes, nor will he decide by what he hears with his ears. (4) But he shall judge the poor with righteousness, and he will decide with uprightness for the humble of the land. He will smite the land with the rod of his mouth, and with the breath of his lips he will slay the wicked. (5) And righteousness shall be the girdle of his loins, and faithfulness the girdle of his waist.

Discussion

This prophecy focuses on (1) the announcement (v. 1), (2) the attributes (v. 2), (3) the administration (vv. 3-5), and (4) the attractiveness (vv. 6-10) of the coming Ruler.

A. *The Announcement of the Coming Ruler* (v. 1). Like the Assyrian forest the stately tree of the Davidic dynasty would also be cut down. Nothing but a stump would remain. So lowly would that stump become that Isaiah does not attach to it the beloved name of David. It is called the stump of Jesse.[24] David's house would be reduced to this condition because of its apostasy.

Just an old stump! But there was yet life in that stump. For ages that stump went unnoticed, virtually hidden from view. The Assyrian empire would never revive; but from the stump of Jesse a shoot would sprout, tender yet vigorous, seemingly weak, yet full of life. Young captures the.irony of the verse in its historical context: "The mighty Assyrian power was about ready to destroy the Davidic kingdom, but actually the Assyrian power would perish, and the Davidic kingdom would arise again."[25]

Who is this future ruler of the house of David? Some Jewish commentators have suggested that Hezekiah is intended, and others Zerubbabel. But the passage could not refer to Hezekiah for he had already been born, and the descriptions here given are not appropriate to Zerubbabel. The ancient Jewish Targum applied the passage to Messiah and in this interpretation is no doubt correct. Matthew apparently had a passage like this in mind when he wrote concerning Jesus: "And he came and dwelt in a city called Nazareth that it might

---

24. The *stump of Jesse* must mean the house of David, for there is only one Jesse in Scripture, David's father.

25. Young, NIC, I, 379 n. 1.

be fulfilled which was spoken by the prophets. He shall be called a Nazarene" (Matt. 2:23). The name Nazarene is related to the Hebrew word *netser*, shoot or twig.

The shoot or twig which would emerge from the stump of Jesse would *bear fruit*. The Davidic dynasty would not continue as a fallen tree, but would truly prosper. The future prosperity of this scion of the house of David is of a spiritual nature, as the rest of the chapter indicates. The blessings about to be described come upon Israel because this Ruler comes from the stump of Jesse.

B. *The Attributes of the Coming Ruler* (v. 2). The Messiah would be abundantly endowed for his mission in this world. The Spirit of Yahweh would rest on him. Isaiah is not speaking of the human spirit, or the spirit of prophecy but the Spirit who is God, and who is the active but unseen presence of God in this world. He is not referring to some temporary endowment of Messiah, but to the abiding presence of the Spirit in his life. The prophet will later return to this theme (Isa. 61:1). The fourth evangelist reports what was said of Jesus and the Spirit in the words: "Upon whom you shall see the Spirit descending, and remaining on him, the same is he who will baptize with the Holy Spirit. And I saw and bare record that this is the Son of God" (John 1:33b-34).[26]

The resting of the Spirit on this Son of David is the basic attribute which qualifies him for his Messianic ministry. The Spirit brings with him, and is the source of, other gifts which are part of Messiah's equipment. Others may have possessed some of these charismatic gifts singly, or in various combinations;[27] but only Messiah possessed all of them. The gifts are grouped in three pairs.

1. Intellectual attributes: wisdom and perception. *Wisdom* suggests the ability to make the right decision in any contingency which might arise. *Perception* is the ability to correctly appraise situations, to see beneath the surface to the reality of things. Jesus as a youth increased in wisdom (Luke 2:52). He also knew what was in the heart of man (John 2:25).

2. Administrative attributes: counsel and might. He has no need of counsellors or wise men who are found in abundance near wise rulers. He is able to formulate long-range plans, and to bring those

---

26. The Spirit is also active in the life of Christ in Matt. 3:16; Luke 2:40; 4:1, 14, 18; John 3:34.

27. The Spirit in the Old Testament equipped craftsmen (Exod. 31:3; 35:31), warriors (Judg. 6:34; 11:29) and prophets (Num. 11:25ff.).

plans to fruition. All authority in heaven and earth has been given unto him (Matt. 28:18).

3. Spiritual attributes: knowledge and the fear of the Lord. It is not knowledge in the abstract, but knowledge of God. The reference is to cognitive as well as experiential knowledge. Jesus declared, "No man knows the Son, but the Father; neither knows any man the Father, save the Son, and he to whom the Son will reveal him" (Matt. 11:27).

The fear of the Lord is the foundation of knowledge (Prov. 1:7), and the heart of Biblical religion. It involves a right understanding of the nature of God and a reverent response to the demands of the deity upon one's life. The fear of the Lord appears in worship as reverential awe, and in everyday life as humble obedience.

C. *The Administration of the Coming Ruler* (vv. 3-5). Four specific functions of the shoot of Jesse are suggested in verses 3-5.

1. He delights in the manifestation of true piety (v. 3). This future Davidic king looks with favor upon those who share his devotion to God. Isaiah uses the bold imagery of the sense of smell. Literally the text reads, *and his smelling with delight will be in the sphere of the fear of the Lord.* The fear of the Lord is like a sweet-smelling sacrifice to him.

2. He judges with righteousness and equity (vv. 3b-4). The primary function of any ruler is to insure justice. Perfect justice is impossible for mere mortals for it is always based upon imperfect knowledge. But the judgment administered by the Ruler envisioned here will not be based on outward appearance or testimony. This Ruler would be omniscient. Jesus knew men's thoughts (Matt. 9:4), and therefore did not need to judge according to the appearance (John 7:24).

The Ruler champions the cause of the poor and the oppressed. Those who find no advocate among the rulers of this world will find perfect equity in his administration. No bribe or coercion by the rich and powerful would hinder the righteous execution of the Ruler's judgment.

3. He shows forth wrath against the wicked (v. 4b). The Davidic Ruler has the power to deal with the incorrigible. Without such power there could be no true justice. His word is the rod which comes down upon the wicked earth.[28] The breath of his lips destroys all opposition. Here is a Ruler who has the power to deal with all who oppose his righteous reign (cf. II Thess. 2:8b).

---

28. *Earth* and *wicked* are parallel. Isaiah views the earth as itself wicked. Cf. Mal. 4:6; Matt. 10:34.

4. He is prepared to deal with any and all opposition (v. 5). There can be no doubt that he will be successful in the administration of his kingdom. He will be able to destroy the wicked and deliver the poor. The Ruler anticipates opposition and therefore girds himself as a warrior.[29]

The Ruler faces his foes girded with righteousness and faithfulness. These two qualities are attributed to God in his judgment activity (Ps. 119:75). Jeremiah speaks of the coming Messiah as being righteous and faithful (Jer. 23:5, 6; 33:15, 16). John joins these two concepts when he describes the return of Christ: "And I saw heaven opened, and behold a white horse: and he that sat upon him was called Faithful and True, and in righteousness he judges and makes war" (Rev. 19:11).[30]

D. *The Attractiveness of the Coming Ruler* (vv. 6-10). Five aspects of the kingdom of the coming Ruler make him attractive to the masses.

1. His will be a peaceful kingdom. Messiah's kingdom differs from all worldly kingdoms. Isaiah announces a day when all hostility between men, between animals, and between men and animals will disappear (vv. 6-8). He paints a verbal picture of Messianic kingdom peace in terms of a complete transformation of nature. Wolf, leopard, lion and bear will submit to the control of a child. Deadly serpents will be harmless. What a beautiful way to depict the moral transformation of the worst of the wicked. The focus of these verses is on God's *holy mountain*, God's kingdom. In God's kingdom men will not defraud, cheat and steal from one another. Rawlinson comments: "Primarily, no doubt, the passage is figurative, and points to harmony among men, who, in Messiah's kingdom, shall no longer prey on one another."[31]

This glorious golden age of peace is attributed to the one who is the root of Jesse.[32] Messiah is the restorer of the Davidic house (Rom. 15:12; Rev. 22:16). The root will not remain inconspicuous in the subsoil. It will grow to a height at which it can become an *ensign*[33] *of the peoples*, i.e., a standard around which all peoples can rally.

---

29. In ancient times disputes were settled in belt wrestling contests, where the adversary who could wrest the belt from his opponent was declared to be the winner. Putting on the belt or girdle came to be a figure for preparing for struggle.

30. Christ is depicted as the righteous Judge in John 5:22; Acts 17:31. He is said to be faithful in Heb. 2:17 and Rev. 1:5.

31. Rawlinson, PC, I, 203.

32. The root of Jesse in v. 10 is equivalent to the shoot and branch of v. 1.

33. A standard erected for the purpose of communication (Jer. 50:2), gathering troops (Isa. 18:3) or assembling fugitives (Jer. 4:6).

2. His is a universal kingdom. The Gentiles will be attracted to this ensign. They are attracted to him apparently because of his stability, and because he alone is the source of true knowledge of Yahweh. Jesus talked about a lifting up which would attract all men (John 3:14; 12:32). The ground at the foot of the cross is level. All racial, national, and social distinctions are meaningless.

3. His is a glorious kingdom. Messiah's place of rest is *glory*. The resting place is where he has settled down to dwell and rule. The reference is to the New Testament Temple in which Christ dwells, i.e., his kingdom or church (Matt. 28:20). The Old Testament Temple had a measure of glory (I Kings 8:11); but the Temple built by Messiah was far more glorious (Hag. 2:7, 9; Isa. 4:5). Christ is the glory of his church now and he will be the glory of the age to come (Isa. 65:17; Rev. 21:22). It is this manifestation of heavenly glory which attracts the Gentiles to the Shoot of Jesse.[34]

4. His will be a united kingdom. Israel as well as Gentiles will rally to the Messianic standard. The citizens of Israel and Judah would be dispersed to the four corners of the earth. But those who were faithful would be gathered anew into one body just as God gathered his people in Egypt under the leadership of Moses (vv. 11, 12). Rawlinson feels that the "first fulfillment" of the prophecy was the return of the Jews from captivity; a "secondary fulfillment" was the gathering of so many Jews from all quarters into the church of Christ (Acts 2:9-41). He allows that there may be "ultimately a further fulfillment in a final gathering together of Israel into their own land."[35] But there is nothing in this context that requires a gathering of Israelites and Jews to Canaan. The passage speaks of the formation of the new Israel of God, and the effects of evangelization on the diaspora.[36] The tribal jealousy which marred old Israel would be a thing of the past (v. 13).[37]

5. His is a victorious kingdom. The united people of God would be able to win great victories in the name of King Messiah. The Philistines,

---

34. Other passages speaking of the Messianic glory: Isa. 55:5; 60:19; Zech. 12:7.

35. Rawlinson, PC, I, 204.

36. *Outcasts* (masculine) of Israel and *dispersed* (feminine) of Judah. "He shall gather together the outcasts and dispersed of both Israel and Judah, both male and female." Rawlinson. PC. I. 205.

37. Young (NIC, I, 397): "The prophets delight to picture as one of the blessings of the Messianic age the healing of the breach between the northern and southern kingdoms."

Edom, Moab and Ammon had all been implacable foes of Old Testament Israel. They symbolize in verse 14 the enemies of Christ and his church. Isaiah employs military metaphors to describe the missionary expansion of the Christian church. No subject of the Prince of Peace would ever attempt to advance his kingdom by use of a blade of steel.

God will remove all obstacles from before his people. The Euphrates River and the tongue of the Egyptian Sea were ancient barriers to the freedom of God's people. God will succeed in bringing about a new Exodus from the world's bondage. He will bring his people safely into the Promised Land (v. 15). Those who survive the Assyrian captivity will find the way out of spiritual bondage by means of the One who is the way, the truth and the life (v. 16).[38] He is the highway which leads to the heavenly kingdom, the New Testament Canaan.

---

38. Other Isaianic passages depicting the deliverance: Isa. 42:16a; 43:19b; 48:21; 49:11.

Chapter Nineteen

SNAPSHOTS FROM ISAIAH (3)

Chapters 13-39 of the Book of Isaiah contain five blocks of material which are sometimes called (1) The Book of Burdens (13-23). (2) The First Book of General Judgment (24-27), (3) The Book of Woes (28-33), (4) The Second Book of General Judgment (34-35), and (5) The Book of Hezekiah (36-39). Five personal Messianic prophecies are found in these chapters. The first is in The Book of Burdens (16:5), the second in The First Book of General Judgment (28:16), and the last three in The Book of Woes (30:19-26; 33:1-2; 33:17).

Prophecy No. 38

JERUSALEM'S IDEAL KING

Isaiah 16:5

The sixth Messianic prophecy in Isaiah is located in the third major division of the book, the Book of Burdens. This section contains judgment oracles against eleven nations ranging from Elam and Media in the east to Egypt and Ethiopia in the southwest. Promises of restoration for Israel and conversion of foreign peoples (e.g., 18:7) are found in this section. One prophecy which may be characterized as personal Messianic is found in the lengthy oracle against Moab.

The Moabites were descendants of Lot and his eldest daughter (Gen. 19:31-37). Their territory was east of the Dead Sea. Under David this region had been conquered and its inhabitants put to forced labor. In the middle of the ninth century B.C. King Mesha[1] of Moab rebelled against Israel. The kings of Israel and Judah tried to suppress this rebellion, but apparently failed (II Kings 3).

Translation of Isaiah 16:1-5

(1) Send a lamb to the ruler of the earth from Sela toward the wilderness unto the mountain of the daughter of Zion. (2) And it shall become like a wandering bird, a nest cast forth shall be the daughters of Moab at the fords of the Arnon. (3) Give counsel, execute justice make your shadow like the night in the midst of noon, hide the outcasts, do not betray the wanderer. (4) Let my outcasts dwell in you, O Moab![2] Be a

---

1. A stele erected by Mesha was discovered in Dibon in 1868. The text is found in Pritchard, ANET, pp. 320-321.

2. Many authorities prefer the rendering of the LXX and Syriac which render this as an appeal by the outcasts of Moab to the inhabitants of Judah.

hiding place for him from the face of the spoiler; for the extortioner has come to an end, violence has ceased, tramplers are consumed out of the land. (5) And a throne shall be established in covenant faithfulness, and one shall sit upon it in truth in the tent of David judging and seeking justice, and hastening righteousness.

Discussion

Isaiah begins by describing a devastating attack against Moab. City after city falls, and the tenderhearted prophet sympathizes with the suffering population of that nation (ch. 15). The leaders of Moab conclude that their only salvation is found in the Davidic dynasty ruling from Zion. The Son of David now rules the earth, and the defeated Moabites recognize him as their king. They send a lamb as a sign of tribute to him. The lamb is sent from Sela (Petra) in Edom where the Moabites have fled for refuge. The ambassadors travel through the wilderness around the southern tip of the Dead Sea to avoid the enemy which now controls the entire eastern side of the Sea (v. 1).

The population of Moab is likened to a bird whose nest has been disturbed. At the Arnon, the border of Moab, the women of Moab will seek refuge, but they will not find it (v. 2).

In verse 3 the Moabites appeal to Judah's king for help. They seek his counsel, for Zion's king is the wonderful counselor (Isa. 9:6). They seek his protective power. If there is to be deliverance Moab must be covered with the shadow of Zion's king. That shadow hides from view, covers, and prevents the enemy from seeing.

Will there be safety for Moab in the shadow of Zion's king? That depends on how the Moabites treat the outcasts of Judah during the present crisis. Four nouns—*spoiler, extortioner, violence, tramplers*—are used to describe the Assyrian adversaries. But that power and all like it would come to an end and would be superseded by a kingdom that is not of this world (v. 4). Moab's faith in this great future will be indicated by the way they treat the worshipers of Yahweh in the present crisis. Isaiah appeals to Moab to allow the outcasts of Judah to take temporary refuge in their land.

The throne of David will survive the ravishing power of Assyria. Isaiah knows not how much time must elapse before that day, but he knows the day will come. The establishment of the throne of David which had tottered throughout the Assyrian crisis would be an act of God's mercy towards his people (cf. II Sam. 7:15). Earthly kingdoms thrive on military might and political sagacity. But the Davidic kingdom is ordered by heaven.

The occupant of that throne will rule from David's *tent*. Why a tent? The words imply that the glorious palaces associated with the Davidic dynasty will be no more. The Davidic dynasty will have a humble rebirth after all the earthly trappings were stripped away. The idea here is very similar to what was observed in Isaiah 11:1.

He who will occupy that throne will reign in truth. His primary role of judging he will carry out with equity and prompt implementation of righteousness. In regard to the Messianic import of this passage Young writes:

> The throne is that of David upon which Christ sits. Insofar, however, as previous kings, such as Hezekiah, could be said to fulfill the terms of this prediction, they may be considered as forerunners and types of Christ.[3]

Prophecy No. 39

THE FOUNDATION STONE

Isaiah 28:16

The fifth main division of the Book of Isaiah begins in chapter 28. This section is sometimes called the Book of Woes because it consists in the main of "woe" oracles directed against Israel and Judah. After a brief warning address to Samaria (28:1-4), Isaiah accuses Judah of following the example of Samaria (28:5-6). Two great sins are singled out for exposure: drunkenness and mockery of God's true prophets (28:7-10). The worldly wise leaders of Judah found Isaiah's message to be childish and unrefined. God would now speak to them, not by his prophet, but by the Assyrian conqueror (28:11-13).

Judah's leaders were negotiating secret security pacts with foreign powers which they believed would save their country from Assyrian exploitation. Isaiah warns them that their refuge (probably Egypt) would prove to be a refuge of lies. The *overflowing scourge* (Assyria) would sweep through Judah destroying all before it. Against this background of the nation's vain and misplaced confidence Isaiah utters one of the grandest Messianic prophecies in his book.[4]

---

3. Young, NIC, I, 464.
4. Young, NIC, II, 284.

Translation of Isaiah 28:16

Therefore thus says the Lord GOD: Behold! I lay for a foundation in Zion a stone, a tested stone, a precious cornerstone, a sure foundation; the one who believes shall not be in haste.

Discussion

The prophecy is introduced with *therefore*. God must act in the interest of his eternal plan for his people. They have chosen to search for security in man-made schemes. Over against their feeble and futile efforts God would intervene decisively in the history of his people.

It is the Lord, *'adhonay*, the Sovereign One who speaks here. He has the power and authority to initiate any course of action which he may deem beneficial for his people.

The prophecy, like the one in 7:14, is introduced by *behold!* This interjection is designed to underscore the wondrous grace and stupendous power which would be involved in the execution of the promise contained here. In Hebrew the word has a suffix and so literally reads, *Behold, I*.[5] Attention is thus focused immediately and forcefully on God.

The tense of the verb is perfect. The stone already had been laid at the time the prophet is writing. The plan of God for the salvation of his people was formulated before the foundation of the earth. What God decreed then was as good as accomplished.

It is a *stone* which God lays as a foundation for the lives of his people. The stone figure has implications of deity. In Genesis 49:24 the "Mighty One of Jacob" is said to be "the stone of Israel." Moses referred to God as Rock (Deut. 32:4). In Isaiah 8:14, 15 both terms, rock and stone, are used of God. The Stone here is God, yet is distinct from God, for he is the One who lays that Stone in Zion. For this reason the Stone was identified by the apostles as being the Messiah (I Peter 2:6f.).

Isaiah makes several statements about the Stone which serve to sharpen the focus of this metaphor.

1. It is a tested stone or a stone of testing. The basic idea of the word *bochan* is that of a stone which has been tested and is approved for use. That stone can be trusted, and because it is reliable, it can be a touchstone for testing men. Some would reject that stone (Ps. 118:22),

---

5. The suffix on the interjection is first person while the verb is third person perfect. Such a change of person is not uncommon in the prophetic books. The thrust of the construction may be expressed as follows: Behold! I am he who has founded.

and some would stumble over it (I Peter 2:8); but to others that stone would become foundational.

2. It is a cornerstone, that special stone which bound together two sides of a building. The conerstone was the most important stone of an edifice, the one which supported the entire building.

3. It is a corner of preciousness or a precious cornerstone. Valuable stones were used in foundations in antiquity (I Kings 5:17; 7:9-11). It would cost God a great deal to place this stone in Zion.

4. It constitutes a firm or fixed foundation.[6] That stone is absolutely unshakable. It cannot be moved. Men may from time to time tremble on the stone, but it will not tremble under them.

God required of the Old Testament saints faith in the stone that he laid in Zion. To *believe* in this context means to accept the stone—the Messiah—as truly laid by God. When one confesses that Jesus is the Christ he is announcing his intention of building his life upon this stone.

Those who build upon the stone will not *make haste*. The rock will not fail. Isaiah is stressing the calmness of the believer in times of crisis. The Septuagint captured the spirit of the passage by rendering *will not be ashamed*. The New Testament has adopted this interpretative reading. *Make haste . . . be ashamed* are closely related. One who is ashamed of a former object of trust hastens away when the pressure mounts.

Prophecy No. 40

THE TEACHER *PAR EXCELLENCE*

Isaiah 30:19-26

In the Book of Woes (Isa. 28-33) the thought of impending disaster is most prominent. Samaria is ripe for judgment (ch. 28), and so is Judah (29:1-4). Blindness and hardness of heart has befallen them (29:9-14). Nonetheless, Judah will experience a wondrous deliverance from the Assyrian invasion (29:5-8), and beyond that, an even more wondrous transformation (29:17-24). In chapter 30 Isaiah stresses the folly of looking to Egypt for aid against Assyria (30:1-8). Reliance is but another manifestation of their stubborn rebellion against God (30:9-11). Such rebellion must be punished (30:12-14). National salvation comes through complete trust in God (30:15). Since Judah has rejected this divine formula for national salvation, God must bring judgment upon them (30:16-18).

---

6. Lit., a founded foundation.

Translation of Isaiah 30:19-26

(19) For a people in Zion shall dwell, (even) in Jerusalem. You shall weep no more. He will be very gracious to you at the sound of your cry. When he hears it, he will answer you. (20) Although the Lord gives to you bread which is affliction and water which is oppression, yet your Teacher will not be hidden any longer; but your eyes shall see your Teacher. (21) And your ears shall hear a word from behind you saying, This is the way; walk in it, when you turn to the right or to the left. (22) Then you shall defile the overlay of your silver images, the exterior of your molten images of gold. You shall cast them away like a menstruous cloth. You will say unto it, Get out! (23) And he will send you rain for your seed which you have sown in the ground, and bread of the increase of the ground, and it shall be fat and plenteous. Your cattle shall graze in that day in broad pastures. (24) The oxen and donkeys which work the ground shall eat salted fodder which has been winnowed with shovel and fork. (25) And upon every high mountain and upon every lofty hill there shall be rivers, streams of water in the day of great slaughter when towers fall. (26) The light of the moon shall be as the light of the sun, and the light of the sun shall be seven times brighter like the light of seven days in the day when the LORD binds up the fracture of his people, and shall heal the wound which he inflicted.

Discussion

In verse 19 Isaiah looks beyond the Assyrian judgment which he has threatened in verses 16-18. The remnant dwells in Zion, God's sacred city. Ultimately those who dwell in Zion shall experience God's true salvation. The gracious God of Judah will listen for some signs of repentance and words of commitment. He will instantly respond. But before that day arrives there must be the discipline of affliction and oppression.

The new age begins with the appearance of a special Teacher. The Hebrew noun in verse 20b is plural, and for this reason the English versions render it *teachers*. The majority of commentaries understand the reference to be to the prophets who would again appear to guide the fortunes of God's people. The verb, however, is singular. This suggests that the plural of excellence is being used. He is the Teacher

279

par excellence, the one who combines in his person all the attributes of a superior Teacher[7] (cf. Joel 2:23).

Israel's divine Teacher will no longer be hidden from view. Throughout Old Testament times the Teacher instructed his people through written law or through surrogate instructors known as prophets. But after the period of national discipline the Teacher himself would be visible to his people.

The Messianic Teacher would provide expert guidance to his people (v. 21). They would hear a voice *behind* them. If pressed too far the language presents a problem. How can they *see* their Teacher with their eyes and at the same time hear a voice behind them? The picture is that of a shepherd who follows his flock and calls out directions to them. The point is that the Teacher's guidance would continue even after the Teacher could no longer be seen. The unseen voice would call the people to repentance and return to the straight and narrow path (cf. Deut. 28:13). The tacit assumption here is that the people will stray and consequently will need the continuing ministry of the Teacher.

Under the influence of the Teacher the people totally repudiate idolatry (v. 22). They would actually come to regard idols as unclean. The idols would be destroyed and cast away. "In the light of the beauty of the grace of God the idols of this world become objects of contempt and disgust."[8]

The Messianic Teacher will bestow gifts of grace upon his people. He (the Teacher) will give to his followers (1) rain which causes the seed to grow; (2) bread which is fat and rich in nourishment, and (3) enlarged pasture for their cattle (v. 23). To those who worked the soil these blessings would symbolize paradise-like conditions. As in Joel 2:23f., abundance of water and agricultural prosperity in a Messianic context points to spiritual blessings which would result from the teaching ministry of Messiah.

Two additional strokes of the artist's brush complete the poetic picture of the agricultural prosperity in the Messianic age. First, the prophet indicates that even the animals will benefit from the prosperity of the age. The work animals will be fed the choicest fodder. The prophet

---

7. The NASB has taken the passage in this way, and translates as follows: "Although the Lord has given you bread of privation and water of oppression, He, your Teacher will no longer hide Himself, but your eyes will behold your Teacher."

8. Young, NIC, II, 359.

then stresses the abundance of water in that age. "On the mountains and hills, where the water could not reach and where cultivation would be extremely difficult, water will be found and the land will be fertile."[9]

The remarkable changes anticipated by Isaiah will come about only after a period of war and slaughter (v. 25b). Probably no one particular slaughter is in view. The basic idea is that God gives peace to his people, but only after he brings upon them periods of wars and judgment.

The Messianic age introduced by the Teacher is to be an age of light. Isaiah makes this point when he says that the moon will become as bright as the sun, and the sun will be seven times brighter than normal (v. 26a). The sevenfold blazing glory of the sun "is simply symbolical language to state the truth that the purposes of God with this world will have been completed and the glory of God will shine forth in all its splendor."[10] When Jesus claimed to be the light of the world he was making a Messianic claim (John 8:12).

The Messianic Teacher would be a healer. The children of Israel received many wounds throughout their national history. Messiah would bind them all up. He is the Great Physician (v. 26b).

Prophecy No. 41

GOD'S NEW GOVERNMENT

Isaiah 32:1-2

In chapter 30 a "woe" is pronounced on those who sought aid from Egypt in the struggle against Assyria (vv. 1-7). This woe is followed by terrible denunciations of Judah for unfaithfulness (vv. 8-17). Yet the situation was not hopeless. If Judah would call upon Yahweh and abandon idolatry God could then continue to be gracious to them (vv. 18-26). The Assyrian king who had dared to harass the people of God would be brought to everlasting death (vv. 27-33).

Chapter 31 commences with another specific warning about depending upon Egypt for help in the struggle against Assyria (vv. 1-3). Judah's true help is Yahweh who would come to the aid of his people (vv. 4-5). In view of what God was about to do for them, Isaiah urged his countrymen to repent (vv. 6-7). This short chapter ends with a very forthright

---

9. Young, NIC, II, 361. Cf. Amos 9:13; Joel 3:18; Ezek. 47:1ff.
10. Young, NIC, II, 363. Isa. 30:26 if pressed literally would contradict Rev. 21:23.

description of the miraculous defeat of the Assyrian army in 701 B.C. (vv. 8-9).

Translation of Isaiah 32:1-4

(1) Behold! For righteousness a king shall reign, and for justice princes shall rule. (2) And a man shall be a hiding place from the wind, and a covert from the rain, as channels of water in a dry place, as the shadow of a heavy rock in a weary land. (3) The eyes of those who see shall not be dim, and the ears of those who hear shall hearken. (4) And the heart of rash men shall discern knowledge and the tongue of stammers shall hasten to speak plainly.

Discussion

Beyond the Assyrian threat Zion will experience a wonderful new era. This unexpected reversal of fortunes is introduced by Isaiah's favorite interjection, *Behold!*

The new era will be possible because of the reign of a very special king.[11] The text emphasizes the righteous purpose of this king's reign.[12] No more would the poor be downtrodden and oppressed. The reign of this king stands in contrast to that of all other kings—to the haughty pretentions of the Assyrian kings, and to the ruthless oppressions of those who ruled Judah.

That 32:1-4 contains a prophecy of Messiah's kingdom is generally admitted. Isaiah did not mistakenly think that the Messianic kingdom would be established immediately after the overthrow of Sennacherib in 701 B.C. He did not regard Hezekiah as a Messianic figure as alleged by some. Isaiah was looking forward in time to one greater than good King Hezekiah. To the extent that Hezekiah sought to be a righteous king he foreshadowed the reign of this righteous one.

It is not only the king himself, but those who serve in positions of leadership subordinate to him that are the epitomy of righteousness. If the king here is Messiah, the *princes* would be the apostles and prophets whose testimony in the New Testament Scriptures is foundational to the establishment and function of the Messianic kingdom.

---

11. The clause is so constructed that the climax is reached in the word *melech*, king.

12. The Hebrew reads literally, for righteousness a king will reign. The preposition *lamedh* (for) can be understood either of two ways: (1) for the purpose of righteousness, or (2) according to righteousness.

The passage emphasizes the truth that after the judgment threatened in the preceding chapter, there will someday arise a royal government which would be perfectly righteous.

The focus is again upon the King in verse 2. It is first stated that he will be a *man*.[13] Elsewhere Isaiah speaks of God himself as the king over his people. The term *'ish* thus emphasizes that the term *king* here is being used Messianically and not theologically. "There was never but *one* man who could be to other men all that is predicted in this verse of the 'man' mentioned."[14]

The King who is man will provide perfect security for his people. He will be (1) a hiding place, (2) a refuge, (3) as channels of water, and (4) as the shadow of a mighty rock. Neither floods, storms or burning heat would harm his subjects. By these comforting figures the prophet means to emphasize the security afforded by the King.[15] Where once there was barrenness, he himself will be like life-giving water (cf. Isa. 55:1; John 4:14; 7:37).

Verses 3-4 outline two of the abundant blessings to attend the reign of the Messianic King.

1. Spiritual insight will be restored in Messiah's kingdom (vv. 3-4a). The generation to which Isaiah preached was obtuse, willfully blind to the truths of God and deaf to his word (Isa. 6:9, 10; 29:10, 11). But to enter Messiah's kingdom men would have to understand and apply God's truths to their lives (Isa. 29:18; 35:5; Matt. 18:16). None in Messiah's kingdom would rashly dismiss the warnings of God's Word.

2. In Messiah's kingdom there would be forthright proclamation of the Word of God (v. 4b). "The tongue of those who hitherto had spoken hesitatingly and inconsistently on moral and religious subjects shall be ready—i.e., prompt and eager—to speak upon them with clearness and elegance."[16]

---

13. Many commentators take the term *'ish* in a distributive sense: and each one will be. Young points out that when *'ish* is used in a distributive sense, it is usually connected with a plural verb. The word *'ish* is used in Zech. 6:12 in the same vague way of one who is clearly the Messiah.

14. Rawlinson, PC, I, 522.

15. Nearly the same epithets which appear here of *man* are used in Isa. 25:4 of God.

16. Rawlinson, PC, I, 522.

Prophecy No. 42

THE KING IN HIS BEAUTY

Isaiah 33:17

In response to an intercessory prayer of Isaiah (33:2-9), God announced that he would arise to intervene on behalf of Judah (33:10). The Assyrian army will be quickly and entirely consumed (33:11-12). Sinners far and near should be moved to repentance by the divine display of power against Assyria (33:13-14). Only a truly righteous man can stand the test of God's judgment fire (33:15, 16).

A transition occurs in verse 17 from the third person to the second person. Isaiah is now addressing those righteous ones about whom he has been speaking in the two preceding verses. Those righteous ones—the remnant—who survive the temporal judgment by the Assyrians will look forward with the eyes of faith to see a glorious king.

Translation of Isaiah 33:17-24

(17) A king in his beauty your eyes shall see, and they shall view a distant land. (18) Your heart will meditate on terror: Where is the scribe? Where is the examiner? Where is the one who lists the towers? (19) An arrogant people you will not see, a people of obscure speech which cannot be heard, stammering lips that are beyond comprehension. (20) Look on Zion the city of our festivals; your eyes shall see Jerusalem, a peaceful habitation, a tent that shall not be moved, its stakes will never be pulled up, nor any of its ropes broken. (21) There the LORD will be a mighty one for us. It will be a place of rivers and wide canals on which no galley with oars will move, no mighty ship will traverse. (22) For the LORD is our Judge, the LORD is our Lawgiver, the LORD is our King; he will save us. (23) Your ropes hang loose, the mast is not secure, the sail is not spread. Then the spoil of abundance is divided; lame men carry off plunder. (24) And no resident will say, I am sick; as for the people who live there, iniquity is forgiven.

Discussion

Concerning the identity of the king who is to appear, Young writes:

The king is not Hezekiah nor any mere human king. The whole context refers to something greater than the bestowal of honor that Hezekiah

284

received (2 Chron. 32:23). It is a king of the redeemed Israel, who reigns when the outward enemy has been punished and when the sinners of Zion have been judged. He is and can only be the Messiah.[17]

The *beauty* of the King is the focus in this prophecy. Recently they had seen their beloved Hezekiah in torn garments and sackcloth. The house of David had been brought to a state of shameful humiliation. But some day the King would appear in worthy apparel, manifesting the glory that should characterize God's vice-regent. The beauty, of course, is spiritual as well as physical. "It is the Messiah in the glory of His wondrous reign over His church that is here in view."[18] The use of the term *beauty* is one of the factors in this prophecy which points to the Messiah. The term is never used of God, but can legitimately be applied to Messiah (cf. Ps. 45:2; Zech. 9:17).

With the *eye* of faith the faithful would see, not only the Messianic King, but the *distant land*.[19] If the King is Messianic, so is the land. Messiah's kingdom stretches far in all directions, even to the distant lands of the Gentiles (cf. Isa. 8:9). This is a way of saying that his kingdom will be universal (Rev. 21:1). In 701 B.C. Sennacherib captured all the fortified cities of Judah save Jerusalem. Hezekiah's kingdom at that point scarcely extended beyond the city limits of Jerusalem. By contrast the future king will rule a realm spacious and wide. What a glorious vision!

In the reign of the future King, Israel will live triumphantly in Jerusalem with no fear from external enemies. Days of submission and payment of tribute to foreign powers will be at an end (v. 18). The sight of ruthless foreigners counting the spoil and numbering Jerusalem's towers[20] will seem like a nightmare which is over. The strange sounding speech of foreign oppressors and rulers will no more be heard in Judah (v. 19).

Zion (Jerusalem) will become a focal point of hope in that day (v. 20). Believers are commanded to *look on Zion*. The King has been mentioned and his spacious realm. Now his capital is in view. That city is the appointed place of worship to God (*the city of our festivals*).

Zion (Jerusalem) will be a peaceful and tranquil city. As in verse 17 the emphasis is on *your eyes shall see*. Does he mean *see* with the eye

---

17. Young, NIC, II, 421.

18. Ibid.

19. The Hebrew *'erets marchaqqim* means, land of distances, i.e., a distant land, rather than a broad land.

20. The reference is probably to the one who made note of the fortresses that the country would be allowed to possess.

of faith? or is he looking forward to the day when faith shall give way to sight? In the previous verse Isaiah spells out what they would not see. They would not see Jerusalem besieged and humiliated. They would see Jerusalem as a city which cannot be shaken. Isaiah uses a figure borrowed from nomadic life to depict the permanence of the place. It will be like a tent which does not have to be moved (v. 20b).

The future Zion finds its stability in the fact that Yahweh, the majestic one,[21] is there. He will be *for us*, i.e., exercising his powerful influence on behalf of his people (v. 21a). Because Yahweh is there, the future Zion will have abundant water. It[22] will be *a place of rivers and wide canals*. The great cities of ancient times were situated beside great rivers. Jerusalem, however, had no major waterways at all. Isaiah foresees a time when that condition would be remedied. He seems to hint that these waterways are not to be interpreted topographically. Isaiah states that these rivers will not be navigable, at least by ships of war. Isaiah here describes the water of life which will flow out of the Messianic Jerusalem (Heb. 12:22).[23]

All that Isaiah has declared about Messianic Jerusalem can be trusted because of the relationship which will exist between God and his people (v. 22). Four aspects of that relationship are mentioned:

1. He is their Judge. Like the ancient Judges of Israel, Yahweh can be relied upon to look after the welfare of his people and to guard them from attacks by hostile nations. Since Yahweh alone is Judge, perfect justice will prevail throughout the land.

2. He is their Lawgiver. Perfect justice must begin with perfect laws. The Messianic community will be governed by divine law issued by Yahweh himself. (Cf. the promise made to Judah in Genesis 49:10.)

3. He is their King. Any doubt as to the identity of the king in verse 17 is now removed. In Messiah is the supreme manifestation of the reign of Yahweh.

4. He is their Savior. God's people can have solid confidence as they face the future.

Messianic Jerusalem will survive all attack. In verse 23 Isaiah depicts Zion as a ship in disarray,[24] a ship which is helpless. Nevertheless, any attack against her is doomed to failure. The citizens of Zion will be

---

21. Others understand *'addir* to emphasize the might rather than majesty of Yahweh.

22. Others think that it is Yahweh himself who is a place of broad waters.

23. Cf. Ezek. 47:1-12; Zech. 14:8; Ps. 46:4.

24. Another view is that the ship represents Assyria which has suffered destruction because it has come too close to Jerusalem.

enriched by the spoils left behind when attackers are overthrown. Even the most humble and handicapped citizen will secure his part of that spoil. Thus the prophet "emphasizes both the abundance of the spoil and the ease with which it may be taken."[25]

Sickness will be absent from Messianic Jerusalem. *No resident will say, I am sick* (v. 24). Sickness in Isaiah is a metaphor for the effects of sin. The citizens of Messianic Jerusalem are those who have been pardoned. Isaiah speaks of a promise of deliverance from a contemporary enemy, "but moves forward to merge this promise with that of complete deliverance from the real enemy of man—sin—under the coming of Messiah."[26] The restoration of Hezekiah after the humiliation of 701 B.C. was a pledge and token of the coming of the glorious future King.

---

25. Young, NIC, II, 426.
26. Jones, WBC, III, 97.

Chapter Twenty

THE MESSIANIC SERVANT (1)

Chapters 40-48 of Isaiah are known as The Book of Cyrus. Israel's grand redemption was to begin when Cyrus the Persian released the Jews to allow them to return to their native land. Cyrus was God's "anointed," the one chosen by God to effect the temporal redemption of his people.

Another divinely commissioned agent, the Servant of Yahweh, would usher in the final spiritual redemption of God's people. He would bring the glad tidings of salvation even to the Gentiles. This Servant is first introduced in 42:1-17.

No small amount of discussion has centered on the identity of the Servant in Isaiah. It is not possible here to digress into a lengthy discussion of the various positions.[1] Some authorities adopt a collective view of the Servant. He is Israel or at least the righteous remnant of Israel. Others view the Servant as an individual. E.J. Young attempted to wed these two views when he wrote:

> The servant is the Messiah (Jesus Christ) conceived as the Head of His people, the Church (or redeemed Israel). At one time the body is more prominent, at another (e.g., chap. 53) the Head.[2]

Without question the term Servant (singular) is used collectively of the people of God at least ten times in chapters 41-48. The national servant is deaf and blind to the things of God (42:19), and desperately in need of redemption from Babylon (48:20) and from sin (44:21f.). In other passages, however, the Servant ministers to Israel, even dies for the sins of Israel. In five poems the Servant, it would appear, is an individual. No person, save Jesus Christ, fulfills the expectations of these poems. Because this great redemptive Servant is so prominent in chapters 49-57 this section of Isaiah has been called The Book of the Servant.

In this chapter three of the Servant poems will be examined, those that speak of (1) his ministry (42:1-17), (2) his success (49:1-13), and (3) his confidence (50:4-11).

---

1. See C.R. North, *The Suffering Servant in Deutero-Isaiah* (London, 1956); and H.H. Rowley, *The Servant of the Lord*. Oxford, 1965.
2. Young, NIC, III, 109 n. 1.

Prophecy No. 43

THE MINISTRY OF THE SERVANT

Isaiah 42:1-17

That this first servant poem is legitimately interpreted individually of the Messiah is proved by the citation of it in Matthew 12:17-21. Jesus is the Servant. In his teaching and healing ministry he fulfilled the predictions made here in Isaiah 42.

Translation of Isaiah 42:1-13

(1) Behold my Servant, I will hold him fast, my chosen one in whom I delight; I will put my Spirit upon him. Judgment to the nations he will bring forth. (2) He will not cry out, nor will he lift up his voice, nor will he cause to be heard his voice in the street. (3) A bruised reed he will not break, and a smoking wick he will not extinguish. According to truth he will bring out judgment. (4) He will not be disheartened nor crushed until he has set judgment on the earth. For his teaching the islands wait. (5) Thus says God, the LORD, the One who created the heavens and stretched them out, who spread out the earth and that which comes out of it, who gives breath to people upon it, and spirit to those who walk on it: (6) I am the LORD! I have called you in righteousness; and I will hold your hand. I will keep you and will make you for a covenant of the people, for a light to the Gentiles, (7) to open blind eyes, to bring out a prisoner from prison, from the dungeon those who sit in darkness. (8) I am the LORD; that is my name! My glory to another I will not give, nor my praise to graven images. (9) As for the former things, behold they have come to pass, and new things I am about to declare; before they spring forth I shall announce them. (10) Sing to the LORD a new song, his praise from the end of the earth, you who go down to the sea and all that is in it, islands and all who live in them. (11) Let the wilderness and its cities shout, the settlements which Kedar inhabits; Let the inhabitants of Sela sing; let them shout from the top of mountains. (12) Let them give glory to the LORD, and announce his praise in the islands. (13) The LORD like a mighty man shall go out, like a man of war he will stir up zeal; he will raise the battle cry, yes he will shout and he will triumph over his enemies.

Discussion

A. *The Description of the Servant* (v. 1a). The Servant enters center stage with verbal fanfare. The interjection *Behold* compels all to turn their attention away from idols and man-made schemes of redemption to the only One who can bring full redemption.

In 48:8 Israel was identified as God's servant. But here Israel is called upon to observe the Servant. The Servant here is a special individual.[3] The term *servant* is an honorific title. It designates one who has been honored by God in being chosen to perform a specific task. Five facts about this Servant are indicated:

1. The Servant has a special relationship to God. He is *my* Servant. God willingly acknowledges him.

2. The Servant is upheld by the Lord in his ministry. God holds him fast in deepest affection.

3. The Servant is described as *my chosen one.* To carry out this mission demanded someone very special, so God chose the Servant.

4. The Servant is beloved by the Lord. He is one in whom God delights. His entire life is an acceptable sacrifice to God. The New Testament uses this expression of Jesus (Matt. 3:17; 17:5).

5. The Servant is empowered by the Spirit of God. The Spirit is said to come *upon him.*[4] The result of this outpouring of the Spirit is that the Servant is fully equipped for his mission.

B. *The Work of the Servant* (vv. 1b-4). The Servant has the task of establishing God's judgment among the nations (v. 1). The judgment is that which God has decreed—his law, standard or norm. "Religion is here conceived of in its judicial aspect, for it has to do with the conduct of men, and its decisions either condemn or justify a man."[5] The judgment which the Servant brings forth to the Gentiles is the Christian system.

Verse 2 gives a triple emphasis to the quiet manner in which the Servant would go about his work. He would not *cry out, lift up his voice,* or *cause his voice to be heard in the street.* What a contrast to the boisterous bragging of wordly conquerors! He would not try to

---

3. The Greek text (Codex Vaticanus) identifies the servant here as Israel, but the Targum thinks Messiah is intended.

4. Cf. Isa. 11:2-4; 48:16; 61:1

5. Young, NIC, III, 11.

force God's judgment (rule, program) upon any one. Violent disputation would not characterize his ministry.[6]

The description of the gentleness of the Servant's work continues in verse 3. The bruised reed and smoking wick are symbols for weak men, men despised by the world and weighed down by its burdens. No soul is unimportant to him! It was upon such bruised reeds and smoking wicks that Jesus pronounced a blessing in the Sermon on the Mount. The mission of the Servant is to give life not extinguish it.

The Servant will promulgate God's judgment *according to truth.* Worldly rulers often establish their will through violence and oppression. Their philosophy too often has been that might makes right, or the end justifies the means. The Servant relies upon the power of truth to establish the judgment (rule, program) of God (cf. Isa. 11:3-4). But he will be successful. He will succeed in causing God's judgment to go forth throughout the world (v. 3b).

The Servant will be equal to the tremendous task which is before him. He will not be *disheartened* (NASB)[7] or *crushed* before he accomplishes his mission. The first verb points to his internal resources and the second to his strength against hostile outside forces. Verse 4 clearly intimates that his work will be opposed, and that he will see discouraging setbacks.

The nature of the Servant's work is indicated in verse 4 in language similar to what was used in verses 1 and 3

v. 1 *Judgment to the nations he will bring forth.*

v. 3 *According to truth he will bring out judgment.*

v. 4 *Until he has set judgment on the earth.*[8]

The term *earth* in verse 4 should be taken in its broadest sense. The Servant's work is universal. The establishment of God's judgment is equivalent to the establishment of his kingdom. The implication here is that the universal sway of the kingdom will not be achieved in one mighty act. The gradual conversion of the heathen will be accomplished through the tireless efforts of the Servant and his servants.

---

6. Matthew gives an interpretative rendering of the first verb in v. 2: He will not *quarrel* (Matt. 12:19).

7. Heb. *yikheh* literally means, grow dim, fade. This is an obvious reflection upon *kehah, smoking* wick in v. 3.

8. The new versions prefer to render *mishpat* in all three verses *justice.* Where God's *judgment* (rule, system) has been established, justice prevails.

Even as the Servant engages in his work the islands of distant seas await his law, i.e., his instruction, his teaching—the Gospel (v. 4b). Moses' law was directed toward the Israelites of the flesh, but Servant's law is intended for all the earth. Historians document a restless dissatisfaction with the religions of the pagan world of the first century. The peoples of distant lands were then and still are today waiting for truth. The missionary implications of this verse are staggering.

C. *The Commitment to the Servant* (vv. 5-9). All the power of the Almighty God of creation stands behind the Servant. Yahweh, the God of Israel, is the Creator. He is the author of life. He gave breath or spirit to all the people who walk upon the face of the earth (v. 5). Not only does this verse explain the power which enables the Servant to accomplish his task, it also points to the reason the program of the Servant must be universal in scope.

The Creator-Covenant God has *called* the Servant. The pronoun *I* is emphatic. Anyone who questions the authority of the Servant will run afoul of the will of God. Calling to service involves (1) selection, (2) delegation, and (3) preparation. This calling was done *in righteousness*. The selection of the Servant was right. Only he would be able to accomplish all that was involved in God's righteous plan. The righteousness of God would be exhibited in the Servant's mission. Both salvation and punishment would be dispensed through him according to principles which are unquestionably right.

The Creator-Covenant God sustains the Servant: *I will hold your hand* (v. 6). The meaning is basically the same as *I will hold him fast* in v. 1. The clause suggests again that the Servant's task would be extremely difficult. He would need this tender assurance of heavenly support. God would watch over the Servant and assure his success.

After describing what he would do for the Servant, God indicates how he would use him in four significant ways:

1. He would be given to be, i.e., appointed to be, *a covenant of the people* (v. 6). The phrase clearly means, a covenant belonging to the people. The term *people* here probably refers to the Jewish people (cf. Acts 26:17, 18). All the blessings of the covenant would be embodied in the Servant. He is greater than Moses who was the mediator of a covenant. The Servant would be the covenant.

2. He would be given as a *light* to the Gentiles. He not only brings light, he is light. Light in Isaiah symbolizes salvation and well-being. He dispels the darkness of superstition, ignorance and sin.

292

3. He would open the eyes of the blind (v. 7). The primary thrust of the passage is not the healing of physical blindness, but the removal of spiritual blindness.

4. He would free those who are bound in a dark prison house (v. 7). The truth proclaimed by Christ sets men free from the prison house of sin.

D. *The Certainty of the Servant's Work* (vv. 8-9). The guarantee that the Servant would succeed in his liberating mission is found in the fact that God's name is Yahweh (v. 8). At the Exodus God revealed the significance of the name Yahweh. He is the eternal one and the God of redemption. God in the distant past proved himself to be a redeemer. Through the Servant he would again redeem his people from bondage.

That God would ultimately redeem his people is underscored by the fact that he would not give his glory to another (v. 8). Yahweh alone has rightful claim to glory and praise. He, therefore, has a vested interest in the successful mission of his Servant.

Still further proof of the certainty of the Servant's successful mission is found in the fact that God's predictive word can be trusted. Isaiah can see *former things*, i.e., the first part of those things which were to come, unfolding before his eyes. The *former things* are the fall of Babylon and the return from captivity. When those events came to pass—and for Isaiah that was a certainty—God's people would have absolute assurance that the *new things*, which he is now relating concerning the Servant, would also come to pass (v. 9).

Prior to the appearance of the Servant, God had been comparatively silent. He was not indifferent to the problems of his people. He *restrained* himself until the time when he would ultimately and decisively speak to the needs of his people through the work of the Servant. The time would come when God would bring forth his final program for the redemption of mankind. Isaiah's figure here is striking. God is likened to a pregnant woman groaning, gasping, panting in anticipation of the moment of deliverance (v. 14).

E. *The Scope of the Servant's Work* (vv. 10-13). The universal work of the Servant is now emphasized. A *new song* celebrating the glorious work of the Servant would be lifted heavenward from one end of the earth to the other. From distant isles, barren deserts and lofty mountains the praise anthems are lifted up (vv. 10-11). Yahweh, the God of redemption, is the object of this praise (v. 12).

The work of the Servant is represented in verse 13 as a great battle. Yahweh, God of redemption, marches forth, probably from heaven, as a great hero (*gibbor*). The verb *to go out* appears to be a technical term for going forth to war.[9] This is the battle which was indicated centuries before in Genesis 3:15. The seed of woman would crush the head of the Serpent. "God the Warrior challenges the Evil One, and fights the fight that will save His own; and this He does through the word of the servant."[10]

Prophecy No. 44

THE SUCCESS OF THE SERVANT

Isaiah 49:1-13

The Servant is featured prominently in Isaiah 49-57 and for this reason these chapters have been given the caption, The Book of the Servant. In the preceding nine chapters the focus was upon Cyrus and the physical deliverance which he would provide for the people of God. In this section Cyrus fades into the background and the Servant of the Lord steps center stage. He will effect a deliverance far greater than that accomplished through Cyrus in 539 B.C. The Servant is a Deliverer infinitely greater than Cyrus, for he will free men from sin and the bondage of death.

Translation of Isaiah 49:1-13

(1) Listen, O islands, unto me, hear this you people from afar: The LORD from the womb has called me, from the loins of my mother he has made mention of my name. (2) He has made my mouth like a sharp sword, in the shadow of his hand he has hidden me; he has made me a polished arrow and has hidden me in his quiver. (3) He said to me, You are my Servant, Israel, in whom I will glorify myself. (4) And as for me, I said, To no purpose I have labored; for nothing and in vain have I spent my strength. Yet surely my judgment is with the LORD, and my work is with my God. (5) And now said the LORD, who formed me from the womb for his Servant, to bring Jacob back to him (but as for Israel, he will not be gathered to him), that I may be honored in the eyes of the LORD, and my God is my strength. (6) And he said, It is too light a thing for you to be my Servant to raise up the

---

9. Young, NIC, III, 127.
10. Ibid.

tribes of Jacob and to restore the preserved of Israel. I will give you for a light for Gentiles to be my salvation to the end of the earth. (7) Thus says the LORD the Redeemer of Israel and his Holy One to him who was despised and abhorred by the nation, to a servant of rulers: Kings will see and arise, princes, and they shall bow down because of the LORD who is faithful, the Holy One of Israel who has chosen you. (8) Thus says the LORD, In the time of favor I have answered you, and in the day of salvation I have helped you that I may keep you, and give you to be a covenant for people, to raise up a land, and to reinhabit desolate inheritances, (9) saying to the prisoners, Go forth, and to those in darkness, Reveal yourselves. Along roads they shall feed, and on every barren hill shall be their pasture. (10) They shall neither hunger, nor thirst; desert heat nor sun will smite them. He who has compassion upon them will guide them, even beside springs of water will he lead them. (11) And I will set all of my mountains for the road, and all of my paths shall be high. (12) Behold these shall come from afar! Behold these from the north and from the west, and these from the land of Sinim. (13) Shout O heavens, rejoice O earth! Let the mountains burst into song! For the LORD will comfort his people and will have compassion on his afflicted ones.

Discussion

Two ideas are prominent in this poem: (1) the task of the Servant (vv. 1-6), and (2) the triumph of the Servant (vv. 7-12).
A. *The Task of the Servant* (vv. 1-6). In various ways the Servant indicates his awareness of the tremendous task which faces him in the world.
1. He indicates his sense of vocation. The Servant speaks with absolute authority commanding distant peoples—Gentiles—to listen to him (cf. 41:1). In the opening verses of his discourse he defends his right to be heard. The Servant has such stature that all men need to hearken to his voice. His message is for all men everywhere. His task is universal in scope.[11]
The Servant entered his vocation by action of Yahweh. The Hebrew word order stresses the fact that it was Yahweh who called the Servant.

---

11. It is not without significance that in 48:20 the people were commanded to declare to the heathen that God had redeemed his servant Jacob. Israel's world-wide testimony to the mighty acts of God set the stage for the universal appeal of the Servant.

He did not usurp power or force his way into such a position of prominence. He was uniquely called to his position, Servant of Yahweh. From the time of birth and even before he was called by Yahweh to fulfill his mission. The phrases *from the womb* and *from the loins of my mother* (v. 1) seem to preclude the collectivistic interpretation of the Servant in this passage.

The Servant is a prophet-like figure. God prepared him for that role by making his mouth like a sharp sword. The words of the Servant would cut like a sword, and pierce like a polished arrow.[12] "I came not," he later would say, "to bring peace on earth, but a sword" (Matt. 10:34). He would cut through hypocrisy, sham and shallow logic to the heart of the eternal issues of life. In Isaiah's day the weapons of God were concealed. The sword was concealed in the shadow of God's hand and the arrow was still in the quiver. The Servant will be hidden until the fulness of time when he would appear on the earth to exercise his prophetic ministry. The Servant is confident of his standing with God. He has, in fact, heard the Father acknowledge him as his own Servant.[13] He is *Israel.* Just as Messiah elsewhere is called David, here he is called *Israel.* Jacob was given the honorable title *Israel* after his successful struggle with the angel of God near the River Jabbok. His descendants were known collectively by this name. The fact that the Servant here is called *Israel* suggests that (1) he would embody all the ideals of God's chosen people; and (2) he would have the same relationship to the New Testament church as Jacob-Israel had to the Old Testament church.

2. The Servant would experience disappointment (v. 4). The words *to no purpose, for nothing, in vain* underscore the apparent futility of his labor. The physical and mental strain of his ministry are captured in the words *I spent my strength.* Those familiar with the life of Jesus of Nazareth will have no trouble identifying the occasions of discouragement, loneliness, and rejection in the days of his flesh.

3. The Servant is confident in his work. The last half of verse 4 expresses his confidence in four ways: (1) The particle *surely* (*'achen*) underscores his confidence. (2) He realizes that the final verdict regarding his work belongs to God. (3) The success or failure of his work is in God's hands. (4) He knows that, in spite of his rejection by men, he has not been abandoned by his Father. He refers to God as *my* God.

---

12. Cf. Heb. 4:12; Rev. 1:16. Young (NIC, III, 269) suggests that the arrow points to the conquest of more distant enemies, while the sword points to victory over foes at hand.

13. Hebrew word order stresses the words *my Servant.*

The confidence of the Servant is again evident in verse 5. He re-affirms his confidence in the fact that God has prepared him from the womb for his work.[14] He is to accomplish two tasks. First, he is to be God's unique Servant. Second, he is to cause Jacob (i.e., the descendants of Jacob) to return to God.[15] In his assignment to bring Jacob to God the Servant would not be entirely successful for *he will not be gathered unto him.*[16]

The Servant expresses confidence that he would be honored in the eyes of Yahweh (v. 5). The Servant would make the effort to bring recalcitrant Israel back to God, and for that effort he would be honored in the sight of God. The exaltation and enthronement of Jesus following his ascension are in view here.

4. The Servant would minister to Gentiles as well as to the house of Jacob (v. 6). It is obvious in this passage that the Servant is sent first to the *tribes of Jacob.* Those tribes, which in the centuries after Isaiah would fall into sin and shame, the Servant would *raise up.* The prophecy has nothing to do with the whole nation of Israel but rather with the remnant—*the preserved of Israel*—those who had been saved from calamity. Those individuals the Servant would *restore* to a right relationship to God.

Raising up and restoring the remnant of Israel would be a task of monumental proportions. Certainly no ordinary servant would or could undertake such a task. But for God's special Messianic Servant even that task is not challenging enough, not significant enough. God says, *my* Servant has an even more challenging responsibility. God has appointed him to be a *light* to Gentiles who walk in spiritual darkness, i.e., total ignorance of God's revelation. Throughout Scripture light and salvation are closely connected. It was with passages such as this in mind that Jesus declared, "I am the light of the world" (John 8:12).

In his address in Pisidian Antioch Paul quoted Isaiah 49:6 as the justification for turning from the Jews to the Gentiles with the Gospel message. The Servant works through Gospel preachers to proclaim his salvation to the ends of the earth. When the Gentiles heard this, they

---

14. Similar language is used in Isa. 44:2, 24 of the entire nation.

15. The Servant here is shown to be an individual and not Israel collectively, for how could Israel bring Israel back to God?

16. Most commentators wish to emend the negative *lo'* (not) and make it read *lo* (to him). It is possible that some scribe mistook these similar sounding forms. The negative, however, can be retained. In this case the clause would indicate the reason for the disappointment evidenced in the preceding verse. The Servant will not succeed in bringing all of Israel back to God.

were glad, and showed their respect for the word of the Lord (Acts 13:48).

B. *The Triumph of the Servant* (vv. 7-13). The Servant would be abhorred by the mass of people. But eventually even kings and princes would recognize the Servant's true dignity and do obeisance to him. In so doing they would recognize the Servant as one especially chosen by the Holy One of Israel (v. 7).

The Servant's triumph is due to the intervention of Yahweh. The verbs *answered* and *helped* (v. 8) are best taken as prophetic perfects, i.e., action so certain of being accomplished that it can be described as having already taken place. God will preserve (the verb is now imperfect = future) the Servant through some unspecified ordeal. From that period of humiliation the Servant will emerge triumphant. That victorious day is here called the *time of favor*,[17] the *day of salvation*, i.e., the time when God shows his favor by providing salvation for the Servant. The resurrection and ascension of Jesus were for him the day of salvation. At the same time those events ushered in an age of salvation for all who will yield to the now exalted Servant (II Cor. 6:2).

The Servant will be triumphant in all aspects of his mission. Six aspects of his triumph are discussed in the passage:

1. As a result of his preservation by Yahweh, he would embody in himself a covenant with God's people (v. 8). On this point see the comments on Isaiah 42:6.

2. He would *raise up* a land (v. 8). That which was desolate would receive life. The Davidic monarchy, which tottered in Isaiah's day, and completely collapsed about a century later, would be restored under the Servant (cf. Amos 9:11).

3. He would give as a grand inheritance the restored land or Davidic kingdom (v. 8). That these promises of restoration and repossession of the land are to be interpreted spiritually can be seen in the following facts: (1) The restoration is a part of the work of the Servant—the Messiah. This fact eliminates any allusion to the restoration from Babylonian captivity which antedated Messiah by some five hundred years. (2) The restoration and repossession of the land foreseen by Isaiah is connected with the concept of a new covenant. The new covenant era would focus on spiritual realities (cf. Jer. 31:31). (3) The New Testament speaks nowhere of any restoration of Jews to physical Canaan. It does, however, emphasize the fact that the Messiah, a son

---

17. In II Cor. 6:2 Paul follows the LXX reading, an accepted time.

of David, now is ruling over his kingdom, and that all citizens of that kingdom have inheritance rights.

4. The Servant would bring about the release of those who were held captive. He would command the prisoners to leave the land of bondage. The Gospel is the good news that releases from sin's bondage. At the same time the Gospel demands that men appropriate for themselves the benefits of God's liberating power. Men must obey the Gospel (II Thess. 1:8). The release of the Jews from Babylonian captivity in 538 B.C. was but one of a series of Old Testament previews of the most glorious redemption ever contemplated by man. This is the liberation provided through the one who said, "You know truth, and the truth will set you free" (John 8:32).

5. He would bring light to those who cower in darkness (v. 9). Darkness in Scripture may depict ignorance, despair, corrupt behavior, or bondage. Here the term seems to have the latter sense, even though the other meanings may also be involved. The verb *reveal yourselves* (*higgalu*)[18] again suggests that the sinner must choose to leave the darkness.

6. The Servant would provide a glorious new life for those who would respond to the Gospel imperative. He likens these redeemed ones to a flock. How well the Good Shepherd will care for that flock!

He will provide pasture for them in abundance. Even the formerly barren hills will sprout grass (v. 9). The Good Shepherd knows where abundant springs of living water are located. He knows when the flock has need of such water and he will lead them to the place of refreshment before the sun can take its deadly toll (v. 10).

The figure of the flock merges in verse 11 to that of a great throng of marching people. Though not stated explicitly, the group seems to be marching toward Zion, the heavenly city. God, through the Servant, does two things for the marchers: (a) He removes the barriers. These barriers are figuratively called *my mountains* (v. 11) because they yield to the power and authority of God. (b) He fills in the pitfalls. This seems to be the meaning of the expression *my paths shall be high* (v. 11).

All over the world the great liberator sets men free from bondage to join the march to the eternal city. Isaiah seems shocked (twice he uses behold!) to see the throng assembling in distant lands of the north, in the isles of the sea, and even in the mysterious land of Sinim which some think is China (v. 12).

---

18. Young suggests, *Show yourselves.* NIV = *Be free;* NASB = *Show yourselves.*

All nature is called upon to rejoice over what God will do in the day of favor. Yahweh will *comfort his people* by all the spiritual blessings he will pour out on them. Prior to the liberation effected by the Servant these people had suffered at the hands of their oppressor. Satan and sin had taken their toll. But on these battered souls God will smile in his mercy. Concerning these afflicted the Servant later would say, "I am come to seek and to save that which is lost" (Matt. 18:11).

Prophecy No. 45

THE CONFIDENCE OF THE SERVANT

Isaiah 50:4-11

As in chapter 49 the Servant of the Lord, unintroduced, speaks in the first person. The soliloquy in 50:4-9 can scarcely be that of Isaiah himself. The humiliation in verse 6 is beyond anything recorded of the writer. The focus here is again upon that individual of whom Isaiah has previously spoken in 42:1-8 and 49:1-12 and about whom he will yet speak in 52:13—53:12.

The passage seems to be unrelated to the opening three verses of chapter 50. If there be any connection at all it is found in this, viz., the same omnipotent God who can clothe the heavens in darkness (v. 3) will equip the Servant for ministry and ultimately vindicate him. This poem further develops the theme of the suffering Servant. In this respect 50:4-9 prepares the heart and mind for the staggering descriptions and explanations of chapter 53.

Translation

(4) The Lord GOD has given to me the tongue of learned ones, to know to help the weary with a word; he will arouse in the morning, in the morning he will awaken for me the ear to hear like learned ones. (5) The Lord GOD has opened for me the ear and, as for me, I did not resist; backward I did not turn. (6) My back I gave to smiters, and my cheeks to those who yank out the hair; my face I did not hide from shame and spitting. (7) And the Lord GOD will help me, therefore I have not been put to shame; therefore I have set my face like flint, and I know that I shall not be ashamed. (8) Near is my Vindicator; who will enter into a lawsuit with me? let us stand together; who is the master of my judgment: let him come near to me. (9) Behold! the

Lord GOD will help me; who is the one who would do me harm? Behold! All of them like a garment become old; a moth shall consume them. (10) Who among you fears the LORD, hearkens to the voice of his Servant, who has walked in darkness and there is no light to him, let him trust in the name of the LORD and lean upon his God. (11) Behold! All of you who kindle a fire, who are girded with sparks; walk in the light of your fire and in the sparks you have kindled. From my hand this was your lot; at the place of sorrow you shall lie down.

Discussion

In this passage the Servant emphasizes his confidence in the preparation (vv. 4-5a), the plan (vv. 5b-6), and the help (vv. 7-9) by God. A. *Preparation by God* (vv. 4-5a). Four times in this poem the Servant refers to the Deity as the Lord God ('*adhonay Yahweh*). The double name "lends a tone of majesty and impressiveness to the Servant's words."[19] The first name points to the sovereignty of God, the second to his covenant faithfulness. As incomprehensible as it may seem to rationalistic man, the heavenly sovereign chose the way of the Servant to bring redemption.

The Servant is fully persuaded that God has given to him the ability to communicate the divine word. He had *the tongue of learned ones*, i.e., a trained tongue, a tongue such as learned or skilled men have. His tongue faithfully conveyed to others what he had learned from his Father. The trained tongue, then, refers to one who is inspired of God's Spirit to communicate the divine word. Here the Servant is pictured as a prophet. Jesus declared: "I speak to the world those things which I have heard of him . . . As my Father has taught me, I speak these things" (John 8:26, 28).

The divine illumination had the purpose of enabling the Servant to speak comforting words to weary souls: *to know to help the weary with a word* (v. 4). The Servant here recognizes this as his mission and expresses confidence in his ability to succeed in that mission. Jesus was the Rest Bringer. He urged all who were weary and heavy laden to come unto him for rest (Matt. 11:28).

He is confident of the source of his teaching. Morning by morning God communicated with the Servant. From time to time God had revealed himself to Old Testament prophets by dreams and visions. This future Servant-Prophet would never experience a time when

---

19. Young, NIC, III, 298.

God is not whispering in his ear. At no time did the Father leave his Son without guidance (John 8:29). The verbs *arouse* and *awaken* stress the thought that divine revelation was the first priority in the life of the Servant.

He is confident that he has correctly apprehended the divine revelation. He is able to *hear like learned ones*, i.e., attentively, respectfully, obediently, anxiously. He would one day declare, "I do always the things that are pleasing to him" (John 8:29).

In the words, *The Lord Yahweh has opened for me the ear* (v. 5a) there is a contrast between the true Servant of God and those who were professed servants, i.e., national Israel. They refused to hear God's Word (48:8). The ear of the true Servant, however, would be perpetually opened to receive God's Word.

B. *The Plan of God* (vv. 5b-6). Unlike some of his prophetic predecessors,[20] he would not inwardly resist (*mariti*) God's leading. The Servant's outward actions matched his inward resolve: *Backward I did not turn* (v. 5). He would not retreat from those obligations laid upon his heart by the Divine Word. He would walk the path of submission to the bitter end.

In verse 6 the Servant offers concrete proof that his professions of faithfulness were not idle boasts. The path of submission led to physical abuse. The language implies a voluntary act on the part of the Servant. He yielded himself to flogging by *smiters*, i.e., those charged with the duty of beating a criminal.[21] Jesus chose to travel to Jerusalem knowing that the Roman scourge awaited him.[22]

The Servant would give his *cheeks to them who yank out the hair* (v. 6). The literal fulfillment of this detail in the life of Jesus cannot be documented in the Gospel records. Pulling out the facial hair, however, was not unknown to the Jews (cf. Neh. 13:25). In the Near East the beard was the symbol of manhood. The plucking of the beard would not only be a painful ordeal, it would be the most degrading of insults.

The Servant did not hide his face *from shame*. The term embraces verbal insults. How cruel were those who executed the sentence! The Servant faced their gibes and taunts with meekness and without a vengeful spirit. Even that most degrading of insults, *spitting*, he bore willingly.

---

20. Moses, Jeremiah, and to some extent Isaiah himself, were reluctant to accept their prophetic commissions. Jonah tried to resign his ministry rather than undertake a mission to Nineveh.

21. Cf. Prov. 10:13; 19:29; 26:3; Isa. 53:5 also refers to this scourging.

22. Matt. 26:67; 27:27-30; John 19:1.

C. The Help of God (vv. 7-9). In these three verses the Servant places in juxtaposition his adversaries on the one hand and his God on the other. He makes a triple declaration of his faith in his Father: *And the Lord Yahweh will help me* (v. 7) . . . *Near is my Vindicator* (v. 8) . . . *Behold! The Lord Yahweh will help me* (v. 9). From these statements the following observations can be deduced:

1. The introductory conjunction *And* serves to bring to the fore the inward thought and conviction of the Servant even in the midst of his intense suffering and humiliation.[23]

2. The Servant has faith in the power of God to intervene on his behalf. He is Lord (*'adhonay*). He is also *Yahweh*, the God of covenant faithfulness. The Father will honor his commitment to the Servant.

3. His God is *near*. He will not have to wait long for the anticipated divine intervention. On the cross he felt forsaken by his Father. That terrible valley of loneliness was a short, albeit necessary, part of the divine wrath which the Servant-Substitute absorbed on the cross. Apart from those moments of separation the Father stood near at hand throughout the redemption ordeal.

4. His God will *justify* him. God is here pictured as the ultimate Judge who finds the Servant innocent of all charges. The Servant's claims will thus be declared to be true, his actions correct, his words faithful. He expects to be fully vindicated by his Father. Condemned as a blasphemer by the Jews and as an anti-government rabble-rouser by the Romans, he was executed between two criminals. Three days later the Servant was vindicated when God raised him from the dead. Forty days after his resurrection he was exalted to such glorious heights that no adversary will dare contend with him before the eternal Judge (v. 8).

5. The intervention by God on behalf of the Servant will be unexpected by the enemies. With the introductory *Behold!* the Servant points out that it is the Sovereign-Yahweh who will in fact help him.

In view of his confidence in divine help the Servant makes a threefold declaration of his determination to carry through on his mission in verse 7.

1. *Therefore I have not been put to shame.* He will not be confounded, confused or dismayed. Through the pressures of indescribable physical pain and ridicule he maintained his composure.

---

23. Young, NIC, III, 301.

2. *Therefore I have set my face as a flint* (v. 7). His face is set so that he will not look right or left. Determination is etched on his brow. With God's help he knew he could face whatever suffering was ahead. The evangelist may have had this passage in mind when he reports that Jesus "set his face stedfastly toward Jerusalem" (Luke 9:51).

3. *And I know that I shall not be ashamed* (v. 7). The Servant knows that he will never have cause to be ashamed of his actions or decisions. Strange they may have seemed to his enemies or perhaps even to his friends. But the Servant had no doubt that he was about his Father's business. He was confident that the shame and reproach heaped upon him would only lead to greater glory.

Being assured of divine aid and ultimate vindication the Servant hurls a triple challenge at his adversaries:

Who will enter into a lawsuit with me? let us stand together (v. 8)

Who is the master of my judgment? let him come near to me (v. 8)

Who is the one who would do me harm? (v. 9)

The first of these challenges is couched in the language of the law court. The Servant fears no legal contest. His defense will quickly silence any opponent who attempts to show that the Servant is not who he claims to be. The second challenge identifies the potential adversary as the *master of my judgment*. This seems to have been an ancient designation for a prosecutor.[24] The last challenging question is stronger than those in verse 8. Who will do me harm, i.e., pronounce sentence against or condemn the Servant? The implication is that the Servant has been pronounced innocent by no less than God himself. To be critical of the Servant under these circumstances would be a direct challenge to God's omniscience.

The speech of the Servant ends with a prophecy of the demise of those who opposed him. This prophecy is introduced with the interjection *Behold*! which underscores the shocking nature of that which the Servant is about to say. The enemies will gradually decay like a garment and be consumed as thoroughly as a moth devours old cloth. The verdict will go against them in the court of divine justice.

D. *Conclusion to the Prophecy* (vv. 10-11). The third Servant poem concludes with an exhortation (v. 10) and a warning (v. 11). The exhortation is addressed to those who fear the Lord and obey the voice of his Servant. When these precious souls are in the darkness of despondency they must continue to trust in the name of God and lean

---

24. Young. NIC. III. 302.

upon him. Only by this means will they be able to exit the darkness. Faith will give way to sight; uncertainty will eventually be illuminated by the further light of God's revelation.

On the other hand, those who *kindle a fire*, i.e., cause strife (cf. James 3:6) will not be able to escape the fire which they themselves have stirred up. Finally they will *lie down at the place of sorrow*, i.e., die with no hope.

Chapter Twenty-One

THE MESSIANIC SERVANT (2)

Two more personal Messianic prophecies are found in the Book of the Servant (Isa. 49-57). The first is the greatest of the Servant poems, Isaiah 52:13—53:12. The focus here is on the Servant's vicarious suffering which secures for others redemption from sin. The last personal Messianic prophecy in this section is a grand invitation to embrace the leadership of Messiah and thus experience all the good things which he has to offer (55:3-5).

The last nine chapters of Isaiah are called the Book of Future Glory. These chapters are filled with general Messianic predictions; but in one passage Messiah speaks personally. This passage (61:1-11), which emphasizes the preaching ministry of Messiah, is regarded as the last of the five Messianic Servant poems in the book.

These three prophecies—the Suffering Servant, the grand invitation and the preaching Servant—are examined in this chapter.

Prophecy No. 46

THE SUFFERING SERVANT

Isaiah 52:13—53:12

Isaiah 53 has been called "the great passional." If the Book of Isaiah is the Mt. Everest of prophetic literature, then surely the fifty-third chapter is the summit of the mountain. Delitzsch called it "the most central, the deepest, and the loftiest thing that Old Testament prophecy, outstripping itself, has ever achieved."[1] Urwick regarded this chapter as "the holy of holies of Old Testament prophecy."[2] The passage depicts very clearly the suffering and death of the Servant of Yahweh. Most commentaries regard the last three verses of chapter 25 as the prelude to the poem of the suffering Servant. Rawlinson describes the sequence of thought in this way: Chapter 52 describes the exaltation of Israel, the collective servant of Yahweh (cf. Isa. 44:1, 21). This brings to the

---

1. Delitzsch, BCOT, Isaiah, II, 303.
2. Cited by Rawlinson, PC, II, 294.

prophet's mind the exaltation of the individual Servant "through which alone the full exaltation of Israel is possible."[3]

The Messianic interpretation of Isaiah 53 was acknowledged by Jewish authorities until the Middle Ages. Almost all Christian leaders until the beginning of the nineteenth century saw in this passage a clear picture of the suffering, death and resurrection of the Messiah. Jews and some Christian scholars now hold primarily to the collective view of the Servant: The Servant is Israel as a whole, or the remnant. The traditional view, however, has much to commend it:

1. The Servant of the Lord here is portrayed in a strongly individualistic way. It takes rich imagination or strong prejudice to see the Servant here as a symbol for Israel, the remnant, the prophets, or any other group.

2. What is said of this individual far exceeds anything which man is capable of accomplishing.

3. The passage is applied directly to Christ in at least seven New Testament passages.[4]

Translation of Isaiah 52:13—53:12

(13) Behold! My Servant will prosper; he will arise, and be lifted up, and be very high. (14) Just as many were astonished over you (so was his appearance disfigured more than men, and his form more than the sons of men) (15) so shall he sprinkle many nations, and kings will shut their mouths because of him. For that which had not been told them they shall see, and that which they have not heard they will comprehend. (1) Who has believed our message, and the arm of the LORD, upon whom has it been revealed? (2) Now he grew up like a tender shoot before him, and like a root from dry ground. He had no form or majesty that we would see him, and no appearance that we should desire him. (3) He was despised and rejected by men, a man of sorrows who knew suffering; and as a hiding of faces from him, he was despised so that we did not esteem him. (4) Surely, our infirmities he carried and our sorrows he bore; but as for us, we regarded him as plagued, smitten by God and afflicted. (5) He was pierced through because of our transgressions, crushed because of our iniquity, the discipline of peace was upon him, and with his wounds

---

3. Rawlinson, PC, II, 280.
4. Matt. 8:17; Mark 15:28; Luke 22:37; John 12:37, 38; Acts 8:32, 33; Rom. 10:16; I Peter 2:24, 25.

we are healed. (6) All we like sheep have strayed, we have each turned to his own way; and the LORD has caused the iniquity of us all to smite him. (7) He was oppressed and afflicted, but he did not open his mouth; like a sheep to the slaughter he was led, and like a ewe before her shearers is silent, so he did not open his mouth. (8) By arrest and judgment he was taken away, and among his generation who took thought that he was cut off from the land of the living; because of the transgression of my people he was smitten. (9) And with the wicked ones his grave was appointed, and with the rich one in his death; because he had committed no violent act, nor was deceit found in his mouth. (10) And the LORD was pleased to crush him, cause him to suffer; when his soul shall place a guilt offering, he shall see a seed, he shall prolong days; and the pleasure of the LORD shall prosper in his hand. (11) From the travail of his soul he shall see and be satisfied through the knowledge of him shall my righteous servant justify the many, and he will bear their iniquities. (12) Therefore I will give him a portion with the great, and with the strong he shall divide the spoil, because he poured out his soul to death, and with transgressors he was numbered; yet he bore the sins of many, and for transgressors he made intercession.

Discussion

The poem of the Suffering Servant contains five units of three verses each. The prophet begins and ends with descriptions of the Servant's ultimate triumph. In between these positive poles he emphasizes the suffering and rejection of the Servant on behalf of the sins of others. A. *The Servant is Triumphant. He will Succeed* (52:13-15). Using his favorite interjection, *Behold!*, Isaiah directs the attention of his readers anew to the Servant of Yahweh. The wise dealing of the Servant is understood at the outset of the passage. The Hebrew verb *yaskil* means to act in such a way as to bring one's task to a successful conclusion. His every action will be intelligent and effective. Whatever humiliation which he might suffer would not be the result of thoughtless mistakes on his part.

The consequences of the Servant's wise dealings are set forth in three verbs: *arise (yarum)*, *be exalted (nissa')*, and *be high (gabhah)*.[5] The same expressions are used of God almighty in 6:1 and 57:15.

---

5. Some have seen in these three verbs an allusion to the resurrection, ascension and enthronement at the Father's right hand.

From obscurity and humiliation he would be exalted high above all others.[6] No person save Messiah is conceived of in the Old Testament as dealing so wisely that he would experience unparalleled exaltation.[7]

Exaltation implies prior humiliation, and that matter is taken up in verse 14 and developed through the entire next chapter. So deep would be his degradation that many would experience a paralyzing astonishment over him. He would be disfigured to the extent that he no longer would appear to be a man (v. 14). The allusion may be to the battered body of the Servant and to the physical contortions which marked his hours of agony. It is as though the prophet is sitting at the foot of Calvary. He sees the Servant hanging on the tree after he had been buffeted, crowned with thorns, smitten, scourged. His face was covered with bruises and blood.

The disfigurement of the Servant is not without purpose. Through his suffering the Servant is able to perform a priestly act of purification: *He will sprinkle many nations* (v. 15). It is taken for granted that one who would perform such purification must himself be pure. Because of his disfigurement others would regard the Servant as impure, a sinner above all men. But the shocking result of his sufferings was the provision of cleansing not only for Israelites according to the flesh, but for all nations.

Kings of Gentile nations would *shut their mouths* out of reverence for the Servant. In contrast to the many—presumably Israelites—who were shocked to stupefication by his suffering, these Gentile kings would pay silent homage to him for the salvation which the Servant would make available to the nations. These kings had never heard the Old Testament prophecies of a coming Savior. They did not have the advantage of centuries of religious ritual pointing to the necessity of vicarious suffering of a perfect Lamb. But in the proclamation of the Gospel they could come to perceive the glorious truth about the suffering of the Servant, viz., that he died for them.

B. *The Servant Rejected. He will be Slighted* (53:1-3). By means of a rhetorical question Isaiah calls attention to the few among his own generation who will believe on the Servant. Two good reasons are given why they should have believed. They should have acknowledged

---

6. Cf. Phil. 2:9-11; Acts 2:33; 3:13, 26.

7. Young, NIC, III, 336.

8. *Yazzeh* is a technical word found in the Mosiac law for the sprinkling of oil, water, or blood in purification rites. Cf. Lev. 14:6, 7; 8:11. Many commentators prefer the reading of the Septuagint, *So shall many nations marvel at him.*

the Servant because of *our message*.[9] Isaiah speaks as representative of the company of Old Testament prophets. In the life of the Servant predictions of the prophets were being fulfilled almost daily, yet the people, for the most part, did not believe. These same people were eye witnesses of the actions of *the arm of Yahweh*, i.e., the power of God. They had witnessed the mighty miracles performed by the Servant in their midst, yet they did not believe (v. 1).

The Servant is rejected superficially. They refused to believe on him because of his humble origins: *He grew up*[10] *like a tender shoot*. His appearance is likened to a "sucker" (*yoneq*) which grows on a tree or plant. Messiah will be a fresh sprout[11] from the stump of the fallen Davidic dynasty. Men regard suckers as useless. They are pruned and cast away. Yet his appearance was *before him*, i.e., before God. The Servant's birth and childhood were under the watchful eye of the Father.

A second figure also underscores the unpromising and unpretentious character of the Servant's appearance on earth. He is likened to a root growing in dry and barren soil which must struggle to maintain its existence. An obscure village, a lowly stable, poor parents, a humble trade, a despised region, a corrupt age and nation—these conditions constitute the *dry ground* out of which the Root emerged. Men of great power and prominence were likened to tall cedars; but in the eyes of most of his contemporaries the Servant was a lowly root (v. 2). "The 'sapling' from the house of David shall become the 'root' out of which his Church will grow (cf. John 15:1-6)."[12]

Nothing about the outward appearance of the Servant attracted men to his cause. The nouns *form* (*to'ar*), *splendor* (*hadhar*) and *appearance* (*mar'eh*) in verse 2 refer to all the obvious qualities that men look for in their leaders. Absalom stole the hearts of the men of Israel by his handsome physique, flashy showmanship and cunning flattery. The Servant would be the exact opposite—quiet, humble, unassuming. He had no regal pomp nor splendor. Only the eye of faith would behold the true glory of the Servant.

---

9. The word *shemu'athenu* is used technically for a prophetic revelation. See Isa. 28:9, 19; Jer. 49:14.

10. Until verse 7 all the verbs are in the perfect state. They are best regarded as prophetic perfects describing actions which are so sure to transpire that they can be described as having been completed.

11. The *sprout* of 11:1, 10 is a different Hebrew word, but it has nearly the same meaning.

12. Rawlinson, PC, II, 294.

The Servant was painfully rejected. He was not just ignored, he was *despised*, i.e., treated with contempt.[13] Their contempt for him was shown in the verbal challenges they hurled at him, the paltry sum they paid for his betrayal, and the treatment they accorded him during the last hours.

He was *rejected* or forsaken. Only a little flock surrounded him. After his incisive sermon on the Bread of Life, many of these "went back and walked no more with him" (John 6:66). In the end, even the apostles forsook him and fled (Matt. 26:56).

The phrase *man of sorrows* (v. 3) may indicate either the subjective result of the rejection of the Servant, or an additional reason for the rejection of him. Perhaps both ideas are involved. Rejection produced sorrow which only led to further rejection. The Servant is a *man* in the most noble sense of that word. Yet the life of this man is filled with *sorrow*. This term embraces bodily suffering, mental anguish, and spiritual discouragement. The sorrows of Christ appear on almost every page of the Gospel records.

Like the expression *man of sorrows*, the expression *acquainted with grief* may indicate both the result of the Servant's rejection and at the same time add an additional reason for that rejection. Literally the word *choli* means *sickness*. By this experience he became acquainted with sickness. Isaiah uses the term *sickness* as a metaphor for sin (cf. 1:5b, 6). On the cross Jesus bore the penalty for sin (I Peter 2:24), and that cross became a stumblingblock to the Jewish people (I Cor. 1:23).

Men hid their faces from him. The griefs and sorrows he bore made him unattractive, repulsive. They treated him as though he had some repulsive disease. Verse 3 ends as it began with emphasis on the word *despised*. The prophet adds to the sad picture this thought: *We did not esteem him*. No one, for a time, truly recognized him for what he was.

C. *The Servant is Wounded: He will Suffer* (53:4-6). His suffering would be on behalf of others. At least twelve times in this and the next three verses Isaiah emphasizes that the Servant's sufferings were vicarious. He suffered to save men from the terrible consequences of sin.

The terms sorrows (*cholayenu*) and griefs (*makh'obhenu*) in verse 4 depict the awful consequences of human sin. The Servant is not a sinner, nor does he become a sinner in order to remove sin. Rather, he removes the consequences of sin. The verbs *carried* (*nasa'*) and *bore*

---

13. The word is used of the attitude of Esau toward his birthright (Gen. 25:34), the people toward Saul's reign (I Sam. 10:27), Michal toward David (II Sam. 6:16), and Goliath toward the armies of Israel (I Sam. 17:42).

(*sebham*) in verse 4 are strong words indicating that he is able to remove the consequences from "us" only by bearing them himself. He, the Righteous One, must pay the price for sins he did not commit. Peter may have had this verse in mind when he wrote, "Our sins he himself has borne in his body upon the tree" (I Peter 2:24).

His suffering was misinterpreted even by those who were sympathetic to him. *We* (the pronoun is emphasized) regarded him as stricken (*nagu'a*) smitten (*mukeh*), afflicted (*me'unneh*) by God (v. 4). The first verb suggests the infliction of some loathsome disease. The sense may be paraphrased thusly: He died for "us" but "we" treated him like he had the plague. Following the popular theology that he who suffers most has sinned most, "we" reached the erroneous conclusion that God had smitten this man (cf. Matt. 27:39, 44).

His suffering was substitutionary. Our transgression (*pesha'enu*), our iniquities (*'avonothenu*) demanded the death penalty from the eternal Judge. He absorbed the punishment rightfully due us.

Matthew applies verse 4 to the healing ministry of Jesus:

> They brought unto him many possessed with demons, and he cast out spirits with a word. He healed all that were sick that it might be fulfilled which was spoken through Isaiah the prophet, He himself took our infirmities and bore our diseases (Matt. 8:16, 17).

A detailed discussion of Matthew's use of the prophetic Scripture lies outside the range of this study.[14] A few observations are appropriate:

1. Sickness and demon possession ultimately are the result of man's sin.[15] In his healing ministry Jesus was demonstrating his power over the consequences of sin. His program for the eradication of sin and death began with his healing ministry and culminated in his crucifixion-resurrection. This paragraph from Ridderbos effectively makes the connection between victory over sin and the healing ministry of Jesus:

> This factual relation between the coming of the kingdom and Jesus' miracles is also brought out not only by the casting out of devils but also by Jesus' other miracles, for they all prove that Satan's power has been broken and that, therefore, the kingdom has come. At the same time it appears that disease is considered to be generally a consequence of Satan's rule and that Jesus' struggle against the Evil One is not fought solely in the field of ethics, but in the whole of the physical domain.

---

14. See Fowler, MBST, I, 81-86; II, 50-53.

15. Sickness, however, is not always the direct consequence of the sins of individuals (John 9:3).

Thus, e.g., in several cases demonic possession is mentioned as the cause of bodily disorders (e.g., Matt. 9:32ff.; 12:22ff.; Mark 9:25); or such possession is mentioned as first in the series of bodily diseases (Matt. 4:24). At the same time Satan is also called the cause of all kinds of physical suffering without any mention of demonic possession. Thus, e.g., in Luke 13:11, 16 where the text speaks of a woman who had 'a spirit of infirmity . . . and was bowed together.' In the 16th verse it says that 'Satan had bound this woman.' Apparently there is no thought of demonic possession here, but Satan is mentioned in a more general sense as the cause of suffering. Not only serpents and scorpions, but also disease and death belong to the enemy's power (*dunamis*) (Luke 10:19)[16]

2. Matthew may want his readers to see that Jesus' suffering really began with his incarnation and continued through his earthly preaching and healing ministry.[17]

3. Matthew may be suggesting that his readers begin to look for more applications of Isaiah's words to Jesus of Nazareth.[18]

4. Matthew's use of this prophecy draws attention to Jesus' perfect command over all human weakness which he can restore to perfect soundness.

His suffering was fatal. Again the emphasis in verse 5 is on the pronoun *he*. What others deserved, he experienced. Two strong participles describe the extent or result of his suffering. He was *pierced through* (*mecholal*) by the thorns, by the nails, and by the spear of the soldier. The participle "expresses a fact that has become completely accomplished."[19] The second participle, crushed (*medhuka'*), denotes being shattered, broken in pieces. "No stronger expression could be found in Hebrew to denote severity of suffering—suffering unto death."[20]

His suffering was redemptive. Isaiah refers to his suffering as chastisement (*musar*).[21] God can only be at peace with sinful man after sin has been chastened. Divine justice had been satisfied, for the wages of sin is death (Rom. 6:23). The death of the Servant was in fact a chastisement designed to enable God and sinful humanity to be reconciled (Eph. 2:15-17; Col. 1:20).

---

16. Ridderbos, CK, pp. 66-67.
17. Fowler, MBST, II, 51.
18. Ibid.
19. Young, NIC, III, 347.
20. Urwick quoted by Rawlinson, PC, II, 296.
21. *Musar* refers to correction, remedial discipline.

Isaiah next refers to the Servant's *wounds*. These marks would result from blows inflicted on him by the hand (Matt. 26:67), the reed (Matt. 27:30), and the scourge (Matt. 27:26). But this suffering procured healing for the sin-sick sons of Adam. Peter alludes to this healing: "He himself bore our sins in his body on the tree, so that we might die to sins and live for righteousness; by his wounds you have been healed" (NIV I Peter 2:24).

His suffering was essential. Collectively, like a stupid flock of sheep the human race had wandered away from the Good Shepherd. Straying sheep are in grave danger. Since the straying here is metaphorical for iniquity, the danger to them comes from God himself. He must punish sin. The human need triggers the divine action. *Yahweh* (the Father) laid upon him (the Servant) the iniquity (i.e., the punishment for iniquity) *of us all* (v. 6). From these words the following observations are in order:

1. God took the initiative in human redemption. "God made him who had no sin to be a sin offering for us, so that in him we might become the righteousness of God (II Cor. 5:21). John declares that the Father "sent the Son to be the propitiation for our sins" (I John 4:10).

2. The Servant absorbs the blow which justly belongs to the straying sheep. The verb *hiphgi'a* means to hit, to strike violently.

3. The provision for redemption is potentially as universal as the predicament of man. The iniquity of *all of us*, all who strayed, is laid upon him.

4. This absorption of the punishment by the Servant has as its ultimate aim the restoration of fellowship with the Father: "For you were like sheep going astray, but now you have returned to the Shepherd and Overseer of your souls" (I Peter 2:25).

D. *The Servant Cut Off: He will be Submissive* (vv. 7-9). Verse 7 focuses on the submissive spirit of the Servant during his trial. He endured patiently in spite of the most difficult circumstances. He was oppressed (*niggas*), as his fathers before him had been oppressed in Egypt (Exod. 3:7). The abuse which Jesus received in the house of the high priest and before Herod is especially in view here. The rest of verse 7 describes how the Servant would deal with this cruel oppression.

1. He would endure voluntarily. The normal inclination is to flee oppression, to resist it, to fight it. But the Servant *suffered himself to be afflicted.*[22] He made no effort to escape.

---

22. Translation of E. J. Young. Rawlinson prefers, *he abased himself.*

2. He endured resolutely. *He did not open his mouth.* What provocation he experienced! If one cannot escape oppression his natural inclination is to cry out to God for help, to plead with the oppressor for relief, to protest his innocence, and to defend his actions. But not the Servant. In Pilate's judgment hall he answered not a word (Matt. 27:12-14). "When he was reviled, he reviled not again" (I Peter 2:23).

3. He would endure innocently as the lamb being led to the slaughter. Most likely it is the slaughter of the Paschal lamb which is intended. It is not the ignorance of the lamb awaiting slaughter that is the point of comparison but the innocence. When John the Baptist called Jesus the Lamb of God (John 1:29) he probably based his language on this verse (cf. I Peter 1:18-19). Philip began at this same Scripture to preach Jesus to the Ethiopian eunuch (Acts 8:32-35).

4. He would endure patiently, like the ewe who had been sheared many times before her shearers. This patient endurance was possible because he knew the cruel oppression was not without purpose.

5. He would endure silently. For the second time the prophet mentions the amazing restraint of the Servant in this ordeal. How easily he could have refuted every charge and thereby confound his accusers! His silence was interpreted as an admission of guilt, and that made his tormentors all the more confident in their foul deeds.

In verse 8 the Servant is condemned to death. He would be *taken away* and *cut off from the land of the living.* The latter verb (*nigzar*) is always used of a violent and premature death. What is not so clear in verse 8 is how his death is connected to his *arrest*[23] and *judgment.* The main interpretations are:

1. *Without* arrest and *without* judgment he was taken away. He was not legally arrested and did not receive a fair trial.

2. From the midst of arrest (confinement, restraint, oppression) and judgment he was taken away by death. He died in the midst of his suffering.

3. By reason of arrest and a judgment he was taken away. He was arrested and then sentenced to die.

Among[24] his contemporaries few gave any serious thought to the significance of his death. In verse 5 it was the suffering only which was

---

23. The noun *'otzer* only occurs four times, each with the idea of restraint or coercion. The verb root has the idea *to restrain, to shut up, keep from, imprison* (cf. II Kings 17:4; Jer. 33:1; 39:15).

24. Following Young and regarding *'eth* as a preposition. On the other hand, the rendering in the KJV and NIV is permissible.

substitutionary; here it is the death itself. In his death he received the stroke or blow due transgressors. Potentially he was the substitution of all transgressors; but in reality his death is only efficacious for *my people*, i.e., those who submit to God in faith and obedience.

In verse 9 the Servant is buried. The original intention of his enemies was to assign his grave to be with the wicked.[25] They intended his burial to be one of dishonor. But that was not to be. As a matter of fact he would be with a rich one[26] in his state of death.

He had *committed no violent act*, i.e., he was not a lawbreaker, nor had he spoken *deceit*. The word for *violent act* (*chamas*) is translated by Peter by *hamartia*, sin (I Peter 2:22). The verse thus becomes an affirmation that Christ was sinless in word and deed.[27]

The fulfillment of verse 9 is clear. Christ died on Golgotha, the common execution ground for Judea. His adversaries intended that he should be buried with the criminals who died with him on that day.[28] Such would have been his fate were it not for the intervention of Joseph of Arimathea, a rich man (Matt. 27:57-60).

E. *The Servant was Exalted: He will be Satisfied* (vv. 10-12). Seven steps in the exaltation of the Servant are evident in this final stanza of the poem.

1. His sacrifice would be acceptable: *Yahweh was pleased* in spite of his innocence *to crush him* and *cause him to suffer*. The second verb intensifies the first and indicates the extent of the crushing. He was crushed to the point of being made sick. These verbs taken together depict the whole range of the suffering of the Servant. All of this was in God's hand, i.e., under his control. It was part of the "determinate counsel and foreknowledge of God" (Acts 2:23). His enemies were only doing what God permitted them to do.

What pleased God about the suffering of the Servant? The fact that a guilt offering[29] had thereby been offered before God. This would make possible the redemption of the fallen sons of Adam. In verse 5

---

25. The verb is best taken impersonally and therefore is properly rendered in English by a passive. Cf. the rendering in NIV.

26. The word translated *wicked* in the previous clause is plural, but *the rich* is singular.

27. Christ affirmed his own sinlessness. It was also attested by Paul, John and the author of Hebrews. See II Cor. 5:21; I John 3:5; Heb. 7:26-28.

28. Rawlinson (PC, II, 297) points out that crucified persons were buried with their crosses near the scene of execution.

29. The essential idea of *'asham* is the payment of restitution. Sin is robbery of God. The sinner owes a debt that must be paid. In Matt. 20:28 Jesus said that he came to give his life a ransom for many.

he was a sin offering; here a guilt offering. *His soul* shall *place* this offering before God. This might mean no more than that he himself offers the offering. Young contends that *his soul* indicates that his very life is to be the oblation.[30]

2. He would survive death (v. 10b). He will *see a seed.* This term obviously is used here in a spiritual sense. The *seed* of a teacher or prophet would be his disciples (John 13:33; 21:4).[31] The resurrection is implicit here. The only way a dead man could see his disciples would be to return from the dead. The passage is reminiscent of Psalm 22:30 where the prophet promised, a *seed* would serve him.

The Servant would survive death to die no more, for *he shall prolong days.* Clearly in the context of resurrection from the dead this expression must point to his eternality. "For we know that since Christ was raised from the dead, he cannot die again; death no longer has mastery over him" (Rom. 6:9 NIV). This theme of the eternality of the Servant should probably be linked to the promise made to David that his throne would endure forever.[32]

3. The Servant would be successful in his mission, for *the pleasure of Yahweh shall prosper in his hand* (v. 10). The pleasure of the Lord is God's ultimate aim for his creation. Under the administration of the resurrected Servant and through his instrumentality[33] this program will *prosper,* i.e., succeed.

4. The Servant would experience personal satisfaction (v. 11). Because of his suffering the Servant *shall see.* The object of the verb is omitted. The reference is most likely to the fact that he would see the fruits and rewards of his ministry. With great satisfaction he would look on the results of his expiatory suffering—the formation of his church which will live with him forever in heaven (Rev. 7:4-17). First the cross, then the crown! The foreknowledge of this triumphant conclusion sustained Christ throughout the ordeal (Heb. 12:2).

5. He would provide abundant salvation (v. 11). He is *righteous,* and thus is in a position to provide this salvation. He will *justify the many,* i.e., he declares that they stand in the right relationship with God. From the standpoint of the guilty sinner the justification is made

---

30. Young, NIC, III, 354.

31. The use of *children* in a spiritual sense of disciples is frequent in the New Testament. See Philemon 10; I Cor. 4:15; Gal. 4:19; I John 2:1.

32. II Sam. 7:13, 16; Ps. 21:4; 89:4; 132:12.

33. The word *hand* may denote ministry as in Num. 36:13 and Haggai 1:3.

possible through knowledge of the Servant.[34] Intimate knowledge of the Servant would involve faith and obedience.

6. The Servant would achieve permanent recognition. He would have *a portion with the great*. Inasmuch as he so willingly and nobly fulfilled his mission, *therefore* God acted on his behalf. The apostle expands on this theme by affirming that God has given him a name which is above every name (Phil. 2:9).

7. The Servant would distribute the spoils of his victory (v. 12). *With the strong he shall divide the spoil*. Some take this clause in a general and metaphorical sense. The Servant is a great conqueror. The dividing of the spoil serves to underscore the greatness of his victory. It is possible, however, that by *the strong* Isaiah means the Servant's disciples. If this be the case, they will share in the spoils of his victory over sin and death. Perhaps a link should be made to Psalm 68:18 and the gifts distributed by Christ at his enthronement.

Chapter 53 closes with a restatement of the reasons for the Servant's exaltation.

1. He died willingly. *He poured out his soul to death*. No man took his life from him.

2. He died submissively. *He was numbered* (i.e., permitted himself to be numbered) *with transgressors*. Jesus quoted this verse and said that its fulfillment was near not long before his arrest in the garden (Luke 22:37).

3. He died vicariously: *Yet he bore the sins of many*. Though counted a sinner by some, yet his ultimate purpose was to pay the price of the sin debt of all who would embrace him.

4. He died victoriously: *and for transgressors he made intercession* (v. 12). Here again the priestly ministry of the Servant is in view. The basis for his intercession is the sacrifice which he himself provided.[35]

Prophecy No. 47

THE GREAT INVITATION

Isaiah 55:3-5

The redemption for sinful mankind was procured by the suffering Servant in Isaiah 53. The following chapter enumerates the blessings

---

34. It is not the Servant's own knowledge, but rather the sinner's knowledge of the Servant which is the condition of justification.

35. On the intercessory ministry of Jesus see Rom. 8:34; Heb. 9:24; I John 2:1.

which will come to God's new covenant people in the Messianic age. Chapter 55 begins with an evangelistic appeal to all who are searching for spiritual realities. The spiritual blessings of the Messiah are depicted under the symbols of water, wine, milk, and bread. All men are invited to come and freely partake.

Translation of Isaiah 55:3-5

(3) For your sake I will make for you an eternal covenant, the faithful mercies of David. (4) Behold! I have given him for your sake as a Witness of peoples, a Prince and a Commander of peoples. (5) Behold! A nation that you do not know, you shall call, and a nation that does not know you shall run to you, for the sake of the LORD your God, the Holy One of Israel, for he has glorified you.

Discussion

The focus is first on a new covenant.[36] There can be little doubt that the Christian covenant is intended (Heb. 9:15). Six features of this covenant are indicated.

1. The covenant is divine in its origin and certain in its prospect. God *will* make a covenant.

2. The covenant is made primarily for the benefit of God's people. *For you* means *for your benefit.*

3. The covenant would be eternal. The context here of spiritual salvation demands that 'olam be given this limitless meaning. The Sinai covenant was meant to be provisional; this covenant would be permanent.

4. The covenant is gracious. It will employ the *mercies* of God promised long before.

5. The covenant reflects God's faithfulness to all of his promises, hence the reference to the *sure* or *faithful* mercies.

6. The covenant pertains to the house of *David.* That is to say, the eternal covenant will center in a descendant of David.

The sure mercies of David, then, are the loving and merciful promises which God made to David of an eternal throne. "The promises to David, rightly understood, involve all the essential points of the Christian

---

36. Elsewhere Isaiah announces this future covenant in 42:6; 49:8; 54:10; 56:4, 6; 59:21 and 61:8.

covenant."[37] The phrase *sure mercies of David* is applied to Christ in Acts 13:34. On the authority of this citation, Isaiah 55:4 can be applied to Messiah. This being the case, four specifics concerning the Messiah are in evidence:

1. Messiah is a gift of God, for he says, *I have given him*, i.e., the Messiah.

2. Messiah is a *Witness*. He bears witness through his life and words to the truth of God (John 18:37). He witnessed a good confession before Pilate (I Tim. 6:13). In a special way he bears witness to Gentiles who have not heard of the sure mercies of David. The Apostle John called him the Faithful Witness (Rev. 1:5).

2. Messiah is a *Prince* (*naghid*). This title is also applied to Messiah in Daniel 9:25. The term stresses his position and authority.

3. Messiah is the *Commander*. This title stresses his function. He is the captain of the Lord's host (Josh. 5:14), the Captain of our Salvation (Heb. 2:10), the leader under whose banner Christians serve (II Tim. 2:3-4).

Verse 5 is a promise addressed to the seed of David of the preceding verse. Messiah will call a nation which heretofore he had not known as his people. This is a way of emphasizing the universality of the future Davidic (Messianic) kingdom. Obviously the seed of David would rule the people of Israel. But other nations as well would own him as their king. This would not be accomplished through military endeavour but by a *call*, the Gospel call. Thus God's kingdom would be enlarged, and Israel's glory would be increased. God has glorified the Messiah (John 17:1; Acts 3:13) in his resurrection, ascension and enthronement.

Prophecy No. 48

THE SERVANT AS PREACHER

Isaiah 61:1-11

The fifth and last of the Servant poems was read by Jesus in the synagogue at Nazareth. When he sat down, the master declared: "Today this Scripture is fulfilled in your hearing" (Luke 4:21 NIV). No doubt therefore can exist that this passage is appropriately considered as a personal Messianic prophecy.

---

37. Rawlinson, PC, II, 329. These promises were that David's seed would sit on an everlasting throne (Ps. 89:2-5, 19-37), triumph over death (Ps. 16:9, 10), give peace to Israel (Ps. 132:15-18), and build a house of God (II Sam. 7:13).

In the preceding chapter Isaiah discussed the future blessings of Zion. In chapter 61 he brings to center stage one last time the one who will bring that blessing. As in two earlier poems Isaiah represents the Servant himself as the speaker (cf. Isa. 49:1; 50:4). In the light of Jesus' declaration in Luke 4, the speaker here must be the Messiah.

Translation of Isaiah 61:1-11

(1) The Spirit of the Lord GOD was upon me because the LORD has anointed me to announce good tidings to the afflicted; he has sent me to bind up those with broken hearts, to proclaim liberty to captives and to prisoners, release; (2) to proclaim a year of the LORD's favor, and a day of vengeance for our God, to comfort all mourners; (3) To appoint to those who mourn in Zion, to give to them a crown in place of ashes, the oil of gladness in place of mourning, a garment of praise in place of a faint spirit; and they shall be called trees of righteousness, the planting of the LORD, that he might glorify himself. (4) And they shall build up the ancient wastes, the former desolations they shall raise up, and they shall restore the waste cities, the desolations of past generations. (5) And strangers shall stand and feed your flock, and the sons of strangers shall be your plowmen and vinedressers. (6) But you shall be called priests of the LORD, and you shall be named ministers of God; the strength of Gentiles you shall eat, and for their glory you shall substitute yourselves. (7) Instead of your shame (you shall have) double, and (instead of) reproach they shall rejoice in their portion. Therefore in their land they shall possess double; they shall possess everlasting joy. (8) For I the LORD am a lover of justice, a despiser of robbery for burnt offering; and I will guide their work in truth, and I will make an everlasting covenant for them. (9) And their seed shall be known among the Gentiles, and their descendants in the midst of the peoples. All who see them shall recognize that they are a seed which the LORD has blessed. (10) I will greatly rejoice in the LORD, my soul shall exalt in my God because he has clothed me in garments of salvation; with a robe of righteousness he shall cover me, like a bridegroom makes splendid his headdress, and a bride adorns herself with her jewels. (11) For as the earth brings forth her bud and as a garden causes that which is sown to spring forth thus will the Lord GOD cause righteousness to spring forth, and praise before all the Gentiles.

Discussion

The last Servant poem stresses three aspects of the Servant and his work: (1) his credentials (v. 1a), (2) his mission (vv. 1b-3) and (3) the blessings which he brings (vv. 3b-10).

A. *The Credentials of the Servant* (v. 1a). The Servant in this passage fills the role of a prophet. For that office he is well equipped, for *the Spirit of Yahweh was upon me.* What was promised in earlier passages of this book (11:2; 42:1; 49:8; 50:4, 5) has now occurred. The Trinitarian thrust of this sentence cannot be ignored. Here is Yahweh, the Spirit and me (Messiah). The emphasis on the pronoun *me* suggests that the speaker is a person of unusual significance.[38]

The Spirit of the Lord is upon the speaker because Yahweh has *anointed* him. The selection of the word *anoint* hints that the speaker is Messiah. Old Testament priests and kings were anointed with oil, but the Servant will be anointed with the Spirit (Luke 3:22; Acts 4:27; 10:38).

B. *The Mission of the Servant* (vv. 1b-3). Seven aspects of the Servant's mission are specified in verses 1b-3:

1. He would proclaim good tidings to the afflicted (v. 1b). The good news is that deliverance from the bondage of sin has become possible. The *afflicted* are those who have been oppressed, beaten down by satanic forces both physical and spiritual.

2. He would *bind up those with broken hearts.* Sin breaks hearts and shatters lives. The Wonderful Counselor speaks words of forgiveness and hope which lift the heart burden. Messiah is the Great Physician.

3. He would *proclaim liberty to captives.* Every fiftieth year—the year of jubilee—all slaves were released (Lev. 25:10, 13; 27:24). The captivity of national Israel in Babylon was a result of sin. That experience was a type of the bondage which is sin and which results from sin. Messiah is the ultimate liberator. The truth he speaks sets men free from the delusions of Satan and the tangled web of sin.

4. He would open the prison to them that are bound. It is not from physical prison that Christ delivers men, but from imprisonment in spiritual darkness.

5. He would proclaim a year of Yahweh's favor. The Gospel age is the antitypical year of jubilee. The Messianic age is the age of grace. All the blessings which God has created for his people are now available.

---

38. Young, NIC, III, 459.

It was at this point in his synagogue reading when Jesus returned the scroll of Isaiah to the minister and sat down. He then remarked, "This day is this prophecy fulfilled in your ears" (Luke 4:21). The age which Isaiah envisioned had arrived. The prophecy began to be fulfilled in the ministry of Jesus. Under his direction believers continue to proclaim the Gospel of liberation.

6. He would proclaim the day of vengeance of God. This he did not do in the Nazareth synagogue, but in other contexts he spoke about the destruction of Jerusalem and the end of the world (Matt. 24, 25). While the day of God's grace lasts for a *year*, his wrath would last but for a *day*. Part of the Christian proclamation is that a day of vengeance is coming upon all who oppose God and his people.

7. He would comfort mourners (vv. 2b-3). Jesus said, "Blessed are they who mourn for they shall be comforted" (Matt. 5:4). The Christian proclamation outlined in verses 1-2 is the means by which the Servant comforts those who mourn over their personal circumstances and the condition of God's people. Isaiah emphasizes the change which would come upon Zion's mourners by pointing out three gifts which God would bestow on his people. First, he would give them a *crown*. The crown which symbolizes joy and victory, would replace the ashes which Jews threw over their heads to demonstrate their sorrow. Second, he would give them the *oil of joy* with which to anoint themselves on festive occasions.[39] Finally, he would give them a *garment of praise*, i.e., God will clothe his people in praise. Such praise is the exact opposite of the faint spirit which characterizes men who are beaten down and oppressed.

C. *The Blessings Brought by the Servant* (vv. 3b-10). Ten blessings which come as a result of the work of the Servant are enumerated in verses 3b-10:

1. God's people will become strong as the oak (v. 3b). The signs of joy will bring about a change in the designation of God's people. They will be called *the oaks of righteousness*. Through the righteousness of God they will have been made towers of strength. God has planted these durable trees for the purpose of glorifying himself. Men praise God when they see the mighty work he does in the lives of his people.

2. Ancient ruins will be restored (v. 4). Those who mourn will build up the *ancient wastes* and *former desolations*. Young captures the thrust of verse 4 when he writes:

---

39. See Song 4:10; II Sam. 12:20; 14:2; Ps. 23:5.

The reference is not merely to the rebuilding of Jerusalem after the exile, for the language is hardly applicable to that, but to the building up of the Church from the ravages sin has made throughout the ages.[40]

3. Gentiles will work for Zion (v. 5). *Strangers* and *the sons of strangers* will serve as Zion's shepherds, husbandmen and vinedressers. Former enemies (*zarim*), now citizens of Zion, dedicate their energies to the work of God's kingdom. The implication here is that Jew and Gentile shall be united in the new covenant Zion (Heb. 12:22).

4. Citizens of Zion will be a priesthood (v. 6a). The Aaronic priesthood would be a thing of the past. All the inhabitants of Zion, including the Gentile converts of the preceding verse, will be called the priests and servants of the Lord. Peter records the fulfillment: "But you are a chosen race, a royal priesthood, a holy nation, a people for possession, that you should proclaim the praises of the One who called you out of darkness and into his marvellous light" (I Peter 2:9).

5. Zion will be nourished by her converts (v. 6b). Priests were entitled under the Law to remuneration for the ministry which they rendered. So the priesthood of the Messianic Zion will be sustained through the generosity of individual converts. The *strength* and *glory* of nations refers to the material contributions of Gentiles. Since the latter decades of the first century, Zion (the kingdom, the church of Christ) has been materially undergirded largely through the gifts of converted Gentiles.

6. Zion will have honor (v. 7a). The condition of Zion in Isaiah's day[41] is described by the words *shame* and *confusion*. When the Servant comes they would receive double honor or glory. Confusion would give way to celebration as the citizens of Zion rejoice in their *portion*, i.e., the privilege of being part of the kingdom of God.

7. Zion will have great joy (v. 7b). The eternal joy is the consequence of the change of status described in the preceding verse, the fact that they will be *in the land* and that they will have a double inheritance to compensate for the years of shame and confusion. *Their land* is the Old Testament way of referring to the Messiah's kingdom. The physical land of Canaan was but a type of that future land of promise. Certainly it is not the intention of Isaiah to teach that the redeemed will live eternally in the land of Palestine!

---

40. Young, NIC, III, 462.

41. It may be that the *shame* and *confusion* describe the condition of God's people during the exile which Isaiah presupposes in chapters 40-66.

8. Zion will live under an everlasting covenant (v. 8). God loves justice and hates injustice. His justice demands that he repay those who serve him. To guarantee the future blessings of his people, God will initiate a new and eternal covenant.

9. Zion will enjoy fame among the nations (v. 9). The seed of God's people, i.e., the individual citizens of Zion, will be recognized by others as having been richly blessed by God. The Jews took note of Peter and John that they had been with Jesus (Acts 4:13).

10. Zion will be clothed in garments of salvation and righteousness (v. 10). The speaker in verse 10 is no longer the Messiah, but the true Israel of God speaking collectively. The saints are filled with joy because Zion has been clothed in garments of salvation and righteousness. This spiritual clothing is likened to that of a bridegroom and a bride. The former wore a grand turban like that of a priest, the latter adorned her bridal gown with jewels. The point is that the spiritual garb which God has supplied to his people is complete, attractive, and praiseworthy.

Verse 11 serves as a fitting conclusion to this prophecy. The coming salvation is sure. Righteousness and praise will spring forth as surely as the plants spring forth from the earth. The saints of God can rest assured that the Messianic age will come.

Chapter Twenty-Two

MICAH AND THE MESSIAH

Micah ministered in the southern kingdom during the reigns of Jotham, Ahaz and Hezekiah (739-686 B.C.). During his ministry Micah saw Samaria fall to Sargon in 722 B.C. The northern kingdom of Israel ceased to exist. Micah saw his own country overrun by Assyrian armies in 701 B.C. Only a last minute miraculous intervention by God saved Judah from total destruction by the armies of Sennacherib.

The thundering preaching and blunt warnings of Micah may seem to have influenced King Hezekiah to undertake one of the most thorough reform movements recorded in the Old Testament.[1] But Micah was more than a prophet of doom. On the other side of judgment he saw a ray of hope. One aspect of that hope was the rise of a ruler from the house of David.

As might be expected, the Messianic expectations of Isaiah and Micah have much in common. Both prophets foresaw:

1. A coming royal hero as God's ultimate answer to the invasion of Assyria.
2. This royal hero will be a scion of the house of David.
3. The birth of this hero will signal the beginning of a special intervention by God.
4. The hero is the embodiment of divine might and authority.
5. The hero will rule over a glorious universal kingdom.

Prophecy No. 49

THE BREAKER

Micah 2:12-13

The Book of Micah opens with an announcement of the coming divine judgment of the covenant people. All of chapter 1 and the first eleven verses of chapter 2 describe this judgment and explain why it is necessary. Chapter 3 also contains messages of threat and punishment against the courts, the false prophets, and the establishment. In the midst of this "desert of doom," 2:12-13 arises "like an oasis of hope."[2] This

---

1. This conclusion is based on Jeremiah 26:18f.
2. Allen, NIC, p. 257.

short salvation oracle serves as a fitting conclusion to the first major division of the Book of Micah.[3]

Translation of Micah 2:12-13

(12) I will surely assemble, O Jacob, all of you, I will surely gather the remnant of Israel. Together I will place them as sheep of Bozrah; like a flock in the midst of its pasture, they will hum with men. (13) The Breaker has gone up before them. They have broken through, have passed through the gate and have gone out thereat; and their King has gone on before them, even Yahweh at the head of them.

Discussion

The two verses of this salvation oracle focus on (1) the flock of God's people (v. 12), and the leader of the flock (v. 13).
A. *The Flock* (v. 12). The oracle is addressed to *Jacob*. As in verse 7 this name is applied to the southern kingdom. In chapter 1 Micah painted a vivid picture of the impending doom of Judah. That picture is further amplified here with two thoughts. First, the ominous phrase *remnant of Israel* suggests a drastic reduction in size of the nation.[4] Also, the verb *gather* suggests that this remnant would be scattered about.

The gathering of the remnant is a divine work. The Hebrew text gives the assurance that this work of gathering will be done. God will once again assume his ancient role as the Shepherd of his people.[5]

God will bring his scattered sheep together. The assembling of the remnant began with the work of Zerubbabel (Ezra 1-2) and Ezra (Ezra 7). These gatherings, however, were but types of the Gospel gathering which is still going on today. While the focus here is primarily on Jewish sheep, Jesus emphasized that he had other sheep which were not of this fold.

---

3. So abrupt is this change of tone that this passage is considered by some to be (1) a misplaced statement by Micah, or (2) an intrusion by someone other than Micah. For a defense of the genuineness of these two verses and the appropriateness of their placement here see Allen, NIC, pp. 300-301.
4. The term *remnant* has qualitative as well as quantitative implications. The remnant consists of those who love and serve God.
5. The Shepherd metaphor is associated with the Exodus in Ps. 78:52f. In Ps. 80:1 God is called Shepherd of Israel. In Ps. 23:1 the concept is individualized.

The success of God's gathering is indicated by the words *as sheep of Bozrah*.[6] The Edomite city of Bozrah was noted for its large flocks of sheep (cf. Isa. 34:6). The great influx of Gentiles helped swell the flock of the Good Shepherd. He gathers them *like a flock in its pasture* or fold. God will supply every need. The activity of the flock is indicated in the words, *they will hum with men*.[7] (v. 12). A great multitude will raise their voices of prayer and praise.

B. *The Leader of the Flock* (v. 13). The gathering of verse 12 is made possible by the coming of a Deliverer who frees God's people from oppressors. He receives three titles. He is first called the *Breaker*. The general import of the verse is clear. The leader breaks through all barriers which confine his people. The specific imagery is not so clear. Perhaps Micah is thinking of the Breaker smashing through the ranks of a besieging army.[8] On the other hand, he may be thinking of God's people imprisoned within a mighty city like Babylon. The Breaker smashes through the gate to release his people. The immediate context suggests yet another picture. The flock of God is pictured in an enclosure. They will rush (LXX) through the opening made for them homeward to their own fold.[9] The Breaker is a conqueror who in the light of other prophecies can be no other than the Messiah.[10]

The coming leader is called *their King*. The Breaker seems to be equivalent to *their King*.[11] The Old Testament speaks of a general and a particular kind of kingship of the Lord.[12] Because he is creator, God is regarded as exercising universal dominion.[13] Yet within this all-inclusive sovereignty, God is said to have been Israel's King in a very special sense.[14] In some passages Yahweh's kingship encompasses both past and future. Other passages look forward to dramatic manifestations of the coming kingship of God.[15] "This expectation of the

---

6. NIV, *like sheep in a pen*.

7. Allen (NIC, p. 302) thinks that this clause further describes the wretched condition of the flock crying out in fear because of *men*, i.e., oppressors.

8. Allen (NIC, p. 303) thinks the reference is to the destruction of the Assyrian armies which besieged Jerusalem in 701 B.C. The theme of God breaking through the ranks of the enemy is found in II Sam. 5:20, 24 in connection with David's victory over the Philistines.

9. Peisker, BBC, V, 205-206.

10. Cheyne, CB, p. 29.

11. Laetsch, BCMP, p. 258.

12. Ridderbos, CK, pp. 4-5.

13. See Exod. 15:18; I Kings 22:19; Isa. 6:5; Ps. 47:2; 103:19.

14. See Num. 23:21; Judg. 8:23; I Sam. 8:7; 12:12; Ps. 48:2; Isa. 41:21.

15. So, e.g., Isa. 40:9-11; 52:7.

future has such a prominent importance in the scope of the prophetic divine revelation that it may be called the center of the whole Old Testament promise of salvation."[16]

Is it legitimate to associate the thought of the future manifestation of King Yahweh with the Messianic expectation? Ridderbos speaks to this point:

> . . . It is true, that the thought of the coming state of bliss in which Jahwe will assume his kingship in the full sense of the word, is often unaccompanied by any mention of the Messiah-King. But the one cannot be separated from the other, because what is said about the coming reign of God has no other reach than that of the prophecies about the messianic kingdom of peace (cf. e.g., Isaiah 9:11; 32). He is the coming ruler of the world (Isaiah 11:9, 10); at least according to some prophecies, his kingship also bears a supernatural character (cf. e.g., Micah 5:1); in short, all that which holds for the coming divine manifestation of the king, also holds for the rule of Messiah-King.[17]

The possessive suffix should not be overlooked. He is *their* king, one of their own. This suffix supports the ancient Jewish tradition here that *their king* refers to Messiah.[18]

The leader is called *Yahweh*. This name emphasizes the role of God as redeemer of his people. Parallelism requires that the King and Yahweh be one and the same person.[19] The name should not be restricted to God the Father. Messiah is deity. He is Yahweh.

Yahweh goes before his people into battle. The verb used here (*'alah*) is a military idiom meaning to lead into battle (cf. I Sam. 29:9). Like a trailblazer *he has gone on before them*. He never asks his people to go where he has not previously gone. He is ever at the *head of them*, in total control of *every situation*.

The Liberator inspires boldness on the part of the flock. Following the lead of their Champion, they will break out of the prison which holds them. They will pass *through the gate*. The city gate in ancient times was a maze of buildings arranged in such a way as to make entrance of an attacker or departure of a captive difficult. The Breaker smashes through the gate to effect the release of the captives.

---

16. Ridderbos, CK, p. 5.

17. Ridderbos, CK, p. 6.

18. Opinions vary on whether Jews regarded the title *Breaker* as Messianic. Pusey affirms that they did; Driver says they applied the term only to Elijah. See Allen, NIC, p. 303.

19. Keil (BCOT, Minor Prophets, I, 148) equates *their king* with Yahweh rather than with the Breaker. It is best to regard the three as names of one leader.

Prophecy No. 50

THE SAVIOR FROM BETHLEHEM

Micah 5:1-15

The Book of Micah is arranged in the proverbial "good news—bad news" pattern. Micah 5:1-6 is the last of a group of three oracles which paint stark contrast between the inglorious present and the glorious future. Allen describes this oracle as "the central peak of the range of oracles in chs. 4 and 5. It presents a longer hope section than any other unit, and points to the fulfillment of royal promise as the key to the greatness of Jerusalem and Israel heralded in the surrounding pieces."[20]

Translation of Micah 5:1-15

(1) Now gather in troops, O daughter of troops, for a siege has been set against us. With the rod he has smitten upon the jaw the judge of Israel. (2) But you, Bethlehem Ephrathah, small to be among the thousands of Judah, from you for me he shall go forth to be ruler over Israel, and his outgoings are from ancient times, even days of eternity. (3) Therefore, he will give them up until the time when she who is with child shall have given birth. And the remnant of his brethren shall return along with the children of Israel. (4) And he shall stand and shepherd in the strength of his God, in the majesty of the name of the LORD his God. And they will remain undisturbed, for now he will be great unto the ends of the earth. (5) And this (one) is Peace. As for Assyria, when he shall come into our land and tread in our palaces, then we will raise up over us seven Shepherds and eight princes of men. (6) And they shall shepherd the land of Assyria with the sword, and the land of Nimrod in her gates. And he shall deliver from the Assyrian when he shall come into our land and when he treads in our border. (7) The remnant of Jacob shall be in the midst of many peoples like dew from the LORD, as showers upon the grass which are not anticipated by men nor awaited by the sons of men. (8) And the remnant of Jacob shall be among the nations, in the midst of many peoples, like a lion in the high places of a forest, like a young lion among the flocks of sheep, which if he pass by treads down and tears and there is

---

20. Allen, NIC, p. 340.

no deliverer. (9) Your hand shall be lifted up over your adversaries, and all of your enemies shall be cut off. (10) And it shall come to pass in that day (oracle of the LORD) that I will cut off your horses from the midst of you, and I will destroy your chariots. (11) And I will cut off the cities of your land, and I will cast down all your strongholds. (12) And I will cut off sorcery from your hand, and soothsayers you will no longer have. (13) And I will cut off your graven images and your pillars from the midst of you; and you shall not worship any more the work of your hands. (14) And I will pluck up your Asherim from your midst, and I will destroy your idols.[21] (15) In wrath and anger I will execute vengeance upon the nations which do not hearken.

A. *The Coming Ruler will Appear only after a Period of National Humiliation.* Micah begins by describing the calamity which must befall the capital and the king. Jerusalem is addressed as *daughter of troops* because she is viewed as a city under attack. Jerusalem is urged to *gather in troops*[22] for self-defense and mutual encouragement.

Israel's judge or king will receive the worst possible insult. He will be struck in the face. What a sorry state to which the house of David will come. It was the primary task of the king to strike with his scepter, as it were, evil doers whether foreign or domestic.[23] Now the judge has become but a whipping boy. He is smitten with a rod. Perhaps Micah is thinking of the war club carried by Assyrian soldiers.[24]

During and after Micah's day Judah was in a state of gradual deterioration. Hezekiah suffered the humiliation of the Assyrian invasion in 701 B.C. Of the seven kings who followed Hezekiah on the throne, only one, Josiah, was great. Even he died an ignominious death at the hands of an invading king. So Micah is predicting this low ebb period for the ruling house of Judah. During the intertestamental period the nation experienced humiliating persecutions by Antiochus, the usurpation of the throne by pretenders from the Hasmonean line, and the reign of the Idumean mad-man Herod the Great. It was "at this time of deepest humiliation and degradation, the Messiah came."[25]

---

21. Or *cities* as in NASB and NIV.

22. NIV *marshal your troops*; NIV margin *strengthen your walls*. Allen gives another meaning to this root: *Now you are gnashing yourself.*

23. Cf. Ps. 2 where Messiah crushes a rebellion with a rod of iron, and Isa. 11:4 where he strikes with the rod of his mouth.

24. Cf. Isa. 10:24; 14:29 where Assyria's attack on Judah is described as striking with a rod.

25. Laetsch, BCMP, p. 271.

B. *The Coming Ruler will be Born in Bethlehem* (v. 2a). All is not lost for the Davidic dynasty. In the very birthplace of David a new and glorious ruler is to be born. This prediction is geographically precise. It is in Bethlehem Ephrathah that he will be born. Ephrathah was either the district in which Bethlehem was located, or an ancient name for the town.[26] The double name distinguishes his birth place from the northern Bethlehem in the tribal area of Zebulun (Josh. 19:15).

The prediction is full of irony. The names Bethlehem (house of bread) and Ephrathah (fruitfulness) are "omens of prosperity[27] in these dark days of Judah. The size of the place is also ironic. Literally, "small in respect of being among Judah's clans." The area would hardly be able to supply sufficient manpower for a unit in the tribal levy. Could the promised Ruler really be coming out of Bethlehem?

When the wise men followed the star of Jerusalem, they sought counsel from King Herod regarding the place for the birth of the promised king. Without hesitation or debate the chief priests and teachers of the law pointed to Bethlehem as the birth place for Messiah. In support of their contention they quoted Micah 5:2 (Matt. 2:1ff.). The people as well as the scholars were expecting Messiah to be born in Bethlehem (John 7:42).

C. *The Coming Ruler will be a Unique Person.* Four points are discussed about him.

1. He would be a committed ruler, for he will come forth *for me*. The words are reminiscent of what God told Samuel over three hundred years earlier when he sent the prophet to Bethlehem to anoint a son of Jesse: "I have provided for myself a king from among his sons" (I Sam. 16:1). So now he promises the rise of a second David, a man after God's own heart, a man who would be totally committed to God.

2. He will be a subordinate ruler for he will be *prince* (v. 2). It may be significant that he is not called *king* here. Perhaps the intention is to suggest his subordination to the divine King. He will rule under God.

3. He will be a theocratic ruler, for he will be prince *over Israel*. Northern Israel was gone and that title had now been assumed by Judah, the remnant of the nation. Already distinctions have been made between the Israel of the flesh and the Israel of faith. Only the latter is the true Israel of God.

---

26. David's father is described as "an Ephrathite from Bethlehem in Judah" (I Sam. 17:12). See Gen. 35:19; 48:7; Ruth 4:11.

27. Allen, NIC, p. 342.

4. He will be an ancient Ruler, for *his outgoings are from ancient times even days of eternity.* Some see in these words no greater significance than the kingly lineage of the Ruler. He can trace his ancestry back to distant times, to David himself.[28] It is best, however, to follow Keil and the older commentators in seeing here an allusion to the pre-incarnate activity of the Messiah.

The term *outgoings*[29] recalls the occasions when this Ruler led his people as a king would lead his people into battle. Throughout early Old Testament history (*ancient times*) this Ruler had been active. In fact, his activities stretch back beyond time to eternity.[30] The Rabbis were not far off when they suggested on the basis of this passage that the Messiah existed in the mind of God before the world began.

D. *The Birth of the Coming Ruler will Signal a New Day for the People of God* (v. 3). In verse 3 Micah makes an application of the promise he has just made.[31] That promise had significance for Israel then in the midst of the Assyrian crisis, and indeed in the midst of smaller crises which followed. If there is to be a glorious Davidic king, he must have a kingdom. That kingdom would be *Israel.* So the fortunes of the nation are intertwined with that of its king.

Micah does not stray far away from the hard times of the present and immediate future. God will in fact abandon his people for a time. He will give them over to their foes. First came the Assyrians. For the most part they dominated Judah from 745 to about 640 B.C. They totally overran the country on at least one occasion (701 B.C.). Next came the Egyptians (609-605 B.C.), the Chaldeans (605-539 B.C.), the Persians (539-332 B.C.), the Greeks (332-165 B.C.), and the Romans. Only for a few short stretches during all those centuries did God's people enjoy any significant measure of freedom from foreign domination.

The birth of a child would signal the end of the period of abandonment. *She who is with child* obviously refers to the mother of the prince.[32] Micah's woman with child is no doubt the virgin of Isaiah 7:14. It would appear that Isaiah's promise of the miraculous birth of

---

28. This view is argued by Allen, NIC, p. 343. He translated *yeme 'olam,* "days of yore" and thinks the expression refers back to the days of David.

29. NIV, *origins.*

30. So Keil (BCOT, Minor Prophets, I, 480): The origin of Messiah before all worlds, and to his appearances in olden times.

31. This transition is indicated by *lachen, therefore.* Yahweh here is referred to in the third person.

32. Others have proposed that the "mother" is the nation personified.

Immanuel uttered over thirty years earlier fueled a popular expectation "too well known to require amplification."[33]

The coming Ruler will bring unity to God's people: *And the remnant of his brethren shall return along with the children of Israel.* That the children of Israel are his brethren according to the flesh is obvious. But who are *the remnant of his brethren?* Former citizens of northern Israel who were now scattered throughout the Assyrian empire? Gentiles? In the light of New Testament teaching the term *brethren* would include those who are of the household of faith (Heb. 2:11). Jesus stressed his kinship with his followers when he said, "For whoever does the will of my Father in heaven is my brother and sister and mother" (Matt. 12:50).

The history of Israel from 931 B.C. forward is the story of the incredible shrinking nation. First the ten northern tribes had broken away from the house of David. That northern kingdom was destroyed in 722 B.C., its citizens scattered across the Assyrian empire. Judah itself had been overrun and thousands of its citizens deported by Sennacherib. About a century after Micah the Babylonian king Nebuchadnezzar would on at least four occasions deport Jews to Babylon. Finally in 587 B.C. Judah itself as a monarchy was destroyed.

Messiah is thus the "chosen brother"[34] in whom resides the hope for all the family of God including the missing *remnant.* About three hundred years before the time of Micah representatives of all the tribes at Hebron had recognized David as being their own flesh and blood. In the future the scattered family of God would recognize their kinship to David's greater son.

E. *The Coming Ruler will be a Mighty Ruler of his People* (v. 4). The figure of the shepherd harks back to the Davidic traditions. David had been taken from the sheep to become the caretaker of the nation (II Sam. 5:2). The leaders of ancient Israel were often called shepherds. But the chief shepherd of the nation was Yahweh himself (cf. 2:12; 4:6-8). Implications of deity are associated with Jesus' claim that he is the good shepherd (John 10:11, 16).[35]

The Shepherd will *stand.* Allen takes this to be a reference to the traditional coronation ceremony in ancient Israel. The royal prince would

---

33. Allen, NIC, p. 345.

34. Ibid.

35. In Hebrews 13:20 he is "that great shepherd of the sheep," in Peter he is "the shepherd and overseer of your souls," and in Rev. 7:17 "the Lamb at the center of the throne will be their shepherd."

stand beside a pillar in the Temple to be anointed (II Kings 11:14). The word *stand*, however, is probably not being used in this technical sense. The idea is that one who is alert and active is standing. So the Shepherd stands to commence his work.

The Shepherd is successful in his work. He *shepherds* his flock. Patience, provision, and protection are all involved in his work. The Shepherd would succeed because he has divine strength: *in the strength of his God*. This is one Ruler who is worthy of the throne.

The Shepherd will manifest in his life and work the *majesty (ge'on)* of God. This shepherd would perform his work *in the name of Yahweh*, i.e., by his authority. This is the Old Testament equivalent of saying that he would have all authority in heaven and on earth (Matt. 28:18). This Shepherd would have a close relationship to the Father who would be in a special sense *his* God. This again is an echo of the covenant made with David and his descendants.[36]

This Shepherd would provide perfect security for his people: *They will remain undisturbed*. Nathan promised David that during his reign God will "plant them so that they can have a home of their own and no longer be disturbed" (II Sam. 7:10). So far the rulers from David's dynasty had not been able to deliver on this promise. But in the powerful reign of the coming Ruler this promise was to be realized. This Shepherd would be famous throughout the world (v. 4). He shall be great to the ends of the earth for that is the extent of his kingdom.[37] What no son of David had ever achieved would be realized in David's greater Son.

The Shepherd will be peace personified, for *this one is Peace* (v. 5). This is but an abbreviation of the title Prince of Peace used by Isaiah (9:6). What a paradox! His kingdom will extend to the ends of the earth, yet the Ruler himself will be Peace. The church of Christ with its unique blend of young and old, rich and poor, Jew and Gentile is the magnificent work of the Prince of Peace.

The Shepherd will provide protection for the flock whenever it is endangered (v. 5). In the age of Messiah no enemy, not even mighty Assyria, would be successful in an invasion of *our land*. Micah here is describing the future security of God's people in terms of eighth-century

---

36. Allen has cited the following passages where *his God* is used in reference to the Davidic dynasty: I Sam. 30:6; I Kings 15:4 (of David); I Kings 11:4 (of Solomon); and II Kings 16:2 (of Ahaz).

37. As in Ps. 2:8 and 72:8 the phrase *ends of the earth* here suggests the universal dominion which was envisioned for the house of David.

threat. Assyria here is a type of all ruthless oppressors who might through the centuries attempt to overrun God's kingdom. Micah apparently envisions some success for the invasion, for the Assyrians will *tread in our palaces.*

To meet this attack God's people will raise up for themselves an abundance of capable leaders—*seven shepherds and eight princes of men* (v. 5). Seven would be enough and eight would be more than enough.[38] God's people would have no lack of leaders in the face of the future Assyrian crisis.[39]

The victory over the enemies of God's people will be complete. The leaders raised up will not only repulse the enemy, they will also invade his territory, *the land of Assyria* and *the land of Nimrod* (v. 6). Nimrod was the founder of the Babylonian empire (Gen. 10:8ff.). In Micah's day the Assyrians were the embodiment of the arrogant spirit of Nimrod. The leaders of God's people will subjugate Assyria and incorporate her territories into the kingdom of God. They will *shepherd,* i.e., assume the role of shepherds, to Assyria. Their victory will extend even to the *gates* of the major cities. Through those gates the soldiers of the Lord will march victoriously.

The *sword* enables God's people to gain the victory over Assyria. Here, as elsewhere in Messianic prophecy, the conquest of one of the historical enemies of Israel becomes a literary mechanism to portray the final victory of God's people over all enemies. It is no mere coincidence that God's Word is likened to a sword in the New Testament (Eph. 6:17).

The victory over the Assyrian in the final analysis, will be the work of the Coming Ruler, Messiah: *He shall deliver from the Assyrian.* No matter what contribution leaders in the kingdom might make to the furtherance of the Gospel, the victory is ultimately, finally and always the Lord's.

F. *The Kingdom of the Coming Ruler will be Glorious* (vv. 7-15). His kingdom will be the *remnant of Jacob* (v. 8). The remnant consists of those sons of Israel who were totally committed to the Lord, the spiritual nucleus of the nation. Yet his kingdom would be universal, for the remnant of Jacob *shall be in the midst of many peoples* (v. 8).

---

38. This so-called x + 1 formula in the Old Testament indicates overabundance.

39. Allen (NIC, pp. 347-348) sees this statement as an empty boast which Micah refutes. According to this view Micah is saying, You cannot save yourselves from the Assyrian; only Messiah can save you.

The context makes it clear that these faithful ones are in the midst of many people because of their triumphant invasion of enemy territory. The reference, then, cannot be to scatterings of the old covenant Israel or Judah as a result of the fall of Samaria or Jerusalem.

His kingdom will be a beneficent one. God's people will bring refreshment and renewal to many peoples. They will be like dew, and even as showers[40] (v. 7) on the barren hearts of men. The simile refers here, as in Deuteronomy 32:2, to the beneficial results of religious instruction. Old Testament Israel was supposed to be a channel of blessing to the world (Gen. 12:3). Only in the Messianic age would this ideal be realized. Solomon had spoken of the refreshing blessing which the Davidic king would bring to the nations (Ps. 72:17). Micah develops that theme and emphasizes that the future Davidic king will fulfill this role through his people. Their message of salvation falls like dew from Yahweh.

His kingdom will be triumphant over all adversaries (vv. 8-9). Two figures are used. The first is that of a powerful lion[41] which fearlessly treads down and tears (v. 8). The strongholds of unbelief, sin and superstition will fall before the lion-like march of men of faith. The second figure is that of a combatant who defeats his opponent. His hand is raised in the sign of victory (v. 9).

The corollary of the triumphs of God's people is the total defeat of all the enemies of God. No one will be able to deliver them[42] from the lion-like tread of God's people (v. 8). The thought here is that God accomplishes the victory over his enemies through the agency of his people. All of the adversaries will be cut off (v. 9). These are but Old Testament ways of declaring that he that believeth not shall be condemned (Mark 16:16).

His kingdom will be a purified kingdom (vv. 9-14). God will purge his people of misplaced trust in horses and chariots, i.e., in carnal weapons (v. 10). They will no longer need the protection of walled cities (v. 11).[43] This kingdom is not of this world. Verse 10 puts the militaristic metaphors in verse 6 in proper perspective.

---

40. The point is not the multiplicity of raindrops symbolizing the increase of the nation as Willis and others have maintained. Micah is not referring to God's blessing on Israel (Calvin, J.M.P. Smith), but to Israel's blessing on the nations (Keil, Allen).

41. Balaam likened the people of Israel to a lion (Num. 23:24; 24:9). Jacob used this figure to describe Judah (Gen. 49:9).

42. The phrase "and none will be able to deliver" is used in connection with God's punishment of his enemies. See Deut. 32:39; Job 10:7; Ps. 50:22; Hos. 5:14.

43. Cf. Zech. 2:4, 5. Allen thinks the allusion is to the capture of forty-six cities by Sennacherib in 701 B.C.

God will purge the land of sorcery and soothsayers (v. 12) who were so prevalent in Micah's day (cf. Isa. 2:6). *Graven images* and *pillars* (II Kings 18:4) associated with pagan worship will be removed (v. 13). The *Asherim* were the emblems of the goddess Asherah. They were made of wood and fixed in the ground. These would be *plucked up* (v. 14) and destroyed along with other idols.[44]

The purification alluded to in verses 10-14 was a process extending over the centuries. In Micah's own day Hezekiah was trying to purge the land. After a serious relapse under Manasseh, Josiah would again attempt to rid the land of all attachment to idolatry. The Babylonian exile was a discipline which helped demonstrate to the Jews the folly of idolatry. These events were but stepping stones to Messiah's kingdom where idolatry would be totally abhorrent.

Those barriers which stand between God and his people will be removed in the future age (vv. 10-14). After that, God deals with the *nations which do not hearken* (v. 15). Implicit here is the idea that the nations will have an opportunity to respond to God in the Messianic age. Nations which do respond positively to God will be blessed as part of the Messianic kingdom. Those who do not so respond will face the wrath, anger, and vengeance[45] of God.

---

44. ASV margin *enemies*; NASB and NIV *cities*. Since the word is parallel to Asherim, it most likely indicates idols of some kind.

45. Cf. II Thess. 1:8 Vengeance is a legal term for actions taken by a great king against vassals who have rebelled against his sovereignty.

Chapter Twenty-Three

HOPE IN THE TWILIGHT OF MONARCHY

In the seventh century before Christ three prophets arose in Judah. Nahum (654 B.C.) concentrated on the destruction of Nineveh. He adds nothing to the Messianic expectation. Zephaniah, the aristocrat, contains no *personal* Messianic prophecy. He does, however, develop several familiar Messianic themes. He paints a vivid picture of the day of Yahweh. Judgment falls first on the idolaters of Jerusalem and Judah (1:14-18) and then on surrounding nations (2:4-15). All is not bleak, however. Zephaniah announced the day when Yahweh would be worshiped by "the nations on every shore" (2:11 NIV). Gentiles would have their language purged from defiling references to idolatry (3:9). Even beyond the rivers of Ethiopia God's people would bring offerings to him (3:10).[1] The universal worship of God in Messianic times "is represented in the forms of the ceremonial of the altar and the offerings of the Old Testament dispensation."[2]

Some of the other great themes in Zephaniah (640 B.C.) which have some Messianic implications are:

1. The purity of future Israel (3:11-13).
2. The great joy (3:14-18).
3. The perfect security (3:15-17).
4. The gathering of the scattered and afflicted (3:19).
5. The restoration of those gathered to their homeland (3:20).
6. The abundant honor of new Israel (3:19b-20).
7. The presence of Yahweh with his people (3:15, 17).

Habakkuk prophesied shortly before the great battle of Carchemish in 605 B.C. In this battle Nebuchadnezzar came to world power by soundly defeating the armies of Pharaoh Necho. In 2:14 Habakkuk quotes Isaiah 11:9, "For the earth shall be filled with the knowledge of Yahweh, as the waters cover the sea." Only, however, in the New Heavens and New Earth will the whole earth be filled with God's glory.[3] This verse, then, has Messianic implications. In chapter three of his book Habakkuk appears to make direct reference to the Messiah.

---

1. Cf. Isa. 19:18-25.
2. Briggs, MP, p. 225.
3. Cf. Laetsch, BCMP, p. 337.

Prophecy No. 51

SATAN PIERCED BY HIS OWN SPEAR

Habakkuk 3:12-15

The third chapter of Habakkuk is a prayer in the form of a psalm to be sung by Levites in the Temple services. This, however, is more than the outpouring of a believing soul; it is the declaration of a prophet. Here Habakkuk describes what the Lord had revealed to him in a vision.

The prayer proper is found in verse 2. The prophet pleads with the Lord to hasten the day of deliverance. Let salvation come "in the midst of years" not in the far distant end of days. In that day of the Lord, may the gracious God not forget to be merciful to his children. Such was Habakkuk's prayer. Versus 3-15 describe the vision which had precipitated the prayer.

The vision describes the advent of the Lord for judgment against his enemies. Such divine advent passages are ultimately Messianic. Briggs remarks: "This advent of Jahveh is the same advent which is ever looked for in the unfolding of the divine side of Messianic prediction."[4] Here "the prophet sees New Testament realities in the mold of Old Testament types and figures."[5] Such passages have not been examined in this study, however, because they do not speak directly of Messiah or differentiate in any way between the work of God and the work of Messiah. They do not make plain the fact that God when he comes will work through his ultimate agent. The justification for including the present passage in this study is the mention of God's anointed in verse 13. In view of (1) the previous usage of that term in the Old Testament, and (2) the context here which seems to depict an eschatological advent of God, it would appear that the Anointed One here is the Messiah.

Habakkuk describes first the majesty of God's advent. In his vision the prophet saw the whole southern horizon from east to west covered with awe-inspiring glory (v. 3). Dazzling light served as a garment, as it were, to veil his power (v. 4). Pestilence and plague go before God to destroy all who would oppose him. God takes his stand in preparation for the final showdown with evil. One look from him causes the

---

4. Briggs, MP, p. 236.
5. Laetsch, BCMP, p. 345.

mountains to heave in earthquake. Great nations, including Midian and Cushan, tremble before him (vv. 6-7).

Why does the Lord come? Not to show his wrath against nature. Rather he comes for the purpose of redeeming his people from the hands of their enemies (v. 8). Yet this salvation will necessitate fierce battle, and the Lord is adequately prepared for that (v. 9). Quaking mountains, storm clouds, and even the deep, were terrified at the presence of the Lord (v. 10). The brightness of God's spears and arrows cause sun and moon to hide themselves in embarrassment (v. 11).

Translation of Habakkuk 3:12-15

(12) In fury you march through the earth, in anger you thresh the heathen. (13) You come forth for the salvation of your people, for the salvation of your Anointed. You smash the head of the house of the wicked, laying bare his foundations up to the neck. Selah. (14) With his own spear you pierce the head of the villagers who sweep forth to scatter me, whose rejoicing is like those who secretly devour the poor. (15) You tread on the sea with your horses, on the restless billows of great waters.

Discussions

For the heathen Habakkuk foresaw a terrifying day as the Lord stalked through the earth (v. 12). There is, however, a twofold deliverance effected by this advent of the Lord. His people would be delivered, and his Anointed, the Messiah. Other references make it clear that the Lord's Anointed would be the leader in the battle against evil.[6] In the fierceness of the struggle he would cry out to his Father for help,[7] and he would be heard.[8]

God's victory is complete. The house of the wicked is demolished— its foundation, its neck (upper parts of the walls) and its head or roof. It is unroofed! No longer would that house protect those within. The house, of course, is here used in the sense of a realm or kingdom.[9] Who, other than Satan, would be the head or roof of that house? Thus in figurative language verse 13 depicts the great victory which God enabled his people, through the Messiah, to win over evil.

6. Gen. 3:15; Num. 24:17-19; Ps. 45:3-5; 110:1-7.
7. Ps. 22:1, 11, 19-21; 40:12, 14.
8. Ps. 110:1; cf. Heb. 5:7-9; Phil. 2:7-11; Eph. 1:20-23.
9. As in II Sam. 7:1-13; I Kings 12:16, 19; 14:10.

In verse 14 Habakkuk speaks for all God's people. He depicts a two-fold attack against *me*, i.e., the people of God collectively. He speaks first of villagers, inhabitants of unwalled areas, rushing against the people of God from without, determined to scatter them. From within the people of God face ruthless men who are determined to devour the poor. These unprincipled men, while nominally part of the kingdom of God, are in reality in league with the devil.

The *head of villagers* (v. 14) is the same as the head of the house of the wicked in the preceding verse, i.e., Satan. He rules over boundless territories, not just the great walled cities of the world. But he is to be pierced through, mortally wounded with his own spear. Satan's weapons by which he intimidated the sons of Adam were sin and death. When the Anointed One became a sin offering (II Cor. 5:21; Isa. 53:6, 11f.) he defeated Satan, crushed his head and rendered him powerless to withstand the Gospel.[10]

In verse 15 Habakkuk speaks of the future deliverance in terms borrowed from the Exodus. God would again make a way, as it were, through the wild waves of opposition for his people.

THE HOPE IN JEREMIAH

Jeremiah was a teenage lad when God called him to the prophetic ministry. The year was 627 B.C. Young King Josiah had already introduced a number of religious reforms. Jeremiah would spend the first eighteen years of his ministry vigorously supporting the efforts of the king to change the direction of the nation.

In 605 B.C. Jeremiah's threats about an enemy from the north materialized. Nebuchadnezzar defeated the armies of Pharaoh Necho at the battle of Carchemish and Babylon became master of the world. In 597 B.C. ten thousand of the leading citizens were deported to Babylon. In 587 B.C. Jerusalem was destroyed and the Judean monarchy came to an end.

Throughout his ministry Jeremiah announced the destruction of Jerusalem. For that message he suffered vicious persecution under the reigns of Jehoiakim (609-598 B.C.) and Zedekiah (597-587 B.C.). Most, but not all, that this prophet said in the way of hope for the future of God's people is found in chapters 30-33. Yet early in his ministry Jeremiah uttered an oracle which is filled with Messianic

---

10. Laetsch, BCMP, p. 349.

implication. The passage (3:11-18) comes in the context of an address to the scattered northern tribes to return to God. In this passage and elsewhere in the book eleven great themes of Messianic prophecy are developed.

1. The return of individuals from the northern tribes to the Lord and to Jerusalem (3:14). Pregnant women and crippled men will be in that number and they will not stumble in the journey (31:5-9).[11] The return of Ephraimites in the days of Josiah (II Chron. 30:10), and later under Ezra (Ezra 2:28, 34) were only hints that some of these scattered sheep would be gathered.

2. The gift of a dedicated leadership following the restoration (3:15). This theme is developed in 23:4 and 33:25-26. The first steps toward the realization of this hope came in the postexilic leadership of men like Zerubbabel, Joshua, Ezra and Nehemiah.

3. The great increase of citizens in the Israel of the future (3:16). In their own pasture the flock will "be fruitful and increase in number" (23:3). God will add to their numbers and "their children will be as in days of old" (30:19-20). The fulfillment of these promises is found in "the increase of the church through Gentile augmentation of Israel."[12]

4. The change in the old covenant worship forms. The ark of the covenant, which figured so prominently in Old Testament worship, would not even be missed (3:16). The ark was gone in post-exilic Jerusalem, but it certainly was missed. Only the spiritual worship taught by Jesus fulfills this prediction.

5. The centrality and exaltation of Jerusalem is a Messianic theme also made prominent by Isaiah (ch. 2) and Micah (ch. 4). Jeremiah predicted that Jerusalem would be called the throne of Yahweh (3:17). The city limits would be expanded to incorporate areas which once were considered unclean (31:38-39). The physical city of Jerusalem was but a type of the heavenly Jerusalem (Heb. 12:22) whose builder and maker is God (Heb. 11:10). This true Jerusalem is the city inhabited by all Christians (Heb. 12:22).

6. Gentiles will abandon their evil ways (3:17), cast aside their idols (16:19-20), and commit themselves to the Lord (4:2; 12:16). While some prominent proselytes to old covenant faith can be named, nothing approaching the magnitude of these predictions occurred until Paul began to carry the Gospel into the Roman empire.

---

11. Prophecies of restoration for both Israel and Judah are found in 30:3; 31:27; 33:7; and 50:4.

12. Payne, EBP, p. 327.

7. The reunification of the house of Israel and the house of Judah (3:18-19). This is the Old Testament way of depicting the one-body theme of the New Testament. Both Peter (I Peter 2:10) and Paul (Rom. 9:25) see in a similar verse in Hosea a prediction of the glorious unity of the body of Christ.

8. The new Israel will be reconciled to God. They will be cleansed (33:8) and thereby receive a new heart (24:7). They will acknowledge God and he will acknowledge them (32:38-39). Some evidence of this change began to be manifested in the post-exilic community (Ezra 1:5); but the final goal of reconciliation could only take place after Calvary.

9. The eternal existence of God's people Israel (31:35-37) is fulfilled in the new Israel of God, (Gal. 6:16), the church of Christ.

10. The multiplication of "the priests, the Levites" (i.e., the Levitical priests) is set forth in 33:18-22. Here Jeremiah takes up a theme introduced by Isaiah (66:21). Conferring upon Gentiles the priestly office in the new Israel fulfills this anticipation (I Peter 2:5, 9).

11. The reversal of the fortunes of Moab (48:47), Ammon (49:6) and Elam (49:39) "in the latter days" may have Messianic implications.[13] The term *latter days* frequently if not always embraces the Messianic age. Christian churches were numerous in the transjordan area. Elamitic Jews were present to hear the Gospel on Pentecost.

Prophecy No. 52

THE SHOOT OF DAVID

Jeremiah 23:5-6

Chapters 21-25 of the Book of Jeremiah contain various political pronouncements of the prophet made during the last half of his ministry. In chapter 22 he deals specifically with the fate of Jehoahaz (vv. 10-12), Jehoiakim (vv. 13-23) and Jehoiachin (vv. 24-30). The shepherds of the nation—the political leaders—were responsible for the impending destruction of Jerusalem and consequent scattering of the flock of God (23:1). Since these leaders had not *visited* the flock to minister to their needs, God would *visit* them in judgment (23:2). The Good Shepherd himself would gather the scattered remnant of his flock. They

---

13. The change in the political fortune of those lands under the Persian government may be the focus of these promises according to Leslie, *Jeremiah*, p. 168.

would return to their land and flourish under his oversight (23:4). He will give them shepherds in abundance who will faithfully tend the flock (23:5).

Translation of Jeremiah 23:5-6

(5) Behold, days are coming (oracle of the LORD) when I will raise up for David a righteous Shoot and he will reign as king and he shall act wisely and execute justice and righteousness in the land. (6) In his days Judah shall be saved, and Israel shall dwell securely; and this is his name by which he will be called, The LORD our Righteousness.

Discussion

The passage speaks of (1) the origin of Messiah; (2) the reign of Messiah and (3) the name of Messiah.

A. *The Origin of Messiah* (v. 5). The Ruler would arise at an unspecific time. *Behold days are coming* is a formula used sixteen times to introduce messages of reassurance. The formula points to the Messianic age.

The appearance of the Ruler is the result of special divine action, for God declares, *I will raise up.* The appearance of the Ruler is not, then, what might be expected in the natural course of events.

The Ruler will come from the royal line of David (cf. II Sam. 7), yet he would have a humble origin. He is called the *shoot,*[14] a tender, delicate plant. This figure describes the helpless years of Christ's infancy. Messiah was implanted in the subsoil of human history by the hand of God. That tender Shoot was destined to become a mighty cedar (cf. Ezek. 17:22, 23).

The Shoot would be *righteous.* All other descendants of David had to confess their sins and ask divine forgiveness. Messiah would be sinless (Isa. 53:9). He did not *become* righteous; he *was* righteous from birth to death.

B. *The Reign of Messiah* (vv. 5b-6a). Seven aspects of the reign of Messiah are indicated in this text.

1. He will reign as king, as a second David. He will have a kingdom, a throne, a scepter, and subjects. In spite of all that his enemies might do, he shall reign. The clear evidence of the New Testament is that Christ is now sitting in his royal throne ruling over his kingdom, the church.[15]

---

14. The term *tsemach* is never used of a twig or branch, but of that which grows directly out of the ground.

15. See Heb. 1:3-13: 10:12-13: Rev. 3:21: I Cor. 15:20-28 and Acts 2:19--34.

2. He shall reign successfully. He shall *reign wisely* (NIV) or *prosper* (KJV). The Hebrew word (*hiskil*) could be translated either way. Both ideas are involved. The Messiah will have the insight and intelligence to bring God's plan of salvation to a successful conclusion (cf. Isa. 11:2).

3. His reign will be characterized by the twin qualities of justice (*mishpat*) and righteousness (*tsedaqah*) which had characterized the reign of David (II Sam. 8:15). Justice and righteousness in the Old Testament are not abstract qualities, but concrete ways of behavior. Frequently, as here, the verb *'asah* (to do, make, execute) is used with one or both of these words. Isaiah called upon men to "preserve justice, and do righteousness" in anticipation of God's coming salvation or deliverance (Isa. 56:1). Jeremiah regarded justice and righteousness as conditions for divine blessings (Jer. 4:2). Certainly those qualities were not obvious in the monarchs contemporary with this prophet (Jer. 22:13, 17). If only the house of David would *do justice and righteousness* God would spare the land (Jer. 22:3).

If any distinction is to be made between *justice* and *righteousness* it is this: *Justice* views the conduct from the standpoint of man, and *righteousness* from the standpoint of God. Thus the man who executes *justice* and *righteousness* is seen by man to be absolutely equitable, and by God to be upright (cf. Jer. 22:3).

4. He will unite Judah and Israel. Ezekiel held out a similar hope (Ezek. 37:19). A few citizens of the northern kingdom joined Jews in returning to Canaan during the Persian period. That was only a dim preview of the glorious unity achieved by Christ in his body the church. The conversion of those who were not God's people (northern kingdom) and their reinstatement as part of the people of God is seen by both Peter (I Peter 2:9) and Paul (Rom. 9:22-26) to be fulfilled in the union of Jew and Gentile in the church.

5. He will bring salvation or deliverance to his people. *In his days Judah shall be saved.* The language suggests one great climatic act of salvation, one so great that it would never have to be repeated. It is a salvation provided for Judah by the Messianic Ruler. Through his ministry, death, and resurrection, Christ made possible deliverance from mankind's greatest Oppressor, Satan himself. The Judah of the Messianic age will be the community of the saved. All those who accept the great Messianic salvation are part of this "Judah."

6. The Ruler will bring security to his people for *in his days . . . Israel shall dwell securely.* The new Israel is secure from condemnation (Rom. 8:1), secure in the salvation provided. No man can pluck a believer out of the hand of Christ (John 10:29).

7. The passage implies that this Ruler will be the true Shepherd with other shepherds serving under him. David was a shepherd, and that term came to be used figuratively of his reign (cf. Ezek. 34:23, 24). The *shepherds* mentioned in verse 4 are best interpreted as a reference to leaders subordinate to Messiah in the church of Christ.[16] The connection with verse 5 and the very magnitude of the promise in verse 4 regarding the work of these shepherds suggest the Messianic interpretation. Christ was the good Shepherd, and leaders within the church are called pastors or shepherds (Eph. 4:11; I Peter 5:1-4).

C. *The Name of the Messiah* (v. 6b). The prophet points out the name by which Messiah will be called, *Yahweh our Righteousness*. The phraseology here is unique in the entire Old Testament: And this is his name which one shall call him. According to Laetsch[17] two facts are underscored by this construction: (1) The name given the Messiah here is not a mere label or tag, but on the contrary, it designates the very nature or essence of the Messiah. He IS righteousness! (2) God desires that mankind should refer to the Messiah the title here given, Yahweh, our Righteousness. This title may not prove the deity of Messiah, but it certainly is beautifully supportive of other passages which do.

The title here given Messiah[18] is very similar to the name of the last king of Judah. *Zedekiah* means, "Yahweh is righteousness." Josiah's son Eliakim assumed this name upon his succession to the throne. That which Zedekiah's name set forth as an ideal would be realized in the time of the Messianic king.[19]

Prophecy No. 53

THE PRIESTLY KING

Jeremiah 30:9, 21

When Jerusalem came under siege by the Babylonians in 588 B.C. Jeremiah was arrested and put in the court of the guard. During those

---

16. Others think these shepherds precede Christ. They have been taken to be the postexilic leaders like Ezra, Nehemiah, and Zerubbabel, or the Maccabees.

17. Laetsch, BCJ, p. 195.

18. Because Jer. 33:16 applies this title to Jerusalem, some say it properly belongs to Israel here. But context strongly supports this as a personal Messianic title, and the Jews so interpreted it in the Targum, Midrash and Talmud.

19. Thompson, NIC, pp. 490-491; Payne, EBP, p. 338. The suggestion of Hengstenberg that Zedekiah presumptuously took his throne name as a result of this passage is most unlikely.

desperate weeks of personal abuse the prophet penned what modern scholars call the book of consolation (chs. 30-33). This is the most consistently optimistic section in the Book of Jeremiah.

Chapter 30 begins with a promise of restoration from the impending exile (v. 3). In verses 4-7 Jeremiah speaks of a period of tremendous distress for the nation, a distress which he likens to the pangs of childbirth. He refers to this as *Jacob's trouble.* Probably the distress began in 733 B.C. with the first deportation of Israelites into the Assyrian empire, and ended in 539 B.C. with the fall of Babylon. Yet God would deliver his people from their distress (v. 8). This deliverance began in 539 B.C. when Babylon fell to Cyrus the Great. Never again would Jacob experience a bondage such as they had experienced under the Babylonians.[20]

Translation of Jeremiah 30:9, 21

(9) But they shall serve the LORD their God, and David their King, whom I will raise up for them. (21) And their Prince shall be of themselves, and their Ruler shall come out of the midst of them; and I will bring him near, and he shall approach me; for who would risk his life to approach me (oracle of the LORD).

Discussion

Three pictures of the coming Messiah are painted in these verses. He will be (1) a Davidic king, (2) a native king, and (3) a priestly king. A. *A Davidic King* (v. 9). In verse 9 Jeremiah is reiterating the prediction of Hosea 3:5. *David* here is not the great king reincarnated or resurrected as some cults affirm. David is Messiah, the son of David. The name is applied to him also by Ezekiel (34:23, 24; 37:24).

1. This king is a liberator. Such is implied in the contrast between verse 8 and verse 9. Whereas before he came God's people suffered humiliating enslavement to foreign powers, after he appears they would serve only him. The first David liberated his people from the menace of the Philistines; but the second David liberated his people from a far greater oppressor.

2. This king is raised up by God. This suggests that his appearance and subsequent enthronement would be quite inexplicable from the

---

20. *Strangers shall no more enslave him.* Even after 539 B.C. Israel was dominated by one foreign power after another. They were never again, however, carried away *en masse* to a foreign land.

human standpoint. Jeremiah is writing at a time when the Davidic dynasty was about to be cut off from the throne. That would not, however, be the end of the story.

3. This king is linked to service to God: *They shall serve Yahweh their God*. How does serving God relate to serving the Davidic king? Various possibilities suggest themselves. (1) They will serve God in the immediate future (after the exile), and David in the more distant future.[21] A time gap would then exist between fulfillment of the two halves of the verse. (2) They will serve Yahweh their God by serving the future Davidic king. (3) God and David are one and the same. The future Davidic king is divine. In this case the sentence should be translated: They shall serve Yahweh their God even David their king.[22]

4. This king has loyal subjects: *They will serve . . . David their king*. To *serve* God means to worship him, to obey him. The word is also used of the service rendered by a servant to his master. The word usually connotes service which results from deliberate choice. The future ruler will not force his rule on anyone.

B. *A Glorious King* (v. 21a). Again in verse 21 the future king comes center stage. As in verse 9, the appearance of this ruler is linked to the overthrow of the oppressors of God's people (v. 20). Four additional facts about the king are brought out here:

1. He will be a glorious one (*'addir*). In the singular this word is used nine times in the Old Testament. Twice it is used as a proper name for Yahweh (Isa. 10:34; 33:21). Twice it is used as an adjective descriptive of God (Ps. 76:4; 93:4). Twice it is used as an adjective to describe the name of God (Ps. 8:1, 9). In the singular the word is never used of a man. The use of *'addir* in Jeremiah 30:21 points strongly to the deity of the coming Ruler.

2. He will be a Jew, for he *shall be of themselves*. By the time of Jeremiah God's people were accustomed to being ruled by foreign rulers. In the future that would no longer be the case.

3. He would *come out of the midst of them*. Some in Jeremiah's day looked for a restoration to power of Jehoahaz who was deported to Egypt, or Jehoiachin who had been carried away to Babylon. The ruler of the future would not return from exile to claim his throne. He would rise to power in the midst of the nation.

---

21. The position taken by the author in JBST, p. 510.
22. Laetsch (BCJ, p. 241) argues that long before Bethlehem, Messiah was worshiped.

4. He would be ruler (*moshel*). He would not be a figurehead leader, a shadow king. He would command respect and demand obedience.

C. *A Priestly King* (v. 21b). The last clause of verse 21 is extremely difficult. The KJV renders: "*Who is this that engaged his heart to approach me?*" The ASV translates, *Who is he that hath had boldness to approach unto me?* To *approach* God means to engage in priestly ministry.[23] The glorious future ruler would be priest as well as king. Regarding this priestly ministry three points are emphasized:

1. His priestly service would be empowered by God, for *I will bring him near.* The sons of Aaron had the right to draw near to God in the Tabernacle and Temple. A special divine act would be necessary to authorize any besides an Aaronide drawing near to God. Just as the budding of a dead rod signified the divine choice of the Levitical priesthood (Num. 17), so the resurrection of Jesus signaled the establishment of a new priestly order.

2. His priestly service is gladly undertaken for *he shall approach.* Once he was properly credentialed for this work, Christ did not hesitate to enter into this service.

3. His priestly service would be successful, for *he shall approach.* In making atonement for sin and intercession for sinners he would succeed in getting through to God the Father.

4. His priestly service is boldly undertaken, for *who would dare to risk his life to approach me?* The one king who tried to usurp the priestly prerogatives and offer incense before the Lord was smitten with incurable leprosy. Yet this glorious Ruler would be priest as well as king. Zechariah a few years later would make crystal clear that Messiah would be priest upon his throne.

Prophecy No. 54

THE NEW THING GOD WILL CREATE

Jeremiah 31:21-22

The background for this prophecy is the same as that for the previous one. The immediate context depicts the heartfelt repentance of Ephraim. God promises to show compassion on Ephraim "my precious son" (vv. 18-20).

Verses 21-22 form a distinct unit within chapter 31. Here Jeremiah does three things. He (1) urges all God's people to return to Canaan;

---

23. Lev. 16:1; Exod. 40:32; Num. 1:51 et. al.

(2) rebukes those who might be inclined to remain in the lands of captivity, and (3) sets forth a remarkable incentive for their return.

Translation of Jeremiah 31:21-22

(21) Erect for yourself road marks, set up guide posts! Set your heart toward the highway, the way you have walked! Return, O Virgin of Israel, return to these your cities! (22) How long will you dillydally, O faithless daughter, for the LORD has created a new thing in the land: A woman shall compass a man.

Discussion

A. *The Exhortation to Return* (v. 21). The entire nation is addressed as the *Virgin of Israel*. What marvelous grace that God can address this faithless wife (3:8) and wayward daughter (31:22) as a *Virgin*. She is urged to mark the road she is traveling into captivity. One day God's people will want to travel that road back home.

Already thousands had been taken away to Babylon, and thousands before them into Assyria. More would follow when Jerusalem was captured just a few months after Jeremiah spoke these words. *Return*, he says, *to these your cities*. Not immediately of course, for no one in his right mind would want to return to that war-ravaged land. In the future, however, when the time was right, all of God's people should return to their native land.

B. *The Reproof for Delay in Return* (v. 22a). Should the virgin daughter reject the invitation to return she would thereby become a *faithless daughter*. The rhetorical question here indicates how utterly incredible it would be for God's people to refuse to return to Canaan.

C. *The Incentive for Return* (v. 22b). In order to encourage God's people to return, Jeremiah points to a stupendous miracle which God would do in the land. Only a verb from the vocabulary of the creation account (*bara'*) is strong enough to depict this divine action. If they fail to return the captives will have no opportunity to share in this great miracle.

What is the new thing which God will create in the land? *A woman shall compass a man*. What woman is this? Most commentators identify her as Israel because the nation has been likened to a virgin in the preceding verse, and a daughter in the present verse. This interpretation would have some merit were it not for the statements which immediately

351

precede and follow. One woman, however, has been mentioned before in the context of Messianic prophecy. Isaiah spoke of a virgin who would give birth to a remarkable son (Isa. 7:14), and Micah spoke of a woman who would bear a child whose birth would mark the end of God's abandonment of Israel (Micah 5:3).

A *man* is mentioned here. The word used is not *'enosh*, a man in his frailty, but *gever*, a man *par excellence*. Who is this man? Most identify the *man* as Yahweh. The virgin daughter of Israel in faith embraces Yahweh. An interpretation which makes *gever* equivalent to Yahweh seems rather strange. The use of the word *gever* and related words in reference to the Messiah, however, is not without parallel (cf. Zech. 13:7).[24]

The woman shall *compass*, i.e., surround, the man. This would be an awkward way of expressing embracement, but a beautiful way of describing the fact that a man child is enfolded in the womb of the woman.

Prophecy No. 55

OLD COVENANTS REAFFIRMED

Jeremiah 33:14-22

Jeremiah's circumstances remain unchanged in chapter 33. He is still in the court of the guard. At God's direction he has purchased a plot of ground beyond the Babylonian siege line in Anathoth. He publicly weighed out the price, and recorded the deed. With the Babylonians about ready to batter down the city gates, the actions of the prophet must have seemed insane. The meaning of the symbolism is stated in verse 15: *Once again houses and fields and vineyards shall be purchased in this land.*

Jeremiah was perplexed by what seemed to be a reversal of the judgment message he had been preaching for forty years. He prayed for clarification (32:16-25). God responded by outlining his plan for the immediate (32:28-35) and distant futures (32:36-41).

Chapter 33 contains the second revelation which Jeremiah received while in the court of the guard. The early part of the chapter is full of great promises, many with Messianic implications (vv. 4-13). As often in the prophets the promises of return from Babylon blend with those of national cleansing. This sets the stage for the last personal Messianic prophecy in the Book of Jeremiah.

---

24. Keil, BCOT, Jeremiah, II, 76. Keil is followed by Payne, EBP, p. 344.

Translation of Jeremiah 33:14-26

(14) Behold, days are coming (oracle of the LORD) when I will raise up the good word which I have spoken concerning the house of Israel and the house of Judah. (15) In those days and at that time I will cause a righteous shoot to spring forth to David; and he will establish justice and righteousness in the land. (16) In those days Judah shall be saved, and Jerusalem shall dwell securely, and this is the name by which she shall be called: The LORD our Righteousness. (17) For thus says the LORD: David shall never lack a man to sit upon the throne of the house of Israel; (18) and the Levitical priests shall never lack a man before me to offer burnt offerings, to burn meal offerings, and to make sacrifice forever. (19) And the word of the LORD came unto Jeremiah, saying, (20) Thus says the LORD: If my covenant of the day and night can be broken so that there will no longer be day and night in their proper times, (21) then my covenant with David my servant shall be broken so that he will have no son to reign upon his throne; and for the Levitical priests, my ministers. (22) As the hosts of the heaven cannot be numbered nor the sand of the sea measured, so will I increase the descendants of David my servant and the Levites, my ministers. (23) And the word of the LORD came unto Jeremiah, saying, (24) Have you not considered what this people have said, saying, The two families which the LORD chose, he has rejected? Thus they despise my people that they no longer regard them as a nation. (25) Thus says the LORD: If my covenant with the day and night shall not stand, if I did not establish the statutes of the heaven and the earth, (26) then shall I reject the seed of Jacob and David my servant, and no longer take from his seed rulers over the descendants of Abraham, Isaac and Jacob. For I will reverse their fortunes and have mercy upon them.

Discussion

This unit contains (1) the repetition of a noteworthy prediction (vv. 14-16), and (2) the covenantal undergirding of this prediction.

A. *The Repetition of a Noteworthy Prediction* (vv. 14-17). Six points are emphasized about this prediction:

1. This prediction is certain of fulfillment: *Behold days are coming.* This formula which in Jeremiah is a Messianic pointer, indicates a certain but indefinite future.

2. This prediction involves good news for the people of God (v. 14): *I will raise up the good word.* This could also be translated, I will

establish the gracious promise. The reference is probably back to the promise of the righteous shoot in 23:5, 6.

3. This prediction involved the whole nation for the good word was spoken to the house of Israel and to the house of Judah. The entire body of God's people would benefit from his coming.

4. This prediction concerns the appearance of a mighty ruler (vv. 15-16). He will appear in the fulness of time, i.e., *in those days and at that time.* He will be a righteous ruler, of humble origins (*a shoot*), and of the line of David.

5. This prediction concerns a mighty deliverance (v. 16). In those days (Messianic age) *Judah shall be saved* and *Jerusalem shall dwell securely.*[25] Physical Judah and Jerusalem never regained political independence. Thus Judah and Jerusalem must be understood here spiritually of the church of Christ, and the deliverance should be regarded as a spiritual blessing.

6. This prediction concerns a glorious name: *Yahweh, Our Righteousness.* In 23:6 this name belonged to the coming ruler. Here the holy city has taken for itself the name of the Redeemer. The righteousness belongs to the coming Ruler. Those who live in this city claim no righteousness of their own. By God's grace alone they have become part of this redeemed community.

B. *The Covenant Undergirding of this Prediction* (vv. 17-26). In these verses Jeremiah stresses five points regarding the covenants made with David and Levi:

1. He reiterates and underscores the promise made to David that he would *never lack a man to sit on the throne of the house of Israel* (v. 17). The prophet was certain that the royal line would survive the impending destruction of Jerusalem. God would honor the commitment which he made to David through Nathan over four hundred years earlier (II Sam. 7:16).[26]

Jeremiah was not prophesying that the line of David would never be removed from the throne. That would contradict what he prophesied elsewhere concerning Jehoiachin: *Write this man childless, a man that shall not prosper in his days; for he shall not be successful in having one of his descendants sit on the throne of David or rule again over Judah* (22:30). Jeremiah also announced the destruction of Jerusalem (22:5-9) and the deportation of the last king of Judah, Zedekiah,

---

25. In 23:6 it was Israel which would dwell securely. The intentional alteration has been made in the earlier prophecy so as to apply it more specifically to the dire straits in which Jerusalem found itself during the Babylonian siege.

26. Cf. I Kings 2:4, David's parting words to Solomon.

the uncle of Johoiachin (21:7). The thought here in 33:17 is that the new Israel would have a throne, and the one to sit on that throne would be a son of David.

Zedekiah, the last Old Testament king of the line of David, was in his last weeks of rule when this passage was penned. He was deposed in 587 B.C. From that time until the ascension of Christ, no one sat on the throne of David. During the intertestamental period some of the Hasmoneans called themselves "king," but they were not universally recognized as such. The Herodian dynasty came to power with Roman backing, but this dynasty was never acknowledged as sitting on the throne of Israel. When the new Israel of God came into being on the day of Pentecost A.D. 30, the sovereign Ruler was a son of David.

2. In verse 18 Jeremiah stresses the commitment made to the Levitical priests. The priestly office as well as the royal will survive the fall of Jerusalem and destruction of the Temple. Under the law of Moses the Levitical priests had exclusive altar rights (Num. 3:10; 16:40; 18:7). The New Testament, however, categorically affirms that the Levitical priesthood has passed away (Heb. 7:11). That priesthood was replaced by a new and better one inaugurated by Christ who was declared by his resurrection to be a priest forever after the order of Melchizedek. Baptized believers are part of a holy priesthood (Heb. 10:19-22).

Taken in a strictly literalistic way verse 18 has failed of fulfillment. No Levitical priests have offered burnt offerings to Yahweh since A.D. 70. Jeremiah did not mean that Levitical priests would function continuously at the Temple in Jerusalem. He himself prophesied that the Temple would be made desolate like Shiloh (Jer. 7, 26). The thought again is that the new Israel would have a priesthood and that priesthood would be the seed of Levi.

The prophecy suggests three ideas: The new Israel would have (1) sacrifices to offer to God continually, (2) a place to offer those sacrifices, and (3) a priesthood to officiate in the offering. The New Testament makes clear that all three elements are part of the new covenant people of God. The church of Christ offers sacrifices to God (Heb. 13:15; Rom. 12:1), has an altar at which to offer those sacrifices (Heb. 13:10), and a priesthood to officiate in the service (I Peter 2:5).

That the prophecies like Jeremiah 33:18 find fulfillment in the priesthood of believers is supported by dozens of verses in the New Testament. Jeremiah declared that the ark of the covenant, so central in Old Testament worship, would not be missed in the Messianic age (3:16). Isaiah spoke of Gentiles serving as Levites in the age to come (Isa. 66:21). It is manifestly impossible for Gentiles to be biologically descended from Levi. David (Ps. 110), Jeremiah (30:21) and Zechariah (6:13) speak of the kingship and priesthood being combined in one person. Such a linkage would be absolutely impossible under the law of Moses.

3. Jeremiah illustrates the permanence of the Davidic and Levitic lines (33:19-21). The covenant made with David and the covenant made with Levi is placed on the same level as the God-ordained succession of day and night.[27] The *covenant with David* refers to the Nathan oracle of II Samuel 7:12-16. The *covenant with Levi* which is also mentioned by Malachi (2:4, 5, 8) is probably a reference to the promises made to Phinehas, the grandson of Aaron, in Numbers 25:13. The argument here is a specific application of that made in 31:35-37. These promises may be diagramed as follows:

PREDICTION		FULFILLMENT	
Seed of Israel Eternal (31:35-37)	> As a Nation	Christ is the Seed of Israel	> Christians are a holy nation
Seed of David Eternal (33:19-21)	> On a Throne	Christ is the Seed of David	> Christians are Christ's Brethren therefore the seed of David.
Seed of Priests Eternal (33:19-21)	> Offering Sacrifices	Christ is Eternal High Priest	> Christians are a priesthood.

4. Jeremiah also speaks here of the multiplication of the Davidic and Levitic lines (33:22). God promised Abraham to make his seed as numerous as the stars of the sky and the sand of the seashore (Gen. 15:5; 22:17). That same promise is now made regarding the descendants of David and the Levites who ministered in the Temple.

Messiah is called David (Hosea 3:5), and his descendants (lit., seed) are mentioned several times (e.g., Isa. 53:10). His descendants or seed would be disciples. Jesus referred to his disciples as his children (John 13:33) and his brethren (Matt. 28:10). The Apostle Paul also spoke of this family relationship (Eph. 3:15). Therefore, the promise of the multiplication of the seed of David is best regarded as fulfilled in the rapid growth of the early church.

A similar line of argument establishes the fulfillment for the promise that the Levites who minister before God will be multiplied. This is but another way of saying that the Old Testament priesthood will be

---

27. This may be an allusion to the covenant made with Noah (Gen. 8:22).

expanded. All members of Messianic Israel would be priests and ministers to the Lord. Even Gentile converts would be part of the priesthood (Isa. 66:20-21). Christians are priests of God (I Peter 2:9; Rev. 1:6; 5:9-10) who offer up sacrifices to God. Christians are also said to reign with Christ (Rev. 5:10; 20:4-6).

5. Two reasons are offered for the reassurance regarding the future of the Davidic and Levitic lines (33:23-24). First, the people of God were beginning to show signs of despair. To them it seemed that God had already cast off the *two families* which he had chosen (v. 23). Judah now was about to be destroyed as Ephraim or Israel had been 135 years earlier.[28]

The second reason for the heavy emphasis on the glorious future of the house of David and Levi was the attitude of the Gentiles. They had nothing but contempt for the people of God in their present condition (v. 23).

The passage closes with yet another strong emphasis on the promises made to his people. He does this in three ways. (1) He links the covenant made with Jacob to that made with David. The very existence of the nation (Jacob) is bound up with the survival of the Davidic line. (2) He links the promise made to David with the names of three great patriarchs through whom God had already revealed his faithfulness. (3) He links the Davidic promises with assurance of restoration. The return from exile would be the pledge of yet greater blessings which were involved in the new covenant age.

Special Note

RACHEL AND HER CHILDREN

Jeremiah 31:15-17 is cited in Matthew 2:18 as a prophecy fulfilled when Herod slaughtered the Bethlehem infants. Though not strictly speaking a personal Messianic prediction, this prophecy is so closely related to the life of Christ that a brief note on it seems appropriate.

In the midst of describing the new and everlasting joy of the Messianic age, Jeremiah abruptly interjects a brief picture of utter woe. Rachel is pictured weeping for her children who *are no more*. It is obvious here that Rachel, the ancestress of the tribe of Benjamin, is depicted

---

28. Others take the two families to be the family of David and the family of Aaron or Levi.

as living on in her descendants. But what is the occasion of her lamentation?

Commentators are all but unanimous in contending that Jeremiah is describing the lamentation of the mothers of Israel when the northern tribes were deported in 722 B.C. or when the Jews were deported to Babylon in 587 B.C. Rachel is comforted in the knowledge that her children would some day return to the land.

How then is the reference to the fulfillment of this prophecy in the Gospel of Matthew explained? Keil lamely replies, "The destruction of the people of Israel by the Assyrians and Chaldeans is a type of the massacre of the infants at Bethlehem. . . ."[29] Matthew is only drawing an analogy between the agony of the mothers of Israel in 722 B.C. (or 587) and the agony of the mothers in Bethlehem. Yet the plain statement of the evangelist is that this passage found its fulfillment in the massacre of the Bethlehem innocents.

Laetsch[30] has pointed out several problems with this common interpretation which may be summarized as follows:

1. Nowhere does Scripture call Rachel the tribal mother of northern Israel.

2. The deportation in 722 B.C. was total. No mothers were left behind to lament the deportation of their sons.

3. No lament is specifically mentioned in connection with Ramah in 587 B.C.

4. Rachel was buried, not in Ramah, but at Bethlehem-Ephrath (Gen. 35:18, 19).

A better interpretation sees Jeremiah 31:15-17 as direct prediction of what was to transpire later at Bethlehem. Rachel is introduced as bewailing her children because her tomb was located at Bethlehem, where the infants would be slain. The mothers, represented by Rachel, would be the first to suffer loss for the sake of Christ. Yet there is comfort for them in verses 16-17.

1. Their labor in bearing children has not been in vain. Their children have not been annihilated by death. They are still part of God's chosen people, even though they have been snatched away from this life prematurely.

---

29. Keil, BCOT, Jeremiah, II, 26.
30. Laetsch, BCJ, pp. 249-250.

2. The children "shall return from the land of the enemy." Death is the great enemy of God's people (I Cor. 15:25, 26). The prophet points to the resurrection as the source of comfort for the bereaved mothers.

3. The mothers are assured that "there is hope in your end." *End* sometimes means "future" (cf. 29:11), and sometimes "posterity" (cf. Ps. 37:38; 109:13; Dan. 11:4). In either case, the hope is centered on the resurrection of those little ones.

4. In the end Bethlehem's children so cruelly murdered will *return to their own land,* i.e., their inheritance. Geographical Canaan was but a pledge and preview of that heavenly Canaan, that new heavens and earth (Heb. 11:14-16), which all those who die in the Lord will claim as their inheritance in the day of resurrection. That this interpretation is correct is supported by the context, which is Messianic from 30:20 through the end of chapter 33. The consolation offered "Rachel" i.e., the mothers of Bethlehem, is offered as a specific example of the kind of comfort which would be available in the future age.

One critical note is important, though the overall meaning of the passage is unchanged. Was the weeping of Rachel to be heard "in Ramah" or "on the heights"? Ramah was one of the cities allotted to Benjamin, about five miles north of Jerusalem. The Masoretic pointing of the Hebrew text suggests that a common noun is intended. This tradition has been followed by the Sinaitic and Alexandrian codices of the Septuagint, Aquila, the Vulgate and the Targum. The reading in Matthew with the proper noun "Ramah" is found also in the Vatican codex of the Septuagint.

If the common noun rendering of Jeremiah 31:15 be proper, then Ramah is left out of the picture entirely. On the other hand, if "Ramah" is the proper rendering the city may be named as indicating the distance to which the lamentation of the mothers was heard. It is also possible that Herod's execution order included all the villages surrounding Jerusalem with Bethlehem marking the southern extremity and Ramah the northern.

Chapter Twenty-Four

THE WITNESS OF THE WATCHMAN

Ezekiel the priest was a contemporary of Jeremiah. When he was twenty-six (in 597 B.C.) Ezekiel was carried away to Babylon with some ten thousand of his fellow captives. In the fifth year of his exile (593 B.C.) Ezekiel experienced his prophetic call (Ezek. 1-3). For the next twenty-two years he ministered to the captives in Babylon. His ministry went through two distinct phases. Prior to the destruction of Jerusalem in 587 B.C. Ezekiel was the prophet of doom. He attempted to smash the delusion that God could never abandon his Temple. After 587 B.C. Ezekiel worked at reconstructing the shattered faith of his people. He then became the prophet of hope (chs. 33-48). In both phases of his ministry this divinely appointed watchman bore witness to his faith in the coming Messiah.

In addition to the texts to be examined in detail in this chapter, the following Messianic themes appear in Ezekiel:

1. The purification and regeneration of Israel by the Spirit of God. Their stoney hearts would be softened (11:19; 36:26). They would walk in God's statutes (11:20). God's Spirit would be put within them (36:27; 37:14). By means of the water of purification God would cleanse his people from former idolatry (36:25).

2. The reversal of the fortunes of Judah, Samaria and Sodom (16:53-61). Sodom here is most likely a prophetic symbol for Gentiles.

3. The reunification of Judah and Israel (16:53-61). This was symbolically portrayed when Ezekiel joined a stick labeled "Judah" to one labeled "Joseph" (37:15-22). A similar passage in the New Testament is applied to the unity of the church of Christ (Rom. 9:25f.; I Peter 2:10).

4. The establishment of an everlasting covenant (16:60-63). The fulfillment is recorded in Hebrews 8. Cf. Jeremiah 31:34.

5. The protection and sustenance provided by the Messianic kingdom for all peoples (17:23-24).

6. The glorious increase in the future Israel and the abundant agricultural blessing of the land. They would dwell securely on their land (28:26). Like a most favored flock they would enjoy good pasture (34:14-16). The number of men and animals would be increased (36:8-11). There would be food in abundance (36:29-30). The desolate land would become like the garden of Eden (36:33-38). With abundant rain fruit would flourish and the land would become "a plantation of renown" (34:26-29).[1]

---

1. Payne (EBP, p. 363) limits the fulfillment to the postexilic community.

7. God will establish a new covenant with his people. It will be a covenant of peace which would make the entire land secure (34:25-28). The land would never again devour its inhabitants (36:12-15). This covenant would be everlasting (37:26).

8. Messianic Israel ruled by the second David would dwell in the land forever (37:25).

9. God would set up his sanctuary in the midst of his people (37:26-28). That sanctuary would be in the very center of the land (48:8-9). In great detail Ezekiel describes that future sanctuary (chs. 40-44) so as to stress its importance in the divine scheme. He seems to be allegorically describing the worship of the New Testament age.[2] Going forth from that Temple the river of life would bring health and fruitfulness to a barren world (47:1-12).

10. The forces of evil attack the people of God, but are completely destroyed (chs. 38-39). Ezekiel seems to be predicting "earth's final, Satan-inspired revolt against Yahweh."[3]

11. The future Israel would be a well-ordered kingdom. Every tribe would have its place (ch. 48). Gentiles would share the inheritance with Jews (47:22-23).

Prophecy No. 56

THE TENDER TWIG

Ezekiel 17:22-24

When King Johoiachin was deported to Babylon in 597 B.C. his uncle Mattaniah was put on the throne by Nebuchadnezzar. Mattaniah took the throne name Zedekiah. Almost immediately after swearing his vassal oath of allegiance to Nebuchadnezzar, Zedekiah began to look to Egypt for deliverance.

The prophecy of the tender twig dates to about 591 B.C., five years before the destruction of Jerusalem. In the immediate context Ezekiel has first related the allegory of the two eagles (17:1-10). He then interpreted this allegory for his readers (17:11-21). A synopsis of the allegory follows:

---

2. See Smith, EBST, pp. 424-487.
3. Payne, EBP, p. 367.

Great Eagle comes to Lebanon.	Nebuchadnezzar came to Judah.
Topmost shoot of a cedar broken off, carried to a land of merchants.	The cedar = the royal family. The topmost twig is Jehoiachin who was carried away to Babylon in 597 B.C.
Seed of the land planted, becomes a vine.	Zedekiah put on the throne.
Vine roots move toward the second great eagle.	Zedekiah's overtures toward Egypt.

The allegory closes with a warning. Pharaoh's army would be of no help in time of war (v. 17). Zedekiah's troops would be slaughtered. Such as survived would be scattered to the winds (v. 21). Zedekiah himself would die in Babylon because he had despised the solemn oath which he had taken in the name of God (vv. 16, 19-21).

Translation of Ezekiel 17:22-24

(22) Thus says the Lord GOD: Moreover I, even I, will take of the top of the lofty cedar, and I will set it; and I will break off from the topmost of its young twigs, a tender one, and I will plant it upon a high and lofty mountain. (23) On the mountain heights of Israel will I plant it; and it shall produce branches and bear fruit, and it shall be a splendid cedar; and birds of every kind will nest under it; they will nest in the shadow of its branches. (24) And all the trees of the field shall know that I the LORD have brought low the high tree, have exalted the low tree, and have dried up the green tree, and I have caused the withered tree to flourish; I the LORD have spoken and done it.

Discussion

This passage speaks of a prince brought back from exile to revive on Israel's soil, the fallen kingdom of his ancestors. Some interpret the passage as referring to Zerubbabel who led the first group of captives home in 538 B.C. He was a descendant of David, a twig from the cedar tree of the royal family. Good reasons, however, exist for regarding the tender twig as a designation for the Messiah.

1. Parallel passages suggest the Messianic character of these verses. Amos 9:11 speaks of the restoration of the fallen hut of David. Isaiah spoke of the beautiful and glorious shoot of the Lord who would appear after the destruction of Jerusalem (Isa. 4:2). (Cf. Isa. 11:1ff. and 53:2).

2. The parable of the mustard seed (Matt. 13:31) bears a striking similarity to the present passage.

3. The Targum and later the Jewish commentator Rashi understood Ezekiel to be referring to the Messianic kingdom.

4. The very extent of the promises themselves seem to warrant the Messianic interpretation.

Three points are stressed by Ezekiel in this allegory of the tender twig: (1) the origin (2) the planting, and (3) the growth of the twig.

A. *The Origin of the Tender Twig* (v. 22a). The tender twig is taken from the very top of the cedar. In the allegory the cedar represents the royal house of Judah. Though Zedekiah's fate was sealed (vv. 19-21), the dynasty of David would not die. The tender twig would be selected by God. The last king of Judah had been selected by Nebuchadnezzar; but the next king would be divinely appointed. This would necessitate credentialing so that the divine choice would be verified by God's people.

B. *The Planting of the Tender Twig* (vv. 22b-23a). The twig is planted as well as selected by God. Here is a reversal of what King Nebuchadnezzar had done. The topmost shoot had been broken off and carried away (vv. 3-4) by the great king of Babylon. Here God takes the topmost shoot and plants it.

God plants the twig on *a high and lofty mountain* (v. 22), *on the mountain heights of Israel* (v. 23). Mt. Zion is most likely intended. Though not physically impressive, Mt. Zion was spiritually preeminent. According to Psalms 2:6 Mt. Zion would serve as the seat of the throne of the divine king. Isaiah (2:2) foresaw the day when Mt. Zion as the center of God's government would be exalted above all the mountains of the earth.

C. *The Growth of the Tender Twig* (vv. 23b-24). In respect to the growth of the twig after the divine implantation, four points are stressed:

1. The growth of the tender twig would be spectacular, for it would *produce branches, bear fruit,* and *become a splendid cedar.* Messiah grows into a stately cedar in the kingdom founded by him.

2. The growth of the tender twig would be beneficial to men, for *birds of every kind will nest in it* (v. 23). The birds represent peoples of all nations who find shelter and sustenance in the kingdom of Messiah.

3. The growth of the tender twig will produce the conviction of its divine origin. The trees of the field symbolize other royal families and the kingdoms which they head. They would be amazed to see the royal house of David resurrected in the glorious cedar, the Messiah.

4. The growth of the tender twig illustrates a basic principle of divine government (v. 24). God humbles what is proud (the tall and green tree) and exalts what is lowly (the low and dry tree).

Prophecy No. 57

THE RIGHTFUL KING

Ezekiel 21:25-27

The year is 590 B.C. The Babylonian destruction of Jerusalem is about four years away. The immediate context contains a series of threats against Jerusalem. Nebuchadnezzar was on his way, and nothing could restrain him.

Translation of Ezekiel 21:25-27

(25) And you, O profane and wicked prince of Israel, whose day is come, in the iniquity of the end; (26) thus says the Lord GOD: The turban shall be removed, and the crown shall be taken off; things will be thrown into confusion; the lowly shall be exalted, and the high shall be brought low. (27) A ruin, a ruin I have made it; this also shall not be until he comes whose right it is, and I will give it to him.

Discussion

Two basic ideas are set forth in these verses: (1) the devastation of the monarchy, and (2) the restoration of the monarchy.

A. *The Devastation of the Monarchy* (vv. 25-27a). God addresses King Zedekiah in verse 25 as the *profane and wicked prince*. He had broken his solemn oath to Nebuchadnezzar. He had refused to listen to God's word. His day of punishment was at hand. The insignia of Zedekiah's royal rank would be removed (v. 26a). *Turban*[5] and *crown* set him apart as king. These would be laid aside. Society would be thrown into confusion.[6] Leadership would no longer reside in the royal family for it would be brought low.

The monarchy would become an utter ruin and cease to exist. Ezekiel thrice used the word *ruin* so as to drive his point home. Zedekiah was

---

5. Some think that the turban was the insignia of the priesthood. The idea is that priesthood as well as kingship would be abolished for a time.

6. Lit., *this not this*. The paraphrase of Lofthouse has been followed. NASB, *this will be no more the same.* NIV, *it will not be as it was.*

to be the last king in Jerusalem for an unspecified amount of time. B. *The Restoration of the Monarchy* (v. 27b). God's people would remain without royal leadership until the rightful ruler would arise. The words, *until he comes* point to the long awaited Messiah.

The coming one would have the right to sit on the throne of David.[7] When Messiah finally came, the crown and turban would be his, for he would be "the culmination of everything to which the Davidic house and the Messianic kingship in Israel have always pointed."[8]

By way of a concluding note to this prophecy it is interesting to observe what Ezekiel goes on to say. The Ammonites would be remembered no more. Israel, however, would have a future, and that future would include the coming of a glorious prince, Messiah.

Prophecy No. 58

THE FAITHFUL SHEPHERD

Ezekiel 34:23-31

Jerusalem has fallen (587 B.C.). Ezekiel has now entered the second phase of his ministry. His primary purpose now is to pick up the pieces of Judah's shattered faith. He wants to direct their attention to the glorious things which God still has in store for his people. In the immediate context (vv. 11-22) God, the Good Shepherd, is pictured gathering his flock from all the countries where they have been scattered due to the negligence of their human shepherds (vv. 1-6). The gathering by the Good Shepherd is a process extending over a long period of time. This is indicated by the fact that even after the flock is pasturing on the mountains of Israel (vv. 13-14), still God searches for the lost sheep (v. 16).

The shepherding of God is kind and just (v. 16). The bullies in the flock would no longer get by with their tactics (vv. 17-22). At this point God announces the rise of a royal shepherd on earth through whom he will shepherd his flock. Does the Messianic Shepherd arise after the period of divine shepherding spoken of in verses 11-22? Does the divine shepherd employ the Messiah-Shepherd to carry out some or all of the shepherding described in verses 11-22? These are hard questions. God began to gather his people in 539-538 B.C. He continued

7. Some think that the words *until he comes whose right it is* reflect Gen. 49:10. See comments on that passage.
8. Taylor, TOTC, p. 165.

to gather and shepherd his flock until the appearance of Messiah-Shepherd. Now God shepherds his flock through Messiah-Shepherd. The situation may be illustrated as follows:

538 B.C.   A.D. 26

SHEPHERDING BY GOD

⇓   ⇓

GATHERING BY   APPEARANCE OF
DIVINE SHEPHERD   MESSIAH-SHEPHERD

Translation of Ezekiel 34:23-31

(23) And I will raise up over them one Shepherd, and he shall feed them, even my servant David; he shall feed them, and he shall be their Shepherd. (24) And I the LORD will be their God, and my servant David prince among them; I the' LORD have spoken it. (25) And I will make a covenant of peace for them, and I will cause the evil beasts to cease from the land; and they shall dwell safely in the wilderness, and sleep in the woods. (26) And I will make them and the areas surrounding my hill a blessing; and I will cause the rain to come in its season; there shall be showers of blessing. (27) And the tree of the field shall give its fruit, and the land shall give its increase, and they shall be safe upon their land, and they shall know that I am the LORD when I have broken the bars of their yoke, and I have delivered them from the hand of those who made them bondmen. (28) And they shall not again be a prey to the nations, nor shall the wild beasts of the earth devour them; but they shall dwell safely, and none shall make them afraid. (29) And I will raise up unto them a famous plantation, and they shall not again be consumed by hunger in the land, neither bear the shame of the nations any more. (30) And they shall know that I the LORD their God am with them, and that they, the house of Israel, are my people (oracle of the Lord GOD). (31) And you my sheep, the sheep of my pasture, are Adam, and I am your God (oracle of the Lord God).

366

Discussion

In Ezekiel 34:23-31 the prophet paints two pictures, one of the Shepherd (vv. 23-24) and the other of his flock (vv. 25-31).

A. *The Shepherd* (vv. 23-24). The future leader is identified in nine ways in verses 23-24.

1. He is to be a *Shepherd*. This term is used to describe both political and religious rulers in the Old Testament. The word connotes the tender caring and thoughtful guidance which a leader should provide. In the verses immediately preceding this prophecy, God assumes the title *shepherd* and establishes the pattern of how faithful shepherds should function. Jesus must have had passages like this in mind when he referred to himself as the Good Shepherd (John 10:14).

2. He is to be *one* Shepherd. Other passages speak of the leaders in the new Israel as *shepherds*. This Shepherd, however, stands out as one of a kind. He is unique. Two inferences seem justified. First, this Shepherd will have supreme authority over other shepherds save God himself. Secondly, this Shepherd will not yield his authority to another. His rule, therefore, must be eternal.

3. He will be a ruler raised up by God. He does not take control of the nation by force, nor is he elected to his office. His authority is God-given. This fact obliges all men to follow his leadership.

4. He is *raised up over them*. The verb in the Hiphil stem has several connotations. It can mean *to erect, raise up* one who has fallen down. In other passages it means *to cause to come forth, to exist*. In this sense God raises up judges (Judg. 2:18), prophets (Jer. 29:15) and priests (I Sam. 2:35). In a third sense, the verb means *to confirm or establish* and in this sense is used of installing one as king. The basic idea is to bring into being what did not previously exist, or exalt that which is of low estate. He who claimed to be Israel's Messiah literally was raised to kingly glory from the lowly estate of servanthood and even death itself. The resurrection completed by the ascension brought Christ to his throne.

5. This ruler will have subjects, for God will raise him up *over them*. The reference is to the remnant gathered by God in the preceding verses. They are the true Israel of God.

6. This ruler will be from the line of David.

7. This ruler will have a unique relationship to God, for he will be *my Servant*. This terminology is often used of David,[9] and signifies one

---

9. At least twenty-two times. Israel or Jacob, i.e., the entire nation is called *my servant* ten times. Moses and Job are called *my servant* six times each. Several others including Isaiah, Eli, Zerubbabel and Abraham also receive this title.

who is in faithful subordination to God. The term is used of Messiah in the Servant poems (Isa. 42-53) and in Zechariah 3:8.

8. The Shepherd would serve the flock faithfully. Twice Ezekiel says that the coming ruler will tend (lit., shepherd) the flock. He adds a similar thought when he says, *he will be their Shepherd.* Whereas others who were shepherds of God's people had with varying degrees fulfilled their roles, this future Shepherd would be ideal.

9. The Shepherd will serve under Yahweh. *I Yahweh, I shall be their God.* The pronoun is emphasized in the Hebrew. The implication is that during the reign of the new ruler men's hearts would be turned toward God in true understanding and commitment as never before. The ruler, *my Servant David,* would be prince among the people. To serve this ruler is one expression of devotion to God.

B. *The Shepherd's Flock* (vv. 25-31). Five points are emphasized about the flock of the Davidic ruler. They will be (1) safe, (2) blessed, (3) free, (4) famous, and (5) confident.

1. Messiah's flock will be safe (v. 25). A new covenant will undergird the Messianic age, a *covenant of peace.* The flock will be safe from evil beasts, by which Ezekiel probably means ruthless oppressors. Even the most dangerous areas of the land—the wilderness and the woods—will be free from ravenous beasts.

The peace depicted here is ultimately a peace with God, not freedom from persecution. When men, however, are confident of eternal life they no longer fear what men can do to the body.

2. Messiah's flock will be blessed (vv. 26a, 27a). The spiritual blessings of the Messianic age are frequently depicted in terms of abundant rain and plentiful harvests.

3. Messiah's flock will be free (vv. 27b-28). They will be totally free. The inhabitants of that blessed and secure land will all know by personal experience that the Lord has delivered them from captivity. He has broken the bars of their yoke and rescued them from the hands of those who had enslaved them. They will be eternally free. The Messianic flock will never fall victim to the beasts of the earth, or adversary nations. They will be confidently free. In their divinely provided security they will manifest a boldness uncharacteristic of sheep. *No one will make them afraid* (v. 28).

4. Messiah's flock will be famous (v. 29). Because of the amazing fertility of the land, Israel will be known far and wide. Famine will be a thing of the past. The inhabitants will never have to suffer the humiliation of having to look to other nations for material assistance.

368

5. Messiah's flock will be confident in their relationship with God (vv. 30-31). They will know that God is with them (v. 30a). They will know that they are God's people (v. 30b), a special creation of God, like Adam (v. 31). "You are a people of God's own possession" (I Peter 2:9).

Prophecy No. 59

THE GREAT REUNION

Ezekiel 37:21-28

The faith of the Jews in the power of their God was shattered when Jerusalem fell to Nebuchadnezzar in 587 B.C. Ezekiel attempted to revive their hope with promises of restoration to their land and to their God. In the immediate context Ezekiel has related his famous vision of the valley of dry bones (37:1-14). Those bones, dead and disjointed, symbolized the sad state of the children of Israel. God would shortly resurrect that dead nation, and breathe new life into them.

Ezekiel was then directed to perform an action parable. He was to write the name *Joseph* on one stick, and the name *Judah* on another. The two sticks were then to be held end to end so that they appeared to be one stick. God's people who had been divided into two separate kingdoms would be reunited in the day of restoration.

Translation of Ezekiel 37:21-28

(21) And say unto them: Thus says the Lord GOD: Behold, I am about to take the children of Israel from among the nations where they went, and I will gather them from round about; and I will bring them into their land. (22) And I will make them one nation in the land, on the mountains of Israel; and one King shall be King to all of them; and they shall no longer be two nations, nor shall they be divided anymore into two kingdoms. (23) They shall not defile themselves anymore with their idols and their abominations and with all their transgressions; and I will save them from all of their sinful backslidings, and I will cleanse them, and they will be my people, and I will be their God. (24) And my servant David will be king over them, and there will be one Shepherd to all of them; and they will walk in my ordinances, and they will keep my statutes, and do them. (25) And they will dwell upon the land which I gave to Jacob my servant, in which your fathers dwelt; and

369

they will dwell therein, they and their sons and their grandsons forever; and David my servant will be prince forever. (26) And I will make a covenant of peace with them—it shall be an everlasting covenant with them; and I will establish them and multiply them, and I will set my sanctuary in their midst forever. (27) And my dwelling place will be over them; and I will be their God, and they will be my people. (28) And the nations will know that I the LORD sanctified Israel, when my sanctuary shall be in their midst forever.

Discussion

This prophecy develops three great themes: (1) the future condition, (2) the future leader, and (3) the future covenant of God's people. A. *The Future Condition of God's People* (vv. 21-23). Seven facts about the future condition of God's people are developed in the first three verses of this passage:

1. God's people will be gathered (v. 21a). This gathering would be made possible because of the repentance of the remnant. The prophecy began to be fulfilled when God stirred up the spirit of Cyrus to release the captives in 538 B.C. Zerubbabel led the first group home, Ezra the second in 458 B.C. Those returnees, however, were but the prelude for the world-wide gathering of God's people through the Gospel call.

2. God's people will be restored to Canaan (v. 21b). The physical land of Canaan was but a type of the inheritance of God's people. Those who have accepted the Gospel have come to Zion, the heavenly Jerusalem (Heb. 12:22).

3. God's people will be unified (v. 22a). The unification is a divine action, for *I will make them one*. Men divide, but only God can unify. They will be *one nation*. Peter speaks of the Christian church as a "holy nation" (I Peter 2:9).

This unity will be made possible because of allegiance to *one King*. If there is one King, there must of necessity be one kingdom. Recognition of the absolute authority of Jesus Christ within his kingdom is the key to Christian unity.

4. They will be committed, for they shall not *defile themselves anymore with their idols* (v. 23). When the remnant returned to Canaan they were, for the most part, cured of their tendency to embrace other gods. Jews scattered throughout the Roman empire were a strong witness to monotheistic faith. Christians were sometimes called "atheists" by their Roman persecutors because they did not worship a visible god.

370

5. They will be saved, for *I will save them from all their sinful back-slidings*. Messiah's people are a saved people. They have experienced the forgiveness of God.

6. They will be cleansed for, *I will cleanse them* (v. 23). They would not only be rescued from the consequence of sin, they would be made pure. In the law cleansing came through ceremonial washing and through sacrifice. So it is through the sacrifice of Christ, and the washing of water by the word (Eph. 5:26) that the sinner receives his cleansing today.

7. They will be a sanctified people, for *they will be my people and I will be their God*. Peter refers to Christians as a people of God's own possession (I Peter 2:9).

B. *The Future Ruler of God's People* (vv. 24-25). The *one king* of verse 22 is now described in more detail. The King is identified as *my servant David*, not David in the flesh, but a scion of the line of David. He is further described as *one Shepherd*. This implies that he would be their spiritual as well as their political leader.

The future leader would rule over the land of Canaan (v. 25a). The physical terrain of Canaan was but a preview of that land (Heb. 11:10) —that better country where Christ reigns supreme. The redeemed people of God would dwell in this land forever—the kingdom of heaven.

The future ruler will *be prince forever* (v. 25b). Such a prophecy could only find its fulfillment in a ruler whose reign cannot be interrupted by death. Only Jesus can fulfill these words.

C. *The Future Covenant with God's People* (vv. 26-27). The constitution for the kingdom age is called a *covenant of peace* (v. 26). It is predicated on the fact that all who enter this kingdom have made peace with God. Unlike the old covenant which anticipated its own abrogation, this covenant is eternal. Under the terms of this new covenant God makes five commitments to his people.

1. He promises them security, for he says, *I will establish them*.

2. He promises to multiply them (v. 26b). The Book of Acts records the spectacular growth of the new Israel of God: three thousand souls (2:41), then five thousand (4:4), then the disciples were multiplied (6:1).

3. He promises to put his sanctuary among them forever (v. 26b). He speaks not of Zerubbabel's Temple which was completed in 516 B.C., nor of Herod's Temple which was destroyed in A.D. 70. Those temples were but previews of the true sanctuary in which Jesus ministers (Heb. 8:2). This promise receives its highest realization first in the incarnation (John 1:14), next in God's inhabitation of the church

371

through the Spirit (II Cor. 6:16), and finally in his tabernacling with redeemed men in the heavenly Jerusalem (Rev. 21:3, 22).

4. He promises to reside with them (v. 27). Perfect harmony will exist between God and his people, for *I will be their God*, and they *will be my people* (cf. II Cor. 6:16).

5. He promises to sanctify them (v. 28). This glorious transformation of Israel's condition would have a profound effect upon the heathen world round about. They would recognize in the lives of the redeemed the power of God to sanctify people. Having recognized this, they would seek admittance to the congregation and fellowship of God's spiritual Israel, the church of Christ.

Prophecy No. 60

THE PRINCE IN THE SANCTUARY

Ezekiel 44-48

The interpretation of the last nine chapters of Ezekiel is extremely difficult. Ezekiel here describes a future Temple, a worship system and reorganization of the land of Canaan. Two basic approaches to these chapters have been proposed, the physical and the spiritual. Those who hold that the details in these chapters are to be interpreted physically (or literally) are themselves divided into two camps. Some believe that Ezekiel is here providing a blueprint for the reconstruction of the Temple and the reorganization of the land in postexilic times. Others think that Ezekiel is predicting a Temple to be constructed during the Millennium. The present writer is committed to the spiritual or symbolic approach to these chapters. The Gospel age is being described under figures meaningful to the original readers of Ezekiel. The church of Christ is the Temple of God (II Cor. 6:16).[10]

Seventeen times in chapters 44-48 there is mention of a Prince (*nasi'*). Jewish commentators regarded this prince as the Messiah. Most Christian commentators have rejected this view for three reasons. The prince (1) offers a sin offering for himself (45:22), (2) has sons (46:15), and (3) is distinct from the priests. While these objections are not without weight, alternative views as to the identity of the Prince are not convincing. He does not appear to be the high priest, although Ezekiel

---

10. See James E. Smith, BSTS, Ezekiel, pp. 428-430. The most thorough discussion of the proper approach to these chapters is found in volume V of *An Old Testament Commentary for English Readers*, ed. John Charles Ellicott, pp. 314-316.

says nothing about that office. Does the Prince symbolize the civil authorities who are committed to the worship of the new age? Is he a scion of the house of David who serves under the Messiah as his vice-regent? Whether one takes a physical or spiritual view of Ezekiel 40-48, the identity of the Prince is problematic.

Much has been made of the fact that the leader in the idealized theocracy is called Prince (nasi') and not king (melech). A number of scholars have stressed the discontinuity between the monarchic institution and Messianic expectation on the one hand, and the figure of the nasi' of chapters 40-48 on the other.[11] But there is no incongruity between a promise of eternal kingship to the Davidic house, and the title nasi'. This is proved by I Kings 11:34 where Solomon is designated nasi'.

There are interesting connotations in the term nasi'. Originally the term designated a tribal leader. Numbers 7 stresses the role of the nasi' as a patron of the liturgy. With the rise of monarchy, the king assumed a liturgical role (II Sam. 6; I Kings 8). From that point on a distinction between nasi' and melech is not in evidence. In Ezekiel nasi' appears several times as a designation of the Davidic head of state.[12]

Why does Ezekiel in these latter chapters prefer the term nasi'? Apparently Ezekiel chooses to limit his view of the king, seeing him only in respect to his relationship to national worship. John Skinner writes:

> National life in its secular aspects, with which the king is chiefly concerned, is hardly touched on in the vision. Everything being looked upon from the point of view of the Temple and its worship, there are but few allusions in which we can detect anything of the nature of a civil constitution.[13]

So the term nasi' stresses the role of the ruler as a religious leader. The term also stresses the unity of the people he rules. A nasi' originally was a tribal leader; a melech ruled several tribes. Though the land over which the Prince rules has space allocated to all the tribes, yet because of their commitment to the worship of the one God and his Prince, they are united as one tribe.

---

11. Zimmerli, Koch, Boehmer, Procksch, and Harford-Battersby.

12. Ezek. 7:27; 12:10, 12; 19:1; 21:25; 34:24. In 7:27 and possibly 32:29 nasi' appears in synthetic parallelism with melech.

13. John Skinner, "Ezekiel" in An Exposition of the Bible (S. S. Scranton, 1907) p. 336. Skinner has a lengthy treatise on "Prince and People" on pages 336-340 of this same volume.

Ezekiel has already indicated that a glorious Ruler will appear in the future age. That Ruler is David, i.e., a descendant of David, or Messiah (34:24; 17:22-24). It would be most unlikely that Ezekiel would now introduce another ruler who would occupy a prominent place subordinate to Messiah. Chapters 40-48 are simply the fulfillment in detail of the poetic visions of chapters 33-37.[14]

In discussing the role of the Prince in Ezekiel 44-48 two points need to be emphasized: (1) the privileges of the Prince, and (2) his responsibilities.

A. *The Privileges of the Prince.* Only the Prince would be allowed to enter the eastern gate of the Temple through which the visible glory of the Lord has passed when he entered the Temple (44:1-3).[15] This indicates that an extraordinary sanctity attached to the Prince. No other human being could use that gate without some degree of profanation. Messiah entered heaven, the true sanctuary, by a way that none other could, on the ground of his own perfect holiness (Rom. 1:4). All others must enter as sinners saved by grace.

The Prince would *eat bread* within the eastern outer gate complex. The terminology *eat bread* refers to the special eating of bread which, under the law, was the prerogative of priests.[16] Under the old system the congregation, including the king, was not allowed to partake of the meal offering (Lev. 2:3) or the shewbread (Lev. 24:9) and certain other bread as well.[17] In the new system envisioned by Ezekiel the Prince would have priestly prerogatives.

The Prince would have a specific inheritance in the future land (45:7, 8). In Ezekiel's symbolic scheme of things, the center of the land would be a rectangle called the *oblation,* a *holy portion* of the land. The ideal Temple and city would occupy this oblation. Here the priests would

---

14. The Messianic identification of the *nasi'* is argued by André Caquot, Kaufman, Gese, Hammershaimb and Baltzer.

15. Others interpret the text to mean that no man including the Prince could pass through that gate. The special privilege of the Prince was that he could "eat bread" within the gatehouse. In either case, the Prince is hereby afforded great honor.

16. Others take *eat bread* as a reference to the eating of that portion of certain meat offerings which was allocated to a worshiper under the law. The terminology *eat bread before the Lord* does occur in this sense in Exod. 18:12 (cf. Gen. 31:54). After the introduction of the law of Moses the terminology *eat bread* in a religious sense is restricted to the sons of Aaron.

17. E.g., the leavened loaves of Passover (Exod. 12:18; Lev. 23:6; Num. 28:17; Deut. 16:3).

live and render their ministration to the Lord. Worship would be central in the new age.

The law of Moses made no special inheritance provision for the kings. Old Testament kings were constantly attempting to expand their personal holdings at the expense of the citizens. Not so in the new age. The Prince (Messiah) would be an integral part of God's plan. He would possess two strips of land bordering the holy oblation on the east and west (48:21-22).

The people would render special tribute to the Prince (45:16). When 45:13-15 is compared to the stipulations of the Mosaic law it becomes clear that "the demands of Ezekiel's Torah surpass those of the earlier or Mosaic Torah in quantity as well as quality."[18] Certainly the liberality of God's people in the Messianic age would "greatly exceed that which was practised at any former time."[19] Such generosity would be expected (required?) of God's people. *All the people of the land shall be held to this offering for the Prince* in Israel (45:16). All offerings would be given to God through the Prince.

The inner eastern gate, unlike the outer eastern gate, would be opened on sabbath and new moon. Through this open gate the Prince would enter as far as its threshold where he would stand worshiping by the posts of the gate (46:1-2). The people were allowed to come to the door of that inner gate. They worshiped behind the Prince. Through the open gate they could observe the priests preparing the sacrifices provided by the Prince (46:3). The coming of the Prince causes the gate to be opened for his subjects to worship from without, *and the gate shall not be shut until evening.* Here again the Prince appears as the leader in worship.

The Prince is accorded honor in that he alone is permitted to enter and leave by the same route, *by the way of the porch of that gate,* on these weekly and monthly worship occasions (46:8-9). All others were required to enter the outer court by either the northern or southern gate, and to leave by the gate on the opposite side. The point here is not so much to prevent crowding and confusion (Keil), but to symbolize that those who truly worship God should leave the experience a new person (46:8-9).

The inner gate of the Temple shall be opened to the Prince (and apparently only to him) on occasions when he might wish to offer

---

18. Plumptre, PC, Ezekiel, p. 414.
19. Ibid.

voluntary burnt or peace offerings unto the Lord (46:12). He surpasses all his people in liberality. so setting them a princely example. His position as Prince affords him special access to God and he practices personal worship seasons above and beyond the stated times of public worship.

B. *The Duties of the Prince.* He provides[20] sacrifices in abundance on behalf of his people (45:17). No mention is made in these chapters of the people bringing sacrifices to the Temple. Apparently sacrifices are offered to the Lord through the Prince. Each sabbath and each new moon he offers before the Lord various sacrifices (46:4-7). This is an entirely new feature for the Mosaic law made no provision in regard to the source from which the festal sacrifices were to be obtained. What has been left to free-will offerings by the people now becomes an established duty of the Prince. The burnt offerings prescribed for the sabbath day are larger than those of the Mosaic law (46:4, 5). The same is true of the sacrifices prescribed for Passover (45:21-24). This suggests that the worship of God is to be conducted by the Prince and people in a more munificent spirit of self-sacrificial liberality.[21]

The sin offering is made more prominent in the new age. On Passover, for example, the sin offering comes before and presumably takes precedence over the Paschal feast proper (cf. Lev. 23:8). This sin offering was to consist of a bullock instead of a he-goat as prescribed in the law of Moses (Num. 28:22). For seven days in the spring at Passover and again in the fall for seven days during Tabernacles the Prince was to prepare each day seven bullocks, seven rams and male goat for a sin offering (45:21-25). Messiah was made to be a sin offering for guilty men (II Cor. 5:21) thus accomplishing all that the animal sin offerings of the old covenant could not accomplish.

The sacrifices offered by the Prince would bring reconciliation to the house of Israel (45:17). The Prince would be a mediator between God and the people. He handed the gifts to the priests whose part it was to offer them up. Plumptre comments: "The combination of the kingly and priestly offices in the person of the prince obviously typified the similar union of the same offices in David's son."[22]

---

20. The verb in 45:17 translated *prepare* in KJV and *provide* in NASB is '*asah*. The verb is frequently used in the technical sense of preparation of sacrifice (e.g., Lev. 5:10; 9:7). It is also used in a more general sense of providing the material for sacrifice (e.g., Lev. 14:30).

21. The sacrifices offered on the new moon (45:6, 7) and Tabernacles (45:25), however, are less than those prescribed by Moses.

22. Plumptre, PC, Ezekiel, p. 414.

During the great annual feasts the Prince was to enter the Temple when the people did, and withdraw from it when they did (46:10). He was an ever attending presence with his people. The law of attendance of the Prince suggests that worshipers should approach God in worship only *with* and *in* and *through* their great mediator, Christ Jesus. *When they go out, he shall go out.* Whether at worship, work or recreation the Prince is in the midst of his people!

The Prince will not oppress his subjects as some of his predecessors on the throne had done. He would not need to do so. His resources will be such that he will not need to forceably dispossess his subjects so as to have an inheritance to give to his sons (46:18). He may give gifts to his servants, but they revert to the Prince in *the year of liberty* (46:16-17). As servants, Christians receive gifts to be used for the building up of the church until the Lord comes. As sons, Christians are joint heirs with Christ!

Chapter Twenty-Five

DANIEL AND THE LATTER DAYS

Daniel was only a teenager when he was made a political hostage by Nebuchadnezzar in 605 B.C. and deported to Babylon. During his lengthy ministry of almost seventy years, Daniel occupied high governmental positions. He was the leading counselor of Nebuchadnezzar. He was made third ruler in the kingdom by Belshazzar. When the Persians conquered Babylon in 539 B.C. Daniel was made one of three presidents of the realm responsible directly, it would seem, to Darius the Mede.

Two passages in Daniel speak personally of the Messiah. In the first Daniel observes one like unto a son of man approaching the Ancient of Days (ch. 7). In the second passage an angel indicates the length of time which must elapse before Messiah appears (ch. 9).

Prophecy No. 61

ONE LIKE UNTO A SON OF MAN

Daniel 7:13-14

In chapter 7 Daniel describes a dream vision which he saw in the first year of the reign of Belshazzar (c. 541 B.C.). The first sight he saw was the great sea—the Mediterranean—whipped into a tumult by the four winds of the heavens (v. 2). The turbulent sea likely represents the constant state of turmoil which exists in the political world.

Daniel next observed four fearsome beasts emerging from the sea. These represented kings or kingdoms which would arise out of the earth (v. 17). The first was a winged lion. Daniel observed the wings plucked from the lion. The beast then assumed a human-like posture (v. 4). From the perspective of Daniel the first world kingdom was the Chaldean or Babylonian (cf. 2:36-38). The swift and powerful Nebuchadnezzar had made himself master of the world at the battle of Carchemish in 605 B.C. Toward the end of his long reign Nebuchadnezzar turned from warfare to construction projects. He lost his beastly characteristics.

The second beast resembled a lopsided bear with three ribs in its mouth (v. 5). This beast symbolized the Medo-Persian empire in which the Persian element dominated the Median. The three ribs *may* symbolize the three greatest conquests of the Medo-Persian empire —Babylonia, Lydia and Egypt.

The third beast resembled a leopard with four wings and four heads (v. 6). The Greek empire is thus symbolized. The wings point to the rapidity of the conquests of Alexander the Great (331-323 B.C.). The four heads probably represent the divisions of the kingdom after the death of Alexander.

For the fourth beast Daniel could find no similitude. It had iron teeth, ten horns (v. 7) and bronze nails (v. 19). It devoured its opposition and crushed them beneath its feet. Daniel's attention was drawn to the emergence of a little horn which uprooted three of the ten hours. The horn is described as having eyes and speaking (v. 8). This horn made war with the people of God and prevailed against them "until the time came that the saints possessed the kingdom" (v. 22).

The interpreting angel explained that the fourth beast was a fourth world kingdom (v. 23). The horns represent ten kings or kingdoms which would arise out of that fourth kingdom. The little horn would arise after the ten. He would be different from them. He would come to power by subduing three of the ten horns or kingdoms (v. 24). He would blaspheme against God, wear out the saints, and "think to change times and laws." For a brief period, three-and-a-half years, the saints of God would be delivered into the power of the little horn (v. 25).

For the most part conservative writers are agreed that the fourth kingdom in Daniel is Rome. No agreement exists, however, on the identity of the ten horns. They have been identified as (1) ten emperors of the Roman empire, (2) ten kingdoms which emerged from the old Roman empire, (3) all the powers which have followed Rome on the stage of history, and (4) a revived Roman empire. The third of these positions is most likely the correct one.

Who, then, is the little horn? Here again striking differences appear. The little horn has been taken to be (1) a particular Roman emperor (Nero or Domitian), (2) the papacy, (3) a personification of the evil of the last day, and (4) the "man of sin," or "antichrist," i.e., some last great persecutor of God's people.

The important point in the passage is that the world powers are destroyed by decree of the sovereign God who rules over all. The first three beasts (Babylon, Medo-Persia, Greece) had their dominion taken away, but their lives were preserved for a time (v. 12). This may be a way of saying that each kingdom was absorbed by, and in a sense continued to live within, the borders of the empire which conquered it.

What is depicted in verses 9-10 seems to be the last judgment on world power. The Ancient of Days, the eternal God, who has witnessed the rise and fall of innumerable governments, sits upon his fiery judgment throne. The white garments depict his absolute righteousness, the hair like wool underscores his eternality. Ten thousand times ten thousand of the heavenly host add to the glory and power of the scene. The *books* were opened. The omniscient God knows all the savage deeds of the beast-like governments which have ruled the world.

Unlike the first four beasts, the fourth was slain, his body destroyed and burned (v. 11). The destruction of the little horn was contemporaneous with that of the fourth kingdom, i.e., Rome. The fourth kingdom is represented as having three stages of existence: (1) the beast stage, (2) the ten horn stage, and (3) the little horn stage. The beast is not finally destroyed until the little horn is destroyed.

In Daniel 7:1-12 the prophet sees what the future holds for the beast-like kingdoms. They enjoy their heyday and then meet their doom. By way of contrast, the prophet sees in verses 12-13 the glorious future of God's kingdom.

Translation of Daniel 7:13-14

(13) I kept observing in the night visions, and behold with the clouds of heaven One like a son of man was coming; and unto the Ancient of Days he came up and they brought him near. (14) And to him was given dominion, glory and a kingdom that all peoples, nations, and tongues might serve him; his dominion is an everlasting dominion that does not pass away, and his kingdom is one which cannot be destroyed.

Discussion

A. *The Establishment of the Heavenly Kingdom* (7:13-14). A new vision begins in verse 13. The events depicted here do not chronologically follow the destruction of the little horn in verse 11. The first twelve verses represent what will take place down here. Verses 13-14 show what will take place up there. The chronological relationship between verses 1-12 and verses 13-14 must be determined by other means.

1. The focus in verse 13 is on a special person, *one like unto a son of man*. A number of commentators see this one as a personification of the people of God. In verse 14 this One receives a kingdom. The explanation given Daniel in verse 22 is that the saints will possess the kingdom. That the *one like unto a son of man* is an individual, however, seems to be suggested by the language of verse 14: all nations serve him. Similar language is used in verse 27.

The nature of this special person is indicated by the title *one like unto a son of man*. He is different from the beastly governments and ruthless kings which were depicted in verses 1-12. He possesses the intelligence and gentleness which God intended human-kind to possess. Daniel, however, stops short of saying that this one *was* a son of man. The prophet could see from other details of the vision that this one was very special. What is said of him could be said of no mere man.

2. Daniel witnessed the one like unto a son of man coming with the clouds of heaven to the Ancient of Days. It is important to note here (1) the direction, (2) the manner, and (3) the glory of his coming.

It was to *the Ancient of Days* that he came. Presumably the Ancient of Days (God) was seen in his heavenly domain (cf. vv. 9-10). The verse could not then be a reference to the second coming, for on that occasion the one like unto a son of man comes *from* the Father. The ascension of the God-man Jesus is most likely being depicted here.

He came *with the clouds of heaven*. Clouds are frequently associated with the presence of deity in the Old Testament. In Acts 1 the ascension of Christ is described as follows: "While they beheld he was taken up; and a cloud received him out of their sight." The apostles witnessed the beginning of his journey back to glory; Daniel in prophetic vision sees the conclusion of that journey.

The glory of his coming is suggested by the words, *they brought him near*. The one like unto a son of man was ushered by the angels into the presence of the Ancient of Days. What a happy welcome that must have been when the Lord of glory returned to the heavenly realms!

3. In the presence of the Ancient of Days the one like unto a son of man is crowned king (v. 14). The Ancient of Days bestowed upon him three gifts, which are in fact three ways of looking at one gift. These are:

a) *Dominion*. God had given only temporary dominion to the beastly kingdoms (v. 6). But to the one like unto a son of man he gives *an everlasting dominion that does not pass away* (cf. v. 27). The reference cannot be to some millennial kingdom of limited duration.

b) *Glory*. His glory is not as the world measures the glory of a kingdom. This is not material glory, but the true glory of the spirit.

c) *A kingdom*. No beastly kingdom will ever conquer this kingdom for *his kingdom is one which cannot be destroyed*.

B. *The Triumph of the Heavenly Kingdom* (vv. 15-28). In response to Daniel's request, an angel explained to him at some length the significance of what he had seen in his night visions (vv. 15-28). The angel pointed out how the heavenly rule of the one like unto a son of man ultimately would affect the *saints*, his followers, on earth. No matter what beastly kingdoms may arise, *the saints of the Most High will receive the kingdom and possess the kingdom forever, for all ages to come* (v. 18).

When will the saints take possession of the kingdom? Several hints are given in the text. They will take possession:

1. At the appropriate time (v. 22).

2. After the Ancient of Days sits in (final?) judgment, and vindicates the saints of God.

3. After a brief time[1] of severe persecution by the "little horn" (v. 25).

4. After the dominion of the "little horn" has been taken away, and his dominion has been totally destroyed (v. 26).

Prophecy No. 62

THE SEVENTY HEPTADS

Daniel 9:24-27

The most important Messianic prophecy in the Old Testament is one given by the angel Gabriel in response to a prayer of Daniel. The prophecy dates to the first year of Darius the Mede, about 538 B.C. Daniel had been studying the books of the prophets. In the writings of Jeremiah he observed that the desolations of Jerusalem would be filled up within seventy years. Counting from 605 B.C. when Nebuchadnezzar first brought his armies against Jerusalem, Daniel realized that the seventy years had almost run their course. Yet Daniel could observe no sign that the promised restoration of Jerusalem was at hand. He went to God in prayer, confessing the sin of his people (vv. 5-15), and calling upon God to smile once again upon the desolate city of Jerusalem (vv. 16-19).

Even while Daniel was praying the angel Gabriel appeared to him again (cf. 8:16). The angel had been dispatched by divine command at the outset of Daniel's supplication to give the prophet understanding regarding the future of his people (vv. 20-23).

---

1. *A time, times and a half time* would be three plus years, roughly half of seven, the number of completeness.

Translation of Daniel 9:24-27

(24) Seventy sevens have been determined concerning your people and your holy city to fill up the transgression, to seal up sins, to make atonement for iniquity, to bring in everlasting righteousness, to seal vision and prophecy, and to anoint the most holy. (25) So you shall know and understand that from the going forth of a word to restore and to build Jerusalem unto Messiah-Prince shall be seven and sixty-two sevens. The street shall be built again and the wall, even in troublous times. (26) But after the sixty-two sevens Messiah shall be cut off and shall have nothing; and the city and the sanctuary the people of the prince that shall come shall destroy; and its end shall be as a flood, and unto the end of the war desolations are determined (27) And he will cause a covenant to prevail for the many one week, and in the midst of the week he will cause sacrifice and oblation to cease; and upon the wing of abominations are desolations even unto the full end, and that determined, shall be poured out upon the one who makes desolate.

Discussion

This difficult passage is placed within an unusual framework of "seventy sevens." The focus of the passage is upon the culmination of God's program for the Jewish people. Five points must be observed here:

A. *The Period of the Seventy Sevens.* Gabriel indicated that seventy sevens (heptads) yet remained before the true deliverance of God's people would take place. Strictly speaking, the Hebrew word can be used of any unit of seven (like dozen is a unit of twelve, and quire a unit of twenty-four). It is obvious that Gabriel did not intend for the "seventy sevens" to be understood here as ordinary weeks of seven days.[2] Seventy weeks of seven days would total 490 days. Daniel lived longer than 490 days (see 10:1) beyond this appearance of Gabriel, yet he says nothing about the fulfillment or non-fulfillment of the stupendous prophecies found in the passage. It is, therefore, clear that the seventy heptads are units of seven years. Whereas westerners think in terms of units of ten years (decades), the Israelites

---

2. The term *shabhu'im* is not the usual feminine form for "weeks." In Dan. 10:2 where this form does mean a seven-day week, the term stands with further qualification, lit., weeks of days. See Payne, EBP, p. 383, n. 56.

organized years into units of seven. Every seventh year the land was to be fallow (Exod. 23:11) and Hebrew slaves were to be set free after seven years of service (Deut. 15:12).

The seventy heptads (490 years) are said to be *determined*. The verb is a *hapax*. i.e., it is only used once in the Old Testament. The idea is that the seventy heptads are preordained and will surely come to pass. Messianic redemption was written on God's calendar.

The seventy heptads are determined *upon your people* and *upon your holy city* (v. 24). Daniel's prayer had pertained to the plight of the holy city and God's people (v. 16). The exile was nearing its end. What did the future hold for the covenant people? The thought here is that the true deliverance of God's people would not come at the end of Jeremiah's seventy years, but within the scope of seventy weeks of years.

B. *The Program for the Seventy Sevens* (v. 24). Six infinitives describe God's program as it pertains to Israel during the seventy sevens.

1. *To fill up[3] the transgression.* Within the 490 year period the people of Israel would commit their final transgression against God. Jesus indicated that the leaders of his generation were about to fill up the measure of the sin of their forefathers (Matt. 23:32). Paul indicated in his first letter to the Thessalonians that the Jews were heaping up their sins to the limit by trying to prevent the preaching of Christ to the Gentiles (I Thess. 2:16).

2. *To seal up sin.[4]* The perfect sacrifice for sin offered by Jesus Christ provided the means by which the sin problem of mankind could be dealt with decisively (Heb. 10:12). After he had made purification for sin the victorious Jesus sat down on the right hand of the Majesty in heaven (Heb. 1:3). The blood of Jesus can cleanse the inner man and thus make possible true service to God (Heb. 9:14).

3. *To make atonement for iniquity.* The necessary sacrifice would be offered and would become the basis upon which iniquity could be forgiven. In Christ there is redemption, the forgiveness of sins (Col. 1:14). His once-for-all-time sacrifice is able to make perfect those who accept it as their own (Heb. 10:12-14).

4. *To bring in everlasting righteousness.* It is obviously God who brings in this righteousness, and he does that through the Messiah.

---

3. Others understand this verb *kala'* to mean *to restrain*. See NIV note. Young (NBC, p. 678) interprets *kala'* to mean seal up, *put away, remove.* Lockhart (MMOT, p. 218) thinks the reference is to the restraint placed upon heathen transgression against Israel.

4. Others understand the verb *hatham* to mean *to seal up,* in the sense of *reserve for punishment.*

This righteousness by its very perpetuity must belong to the age of Messiah.[5] Through faith in Christ a righteousness from God apart from the law has been made known (Rom. 3:21-26; cf. 14:17). The goal of every believer is to seek first the kingdom of God and his righteousness (Matt. 6:33).

5. *To seal up vision and prophecy.*[6] On two occasions Jesus cited the prophecy in Isaiah 6:9, 10 regarding the obtuseness of the Jews. They heard, but did not understand; they saw but did not perceive. Paul cited the same prophecy as justification for turning from the Jews to the Gentiles (Acts 28:25-27). The sealing of vision and prophecy in their midst—the failure to understand that the long awaited Messiah was ministering in their midst—was one of the penalties suffered by the Jewish nation because of their hardness of heart.[7]

6. *To anoint the most holy.*[8] The expression could refer to the anointing of the most holy person,[9] the anointed one *par excellence*, the Messiah. At his baptism the Holy Spirit descended on him in bodily form like a dove (Luke 3:22). Peter was apparently referring to this incident when he declared that "God anointed Jesus of Nazareth with the Holy Spirit and power" (Acts 10:38).

In summary, it is clear that all six objectives stated in verse 24 were accomplished by the time Jesus of Nazareth ascended to heaven in A.D. 30, or shortly thereafter.

C. *The Focal Point of the Seventy Sevens* (vv. 25-27). Verse 25 speaks of two great events which were on God's agenda and the time interval between them. When Daniel was told to *know and understand* this information he is being encouraged to have absolute confidence that both of these important events would transpire.

The angel spoke of the *going forth of a word to restore and to build Jerusalem.* The assumption is generally made that the reference here is to the decree of some Persian king. Commentators are sharply divided in their opinions about which Persian decree is intended. The

---

5. Lockhart, MMOT, p. 218.

6. Lit., vision and prophet. Young thinks these two terms represent the Old Testament dispensation. The prophetic institution was typical of Christ. In Christ this method of revelation ceased and in this sense vision and prophecy were sealed up.

7. Young (PD. p. 200) thinks the sealing refers to the fulfillment of prophecies in Christ. Others see in the sealing the termination of the prophetic office.

8. The KJV supplies the noun *place*. NIV leaves the question open as to whether *place* or *one* is to be supplied. Literally the phrase means *a holiness of holiness*.

9. In I Chron. 23:13 the high priest is called "most holy." The expression, therefore, is appropriate to a person.

word dabhar (KJV, *commandment*) in verse 25 is the same word used in verse 23 for the directions which God had given the angel Gabriel. This raises the possibility that the *word* to restore and to build Jerusalem was not that of any Persian king, but rather a commandment of God himself.[10]

Most likely it was Ezra the Scribe who issued the word to restore and to build Jerusalem in the spring of 457 B.C. (See the Special Study at the conclusion of this chapter). This is the *terminus a quo* of the passage. Counting from that date *seven sevens and sixty two sevens of years* would elapse before the appearance of Messiah-Prince. Seven sevens of years are equal to 49 years; sixty-two sevens is equal to 434 years. The prophecy may be diagrammed as follows:

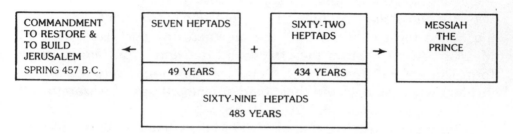

Subtracting 483 years from the starting point of 457 B.C. the year A.D. 27 is reached. In the modern system of counting years there is no year zero. Hence the year A.D. 27 must be reduced by one for chronological accuracy. According to Daniel, Messiah-Prince would appear in A.D. 26. It is surely more than a coincidence that the baptism of Jesus occurred in A.D. 26.[11] At that time John introduced him to the nation as their Messiah, the Lamb of God who would take away the sin of the world.

At some point during the sixty-nine sevens *the street shall be built again, and the wall, even in troublous times* (v. 25). The reference is to the rebuilding of Jerusalem. Most likely the angel meant for Daniel to understand that the first seven sevens (49 years) would be devoted

---

10. Young (NBC, p. 679) recognizes that the *commandment* is a divine word, yet insists that "the effects of the going forth of this word appeared in human history and this was during the first year of Cyrus, when he permitted the Jews to return to their land."

11. According to Luke 3:1ff. it was the fifteenth year of the reign of Tiberius Caesar that John began his ministry. Finegan (HBC, pp. 259-69) dates the baptism of Jesus to November, A.D. 26.

to the rebuilding of Jerusalem. Counting forty-nine years from 457 B.C. (the word to rebuild) brings one to 407 B.C. The major efforts toward reconstruction of the city occurred when Nehemiah successfully rebuilt the walls around 445 B.C.

D. *The Death of the Messiah* (v. 26). Verse 26 mentions two events which would transpire after the expiration of the sixty-two sevens. The first is the death of Messiah; the second is the fate of Jerusalem. Verse 26 does not state, nor should it be inferred from the passage, that these two events occur during the seventieth heptad.

1. After his appearance at the end of sixty-two sevens (483 years) the Messiah would be *cut off*. This term is best taken as a reference to the premature and violent death of the Messiah.[12] Here, as in Isaiah's Servant poems, Messiah and suffering are linked. A gap of time between the appearance of the Messiah and the death of Messiah is suggested by the adverb *after*. How long that time interval would be cannot be determined from verse 26 alone.

When he is cut off Messiah *shall have nothing*.[13] This expression points to the utter rejection of Messiah, both by God and by men. He died without physical posterity, not having achieved success as a ruler. Over his sole possession the soldiers gambled at Golgotha.

2. Verse 26 mentions the fate of *the city and the sanctuary,* i.e., Jerusalem and the Temple. Both are to be destroyed by *the people of the prince that shall come*. This prince is to arise after the anointed one has been cut off.[14] This verse certainly suggests that this terrible fate befalls the city because the Messiah has been cut off. The destruction of Jerusalem by the Romans in A.D. 70 is clearly prophesied here. The prolonged agony of the fall of the city is indicated by the words *unto the end of the war desolations are determined*. God has decreed this violent end for Jerusalem. This interpretation of the latter half of verse 26 fits well with the predictions which Jesus made concerning the destruction of Jerusalem in Matthew 24.

---

12. Both the Syriac and Vulgate support the interpretation that Messiah would be killed.

13. Lit., *there is not to him*. KJV saw the expression as a reference to the vicarious suffering of Christ and rendered it, *not for himself.*

14. Some think this prince is the same one who is cut off, i.e., Christ. The people of the prince would be the armies which he sent against Jerusalem. Payne (EBP, p. 387) seems to endorse the variant Hebrew and versional reading, *And the city and the sanctuary shall be destroyed along with the Prince that is to come,* viz., Messiah.

E. Further Details Regarding Messiah's Ministry and the Fall of Jerusalem (v. 27). The focus in verse 27 is on the crucial events of the seventieth seven. There is no reason to assume that this period of seven years is separated from the previous sixty-nine. Gabriel has already made two points relative to the Messiah: (1) he is to appear within sixty-nine heptads of the issuance of a decree to rebuild Jerusalem, and (2) he is to be cut off at some point after the seven plus sixty-two sevens. But what of Messiah's ministry? What would he accomplish after his appearance? Daniel addresses this question in verse 27.

Messiah will *cause a covenant to prevail* for one heptad (seven years). By his life, death, resurrection, and the pouring out of his Spirit upon the apostles the Messiah inaugurated a new covenant. For 3-1/2 years he proclaimed the gospel of the kingdom to Israel (cf. Isa. 42:1-4). After his ascension the covenant continued to be confirmed to Israel through the preaching of the apostles. This open message terminated with the stoning of Stephen after which the church scattered (Acts 8:1). In that same year (A.D. 33/34) Paul was converted to Christianity.[15]

In the midst of the seventieth heptad (i.e., after 3-1/2 years) Messiah would *cause sacrifice and oblation to cease*. It is clear from the Book of Hebrews that it was by his death that Messiah brought about the cessation of the Old Testament sacrificial systems (cf. Heb. 8:13). The Temple veil was rent (Matt. 27:51). Typical sacrifice ceased once for all time (Heb. 9:12).

Further details are given regarding the destruction of Jerusalem by the Roman armies. The last half of verse 27 is difficult to translate and interpret, but these points are more or less clear:

1. One shall come who makes desolate. Most likely this is a reference to the Roman prince Titus.

2. He will come *upon the wing of abominations*. This is probably a reference to the pinnacle of the Temple. Even the highest point of the Temple (the wing) will be overrun and desecrated by the invader.

3. He will succeed in making the Temple area *desolate*.

4. The one who makes the Temple desolate will meet his doom when the *full end* shall be poured upon the one who makes desolate.

5. The doom of the Roman destroyer is *determined* by God.

---

15. Payne, EBP, p. 388 and Finegan, HBC, pp. 320-321.

Special Study

THE INTERPRETATION OF THE SEVENTY HEPTADS

The interpretation of Daniel 9:24-27 is notoriously difficult. It baffles the acumen of the wisest scholar.[16] Three main approaches to the passage have been championed.

A. *The Liberal Position.* A representative exponent of the liberal position is J. A. Montgomery in the *International Critical Commentary.* Montgomery interprets the command to rebuild Jerusalem to be Jeremiah's word at Jerusalem's fall in 586 B.C. The first seven weeks (49 years) conclude with the return of the Jews to their homeland in 538 B.C. The sixty-two heptads (434 years) are counted from 538 B.C. and terminate in 171 B.C. with the appearance of Jeshua the anointed one. The Messiah who is cut off is Onias III. The Prince who would come against Jerusalem is Antiochus who continued to make war against the Jews until his death in 164 B.C. Antiochus had a covenant with the Hellenistic Jews (168-165 B.C.) which he broke after 3-1/2 years when he defiled the Temple with idols. The seventieth heptad ends with the victory of the Maccabees over the Greek invaders.

This approach to the passage has the following defects:

1. An inadequate starting point for the decree to restore Jerusalem.

2. The failure to do justice to the terminology "Messiah-Prince."

3. Counting from 538 B.C. the sixty-two heptads (434 years) terminate more than sixty-five years after the period of Antiochus' tyranny. Montgomery must postulate an error in calculation on the part of the author of Daniel.

DIAGRAM OF THE LIBERAL VIEW

586 B.C. | 7 SEVENS (49 YEARS) | 538 B.C. | 62 SEVENS (434 YEARS) | 171 B.C. | WRITER MADE AN ERROR | 104 B.C.

ONIAS KILLED 171 B.C.

---

16. Lockhart, MMOT, p. 217.

B. Traditional Interpretation. This view is represented by E. B. Pusey, *Daniel the Prophet,* an excellent commentary which has been reprinted in the Barnes Notes series. Pusey starts counting the seventy sevens from 458 B.C., the decree of Artaxerxes to Ezra. The first forty-nine years, which include the work of Nehemiah, terminate in 409 B.C. The anointed one is Christ who was baptized in A.D. 26 and immediately thereafter began his Messianic ministry. He was cut off by his death on the cross. The prince who is to come in judgment on Jerusalem is Christ or Titus who acts as an agent for Christ. The covenant to be made firm is Christ's new testament. The Old Testament sacrificial system ended in the midst of the seventieth week when Christ died on the cross (A.D. 30). The seventieth seven ends with the stoning of Stephen, Jewish rejection of the New Testament, and the call of Paul (A.D. 33).

The main weakness of the traditional interpretation is that the destruction of Jerusalem foretold in verses 26-27 must be removed from seventy sevens. The seventieth heptad ended in A.D. 33; but the destruction of Jerusalem did not occur until thirty-seven years later.

While the implication may be present that the seventy heptads terminate in the destruction of Jerusalem, the passage does not directly affirm such to be the case. The word *determined* in verses 26-27 may suggest that what would happen during the seventy heptads would seal the fate of Jerusalem, and of the Roman armies which would attack Jerusalem. Taken this way, the passage would not be saying that the desolations would take place during the seventy heptads, but only that they would be determined during that period.

DIAGRAM OF THE TRADITIONAL VIEW

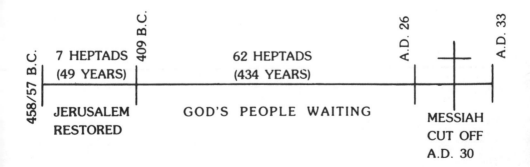

C. The Symbolic Interpretation. H. C. Leupold in his *Exposition of Daniel* is a modern representative of the symbolic interpretation of Daniel 9:24-27. According to this view, the seven heptads, sixty-two heptads and one heptad are periods of time but are not to be computed in terms of literal years. Lockhart[17] addresses the hermeneutical issues as follows:

> There is no good reason for not understanding the prophet to use the seven weeks, the sixty-two weeks, and other periods elsewhere according to the simple figure of synechdoche, a definite for an indefinite. The object of the prophecy is not to set dates; for that . . . is too precise to accomplish the true ends of prophecy . . . . Either weeks or days used in a prophecy like this would most naturally convey to the Jewish reader the idea of periods of definite lengths in the mind of God, but presumably much longer than literal weeks or days. There is no good reason for assuming that the Jewish mind would ever imagine that a day stood for a year, or that a week stood for seven years.

Leupold thinks the decree to restore Jerusalem was that of Cyrus in 538 B.C. The first seven heptads end with the incarnation of Christ. The sixty-two heptads is the period of the church age. Messiah being cut off refers to the end of the progressive expansion of the church. The Prince who is come is Antichirst who enslaves the masses. He breaks his covenant and causes sacrifice (i.e., church worship) to cease. The seventieth week ends with God's final judgment.

DIAGRAM OF THE SYMBOLIC VIEW

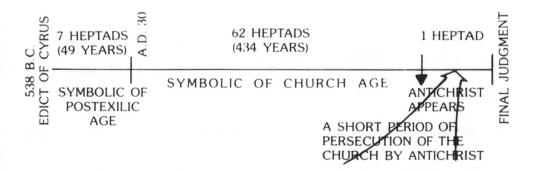

17. Ibid., p. 221.

Weaknesses in the symbolic interpretation are as follows:

1. The failure to recognize that the blessings promised in verse 24 were abundantly fulfilled in the first advent of Christ.

2. The failure to recognize Messiah, the main figure in the passage, as the subject of verse 27. The introduction of an eschatological antichrist into the passage is rather abrupt.

3. The failure to do justice to the prediction that the "Messiah shall be cut off." This is taken by Leupold to be a reference to massive defections of Christians in the last days. The phrase more naturally refers to the death of Christ.

4. Placement of the sixty-two heptads after the appearance of Messiah flies in the face of the language. The angel clearly is saying that the seven heptads plus sixty-two heptads must elapse before Messiah appears.

5. The application of the building of streets and wall (v. 25) to the building up of the church is forced. This interpretation makes the angelic prophecy unresponsive to the immediate concern of Daniel which was that Jerusalem was desolate (vv. 16-17).)

D. *The Dispensational Interpretation.* The dispensational interpretation of Daniel 9:24-27 is represented by A. C. Gaebelein, *The Prophet Daniel.* Gaebelein regarded the years in this passage as prophetic years of 360 days each. The total number of prophetic days is first computed, and then that figure is divided by 365 to determine the number of solar years involved.[18]

The seventy heptads begin in 444 B.C. with the decree of Artaxerxes to Nehemiah. The seven plus sixty-two heptads end with the triumphal

DIAGRAM OF THE DISPENSATIONAL VIEW

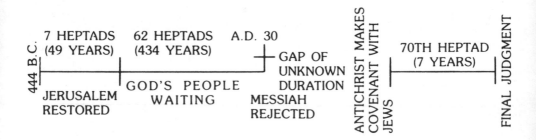

18. This theory was originally worked out by Sir Robert Anderson. Some more recent dispensational writers question the validity of the 360-day prophetic year theory. See Culver, DLD, p. 145.

entry in A.D. 30. Messiah is then cut off by his crucifixion. The prince that shall come is Titus the Roman. The seventieth heptad is yet future. Antichrist will make a covenant with regathered infidel Jews. After 3-1/2 years he will break his covenant and will desecrate the Temple. The seventieth week ends with God's final judgment. According to this view the promises made in verse 24 were not fulfilled at the first coming.

The weaknesses of the dispensational interpretation are as follows:

1. The mathematical gymnastics which most in this school perform in order to convert "prophetic years" into solar years. Daniel understood Jeremiah's prophecy of seventy years of desolation for Jerusalem as ordinary years (9:2). Furthermore, extra months were periodically inserted into the year to bring the lunar calendar into harmony with the seasons. This would mean that over a long period of time the 360 day year with extra months added periodically, would be equivalent to a 365 day year.[19]

2. The failure to recognize that the promises in verse 24 are blessings flowing from the first coming of Christ.

3. The separation of the seventieth heptad from the first sixty-nine. The existence of a gap of two thousand years is a strange intrusion into the text.

4. The double identity of the "prince who is to come" is strange. In verse 26 he is Titus, the general who destroyed Jerusalem in A.D. 70. This prince who is to come is said to be the subject of verse 27, but is now identified as the Antichrist who has not yet appeared.

5. Identifying the "prince" as the subject in verse 27 does not appear to be the most natural reading, for the word occupies only a subordinate position in verse 26 where it is not even the subject of a sentence.

6. Scripture does not so much as even hint of any covenant to be made by Antichrist, or any covenant to be confirmed by him.

Special Study

THE DATE OF THE DECREE TO
REBUILD JERUSALEM

The seventy heptads are to be counted from a decree or word to restore and to build Jerusalem. Commentators generally assume that

---

19. Finegan, HBC, p. 36.

the decree of some Persian king is intended. Four Persian decrees have been mentioned as possible:

1. The decree of Cyrus in 538 B.C. This decree is defended by such able scholars as E. J. Young and H. C. Leupold. Certainly the prophet Isaiah linked Cyrus to the restoration of the Jews to their homeland. It is generally conceded, however, that Cyrus did not specifically authorize the rebuilding of Jerusalem, and especially the walls of that place. A city which once had walls could not be spoken of as having been "built" without the rebuilding of those walls. The proof that Cyrus did not authorize the rebuilding of Jerusalem is found in Ezra 4:17-22. Had King Artaxerxes found in the royal archives an edict by Cyrus permitting the Jews to restore Jerusalem, he would hardly have given orders that the attempt to rebuild the city in his day must cease.[20] The Jews defended their right to rebuild the Temple in the second year of Darius by appealing to the decree of Cyrus. They claimed no right, on the basis of his decree, to rebuild anything other than the Temple itself (Ezra 5:11-17).

2. The decree of King Darius in 520 B.C. might be mentioned. This decree (Ezra 6:1-12) reconfirmed the earlier decree of Cyrus regarding the Temple but said nothing of the city itself or its walls. For this reason this second Persian decree has found few defenders.

3. A decree by the Persian Artaxerxes in 458/457 B.C. allowed Ezra to return to Jerusalem with sweeping powers to enforce the law of God (Ezra 7:11-26). A rather lengthy citation of this decree is contained in the record, but it makes no mention of rebuilding Jerusalem. Nonetheless, this decree is defended by some as the *terminus a quo* for the prophecy of the seventy heptads.

4. In 445 B.C. the same king Artaxerxes granted permission to Nehemiah to return to rebuild the walls of Jerusalem. He even authorized a requisition of timber from the royal forest to assist in the project. Many commentators defend this decree as the *terminus a quo* of the seventy heptads. There are problems with this starting point. First, there is the language of the prophecy itself: *From the going forth of a word to restore and rebuild Jerusalem.* The language seems to imply initiative on the part of the one who issued this word. Yet the initiative in 445 B.C. was on the part of Nehemiah. King Artaxerxes simply responded to the request of his faithful cupbearer. Furthermore, those

---

20. Compare the reaction of Darius when he discovered after searching the archives that Cyrus had given permission for the Temple to be rebuilt. Ezra 6:1-12.

who start counting the seventy heptads in 445 B.C. must resort to complicated conversions of lunar years to solar years in order to make the prophecy fit the known chronology of the life of Jesus of Nazareth. Ancient peoples intercalated months into their lunar calendar from time to time to bring the lunar year into harmony with the seasons. The net result was that over the long haul, the "years" of the Hebrews were just as long as solar years. It cannot be demonstrated from any prophecy involving years in the Bible that the writer intended solar years of 360 days to be understood.

So problems arise with accepting any of the Persian decrees as the prophetic command to restore and to build Jerusalem. But then nothing in the text compels the view that a royal edict is in view here. In fact there is a hint in the text that something other than a Persian edict is intended. The same Hebrew word is used of the commandment or word to restore and build Jerusalem in verse 25 as is used of the divine command to the angel Gabriel in verse 23. This suggests that the commandment to restore and to build Jerusalem came from God, not the Persian monarch. If it be argued that the commandment came from God *through* the Persian ruler, then the obvious question is, Where is the evidence that such is the case? Why could not God have issued his commandment regarding Jerusalem through someone else, through perhaps some leader of the Jewish people?

Can an occasion be pinpointed when God, through a Holy Spirit inspired man, commanded his people to rebuild Jerusalem? Ezra 4 contains a topical summary of hostile actions taken against Jewish attempts to rebuild their Temple and their capital. When the Jews attempted to rebuild their Temple during the reigns of Cyrus and Darius, the enemies "hired counselors to work against them and to frustrate their plans" (Ezra 4:5). In the days of King Ahasuerus (Xerxes) "they filed an accusation against the people of Judah and Jerusalem" (Ezra 4:6). A letter to King Artaxerxes (464-424 B.C.) is quoted in Ezra 4. This letter is of crucial importance in determining the occasion for the divine commandment to restore and rebuild Jerusalem.

In their letter to the Persian king the enemies make several important comments about recent developments among the Jews:

1. Jews had "come up to us from you" (v. 12). This implies that some official delegation recently had come back from the lands of the captivity.

2. These Jews had gone to Jerusalem (v. 12).

3. They were building the city (v. 12).

4. They were restoring the walls and repairing the foundations (v. 12).

King Artaxerxes searched the archives and found that Jerusalem had a history of rebellion and sedition. He fired back a letter to local officials ordering that the Jerusalem project cease "until I give permission" (v. 21). The local officials went immediately to Jerusalem "and compelled them by force to stop" (v. 23).

Biblical history provides two occasions when delegations returned from Babylon during the reign of King Artaxerxes. Ezra led the first group back from Babylon in 458 B.C.[21] (Ezra 7). Ezra was given extensive powers to enforce the law of Moses; but he was *not* given permission to rebuild the walls of Jerusalem. Twelve years later Nehemiah, a cupbearer to this same Artaxerxes, returned as governor of Judea with royal permission to rebuild the city (Neh. 1).

These historical data furnish the clue to the point at which a divine command was issued to restore and to build Jerusalem. The first attempt to rebuild Jerusalem came shortly after Ezra and his group returned to Jerusalem. Though Scripture nowhere so states explicitly, it is surely reasonable to believe that *Ezra* must have issued the first command to rebuild Jerusalem. The situation can be diagramed as follows:

457 B.C.	445 B.C.
ATTEMPT TO REBUILD JERUSALEM	SUCCESS IN REBUILDING JERUSALEM
EZRA THE LEADER	NEHEMIAH THE LEADER
ARTAXERXES ORDERED THE WORK TO CEASE	ARTAXERXES ENCOURAGED THE WORK TO PROCEED

Biblical data furnish further clues which help to pinpoint the year of Ezra's commandment. Ezra arrived in Jerusalem in the fifth month of the seventh year of King Artaxerxes (Ezra 7:7-8). On the modern calendar this would be August 4, 458 B.C. Ezra was confronted almost immediately with a monumental problem. Many leaders of the nation had intermarried with pagan women. It was not until March of the following year (Ezra 10:17) that this problem was solved. Burdened as he was with the intermarriage problem, it is most unlikely that Ezra would have issued any directive to rebuild Jerusalem until at least the spring of 457 B.C.

---

21. Finegan, HBC, p. 213. "Departure from Babylon on the first day of the first month was on April 8, 458; arrival in Jerusalem on the first day of the fifth month was on August 4, 458 B.C."

Chapter Twenty-Six

MESSIAH: THE TEMPLE-BUILDER

Cyrus the Great conquered Babylon in October 539 B.C. He was greeted as a liberator by the peoples who had been held captive there by Nebuchadnezzar and his successors. Not long after Cyrus conquered Mesopotamia he issued a decree allowing captive peoples to return to their native lands. Two copies of his decree as it affected the Jews are contained in the Book of Ezra. The official copy of the decree is in Aramaic (Ezra 6:3-5), the popular paraphrase is in Hebrew (1:1-4). From Scriptural data the date of the edict cannot be pinpointed. Most likely it was issued late in 538 B.C.

About fifty thousand were part of the first wave to make the trip back to Canaan. This group was led by Zerubbabel, a governor who was descended from David, and Joshua (or Jeshua) the high priest. That the group was motivated primarily by religious devotion is suggested by the fact that the first order of business upon arrival in the land was the collection of a substantial free-will offering for reconstructing the house of God.

In the seventh month[1] of the year of return an altar was erected on the site of the ancient Temple in Jerusalem. The regular sacrificial service was revived, the feast of Tabernacles was observed, and plans were formulated to proceed immediately with the reconstruction of the Temple. The older generation which had seen the first Temple was moved to tears by the comparison between the former glorious structure and the humble foundations of the new structure (Ezra 3:8-13).

From the moment the Jews returned home they faced opposition from peoples of surrounding countries (Ezra 3:3). The first ploy of the adversaries was to request permission to help in the Temple project (Ezra 4:1-2). Zerubbabel would have no part of this. The people of the land, as the adversaries were called, were offended by this rebuff. They "weakened the hands of the people, and troubled them in building" (Ezra 4:4). They even went to the trouble of hiring legal counsel to work against the Jews in the Persian court throughout the reigns of Cyrus, his son Cambyses, and into the reign of Darius (Ezra 4:5).

The opposition succeeded in intimidating the Jews to the point where all Temple construction efforts ceased. After some sixteen years God raised up two prophets to stir his people to action.

---

1. Unfortunately the text does not give the year. Presumably it was still the first year of Cyrus, 538-537 B.C. The seventh month would roughly correspond to October, 538 B.C.

Cyrus was followed on the throne by his son Cambyses who reigned for eight years. Cambyses died under mysterious circumstances while on a campaign in Egypt. One of his generals, Darius Hystaspes seized the throne. Rebellions against the new king broke out throughout the empire. Against this backdrop of international upheaval and political uncertainty the prophets Haggai and Zechariah arose to stir up God's people with promises of a glorious future. For both prophets the reconstruction of the Temple was a prelude to the Messianic age.

Prophecy No. 63

THE DESIRE OF ALL NATIONS

Haggai 2:6-9

Haggai began his short ministry of less than six months in August 520 B.C. Four of his messages are recorded in the book that bears his name. In his first message he rebuked the people for their indifference to the Temple project and exhorted them to resume the work immediately (1:1-11). Zerubbabel, Joshua, and all the people enthusiastically responded to Haggai's message and the work resumed. About a month after the renewal of the work, the prophet spoke to encourage the Temple builders. Haggai pulls back the curtain to reveal the glorious future of the era of the second Temple.

There can be no doubt that Haggai 2:6-9 is Messianic. Legitimate questions have been raised about whether or not the passage involves the Messiah personally. The older Christian and Jewish commentators concluded that it does bear witness to the coming Messiah; but most modern commentators have abandoned the personal Messianic interpretation.

Translation of Haggai 2:6-9

(6) For thus says the LORD of hosts: Yet again, once more, it is a little while, I will shake the heavens and the earth, the sea and the dry land. (7) And I will shake all the nations, and the Desire of all Nations shall come; and I will fill this house with glory, says the LORD of hosts. (8) Mine is the silver and mine is the gold (oracle of the LORD of hosts). (9) Greater shall be the glory of this latter house, than the former says the LORD of hosts, and in this place I will give peace (oracle of the LORD of hosts).

Discussion

Three main ideas are developed in this passage: (1) the preparation for the Messianic age, (2) the appearance of the Messiah, and (3) the result of Messiah's coming.

A. *The Preparation for the Messianic Age* (vv. 6-7a). Haggai is attempting to help his audience see the big picture. He wants them to realize that the rebuilding of the Temple will prepare the way for the glorious age which had been anticipated for centuries. He speaks of the preparation for the Messianic age as a great shaking. From the time of the appearance of God on Mt. Sinai, earthquake was used as a symbol for supernatural intervention. The severe earthquake in the eighth century B.C. by which Amos dates his ministry (Amos 1:1) reconfirmed this association. Isaiah,[2] Joel (3:16) and Ezekiel (38:20) also link earthquake with divine intervention.

Five facts about this preparatory shaking are underscored in this text:

1. The preparatory shaking is a repetition of what took place previously. The preposition *yet* (*'od*) generally retains its primary sense of repetition,[3] especially when connected to a temporal term or phrase as here. The writer of Hebrews identified this former shaking with what took place at Sinai. Haggai is now holding out to the faith of his despondent people the prospect of a new era which was to be prefigured by their present Temple. When Haggai speaks here and in verse 22 of commotions of nature ushering in the new dispensation he speaks according to the usage of the Hebrew poets by whom divine interposition is frequently depicted in coloring borrowed from the incidents of the Exodus period.[4]

2. This preparatory shaking would occur but once again, for the prophet said, *Yet again, once more*. Only one more time would God reveal himself in the mighty way which he did at Sinai. There he revealed his mighty power and his holy law; there he entered into covenant with his people. The new revelation and the attendant covenant would be *once for all time* (*hapax* in Heb. 12:26). Pusey captures the significance of the first two Hebrew words of Haggai's oracle:

---

2. Isa. 2:13-21; 13:13; 29:6.
3. Keil, BCOT, Minor Prophets, II, 191.
4. See Hab. 3:3-15; Ps. 18:7-15; 93; 97.

By the word *yet* he looks back to the first shaking of the moral world, when God's revelation by Moses and his people broke upon the darkness of the pagan world . . . ; *once* looks on and conveys that God would again shake the world, but *once* only, under the one dispensation of the Gospel, which should endure to the end.[5]

3. This preparatory shaking will begin in a very short time, for Haggai says, *it is a little while.* But how long is "a little while"? Some think that this shaking would begin within a very few years in the vicissitudes of the Persian empire.[6] A series of movements would soon begin which would culminate in the advent of Messiah.

4. The preparatory shaking would be universal in scope, for God would shake *the heavens, the earth, the sea and the dry land.* At the first shaking in connection with the Exodus and Mt. Sinai signs of divine intervention were obvious. The ten plagues shook Egypt and the religious establishment which guided that nation. The parting of the Red Sea, the pillar of fiery cloud, the shaking earth at Sinai, the meat and manna provided in the wilderness are just a few of the mighty miracles which literally shook the world of the fifteenth century B.C.[7] Haggai must be anticipating another shaking of similar magnitude—a cluster of supernatural signs so spectacular that no reasonable person could doubt that the unseen God had once again intervened in history to reconstitute his people and to redirect their affairs.

According to the writer of Hebrews the prophecy of Haggai has to do with the shaking of all created things so that the eternal things of the spirit would be made the more obvious. Hebrews points out that at the establishment of the Sinaitic covenant, only the earth was shaken to introduce it, but at the inauguration of the New Covenant heaven and earth and all things are to be shaken. Any thing that stands in the way of the triumph of Messiah's kingdom will be removed. His is a kingdom that cannot be shaken.[8]

The birth of Jesus was heralded by the shaking of nature: the star in the east, the angelic appearance to the shepherds, not to mention the heavenly announcements to Mary, Joseph, Zecharias and Elizabeth. The miracles performed by Jesus during his ministry spread his fame

---

5. Pusey, MPC, II, 309.

6. Keil, BCOT, Minor Prophets, II, 191. See also Perowne, CB, p. 36. Pusey and others think the shaking began with the coming of Christ.

7. See Hab. 3:6; Judg. 5:4-5; Ps. 68:8, 9; Exod. 19:16-18; Ps. 77:15ff.

8. Dan. 2:35, 44; Matt. 21:44; Heb. 12:27.

far and wide. Note the superiority of his miracles to those associated with the Exodus:

a) Moses healed only one person, and that only through intercessory prayer. Jesus healed all manner of sickness by command and touch.

b) Moses led the people through the Red Sea on dry land, but Jesus could walk on top of the water.

c) Moses announced the arrival of the manna and meat in the wilderness, but Jesus on two occasions multiplied a small quantity of food to feed thousands.

d) In support of Moses the earth opened to swallow up adversaries. In support of Jesus graves opened to temporarily release the dead.

e) Moses was buried by God atop Mt. Nebo, but Jesus walked out of his own sepulcher three days after he was interred.

f) The shaking of earth and blackness which marked the giving of the law on Sinai were matched by the earthquake and mid-day darkness associated with the death of Jesus on the cross. The fire atop Sinai is matched by the cloven tongues of fire which Jesus sent upon the waiting apostles on the day of Pentecost.

g) Moses ascended the mount into the presence of God, but Jesus ascended into heaven itself.

The convulsions in the heaven, earth, sea and dry land, in accordance with the more spiritual character of the new era were to occur not so much in the physical as in the moral sphere. Nonetheless the convulsions in the physical realm are not to be excluded.

5. The shaking would involve the nations of the world (v. 7). The verb *shake* is used of the political and social disturbances brought about by Babylon (Isa. 14:16f.), the overthrow of Gog (Ezek. 38:14-23), the humbling of Egypt (Exod. 12:33), and the destruction of Pharaoh's army (Ps. 68:7f.). Haggai is not talking about the conversion of the nations, but of the political and spiritual agitations which created in the hearts of the heathen a longing for the Prince of Peace.

The Jews in Haggai's day hesitated about going forward with the Temple work because they feared the superpower, Medo-Persia, which was in turn influenced by the Samaritan adversaries. The Prophet assures these workers that this and other world-powers are to fall before Messiah. They have no need to fear.

This theme of the upheaval of nations is taken up again in the closing verses of Haggai. The writer of Hebrews condenses the two references (2:6, 7 and 2:21, 22), implying that it was one and the same shaking. The first passage (2:6, 7) depicts the beginning of the shaking process and the second the end of the process. "The shaking began introductory to the first advent; it will be finished at the second."[9]

6. The shaking has the purpose of removing all that opposes the kingdom of God.

7. This shaking is progressive and continuous. Hengstenberg comments: `

> We must not by any means suppose that the prophecy reached its completion with the first manifestation of Christ. Its fulfillment must rather be progressive, so long as the antithesis of earthly power, in opposition to the kingdom of God on earth, continues; therefore until the establishment of the kingdom of glory.[10]

B. *The Coming of the Messiah* (v. 7b). In connection with, and as a result of, the shaking of the nations the Desire of all Nations would come. This traditional Christian and Jewish understanding of the passage has been abandoned by nearly all modern commentators and translators. Nonetheless, something can be said in defense of this interpretation of the text. See the special study at the conclusion of this chapter.

The term *chemdat* (desire of) was used in I Samuel 9:20 of Saul. All the desire of Israel—all the hopes of the nation for a successful monarchy—were fixed on him. He who will reign in that kingdom will not simply be the desire of Israel, but of all nations. Though of Jewish ancestry, he would be a king eagerly embraced by all men.

How is the concept of the Desire of all Nations to be reconciled with Isaiah 53:2 which says that the Servant would have no beauty that one should *desire* (*nechmedehu*) him? What is implied here is not that nations definitely desired *him,* but that he is the only one who could satisfy the yearnings which they all felt for a Savior. In Isaiah 53 it is the Jews as a nation who do not desire him because of his lowly origins, here it is the Gentiles who are particularly in view. Both Job (19:25-27; 33:23-26) and Abraham (John 8:56) *desired* him.

Messiah may be described as realizing in himself at his coming the desires (the noun expressing collectively the plural) of all nations; whence the verb is plural. He is the embodiment of the good things to come, unto whom shall be "the gathering of the people" (Gen. 49:10). The announcement of his birth was "good tidings of great joy to all people" (Luke 2:10).

C. *The Results of Messiah's Coming* (vv. 7-8). Three promises are attached to the coming of Messiah:

---

9. Jamieson, Fausset and Brown, CCEP, IV, 655.
10. Hengstenberg, COT, p. 584.

1. God declares that he will fill the Temple with glory. The term *glory* (*kabhad*) can signify material embellishment,[11] or it can point to the presence of God. Isaiah spoke often of the glory which would characterize the Messianic age. In that day men would see the glory of God (Isa. 35:2). The voice in the wilderness would prepare the way for the glory of the Lord (Isa. 40:5). God's glory would be seen upon Messianic Jerusalem (Isa. 60:2). All nations and tongues would gather to see God's glory (Isa. 66:18). In Zechariah Messianic Jerusalem is filled with the glory of God's presence (2:5).

It is *this house* which is to be filled with glory. The glory which is said to fill the Old Testament holy places is that of God's personal presence. A glorious cloud of God's glory filled the Tabernacle.[12] When Solomon finished praying at the dedication of the Temple "the glory of the Lord filled the house" (II Chron. 7:1).[13] Ezekiel saw the glory of God leave that Temple (11:23), but he foresaw a future Temple wherein God's glory would reside (Ezek. 43:4; 44:4).

What is signified by *this house*? Certainly the Temple, but what Temple? It is clear from Haggai that the term refers to the Temple past, present and future. Haggai anticipates a glorious future for the Temple, a glory which was not obvious in the humble beginnings of the second Temple. Haggai does not promise that the house will be filled with glory immediately after it is completed (as was Solomon's Temple). First must come the shaking of the nations, then the coming of the Desire of Nations, and then the glorious filling of the Temple.

Indirectly Haggai is announcing the appearance of Messiah during the days of the second Temple. This passage was so interpreted by many Jewish leaders.[14] Rabbi Akiba was induced by this prophecy to acknowledge Bar-Cochbah as Messiah after the destruction of the Temple in A.D. 70.

When baby Jesus was presented by his parents in that second Temple[15] the aged Simeon identified him as "a light for revelation to the Gentiles and for *glory* to . . . Israel" (Luke 2:32). Jesus claimed a special relationship to that Temple when he called it "My Father's house." When he purged the Temple on two occasions, and when he taught in the Temple precincts he brought glory to the place. "As the first temple

---

11. Hengstenberg (COT, p. 587) restricts *glory* here to material embellishment of the Temple. He cites Isa. 60:13, "The glory of Lebanon shall come to you."

12. Exod. 40:34, 35; Num. 14:21.

13. See also I Kings 8:11; II Chron. 5:14.

14. See Josephus, *Wars* VI.v,4; Tacitus, *Hist.* 5:13.

15. The Jews never regarded Herod's Temple as a third Temple. It was in fact a refurbishing and enlargement of Zerubbabel's Temple.

was filled with the *cloud* of glory, the symbol of God (I Kings 8:11; II Chron. 5:14), so the second temple was filled with the 'glory' of God (John 1:14) *veiled* in the flesh (as it were in the cloud) at Christ's first coming. . . ."[16]

2. God claims possession of the world's gold and silver (v. 8). The workers to whom Haggai spoke were disappointed that they could not embellish the Temple with precious metals as did Solomon. In Solomon's day gold had been so plentiful that silver counted for little (I Kings 10:21). But now the Persians had inherited the world's wealth. The sixth century community of believers in Judea had few resources to contribute to the Temple project. Some who had seen the earlier sanctuary were making adverse comparisons (Hag. 2:3). God assures the workers that he already possesses silver and gold (v. 8). He could adorn the Temple with these precious metals if he so chose;[17] but he chose rather to adorn it with a glory far more precious.

3. God announces that the latter glory of the Temple will be greater than the former glory (v. 9). "Haggai knows of only one house, whose glories vary. The glory of God's dwelling place among His people shall in the latter days far exceed the first glory of His temple in the days of Solomon."[18]

In Haggai's day three stages in the history of the glorification of *this house* (God's Temple) yet remained. Early in 19 B.C. Herod the Great began to rebuild Zerubbabel's Temple. He enlarged it and gave it an

THIS HOUSE

FORMER GLORY (Hag. 2:3)	R U I N S	PRESENT NON-GLORY	FUTURE GLORY	LATTER GLORY
⇦		⇦	⇦	⇦
Days of Solomon (960-587 B.C.)		Days of Zerubbabel (516-20 B.C.)	Days of Herod	Days of Messiah
⇦		⇦	⇦	⇦
Physical Glory		Physical Non-Glory	Physical Glory	Spiritual Glory
First Temple (Type)		Second Temple (Type)	Third Temple (Type)	Fourth Temple (Antitype)

16. Jamieson, Fausett and Brown, CCEP, IV, 656.

17. Ezra 6:8-12 records how Darius ordered the cost of the Temple project to be financed from royal revenue in the region. This financial aid probably arrived just after Haggai made his claim that all silver and gold belonged to God.

18. Laetsch, BCMP, p. 397.

external glory that exceeded that of Solomon's Temple. *This house received its physical glorification through the agency of Herod.*[19]

The second stage of the glorification of the Temple came when God incarnate visited the place. In his face was given "the light of the knowledge of the glory of God" (II Cor. 4:6). During part of his ministry this one sat daily in the Temple teaching (Matt. 26:55). He was the Lord of that Temple (John 2:13-22) and as such was superior to it (Matt. 12:6).

The third stage in the glorification of *this house* (God's Temple) occurred when Messiah built a new Temple of living stones (Eph. 2:19-22) to be a habitation of God's spirit in the new covenant age. This Messianic Temple is greater than that of Solomon, Zerubbabel, or even Herod in at least six ways as the following chart illustrates:

A COMPARISON OF TEMPLES

	OLD COVENANT TEMPLES	NEW COVENANT TEMPLES
Builder	Solomon: A Backslider Zerubbabel: A Governor Herod: A Madman	Messiah: Son of God and Sinless son of man. One greater than Solomon or the physical Temple.
Worship	Animal sacrifice, incense	Worship in spirit and truth.
Dimensions	Comparatively small structures.	World-wide in scope.
Materials	Gold, silver, fine timber, huge stones made ready at the quarry = PHYSICAL	Living stones, precious souls carved out of the quarry of life = SPIRITUAL
Influence	Mostly local	Universal
Duration	Solomon's Temple: 381 yrs. Zerubbabel's Temple 495 yrs. Herod's Temple: c. 75 yrs.	Eternal

4. *In this place I will give peace* (v. 8). In the term *peace (shalom)* all the hopes of the Messianic age are encompassed.[20] The word does not simply point to the resolution of hostilities, but to the total well-being of mankind. It is a divinely provided peace, a peace which surpasses understanding (Phil. 4:7). It is through Shiloh the Rest Bringer (Gen. 49:10) that this peace is made a reality.

---

19. The Rabbis applied Haggai 2:9 to the greater glory of Herod's Temple or to the fact that the second Temple stood longer than the first. Some Rabbis applied the verse to a Temple yet to be built.

20. Other prophecies of an ideal peace: Ezek. 34:25, 26; Micah 4:3-4; Zech. 8:12.

The peace would be manifested *in this place*, i.e., in Jerusalem.[21] In that city, the earthly capital of God's people, Messiah initiated the greatest peace movement of all history, for "he made peace through the blood of his cross" (Col. 1:20). This peace begins when obstacles are removed which stand between a just God and sinful men (II Cor. 5:18, 19). Reconciliation to God creates peace in the forgiven sinner's own heart.[22] "First peace between God and man, then between man and God, then between man and man."[23]

Prophecy No. 64

GOD'S SIGNET

Haggai 2:21-23

Haggai's last two sermons were delivered on the same day, about two months after the great prophecy discussed above. The last message was one of encouragement to Zerubbabel, the devout governor who was spearheading the Temple project. The message is full of optimism and confidence in God's power. Nothing in heaven or earth can withstand him.

Translation of Haggai 2:21-23

(21) Say unto Zerubbabel governor of Judah: I am about to shake the heavens and the earth. (22) And I will overthrow the throne of kingdoms, and I will destroy the strength of the kingdoms of nations, and I will overthrow chariots and riders; and horses and their riders shall go down, each man by the sword of his brother. (23) In that day (oracle of the LORD of hosts) I will take you Zerubbabel son of Shealtiel my servant (oracle of the LORD) and I will make you like a signet for I have chosen you (oracle of the LORD of hosts).

Discussion

The shaking mentioned in verse 21 is the preparatory shaking mentioned in verses 6-7 and discussed above. Verse 22 amplifies that

---

21. Since the name Jerusalem probably means "city of peace," the prophet is making a play on the word. There also is assonance between the word for peace (*shalom*) and place (*maqom*).

22. Acts 10:36; Rom. 5:1; 14:17; Eph. 2:13-17; Phil. 4:7.

23. Jamieson, Fausett and Brown, CCEP, IV, 656.

prediction a bit. The divine "I wills" are striking. Behind the upheavals of human government God is working out his program. Four points of amplification emerge:

1. The throne of kingdoms is to be overthrown. This may be a reference to the convulsions of the Persian Empire, some of which were beginning even as Haggai spoke.

2. The strength of the kingdoms of nations is to be destroyed. Not just the Persian empire, but all heathen kingdoms will fall.

3. The finest military forces will be overthrown.

4. The enemies will turn on and destroy themselves. God works through others to accomplish his purposes. It is, nonetheless, he who is working.

In that day when world kingdoms had been brought low, God would begin to act decisively for his people. He would do four things:

1. God would select a ruler for his people and indeed, a ruler for all the world. That seems to be the basic connotation of the verb *take* in verse 23.

2. The focal point of this divine intervention in world history would be Zerubbabel. It is not Zerubbabel personally who is intended, but one from his line.[24] Just as Messiah is sometimes called David (e.g., Hosea 3:5), so here he is called Zerubbabel.

3. Zerubbabel would be God's *signet*. The signet ring was one of man's most precious possessions. With it documents were signed. To have in one's possession the signet of the king gave one enormous powers. This promise of great authority is tantamount to a commitment to restore the throne of Judah and the royal family of David of which Zerubbabel was the most prominent representative.[25] Jesus once said: "All authority in heaven and in earth has been given unto me.

4. For his future role in the kingdom Zerubbabel had been *chosen* by God. "As Abram and David and Solomon were selected, so Zerubbabel falls into line in the noble succession of the chosen ones in whose seed the promises find their highest fulfillment (Matt. 1:12, 13).[26]

---

24. Keil (BCOT. Minor Prophets, II, 214): "The promise did not apply to his own particular person, but rather to the official post he held." Liberalism sees here an expectation that Zerubbabel would be crowned king. Payne (EBP, p. 446) finds the fulfillment in the resurrection of Zerubbabel at the last day!

25. The language here is all the more significant in view of what is said in the rejection of the next-to-last king of Judah. "As I live . . . though Coniah the son of Jehoiakim king of Judah were the signet upon my right hand, yet I would pluck you thence" (Jer. 22:24).

26. McIlmoyle, NBC, p. 747.

Special Study

THE DESIRE OF ALL NATIONS

It has been said that grammatical and contextual considerations rule out the personal Messianic interpretation of Haggai 2:7. McIlmoyle comments:

> Much as the heart . . . would wish to follow ancient Jewish expositors and find a personal reference here to the Messiah, and great as would be the truth that would be thus expressed the difficulty in so rendering the words seem insuperable.[27]

The difficulty of rendering the verse *the Desire of all Nations shall come* is obviously not "insuperable." At least one great English translation—the King James Version—has so rendered the text. Nonetheless, a translation problem does exist here which must be addressed.

For those who do not know the Hebrew language, a word for word literal translation will illustrate the problem. The clause in question begins with a *vav* consecutive which is rendered in English by the conjunction *and*. The Hebrew conjunction is attached to the verb. The verb is plural and would ordinarily be translated, *they shall come*. Standing third in the clause is a noun which is regarded by most as the subject of the clause. The noun is singular and in what Hebrew grammarians call the construct state. This form would ordinarily be translated *the precious one of* or *desire of.* The last two words in the disputed clause are a noun and its modifier which all agree should be rendered, *all nations.* The word for word translation would then be: And-they shall come the-precious-one-of all nations.

The sentence as constructed above obviously makes no sense. How is it to be interpreted? Some have proposed that the noun *chemdat* (*desire of*) is not the subject of the verb but rather an accusative of specification indicating direction. This yields the interpretation, "And they (the nations) shall come (to) the desire of all nations (Christ)." No one can fault this understanding of the second word of the clause. A variation of this approach is found in the NASB: "they will come with the wealth of all nations." Here *chemdat* is regarded as an accusative specifying manner.

The testimony of the ancient versions is not harmonious on Haggai 2:7. The Septuagint and Syriac make the subject a plural and thus

---

27. McIlmoyle. NBC. p. 746.

support the rendering, the *precious things of the nations shall come.* The Vulgate, on the other hand, supports the singular understanding of the subject: the Desire of all Nations shall come. Rabbis prior to the time of Jerome also looked upon the subject here as a singular referring to Messiah.

Most commentators, however, regard *chemdat* as the subject of the plural verb. How do they reconcile a singular subject with a plural verb? By regarding the subject as a collective noun which is rendered in English by a plural.[28] Some understand *chemdat* to refer to the treasure of the Gentiles,[29] or to the precious Gentile souls who would come to Jerusalem.[30] The problem with this approach is that other examples of *chemdah* used collectively are wanting.[31] If the intent of the writer was to say that the shaking of the nations would result in the bringing of their treasures to Jerusalem, why did he not use the *hiphil* (they shall bring) form of the verb?[32]

Can the singular *chemdat* be the subject of the plural verb? Is there something to be said in behalf of the King James rendering?

The word *chemdah* is used some twenty-five times in the Old Testament. In the singular it is used to describe the Land of Promise (Jer. 3:19; 12:10; Zech. 7:14; Ps. 106:24), houses (Ezek. 26:12), valuable objects[33] and people. All the *desire of Israel* was focused on Saul (I Sam. 9:20). The "King" of Daniel 11:37 had no concern for the *desire of women.* This may be a reference to the ruthless attempt of King Herod to slay the infant Christ. He was the Desire of women in that *every* Jewish girl hoped some day to give birth to Messiah. In the plural form the word *chemdah* is used of Daniel,[34] and possibly of Esau.[35]

---

28. The majority of commentators explain the text in this way. Among them are Calvin, McCurdy, Hengstenberg, Clarke, Keil, Moore and Ellicott.

29. JB: "The treasures of all the nations shall flow in"; NEB: "The treasure of all nations shall come hither"; ASV: "The precious things of the nations shall come."

30. NIV: "The desired of all the nations shall come."

31. Gesenius-Kautzsch insists that the noun be emended to a plural. This would be a strange and unnecessary proposal if *chemdat* could be construed as a collective.

32. It is not true, as some have argued, that the verb *bo'* cannot refer to objects and must therefore refer to persons or a person. This verb is used of trees coming to adorn the Temple in Isa. 60:13, of gold and silver (Josh. 6:19) and incense (Jer. 6:20).

33. Jer. 25:34; Hos. 13:15; Nah. 2:10; II Chron. 32:27; Isa. 2:16; II Chron. 36:10; Dan. 11:8.

34. Dan. 9:23; 10:11. The plural of intensity is used. Daniel was a man greatly desired.

35. In Gen. 27:15 it is unclear whether *chemdot* refers to the garments of Esau or to Esau himself as one greatly desired by his father.

The above evidence on the usage of *chemdah* in the Old Testament certainly does not preclude a personal reference. The Desire of all Nations could be a person, that one person who would fulfill the aspirations of all nations.

But how can the grammatical difficulty of the singular noun and plural verb be explained? First, it should be recognized that while the construction here is unusual, it is not unique. In Amos 6:1 for example the verb is plural (they shall come) while the subject is singular (the house of Israel). In Haggai 1:2 the verb is plural (they said) and the subject is singular in Hebrew (this people). The reverse of the situation here, where the subject is plural and the verb singular is not uncommon in the Hebrew Bible. The name *'elohim* (God), for example, is plural, and yet when it refers to the one true God the verb is singular. Grammarians refer to this as the plural of majesty or plural of intensification. Perhaps the plural verb in Haggai 2:7 serves to emphasize the multifaceted character of that single individual who was the Desire of all Nations.[36] There is also this consideration: When two nouns stand together, of which one is governed by the other, the verb sometimes agrees *in number* with the latter, though it really has the former as its nominative. In this case, the verb *come* is made *in number* to agree with *nations*, though really agreeing with *the desire*.

---

36. Pusey (MPC, II, 312) suggests that the singular object of desire (the Messiah) contains in himself many objects of desire. He was God and man; he was prophet, priest and king.

Chapter Twenty-Seven

A PRIEST UPON HIS THRONE

The priest Zechariah began his prophetic ministry in 520 B.C. two months after Haggai preached his first sermon. The focus of both men was the same, and they can be viewed as conducting a joint ministry. Completion of the Temple was the priority underscored by these two prophets. Long after the voice of Haggai was silenced by death, Zechariah continued to describe in spectacular apocalyptic imagery the future of God's people.[1]

Zechariah's contribution to the Messianic expectation is considerable. First, he built on the Messianic hope of the former prophets. That is to be expected. But he did more. He provided for his readers a terse summary of God's previous revelations on this great theme. Baron observes:

> This indeed is one reason why this short prophetic book of only fourteen chapters is so marvellously rich in its contents; for, in addition to new Divine communications granted to this priest-prophet, we have in it, as it were, an inspired condensation, or summary, of the great prophecies and promises contained in the earlier prophets.[2]

Prophecy No. 65

THE PROMISE OF NEW PRIEST

Zechariah 3:8-10

The prophecy now to be examined grows out of the fourth in a series of eight visions related by Zechariah. The visions date to about 519 B.C. In this vision Joshua the high priest is standing before the angel of the Lord as the representative of Israel (v. 1).[3] Satan acts as prosecuting attorney. Joshua stands silently guilty dressed in filthy garments (v. 3). He personally is unworthy to continue in the priestly office. The nation which he represents is unworthy to play any role in God's program. Nonetheless, Satan is reprimanded for his attack against Joshua. After all, God had *chosen* Jerusalem. He had rescued his people from the fires of captivity (v. 2).

---

1. Zechariah's ministry may have extended as late as 480 B.C. in which case he preached for over forty years.
2. Baron, VPZ, p. 315.
3. Cashdan, Perowne, and Baldwin think this is a judicial scene. Joshua the defendant is on trial. Deane, Laetsch and Unger see Joshua standing before the Lord in the performance of his ministerial function.

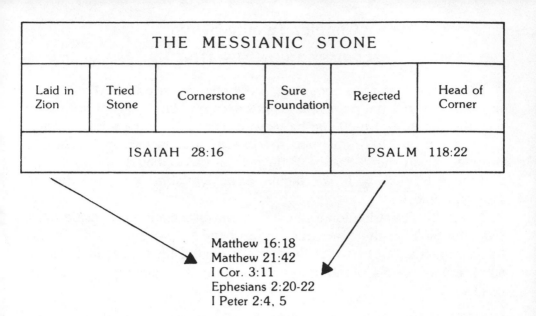

THE MESSIANIC STONE

Laid in Zion	Tried Stone	Cornerstone	Sure Foundation	Rejected	Head of Corner
ISAIAH 28:16				PSALM 118:22	

Matthew 16:18
Matthew 21:42
I Cor. 3:11
Ephesians 2:20-22
I Peter 2:4, 5

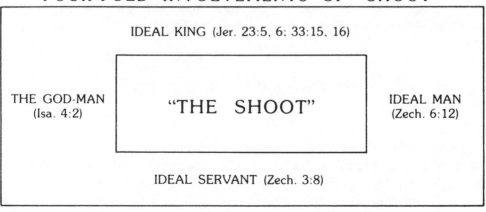

FOUR-FOLD INVOLVEMENTS OF "SHOOT"

IDEAL KING (Jer. 23:5, 6; 33:15, 16)

THE GOD-MAN (Isa. 4:2)   **"THE SHOOT"**   IDEAL MAN (Zech. 6:12)

IDEAL SERVANT (Zech. 3:8)

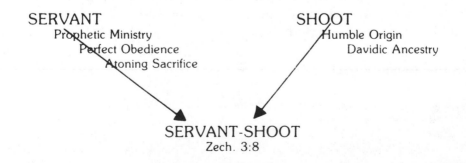

SERVANT
Prophetic Ministry
Perfect Obedience
Atoning Sacrifice

SHOOT
Humble Origin
Davidic Ancestry

SERVANT-SHOOT
Zech. 3:8

412

Joshua (and the people he represents) is to be cleansed and re-instated. This is symbolized by the removal of the filthy garments and donning of the festal robes worn by high priests on the most holy occasions (vv. 4-5). God promises Joshua that if he is faithful in his priestly ministrations he would continue in office and have access through prayer to the very throne room of God himself (v. 7).

Baron refers to the prophecy which follows as "one of the richest and most beautiful Messianic passages in the Old Testament" and at the same time as "a terse summary of glorious announcements concerning the coming Redeemer in the 'former prophets.'"[4]

Some emminent Jewish commentators see here only a promise to Zerubbabel.[5] In support of the Messianic interpretation, however, the following points can be made:

1. The oldest Jewish commentators see here and in Zechariah 6 a reference to the Messiah.

2. The passage uses the title "Shoot" which is elsewhere (Jer. 23:5; Isa. 4:2) used of Messiah.

3. The focus here is on one who would come in the future, not Zerubbabel or some other contemporary of the prophet: "I *will bring* my Servant, the Shoot."

4. The notation that God would remove the iniquity of the land in one day. This statement would be hard to reconcile with any interpretation other than the Messianic.

Translation of Zechariah 3:8-10

(8) Hear now, O Joshua the high priest, you and your companions who are sitting before you, for they are men of a sign; for behold I am about to bring forth my Servant the Shoot. (9) For behold the Stone which I have placed before Joshua, upon one Stone are seven eyes. Behold I am about to make its engraving (oracle of the LORD of hosts) and I will remove the iniquity of that land in one day. (10) In that day (oracle of the LORD of hosts) you shall call each man to his neighbor under a vine and under a fig tree.

---

4. Baron, VPZ, p. 107.

5. Rashi and Kimchi. To acknowledge the Shoot here as Messiah would require a similar identification in 6:12. This would necessitate an admission that the Messiah would be priest as well as king.

Discussion

The cleansed and reinstated high priest and the priests who served under him were *men of a sign*, i.e., men of portent, omen, and significance.[6] In their persons, office and duties Joshua and his fellow priests were types prefiguring the New Testament priesthood. The prophetic significance of these men is further underscored by the words *for behold*. These words point forward to that not-too-distant day when God himself would *bring forth* the long-awaited Messiah.[7] The language also suggests that "the type . . . would continue until the coming of the anti-type, the order foretokening the Messiah would not cease until he came, and hence they could go on in the erection of the temple, in which these priests were to minister."[8]

In verses 8-9 the Messiah is given three names. He is *my Servant*. He is so called because of his willing, patient and perfect obedience to his Father. In prophecy the term *servant* is used with both royal and priestly connotations.[9]

Messiah is called *Shoot* (*tsemach*). Throughout the ages commentators have consistently given to this word a Messianic interpretation.[10] The name is first used in Isaiah 4:2. By the time of Zechariah the term had become a proper name. *Shoot* points to the mysterious origin of Messiah and the gradual development of his character.[11] The combination *my Servant Shoot* may be a reminiscence of the expression in Ezekiel 37:24, "my servant David."

He is called *the Stone*. The stone is linked to the Servant by the word *for* (*ki*). The stone is significant for it is introduced by the interjection *behold*. Whether the stone had been present before Joshua throughout the vision, or is now at this point placed before him by God cannot be determined. Whether or not this was the foundation stone of

---

6. This terminology is elsewhere used of individuals who arouse attention to a coming event by their symbolic names (Isa. 8:1-4, 18) or actions (Isa. 20:3).

7. Keil, Pusey and Wright feel that the words *men of sign* point backward to the previous incidents in the vision as well as forward to what is related in verse 9. The deliverance and cleansing of Joshua would then be typical of a greater salvation which was now to be revealed to the prophet.

8. Moore, COZ, p. 67.

9. Cf. the Servant prophecies of Isa. 42:1-17; 49:1-13; 50:4-11; 52:13—53:12. Also see Ezekiel 34:23.

10. Even the Jewish commentator Kimchi, who denies the Messianic identification here, admits that this is a Messianic title in Isa. 4:2 and Jer. 23:5.

11. Cf. Jer. 23:5; 33:15 where the same word is used; and Isa. 11:1 and 53:2 where the same concept occurs.

the second Temple as some suggest also cannot be determined. It is not, however, until the symbolic aspects of the vision are explained that any reference is made to the stone. That the stone symbolizes the Messiah is indicated by the connection made with the previous verse, and by what is said about this stone in the present verse. This is, as Baron observes, "a terse summary of well-known predictions in the former prophets, in the light of which we must interpret the passage."[12] Like Servant and Shoot in the previous verse, Stone is a well-known Messianic title carried over in these visions of Zechariah from the former prophets (cf. Isa. 28:16; Ps. 118:22). Three points are emphasized:[13]

1. This is a unique stone, for on *one stone* are seven eyes. The stone points to a single individual.

2. The stone has *seven eyes* upon it. Are these the seven eyes of God (Zech. 4:10) watching over the Messiah? (cf. I Kings 8:29). Perhaps. But it is better to regard the eyes[14] as sculpted on the stone itself.[15] Seven is the number of perfection. The eye is the symbol of intelligence. The seven eyes would then symbolize the omniscience of the Messiah.[16]

3. The stone is to be *engraved*. Probably the engraving is something in addition to the *eyes*. The same idiom is used of carving precious wood and stone for the Temple. The engraving would thus be what makes this Stone precious and suitable to use as the cornerstone of the future Temple (I Peter 2:6). The prophet has already alluded to the wounds to be inflicted on God's Servant (Isa. 53). Those wounds, which make him so ugly to the eyes of the world, make him precious to the believer. That wound by men was in reality an engraving by God.

That the Stone symbolizes Messiah can be seen by the results of this deep cutting or engraving: *I will remove the iniquity of that land.*[17] The engraving of the Stone made possible the forgiveness of sins. From

---

12. Baron, VPZ, p. 114.

13. Leupold (EZ, p. 77) lists nine interpretations of the stone. The personal Messianic view is defended by Unger, Wright, and Pusey.

14. Baldwin (TOTC, pp. 117-118) takes the word 'ayin to mean "well," not "eye." She thinks the idea is that seven wells of water spring forth from the rock.

15. Cashdan (SBB, p. 203) refers to a stone marked with seven eyes which was found at Gezer.

16. Cf. the eyes on the wheels of the throne chariot of God (Ezek. 1:18; 10:12) and the Lamb having seven eyes in Rev. 5:6. Baron, following Wright, thinks the reference is to the sevenfold plentitude of the one Spirit of Yahweh mentioned in Isa. 11:2.

17. That these words relate to the work of Messiah is argued by Wright (ZHP, p. 71) as follows: "As the section begins (v. 8) with a distinct promise of the Messiah's coming, and closes (v. 10) with a statement of the result of that coming to Israel, it is only natural to view the middle portion as having reference to the same event."

this it can be seen that the visionary cleansing of Joshua was symbolic of the future cleansing of Israel.

That land spoken of by the prophet refers primarily to the land of Israel. The land of Israel in the Old Testament is typical of the kingdom of Messiah which includes Jews and Gentiles. Already Zechariah has referred to the Gentiles who will be joined to the God of Israel in the Messianic age (2:11).

This cleansing of the land of Israel was to take place *in one day.* Rashi, the most popular Jewish commentator, confesses that he does not know what day this is. Christian commentators, however, see here the Messianic day of atonement, Calvary day, when Jesus gave his life a ransom for many. The *one day* of Zechariah is equivalent in meaning to the *once for all* so often emphasized in Hebrews (7:27; 9:12; 10:10.

Verse 10 is a brief allusion to the wonderful age of peace which would be ushered in by the Servant, the Shoot, and the Stone. Sitting peacefully under one's vine or fig tree is prophetic picture of tranquility. The forgiveness of sins makes possible, first peace with God, and then peace with one's fellow man. The Talmud (*Yoma* 7:4) indicates that once the high priest had performed his solemn duties on the day of atonement he was escorted home in a festive manner. Maidens and youths went forth to their gardens and vineyards with songs and dances. Universal gladness closed the festival of that solemn day. In similar fashion once the solemn high priestly duties on the cross, the resurrection and ascension were completed a day of gladness and joy was ushered in.

Prophecy No. 66

THE REIGNING PRIEST

Zechariah 6:12-13

Sometime in 519 B.C. a delegation of Jews from Babylon arrived in Jerusalem with gifts for the Temple reconstruction project. Zechariah was told to meet this delegation. He was told to take some of the silver and gold which they brought and to fashion crowns.[18] He was then to

---

18. It is not clear why the plural is used. Some think in terms of two circlets intertwined to form a single crown. Others suggest that two separate crowns were placed on the head of Joshua. Baron (VPZ, p. 190) comments: "The plural *'ataroth* is used in Job 21:36 for one crown, and what most probably is meant is a single splendid royal crown consisting of a number of gold and silver twists or circlets woven together. Cf. Rev. 19:9, 12."

perform a symbolic crowning of Joshua the high priest. The mitre normally worn by the high priest (3:5) is never called a crown. The crown is a symbol of royal dignity. The significance of the coronation was declared by Zechariah in a message given him by the Lord.

Concerning the Messianic import of this passage Wright observes:

> No plainer prophecy could have been uttered as to the coming of the Messiah, or as to the offices he was to fill. Even those commentators who are least inclined to admit definite Messianic predictions have been constrained to acknowledge that Messiah is here spoken of.[19]

In chapter 3 the high priest Joshua was said to be a typical person. Joshua personally could not have exercised royal power under the Old Covenant for that was reserved for the house of David. The crowning of Joshua was a prophetic drama predictively portraying the conferring of kingly power on Messiah.

Translation of Zechariah 6:12-13

(12) And you shall say unto him: Thus says the LORD of hosts: Behold! a man, Shoot is his name and he shall shoot up out of his place; and he shall build the Temple of the LORD. (13) Yes he himself shall build the Temple of the LORD, and he shall bear glory and he shall sit and rule upon his throne and he shall be a priest upon his throne and peaceful counsel shall be between the two of them.

Discussion

Regarding this passage Baron remarks:

> This is one of the most remarkable and precious Messianic prophecies, and there is no plainer prophetic utterance in the whole Old Testament as to the Person of the promised Redeemer, the offices He was to fill, and the mission He was to accomplish.[20]

The prophecy speaks of the promise, the work, the glory and the offices of the Messiah.

A. *The Promise of Messiah.* The symbolic crowning of Joshua pointed forward to a glorious future leader. The prophet dramatically introduces this person with the words, Behold the man! Some five centuries

---

19. Wright, ZHP, p. 149.
20. Baron, VPZ, p. 190.

later these very words were used by Pilate when Jesus was led forth to die. Four aspects of the Messianic character are introduced by the word *Behold!* as is indicated in the following diagram.

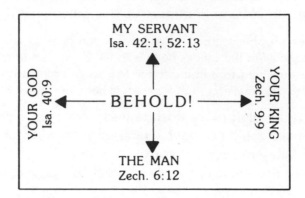

The *man* here is not Zerubbabel, for he is not so much as mentioned in the chapter. Nor is the *man* Joshua, for the words are addressed to him. Besides, the priest under the law could never wear a royal crown. *Behold the man* does not signify that the person so designated was actually present, but rather that he was symbolically represented in the person of Joshua the high priest. The most ancient Jewish interpretation is found in the Targum of Jonathan where the verse is paraphrased thus: "Behold the man; Messiah is His name. He will be revealed, and He will become great and build the Temple of God.[21]

The name of the man is said to be *Shoot* (*tsemach*). This name, already employed in 3:8, has deep roots in the Messianic vocabulary. The word is associated with promises made to David. The house of David, once a great cedar (Ezek. 17:3), was nothing but a stump in Zechariah's day. Nonetheless, out of the stump of Jesse (David's father) God would bring forth new growth (Isa. 11:1).

The Shoot would shoot up *out of his place.*[22] The expression "presupposes the lowliness from which he will rise by degrees to glory."[23] He would not descend from heaven in visible glory, but "shall grow up out of the earth, in lowly humiliation."[24] A lowly village, a lowly

---

21. Some later Jewish commentators (Rashi, .Iben Ezra, and Kimchi) identified the man as Zerubbabel.

22. Literally, from under him. The expression is used elsewhere only in Exod. 10:23 where it means "out of his own place."

23. Baron, VPZ, p. 194.

24. Moore, COZ, p. 96.

trade, and thirty years of obscurity are involved. Wright summarizes the meaning this way: "Thus in this one significant sentence the lowly origin of the Messiah on the one hand, and His royal dignity on the other, are both not obscurely referred to."[25]

B. *The Work of Messiah.* The Messiah's work is indicated in the words, *and he shall build the Temple of Yahweh; yes, he himself shall build the Temple of Yahweh.* This repetition underscores the certainty of the promise and the greatness of the task. The emphasis on the pronoun *he* directed attention away from Joshua, Zerubbabel and their Temple reconstruction project, to the infinitely more important task of a future Priest-King. The physical house built by Solomon and rebuilt by Zerubbabel (Zech. 4:9) was but the earthly model of the true Temple referred to in I Peter 2:5. At the time this prophecy was given Temple reconstruction was nearing completion. The statement that the Shoot— Messiah—would build the Temple was so shocking that it had to be repeated for emphasis.

The concept that the people of God collectively constitute the Temple of God is a truth which is certainly not beyond the grasp of perceptive Old Testament saints. Even Solomon realized that God did not dwell in temples made with hands; he dwelt in the midst of his people (I Kings 8:27; II Chron. 2:5).

MESSIAH—A TEMPLE BUILDER

DAVID'S SON A TEMPLE BUILDER	DAVID'S SHOOT A TEMPLE BUILDER	DAVID'S LORD A TEMPLE BUILDER
(II Sam. 7:13)	(Zech. 6:12)	(John 14:23; Matt. 16:18)
——— SPOKEN ———	——— SPOKEN ———	——— SPOKEN ———
BEFORE CON- STRUCTION OF THE FIRST TEMPLE	BEFORE RECONSTRUC- TION OF THE TEMPLE	BEFORE DESTRUCTION OF THE TEMPLE

C. *The Glory of Messiah.* Messiah's glory is indicated by the clause, *and he shall bear glory.* The crown upon Joshua's head symbolized the royal honor and glory which would characterize Messiah. The word *glory (hod)* is used to indicate royal honors.[26] It is used often of the special glory of God.[27] Messiah is said to *bear* the glory. Glory was bestowed

---

25. Wright, ZHP, p. 149.

26. Jer. 22:18; Ps. 21:5; Dan. 11:21.

27. Ps. 8:1; 45:3; 148:13; Hab. 3:3. Pusey goes too far when he asserts that the word is used almost always of God's glory.

upon him by the Father and is therefore regarded as a precious treasure to be carried.[28]

The New Testament sheds light on the *glory* of the Messiah. He manifested his glory in his first miracle at Cana (John 2:11) and in his transfiguration (Luke 9:32). After his suffering he entered into glory (Luke 24:26) like that which he had with the Father before the world began (John 17:5).

D. *The Offices of Messiah.* Two offices of Messiah are depicted here. First, he will be king, for *he shall sit and rule upon his throne.* The verb *sit* points to the permanence of his office, the verb *rule* to his success. *His throne* is God's throne, the throne upon which David and his dynasty had been enthroned. That throne was located in Jerusalem for 427 years (1004-587 B.C.). That physical throne was but a replica of the true throne of God in the heaven of heavens. There the greater son of David sat down after his death, burial and resurrection.

The Messiah will also be *priest upon his throne.* The high priest had no throne in the Old Testament economy. His duty was to stand in service before the Lord, not sit upon a throne.[29]

A rigid distinction between kingly and priestly offices was enforced under the Old Testament economy. The former was confined to the house of David, the latter to the house of Aaron. King Uzziah attempted to enter the Holy Place of the Temple to offer incense and was smitten with leprosy (II Chron. 26:16-21). Under the Old Testament Joshua the high priest could not wear a crown. His coronation was an act of prophetic symbolism pointing to the Messianic priest-king (Heb. 7:1-3).

Wardlaw draws attention to the fact that it was the high priest and not the governor who was selected to wear the crown. Thus, "it is the priest that is to wear the regal, not the prince to wear the sacerdotal. This has the important meaning—that it was to be by the execution . . . of His priestly work, that He was to obtain, in reward, His kingly crown."[30]

Joshua has already been told in 3:8 that he and his fellow Aaronic priests were types (lit., men of a sign) of that future Priest. Thus

> there could be no shadow of a possibility of his understanding this new and fuller message about the Priest-King in the 6th chapter as referring to himself beyond the fact that in his official capacity as high priest he (like all the other priests of the House of Aaron) foreshadowed the

---

28. Cf. Num. 27:20; Dan. 11:21; I Chron. 29:25 where glory (hod) is given by a superior to a subordinate.

29. Cf. Judg. 20:28; Deut. 17:12.

30. Quoted by Collins, NBC, p. 753.

Person and office of the One who should be the true and only Mediator between God and man.[31]

The expression *peaceful counsel shall be between the two of them* (v. 13) is difficult. Neither the numeral nor its masculine plural suffix is connected grammatically with a definite stated antecedent in the Hebrew. The meaning of the expression must be determined by implication and context. Two views deserve consideration.

Hengstenberg and others have proposed that the reference is to the harmony which would exist between kingly and priestly offices as they would be combined in the person of the Messiah. The *counsel* of peace points to the plan devised by the Messiah in his double role as king and priest whereby peace and salvation would be secured for the people of God.[32] According to this view the beneficial cooperation between Zerubbabel (royal family) and Joshua (the high priest) is the backdrop for the prediction of the perfect harmony between the two offices.

Pusey, Wright and others propose that the peaceful counsel is between the priest-king and Yahweh. Both Yahweh and the Messiah are clearly mentioned in the verse. The unity of Messiah and his Father in the salvation of mankind is a major emphasis in the New Testament.[33]

The words *peaceful counsel* point then to the harmony between the Father and Messiah. But the word *peace* by itself would have conveyed that thought. "The word used here signifies a *counsel planning or procuring* peace."[34] The Father and Son are united in planning *peace,* i.e., well-being or salvation, for others (cf. Eph. 2:14, 16, 17).

The results of Messiah's coming are indicated in verse 15. Gentiles will recognize him as Lord and will come to labor in his spiritual Temple, for *those afar shall come and build in the house of the Lord* (v. 15). The deputation from Babylon which had brought an offering of silver and gold for the physical Temple provided the occasion for this prediction of a future glorious Temple to which even Gentiles would bring their gifts.[35] It is, however, important to note this distinction: whereas the nations will build *in* the Temple, it is the Messiah himself who is the Temple-builder.

---

31. Baron, VPZ, p. 192.
32. Cf. Moore (COZ, p. 98): In the exercise of the one office he purchases redemption, by the other he applies it; by the one he expiates sin, and by the other extirpates it.
33. John 6:38; 10:15-18; 3:16-17; Col. 1:19-20.
34. Baron, VPZ, p. 201.
35. Cf. Isa. 2:2-3; 60:1-7; Micah 4:1-2.

The appearance of the Messianic Temple-builder, and the influx of Gentile laborers would establish the truth of this prophetic utterance: *You shall know that the Lord has sent me unto you* (v. 15). Only those, however, who hearkened to the voice of God would be able to share in the blessings of the Messianic age (v. 15).

The crowning of Joshua itself was a transitory typical act, the important thing was that a memorial of this significant act be preserved (v. 14). According to Jewish tradition the crowns were hung in the windows in the height of the Temple. Every priest who entered that sacred sanctuary would thereby be reminded of God's commitment to send the priest-king who would build the true Temple of God.

Chapter Twenty-Eight

PORTRAITS OF THE COMING PRINCE

The last six chapters of Zechariah are notoriously difficult to interpret. These chapters were written some time after the completion of the Temple in 516 B.C. They appear to be organized in two cycles of three chapters. Both cycles contain predictions concerning the future of the people of God from the time of Alexander the Great to the Messianic age. The personal Messianic prophecies in these chapters are five in number. They seem to focus on the final week of Messiah's earthly ministry.

Prophecy No. 67

THE PRINCE OF PEACE

Zechariah 9:9-11

Chapter 9 opens with a description of an invasion from the north. Hadrach, Damascus, Hamath, Tyre, Sidon and the Philistine city states fall to the mighty conqueror (vv. 1-5). As a result of this invasion a mongrel race would come to inhabit Ashdod. The pride of the Philistines would be cut off (v. 6). Once humbled the Philistines would be ripe for conversion. They would give up their abominations. Some of them would become leaders among the people of God (v. 7).

Most likely Zechariah is prophetically describing the campaign of Alexander the Great in 332 B.C. The Macedonian king bypassed Jerusalem as he made his way to Egypt and again as he returned through Palestine on his way to the heart of the Persian empire. Josephus (Ant. XI.viii,5) records the fulfillment of verse 8.

In contrast to the militarism of Alexander the Great, Zechariah speaks of a beautiful and gentle Ruler who will arise in Israel. "If there ever was a true picture of the Messiah-King and His kingdom, it is this."[1]

The Messianic import of Zechariah 9:9-10 is now almost universally acknowledged. Moore writes: "That this passage applies to Christ is beyond all refutation."[2] Four points support the Messianic application:

1. Pages could be filled with quotations from ancient Jewish sources in which this passage is applied to Messiah.[3]

---

1. Baron, VPZ, p. 304.
2. Moore, COZ, p. 145.
3. See Pusey (MPC, II, 402-406) for an extensive collection of citations. Iben Ezra, the one noted exception among Jewish commentators, lamely applies the passage to Nehemiah.

2. The Gospel writers apply this passage to Jesus (Matt. 21:4, 5; John 12:15).

3. The passage contains expressions from older Messianic prophecies.

4. The passage can be consistently applied to none other than Messiah.

Translation of Zechariah 9:9-11

(9) Rejoice greatly, O daughter of Zion! Shout, O daughter of Jerusalem! Behold! your King shall come to you! He is righteous and endowed with salvation, lowly and riding upon a donkey, even upon a foal of a she-ass. (10) And I will cut off chariot from Ephraim and horse from Jerusalem, and the battle bow shall be cut off. And he will speak peace to the nations, and his rule shall be from sea unto sea, and from the river to the ends of the earth. (11) Also you in the blood of your covenant I have sent forth your prisoners from the pit wherein there is no water.

A. *The Promise of His Coming* (v. 9a). The daughter of a place is the population of that place personified as a female. The daughter of Zion/Jerusalem is urged to give a glorious shout because of what is about to happen. The coming of Messiah was a joyous anticipation in ancient Israel.

1. It is a king who is promised. As Zechariah penned these words no one had occupied the throne of Israel for over seventy years. There is no indication that Zerubbabel, who was of the royal line, had any royal ambition. This promised king must be Messiah. "The kingly office of the Messiah which was conferred upon him for the accomplishment of the work of redemption, is often alluded to as ground for rejoicing."[4]

The coming one is called *your king,* i.e., a king of your own race. It does not say *a* king, but *your* king. He is your rightful king, the long-promised and long expected ruler from the family of David.

Zion (the people of God) is promised that Messiah-King would *come.* In one sense he is *of Zion,* for he is uniquely *their* king. In another sense he is not of Zion, for he would come *to* Zion apparently from outside Zion. As man he was born of Zion; as God in the flesh, he *came* to her. Speaking of Zion, Zechariah declares that Messiah-King will come *to you.* The phrase often has the connotation, *for your sake.*

_____

4. Moore, COZ, p. 146. See Ps. 2 for example.

He comes for the sake of his people to be their Teacher, Prophet, King, High Priest, and Perfect Sacrifice.

B. *The Character of the Messiah* (v. 9b). The ground for the rejoicing is said to be the character of the king and the nature of his kingdom. Four statements are made about his character:

1. He is *righteous*.[5] The word can mean *triumphant*; but here *tsaddik* refers to the quality of impartiality in judgment. "The righteousness here referred to is not his priestly, but his kingly righteousness, that rigorous justice of his reign in virtue of which no good should be unrewarded and no evil unpunished."[6] His decisions are altogether righteous. This title is appropriate to him "who did no sin, neither was guile found in his mouth" (I Peter 2:22).

2. He is *endowed with salvation*. The Niphal participle *nosha'* here has occasioned much discussion. The form could be rendered (1) as a passive, or (2) as a reflexive. In the former sense, the Messiah would be *saved*,[7] i.e., delivered from the power of death. In the latter sense, the Messiah would show himself to be a savior.[8] This understanding of the participle is reflected in the ancient versions (the Septuagint, Targum, Syriac and Vulgate) which render *nosha'*, *savior*.

3. He is *lowly*. The word *'oni* refers to lowliness of outward circumstances. The Septuagint, Targum and Syriac seem to have regarded *'oni* as equivalent to *'anav* which refers to lowliness of disposition, i.e., meekness. Matthew (21:5) seems to endorse the Septuagint rendering. The word *'oni* also has the connotation of *afflicted*, and some would argue this is the only legitimate rendering of the word.[9] If so, then the king's victory would be gained through personal humiliation and affliction (cf. Isa. 53). What a paradox!

Is it not incongruous that the people would be called upon to rejoice over the approach of such a lowly one? "Had this august king been as sorrowless as he was sinless, had he been a robed seraph or a crowned monarch, the poor and suffering could never have approached him with confidence, for he could not have sympathized with them in their

---

5. This attribute is assigned to Messiah also in Isa. 53:11; Jer. 23:5 and 33:11.

6. Moore, COZ, p. 146.

7. This is taken by Keil to mean that he is "upheld by God," and by Deane and Hengstenberg to mean that he is "endowed with salvation." Compare the use of this form in Deut. 33:29; Ps. 33:16. Wright (ZHP, p. 234) points to Ps. 2 where Messiah has already been depicted as "saved."

8. Unger, UBCZ, p. 162.

9. Hengsenberg, Keil, Wright, and Baron.

sorrows."[10] But crushed souls can rejoice that this king can be touched with the feeling of their infirmities. For this reason the lowly king can be enthusiastically welcomed.

4. He presents himself to his people by *riding upon a donkey*. In ancient times men of distinction rode on donkeys (Judg. 5:10; 10:4). After Solomon's day the horse became the royal animal and the animal of war. From that time on the donkey came to be regarded more lowly than the horse. The animal was also used for peaceful purposes, and is thus a symbol of peace.

The prophet becomes even more specific when he identifies the donkey as a *foal*. The donkey was a young animal, not yet ridden, but still running behind its mother.[11] The use of such an untrained colt was even less honorable than that of a full-grown animal. Under the law of Moses animals devoted to the service of God were to be animals which had not previously been used in the service of man.[12] That such an animal was employed by Jesus upon his entry into Jerusalem indicates two things: (1) he viewed himself as involved in the special service of his Father; and (2) he wished to claim by this action parable that he was the long awaited Messiah.

Jewish commentators have had difficulty reconciling this prophecy with those which speak of Messiah as a mighty conqueror. Some Rabbis met the difficulty by exalting the dignity of the donkey. One Rabbi is reported to have boasted to a Gentile monarch that Messiah's donkey would have a hundred colors.[13] Other Rabbis took a different approach. They argued that the prophets were speaking of two Messiahs. The mighty conqueror was Messiah ben David; the suffering Messiah was dubbed Messiah ben Joseph. Still another approach was to make the prophecy conditional. If Israel were righteous, Messiah would come on the clouds as in Daniel 7; if they were not righteous he would come lowly, riding on a donkey.

The exact agreement between the arrangements made by Jesus at his triumphal entry and this prophecy is made especially clear by Matthew (21:1-7). Jesus ordered not only the donkey's foal upon which he rode into Jerusalem to be brought, as Mark, Luke and John relate, but a she-ass and a foal with her. The purpose of this unusual arrangement was to set forth Zechariah's figurative description with greater

10. Moore, COZ, p. 148.
11. The Hebrew word is plural—the plural of species as in Judg. 14:5; Gen. 37:31 and Lev. 4:23.
12. Num. 19:2; Deut. 21:3; I Sam. 6:7.
13. Cited by Wright, ZHP, p. 239.

completeness. John states that the disciples only understood the fulfillment after Jesus was glorified (John 12:16).

What a striking fulfillment of the prophecy of Zechariah. The triumphal entry, however, is not the main point of the prophet. Wright explains:

> The prophecy would have been as truly and really fulfilled if the triumphal procession of Palm Sunday had never taken place. That single incident in the life of our Lord is not the point which the prophet had in view. It was rather the whole of the Savior's life, the entire series of events connected with Christ's first advent which was presented in one striking picture.[14]

What then was the significance of the triumphal entry as it relates to this passage? Jesus arranged this procession into Jerusalem as a symbolic action declaring two things: (1) that Zechariah 9:9-10 was Messianic in the most complete sense; and (2) that Jesus was the fulfillment of Israel's Messianic hope.

C. *The Nature of His Kingdom* (v. 10). Four conclusions regarding Messiah's kingdom are grounded in this prophecy:

1. His kingdom is united, for Ephraim and Judah will both be part of it. Not since the days of Solomon had Ephraim and Judah been part of one kingdom.[15] Social, political, economic and racial barriers all break down in Messiah's kingdom.

2. His kingdom will be peaceful. As a consequence of his coming Yahweh[16] will *cut off* from his people chariot, horse and battle bow. The verb *cut off* suggests a decisive action by which the instruments of war are eliminated. The implications of Zechariah's declaration are far reaching.

a) Messiah will be a king unlike any to ever rule in Israel or among the Gentiles. His strength will not be measured in terms of arms and armies. This is but a concrete illustration of the fact that his kingdom would not be of this world.

b) It is God who compels his people to disarm. Most likely the prophet means to imply that through the example of Messiah—through his teaching, as well—those who owned him as king would be compelled

---

14. Wright, ZHP, p. 239.

15. The New Testament regards the physical Israel of the first century as consisting of twelve tribes (Acts 26:7). The spiritual Israel is also spoken of figuratively as consisting of twelve tribes: James 1:1; Rev. 7; 21:12; Matt. 19:28.

16. The change to first person in the verse should be noted. Others conclude that Yahweh is working through the person of Messiah.

to lay down their arms. The revolutionary teaching of Messiah cannot be taken seriously without resulting in a fundamental change in attitude toward one's enemies.

c) The cutting off of chariot, horse and battle bow suggests a rebirth of militarism in Israel before the advent of Messiah. The Jews in Zechariah's day were not armed. They may have dreamed of rebellion against the Persians, but they had no strength to resist. But elsewhere Zechariah alludes to mighty battles which would in the future be fought with the Greeks (9:13ff.). Some time must, then, elapse before Messiah would come—the fall of Persia, the rise of the Greek kingdom, and Jewish rearmament. Then would come a decisive disarmament, or a loss of independence. Such was the condition of Judea and Galilee when Jesus rode into Jerusalem. Save for a single sword, those who rallied to his cause were weaponless.

3. His kingdom would be universal, for *he will speak peace to the nations* (v. 10). The Old Testament Joshua marched his armies across the Jordan against the Gentiles entrenched in their towns. The New Testament Joshua uses the disarmament of his people as the means of spreading their influence to Gentile nations. Instead of making war against Gentiles, he makes a unilateral declaration of peace.[17]

4. His kingdom is extensive, for his dominion extends from *sea to sea*. Zechariah here is quoting Psalm 72:8, and in so doing he underscores the Messianic thrust of that Psalm. By comparison with this Psalm and other passages, the expression *sea to sea* is found to express absolute universality, being equivalent to the known world.[18]

A second expression further underscores the universality of Messiah's kingdom: *from the River to the ends of the earth. The River* here, as usual, denotes the Euphrates which was the most remote northeastern boundary of the promised land (Gen. 15:18; Exod. 23:31). Messiah's kingdom would include all the territory ruled by Solomon (I Kings 4:21) and more, for it would extend from the Euphrates to the *ends of the earth.* Jesus asserted his world-wide dominion when he instructed his disciples to bear witness of him unto the uttermost parts of the earth (Acts 1:8).

D. *The Redemption of the Coming Ruler* (v. 11). In the Messianic age God would send forth to freedom those who were prisoners in a

---

17. In Isa. 52:7 he speaks peace to his own people; in Micah 5:5 he speaks peace to Gentiles.

18. Moore, COZ, p. 150. Cf. Amos 8:12; Micah 7:12. The two seas are not the Dead Sea and the Mediterranean as supposed by some.

pit where there is no water. In such a pit the captive would inevitably perish if he were not drawn out.[19]

Who are these prisoners? Verse 11 is most naturally addressed to the daughter of Zion, the whole remnant of the covenant people. They are in a blood covenant relationship with the Lord. It is because of this covenant that God sends them forth from the pit. The covenant here mentioned may be the covenant of Sinai which was sealed with blood (Exod. 24:5ff.) or the covenant with Abraham (Gen. 15:9-12, 17ff.). Through Messiah God will speak peace to Gentiles; but he will not forget the children of Abraham.

What is the pit in which these blood covenant people are held captive? Some would say that the pit is a metaphor for the Babylonian captivity. But since the context here is Messianic the bondage here spoken of must be spiritual rather than physical. What better picture could be painted of the hopeless condition of the sinner?

Though verse 12 properly introduces another paragraph, it contains some thoughts appropriate to the conclusion of the prophecy under consideration. Those in Babylonian captivity are apparently addressed. They are urged to *return to the stronghold*. Is this a reference to the promised land as some suppose? or a reference to God, who is the strength and sure refuge of his people (cf. Joel 3:1-6)? These captives are described as *prisoners of the hope*. This is the only place in the Hebrew Bible where the word for hope has the article. He makes reference to that special hope which has been the subject of study in this volume. Paul spoke of it as *the hope of Israel* (Acts 26:6, 7; 28:20). That Old covenant hope is the same as the *blessed hope* of Titus 2:13.

FULFILLMENT OF ZECHARIAH 9

Prediction	*Fulfillment*
1. Uniquely Zion's King.	1. Born King of the Jews; Given the throne of David.
2. Came to Zion.	2. He came unto his own (possession, estate).
3. He would be righteous.	3. He did no violence nor was deceit found in his mouth; he loved righteousness and hated iniquity.
4. Poor/Afflicted.	4. He had no place to lay his head.
5. Savior/Saved.	5. He became a savior when God saved him from death (Rom. 1:3; Phil. 2:8; Heb. 5:9).

---

19. Here is an evident allusion to the story of Joseph (Gen. 37:24).

Prophecy No. 68

THE TETRA-TITLED RULER

Zechariah 10:4

As noted before, the last six chapters of Zechariah were written after the rebuilding of the Temple. Following his description of the gentle Messiah-King riding upon a donkey, Zechariah predicted the mighty victories of the Jews over their future Greek oppressors (9:13-17). The Greek rulers who would control Palestine for a century and a half are called in 10:3 *shepherds* and *he-goats*[20] They are smashed when Yahweh[21] mounts his battle horse, a revived Judah, and rides forth to do battle with all his enemies (10:3). This prophetically describes the thrilling victories which the Jews under the leadership of Judas Maccabee and his brothers, won over the huge armies of the Syrian-Greek kings.

In support of the Messianic interpretation of the verse the ancient Jewish Targum can be cited. Baron regards this verse as "one of the richest Messianic prophecies in the Old Testament."[22] Nevertheless, the Messianic character of this verse is not admitted by many eminent evangelical scholars.[23]

Translation of Zechariah 10:4

From him shall be the Corner, from him shall be the Nail; from him shall be the Battle-bow; from him shall go forth he that will exercise all rule.

Discussion

The verse speaks first of the *origin of Messiah*. He *goes forth . . . from him*. From whom? Most likely the antecedent of the singular pronominal suffix is Yahweh.[24] Others have suggested that the antecedent

---

20. For the term *shepherd* used of foreign rulers see Isa. 44:28; Jer. 25:32ff. and Nahum 3:18. For *he-goats* used of a leader or chieftain see Isa. 14:9 and Ezek. 34:17.

21. Others think the rider is Messiah who is mentioned in the next verse. Christ rides a battle horse in Rev. 6:2 and 19:14.

22. Baron, VPZ, p. 345.

23. Wright (ZHP, p. 275) states that the Messianic interpretation "cannot be defended on any rational principles of exegesis."

24. Cf. Wright (ZHP, p. 274): "It would be doing violence . . . to the syntax, without any necessity whatever, to refer the pronoun of the 3rd pers. singular . . . to any other than to Jahaveh." Keil objects to this interpretation, but on insufficient grounds.

is Judah, but Judah throughout the passage is treated as a plural. In no other passage is it said of Messiah in the Old Testament that he was to come forth from God, although this is implied in several passages.

Messiah is here called the Corner (*pinnah*). This is equivalent to the cornerstone of Isaiah 28:16 (cf. Ps. 118:22). If the people of God are viewed as a sacred edifice, he is the foundation. Tribal leaders were called corners (*pinnot*) in the period of the Judges (Judg. 20:2; I Sam. 14:38). Isaiah referred to certain princes collectively as the *corner* of the tribes of Egypt (Isa. 19:13). The Christian cannot forget the fact that in the New Testament the figures of the foundation stone and head stone of the corner are applied to Christ (Matt. 21:42; Acts 4:11; I Peter 2:4-8).

The title Corner underscores two great qualities about Messiah. First, he is the *foundation* of that glorious Temple which the Divine Architect is fashioning for his own eternal habitation through the Spirit. This accounts for the marvelous endurance of the church of Christ through the ages. As the Corner he is also the *unifier* of his people. The cornerstone was cut at right angles. It bound the two walls of a structure together. So it was Christ who broke down the legal and ceremonial barrier separating Jews and Gentiles so that they might both unite as one building to the glory of God (Eph. 2:14, 15).

Messiah is called *the Nail* (*yated*). The word is used of (1) a stake that fastens the cord of a tent[25] and (2) a hooked peg used for hanging arms and utensils on a wall.[26] In this latter sense the word is used by Zechariah. This passage is an obvious allusion to Isaiah 22:23-25. In this passage Isaiah predicts the elevation of Eliakim[27] a son of David:

> And I will fasten him as a nail to a sure place . . . and they shall hang upon him all the glory of his father's house, the offspring and the issue, all the vessels of cups, even to all the vessels of flagons (Isa. 22:23-24).

The usage of the nail figure brings out the two dimensions of the Messiah. First, the Messianic Nail is a burden bearer. All the saints of the household of faith may hang their burdens on him. The thought here is that of reliability. Second, from this Nail all the precious possessions of the household of faith are displayed. Easterners hung all the precious

---

25. Cf. Exod. 27:19; 35:18; Judg. 4:21-22.

26. Cf. Ezek. 15:3.

27. Baron (VPZ, p. 352) contends that the prophecy concerning Eliakim a son of David "merges into *the* Son of David, the Messiah, in whom all the promises given to the Davidic house finally center and are being fulfilled."

vessels of their house from a nail or peg so that all who entered might admire the material possessions of the home. The Christian dedicates to Christ all that is of value in his life. Every talent, every treasure is offered to him, is hung on him, as it were.

Messiah is called the Battle-bow (*qeshet milchama*). He is a warrior fighting for and with his people. The title calls to mind the scenes of Messianic triumph depicted in Psalms 45:5 where Messiah sends forth his sharp arrows into the heart of the king's enemies. This is the Old Testament equivalent to the concept that Christ is the Captain of the Christian's salvation. He has fought the battle, he is fighting the battle, and he shall finally and for all time crush the foe when he returns (II Thess. 1:7-10; Rev. 19:11-16).

The exact meaning of the last phrase of Zechariah 10:4 is difficult to ascertain. The Hebrew construction is unusual, and this has resulted in conflicting translations and interpretations. The translation *he that will exercise all rule* was suggested by Baron. The Hebrew more literally reads, *every noges together*. The term *noges* is used in the Old Testament for a taskmaster or exactor. Here, however, the term must have a more positive connotation.[28] It seems to be used in the more general sense of *ruler* as in Isaiah 3:12 and 60:17. A *noges* is an absolute ruler, one who demands total submission to his authority. The word *together* at the end of the phrase would suggest that all sovereignty would reside in this future Ruler.

---

28. Baron (VPZ, p. 356): "That *noges* is here used in a *good* sense is pretty generally admitted by lexicographers and commentators."

Chapter Twenty-Nine

THE REJECTED SHEPHERD

This entire chapter is devoted to one lengthy Messianic prophecy, the sixty-ninth to be treated in this study. Zechariah 11 opens with a description of a desolating judgment which sweeps across the whole land of Palestine. This physical desolation is the result of an invasion by some unnamed enemy. The trees of Labanon are devoured by fire. The thickets of the Jordan are destroyed and the lions who live therein howl. While the focus here is on the devastation of the land, it is obvious that the people of the land suffer too.

The Roman invasion of Palestine is most likely the focus of verses 1-3. But is this a metaphorical description of the coming of the Romans *prior to* the coming of Christ, or *subsequent to* his rejection? Moore contends for the former view in these words:

> This metaphor describes the storm of invasion, bloodshed and oppression that should roll over Palestine after the glorious Maccabean era, and before the coming of the Messiah. . . . The reference is to that desolating storm of civil war that caused the calling in of the Romans, whose legions swept like a whirlwind of steel over the land, and finally prostrated every vestige of independent authority . . . and humbled the whole land beneath the mighty power of Rome.[1]

Other commentators (e.g., Unger) defend the view that the Roman judgment against Judea subsequent to the rejection of the Good Shepherd (Messiah) is the focus of verses 1-3.

The Messianic character of this prophecy is conceded even by those who are not inclined to find many prophecies of Christ in the Old Testament. Of course, some rationalistic expositors regard the passage, not as predictive, but as descriptive of something which happened before the destruction of the first Temple. The context of Zechariah 9-14 demands that this passage be regarded as predictive. The Talmud itself and a number of respected Jewish commentators apply the passage to the days of the second Temple. It would scarcely serve any useful purpose in Zechariah's day to depict past history, even recent history, by obscure symbols. So the passage must be regarded as predictive.

Jewish commentators and some eminent Christian commentators see in Zechariah 11 a depiction of the dealings of God and Israel during the whole period of the second Temple (516 B.C.-A.D. 70). This approach is based on the observation that the two preceding chapters

---

1. Moore, COZ, p. 171.

embrace the whole period of the second Temple from Alexander the Great to Christ. Therefore, it is argued, chapter 11 must be similarly comprehensive.

Good reasons, however, exist for viewing Zechariah 11 as a prophetic depiction of the rejection of Christ: First, the state of God's people depicted here answers exactly to the condition of the Jewish nation immediately preceding the destruction of the second Temple. What is depicted here does not correspond to their condition and experience during the whole, or even the greater part, of their history after re-building the Temple. Furthermore, the principal object of the greatest prophecies in the two immediately preceding chapters was Messiah. Finally, the New Testament clearly links this prophecy to events in the life of Christ.

Translation of Zechariah 11:4-14

(4) Thus said the Lord my God: Feed the flock of slaughter (5) whose possessors slay them, and regard themselves not guilty; and they that sell them say, Blessed be the LORD, for I am rich; and their own shepherds do not pity them. (6) For I will no more pity the inhabitants of the land, (oracle of the LORD); but behold I will deliver the men each into the hand of his neighbor, and into the hand of his king; and they shall smite the land, and out of their hand I will not deliver them. (7) So I fed the flock of slaughter, yea the poor of the flock. And I took unto me two staves: the one I called Beauty, and the other I called Bands, and I fed the flock. (8) And I cut off three shepherds in one month, and my soul loathed them and also their soul abhorred me. (9) And I said, I will not shepherd you! The one that dies, let it die; the one that is cut off, let it be cut off, and let the rest eat each the flesh of another. (10) And I took my staff, Beauty, and I cut it in two, to break my covenant which I made with all the peoples. (11) And it was broken in that day and the poor of the flock who kept me knew that it was the Word of God. (12) And I said unto them, If it seems good in your eyes give my wages, and if not, desist. And they weighed out my hire thirty silver pieces. (13) And the LORD said unto me, Cast it unto the potter, the goodly price with which I was evaluated by them. And I took the thirty silver pieces and cast it in the house of the LORD unto the potter. (14) And I cut in two my second staff, Bands, to break the brotherhood between Judah and Israel.

Discussion

The prophecy of the rejected Shepherd has three main divisions: (1) the commission and explanation by the Lord (vv. 4-6); (2) the symbolic dramatization of the ministry of the Good Shepherd (vv. 7-9); and (3) the symbolic termination of the ministry of the Good Shepherd (vv. 10-14).

A. *The Commission and Explanation by the Lord* (vv. 6-9).

1. The prophet's *commission* is short and to the point: *Feed the flock of slaughter!* The flock is Israel. The prophet is to assume the role of a shepherd to this flock. Concerning this commission five observations are in order:

a) This is a genuine commission laid upon the prophet to be acted out before his contemporaries. What is here recorded is not an allegory (Baldwin) or an inner visionary experience (Leupold) but a minidrama acted out by the prophet to a restricted audience for a limited time (Unger). Zechariah's actions here are comparable to the symbolic crowning of Joshua in 6:9-15.

b) The commission is urgent. The nation faced a terrible judgment from the north (vv. 1-3). God must make one last effort to reach his people and rescue them from judgment.

c) The commission is prophetic. It does not concern Zechariah's ministry to his contemporaries. He is here to portray the divine Shepherd who, according to Ezekiel 34, attempts to seek, save, strengthen and heal his people.

d) The commission is Messianic. According to Ezekiel 34 the work of the Good Shepherd would culminate in the one Shepherd from the house of David, i.e., the Messiah. The Good Shepherd became flesh and dwelt among men.

e) The commission is in one respect, shocking. In contrast to the glorious promises which the Lord elsewhere holds out for Judah in this book, here he depicts the nation as doomed. The inhabitants are the *flock of slaughter*, i.e., the flock which is destined for slaughter. By no stretch of imagination would this terminology be appropriate for the generation to whom Zechariah preached. Some future generation of their descendants, however, would be so victimized by native leaders and foreign oppressors that they could be referred to as the *flock of slaughter*.

2. In verses 5-6 the Lord offers an explanation for the sad condition of the flock. *Their possessors* (lit., buyers) *slay them* and hold themselves guiltless in so doing. Those who sell the sheep into the hands

of their enemies rejoice over the personal enrichment they receive from the transaction.[2] What a tragedy! Their own shepherds do not pity them.

In the latter part of the sixth century Judea was blessed with dedicated leadership. Therefore, Zechariah must be talking about a group of national leaders who would arise in the future. The available sources do not furnish any likely candidates for the fulfillment of this prediction until the second century B.C. The priestly family became thoroughly corrupt. The high priesthood was politicized and sold to the highest bidder by the Syrian-Greek kings. The successors of these worldly-minded priests and their supporters became the Sadducees of the New Testament era. Rising to oppose the corruption of these leaders was a populist party called Pharisees or Separatists. By the time of Christ this party too had lost sight of spiritual values. The Pharisees were guilty of avarice. They enriched themselves by exploitation of their fellows, "yet they had the bare-faced hypocrisy to thank God for their ill-gotten wealth, and because they were not punished, they imagined they might persevere with impunity."[3]

What a calamity! The Jewish authorities had no consideration for the flock of slaughter. Yet an even worse fate awaited the flock. They would be abandoned by the Good Shepherd. The circumstances of the divine rejection are described in four statements of antagonism.

a) *For I will no more pity the inhabitants of the land* (v. 6). What purpose does the conjunction serve? Does verse 6 give the reason for the mistreatment of the flock, or the reason for the efforts of the Good Shepherd to reclaim the flock? Defending the latter view Moore contends:

> V. 6 gives the reason for making this last effort to save them: their wickedness could no longer be borne, but must be arrested either by penitence at the call of Christ, or punishment at the sword of the Romans.[4]

The former interpretation of the conjunction would be explained thus: The abuse of the flock by the "buyers and sellers" was possible only because God had withdrawn his protective care of the flock. To show pity, spare or have compassion (*yachmal*) in the Old Testament means to spare one from suffering, calamity or judgment.[5] God is then saying that the

---

2. What is depicted here goes beyond the accusation of negligence hurled at pre-exilic "shepherds" by Jeremiah (50:6-7).

3. Henderson, BTMP, p. 420.

4. Moore, COZ, p. 173.

5. I Sam. 15:3; II Sam. 21:7; Jer. 50:14.

reason for the pitiful condition of the flock described in the preceding verse is that he will no longer hold back or restrain the forces of judgment.

The first statement of antagonism is reinforced by *neum Yahweh, oracle of Yahweh*. Prophets used this terminology to make the strongest possible claim to inspiration. It may be utterly incredible that God would cease to have compassion on his people, but that is exactly what he had spoken.

b) *But, behold, I will deliver the men, each into the hand of his neighbor* (v. 6). The Hebrew construction is very emphatic: the interjectional adverb *hinneh* plus the separate pronoun *'anokhi* plus a participle. What is announced here is the exact opposite of exercising compassion. Instead of delivering his people from calamity, God delivers them over to it. The verb *deliver* has a double object: *men* (plural) and *each* (singular). This individualizing of the plural emphasizes the thoroughness of the action expressed by the verb.

The inhabitants of Judea would be delivered over to mutual strife and antagonism (*each into the hand of his neighbor*). Josephus bears testimony to the insane factional strife in Jerusalem for some months prior to the fall of that city to the Romans in A.D. 70. More Jews died by Jewish swords than by the hand of Romans.

c) *I will deliver the men, each . . . into the hand of his king* (v. 6). The king here is not that humble ruler whom Zechariah depicted riding into Jerusalem on a donkey (9:9). That ruler would be rejected as the present passage clearly shows. *His king* must be understood as referring to the king of Judah's own choice. The *king* must be a foreign ruler, for the Jews in Zechariah's day had no king, and Zechariah never speaks of any native king except Messiah. The king into whose hands the Jews are delivered must be that king which they embraced when they rejected the rule of the Good Shepherd. "We have no king but Caesar," they cried in Pilate's judgment hall (John 19:15). Within forty years of that day the Jewish people, their holy city and Temple were crushed by Caesar's hand.

d) *And they shall smite the land* (v. 6). The reference must be to the armies of the king. The verb *smite* (*kittet*) has the connotation of beating to pieces as if with repeated blows of a hammer.[6] Thus did the relentless Romans crush the Jewish state.

---

6. Unger (UBCZ, p. 193) cites II Kings 18:4; II Chron. 34:7; and Isa. 2:4.

e) And . . . I will not deliver them (v. 6). The conscious decision of the Good Shepherd to have no compassion on the flock results in his inaction in their hour of need. (No divine intervention would halt the factional warfare within, nor bring to naught the power of Rome without.)

B. *The Symbolic Dramatization of the Ministry of the Good Shepherd* (vv. 7-9). Twice in verse 7 Zechariah affirms that he did what most critics deny that he did. He claims to have *fed* or tended the flock. The prophet performed a symbolic act for the people of his generation. Thus he visually set forth the future ministry of Messiah the Good Shepherd, who tenderly cared for the flock of God even to the point of being willing to lay down his life for the sheep.

The object of the ministry of the Good Shepherd is described in two ways. First, the Good Shepherd (impersonated by Zechariah) feeds the *flock of slaughter*. History records that thousands of Jews died in the wars against the Syrian-Greeks and later under the Herodian rulers. From roughly 200 B.C. (some 300 years after this prophecy) the inhabitants of Judea could appropriately be called *the flock of slaughter*. But the focus here is on what would happen to this flock as a result of the rejection of the Good Shepherd. More than a million died during the course of the war with Rome and the siege of Jerusalem in A.D. 70.

The Good Shepherd's ministry was especially aimed at the *poor of the flock*. The term 'oni embraces the "afflicted" or "wretched" among the covenant people—those destitute of worldly goods but full of faith. Here is summed up the blessed fruit of the labors of the Good Shepherd. The masses and their leaders would prove obstinate. But in the midst of the nation there would be those who chose life. Christ assumed the work of feeding the Jewish flock in order that he might save that remnant which was waiting for Messianic redemption. John 1:11 succinctly sets forth the fulfillment:

> He came unto his own, and they received him not. But as many as received him, to them gave he the right to become children of God, even to them that believe on his name.

From the ranks of the common people (Mark 12:37) came those who believed. They were the poor of the flock. The Good Shepherd fed them all; but the poor of the flock were his special concern.

In symbolically tending the flock, Zechariah made use of two staves. The Eastern shepherd normally carried a rod to beat away wild animals

438

and a crooked staff to retrieve straying sheep (cf. Ps. 23:4). The two staves were given names which symbolized the treatment which the people of God had received from the Good Shepherd.

The first staff signified the Good Shepherd's loving and gracious care of the flock. It was called *no'am,* a word which could be translated any one of the following ways: Pleasantness, Graciousness, Beauty, Delight. The first staff symbolized the favor with which God caused the Jews to be regarded and their rights respected until the work of redemption was completed. The record bears witness to this favored position of Israel. Alexander, Antiochus and Pompey were each restrained from destroying Judea. But once the Good Shepherd in the flesh was rejected this mystic staff was broken and the power of Rome crushed Judea and permanently destroyed the Temple.

The second staff signified the unity of the people under their Good Shepherd. It was called *chobhelim,* Bands, i.e., the ties which bound God's people together as one people until the coming of Christ.

A key element in the ministry of the Good Shepherd was the rejection of the undershepherds. That the undershepherds were ruthless, greedy, hypocritical and totally unworthy of a position of leadership among the people of God has already been indicated in verse 5. It must be stressed that Zechariah is not referring to the "shepherds" of his own day, a leadership which was dedicated to the Lord. He speaks of that generation of leaders who would be on the scene when the Good Shepherd appeared in the flesh.

Commentators have exercised themselves no small bit in attempting to identify the *three* shepherds who would be cut off (v. 8). More than forty proposals have been made. These interpretations fall into four categories which may be outlined as follows:

(A) The three shepherds are three individuals.
    (1) Three Gentile rulers.
        (a) Three Gentile rulers during the intertestamental period.[7]
        (b) Three Roman emporers.[8]
    (2) Three Israelite/Jewish leaders.
        (a) Three leaders prior to the time of Zechariah.[9]
        (b) Three leaders during the intertestamental period.[10]

---

7. E.g., Wright: Antiochus Epiphanes, Antiochus Eupator and Demetrius during the period 172-141 B.C.

8. E.g., Kalmet: Galba, Otho, Vitellius.

9. E.g., Ewald: Zechariah, Shallum, Menahem, kings of the fallen kingdom of Israel: Kimchi: Jehoahaz, Jehoiakim and Zedekiah, kings of the fallen kingdom of Judah.

10. E.g., Abarbanel: Judas, Jonathan, and Simon.

(B) The Three shepherds are three world powers.[11]
(C) The Three shepherds are three classes of rulers.[12]
(D) The number three is used figuratively to indicate completion. The Good Shepherd would remove from power all unworthy rulers.[13]

Perhaps by three shepherds nothing more is meant than the three types of leaders already described in verse 5, viz., *possessors, sellers,* and *shepherds*. It is, however, a matter of record that when the Good Shepherd came in the flesh the flock was largely controlled by three classes of shepherds: (1) the priests or Sadducess, (2) the Rabbis of the Pharisaic sect, and (3) the civil rulers of the Herodian line. That these three classes of shepherds shared a hatred for Christ is documented on almost every page of the Gospel record. All three classes shared responsibility for his crucifixion.

During his ministry the Good Shepherd *cut off* the undershepherds. The verb does not necessarily indicate destroying or executing, but rather points to rejection, disavowal or repudiation. His blistering sermons aimed at the "shepherds" (e.g., Matt. 23) cut them off. He silenced the Pharisees, Sadducees and Herodians in public debate. His masterful teaching displaced that of the Rabbis. His priestly work on Calvary rendered the ministrations of Aaron's sons purposeless. In his resurrection he received all authority and thereby superseded any civil leader of his day.

The three shepherds would be cut off in *one month*. A month is long when compared with that which Zechariah elsewhere figuratively described as *one day* (3:9), but brief as contrasted with other periods of time.[14] The symbolic *one month* finds fulfillment in (1) the brief, three plus year ministry of Christ during which he sought to rescue the flock from the tyranny of their "shepherds"; or (2) the period of gradual transition from the old to the new dispensation.[15]

A further development in the ministry of the Good Shepherd is indicated in verse 8b. The flock did not appreciate the fact that their unworthy shepherds had been "cut off" by the Good Shepherd. The

---

11. E.g., Keil: Babylon, Medo-Persia and Macedonia.

12. E.g., Hengstenberg: civil authorities (rulers), priests and prophets.

13. Baldwin, TOTC, p. 183.

14. Other views of the *one month*: (1) a literal month of thirty days; (2) a month of years, i.e., thirty years. Adequate fulfillment of neither of these interpretations has been offered.

15. Moroe, COZ, p. 177.

flock did not immediately embrace him, but on the contrary, became antagonistic toward him.

The antecedent of the pronoun in the last half of verse 8 is ambiguous. Grammatically, the antecedent would naturally be supposed to refer to "the three shepherds" spoken of in the previous part of the verse. For the following reasons, however, it is best to regard the latter half of verse 8 as referring to the mutual antagonism between the Shepherd and the flock:

First, without question verse 9 refers to the abandonment of the entire flock. The last half of verse 8 would set forth the reason for this abandonment. Second, the verb in the original cannot be rendered as a pluperfect, as if the second clause of verse 8 referred to some action performed by the shepherds previous to their having been "cut off."[16] Finally, it is not likely that the prophet be supposed to speak of his being wearied with the acts of the shepherds after he had actually cut them off.

The Good Shepherd became weary with the flock. Literally, *My soul (I) became short at them* (v. 8). Even the patience of God is not inexhaustible! This weariness did not arise from any reluctance on his part to perform the task of tending the flock. His weariness was solely occasioned by the conduct of the sheep.

The flock grew increasing hostile toward the Good Shepherd. They *loathed* him. This verb *bachal* has the connotation of feeling extreme nausea.[17] They had utter disgust for him. In his Galilean ministry Jesus reached the height of popularity when he fed the five thousand. When he preached his sermon on the Bread of Life shortly thereafter (John 6), the multitude deserted him. His brief moment of triumph on Palm Sunday was followed by rejection, ridicule and a humiliating death.

Impersonating the Good Shepherd, Zechariah declares *I will not shepherd you*. All his tender care with which he had watched over the flock would come to an end. He had rescued his flock time and again during the intertestamental period from the ruthless oppressors. Now there would be no more divine intervention. "By withholding his leadership the shepherd abandoned the people to the consequences of their rejection of him: death and mutual destruction. He simply lets things take their course."[18] Payne sees the fulfillment in the end of the independent Jewish kingdom by Pompey's occupation of Jerusalem.[19]

---

16. Wright, ZHP, p. 321.
17. Unger, UBCZ, p. 196.
18. Baldwin, TOTC, p. 184.
19. Payne, EBP, p. 463.

The general declaration of divine antipathy is quickly amplified. Sheep which are in the process of dying are abandoned to death. *Let it die* expresses a resolution within the heart of the Good Shepherd. Sheep which are *cut off*, i.e., disowned, are allowed to remain in that condition. A sheep cut off from the flock had no chance of survival. A third jussive announces the determination of the Shepherd to give the remainder of the flock over to cannibalism. They would devour one another like ferocious beasts[20] (v. 9).

C. *The Termination of the Ministry of the Good Shepherd* (vv. 10-14). The last movement within the prophecy underscores by three symbolic actions the fact that the ministry of the Good Shepherd had come to an end.

1. He breaks the first staff (vv. 10-11). In fact, he chopped it to pieces (*gada'*). This staff was named Graciousness (cf. v. 7) and symbolized God's gracious protection of his people. Since the restoration from Babylon God had tended his flock with this staff. The grace period, however, would not last forever.

The action of the prophet (portraying the Good Shepherd) is immediately explained. God had broken a covenant which he had *with all the peoples*, i.e., Gentile nations (v. 10). This was not a covenant made with them for their own good, but rather one made with them for the good of the people of Israel. It was an ordinance whereby the nations had been restrained, at least partially, in their assaults against Israel. By virtue of this "covenant" when the nations acted injuriously toward Israel they met with appropriate chastisement from God.[21]

During the period of the second Temple Judea fared tolerably well under the Persians. Alexander the Great spared Jerusalem when he marched to Egypt in 332 B.C. After the death of Alexander Judea came under the control of the Ptolemies, Greek rulers of Egypt. It would appear that for the most part this was a tranquil period for the flock of God. In 198 B.C. the Seleucids, Greek rulers of Syria, gained control of Judea. During this period there were some humiliating times for the flock. The Temple was ransacked on occasion. But even during this period the record underscores the gracious protection provided by the Good Shepherd. One massive Greek army after another was

20. Note the parallel with v. 14. Payne (EBP, p. 463) sees in this verse a reference to the internal leadership struggles which preceded the coming of Christ, whereas v. 14 refers to strife which followed rejection of Christ.

21. Cf. Hosea 2:18 where God has a covenant with the beasts of the field on behalf of Israel.

defeated by woefully outnumbered Jewish patriots. The Roman annexation of Judea was largely peaceful. Roman rule, while bitterly resented by the Jews, did allow freedom of worship.

The fulfillment is described by Unger in the following words:

> This stern action in telling fashion portrays the exhaustion of the good Shepherd's patience and His giving the nation over to judgment and the manifestation of divine wrath in the invasion of Roman armies and the terrible sufferings ensuing in the destruction of the city of Jerusalem and the polity of the ancient people of God.[22]

The *poor of the flock*—the faithful few, the spiritual minority—would listen to (lit., watch, observe) the Good Shepherd. They knew he was speaking the word of God. They realized that God's gracious restraining providence which kept Gentile nations on a leash had been removed (v. 11).

2. He requests his wages (vv. 12-13). In verse 12 the Good Shepherd makes a request for wages. Concerning this request the following points need to be noted.

a) The persons addressed in this request. The Good Shepherd directs his request for wages to *them*. The nearest antecedent would be the poor of the flock who recognize in the actions of the Good Shepherd the word of God. In view of the response, however, it is hardly likely that the poor of the flock are those being addressed. The same third masculine pronoun was used in verse 8 (*my soul was weary of them*), and the use there is also ambiguous (see on verse 8). Most likely it is the entire flock which is being addressed.

b) The tone of the request: *If it seems good in your eyes.* In view of the way the flock has shown contempt for their divine Shepherd, the request is stated hypothetically.[23] Real doubt existed as to whether or not the flock would acknowledge any obligation to him. The Shepherd cannot compel the flock to love and appreciate him. The choice is theirs.

c) The purpose of the request. The Good Shepherd was no mercenary. He was not interested in personal remuneration. His request for wages served a twofold purpose: (1) to reinforce to the flock the fact that his services were now at an end; and (2) to arouse in them a realization of the seriousness of their plight.

---

22. Unger, UBCZ, p. 197.

23. Moore (COZ, p. 179) sees this expression as "one of indignant contempt, with an intimation that to retain that reward was a far more costly thing than to bestow it."

d) The appropriateness of the request. It cannot be thought strange that the Good Shepherd requests wages. The flock here, after all, is not a group of amoral dumb beasts. The flock consists of free moral agents committed to God by solemn covenant. That which the Good Shepherd requests is that which he had deserved all along—Israel's faith, stedfastness, holiness, love and praise.

e) The occasion of the request. Under the law of Moses wages were to be paid daily. One was never to have to ask for his wages. Yet Israel paid the Divine Shepherd the wages of obedient love only spasmodically. The incarnation was the culmination of the Good Shepherd's efforts to collect his rightful wages. Every sermon he preached, every miracle he performed, every tender word he spoke called upon Israel to render appropriate wages to the divine Shepherd.

The flock responded to the request of the Good Shepherd in a most surprising way. They *weighed out* his wages (v. 12). They owed him an incalculable debt, yet they have the audacity to attempt to reimburse him with finite resources. They did not wish for him to receive one cent more than he deserved!

Thirty pieces of silver was the price of a slave under the law (Exod. 21:32). The Good Shepherd was worth no more to them than a common slave. The flock intended for this sum to demonstrate their scorn and hatred for him (v. 12). It would have been better had they given him nothing.

The insult by the flock provokes a direct response from the Lord (v. 13). He spoke directly to the prophet. All that Zechariah had done in verses 7-12 in his dramatic role as Good Shepherd met with divine approval. Now the Divine director shouts down further instructions for the prophetic actor. The Lord's words indicate his total disgust in three ways:

a) By the action verb which is used. Zechariah is to *fling or cast away* (*hashlichehu*) the treasure tainted by mockery (v. 13). The verb is used of flesh thrown to the dogs (Exod. 22:31), of a corpse cast out without burial (Jer. 26:23; 36:30), of idols flung to the moles and to the bats (Isa. 2:20), and of an unwanted infant abandoned to death (Ezek. 16:5).

b) By the directional phrase. The silver is to be flung *unto the potter*,[24] one of the lowest of the laboring classes. One would expect that wages

---

24. There is no reason to follow the lead of the LXX and render the word *foundry* or *furnace*. So also the renderings of the Syriac and Targum (*treasury*) and Vulgate (*sculptor*) are to be rejected. The article on *potter* is generic.

paid to the Good Shepherd would be deposited in the Temple treasury; but such was not the case with this ignominious silver. Dishonorable gains of any kind were not to be brought into that treasury (Deut. 23:18), much less this paltry sum offered to the Good Shepherd in derision and mockery.

The directional phrase has received a variety of explanations, of which the following are representative:

(1) *To the potter* is an idiomatic way of saying, cast the silver to the ground (Hofmann) or to an unclean place.[25]

(2) The potter is God himself (Kliefoth).

(3) The potter represents one of the lowliest of the working class. The sum of money is fit only for such a lowly one.

(4) The potter was one who makes pots for the Temple (Hengstenberg, Baldwin).

c) By the evaluative clause. The Lord refers sarcastically to the thirty pieces of silver as the *goodly price with which I was evaluated by them.* It is important to note here how the Lord identifies with the Good Shepherd.

Following the instructions of the Lord, Zechariah continued his mini-drama (v. 13b). He did three things:

(1) He took the thirty pieces of silver, but only for the purpose of demonstrating the divine disgust with the evaluation.

(2) He flung or cast the silver pieces in the house of the Lord. The implication is that it was here that the paltry sum had been offered. Wright comments:

> . . . . the temple was the place where the people of the covenant, the Israel of God, were wont to assemble to present themselves before the Lord. In that holy place the awful repudiation on the part of the nation of him who was the Shepherd of Israel was to be publicly made known. . . . In the place where the solemn covenant between Jahaveh and his people had so often been ratified by sacrifices, the fearful divorce between the people of Israel and himself was to be declared.[26]

(3) He flung the silver *unto the potter.* Was a potter present in the

---

25. This theory is based on two assumptions: (1) that *the potter* is an allusion to the potter in Jeremiah 18:2 and 19:1; and (2) that this potter had his pottery in the valley of Hinnom, an unclean place (II Kings 23:10).
26. Wright, ZHP, p. 330.

Temple when Zechariah performed his symbolic action?[27] Did he merely announce as he flung it down that this money was to go to the potter? Either interpretation is possible. Normally money found in the Temple would be placed in the Temple treasuries. By casting down the silver the prophet signifies that it is tainted. Temple officials could not use it (cf. Deut. 23:18). By one means or the other the prophet made clear that the thirty pieces of silver would wind up in the possession of a potter.

3. He breaks the second staff (v. 14). Zechariah next cuts to pieces his second staff, *Bands*. All relations between the Good Shepherd and Israel now comes to an end. This staff symbolized the religious and social ties which bound Israel together as a nation. The chopping up of the second staff signified the future disolution of the *brotherhood of Judah and Israel*.

After the death of Solomon in 931 B.C. the northern tribes renounced their allegiance to the house of David and formed a kingdom of their own known as Israel or Ephraim. The reunification of the sister king-doms was one of the key themes among the Old Testament prophets (cf. Ezek. 37:15-28). That reunification did in fact take place after the return from Babylonian exile. During the intertestamental period Ephraim and Judah fought side by side against the sons of Greece (Zech. 9:13; 10:5-7). That unity which the people of God knew in Zechariah's day would be broken up because the Good Shepherd was rejected. To break *the brotherhood of Judah and Israel* brings to mind that earlier schism in the days of Rehoboam.

How was the symbolic rupture of the unity of Israel and Judah actually fulfilled? Not in the formation of two rival religious communities. There is no hint here of an Israel after the spirit (Judah) and an Israel after the flesh (Ephraim) which determines to have no part of the Messianic son of David. The fulfillment is found in the suicidal party spirit which ripped asunder the Jewish people in A.D. 70 at the end of the second Temple era.

Matthew 27:3-10 cites verses 12 and 13 of this passage as a direct prophecy of Jesus Christ. The priests paid thirty pieces of silver to Judas for information which led to the arrest of Jesus. This was the price

---

27. Cf. Baldwin (TOTC, p. 185): "Potters were connected with the Temple because the sacrifice ritual needed a continual supply of new vessels. A guild of potters may have been minor officials at the Temple." Also Payne (EBP, p. 463): "A potter must have been there in the temple, perhaps delivering vessels. . . ."

at which those representatives of the Jewish nation valued the services of the Lord. "As one of the chosen twelve, Judas in this incident can be regarded as a representative of Christ."[28] The priests would not allow this blood money to be put in the Temple treasury. They immediately took the money and purchased a field from a potter where strangers might be buried.

Some have objected that a discrepancy exists between this prophecy and the Gospel narrative. In the former the thirty pieces of silver were weighed as wages for the Shepherd, whereas in the Gospel narrative they were paid to Judas for betraying Jesus. Keil has an excellent response to this objection:

> The payment of the wages to the shepherd in the prophetical announcement is simply the symbolical form in which the nation manifests its ingratitude for the love and fidelity shown towards it by the shepherd, and the sign that it will no longer have him as its shepherd, and therefore a sign of the blackest ingratitude, and of hard-heartedness in return for the love displayed by the shepherd. The same ingratitude and the same hardness of heart are manifested in the resolution of the representatives of the Jewish nation . . . to put Jesus . . . to death, and to take him prisoner by bribing the betrayer. The payment of thirty silverlings to the betrayer was, in fact, the wages with which the Jewish nation repaid Jesus for what He had done for the salvation of Israel; and the contemptible sum which they paid to the betrayer was an expression of the deep contempt which they felt for Jesus.[29]

One detail in Matthew's use of this passage has perplexed commentators through the years. Why does Mathew attribute to Jeremiah words which are obviously taken from Zechariah? Various proposals have been made: (1) Matthew experienced a lapse of memory; or (2) quotes from an original prophecy of Jeremiah which is now lost; or (3) blends Zechariah's prophecy with that of Jeremiah 18:2 and 10:11. The most satisfactory interpretation, however, is that Jeremiah originally stood at the head of the collection of prophetic books. Matthew is thus citing a *section* of the sacred canon, not an individual book.

In summary, the chief points made by Zechariah in this prophecy are as follows:

1. Before a second destruction of Jerusalem the Good Shepherd would manifest himself to Israel.

---

28. Wright, ZHP, p. 341.
29. Keil, BCOT, Minor Prophets, II, 373-374.

2. Both the leaders and the people would reject him.

3. A remnant would accept his teaching as the Word of God.

4. The Good Shepherd would be valued at the price of a common slave.

5. In consequence of rejecting the Good Shepherd, national Israel would be delivered over to Gentile powers from without and to civil strife within.

Chapter Thirty

PIERCED AND SMITTEN

The last three chapters form a distinct unit in the Book of Zechariah. This is indicated by the use of the opening verse which begins, *the burden of the word of Yahweh.* The theme of this section is the invincibility of Jerusalem. The phrase *in that day* is used in these three chapters sixteen times. This indicates that all the prophecies in these chapters relate to the same period, the Messianic age.

Two personal Messianic prophecies are yet to be explored in Zechariah. These are the prophecies of (1) the Pierced One (12:10), and (2) the Smitten Shepherd (13:17).

Prophecy No. 70

THE PIERCED ONE

Zechariah 12:10

The opening paragraph of chapter 12 (vv. 1-9) describes a vicious, but unsuccessful attack against Jerusalem. But which Jerusalem? The physical city which had not even been rebuilt in Zechariah's day, or its antitype, the Jerusalem of Hebrews 12:22? Zechariah must have been familiar with Daniel's prophecy concerning the future destruction of physical Jerusalem following the death of Messiah (Dan. 9:26). The previous chapter closed with a similar picture: Messiah rejected, and Gentile nations coming against the people of God. In the first paragraph of chapter 12 Zechariah must have been talking about that future Jerusalem, the New Testament Jerusalem, the church of Christ. Collins comments:

> In this picture of the impregnable city Jerusalem represents the Church. The literal Jerusalem was to be laid waste by the Romans, as it had been on former occasions by other enemies; but the spiritual Jerusalem shall never know defeat by the 'gates of hell.'[1]

According to Chambers the remainder of chapter 12 is designed to show "how the covenant people become such, how the church . . . commences the Christian life, and obtains a title to the divine protection" mentioned in the preceding paragraph.[2] The inhabitants of the invincible Jerusalem are those who have experienced a genuine

---

1. Collins, NBC, p. 760.
2. Chambers, CHSL, p. 95.

conversion. This conversion was triggered by looking on one who was pierced.

Controversy has raged around the simple prediction of verse 10. Jewish commentators have done their best to deny this text to that One who suffered and died for the sins of his people. If the obvious meaning of this verse be admitted, here is a real prophecy of a suffering, yet divine Messiah. Some rationalist Christian writers have played down the New Testament citations of the verse and joined Jewish scholars in their interpretation of the passage.

That Zechariah 12:10 is a Messianic prophecy is indicated by the following considerations.

1. The ancient Jewish synagogue identified the *one who is pierced* here as Messiah ben Joseph. This interpretation is at least as old as the Talmud.[3]

2. The New Testament twice quotes the verse, identifying the one who is pierced as Christ (Rev. 1:7; John 19:37).

3. The piercing of no other than Messiah could account for the intense mourning described in this passage.

4. The one who is pierced is Yahweh, yet is distinguished from Yahweh. No one save Messiah the God-man could fulfill the terms of the prophecy.

To escape the theological implications of this prophecy, Jewish expositors have raised the following arguments which must be answered:

1. The verb *daqar* means to grieve or insult rather than pierce. The Septuagint has so rendered the verb. Answer: The word *daqar* is never used in the Old Testament in the sense of grieve or insult, but always in the sense of literal piercing (e.g., 13:3). The mourning to take place is likened to that which resulted from the literal piercing to death of Josiah at Megiddo.

2. The pronoun is actually *him* rather than *me*. Hence the one pierced is a mere man. Answer: Manuscript study indicates that the third person reading was at first only a marginal reading which in later manuscripts crept into the text. Many of the most able Jewish authorities admit that the first person reading is the true reading.

The evasions are utterly inadmissable. The text clearly affirms that the Jews would look on Yahweh whom they had pierced through to death. This prophecy can only be interpreted in the light of the cross.

---

3. *Sukk.* 52a. Later Jewish scholars such as Rashi and Kimchi departed from the Messianic interpretation by attempting to identify the pierced one as the Jews slain in the Gentile attack against Jerusalem.

The earliest Jewish sources recognized the fact that Messiah would suffer and die and thereby provide in some way an atonement for sin.[4] As the controversy with Christians over the Messiahship of Jesus heated up, the Rabbis began to argue for two Messiahs—one who would suffer, and one who would reign.

Translation of Zechariah 12:10

And I shall pour out upon the house of David and upon the inhabitants of Jerusalem the spirit of grace and supplication; and they shall look unto me whom they have pierced, and they shall mourn over him like the mourning over an only son, and as one bitterly laments shall be bitterly remorseful over him like one is bitter over a first born son.

Discussion

This verse has three points of emphasis: (1) the outpouring of God's spirit, (2) the looking upon one who was pierced, and (3) the mourning over the terrible sin.

A. *The Outpouring of God's Spirit.* Zechariah looks forward in this verse to the age of the Holy Spirit. Concerning this blessed age several points are stressed:

1. The spirit is poured out. The same verb is used in Joel 2:28.[5] The fullness and abundance of the gift of the spirit is thus indicated.

2. It is God who pours out his spirit. Thus, the divine source of the outpouring is indicated.

3. The beneficiaries of the outpouring are listed next. The Spirit is to be poured out on *the house of David.* This seems to be a designation for the rulers of the people. The prophets always regarded the house of David as the lawful rulers of the nation. The spirit is also to be poured out on *the inhabitants of Jerusalem.* Here, as in Joel 2:28, it is the entire population and not just the royal family, the leadership, which receives this blessing. Wright observes that "Jerusalem is used as a designation for the whole people, and is pointed out as the place where the penitential sorrow was first to be manifested."[6]

The outpouring of the Spirit should not be limited to the Jews living in the physical city of Jerusalem. *Jerusalem* here represents the new

---

4. Wright, ZHP, p. 391.
5. See Ezek. 39:29; Isa. 44:3. Cf. Ezek. 36:26, 27.
6. Wright, ZHP, p. 384.

covenant people of God. *House of David* represents the leadership of that new covenant city. All who hold citizenship in that Jerusalem which is from above (Phil. 3:20; Gal. 4:26) have looked upon the pierced one and experienced penitential mourning.

4. The results of the outpouring are summed up in the words (1) grace and (2) supplication. That which is *poured out* is the *spirit of grace*. The convicting Spirit is a result of God's grace.[7] He also communicates God's grace to sinful men through the Word of God.

The message of grace leads guilty men to make supplication for pardon, hence the Spirit is called the *spirit of supplication*. The thought in the verse can be diagramed as follows:

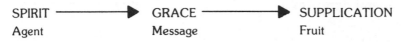

SPIRIT	→	GRACE	→	SUPPLICATION
Agent		Message		Fruit

B. The Looking. The words *they shall look unto me whom they have pierced* have occasioned no little dispute among commentators. Several points need exploration:

1. The *reason* for the looking. Men shall look to Messiah as a consequence of the outpouring of the spirit.

2. The *subject* of the looking. All commentators admit that the third person plural pronoun refers to the inhabitants of Jerusalem and the house of David upon whom the Spirit has been poured out.

3. The *nature* of the looking. The verb is *nabhat*. It signifies no ordinary look or passing glance. The verb connotes trusting hope and longing. The same verb is used in Numbers 21:9 where Israel was to look to the brazen serpent for salvation from physical death. Zechariah may be suggesting that the one upon whom Israel looked in the future would be an antitypical bronze serpent.

4. The *object* of the looking is indicated by a pronoun and a modifying clause: *unto me whom they have pierced.* The first person singular pronoun makes it clear that the object of the looking is deity.[8] The one who pours out the spirit is the one upon whom they look. At the very least this passage must have been taken to refer to "one who stood in an intimate connexion with Jahaveh."[9] Those who were truly perceptive may have recognized in this shift of pronouns a hint that Yahweh himself would be manifested in the flesh.

---

7. Moore (COZ, p. 197) takes the expression *spirit of grace* to mean, the spirit which awakens gracious affections in the hearts of men.

8. Whereas a few MSS have *him*, the first person pronoun has the support of all the ancient versions and the great majority of Hebrew MSS, including all the better ones.

9. Wright, ZHP, p. 386.

In John 19:37 the verse is given an interpretative paraphrase: They shall look *on him*. John has made an *application* of the prophecy in the light of fulfillment (as far as the piercing is concerned) to Jesus. John knew that in its Old Testament context the first person was used, and that the pronoun referred to Yahweh. But this Apostle believed that Jesus was the Word made flesh, the only begotten of the Father. As he witnessed that piercing of Christ he realized he was witnessing the fulfillment of the piercing aspect of this prophecy.

The deity upon whom they looked is said to have been pierced through (*daqar*). The verb means "to pierce" or "thrust through with spear or lance" (cf. 13:3), and points to the climax of the savior's sufferings. As God is here the speaker, this passage has always been a stumbling block to the Jews, for how could God experience piercing? Certainly the Jews had pierced the Lord through metaphorically by their rebellion and ingratitude throughout their history. They pierced him literally in the crucifixion.

The subject of the verb *pierced* is another third person plural pronoun. The natural antecedents of this pronoun are the phrases *the house of David* and *the inhabitants of Jerusalem*. Jewish commentators and some critics attempt to make the heathen who attack Jerusalem earlier in the passage the antecedent. According to this interpretation the mourning is over Jews who fell in the defense of their city. Thus: They (the house of David and inhabitants of Jerusalem) shall look upon him (fellow Jews) whom they (the heathen) have pierced. This interpretation reveals the desperation of the interpreters who are determined to eliminate any prediction of Messiah's death at the hands of his own people.

It was a Roman soldier who drove a spear through his side; Roman soldiers also pierced his brow with thorns, and his hands and feet with nails. But *responsibility* for the actions fell immediately upon the Jews (Acts 2:23) and ultimately upon all sinners. The Roman soldier was but a representative of all sinful men.

5. The *occasion* of the looking. Keil is no doubt correct when he says that the rejection and consequent crucifixion of the Lord is the event which is in view here. The Apostle John (19:37) applies the passage to the piercing of the Savior's side by the soldier after he was dead. Wright comments:

> The incident itself was . . . an illustration and example of what is here referred to. . . . The piercing of Christ's side with the lance was regarded

by St. John as the final act of indignity done to our Lord, as in fact the summing up of the rejection and death here darkly predicted.[10]

C. *The Mourning.* The looking upon the Pierced One results in great mourning. The mourners are identified by the third person masculine plural pronoun: *they shall mourn.* The reference is to those who (1) have looked upon the pierced one and (2) who have experienced the outpouring of God's spirit.

The object of the mourning is described by a third person masculine singular pronoun: they shall mourn over *him.* Baron comments on the significance of this pronoun:

> But just as the words 'they shall *look unto me,'* set forth the essential oneness of the Pierced One with Jehovah, so does the sudden transition in the same verse from the first person to the third, and the words, 'they shall mourn *for Him'* teach us that, as to His person, He is yet *distinct* from God.[11]

On the basis of this passage the Rabbis invented the concept of two Messiahs. Messiah ben Joseph would be born in poverty, would be acquainted with ills, would lose his life fighting for his people in the great contest against Gog and Magog. Messiah ben David, on the other hand, would be a mighty conqueror who would establish his kingdom and rule in it forever. This two-Messiah theory seems to have sprung up after the Christian era, in order to explain in some way the prophecies adduced by Christians in proof of the Messiahship of Jesus.[12]

The national mourning spoken of in this chapter was primarily fulfilled when the people who beheld the death of Jesus and the signs that followed smote their breasts in grief (Luke 23:48). A few days later many of those Jews were pricked in their hearts by Peter's sermon, as the Apostle painted a verbal picture of his death. Time and again throughout Christian history when men have been confronted with the crucifixion of Christ they have responded with heart-felt repentance. The depth and intensity of the mourning is indicated by two similes: (1) as for the mourning for an only son or (2) a firstborn son. Mourning for an only son was proverbial for the magnitude of grief.[13]

---

10. Wright, ZHP, pp. 387-388.
11. Baron, VPZ, pp. 447-448.
12. Wright, ZHP, p. 389.
13. Cf. Jer. 6:26; Amos 8:10. The terms *only son* and *firstborn* are prophetically appropriate to describe the one who was "the firstborn of all creation" (Col. 1:15) and the only begotten of the Father (John 1:14).

The remaining verses of chapter 12 underscore the extent of the mourning. It will be both universal and individual:

1. The mourning will be manifest both in Jerusalem and throughout the land.

2. The mourning in Jerusalem will be like that experienced when the beloved king Josiah was slain in the valley of Megiddo (v. 11).

3. The mourning would particularly affect the royal and priestly families, the house of David and the house of Levi. Wright observes:

> The prophet names specially the royal and priestly families in order to intimate that in the crime of the nation, in the murder of the great martyr, to which reference is made, these families should bear a part, and that they, therefore, should have a special share in the great penitential mourning.[14]

4. The mourning would reach into even the lowliest branches of the royal (*house of Nathan*)[15] and priestly (*house of Shimei*)[16] families.

5. The mourning would reach into the private quarters of the wives in these families.[17]

6. All the rest of the families of the land would also share in the mourning (v. 14).

The mourning over the Pierced One has a continuous fulfillment. The Book of Acts attests to the conversion of thousands of Jews in Jerusalem, Judea and the Roman Empire (Acts 21:20). Through the Gospel they had been awakened to a sense of guilt over their role in the crucifixion of their Messiah. Gentiles, however, as well as Jews were responsible for the death of Christ. They, no less than Jews, mourn over the one they have pierced when they see him verbally portrayed on the cross in the Gospel.

Prophecy No. 71

THE SMITTEN SHEPHERD

Zechariah 13:7

Chapter 13 continues to describe the changes which would characterize the Messianic age. For those penitent mourners who were described

---

14. Wright, ZHP, pp. 399-400. A number of priests (house of Levi) were among the earliest believers (Acts 6:4). Certain brothers of Jesus (house of David) were among the foremost believers after Pentecost.

15. See II Sam. 5:14 and Luke 3:31.

16. Shimei was the grandson of Levi. See Exod. 6:17; Num. 3:17, 18, 21.

17. Weeping women are mentioned prominently in the Passion narrative (Luke 23:27; John 19:25; 20:11; Mark 16:47).

in the closing verses of chapter 12, a fountain for cleansing will be opened. In that future age the old attraction to idolatry will not be in evidence. The very names of the idols would be cut off. False prophets filled with the unclean spirit would be removed from the land (v. 2). So great would be the commitment to pure doctrine that a man's parents would rise up against him should he try to prophesy in the name of some false god (v. 3). Those who had engaged in false prophecy would be ashamed of everything connected with the former life style, especially the lacerations which were part of pagan self-mutilation (vv. 4-6).

From the wounding of a false prophet in the house of his friends (13:6) Zechariah turns to one who would be treated like a false prophet. He would be smitten even unto death. His death would result, however, in the purification of a remnant and the punishment of the whole nation.

In 13:7 the Pierced One of 12:10 and the rejected Shepherd of chapter 11 are brought together. It is through the death of this special person that the new age of cleansing and consecration can be ushered in.

REJECTED SHEPHERD Ch. 11	PIERCED ONE 12:10	SMITTEN SHEPHERD 13:7
(1) Protective grace withdrawn—invasion by northern power. (2) Disunity of flock. (3) Poor of flock knew it was word of God.	Penitent mourning. Fountain of cleansing opened (13:1).	(1) Flock scattered. (2) 2/3 cut off. (3) 1/3 refined.

In chapter 11 the Good Shepherd assumed pastoral charge of the flock but was rejected by them. In chapter 12 the divine Shepherd of Israel was pierced through to the death. Were the purposes of God thus frustrated by the folly of man? The prediction in chapter 13 makes clear that the hand of God was in it all. He worked through the evil designs of men to accomplish his own divine purposes.

That Zechariah 13:7 is a Messianic prophecy is indicated by the following considerations:

1. The obvious connection between the rejected Shepherd of chapter 11, the Pierced One of 12:10 and the smiting of this Shepherd.

2. The language of the passage which points to a man who was God's equal.

3. The citation of part of the verse in Matthew 26:31, 32 in reference to the arrest of Christ by his enemies.

Translation of Zechariah 13:7

O sword, arouse yourself against My Shepherd even against the Man My equal (oracle of the Lord of hosts). Smite the shepherd and the flock will be scattered and I will cause my hand to return over the little ones.

Discussion

A. *The Call for the Smiting.* In the first half of the verse attention is focused on (1) the instrument, and (2) the instigator of the act of retribution herein described.

1. The instrument of retribution is a *sword.* This prophecy is not intended to portray the *manner* of Christ's death, but the *reason* for it. The term *sword* is symbolical. There are three dimensions to this symbolism. First, a sword symbolizes any kind of instrument which inflicts death.[18] Second, the sword is the symbol of judicial power. The taking of life is the ultimate power divinely bestowed upon the state. The sword was selected as the symbol for this, the ultimate judicial function (cf. Rom. 13:4). Finally, the sword is the symbol of divine wrath. The prediction, then, asserts that the Shepherd (1) would die (2) a judicial death (3) by means of the sword of divine wrath.

It is not the sword of Caiaphas which is being addressed, nor the sword of the priests, nor Pilate, nor the Romans, but the sword of righteous retribution for the sins of the world. Moore comments:

> The sheep had deserved the blow, but the shepherd bares his own bosom to the sword, and is wounded for the sins of his people, and bears those sins in his own body on the tree. The vicarous nature of the atonement is therefore distinctly involved in this passage.[19]

In this passage the sword is personified (cf. Jer. 47:6, 7). It is called upon to rouse itself to execute divine justice.

2. The instigator of the retribution is the Lord. The imperative shows that it is God's will being exercised. The crucifixion of Christ to which this prophecy refers, results from the determinate counsel and foreknowledge of God (Acts 2:23) as well as the malice of men. God was making his soul "an offering for sin" (Isa. 53).

---

18. Cf. Exod. 5:21: II Sam. 12:9: Isa. 27:1
19. Moore, COZ, p. 213.

B. The Victim of this Smiting. The sword of divine justice does not fall upon the wicked, but upon one who stands in the closest possible relationship to Yahweh. The Shepherd who is smitten here is the same as the Lamb of God who is pierced through for transgressions in Isaiah 53. The victim is here described three ways:

1. He is called *my shepherd.* This is not the foolish shepherd of 11:15-17, nor the wicked shepherds who would oppress Israel (11:5). This is the Shepherd of Yahweh who was impersonated by Zechariah in chapter 11. He is called *my* shepherd, for he is specially called and appointed by Yahweh to this office. He is in the fullest sense the representative of Yahweh, in and through whom the shepherd relationship between God and Israel reaches its climax.

2. He is the man (*gever*). The word signifies man *par excellence.* This is the man (*gever*) encompassed by a woman in Jeremiah 31:22. The humanity of Messiah is thus indicated. He was to be a man with all the human sympathies and emotions.

3. He is *my fellow* ('*amiti*). The word occurs only here and in Leviticus where it is usually rendered *neighbor.* It implies one united to another by possession of common nature, rights and privileges.[20] No owner of a flock would call a hireling his '*amit.* It is not likely that God would apply this epithet even to the most godly among men whom he might appoint as shepherd over the nation. Only one man could be denominated God's equal, and that is Messiah.

C. The Results of the Smiting. Two results follow upon the smiting of the Shepherd:

1. The scattering of the sheep. The sheep are the Jewish people, who rejected him as Shepherd. The dispersion of the Jews and their denationalization were results of the smiting of the Shepherd. Even the *poor of the flock* (11:11), the apostles and close followers, initially fled away from the cross. It was to the dispersion of the disciples after his arrest that Jesus himself applied this prophecy in Matthew 26:31.

2. The gathering of the little ones. The sheep may be scattered; but mercy was reserved for a portion of the flock. "The Lord would *turn back his hand*,[21] outstretched in anger against the flock considered as a whole, in love and chastening grace upon the lowly and the humble."[22] It is not without significance that Jesus referred to his disciples as the *little flock* (Luke 12:32). Collins remarks:

---

20. Deane, PC, Minor Prophets, III, 148.

21. Unger (UBCZ, pp. 233-234) denies that this idiom is ever used in the positive sense of protection.

22. Wright, ZHP, p. 441.

The Shepherd was smitten as the substitute of the flock, and for His sake the scattered sheep were to be re-gathered and lovingly protected by the very hand that had wielded the sword against the Shepherd.[23]

The regathering began when Jesus met with his disciples in Galilee following the resurrection (Matt. 26:32; Mark 14:28). The Great Commission sent those disciples forth on a mission to assemble, by the preaching of the Gospel, the scattered sheep of Israel and the other sheep which were not of that fold.

The remaining verses of chapter 13 further depict the results of the smiting of the Shepherd. Two-thirds[24] (lit., a double portion)[25] of those who live *in the land* of Israel would be *cut off* from the Shepherd and thus would die (v. 8). The reference is, no doubt, to those who rejected the claims of Messiah. Upon that generation of Jews who so callously rejected the claims of Christ and so forcefully embraced Caesar, wrath came to the uttermost (I Thess. 2:16). Over a million, one hundred thousand Jews died in the siege of Jerusalem by Titus. Another six hundred thousand perished in the revolt by Bar Cochba not long after. The whole land of Judea was reduced to a desert.

The third[26] which embraced the smiting—Jewish believers—would pass through the purifying fires of persecution. In their distress they would call on God, and God would respond (v. 9). The Israel of God, assembled under Gospel preaching, enjoyed all the privileges of the Old Covenant Israel and more.

---

23. Collins, NBC, p. 761.

24. In Ezek. 5:12 the nation is also divided into three parts which would suffer judgment.

25. The vocabularly of inheritance. Death claims two-thirds of the inheritance claimed by the Shepherd. Cf. II Sam. 8:2 where David executed two-thirds of the captive Moabites.

26. The expression is symbolic of *a few*; it does not describe the exact proportion of the remnant that would escape.

Chapter Thirty-One

MALACHI AND THE MESSIAH

The last Old Testament prophet appeared upon the scene about 432 B.C. The relationship between his ministry and that of Ezra and Nehemiah cannot precisely be determined. Malachi has been called the prophet of debate because of his style of (1) making accusations, (2) placing imaginary objections in the mouths of his audience, and then (3) answering those objections.

Two personal Messianic prophecies are found in the final book of the Old Testament. He appears here as (1) the messenger of the covenant and (2) the Sun of Righteousness.

Prophecy No. 72

THE MESSENGER OF THE COVENANT

Malachi 3:1

In 2:17 Malachi leveled this accusation at his audience: *You have wearied the Lord with your words!* What words? The age-old complaint that the Lord seems to smile upon those who do evil. The people of Judea apparently regarded material prosperity as proof positive of divine favor. The people are then said to ask, *Where is the God of judgment?* Either evil was pleasing to God or there is no God of justice.

Translation of Malachi 3:1-4

(1) Behold, I am about to send my messenger and he shall prepare a way before me. Then suddenly he shall come unto his Temple, the Lord whom you are seeking; the Messenger of the Covenant whom you are desiring, behold he comes, says the LORD of hosts. (2) But who can endure the day of his coming? Who can stand when he appears? For he will be like the fire of a refiner and like soap of a launderer. (3) And he will sit as a refiner and purifier of silver; he will purify the sons of Levi and refine them like gold and silver. Then the LORD will have those who bring an offering in righteousness. (4) Then the offering of Judah and Jerusalem shall be acceptable to the LORD as in days of old, as in former years.

Discussion

Three points are emphasized in this prediction: (1) the preparation for his coming; (2) the promise of his coming; and (3) the purpose of his coming.

A. The Preparation for his Coming (v. 1a). In two ways verse 1 points to the preparation which would be made for the advent of Messiah, by (1) the announcement of God, and (2) the actions of a messenger.

1. The announcement by God: Behold! *I am about to send my messenger.* This announcement is viewed as startling and unexpected for it is introduced with *behold*. Literally the text reads, *Behold me*, i.e., here I am, about to send my messenger.

This announcement pertains to a divine action. The use of the present participle—*am sending*—"indicates that something is being set in motion that will keep on going without interruption until it is accomplished."[1] The divine plan was already in motion. The coming of the Lord was imminent.

The announcement is that one called "my messenger"[2] is being sent in advance of the coming of the Lord. The word *messenger* may be translated *angel*, but it is not likely that a celestial messenger is intended. Prophets were messengers of God (cf. I Sam. 2:27ff.; Haggai 1:13), and priests as well (Mal. 2:7).

Who is this special messenger? Malachi does not say who he is, where he is from, nor when he will come. This prophecy, however, seems to be a further development of the prediction in Isaiah 40:3-5 of one who would prepare the way of the Lord. This passage may also be linked to Malachi 4:5 which indicates that Elijah would come before the day of the Lord. Fortunately these three related passages are explained in the New Testament. The Gospel writers affirm that John the Baptist is the messenger of Isaiah and the Elijah of Malachi (Matt. 3:1-3; Mark 1:3; Luke 3:4). John himself used the language of Isaiah to identify himself as the voice in the wilderness (John 1:19-23). Before his birth, an angel announced to his father that John would go before the Lord in the spirit and power of Elijah (Luke 1:17, 76). Jesus identified John as the Elijah who would come (Matt. 11:14; 17:12f.). From all of this it is clear that John the Baptist was the fulfillment of the promise of a preparatory messenger.

2. The action of the messenger. He would prepare the way before the Lord. Messengers ran before dignitaries to alert villages along the travel route of their approach. Every obstacle—holes in the road, rocks, trees—had to be removed (cf. Isa. 40:3-5).[3] Every care was

---

1. Delaughter, MMDL, p. 106.
2. The name Malachi means "my messenger."
3. The verb *pinnah* means, to turn away, turn aside, put out of the way, thus remove or clear.

exercised to see that the coming one was greeted with a reception befitting his station. The higher the position of the dignitary, the more illustrious the messenger who preceded him.

The mission of John was to prepare the way before the speaker—*me*—God himself. As befitting the ultimate concerns of that Coming One, John's preparation was moral and spiritual in nature. Repentance is the road which leads men to God and allows him to come to men. John preached repentance and introduced a baptism of repentance. When the Messiah appeared, John presented him to his people.

B. *The Promise of his Coming* (v. 1b). The skeptics of Malachi's day were asking, Where is the God of judgment? God now responds, He is nearer than you might think. Even though a messenger is sent to prepare the way for this one who comes, his coming is still unexpected. He would *suddenly* come. Baldwin points out that suddenness was usually associated with a calamitous event, and hence the word here is ominous.[4] The announcement of his birth and that of his forerunner were unexpected. Herod the Great was surprised and disturbed when the wise men came seeking a new-born king (Matt. 2:3). Christ's appearance at the Jordan was also unexpected.

Three clues are given with regard to the identity of the Coming One in verse 1.

1. He is *the Lord* (*ha-'adon*). This title emphasizes the Lordship of God. He owns the world and is its boss.

2. He is the one they were seeking. They were seeking the God of judgment (2:17). His coming, then, would meet the challenge of the cynics to do something about the injustice in the world. Believers as well as skeptics, however, longed for the coming of this one. He was the focal point of all the hopes and aspirations of Old Testament saints.

3. He is the rightful owner of the Temple, for he comes to *his Temple*. This again points to the deity of the Coming One. Some (e.g., Laetsch) take the term Temple to be a symbol for the people of God; others think the physical Temple is intended. Perhaps both are involved. The physical Temple was but a type of the true Temple, the congregation of believers. Jesus was presented in the Temple when he was an infant (Luke 2:22ff.), he visited the Temple at age twelve (Luke 2:41ff.) and several times during his ministry.[5]

4. He is *the messenger of the covenant*. This title appears only here.

---

4. Baldwin, TOTC, p. 243.
5. Luke 20:1; John 2:13; 5:1ff.; 7:14ff.

It harks back to the angelophanies (Christophanies?) of earlier times.[6] New Testament authority identifies the messenger of the covenant as Jesus Christ.[7]

Of which covenant is Messiah messenger? Keil thinks that the reference is to the old covenant. Most seem to think that the new covenant is intended. Packard thinks that Messiah was to be messenger of both old and new covenants. Just as the angel of the Lord was instrumental in establishing the Mosaic covenant (Exod. 3:2; cf. Isa. 63:9), so he would be needed also to institute the new covenant (Jer. 31:31; Ezek. 37:26).[8] This verse may also contain a reference to the covenant with Levi (2:4, 8) which the priestly "messengers" had failed to observe. The future Messenger would establish a new covenant and a new priesthood.[9]

5. He is the one in whom the people delight. Is this a statement of fact alluding to the persistent hope and expectation of the Old Testament saints? or is this said sarcastically? They professed to delight in the coming of Messiah, but in reality, they were only going through the motions. Even if they were sincerely anticipating him it is clear that they had the wrong concept of his coming.

One fact is clear: Messiah was coming! The certainty of his coming is underscored by the second use of *behold* in the verse. Ready or not, he *was* coming.

C. *The Purpose of his Coming* (vv. 2-4). The Messiah, according to this passage, comes for two reasons: (1) to purify, and (2) to punish.

1. Purification. Malachi's audience expected the Lord to come to judge the heathen. By means of an ominous question (*who can endure the day?*) the prophet warns that Jews too will undergo a searching ordeal. The second question, *Who can stand?*, is borrowed from battle imagery[10] and means, who will stand his ground? "The prophet suggests that no one will pass the penetrating tests which the Lord will impose."[11]

Some consolation could be taken from the two similes which are used to describe the work of Messiah when he comes. He is likened to (1) the fire of a refiner[12] and (2) the soap of a launderer. His work

---

6. Gen. 16:7; Exod. 3:2f.; 23:20-23; Judg. 6:11ff.; 13:21-22.
7. Heb. 8:7-11; 12:24; 13:20; Matt. 26:28.
8. Baldwin, TOTC, p. 243.
9. Wolf, HM, p. 99.
10. II Kings 10:4; Amos 2:15.
11. Baldwin, TOTC, p. 243.
12. Cf. Zech. 13:9. Other Scriptures referring to this refining process: Isa. 1:21-27; 4:2-7; Jer. 9:7; Matt. 3:10-12; I Cor. 3:13-15.

then is to refine and purify. These similes indicate that the judgment process was not designed for total destruction. The dross of sin will be burned out and the filth washed away.

In verse 3 Malachi picks up his first metaphor and develops it and applies it specifically to the *sons of Levi*. Messiah *will sit as a refiner*, i.e., he will carry out the process with precision and care. "The Lord exercises a watchful eye, pours in his tears of love, and performs the work with a steady hand. The fires are not permitted to become too hot nor is the process left incomplete."[13] The words *refiner* and *purifier* in this verse are participles which suggest that the work goes on continually. The priests had been largely responsible for the apathy and cynicism which gripped the nation in the fifth century B.C. These priests regarded Temple service as despicable (Mal. 1:7, 10, 12). They could hardly look forward to the coming of the Master. Cleansing would begin at the house of God.

One thinks naturally of the double cleansing of the Temple. Jesus aimed much of his teaching at the religious leaders of his day. Finally, the old Levitical priesthood was replaced by the priesthood of believers. Only Aaronic priests who submitted to the authority of the high priest after the order of Melchizedek could qualify for priestly service under the new covenant (Acts 6:7).

The cleansed New Testament priesthood would present before the Lord *offerings in righteousness*. The idea here is that the worship in the Messianic age would flow from humble and righteous hearts.[14] The Lord will delight in the worship of the New Covenant Judah and Jerusalem as he did the worship in the days of Moses.[15]

The prophet does not necessarily expect that the Mosaic ritual is to last for ever. Malachi uses terms with which the Jews were conversant to express the worship of the new covenant. In the New Testament church foreseen by Malachi there is no special priestly caste. Every believer is a royal priest (I Peter 2:5, 9) who is capable of offering up spiritual sacrifices to God (Phil. 4:18).

2. Punishment. Messiah comes also to judge the wicked. He will bear witness against the evil doers by bringing judgment upon them (v. 5).

The prophecy closes with an assurance that the things here predicted will surely come to pass. God does not change; he is true to

---

13. Delaughter, MMDL, p. 111.

14. Others take *offerings in righteousness* to refer to the unblemished condition of the sacrificial animal.

15. The ancient days could also refer to the age of David and Solomon.

his word. The very survival of the descendants of Jacob proves that God keeps his promises. The implication, then, is that God's promises about the coming Messiah would also be honored, Christians bear testimony to the world that God did keep those promises (v. 6).

Prophecy No. 73

THE SUN OF RIGHTEOUSNESS

Malachi 4:2

In the closing section of his book Malachi addresses two very different groups of people. He speaks first to those who had become cynical about service to God. They no longer believed that it paid to serve God (3:13-15). A second group, the believers, encouraged one another in those skeptical days. Malachi reminds them that God has taken note of them and will have compassion upon them in the day of judgment (3:16, 17). In that day the advantages of being a child of God would be obvious to everyone (3:18) for the wicked would be totally consumed in the judgment fires.

Is the expression *Sun of Righteousness* in 4:2 a Messianic title? Some see here only a figure of speech for the righteousness of Yahweh. His righteousness will shine like the sun in some future day. There are, however, good reasons for regarding the expression as a personal Messianic title:

1. The Messiah is the star out of Jacob in Numbers 24:17.
2. Messiah is called a great light (Isa. 9:2) and a light to the Gentiles (Isa. 42:6; 49:6).
3. Messiah is called the Lord our righteousness (Jer. 23:6).
4. When Zacharias prophesied concerning his son John he tied together Malachi 4:2 and Isaiah 9:2.

> And you, child, shall be called the prophet of the Highest, for you shall go before the face of the Lord to prepare his ways. To give knowledge of salvation unto his people by the remission of their sins, through the tender mercy of our God; whereby the dayspring from on high hath visited us, to give light to them that sit in darkness and in the shadow of death, to guide our feet into the way of peace (Luke 1:76-79).

Verse 76 is an obvious allusion to Malachi 3:1. Furthermore, the angel cited the book of Malachi in his prior description of the mission of Zacharias' son (Luke 1:17). This makes it likely that the *dayspring*

465

from on high in Luke 1:78 is Zacharias' allusion to the Sun of Righteousness.

5. Other New Testament passages seem to be based on the sun image:

> Wherefore he says, Awake you sleeper, and arise from the dead, and Christ shall give you light (Eph. 5:14).

> We have also a more sure word of prophecy whereunto you do well that you take heed, as unto a light that shines in a dark place, until the day dawns, and the day star arise in your hearts (II Peter 1:19).

> And the city had no need of the sun, neither of the moon, to shine in it, for the glory of God illuminated it, and the Lamb is the light thereof (Rev. 21:23).

Translation of Malachi 4:2

But to you who fear my name the Sun of Righteousness shall rise with healing in its wings. And you shall go out and leap like calves of the stall.

Discussion

With regard to the manner of Messiah's work the passage is suggestive. The sun image suggests quiet permeation, impartiality, and universality. The beneficiaries of Messiah's work are *You who fear my name.* The blessing which is provided by the Sun of Righteousness is designated as being the possession of those who fear and reverently worship the name of Yahweh.

The objective of Messiah's word is summed up in the word *righteousness.* He is coming to make possible the right relationship between God and man and between man and his brother. The dark night of oppression, violence, and hatred will give way to a new day which can be characterized by the word *righteousness.*

The Sun of Righteousness would provide healing, for it rises with *healing in its wings.*[16] The rays of this Sun would radiate healing for broken hearts and perplexed minds. Just as the sun awakens nature to new life each spring, even so would the Sun of Righteousness awaken the righteous to new life.

---

16. The figure of the winged sun may have been suggested to the prophet by the winged solar disc of Egypt, Babylon, Assyrian and Persia.

The rise of the Sun of Righteousness will inaugurate a new day for the people of God.[17] It will mean a day of joyous freedom. The righteous will break into life and energy like young calves leaping from the dark pen into early morning sunshine. By this happy figure Malachi is suggesting that God's people will experience freedom after oppression, joy after gloom and vigor after vicissitudes.

It will mean a day of victory over oppression. The wicked, reduced to ashes by the burning judgment, shall be trampled under foot. The oppressed will be victorious over the oppressors.

---

17. Although not mentioned in verse 1, the sun may be there in the mind of the prophet as the symbol of the blazing fire that brings destruction to the wicked.

Appendix I

JEWISH MESSIANIC EXPECTATION IN THE APOCRYPHA AND PSEUDEPIGRAPHA

SOURCE	APPROX. DATE	SUMMARY
Sibylline Oracles 3:652	140 B.C.	A king from the sunrise sent by God to bring peace to every land.
Enoch 88-90	135-106 B.C.	In a symbolic portrayal of the history and destiny of the chosen people, a white bullock is generally thought to denote the Messiah.
I Maccabees 14:41	110 B.C.	May be a hint of Messianic hope in the reference to the coming of the "faithful prophet."
Testaments of the Twelve	109-106 B.C.	Messiah is descended from Levi, and is a priest (Reuben 6:7-12; Levi 8:14; 18; Judah 24:1ff.), and from Judah (Judah 24:5f.; Naphtali 4:5). He is sinless with power over evil spirits. He brings sin to an end.
Enoch 37-71	94-64 B.C.	Messiah is pre-existent Son of Man, judge, ruler, champion, and revealer. Besides "Son of Man" he is called "the elect One" and "the righteous." "Messiah" or "His Anointed" occurs in 48:10 and 52:4.
Psalms of Solomon esp. 17, 18	60 B.C.	Full and clear evidence of the idea of Messiah. He is Davidic, endowed with power from God. He is to conquer the nations and purge Jerusalem of sin. Called "His Anointed" and "the Lord's Anointed."
Sibylline Oracles 3:46-50	50 B.C.	A "holy prince" who is to reign over the whole earth for all ages. Judgment follows.
IV Esdras 7:27ff.; 12:32; Ch. 13	50 B.C.	Messiah comes from the sea, flying with the clouds of heaven; yet he is the anointed one, the seed of David, "My Son, the Man." He executes vengeance on God's enemies, gathers dispersed of Israel, rules for 400 years. Then Messiah and all flesh dies. This is followed by the general resurrection, judgment, and a new world.

JEWISH MESSIANIC EXPECTATION IN THE
APOCRYPHA AND PSEUDEPIGRAPHA

SOURCE	APPROX. DATE	SUMMARY
Zadokite Fragment	18-8 B.C.	A "Teacher of righteousness" has already appeared (1:7) and a Messiah is expected (2:10; 8:2; 9:10, 29; 15:4; 18:8) who is to arise "from Aaron and Israel."
Apoc. of Baruch 29f.	Before A.D. 70	Messiah is revealed mysteriously from heaven whither he returns in glory. He has a passive role. Materialistic concept.
Apoc. of Baruch 39f.; 72ff.	Before A.D. 70	Messiah is the warrior slaying his enemies and ruling over Gentiles. Influence of Isaiah 11 is marked.
Apoc. of Baruch 70:9	Before A.D. 70	The phrase "my servant Messiah" is used.
Sibylline Oracles 5:108	A.D. 130	A king sent by God who destroys Antichrist.
Sibylline Oracles 5:414ff.	A.D. 130	A "blessed man" from the plains of heaven destroys evil-doers and sets up a new Temple.

Appendix II

MESSIANIC PRETENDERS

Information gleaned from the articles under the caption "Messiah, Pseudo" in McClintock and Strong, *Cyclopedia*, and in Hastings, *Encyclopedia of Religion and Ethics*.

NAME	DATE A.D.	LOCATION	NOTES
1. Theudas	44	Palestine	Slaughtered by Romans when he gathered his followers to attempt to divide the Jordan. Cut off his head and carried it to Jerusalem. *Ant.* XX.v.1; Acts 5:36.
2. The Egyptian	1st cent.	Palestine	Gathered 30,000 on Mt. of Olives with promise he would command the walls of Jerusalem to fall. He was slaughtered by the Romans. *Ant.* XX.viii.6 *Wars* II.xiii.5; Acts 21:38.
3. Anonymous	1st cent.	Palestine	Slain by Festus when he was preparing to lead his followers into the wilderness. *Ant.* XX.viii.10
4. Menachem	1st cent.	Palestine	Seized Masada; captured Jerusalem from Agrippa; assassinated by his followers.
5. Simon Magus	1st cent.	Palestine	Samaritan. Converted to Christianity.
6. Dositheus	1st cent.	Palestine	Founded a Samaritan sect which lasted until the sixth cent.
7. Bar Cochba	2nd cent.	Palestine	Called Messiah by R. Akiba. Commanded an army of 500,000. After some fifty campaigns he was killed in battle.
8. Moses Cretensis	434	Crete	Promised to lead followers dryshod to main land. Many who hurled themselves into the sea drown.
9. Dunaan	520	Arabia Felix	Called himself the son of Moses. Oppressed Christians. Taken prisoner and executed by an Ethiopian general.

NAME	DATE A.D.	LOCATION	NOTES
10. Julian	529	Palestine	Jews and Samaritans acknowledged him as king. Crushed by emperor Justinian.
11. Isaac ben Yakub Abu Isa	7th cent.	Isfahan	Sudden cure from leprosy was his call. Killed in battle with the Khalif.
12. Yudghan	8th cent.	Hamadan	Called "the Shepherd." Follower of Abu Isa. Claimed to be a Prophet, that he would return from dead.
13. Serenus	720	Syria	Promised to restore Jews to Holy Land. Influence spread as far as Spain. When arrested by the Khalif he renounced his claims as a joke.
14. Anonymous	1137	France	He and followers put to death.
15. Anonymous	1138	Persia	Vast army. Killed by Persians. His followers shamefully treated.
16. Anonymous	1157	Spain	Resulted in destruction of nearly all Jews in Spain.
17. David Alroy	1160	Persia	Practiced magic. Large following. Promised to lead Jews to promised land. Killed by his father (?).
18. Anonymous Arabian	1172	Yemen	Pretended to work miracles. Beheaded at his own request. His return to life was to prove his claims.
19. Anonymous	1173	Beyond the Euphrates	Claimed to have been healed of leprosy in one night.
20. Anonymous	1174	Persia	A magician who seduced many common people and brought the Jews much tribulation.
21. David Almasser	1176	Moravia	Pretended he could make himself invisible. Taken, put to death. Heavy fine put on Jews.

MESSIANIC PRETENDERS

NAME	DATE A.D.	LOCATION	NOTES
22. David el-David	1199	Persia	Learned man, great magician. Raised an army, captured, escaped, recaptured and beheaded. Many followers were butchered.
23. Abraham ben Samuel Abulafia	1285	Sicily	Attempted to convert the pope to Judaism. Imprisonment and miraculous escape. Millennium to begin in 1290. Disappeared from history.
24. Joseph Jikatilla	13th cent.	Medinaceli	Disciple of Abulalia
25. Samuel	13th cent.	Medinaceli	Disciple of Abulalia
26. Nissim ben Abraham	13th cent.	Avila	Proclaimed 1295 as beginning of Millennium. Mystic crosses appeared on garments of his followers on appointed day and they converted to Christianity.
27. Moses Botarel	14th cent.	Cisneros	Little impact.
28. Asher Lammlein	1502	Istria	Messiah to appear that year if people would prepare themselves. Fasting, prayer and alms giving practiced by Jew and Christian alike. Prophet disappeared.
29. Jacob Carson	14th cent.	Spain	Little impact.
30. David Reubeni	1524-25	Arabia	Jewish ambassador at the court of the relentless Jewish persecutor John III of Portugal. Jews attributed to him miraculous powers. Travelled widely in Spain and Italy. Died in Inquisition.
31. Solomon Molkho	1525-32	Portugal Turkey	Abandoned Christianity under influence of Reubeni. His disciples regarded him as divine. Foretold Messiah in 1540. Hailed as prophet by pope and Jews. Later executed in Inquisition.

NAME	DATE A.D.	LOCATION	NOTES
32. Isaac ben Solomon Ashkenzal Luria	1534-72	Safed	Founder of kabbala. Ascetic and mystic. Regarded himself as forerunner of Messiah.
33. Hayyim Vital Calabrese	1543-1620	Safed	Disciple of Luria. Claimed to be Messiah ben Joseph, precursor of Messiah ben David.
34. Abraham Shalom	1574		Claimed to be Messiah ben David. Rival of Vital.
35. Shabbathai Sebi	1621-1676	Smyrna, Constant.	Most influencial of all pseudo-Messiahs. Kabbalists expected Messiah in 1648. Proved he was Messiah by uttering the Name of God. Called king of kings. Tribute poured in to Smyrna. Embraced Muhammadanism to save his life, thereby lost his influence in Jewry.
36. Anony-mous	1615	East Indies	Followed by Portuguese Jews who were scattered over that country.
37. Anony-mous	1624	Low Countries	Declared himself to be Messiah of the family of David of the line of Nathan. Promised to destroy Rome, and to overthrow the kingdom of Antichrist and the Turkish empire.
38. Nehemiah ha-Kohen		Constan-tinople	Posed as forerunner of Messiah. Refused to endorse Messianic claims of Shabbathai; denounced him as a traitor to the Sultan. Converted to Muhammadanism.
39. Jacob Querido	17th cent.		Brother of Shabbathai's fourth wife. Taught that world had to become totally evil before the Millennium. Practiced licentious-ness.
40. Berehiah	1695-1740		Son of Querido.

MESSIANIC PRETENDERS

NAME	DATE A.D.	LOCATION	NOTES
41. Miguel Cardoso	1630- 1706		Prophets of Shabbathai who attempted to step into his place when he died.
42. Mordecai Mokiah	1682		
43. Lobele Prossnitz	d. 1750	Germany, Austria	
44. Judah Hasid	18th cent.	Europe	Led a group of followers to Jerusalem, but died shortly after arriving.
45. Ari Shocher	1850	Yemen	Bedouins attracted by his miracles. Lived in princely style. Assassinated. Said to have appeared in another form after his death.
46. Jekuthiel	1870	Germany	A letter announced to a German synagogue that he was about to assume his throne as Messiah. Would enter Berlin to punish Jews who refused to believe. Never showed up.

Appendix III
SUMMARY OF PERSONAL MESSIANIC PROPHECY

No.	Reference	Speaker	Form	Vss.	Approx. Date B.C.
1.	Genesis 3:15	God	Curse	1	?
2.	Genesis 9:26-27	Noah	Patriarchal Blessing	2	?
3.	Genesis 12:3; 18:18; 22:18; 26:4; 28:14	God	Blessings	5	2000
4.	Genesis 49:10-12	Jacob	Patriarchal Blessing	3	1860
5.	Numbers 24:16-24	Balaam	Oracle	9	1407
6.	Deuteronomy 18:15, 18	Moses	Discourse	2	1407
7.	Deuteronomy 32:43	God	Song	1	1407
8.	I Samuel 2:10	Hannah	Prayer/Hymn	1	1075
9.	I Samuel 2:35-36	Man of God/God	Oracle	2	1065
10.	II Samuel 7:12-16	Nathan/God	Oracle	5	1000
11.	Psalm 89	Ethan	Psalm	51	930
12.	Psalm 132	Anonymous	Psalm	8	960
13.	Psalm 8	David	Psalm	4	1000
14.	Psalm 40	David/Christ	Psalm	17	1000
15.	Psalm 118	David/Christ	Psalm	24	1000
16.	Psalm 78:1-2	God	Psalm	2	1000

475

SUMMARY OF PERSONAL MESSIANIC PROPHECY

No.	Reference	Speaker	Form	Vss.	Approx. Date B.C.
17.	Psalm 69	Messiah/Asaph	Psalm	36	1000
18.	Psalm 109	David/Christ	Psalm	30	1000
19.	Psalm 22	David/Christ	Psalm	31	1000
20.	Psalm 2	David	Psalm	12	1000
21.	Psalm 16	David/Christ	Psalm	11	1000
22.	Psalm 102	Anonymous/Christ	Psalm	27	580
23.	Psalm 45	Sons of Korah	Psalm	17	950
24.	Psalm 110	David	Psalm	7	1000
25.	Psalm 72	Solomon	Psalm	19	950
26.	Psalm 68	David	Psalm	23	1000
27.	Job 9:33; 16:19-21; 17:3; 33:23-28	Job/Elihu	Discourse	11	?
28.	Job 19:23-27	Job	Discourse	5	?
29.	Joel 2:23	Joel/God	Oracle	5	830
30.	Hosea 1:10—2:1	Hosea	Oracle	3	750
31.	Hosea 3:5	Hosea	Oracle	1	750
32.	Hosea 11:1	Hosea/God	Oracle	1	750
33.	Isaiah 4:2-6	Isaiah	Oracle	6	734

SUMMARY OF PERSONAL MESSIANIC PROPHECY

No.	Reference	Speaker	Form	Vss.	Approx. Date B.C.
34.	Isaiah 7:14-16	Isaiah	Oracle	3	734
35.	Isaiah 8:17-18	Isaiah/Messiah	Oracle	2	734
36.	Isaiah 9:1-7	Isaiah	Oracle	7	734
37.	Isaiah 11:1-16	Isaiah	Oracle	16	734
38.	Isaiah 16:5	Isaiah	Oracle	5	701
39.	Isaiah 28:16	Isaiah	Oracle	1	701
40.	Isaiah 30:19-26	Isaiah	Oracle	7	701
41.	Isaiah 32:1-2	Isaiah	Oracle	2	701
42.	Isaiah 33:17	God	Oracle	1	701
43.	Isaiah 42:1-17	Isaiah/God	Oracle	17	690
44.	Isaiah 49:1-13	Isaiah/Messiah	Oracle	13	690
45.	Isaiah 50:4-11	Isaiah/Messiah	Oracle	8	690
46.	Isaiah 52:13—53:12	Isaiah	Oracle	15	690
47.	Isaiah 55:3-5	Isaiah/God	Oracle	3	690
( )	Isaiah 59:20-21	Isaiah/God	Oracle	2	690
48.	Isaiah 61:1-11	Isaiah/Messiah	Oracle	11	690
49.	Micah 2:12-13	Micah/God	Oracle	2	700
50.	Micah 5:1-5	Micah	Oracle	5	700
51.	Habakkuk 3:12-15	Habakkuk	Oracle	4	615
52.	Jeremiah 23:5-6	Jeremiah	Oracle	2	595

SUMMARY OF PERSONAL MESSIANIC PROPHECY

No.	Reference	Speaker	Form	Vss.	Approx. Date B.C.
53.	Jeremiah 30:9, 21	Jeremiah	Oracle	2	588
54.	Jeremiah 31:21-22	Jeremiah	Oracle	2	588
55.	Jeremiah 33:14-26	Jeremiah/God	Oracle	13	588
56.	Ezekiel 17:22-24	Ezekiel/God	Oracle	3	591
57.	Ezekiel 21:25-27	Ezekiel/God	Oracle	3	590
58.	Ezekiel 34:23-31	Ezekiel/God	Oracle	9	585
59.	Ezekiel 37:21-28	Ezekiel/God	Oracle	8	585
60.	Ezekiel 44-48	Angel	Vision	19	572
61.	Daniel 7:13-14	Daniel	Vision	2	541
62.	Daniel 9:24-27	Gabriel	Discourse	4	538
63.	Haggai 2:6-9	Haggai/God	Oracle	4	520
64.	Haggai 2:21-23	Haggai/God	Oracle	3	520
65.	Zechariah 3:8-10	Zechariah/God	Oracle	3	519
66.	Zechariah 6:12-13	Zechariah/God	Oracle	2	519
67.	Zechariah 9:9-11	Zechariah/God	Oracle	3	515
68.	Zechariah 10:3-4	Zechariah	Oracle	1	515
69.	Zechariah 11:4-14	Zechariah/God	Action Parable	11	515
70.	Zechariah 12:10	Zechariah/God	Oracle	1	515
71.	Zechariah 13:7	Zechariah/God	Oracle	1	515
72.	Malachi 3:1	Malachi/God	Oracle	1	432
73.	Malachi 4:2	Malachi/God	Oracle	1	432

Appendix IV

OLD TESTAMENT NAMES, TITLES AND EPITHETS FOR THE MESSIAH

*A name or title taken directly from Scripture. Scriptures cited for each name are not exhaustive.

1. Advocate* (Job 16:19)
2. Angel* (Messenger) (Job 33:23)
3. Anointed* (I Sam. 2:19; Ps. 2:2)
4. Battle-bow* (Zech. 10:4)
5. Bethlehem's Ruler (Mic. 5:2)
6. Breaker* (Mic. 2:13)
7. Commander* (Isa. 55:4)
8. Cornerstone* (Ps. 118:22; Isa. 28:16)
9. Covenant of the People* (Isa. 42:6)
10. Crusher (Gen. 3:15)
11. David* (Hosea 3:5; Jer. 30:9)
12. Desire of all Nations (Hag. 2:7)
13. Eternal One (Ps. 102:25-27)
14. Eternal Priest (Ps. 110:4)
15. Everlasting Father* (Isa. 9:6)
16. Faithful Priest* (I Sam. 2:35)
17. Firstborn* (Ps. 89:27)
18. Forsaken Sufferer (Ps. 22)
19. Foundation* (Isa. 28:16; Zech. 10:4)
20. God* (Ps. 45:6, 7)
21. Head* (Hosea 1:11; Mic. 2:13)
22. Healer (Isa. 42:7)
23. He who Comes* (Ps. 118:26)
24. Horn of David* (Ps. 132:17)
25. Immanuel* (Isa. 7:14)
26. Interpreter* (Job 33:23)
27. Israel* (Hosea 11:1; Isa. 49:3)
28. King* (Ps. 2:5; Hosea 3:5)
29. Lamp for David* (Ps. 132:17)
30. Last* (Job 19:25)
31. Launderer (Mal. 3:2)
32. Leader (Isa. 55:4)
33. Liberator (Isa. 42:7)
34. Light* (Isa. 9:2)
35. Light to the Gentiles* (Isa. 42:6; 49:6)
36. Lord* (ha'adon) (Mal. 3:1)
37. Man* (Zech. 6:12; 13:7)
38. Man of Sorrows* (Isa. 53:3)
39. Mediator* (Job 33:23)
40. Messenger of the Covenant* (Mal. 3:1)
41. Messiah-Prince* (Dan. 9:25)
42. Mighty God* (Isa. 9:6)
43. Mighty Hero* (Ps. 45:3)
44. My Equal* (Zech. 13:7)
45. Nail (peg)* (Zech. 10:4)
46. Our Peace* (Mic. 5:5)
47. Parable Teller (Ps. 78:1-2)
48. Pierced One (Zech. 12:10)
49. Poor and Afflicted* (Ps. 69:29)
50. Priestly Ruler (Jer. 30:21; Zech. 6:13)
51. Prince* (Ezek. 37:25; 44-48)
52. Prince of Peace* (Isa. 9:6)
53. Proclaimer of Good Tidings (Isa. 61:2)

54. Prophet like Moses (Deut. 18:15, 18)
55. Redeemer* (Job 19:25; Isa. 59:20)
56. Refiner (Mal. 3:2)
57. Refuge* (Isa. 32:1)
58. Rejected Shepherd (Zech. 11)
59. Rejected Stone (Ps. 118:22)
60. Righteous Shoot (Jer. 23:5; 33:15)
61. Root out of Dry Ground (Isa. 53:2)
62. Ruler of all Nature (Ps. 8:5-8)
63. Ruler of the Earth (Isa. 16:5)
64. Scepter* (Num. 24:17)
65. Second Moses (Hos. 1:11)
66. Seed of Abraham (Gen. 12:3; 18:18)
67. Seed of David (II Sam. 2:12)
68. Seed of Woman (Gen. 3:15)
69. Servant* (Isa. 42:1; 49:3, 6)
70. Shade* (Isa. 32:2)
71. Shelter* (Isa. 32:1)
72. Shepherd* (Ezek. 34:23; 37:24)
73. Shiloh* (Gen. 49:10)
74. Shoot* (Zech. 3:8; 6:12)
75. Shoot from the Stump of Jesse* (Isa. 11:1)
76. Shoot of Yahweh* (Isa. 4:2)
77. Sign and Wonder (Isa. 8:18)
78. Signet* (Hag. 2:23)
79. Son of God (II Sam. 7:14; Ps. 2:7)
80. Son of Man* (Ps. 8:4; Dan. 7:13)
81. Star* (Num. 24:17)
82. Stone* (Zech. 3:9)
83. Substitutionary Sufferer (Isa. 53)
84. Sun of Righteousness* (Mal. 4:5)
85. Teacher* (Isa. 30:20)
86. Teacher for Righteousness* (Joel 2:23)
87. Tender Shoot* (Isa. 53:2)
88. Tender Twig* (Ezek. 17:22)
89. Temple Builder (Zech. 6:12)
90. Tent Dweller (Gen. 9:26, 27)
91. Tested Stone* (Isa. 28:16)
92. Trailblazer (Ps. 16:11)
93. Victor (Ps. 68:18)
94. Volunteer (Ps. 40:7)
95. Water of Life (Isa. 32:2)
96. Witness* (Job 16:19)
97. Witness to the Peoples (Isa. 55:4)
98. Wonderful Counselor* (Isa. 9:6)
99. Yahweh our Righteousness* (Jer. 23:6)
100. Zerubbabel* (Hag. 2:23)

Appendix V

THE BASIS OF MESSIANIC INTERPRETATION

Column One indicates the number of the prophecy as discussed in the preceding pages. One passage—Isaiah 59:20-21—is unnumbered because it is not discussed in this work. The columns to the right of the Summary column are explained as follows:

1. Exegetical logic: Something in the passage itself which if pressed literally would compel or strongly suggest a personal Messianic interpretation. Absence of an X in this column does not imply that the passage is antithetical to a personal Messianic interpretation. In these passages only external insight provided by the New Testament provides a clue as to the true meaning of the text.

2. Early Jewish Interpretation is defined as interpretation which is Talmudic or earlier. Appendix IX of Edersheim's *Life and Times of Jesus the Messiah* provides a convenient summary of Old Testament passages Messianically applied in Rabbinic writings.

3. New Testament allusions to prophecies are hard to nail down. Included here are key phrases, names or titles used in the Old Testament and cited in the New but without any apostolic exegesis.

4. New Testament exegesis requires specific statements interpreting the Old Testament passage, or statements regarding the Messianic fulfillment of same.

5. A.J. Maas (*Christ in Type and Prophecy*, 1893) has been used to check the opinions of Church Fathers regarding the Messianic import of the various passages.

6. Sometimes a passage can be identified as a Messianic prophecy because it builds on earlier themes which can be established on other grounds as Messianic.

THE BASIS OF MESSIANIC INTERPRETATION

NO.	REFERENCE	SUMMARY	EXEGETICAL LOGIC	EARLY JEWISH INTER.	NEW TESTAMENT ALLUSION	NEW TESTAMENT EXEGESIS	CHURCH FATHERS	AMPLIFICATION OF EARLIER THEMES
1.	Gen. 3:15	One from the ranks of the seed of woman will crush the head of Serpent.	X	X	X		X	
2.	Gen. 9:26f.	God to come and dwell in the tents of Shem.	X	X	X		X	
3.	Gen. 12:3; 18:18; 22:18; 26:4; 28:14	All nations of the earth to be blessed through the seed of Abram, Isaac and Jacob.	X	X	X	X	X	X
4.	Gen. 49:10ff.	Leadership among the tribes will not depart from Judah until Shiloh comes and to him shall be the obedience of the peoples.	X	X	X		X	
5.	Num. 24:16-24	In the distant future a powerful Ruler would arise in Israel who would crush the enemies of God's people.	X	X	X		X	
6.	Deut. 18:15-18	A prophet like unto Moses is to arise and God will require strict obedience to his words.	X		X	X	X	
7.	Deut. 32:43	The angels of heaven are commanded to rejoice at the time God sends forth his Firstborn into the world.			X			
8.	I Sam. 2:10	God will judge the ends of the earth but he will give strength to his anointed.	X	X			X	

THE BASIS OF MESSIANIC INTERPRETATION

NO.	REFERENCE	SUMMARY	EXEGETICAL LOGIC	EARLY JEWISH INTER.	NEW TESTAMENT ALLUSION	NEW TESTAMENT EXEGESIS	CHURCH FATHERS	AMPLIFICATION OF EARLIER THEMES
9.	I Sam. 2:35-36	A faithful priest is to arise who will dispense the blessings of priesthood to others.	X					
10.	II Sam. 7:12-16	The seed of David will sit upon an eternal throne and will build the house of God.	X		X		X	X
11.	Psalm 89	In spite of all appearance to the contrary, God's covenant with David is irrevocable.	X	X				X
12.	Psalm 132	God has chosen David and Zion.	X		X			X
13.	Psalm 8	The Son of Man, made for a time to be lower than angels, is exalted as ruler over all creation.			X	X	X	
14.	Psalm 40	Christ volunteers to enter the world, he suffers, but is delivered.				X	X[1]	X
15.	Psalm 118	Christ survives the power of death to become the chief cornerstone.				X	X	X
16.	Psalm 78:1-2	God announces that he will speak to his people in parables.				X		

THE BASIS OF MESSIANIC INTERPRETATION

NO.	REFERENCE	SUMMARY	AMPLIFICATION OF EARLIER THEMES	CHURCH FATHERS	NEW TESTAMENT EXEGESIS	NEW TESTAMENT ALLUSION	EARLY JEWISH INTER.	EXEGETICAL LOGIC
17.	Psalm 69	Because of his zeal for the house of God, Christ is hated and abused. His enemies will receive their just dues.	X	X	X			
18.	Psalm 109	The betrayer of the Christ will suffer a terrible fate.	X	X	X			
19.	Psalm 22	After unparalleled suffering, Christ conquers death to re-join his brethren.	X	X	X		?	X
20.	Psalm 2	In spite of opposition, Christ is installed as King on Zion; he rules to the ends of the earth.	X	X	X		X	X
21.	Psalm 16	Christ not allowed to see corruption in Sheol.	X	X	X			X
22.	Psalm 102	Though suffering severe persecution, Christ, the creator, is eternal.		X			X	
23.	Psalm 45	Christ is God and he has been anointed by God to sit upon an eternal throne. His people are his lovely bride.					X	X
24.	Psalm 110	Christ is a priest-king who sits at the right hand of God ruling over all men.	X	X	X		X	X
25.	Psalm 72	Christ reigns over a universal and righteous kingdom.	X	X			X	X
26.	Psalm 68	God wins a great victory, then ascends back on high.		X	X		X^2	

THE BASIS OF MESSIANIC INTERPRETATION

NO.	REFERENCE	SUMMARY	AMPLIFICATION OF EARLIER THEMES	CHURCH FATHERS	NEW TESTAMENT EXEGESIS	NEW TESTAMENT ALLUSION	EARLY JEWISH INTER.	EXEGETICAL LOGIC
27.	Job 9:33; 16:19-21; 17:3; 33:23-28	Job longs for a mediator, interpreter, advocate and witness.				?		X
28.	Job 19:23-27	Job prophesies that his Redeemer will ultimately stand upon the earth, and he (Job) will see him.		X				X
29.	Joel 2:23	A wonderful Teacher will arise who will usher in an age of great abundance.		X			X	X
30.	Hosea 1:10—2:1	A second Moses will lead God's people out of bondage into a glorious new era.	X		X			X
31.	Hosea 3:5	After the exile they will serve Yahweh their God and David their king.	X				X	X
32.	Hosea 11:1	God calls his son, the second Israel, out of Egypt.			X			
33.	Isa. 4:2-6	The beautiful and glorious Shoot of Yahweh will be the pride of the remnant of Israel.					X	X
34.	Isa. 7:14-15	A virgin will conceive and bear a son who will be called Immanuel.		X	X			X

THE BASIS OF MESSIANIC INTERPRETATION

NO.	REFERENCE	SUMMARY	EXEGETICAL LOGIC	EARLY JEWISH INTER.	NEW TESTAMENT ALLLUSION	NEW TESTAMENT EXEGESIS	CHURCH FATHERS	AMPLIFICATION OF EARLIER THEMES
35.	Isa. 8:17-18	Messiah waits for the time of his coming. He and his "children" are signs and wonders in Israel.			X	X		
36.	Isa. 9:1-7	A wondrous child from the house of David will bring a day of great light to the region of Galilee.	X	X	X	X	X	
37.	Isa. 11:1-16	A Shoot from the stem of Jesse will have an abundance of God's Spirit. He will usher in a righteous and peaceful era.	X	X	X	X	X	X
38.	Isa. 16:5	Downtrodden peoples will look to the house of David for justice and lovingkindness.	X					X
39.	Isa. 28:16	God is going to lay in Zion a tested stone, a costly corner-stone.		X	X	X	X	X
40.	Isa. 30:19-26	The people of God will see their divine Teacher and will enjoy as a result abundant blessing.	X	X				X
41.	Isa. 32:1-2	A leader of the future will be a shelter from the storm, like water in a dry place.	X					
42.	Isa. 33:17	The eyes of the people of God would see the King in his beauty.	X					

THE BASIS OF MESSIANIC INTERPRETATION

NO.	REFERENCE	SUMMARY	AMPLIFICATION OF EARLIER THEMES	CHURCH FATHERS	NEW TESTAMENT EXEGESIS	NEW TESTAMENT ALLUSION	EARLY JEWISH INTER.	EXEGETICAL LOGIC
43.	Isa. 42:1-17	God's Servant brings forth justice to the nations. He is a covenant to the people and a light to the nations.	X	X	X	?	X	X
44.	Isa. 49:1-13	The Servant is divinely appointed to teach. His mission: to raise up the tribes of Jacob and to be a light to the Gentiles.	X	X			X	X
45.	Isa. 50:4-11	The Servant is a capable teacher. He endures scourging, spitting.	X					X
46.	Isa. 52:13—53:12	The Servant is rejected, suffers for the sins of others, dies but then sees his seed.	X	X	X	X	X	X
47.	Isa. 55:3-5	A son of David to be made a witness, leader and commander for the peoples.	X	X		?		X
( )	Isa. 59:20-21	A Redeemer will come to penitent Zion.	X	X	X		X	X
48.	Isa. 61:1-11	Messiah has been anointed by the Spirit to proclaim good news.	X	X	X	X	X	X
49.	Micah 2:12-13	The divine Breaker leads the people of God out of bondage.	X		X		X	X

THE BASIS OF MESSIANIC INTERPRETATION

NO.	REFERENCE	SUMMARY	EXEGETICAL LOGIC	EARLY JEWISH INTER.	NEW TESTAMENT ALLUSION	NEW TESTAMENT EXEGESIS	CHURCH FATHERS	AMPLIFICATION OF EARLIER THEMES
50.	Micah 5:1-5	A glorious Ruler will go forth from Bethlehem to shepherd the people of God and give them victory over enemies.	X	X	X	X	X	X
51.	Hab. 3:12-15	Yahweh comes forth for the salvation of his anointed and in so doing strikes through the head of the house of evil.	X		X	X		X
52.	Jer. 23:5-6	God will raise up for David a righteous Branch who will act wisely and execute righteousness and justice in the land.	X	X	?			X
53.	Jer. 30:9, 21	Upon return from exile God's people will serve David their king who will enjoy priestly prerogatives.	X	X				X
54.	Jer. 31:21-22	God will create a new thing in the land: a woman shall encompass a man.	X	X			X	X
55.	Jer. 33:14-26	Promises made to David and Levi are irrevocable.	X	X	?			X
56.	Ezek. 17:22-24	A tender twig from house of David becomes a stately cedar with birds of every kind nesting under it.	X	X	?		X	X
57.	Ezek. 21:25-27	The crown is removed from the last king of Judah until he comes whose right it is.	X					X

NO.	REFERENCE	SUMMARY	EXEGETICAL LOGIC	EARLY JEWISH INTER.	NEW TESTAMENT ALLUSION	NEW TESTAMENT EXEGESIS	CHURCH FATHERS	AMPLIFICATION OF EARLIER THEMES
58.	Ezek. 34:23-31	God will set over those who return from Babylon one shepherd, viz., "my servant David."	X		X			X
59.	Ezek. 37:21-28	God's people will be united and will have one king, "my servant David."	X		X			X
60.	Ezek. 44-48	A Prince in the future age will be accorded honor. Through him sacrifices will be offered to God.	X	X				
61.	Dan. 7:13-14	One like unto a son of man goes before the Ancient of Days to receive an everlasting kingdom.	X	X	X	X	X	X
62.	Dan. 9:24-27	After 69 heptads of years Messiah will appear, be cut off, cause sacrifice and oblation to cease.	X	X	?		X	X
63.	Haggai 2:6-9	After the shaking of the nations the Desire of all Nations shall come to fill the Temple with glory.	X	X		X		X
64.	Haggai 2:21-23	Zerubbabel to be made God's signet in the day when the thrones of kingdoms are overthrown.	X					X
65.	Zech. 3:8-10	My Servant the Shoot is symbolized by Joshua the high priest and by an engraved stone.	X	X			X[3]	X

THE BASIS OF MESSIANIC INTERPRETATION

NO.	REFERENCE	SUMMARY	EXEGETICAL LOGIC	EARLY JEWISH INTER.	NEW TESTAMENT ALLUSION	NEW TESTAMENT EXEGESIS	CHURCH FATHERS	AMPLIFICATION OF EARLIER THEMES
66.	Zech. 6:12-13	A man whose name is Shoot shall build the Temple of the Lord. He will be a priest-king.	X	X			X[3]	X
67.	Zech. 9:9-11	Zion's king is coming riding upon the foal of a donkey.	X	X		X	X	X
68.	Zech. 10:3-4	God will send one who is the cornerstone, the tent peg, the battle bow and who possesses all sovereignty.	X	X				X
69.	Zech. 11:4-14	Thirty pieces of silver thrown to the potter in the house of God.	X	?[4]		X	X	X
70.	Zech. 13:7	The sword of divine justice smites the Shepherd and the sheep are scattered.	X	X		X	X	X
71.	Mal. 3:1	My messenger will clear the way before me and the Lord will suddenly come to his Temple.	X	X	X	X	X	X
72.	Mal. 4:2	The Sun of Righteousness will arise with healing in his wings.	X	X	X		X	X

Notes:
1. The Church Fathers apply Ps. 40 to the Messiah speaking partially in his own name, partially in the name of his followers.
2. Early Rabbinic literature assigns at least v. 31 to the Messianic age.
3. General agreement exists among the Fathers on the Messianic thrust of the message, but most take the term *shoot* in its literal application to refer to Zerubbabel. The passage was regarded as typically Messianic.
4. The majority Jewish opinion is against the Messianic interpretation, but there are exceptions.

490

Appendix VI

MESSIANIC PROPHECY CITED IN THE NEW TESTAMENT

	OT REF.	INDICATION OF FULFILLMENT	SPEAKER	GIST OF PROPHECY
1. Matt. 1:23	Isa. 7:14	Now all this happened that what was spoken by the Lord through the prophet might be fulfilled.	Matthew	Virgin Birth
2. Matt. 2:6	Mic. 5:2	For so it has been written by the prophet.	Scribes	Born in Bethlehem
3. Matt. 2:15	Hos. 11:1	That what was spoken by the Lord through the prophet might be fulfilled.	Matthew	To come out of Egypt
4. Matt. 2:18	Jer. 31:15	Then that which was spoken through Jeremiah the prophet was fulfilled.	Matthew	Women weeping over infants slain by Herod
5. Matt. 3:3	Isa. 40:3	For this is the one referred to by Isaiah the prophet.	Matthew	Preaching of John
6. Matt. 4:15f.	Isa. 9:1f.	This was to fulfill what was spoken through Isaiah the prophet.	Matthew	Galilean ministry
7. Matt. 8:17	Isa. 53:4	He cast out the spirits with a word and healed all who were ill in order that what was spoken through Isaiah the prophet might be fulfilled.	Matthew	Healing ministry
8. Matt. 11:4f.	Isa. 35:5f., 61:1	Go and report to John the things which you see and hear.	Jesus	Healing and preaching ministry
9. Matt. 11:10	Mal. 3:1	This is the one about whom it was written . . .	Jesus	John the Baptist

491

MESSIANIC PROPHECY CITED IN THE NEW TESTAMENT

	OT REF.	INDICATION OF FULFILLMENT	SPEAKER	GIST OF PROPHECY
10. Matt. 12:18-21	Isa. 42:1-4	He healed them all in order that what was spoken through Isaiah the prophet might be fulfilled.	Matthew	Compassion of Jesus for weak people
11. Matt. 12:40	John 1:17	As Jonah was three days and three nights in the belly of the sea monster. so shall the son of man be three days and three nights in the heart of the earth.	Jesus	Burial and Resurrection
12. Matt. 13:14f.	Isa. 6:9f.	In their case the prophecy of Isaiah is being fulfilled.	Jesus	The spiritual dullness of his audience
13. Matt. 13:35	Ps. 78:2	So that what was spoken through the prophet might be fulfilled.	Matthew	Teaching in Parables
14. Matt. 15:8f.	Isa. 29:13	Rightly did Isaiah prophesy of you.	Jesus	Hypocrisy of his audience
15. Matt. 21:5	Zech. 9:9	Now this took place that what was spoken through the prophet might be fulfilled.	Matthew	Triumphal entry
16. Matt. 21:9	Ps. 118:26f.	Implied	Matthew	Triumphal entry
17. Matt. 21:16	Ps. 8:2	Implied	Jesus	Triumphal entry
18. Matt. 21:42	Ps. 118:22	Implied	Jesus	Rejected stone
19. Matt. 23:39	Ps. 110:1	Then how does David in the Spirit call him Lord?	Jesus	Enthronement
20. Matt. 24:30	Dan. 7:13	Implied	Jesus	Coming with clouds
21. Matt. 26:31	Zech. 13:7	Implied	Jesus	Shepherd smitten

MESSIANIC PROPHECY CITED IN THE NEW TESTAMENT

	OT REF.	INDICATION OF FULFILMENT	SPEAKER	GIST OF PROPHECY
22. Matt. 26:64	Ps. 110:1	Implied	Jesus	Enthronement
23. Matt. 26:64	Dan. 7:3	Implied	Jesus	Coming with clouds
24. Matt. 27:9f.	Zech. 11:12f.	Then that which was spoken through Jeremiah the prophet was fulfilled.	Matthew	Thirty pieces of silver
25. Matt. 27:34	Ps. 69:21	Implied	Matthew	Wine mingled with gall
26. Matt. 27:43	Ps. 22:18	Implied	Matthew	Casting lots for his garments
27. Matt. 27:43	Ps. 22:8	Implied	Matthew	Mockery on cross
28. Matt. 27:46	Ps. 22:1	Implied	Matthew	Christ forsaken
29. Mark 1:2	Mal. 3:1	Implied	Mark	John the Baptist
30. Mark 1:3	Isa. 40:3	Implied	Mark	John the Baptist
31. Mark 4:12	Isa. 6:9	Implied	Mark	The spiritual dullness of his audience
32. Mark 7:6	Isa. 29:13	Rightly did Isaiah prophesy of you hypocrites.	Jesus	Hyprocrisy of his audience
33. Mark 11:9	Ps. 118:25	Implied	Mark	Triumphal entry
34. Mark 12:10f.	Ps. 118:22f.	Implied	Jesus	Rejected stone
35. Mark 12:36	Ps. 110:1	Implied	Jesus	Enthronement

MESSIANIC PROPHECY CITED IN THE NEW TESTAMENT

	OT REF.	INDICATION OF FULFILLMENT	SPEAKER	GIST OF PROPHECY
36. Mark 13:26	Dan. 7:13	Implied	Jesus	Coming with clouds
37. Mark 14:27	Zech. 13:7	You will fall away because it is written . . .	Jesus	Shepherd smitten
38. Mark 14:62	Dan. 7:13	Implied	Jesus	Coming with clouds
39. Mark 14:62	Ps. 110:1	Implied	Jesus	Enthronement
40. Mark 15:24	Ps. 22:18	Implied	Mark	Casting lots
41. Mark 15:34	Ps. 22:1	Implied	Mark	Christ forsaken
42. Luke 1:17	Mal. 4:6	Implied	Zacharias	John the Baptist
43. Luke 1:76	Mal. 3:1	Implied	Zacharias	John the Baptist
44. Luke 1:79	Isa. 9:1f.	Implied	Zacharias	Galilean ministry
45. Luke 2:32	Isa. 42:6, 49:6	Implied	Simeon	Light to Gentiles
46. Luke 3:4f.	Isa. 40:3	Implied	Luke	John the Baptist
47. Luke 4:18f.	Isa. 61:1f.	Today is this Scripture fulfilled in your hearing.	Jesus	Gospel preaching
48. Luke 7:27	Mal. 3:1	This is the one about whom it is written . . .	Jesus	John the Baptist
49. Luke 8:10	Isa. 6:9	Implied	Jesus	The dullness of his audience
50. Luke 19:38	Ps. 118:26	Implied	Luke	Triumphal entry
51. Luke 20:17	Ps. 118:22	Implied	Jesus	Rejected stone
52. Luke 20:42f.	Ps. 110:1	David calls him (Messiah) Lord.	Jesus	Lordship of Christ

MESSIANIC PROPHECY CITED IN THE NEW TESTAMENT

	OT REF.	INDICATION OF FULFILLMENT	SPEAKER	GIST OF PROPHECY
53. Luke 22:37	Isa. 53:12	For I tell you, that this which is written must be fulfilled in me . . . for that which refers to me has its fulfillment.	Jesus	Classed among criminals
54. Luke 22:69	Ps. 110:1	Implied	Jesus	Enthronement
55. Luke 23:34	Ps. 22:18	Implied	Luke	Casting lots
56. John 1:23	Isa. 40:3	I am the voice of one crying in the wilderness . . . as Isaiah the prophet said.	John the Baptist	John's preaching
57. John 2:17	Ps. 69:17	His disciples remembered that it was written . . .	John	Zeal for the house of God
58. John 6:45	Isa. 54:13	Implied	Jesus	Those taught of God come to Christ
59. John 7:42	Ps. 89:4 Mic. 5:2		People	Christ the seed of David from Bethlehem
60. John 12:13	Ps. 118:25f.	Implied	John	Triumphal entry
61. John 12:15	Zech. 9:9	Implied	John	Triumphal entry
62. John 12:38	Isa. 53:1	That the word of Isaiah the prophet might be fulfilled.	John	Non-belief of his audience
63. John 12:40	Isa. 6:10	These things Isaiah said because he saw his glory, and he spoke of him.	John	The dullness of his audience
64. John 13:18 cf. Jn. 17:12	Ps. 41:9	That the Scripture may be fulfilled.	Jesus	Betrayal by Judas

495

MESSIANIC PROPHECY CITED IN THE NEW TESTAMENT

	OT REF.	INDICATION OF FULFILLMENT	SPEAKER	GIST OF PROPHECY
65. John 15:25	Ps. 35:19 69:4	They have done this in order that the word may be fulfilled that is written in their law.	Jesus	Hated Christ without cause.
66. John 19:24	Ps. 22:18	That the Scripture might be fulfilled.	John	Garments divided
67. John 19:28	Ps. 69:21	Jesus, knowing that all things had already been accomplished, in order that the Scriptures might be fulfilled, said . . .	John	Offered wine on the cross
68. John 19:36	Exod. 12:46 Num. 9:12 Ps. 34:20	For these things came to pass that the Scripture might be fulfilled.	John	No bone broken
69. John 10:37	Zech. 12:10	Ditto	John	Look on Pierced One
70. Acts 1:20	Ps. 69:25 Ps. 109:8	The Scriptures had to be fulfilled which the Holy Spirit foretold by the mouth of David concerning Judas.	Peter	Judas to be replaced
71. Acts 2:16-21	Joel 2:28-32	This is what was spoken through the prophet Joel.	Peter	Outpouring of the Spirit
72. Acts 2:25-28	Ps. 16:8-11	David says of him (Christ) . . .	Peter	Christ could not undergo decay in the grave
73. Acts 2:34-35	Ps. 110:1	Implied	Peter	Enthronement
74. Acts 3:22-23	Deut. 18:15, 19	Implied	Peter	Prophet like Moses

MESSIANIC PROPHECY CITED IN THE NEW TESTAMENT

	OT REF.	INDICATION OF FULFILLMENT	SPEAKER	GIST OF PROPHECY
75. Acts 3:25	Gen. 22:18	Implied	Peter	All nations blessed in seed of Abraham
76. Acts 4:11	Ps. 118:22	He (Christ) is the . . .	Peter	Rejected stone
77. Acts 4:25	Ps. 2:1	Implied	Church	Opposition to Christ
78. Acts 7:37	Deut. 18:15	Implied	Stephen	Prophet like Moses
79. Acts 8:32f.	Isa. 53:7-9	Implied	Philip	Suffering Servant
80. Acts 13:33	Ps. 2:7	That God has fulfilled this promise to our children in that he raised up Jesus, as it is written in the second Psalm.	Paul	Christ God's Son
81. Acts 13:34	Isa. 55:3	And as for the fact that he raised him up from the dead . . . he has spoken in this way:	Paul	Christ the fulfillment of the sure mercies of David.
82. Acts 13:35	Ps. 16:10	Therefore he also says in another place:	Paul	Christ not to undergo decay in the grave
83. Acts 13:47	Isa. 49:6	For this the Lord has commanded us . . .	Paul	Through Paul Christ becomes a light to the nations
84. Acts 15:16-18	Amos 9:11f.	And with this the words of the prophets agree, just as it is written:	James	Davidic dynasty restored. Gentiles converted

MESSIANIC PROPHECY CITED IN THE NEW TESTAMENT

	OT REF.	INDICATION OF FULFILLMENT	SPEAKER	GIST OF PROPHECY
85. Rom. 9:25f.	Hos. 2:23, 1:10	Implied	Paul	Gentiles become people of God.
86. Rom. 9:33, 10:11	Isa. 28:16	Implied	Paul	Stone of stumbling
87. Rom. 10:13	Joel 2:32	Implied	Paul	Calling on the name of the Lord
88. Rom. 11:8	Isa. 29:10	Implied	Paul	Hardening of Israel
89. Rom. 11:9f.	Ps. 69:22f.	Implied	Paul	Judgment on hardened Israel
90. Rom. 11:26	Isa. 59:20f.	Implied	Paul	Deliverer from Zion
91. Rom. 11:27	Isa. 27:9	Implied	Paul	Forgiveness of sins
92. Rom. 14:11	Isa. 45:23	Implied	Paul	Final judgment
93. Rom. 15:9	Ps. 18:49	Implied	Paul	Gentiles praise God
94. Rom. 15:10	Deut. 32:43	Implied	Paul	Ditto
95. Rom. 15:11	Ps. 117:1	Implied	Paul	Ditto
96. Rom. 15:12	Isa. 11:10	Implied	Paul	Gentiles hope in the root of Jesse
97. Rom. 15:21	Isa. 52:15	Implied	Paul	Gospel preached to those without understanding

MESSIANIC PROPHECY CITED IN THE NEW TESTAMENT

	OT REF.	INDICATION OF FULFILLMENT	SPEAKER	GIST OF PROPHECY
98. I Cor. 15:27	Ps. 8:7	Implied	Paul	All things put under his feet
99. I Cor. 15:54	Isa. 25:8	Implied	Paul	Death swallowed up in victory
100. I Cor. 15:55	Hos. 13:14	Implied	Paul	Death no more sting
101. II Cor. 6:2	Isa. 49:8	Implied	Paul	Now is the day of salvation
102. II Cor. 6:16	Ezek. 37:27	Implied	Paul	God to dwell with his people
103. II Cor. 6:18	Hos. 1:10 Isa. 43:6	Implied	Paul	Christians are sons of God
104. Gal. 3:8, 16	Gen. 12:3, 13:15, 17:8	The Scripture foreseeing that God would justify the Gentiles by faith preached the Gospel beforehand to Abraham, saying	Paul	All nations to be blessed in Abram
105. Gal. 4:27	Isa. 54:1	Implied	Paul	Jerusalem is the mother of us all
106. Eph. 2:17	Isa. 57:19	Implied	Paul	Preached peace to Jew and Gentile
107. Eph. 4:8	Ps. 68:18	To each one of us grace was given . . . therefore it says:	Paul	Ascension
108. Eph. 5:14	Isa. 26:19, 51:17, 52:1, 60:1	Implied	Paul	Regeneration

MESSIANIC PROPHECY CITED IN THE NEW TESTAMENT

	OT REF.	INDICATION OF FULFILLMENT	SPEAKER	GIST OF PROPHECY
109. Heb. 1:5	Ps. 2:7	Implied	?	Messiah God's Son
110. Heb. 1:5	II Sam. 7:14	Implied	?	Ditto
111. Heb. 1:6	Deut. 32:43	And when he again brings the firstborn into the world he says:	?	Angels worship him when he entered the world
112. Heb. 1:8f.	Ps. 45:6f.	But of the Son he says:	?	Deity of Christ
113. Heb. 1:10-12	Ps. 102:25-27	Ditto	?	Son is creator, eternal
114. Heb. 1:13	Ps. 110:1	Implied	?	Enthronement
115. Heb. 2:6-8	Ps. 8:4-6	Implied	?	All things subject to the Son
116. Heb. 2:12	Ps. 22:22	He is not ashamed to call them brethren saying:	?	Christ a brother to the redeemed
117. Heb. 2:13	Isa. 8:17f.	Implied	?	Messiah puts his trust in God
118. Heb. 5:5	Ps. 2:7	He (God) said to him (Messiah)	?	Messiah God's Son
119. Heb. 5:6	Ps. 110:4	Implied	?	Eternal Priest
120. Heb. 7:17, 21	Ditto	Implied	?	Ditto
121. Heb. 8:8-12	Jer. 31:31-34	Implied	?	New Covenant

MESSIANIC PROPHECY CITED IN THE NEW TESTAMENT

	OT REF.	INDICATION OF FULFILLMENT	SPEAKER	GIST OF PROPHECY
122. Heb. 10:5-9	Ps. 40:6	When he (Christ) comes into the world he says:	?	Christ replaces sacrificial system
123. Heb. 10:13	Ps. 110:1	Implied	?	Enthronement
124. Heb. 10:16f.	Jer. 31:33f.	Holy Spirit bears witness to us.	?	New Covenant
125. Heb. 10:37f.	Hab. 2:3f.	Implied	?	He comes in a little while
126. Heb. 12:26	Hag. 2:6	Implied	?	The final shaking
127. I Peter 2:6	Isa. 28:16	Implied	Peter	Cornerstone laid in Zion
128. I Peter 2:7	Ps. 118:22	Implied	Peter	Rejected stone
129. I Peter 2:8	Isa. 8:14	Implied	Peter	Stone of stumbling
130. I Peter 2:10	Hos. 1:10 2:23	Implied	Peter	Gentiles to become people of God
131. I Peter 2:22	Isa. 53:9	Implied	Peter	Sinless Christ

Bibliography

Ahlström, G. W. *Joel and the Temple Cult of Jerusalem.* Leiden: Brill, 1971.

Alexander, Joseph A. *The Psalms, Translated and Explained.* Grand Rapids: Baker, 1975.

Allen, Leslie C. *The Books of Joel, Obadiah, Jonah and Micah,* (The New International Commentary.) Grand Rapids: Eerdmans, 1975.

Andersen, Francis I. *Job, An Introduction and Commentary,* (Tyndale Old Testament Commentaries). Downers Grove, IL: InterVarsity, 1976.

Baldwin, Joyce. *Haggai, Zechariah and Malachi,* (Tyndale Old Testament Commentaries.) Downers Grove, IL: InterVarsity, 1972.

Barnes Albert. *Notes on the New Testament* and *Notes on the Old Testament.* Grand Rapids: Baker, 1961.

Barnes, W. E. *The Psalms* (Westminster Commentaries, 2 vols.) London: Methuen, 1931.

Baron, David. *Rays of Messiah's Glory.* Grand Rapids: Zondervan, n.d.
_____. *The Visions and Prophecies of Zechariah.* Grand Rapids: Kregel, 1972.

Becker, Joachim. *Messianic Expectation in the Old Testament.* Trans. David Green. Philadelphia: Fortress Press, 1977.

Beecher, W. J. *The Prophets and the Promise.* Grand Rapids: Baker, 1963.

Berkhof, Louis. *Principles of Biblical Interpretation.* Grand Rapids: Baker, 1950.

Bonar, Andrew A. *Christ and His Church in the Book of Psalms.* Grand Rapids: Kregel, 1978.

Borland, James. *Christ in the Old Testament.* Chicago: Moody, 1978.

Bright, John. *The Authority of the Old Testament.* Nashville: Abingdon, 1967.

Briggs, Charles A. *Messianic Prophecy.* New York: Scribner, 1886.

Brown, Raymond E., J. A. Fitzmyer, and R. E. Murphy, eds. *The Jerome Bible Commentary.* Englewood Cliffs, NJ: Prentice-Hall, 1968.

Bruce, F. F. *The Epistle to the Hebrews* (The New International Commentary). Grand Rapids: Eerdmans, 1968.

Callaway, T. W. *Christ in the Old Testament.* New York: Loizeaux, 1950.

Carnell, E. J. *The Case for Orthodox Theology.* Philadelphia: Westminster, 1959.

Cashdan, E. "Haggai, Zechariah, Malachi" in *The Twelve Prophets* (Soncino Books of the Bible). London: Soncino, 1961.

Chambers, T. W. "Zechariah" in *Commentary on the Holy Scriptures . . . by John Peter Lange*. Trans. and ed. Philip Schaff. Grand Rapids: Zondervan, n.d.

Charles, R. H. *A Critical and Exegetical Commentary on the Book of Daniel*. Oxford: Clarendon, 1929.

Cheyne, T. T. *Micah* (The Cambridge Bible for Schools and Colleges). Ed. J. J. S. Perowne. Cambridge: University Press, 1882.

Clarke, Adam. *The Holy Bible . . . with Commentary and Critical Notes*. 5 vols. New York: B. Waugh and T. Mason, 1833.

Cohen, A. *Psalms* (Soncino Books of the Bible). London: Soncino, 1964.

Collins, G. N. M. "Zechariah" in *The New Bible Commentary*. Eds. F. Davidson, A. M. Stibbs and E. F. Kevan. Grand Rapids: Eerdmans, 1953.

Cullman, Oscar. *Christology of the New Testament*. Philadelphia: Westminster, 1963.

Culver, Robert D. *Daniel and the Latter Days*. Chicago: Moody, 1954.

_____. "The Old Testament as Messianic Prophecy," *Bulletin of the Evangelical Theological Society*. (1964):91-97.

Davison, John. *Discourses on Prophecy*. London: Parker, 1882.

Davison, W. T. "Psalms, Book of," in Vol. IV of *Dictionary of the Bible*. Ed. James Hastings. Pp. 145-162.

Deane, W. J. *Minor Prophets*, 3 vols. in *The Pulpit Commentary*, eds. H. D. M. Spence and Joseph S. Excell. New York: Funk and Wagnalls, n.d.

Delaughter, Thomas J. *Malachi, Messenger of Divine Love*. New Orleans: Insight Press, 1976.

Delitzsch, Franz. *Messianic Prophecies in Historical Succession*. New York: Charles Scribner's Sons, 1891.

_____. *Commentary on the Epistle to the Hebrews*. Trans. Thomas Kingsbury. 2 vols. Grand Rapids: Eerdmans, 1952.

Dewart, Edward H. *Jesus the Messiah in Prophecy and Fulfillment*. Cincinnati: Cranston and Stowe, 1891.

Dickson, David. *Commentary on the Psalms*. 2 vols. Minneapolis: Klock and Klock, 1980.

Eadie, John. *Commentary on the Epistle to the Galatians*. Minneapolis: James and Klock, 1977.

Edersheim, Alfred. *The Life and Times of Jesus the Messiah*. 2 vols. London: Longmans, 1915.

_____. *Prophecy and History in Relation to the Messiah*. Grand Rapids: Baker, 1955.

Edghill. E. A. *An Enquiry into the Evidential Value of Prophecy*. London: Macmillan, 1906.

Elliott. G. M. "Future Life in the Old Testament," *The Seminary Review* 3(1957):41-93.

Ellison, H. L. *The Centrality of the Messianic Idea in the Old Testament*. London: Tyndale, 1953.

Emmet, C. W. "Messiah" in Vol. XIV of *The Encyclopedia of Religion and Ethics*. Ed. James Hastings. New York: Scribner's Son, n.d. Pp. 570-581.

Fairbairn, Patrick. *This Interpretation of Prophecy*. London: Banner of Truth, 1964.

Finegan, Jack. *Handbook of Biblial Chronology*. Princeton: University Press, 1964.

Fowler, Harold. *Matthew* (The Bible Study Textbook Series, 3 vols.). Joplin, MO: College Press, 1968-1972.

Geisler, Norman. *Christ: the Key to Interpreting the Bible*. Chicago: Moody, 1975.

Girdlestone, R. B. *The Grammar of Prophecy*. London: Eyre and Spottiswoode, 1901.

Goldman. S. *Samuel* (Soncino Books of the Bible). London: Soncino Press, 1964.

Goodspeed, G. S. *Israel's Messianic Hope to the Time of Jesus*. London: Macmillan, 1900.

Gordis, Robert. *The Book of God and Man: A Study of Job*. Chicago: University Press, 1965.

Heavenor, E. S. P. "Job" in *The New Bible Commentary*. Eds. F. Davidson, A. Stibbs and E. F. Kevan. Grand Rapids: Eerdmans, 1953.

Heinisch, Paul. *Christ in Prophecy*. Trans. William G. Heidt. Collegeville, MN: Liturgical Press, 1956.

Henderson, E. *The Book of the Twelve Minor Prophets*. Andover: Draper, 1864.

Hengstenberg, E. W. *Christology of the Old Testament*. Grand Rapids: Kregel, 1970.

Horne, T. H. *An Introduction to the Critical Study and Knowledge of the Holy Scriptures*. 2nd. ed. New York: Robert Carter, 1872.

Huffman, Jasper A. *The Messianic Hope in Both Testaments*. Butler, IN: Higley, 1945.

Hughes, Philip E. *Interpreting Prophecy*. Grand Rapids: Eerdmans, 1976.

Jamieson, Robert, A. R. Fausset and David Brown. *A Commentary, Critical, Experimental, and Practical on the Old and New Testaments*. 5 vols. Philadelphia: Lippincott, n.d.

Jenni, E. "Messiah, Jewish" in Vol. K-Q of *The Interpreter's Dictionary of the Bible*. Ed. George Buttrick. New York: Abingdon, 1960. Pp. 360-365.

Jocz, J. "Messiah" in Vol. IV of *The Zondervan Pictorial Bible Encyclopedia*. Ed. Merrill C. Tenney. Grand Rapids: Zondervan, 1975.

Jones, Kenneth E. "Isaiah" in *The Wesleyan Bible Commentary*. Ed. Charles W. Carter. Grand Rapids: Eerdmans, 1969.

Kaiser, Walter C. *The Old Testament in Contemporary Preaching*. Grand Rapids: Baker, 1973.

Keil, C. F. and F. Delitzsch. *Biblical Commentary on the Old Testament*. Trans. James Martin. Grand Rapids: Eerdmans, 1959.

Keith, Alexander. *Evidence of the Truth of the Christian Religion Derived from the Literal Fulfillment of Prophecy*. London: Ward, Lock and Co., n.d.

Kirkpatrick, A. F. ed. *The Book of Psalms*(The Cambridge Bible for Schools and Colleges). Cambridge: University Press, 1910.

_____. *The Doctrine of the Prophets*. 3rd ed. London: Macmillan, 1923.

Kitto, John ed. "Messiah" in Vol. II of *A Cyclopaedia of Biblical Literature*. New York: Mark H. Newman, 1846. Pp. 330-332.

Kligerman, Aaron. *Messianic Prophecy*. Grand Rapids: Zondervan, 1957.

Laetsch, Theodore. *Bible Commentary: The Minor Prophets*. St. Louis: Concordia, 1956.

_____. *Bible Commentary: Jeremiah*. St. Louis: Concordia, 1965.

Lenski, R. C. N. *The Interpretation of St. Paul's Epistles to the Galatians, Ephesians and Philippians*. Minneapolis: Augsburg, 1961.

Leslie, Elmer A. *Jeremiah, Chronologically Arranged, Translated and Interpreted*. New York: Abingdon, 1954.

Leupold, H. C. *Exposition of Zechariah*. Grand Rapids: Baker, 1965.

_____. *Exposition of Isaiah*. 2 vols. Grand Rapids: Baker, 1968-71.

_____. *Exposition of Psalms*. Grand Rapids: Baker, 1974.

_____. *Exposition of Genesis*. Columbus, OH: Wartburg, 1942.

Lewis, C. S. *Reflections on the Psalms*. New York: Harcourt, Brace and World, 1958.

Lockhart, Clinton. *The Messianic Message of the Old Testament*. Joplin: College Press, n.d.

Lockyer, Herbert. *All the Messianic Prophecies of the Bible*. Grand Rapids: Zondervan, 1973.

Longenecker, Richard N. *The Christology of Early Jewish Christianity*. Naperville, IL: Allenson, 1970.

Maas, A. J. *Christ in Type and Prophecy*. 2 vols. Cincinnati: Benziger, 1893-96.

McClintock, John and James Strong, eds. "Messiah" in Vol. VI of *Cyclopaedia of Biblical, Theological and Ecclesiastical Literature*. Grand Rapids: Baker, 1969.

McCullough, W. Stewart. "The Book of Psalms" in *The Interpreter's Bible*. Ed. George Buttrick. New York: Abingdon, 1952.

McGarvey, J. W. *New Commentary on Acts of Apostles*. 2 vols. in one. Cincinnati: Standard, n.d.

McIlmoyle, J. "Haggai" in *The New Bible Commentary*. Eds. F. Davidson, A. M. Stibbs and E. F. Kevan. Grand Rapids: Eerdmans, 1953.

Mack, Edward. *The Christ of the Old Testament*. Richmond: Presbyterian Committee of Publication, 1926.

M'Lean, Daniel. *The Gospel in the Psalms*. Edinburgh: Andrew Elliot, 1875.

Martin, R. A. "The Earliest Messianic Interpretation of Genesis 3:15," *Journal of Biblical Literature* 84(1965): 427.

Meyrick, Frederick. "Prophet" in Vol. III rev. ed. of *Dr. William Smith's Dictionary of the Bible*. Ed. H. B. Hackett. Boston: Houghton Mifflin, 1881. Pp. 2590-2602.

Mickelsen, A. Berkeley. *Interpreting the Bible*. Grand Rapids: Eerdmans, 1963.

Milligan, Robert. *Epistle to the Hebrews*. Cincinnati: Chase and Hall, 1875.

Moore, T. V. *A Commentary on Zechariah*. London: Banner of Truth, 1958.

Mowinckel, Sigmund. *He that Cometh*. Trans. G. W. Anderson. New York: Abingdon, 1954.

North, C. R. *The Suffering Servant in Deutero-Isaiah*. 2nd ed. London: 1956.

Orelli, C. von "Messiah, Messianism" in Vol. VII of *The New Schaff-Herzog Encyclopedia of Religious Knowledge*. Ed. Samuel M. Jackson. Grand Rapids: Baker, 1950. Pp. 323-329.

Payne, Barton. *Encyclopedia of Biblical Prophecy.* New York: Harper and Row, 1973.

Peake, A. S. *Jeremiah* (The Century Bible, 2 vols). Edinburgh: T. and T. Clark, 1910-12.

Peisker, Armor D. "Micah" in *Beacon Bible Commentary.* Kansas City: Beacon Hill, 1966.

Perowne, J. J. Steward. *The Book of Psalms.* 2 vols. in one. Grand Rapids: Zondervan, 1976.

Perowne, T. T. *Haggai and Zechariah* (Cambridge Bible for Schools and Colleges). Cambridge: University Press, 1886.

Pinnock, Clark. *Truth on Fire.* Grand Rapids: Baker, 1972.

Plummer, Alfred. *An Exegetical Commentary on the Gospel According to St. Matthew.* Grand Rapids: Eerdmans, 1956.

Pritchard, James. *Ancient Near Eastern Texts.* 3rd ed. Princeton: University Press, 1969.

Pusey, E. B. *The Minor Prophets with Commentary.* 2 vols. New York: Funk and Wagnalls, 1885.

Ramm, Bernard. *Protestant Biblical Interpretation.* Boston: W. A. Wilde, 1950.

Rawlinson, George. *Isaiah* (The Pulpit Commentary, 2 vols.). Ed. H. D. M. Spence and Joseph S. Excell. New York: Funk and Wagnalls, n.d.

Reich, Max I. *The Messianic Hope in Israel.* Philadelphia: Pinerbook Book Club, 1940.

Reichert, V. E. *Job* (Soncino Books of the Bible). London: Soncino Press, 1964.

Ridderbos, Herman. *The Coming of the Kingdom.* Philadelphia: Presbyterian and Reformed, 1962.

Riehm, Edward. *Messianic Prophecy, Its Origin, Historical Growth, and Relation to the New Testament.* Edinburgh: T. & T. Clark, 1900.

Rowley, H. H. ed. *Job* (The New Century Bible). Greenwood, SC: Attic Press, 1970.

_____. *Biblical Doctrine of Election.* London: Lutterworth, 1950.

_____. *The Relevance of Apocalyptic.* London: Lutterworth, 1944.

_____. "The Book of Job and its Meaning," in *From Moses to Qumran.* New York: Association, 1963.

_____. *The Servant of the Lord.* Oxford, 1965.

Sampey, John R. "Psalms, Book of," in Vol. IV of *The International Standard Bible Encyclopedia.* Ed. James Orr. Grand Rapids: Eerdmans, 1947. Pp. 2487-2494.

Silver, Abba. *A History of Messianic Speculation in Israel.* Boston: Beacon Press, 1959.

Smith, James E. *Jeremiah and Lamentations* (The Bible Study Textbook Series). Joplin: College Press, 1972.

_____. *Ezekiel* (The Bible Study Textbook Series). Joplin: College Press, 1979.

Smith, John Pye. *The Scripture Testimony to the Messiah.* 6th ed. 2 vols. Edinburgh: William Oliphant, 1871.

Smith, R. Payne. *Samuel* (The Pulpit Commentary, 2 vols.). Ed. H. D. M. Spence and Joseph S. Excell. New York: Funk and Wagnalls, n.d.

Spurgeon, C. H. *Treasury of David.* 7 vols. New York: Funk and Wagnalls, 1892.

Sutcliffe, Edmund. *Future Life in the Old Testament.* 2nd ed. Westminster, MD: Newman Bookshop, 1947.

Taylor, John B. *Ezekiel, An Introduction and Commentary* (Tyndale Old Testament Commentaries). Downers Grove, IL: InterVarsity, 1969.

Terry, Milton. *Biblical Hermeneutics.* New York: Eaton and Mains, 1890.

Unger, Merrill F. *Unger's Bible Commentary, Zechariah.* Grand Rapids: Zondervan, 1963.

Urquhart, John. *The Wonders of Prophecy.* 4th ed. New York: Gospel Publishing, n.d.

Vos, Geerhardus. *Biblical Theology.* Grand Rapids: Eerdmans, 1948.

Wiley, H. Orton. *The Epistle to the Hebrews.* Kansas City: Beacon Hill, 1959.

Wilmot, John. *Inspired Principles of Prophetic Interpretation.* Swengel, PA: Reiner, 1965.

Wilson, T. Earnest. *Messianic Psalms.* Neptune, NJ: Louizeaux, 1978.

Wolf, Herbert. *Haggai and Malachi.* Chicago: Moody, 1976.

Wolff, Hans W. *Hosea* (Hermeneia). Trans. Gary Stansell. Philadelphia: Fortress, 1974.

Wright, C. H. H. *Zechariah and His Prophecies.* New York: Dutton, 1879.

Young, E. J. "Daniel" in *The New Bible Commentary.* Eds. F. Davidson, A.M. Stibbs, and E. F. Kevan. Grand Rapids: Eerdmans, 1953.

_____. *The Book of Isaiah* (The New International Commentary, 3 vols.). Grand Rapids: Eerdmans, 1965-72.

_____. *The Prophecy of Daniel.* Grand Rapids: Eerdmans, 1953.

Zollars, E. V. *The King of Kings.* Cincinnati: Standard, 1911.

Index of Scriptures

Topical Index

Use the Topical Index in conjunction with the Index of Scriptures (beginning on page 509) to obtain reference pages.

After the exile	Hosea 3:5
After the fall of the Greek kingdom	Num. 24:20-24
After 69 heptads	Dan. 9:25
After a preparatory messenger	Mal. 3:1

C. The Place of his Birth — Micah 5:2

D. The Circumstances of his Birth

Angelic praise	Deut. 32:43
Angels, made lower than	Ps. 8:5
Infants, slaughter of	Jer. 31:15
Virgin birth	Isa. 7:14

E. The Significance of his Birth

Election	Isa. 8:17; 42:14
End of Israel's abandonment	Micah 5:3
Raised up by God	Deut. 18:15, 18
Sign	Isa. 7:14
Son of man	Ps. 8:4; Dan. 7:14

F. Messiah's Childhood

Called out of Egypt	Hosea 11:1
Committed from birth	Ps. 22:9-10; Isa. 49:1, 5
Humble diet	Isa. 7:15
Root out of dry ground	Isa. 53:2
Tender shoot	Isa. 4:2; Jer. 33:15; Ezek. 17:22; Zech. 3:12

G. The Longing for his Coming — Isa. 8:17; 42:14

IV. THE OFFICES OF MESSIAH

A. Prophet

Announces good tidings	Ps. 40:9-10; Isa. 61:1-2
Like Moses	Deut. 18:18

B. Priest

Approaches God	Jer. 30:21
Intercession	Isa. 53:12; Ps. 16:4
Offers guilt offering	Isa. 53:10
Order of Melchizedek	Ps. 110:4
Priest forever	Ps. 110:4
Priestly house	I Sam. 2:35
Priestly obedience	I Sam. 2:35
Priest upon his throne	Zech. 3:13

C. Teacher

Appears in Galilee	Isa. 9:1
Islands wait for him	Isa. 42:4
Mouth a sharp sword	Isa. 49:2
Parables	Ps. 78:2
Teacher for righteousness	Joel 2:23
Tutorial guidance	Isa. 30:21
Visible	Isa. 30:20

D. Shepherd

Feeds the flock	Isa. 49:9, 10
Guides the flock	Isa. 49:10-11
One shepherd	Ezek. 34:23
Shepherds in strength of God	Micah 5:4
Smitten shepherd	Zech. 13:7

E. King

Anointed	I Sam. 2:10; Ps. 2:6; 45:6; 89:52; 132:17; Dan. 9:24
Beauty	Isa. 33:17
Corner/cornerstone	Ps. 118:22; Zech. 10:4; Isa. 28:16
Crown	Ps. 132:18
David	Jer. 30:9; Ezek. 34:23, 24; 37:24-25; Hosea 3:5
Covenant with	II Sam. 7:13, 16; Ps. 89:3-4, 29, 34-38; 132:12; Isa. 55:3; Jer. 33:20-21, 25-26
Horn of	Ps. 89:25
House of	II Sam. 7:16
Never to lack a man	Jer. 33:17
Shoot	Ps. 132:17; Isa. 11:1; Jer. 23:5; 33:15
Tender twig	Ezek. 17:22-23
Tent of David	Isa. 16:5
Divine aid	I Sam. 2:10; Isa. 42:1, 6
Enthroned	Ps. 2:6; 110:1
Firstborn	Ps. 89:28
Government	Isa. 9:6-7; Ezek. 37:26
Horn of anointed	I Sam. 2:10
Prince	Jer. 30:21
Righteous rule	Isa. 9:7; 11:5; 16:5; 32:1

Scepter	Num. 24:17; Ps. 45:6
Shiloh	Gen. 49:10
Signet	Haggai 2:23
Star	Num. 24:17
Strong rod	Ps. 110:2
Universal ruler	Gen. 49:10; Num. 24:19; Ps. 2:8; 8:6-8; 22:27-29; 72:8-11; Isa. 16:1, 42:10-12; Ezek. 17:23; Zech. 9:10

F. Other Offices

Advocate	Job 16:19
Bondsman	Job 17:3
Counselor	Isa. 9:6
Deliverer	Hosea 1:11
Father	Isa. 9:6
Judge	Isa. 33:22
Mediator	Job 9:33; Isa. 49:8; 55:3; 61:8; Ezek. 34:25; 37:26
Redeemer	Job 19:25
Servant	Isa. 42:1; 49:3, 5-7; 50:10; 52:13; 53:11; Ezek. 34:23-24; 37:23; Hag. 2:23; Zech. 3:8
Warrior	Ps. 45:3-5; Isa. 42:13
Witness	Job 16:19; Isa. 55:4

V. THE CHARACTER OF MESSIAH

Commitment to God	Ps. 16:1-2; 40:6-8; 118:6-7; Isa. 11:2-3; Zech. 3:13
Confidence in God	Isa. 49:4-5
Delight in the saints	Ps. 16:3
Endowed with salvation	Hab. 3:13; Zech. 9:9
Eternal	Job 19:25; Ps. 16:11; Isa. 9:6-7; Ezek. 37:25; Dan. 7:14
Faithful	Isa. 11:5
Gentle	Isa. 42:2-3
Innocent	Isa. 53:9
Lowly	Zech. 9:9
Mighty	Isa. 9:6; 11:2
Peaceable	Micah 5:5

Righteous

Ps. 45:7; Isa. 9:7; 11:5; 32:1; 53:11; Jer. 23:6; 33:15; Zech. 9:9; Mal. 4:5

Spirit filled

Isa. 11:2; 42:1; 61:1

Wise

Isa. 9:6; 11:2; Jer. 23:5; Zech. 3:9

Wrathful

Ps. 2:12

VI. THE WORK OF MESSIAH

Atonement

Ps. 118:27; Isa. 53:4-5, 11-12; Dan. 9:24, 27; Zech. 3:9

Bring back Jacob

Isa. 49:5

Cause a covenant to prevail

Isa. 42:6; 49:8; Dan. 9:27

Champion the cause of truth

Ps. 45:4; Isa. 11:5; 42:3

Deliver from attack

Micah 5:6

Discouraged in his work

Isa. 49:4

Establish righteousness

Ps. 22:31; 45:4; 72:1-7; Isa. 11:4-5; 16:5; 61:10-11; Jer. 33:15; Ezek. 37:24; Dan. 9:24

Judge the afflicted

Ps. 72:4

Justify many

Isa. 53:11

Lead in worship

Ezek. 44:1-3; 46:1-2, 8-9; 45:16-17

Liberate captives

Isa. 9:4; 42:7; 49:9; Zech. 9:11

Light to the Gentiles

Isa. 9:2; 42:6, 16; 49:6; 55:5; 61:9, 11

Make straight paths

Isa. 42:15-16

Open blind eyes

Isa. 42:7, 16

Redeem from bondage

Hosea 1:11; Micah 2:13

Refine the Levites

Mal. 3:2-3

Restore the land

Isa. 49:8

Save the needy

Ps. 72:4, 12, 13

Seal vision and prophecy

Dan. 9:24

Sign and wonder

Isa. 8:18

Unify the people

Hosea 1:11; Micah 5:3; Isa. 49:12; 61:5-6

Victory over enemies

Ps. 2:9; 45:5; 72:4; 110:2; Num. 24:17-18; I Sam. 2:10; Gen. 3:15; Isa. 42:13; Micah 5:6, 8-9; Hab. 3:13-14

519

VII. THE DEITY OF MESSIAH

Appear on earth	Job 19:25
Come to his Temple	Mal. 3:1
Creator	Ps. 102:25
God	Ps. 45:6; Isa. 9:6
Immanuel	Isa. 7:14
Preexistence	Micah 5:2
Son of God	II Sam. 7:14; Ps. 2:7, 12; 89:27; Isa. 9:6; Hosea 11:1
Yahweh	Hosea 3:5; Micah 2:13

VIII. THE SUFFERINGS OF MESSIAH

Abused	Ps. 40:12
Accused	Ps. 109:2-5
Afflicted/poor/needy	Ps. 22:24; 40:17; 69:9; 109:30; Isa. 53:7
Agony	Ps. 22:14-15; 102:3-11, 23-24; Isa. 53:10
Appearance/disfigurement	Isa. 52:13-14; 53:2
Arrest/judgment	Isa. 53:8
Betrayal	Ps. 109:6-19
Burial	Isa. 53:9
Chastened	II Sam. 7:14; Ps. 118:18
Cut off	Dan. 9:26
Death	Isa. 53:8, 12
Despised/abhorred	Isa. 49:7
Fate of his adversaries	Ps. 40:14-15; 69:22-25, 27-28; 118:7, 10-12; 132:18; Dan. 9:26-27; Zech. 11:8, 14
Forsaken	Ps. 22:1; 69:8, 20
Garments divided	Ps. 22:18
Groaning	Ps. 22:1; 102:5
Heel bruised	Gen. 3:15
Humiliation	Isa. 49:7
Knocked back	Ps. 118:13
Loneliness	Ps. 102:6-9
Misunderstood	Isa. 53:4
Numbered with transgressors	Isa. 53:12
Opposition	Ps. 2:1-4; 22:12-13, 16; 69:4, 14, 19; 109:28; Zech. 11:8
Petition	Ps. 22:2, 19-21, 24; 40:1-2, 11, 13-17; 69:1-3, 6, 13-18, 29; 109:21, 26; 118:5, 21

IX. THE EXALTATION OF MESSIAH

X. THE KINGDOM OF MESSIAH

Growing kingdom	Isa. 9:3; Hos. 1:10; Micah 2:12
Joyous kingdom	Isa. 9:3; 42:10-12; 61:3, 7
Peaceful kingdom	Ps. 72:2, 7; Isa. 9:5-7; 49:13; Ezek. 34:25; Micah 5:10-11; Haggai 2:9; Zech. 3:10; 9:10
Priestly kingdom	Isa. 61:6
Purified kingdom	Isa. 32:3-8; Ezek. 37:23; Micah 5:12, 14
Redeemed kingdom	Jer. 23:6; 33:16; Ezek. 34:27, 28
Restored kingdom	Isa. 61:4
Safe kingdom	Jer. 23:6; 33:16; Ezek. 34:27-28; Micah 5:4-5
Spiritual kingdom	Isa. 61:8; Ezek. 34:30, 31; 37:24, 27
Unified kingdom	Ezek. 37:21-22, 24; Micah 2:12